TOURING
BRITAIN
—AND—
IRELAND

PUBLISHED BY
THE AUTOMOBILE ASSOCIATION, FANUM HOUSE, BASINGSTOKE, HAMPSHIRE RG21 2EA

The way to the far north west – the Kylesku road bridge in the
Scottish Highlands

© The Automobile Association 1991

Reprinted 1993

Text by Valerie Shepard and Peter Wenham

Mapping produced by the Cartographic Department of The Automobile
Association. The atlas pages have been compiled and produced from the
Automaps database utilising electronic and computer technology.

Typeset by Microset Graphics Ltd, Basingstoke, Hampshire

Reproduction by Scantrans Pte, Ltd, Singapore

Printed and bound in Spain by Graficromo S.A.

Published by The Automobile Association, Fanum House, Basingstoke,
Hampshire RG21 2EA

CONTENTS

ABOUT THIS BOOK

JOURNEY PLANNING

KEY MAP AND NATIONAL GRID

MAP SYMBOLS

GAZETTEER, FEATURES and TOURS

Tour pages are highlighted in blue

Deepest Cornwall	18
Riches of Land and Sea	20
Cornish Castles to Drake's Devon	22
DARTMOOR	24
From Dartmoor to Dartmouth	26
Bude, Barnstaple and Bideford	28
Tradition and Serenity	30
EXMOOR	32
Cider, Lace and Wool	34
The Kingdom of Wessex	36
A Thousand Years of Royal Connections	38
NEW FOREST	40
A World of Difference	42
Between War and Peace	44
The North and South Downs	46

1

2

Around the Ashdown Forest	48	Historic East Anglia	96
SUSSEX DOWNS	50	Songs, Ships and Sea	98
From Oast to Coast	52	Around Cardigan Bay	100
By the Channel	54	Wool and Water	102
Across the Landsker	56	SHROPSHIRE HILLS	104
PEMBROKESHIRE	58	The Welsh-English Borders	106
Rivers and Castles	60	Historic Shropshire	108
Valleys of Song	62	Rural and Industrial Heritage	110
Around the Severn Estuary	64	It's Not All Grey	112
Salisbury Plain and The Cotswolds	66	Rutland: Gone But Not Forgotten	114
From Prehistory to Silicon Chips	68	Fenland, Flowers and Fruit	116
The Prosperous Home Counties	70	Saints and Sand-Dunes	118
LONDON	72	NORFOLK BROADS	120
Outer London	74	The City and The Broads	122
Essex: Town and Country	76	Sacred Sites and Sandy Shores	124
From Boudicca to John Constable	78	Land of the Eagle	126
Mountains and Waterfalls	80	SNOWDONIA	128
BRECON BEACONS	82	Deeside and Merseyside	130
The Marches	84	Salt, Cotton and Pottery	132
Land of the Lower Severn	86	Caves, Crags and Spas	134
Statesmen, Scholars and the Bard	88	PEAK DISTRICT	136
CHILTERNS	90	City and Countryside	138
Town and Country Together	92	Treasures of Eastern England	140
From the Cam to the Ouse	94	Peaceful Lincolnshire	142

LINCOLNSHIRE WOLDS	144
The Independent Isle of Man	146
Lancashire By Sea	148
Cotton, Cloth and Co-ops	150
YORKSHIRE DALES	152
Yorkshire, Rural and Urban	154
York Minster to the Humber Bridge	156
Humberside: Fishing and Farming	158
Peaceful Lakes and Rugged Fells	160
The Lakes: Preserving the Balance	162
LAKE DISTRICT	164
Fells and Falls	166
Dale and Rail	168
From James Herriot to James Cook	170
Coasts, Cliffs and Cascades	172
NORTH YORK MOORS	174
Southernmost Scotland	176
The Galloway Hills	178
The Hinterland of Dumfries	180
Carlisle to Hawick	182
Hadrian's Wall and Hexham	184
NORTHUMBERLAND	186
Newcastle and Tyneside	188

Isles of the South West	190
The Lochs and Isles of Strathclyde	192
Arran, South Kintyre and Gigha	194
Ballads and Verse	196
An Industrial Heritage	198
GLASGOW	200
The Lowlands	202
EDINBURGH	204
Tweed and Wool	206
Cattle, Kippers and Castles	208
Iona, Staffa, Coll and Tiree	210
Oban and the Island Of Mull	212
Lochs and Gardens	214
Gateway to the Highlands	216
TROSSACHS	218
The Forth Valley	220
Golf Courses and Golden Villages	222
The Small Islands and Southern Skye	224
The Road to The Isles	226
Peaks and Glens	228
The Highlands	230
A Royal Progress	232
CAIRNGORMS	234

6

8

Mountains and Coastline	236
Romantic Memories	238
Wester Ross	240
The Great Glen	242
Battles, Birds and Castles	244
Whisky Galore!	246
The Moray Coast	248
Wilderness and Water	250
NORTH WEST HIGHLANDS	252
Dornoch Firth	254
The Far Highland	256
Crofter's Country	258
Castles and Creels	260
Outer Hebrides	262
The Orkneys Islands	264
The Shetlands Islands	266
Guernsey	268
CHANNEL ISLANDS	270
Jersey	272
Western Ireland	274
Northern Ireland	276
South-West Ireland	278
South-Eastern Ireland	280
Index	282
Acknowledgements	288

Typical Cotswold houses by the River Eye, Lower Slaughter

10

9

1 Carn Galver mine at St Just, Cornwall

2 Bucklers Hard on the beautiful Beaulieu River

3 Knole Palace at Sevenoaks in Kent

4 A mill at Thurne in eastern Norfolk

5 The rack-and-pinion Snowdon Mountain Railway

6 Bride Stones on the moors in West Yorkshire

7 The 12th-century Lanercost Priory, Cumbria

8 The Forth rail bridge, Lothian

9 The Highlands' Kyle of Lochalsh to Kyleakin ferry

10 The 14th-century Urquhart Castle, overlooking Loch Ness

ABOUT THIS BOOK

TOURING Britain and Ireland is a new kind of touring book for the 1990s. It has been designed for the motorist who enjoys exploring new places and wants to get the most out of whatever part of the country he finds himself in. For the first time a complete road atlas of Britain and Ireland with comprehensive touring information has been put together in a single volume.

PLACES TO VISIT
Red symbols and type on the atlas highlight the numerous places of interest to be found all over the country and every page of mapping is accompanied by descriptions of selected places to visit in that area. The corresponding symbols are also shown in the text for easy identification and there is a map reference with every entry so it can be quickly found on the map. Map references are explained in detail on page 14 and there is a key to the symbols on page 16.

Opening times are not given in this book. Always remember to check the latest details in advance when making a special visit to avoid disappointment.

PAGE FINDER

This diagram, positioned near the title, appears on every spread featuring an atlas page. The numbers on the diagram indicate the page numbers of adjoining maps, and, together with the arrows, show where they join with the map currently being used.

TOURS
An important feature of this book is the motor tours. These are highlighted in yellow on 49 of the atlas pages and their route is fully described in the accompanying text, although the large scale of the mapping means there is no need for complex route directions. These tours have been carefully planned to take in the best of an area and can either be followed in their entirety or used as a basis for further exploration.

SPECIAL FEATURES
Finally, 23 special double page features are devoted to some of the most popular and attractive touring areas of Britain, including all the National Parks of England and Wales. The three great cities of London, Edinburgh and Glasgow are also given special treatment. These features are positioned throughout the book as near as possible to the relevant page of mapping, but can quickly be found by referring to the contents page.

INDEX
The index at the back lists all the places to visit that are described in the book.

JOURNEY PLANNING

THE maps shown on the following pages at a scale of 22 miles to the inch enable easy planning of 'how to get there' routes, and are also a guide to the main roads in your selected touring area.

PLANNING A ROUTE
The principal routes can be used to plan a long journey in advance and although motorways are generally the fastest means of getting across the country, there are usually good alternative roads if required. A more detailed route can be worked out by studying the atlas pages. Remember to take a note of road numbers and directions before setting off.

BEFORE YOU GO
When you are embarking on a long journey it is important to set out feeling confident and alert. If you are staying away from home for any length of time it is a good idea to jot down a check-list the night before and run through it just before leaving: gas; water; electricity; pets; security; milk and papers cancelled, etc.

Remember to check the car as well, particularly the lights and tyres.

A long journey with small children can be a nightmare. Some books, games or, best of all, a toy cassette player and some story tapes can all help to stop tears in the back seat.

The scenic Whinlatter Pass and Bassenthwaite, Cumbria

ON THE ROAD
If you are on the motorway, the service areas are probably the best solution for lunch or snack breaks, particularly if you are with children. However, the pages of this book may well suggest a small town or village for a more enjoyable break, perhaps combined with a visit to a place of interest.

ARRIVING
Scanning the airwaves on the car radio may well find you a local radio station which will give you the latest local news, weather and traffic reports. If you require accommodation, look for Tourist Information Centre signs. They carry lists of hotels, bed and breakfast establishments, camping and caravan sites as well as ticket and time details for local tourist attractions.

TOURING
Show courtesy and care when touring on the road. In wilderness areas sheep stray freely and on some roads in Scotland cars can only be passed in special, signed passing bays. Check that your raptures with the landscape are not holding up local people on urgent business. Keep a full tank too in remote areas; petrol stations can be far apart and keep short hours. Whatever you do, never drink and drive.

To the Pass of Bealach-Na-Ba, Highlands

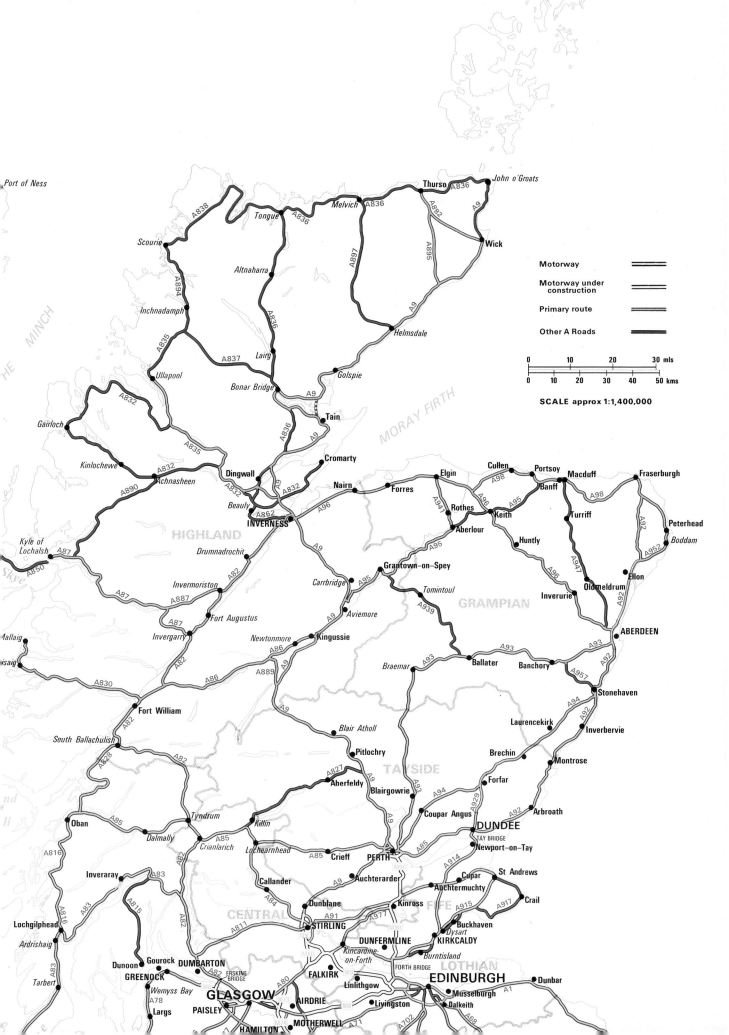

Port of Ness

THE MINCH

Scourie

Tongue   A836   Melvich   A836   Thurso   A836   John o'Groats

A838

Inchnadamph

A894

Altnaharra

A897

A882   A9

Wick

A895

Helmsdale

A9

Lairg

A835   A837

Ullapool

Bonar Bridge

Golspie

Gairloch

A832

A9

A835

Kinlochewe

A832

Achnasheen

A890

Dingwall

A862

Cromarty

Tain

A836

MORAY FIRTH

A832

Nairn

Forres

Elgin

Cullen   Portsoy   Macduff   Fraserburgh

A98

A98

Banff

A96

A941   Rothes   A95   Keith

Turriff

A92   Peterhead

Kyle of
Lochalsh

A87

A850

Skye

Beauly

INVERNESS

HIGHLAND

Drumnadrochit

A82

A9

Aberlour

Huntly

A95

A96

A947   Oldmeldrum   Ellon

A952   Boddam

Invermoriston

A887

Grantown-on-Spey

Carrbridge

A95

Tomintoul

A939

Inverurie

A96

A92

Fort Augustus

A87

Aviemore

GRAMPIAN

ABERDEEN

Mallaig

Invergarry

Newtonmore   A86   Kingussie

A93

A889   A9

A82

A86

Braemar   A93   Ballater   Banchory   A957

A93

A92

Stonehaven

A94

Fort William

A82

Blair Atholl

Laurencekirk

A92

Inverbervie

South Ballachulish

A828

Pitlochry

Brechin

Montrose

A82

A827

Aberfeldy

Forfar

A94   A929   A92   Arbroath

Oban

A85

Tyndrum

Killin

Blairgowrie

Coupar Angus

A9

Dalmally

A85   Crianlarich

Lochearnhead

A85   Crieff

PERTH

DUNDEE   TAY BRIDGE   Newport-on-Tay

A816

A82

A85

A914

A83

Inveraray

Callander

A84

A9   Auchterarder

Cupar   St Andrews

Auchtermuchty

A915   A917   Crail

A815

Dunblane

Dunoon   Gourock   DUMBARTON

A816

Lochgilphead

A811

STIRLING

CENTRAL

A91

Kinross

A977

FIFE

Buckhaven

Dysart

Ardrishaig

A83

DUNFERMLINE

KIRKCALDY

Kincardine-on-Forth

Burntisland

Tarbert

GREENOCK

Wemyss Bay

ERSKINE BRIDGE

FORTH BRIDGE

LOTHIAN

EDINBURGH

Dunbar

A78

GLASGOW

FALKIRK

Linlithgow

Musselburgh

A1

Largs

PAISLEY

AIRDRIE

Livingston

Dalkeith

A702

A68

HAMILTON   MOTHERWELL

A71

HULL
Goole
PONTEFRACT
WAKEFIELD
HUMBER BRIDGE
Barton-upon-Humber
Immingham
Thorne
SCUNTHORPE
GRIMSBY
CLEETHORPES
BARNSLEY
DONCASTER
Brigg
Glossop
ROTHERHAM
Bawtry
Market Rasen
Gainsborough
SHEFFIELD
Louth
WORKSOP
Mablethorpe
Buxton
Bakewell
CHESTERFIELD
LINCOLN
Horncastle
Matlock
MANSFIELD
Skegness
ALFRETON
NEWARK-ON-TRENT
LINCOLNSHIRE
Ashbourne
Sleaford
BOSTON
THE WASH
Uttoxeter
DERBY
NOTTINGHAM
GRANTHAM
Hunstanton
Wells-next-the-Sea
Sheringham
Cromer
Holt
BURTON UPON TRENT
LOUGHBOROUGH
Bourne
Spalding
Fakenham
North Walsham
Lichfield
Ashby-de-la-Zouch
Melton Mowbray
KING'S LYNN
Tamworth
Oakham
LEICESTER
Stamford
Wisbech
Swaffham
Dereham
NORWICH
Acle
Caister-on-Sea
GREAT YARMOUTH
Uppingham
PETERBOROUGH
Downham Market
NORFOLK
HINCKLEY
NUNEATON
Market Harborough
CORBY
March
Attleborough
LOWESTOFT
Chatteris
Bungay
Beccles
COVENTRY
KETTERING
Ely
Thetford
Diss
LEAMINGTON SPA
Warwick
Huntingdon
CAMBRIDGESHIRE
Daventry
NORTHAMPTON
Newmarket
BURY ST EDMUNDS
Stratford-upon-Avon
St Neots
CAMBRIDGE
SUFFOLK
Saxmundham
Towcester
BEDFORD
Biggleswade
Haverhill
BANBURY
MILTON KEYNES
Ampthill
Sudbury
IPSWICH
Brackley
Royston
Baldock
Felixstowe
Chipping Norton
Leighton Buzzard
HITCHIN
STEVENAGE
BISHOP'S STORTFORD
Halstead
Harwich
Stow-on-the-Wold
Bicester
LUTON
Puckeridge
Braintree
COLCHESTER
DUNSTABLE
AYLESBURY
Great Dunmow
Witney
Ware
Hertford
HARPENDEN
HARLOW
CLACTON-ON-SEA
OXFORD
Thame
Hatfield
ST ALBANS
EPPING
CHELMSFORD
Abingdon
HIGH WYCOMBE
Amersham
WATFORD
ESSEX
Faringdon
Beaconsfield
BRENTWOOD
Northolt
Tottenham
MAIDENHEAD
SLOUGH
EALING
LONDON
SOUTHEND-ON-SEA
READING
WINDSOR
DARTFORD TUNNEL
Tilbury
HEATHROW AIRPORT
KINGSTON-UPON-THAMES
DARTFORD
GRAVESEND
Sheerness
Hungerford
NEWBURY
STAINES
Swanley
Bromley
ROCHESTER
GILLINGHAM
MARGATE
CHERTSEY
Orpington
CHATHAM
RAMSGATE
CROYDON
Wrotham
Faversham
EPSOM
BASINGSTOKE
LEATHERHEAD
CANTERBURY
Sandwich
REIGATE
SEVENOAKS
MAIDSTONE
Andover
GUILDFORD
DORKING
Redhill
DEAL
FARNHAM
TONBRIDGE
KENT
ASHFORD
Alton
East Grinstead
SURREY
Gatwick
CRAWLEY
Stockbridge
Sutton Scotney
DOVER
TUNBRIDGE WELLS
WINCHESTER
Liphook
Hythe
FOLKESTONE
SALISBURY
HORSHAM
Romsey
Petersfield
Midhurst
WEST SUSSEX
EASTLEIGH
Rye
New Romney
Uckfield
SOUTHAMPTON
EAST SUSSEX
Lewes
Lyndhurst
CHICHESTER
Arundel
HOVE
BRIGHTON
HASTINGS
FAREHAM
WORTHING
BEXHILL-ON-SEA
PORTSMOUTH
BOGNOR REGIS
Cowes
EASTBOURNE
RYDE
CHRISTCHURCH
Freshwater
Newport
Isle of Wight
Sandown
Shanklin

KEY MAP AND NATIONAL GRID

ONE of the features of AA mapping is the use of the National Grid system. Britain is divided into 100 kilometre grid squares, each of which is identified by a set of two letters as shown, circled in blue, on this map. These 100 kilometre squares are sub-divided into smaller squares by grid lines numbered 0-9 along the bottom and up the left hand side of the atlas pages.

FINDING PLACES OF INTEREST

For easy reference to the accompanying atlas page, a four-figure number is given with each place of interest described in the text. The four figures of this map reference are arranged so that the first and third are in a bolder type than the second and fourth.

The first figure shows which number along the bottom to locate, and the third figure which number up the left hand side. Where these intersect indicates the square in which you will find the place name.

However, to pinpoint a place more accurately, use the second and fourth numbers as well. The second will tell you how many imaginary tenths along the bottom line to go from the first number, and the fourth how many tenths up the line to go from the third number. The place will be found where these two lines intersect. For example, Skegness, Map ref **5663**, is located within grid square 56. Its exact location is **5663**.

If you find you get the numbers confused, it might

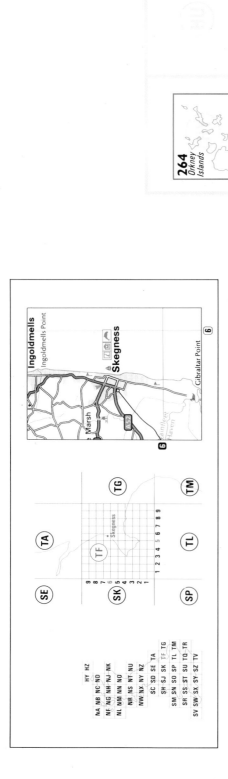

		HY	HZ	
NA	NB	NC	ND	
NF	NG	NH	NJ	NK
NL	NM	NN	NO	
NR	NS	NT	NU	
NW	NX	NY	NZ	
	SC	SD	SE	TA
	SH	SJ	SK	TF	TG
SM	SN	SO	SP	TL	TM
SR	SS	ST	SU	TQ	TR
SV	SW	SX	SY	SZ	TV

266
Shetland Islands

264
Orkney Islands

262
Outer Hebrides
Stornoway

256 **258** **260** Thurso

250 **254**

240 **242** **244** Inverness **246** **248**

238 **224** Portree **228** Fort William **230** **232** **236** Aberdeen

226

210 *Coll and Tiree* **212** **214** Oban **216** **220** Perth **222** Dundee

190 **192** **196** **198** Glasgow **202** **206** Edinburgh **208**

Ingoldmells
Ingoldmells Point

Skegness

Gibraltar Point

SE   TA

SK   TF   TG

SP   TL   TM

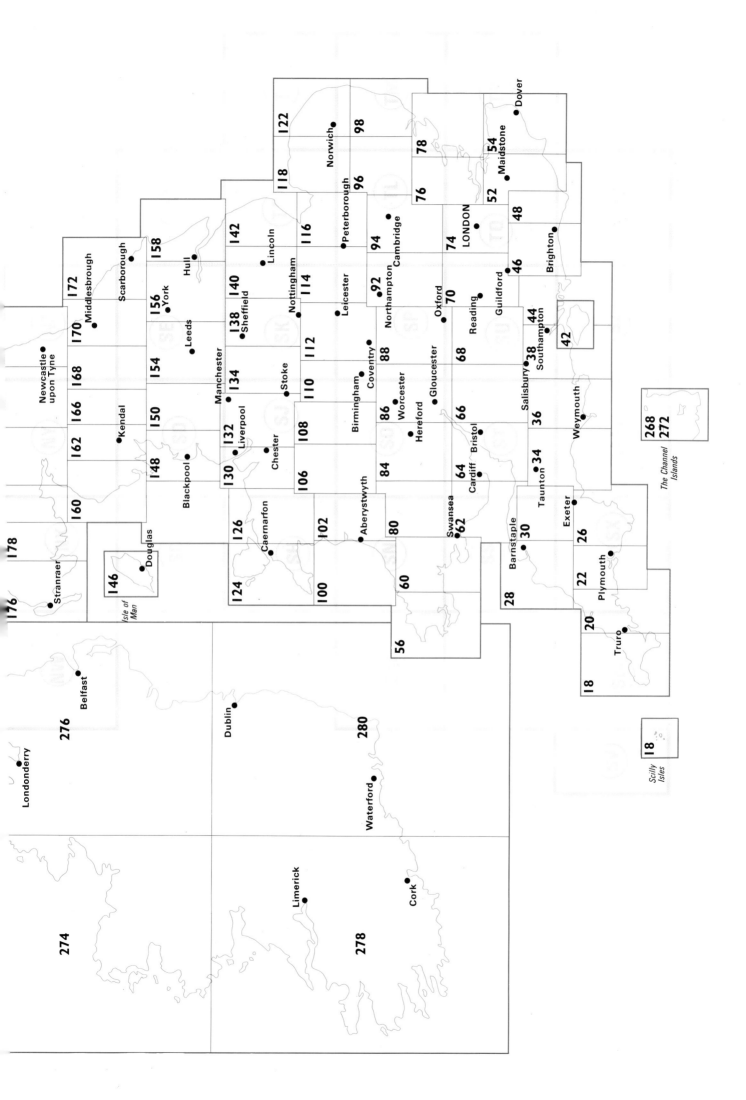

MAP SYMBOLS

MOTORING INFORMATION		TOURIST INFORMATION	
M4 — Motorway with number	— V — Vehicle ferry – Great Britain	ℹ Tourist Information Centre	⁖ Hill fort
Motorway junction with and without number	CHERBOURG V Vehicle ferry – Continental	ℹ Tourist Information Centre (summer only)	Roman antiquity
3 Motorway junction with limited access	— H — Hovercraft ferry	Abbey, cathedral or priory	Prehistoric monument
S Motorway service area	⊕ Airport	Ruined abbey, cathedral or priory	× Battle site with year
Motorway and junction under construction	H Heliport	Castle	Preserved railway/ steam centre
A4 Primary route single/dual carriageway	Railway line/in tunnel	Historic house	Cave
S Primary route service area	Railway station and level crossing	Museum or art gallery	Windmill
A1123 Other A road single/dual carriageway	AA AA Shop – full services	Industrial interest	Golf course
B2070 B road single/dual carriageway	AA AA Roadside Shop – limited services	Garden	County cricket ground
Unclassified road single/dual carriageway	AA AA Port Shop – open as season demands	Arboretum	Rugby Union national ground
Road under construction	AA telephone	Country park	International athletics stadium
Narrow primary, other A or B road with passing places (Scotland)	BT telephone in isolated places	Agricultural showground	Horse racing
Road tunnel	Urban area/village	Theme park	Show jumping/equestrian circuit
Steep gradient (arrows point downhill)	628 ▲ Spot height in metres	Zoo	Motor racing circuit
Toll Road toll	River, canal, lake	Wildlife collection – mammals	Coastal launching site
5 Distance in miles between symbols	Sandy beach	Wildlife collection – birds	Ski slope – natural
	County boundary	Aquarium	Ski slope – artificial
	National boundary	Nature reserve	★ Other places of interest
	Tour routes	RSPB RSPB site	Boxed symbols indicate attractions within urban areas
		Nature trail	National Park (England & Wales)
		····· Forest drive	National Scenic Area (Scotland)
		– – – National trail	Forest Park
		AA viewpoint	Heritage Coast
		Picnic site	Blue flag beach

TOURING
BRITAIN
—AND—
IRELAND

GAZETTEER • TOURS • FEATURES

A peaceful stretch of the River Tweed near Innerleithen, Borders

DEEPEST CORNWALL

Blessed by the mild climate of the Gulf Stream and cursed by the perils of the sea, Cornwall stretches out into the Atlantic. The miles of cliffs and coves of Land's End, the Lizard and St Ives are some of the most beautiful in the country.

In contrast, the desolate hinterland, exploited by man since earliest times, still bears the scars of the harsh, and temporary, prosperity brought by the mining industry in the last century.

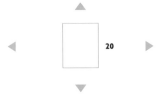

TOUR

THE LAND'S END PENINSULA
46 MILES

The tour begins in Penzance, hugging the coast towards Newlyn and Mousehole. While not quite rivalling St Ives' artistic connections, Newlyn has long been a haunt of landscape painters.

Mousehole, a delightful fishing village approached by narrow roads, came tragically to nationwide attention in 1981 when its lifeboat was lost with all hands as it attempted a rescue in terrible conditions.

From Mousehole the route turns inland, onto the B3315, although it is worth the short detour back to the coast to experience the beauty of Lamorna Cove.

Continuing south west, at Trethewey a left turn leads back to the coast up a steep hill to the cliff-top car park of the Minack Open Air Theatre. The cliff forms a natural

Porthminster, the more sheltered of St Ives' beaches, is popular with families

amphitheatre, and the sea forms a superb backdrop to the performances which take place most evenings during the summer.

Next stopping point on the tour is Land's End – the most westerly tip of the English mainland – from whose spectacular granite cliffs the Isles of Scilly can be seen on a clear day. The 200-acre site has recently been developed with exhibitions tracing the origins of the region, its flora and fauna.

Passing Sennen, the road winds north towards St Just, a large former tin-mining village. The shallow amphitheatre by the clock tower was used in the Middle Ages for performances of miracle plays.

Following the curve of the coastline, the route passes through villages which previously depended on the tin-mining industry for survival. Inland is an area full of prehistoric monuments. Reaching Zennor, the private Wayside Museum is full of intriguing objects reflecting every aspect of local life from 3,000BC to the date of its foundation in 1935. A carved bench-end in the church depicts the mermaid of Zennor, reputed to have lured the squire's son to live with her on the sea-bed.

The road climbs on towards St Ives, giving an extensive view across the bay. The town is almost inaccessible to cars, so it is best to park at Lelant Station and use the train service provided. This picturesque fishing port has attracted many artists and sculptors, including Dame Barbara Hepworth and potter Bernard Leach. Examples of Dame Barbara's work are on display at the house in which she lived from 1949 until her death in 1975. Her *Madonna and Child* can be seen in the Lady chapel of the church of St Ia.

From St Ives the route passes through Lelant on its way back to Penzance. After Crowlas, a left turn heads towards Marazion and St Michael's Mount. Originally the site of a Benedictine chapel established by Edward the Confessor, the spectacular castle, set on a rock, dates from the 14th century. Visitors must cross the tidal causeway on

foot or take a sailing boat, before climbing to the top of the castle, 200ft above the sea to enjoy the view and the fine contents.

Finally back in Penzance, the tour ends with the opportunity to reflect on the history and development of the area from prehistoric times to the present in the Penlee House Museum and Art Gallery. Visitors also enjoy examples of locally painted work. Opposite the famous Admiral Benbow Inn stands Roland Morris's Maritime Museum, full of treasure recovered from wrecks.

SELECTED PLACES TO VISIT

✕ ☀ ♦ FALMOUTH
Map ref 8032
Blessed by a mild climate and a superb location overlooking the bay, Falmouth has long been a popular holiday destination. Pendennis Castle contains an exhibition explaining the coastal defences.

★ FLAMBARDS THEME PARK
Map ref 6725
Flambards Theme Park has three main all-weather attractions: reconstructed Victorian village, Britain in the Blitz (a full-scale street, complete with sound effects) and the Aero Park, which has been developed from the display of flying machines with which the site began as a tourist attraction.

☐ ✕ FOWEY
Map ref 1251
Much of the beautiful coastline to the east and west of Fowey is owned by the National Trust, starting from Gribbin Head.

St Catherine's Castle – one of the fortresses built by Henry VIII – was restored in 1855 after falling into disrepair and is worth a visit.

❀ GLENDURGAN
Map ref 7727
Glendurgan Garden, set in a valley above the River Helford, is now maintained by the National Trust. An informal landscape contains trees and shrubs from all over the world, and a walled garden.

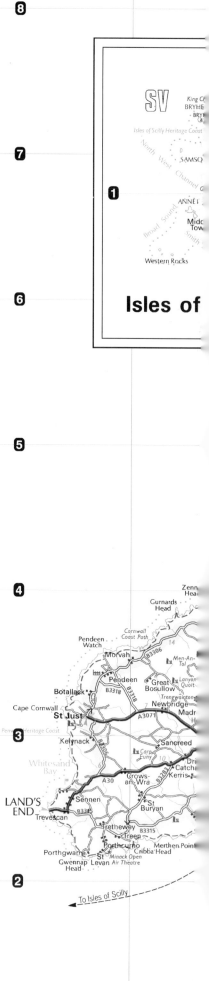

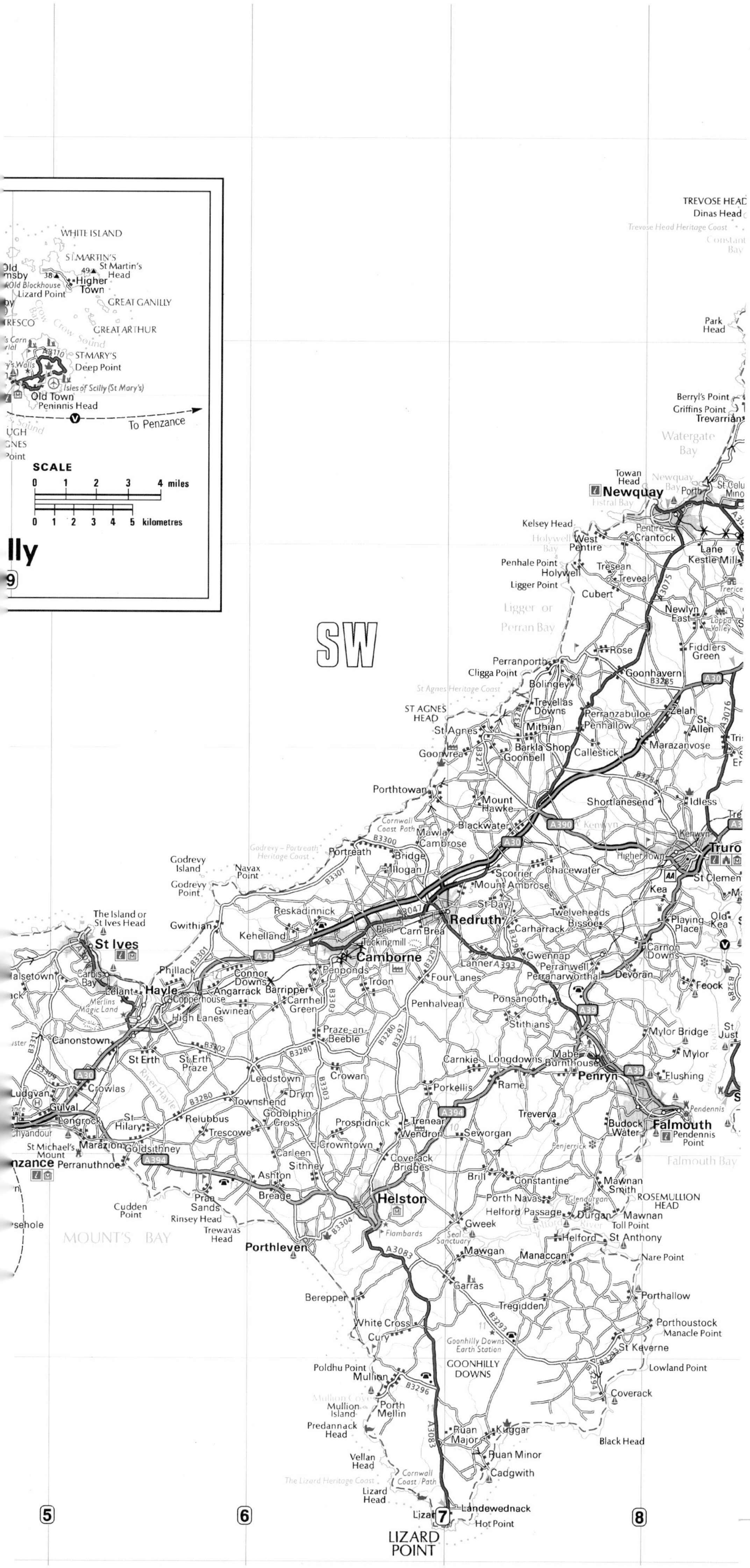

Map (Deepest Cornwall)

SCALE
0 1 2 3 4 miles
0 1 2 3 4 5 kilometres

lly

To Penzance

Isles of Scilly (St Mary's)
Old Town
Peninnis Head
WHITE ISLAND
ST.MARTIN'S
St Martin's Head
Higher Town
GREAT GANILLY
GREAT ARTHUR
ST.MARY'S
Deep Point
TRESCO
Old Blockhouse
Lizard Point

Map place names:

TREVOSE HEAD
Dinas Head
Trevose Head Heritage Coast
Constant Bay
Park Head
Berryl's Point
Griffins Point
Trevarrian
Watergate Bay
Towan Head
Newquay
Fistral Bay
Newquay Bay
St Columb Minor
Kelsey Head
West Pentire
Crantock
Lane
Kestle Mill
Holywell Bay
Penhale Point
Holywell
Ligger Point
Tresean
Treveal
Cubert
Ligger or Perran Bay
Newlyn East
Lappa Valley
Fiddlers Green
Rose
Perranporth
Cligga Point
Goonhavern
St Agnes Heritage Coast
Bolingey
Trevellas Downs
Perranzabuloe
Penhallow
Zelah
St Allen
ST AGNES HEAD
St Agnes
Mithian
Marazanvose
Goonrea
Barkla Shop
Goonbell
Callestick
Idless
Porthtowan
Mount Hawke
Shortlanesend
St Kenwyn
Truro
Cornwall Coast Path
Mawla
Blackwater
Godrevy – Portreath Heritage Coast
Cambrose
Portreath
Bridge
Milogan
Scorrier
Chacewater
Higher town
St Clement
Godrevy Island
Navax Point
Godrevy Point
Reskadinnick
Mount Ambrose
St Day
Twelveheads
Bissoe
Kea
Old Kea
Playing Place
The Island or St Ives Head
Gwithian
Redruth
Carharrack
Carnon Downs
St Ives
Kehelland
Tuckingmill
Carn Brea
Gwennap
Feock
Carbis Bay
Lelant
Connor Downs
Camborne
Lanner
Perranwell
Perranarworthal
Devoran
Mylor Bridge
Mylor
Hayle
Phillack
Angarrack
Barripper
Penponds
Four Lanes
Troon
Copperhouse
Carnhell Green
Gwinear
Penhalvean
Ponsanooth
Stithians
Mabe Burnthouse
Flushing
High Lanes
Praze-an-Beeble
Crowan
Longdowns
Penryn
St Just
Canonstown
St Erth
St Erth Praze
Leedstown
Drym
Carnkie
Rame
Treverva
Budock Water
Pendennis Point
Ludgvan
Crowlas
Townshend
Porkellis
Penzance
Gulval
St Hilary
Godolphin Cross
Prospidnick
Trenear
Wendron
Seworgan
Falmouth
Pendennis Point
Longrock
Relubbus
Trescowe
Crowntown
Constantine
Mawnan Smith
Falmouth Bay
Marazion
Goldsithney
Carleen
Sithney
Brill
Porth Navas
ROSEMULLION HEAD
Mawnan
St Michael's Mount
Perranuthnoe
Ashton
Breage
Helston
Helford Passage
Durgan
Mawnan
Nare Point
Cudden Point
Praa Sands
Rinsey Head
Trewavas Head
Gweek
Helford
St Anthony
Toll Point
MOUNT'S BAY
Porthleven
Berepper
Mawgan
Manaccan
Porthallow
Garras
Tregidden
Porthoustock
Manacle Point
White Cross
Cury
Goonhilly Downs Earth Station
St Keverne
Poldhu Point
GOONHILLY DOWNS
Lowland Point
Mullion
Coverack
Mullion Island
Porth Mellin
Predannack Head
Ruan Major
Kuggar
Black Head
Vellan Head
Ruan Minor
Cadgwith
The Lizard Heritage Coast
Cornwall Coast Path
Lizard Head
Landewednack
Lizard
Hot Point
LIZARD POINT

5 6 7 8

DEEPEST CORNWALL

HELSTON
Map ref 6627
Helston is famous for its annual Floral Dance.

The Folk Museum captures the atmosphere of the busy market town through the centuries.

NEWQUAY
Map ref 8161
There have been settlements here since Iron and Bronze Age times, but Newquay's development into the largest resort on Cornwall's north coast has largely been the result of the coming of the railway in 1875. Fishing is still an important activity for this busy town.

POOL
Map ref 6741
At Pool, near Camborne, Cornish Engines have beam engines which were used to pump water from more than 2,000ft below. Once used for winding men and ore, they are now preserved by the National Trust.

★ SEAL SANCTUARY
Map ref 7026
The Seal Sanctuary and Marine Rescue Centre at Gweek is devoted to caring for sick and injured seals. The centre also has an aquarium and exhibition centre.

TRELISSICK GARDEN
Map ref 8339
A beautiful woodland park of 370 acres overlooking the Falmouth estuary. Trelissick Garden is particularly noted for its camellias, magnolias and hydrangeas. The location and sheltered nature of the garden allows many unusual and exotic plants to be grown. The park offers spectacular views from walks through beech and oak trees.

TRURO
Map ref 8244
The county town of Cornwall has been a cathedral city since 1880, when Prince Edward – later to be Edward VII – laid the foundation stone. In medieval times it was a centre for the export of mineral ore, and a stannary town to which smelted tin was brought for quality tests and the imposition of taxes.

The mineral collection in the County Museum and Art Gallery's Rashleigh Gallery is unrivalled. The museum also features Cornish wildlife, pottery, pewter, Japanese ivories and a marble bust of Richard Trevithick – inventor of the beam engine so crucial to the local mining industry. In the art gallery are paintings by John Opie, the local 18th-century artist.

The gracious Georgian homes of the prosperous merchants are an attractive feature of the town.

WENDRON
Map ref 6731
At Wendron visitors can explore the Poldark tin mine and learn the details of Cornish mining history.

RICHES OF LAND AND SEA

Tin, china clay, dairying and fishing have long been the mainstays of the central Cornish economy. From the beauty of Falmouth estuary in the south west to the majesty of Bodmin Moor in the north, the varied landscape proves a magnet to visitors from near and far.

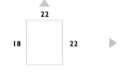

SELECTED PLACES TO VISIT

BODMIN
Map ref 0767

Little remains of the 10th-century priory of St Petrock, but Bodmin has the county's largest parish church – dedicated to the same saint – whose bones are said to be in the ivory Bodmin Casket displayed in the south aisle.

On the summit of the Beacon above the town is a 144ft obelisk commemorating the distinguished soldier Lieutenant-General Sir Walter Raleigh Gilbert.

The Duke of Cornwall's Light Infantry Museum features pictures and relics of the major campaigns of the regiment from 1702 to 1945.

CHARLESTOWN
Map ref 0351

To the east of St Austell lies the unspoilt 18th-century village of Charlestown, which is still a working port. Its Shipwreck and Heritage Museum contains a remarkable collection of recovered articles and tableaux showing rural Cornish life.

LANHYDROCK
Map ref 0863

South of Bodmin is Lanhydrock, a 17th-century house largely rebuilt after a fire in 1881. The north wing with a 116ft picture gallery and gatehouse are unchanged, and the gardens are beautiful all year round.

LANREATH
Map ref 1857

Cornish rural heritage is the theme of the Lanreath Farm and Folk Museum, with a large collection of farming, dairy and agricultural exhibits, as well as demonstrations of local crafts.

LOOE
Map ref 2553

The town sits astride the River Looe, which originally divided the community into two separate

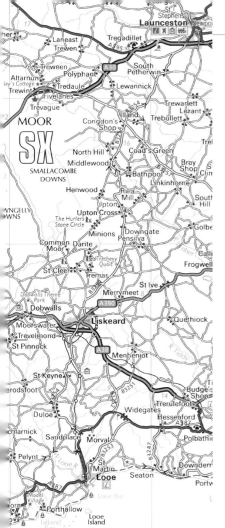

settlements. From the town expeditions fish for shark in the Channel. Cruises also run to the bird sanctuary on Looe Island.

The town has many ancient buildings, including the Guildhall which houses the old stocks and pillory in the museum.

🏛 MEVAGISSEY
Map ref 0144

Relics of the fishing industry – so important to this attractive village – can be found in the Folk Museum, together with examples of other local crafts and industries.

Enthusiasts will find the World of Model Railways a paradise.

MONKEY SANCTUARY
Map ref 2855

About three miles east of Looe visitors can have a close encounter with primates at the Murrayton Monkey Sanctuary, home to the rare Amazon Woolly monkey.

🚂 NEWLYN EAST
Map ref 8256

The Lappa Valley narrow gauge steam railway makes a round trip of some two miles, stopping at East Wheal Rose Halt for visitors to explore an old silver and lead mine. A five-acre pleasure garden is accessible only by the train.

🐦 PADSTOW
Map ref 9175

A taste of the exotic can be enjoyed at the Padstow Tropical Bird Gardens. There is a walk-in tropical house where birds fly freely, and a butterfly house where the lifecycle of the butterfly can be observed. The garden contains many species of sub-tropical plants.

🏛 PENCARROW
Map ref 0471

Between Bodmin and Wadebridge is Pencarrow, a Georgian mansion containing many fine contemporary paintings, furniture and china. The 50-acre woodland garden has trails, a pets' corner and a craft centre.

★ POLPERRO
Map ref 2051

Polperro was once the haunt of smugglers, whose exploits are commemorated in a Smugglers' Museum.

East of Polperro on the main road is the Land of Legend and Model Village.

★ PROBUS
Map ref 9147

On the road from Truro to St Austell lies Probus – Cornwall County Council's demonstration garden and centre for rural studies.

Originally part of the Trewithen estate, the garden features permanent displays of different garden layouts, showing the effect of climate. Guidance is available on selecting plants and propagating them, with the emphasis on the choice of the right tree, shrub or flower for a particular environment. Included in the garden are

geological displays and an outdoor exhibition of sculpture.

Trewithen House and its gardens were created in 1720 and have been lived in continuously by the same family. A video presentation and guided tour explain the history of the house. The famous garden is noted for its superb displays of magnolias, camellias and rhododendrons, as well as a large number of rare and exotic trees and shrubs.

⚔ RESTORMEL CASTLE
Map ref 1061

Restormel Castle stands above the ancient stannary of Lostwithiel. Much of what remains is 13th century, including its splendid round keep.

⚔ ST MAWES
Map ref 8433

Above the Carrick Roads stands St Mawes Castle; facing Pendennis Castle in Falmouth, built by Henry VIII in 1540. No invader was ever so adventurous as to put the fortress to the test. The harbour below the

castle is popular with yachts as well as fishermen.

🏛 TRERICE
Map ref 8458

Trerice is a charming small Elizabethan manor house, which has fine fireplaces and plaster ceilings. A small museum in the barn traces the development of the lawn mower.

🏛 WHEAL MARTYN MUSEUM
Map ref 0055

The Wheal Martyn Museum gives the visitor a fascinating opportunity to see exactly how a clayworks operated: the old site has been restored as an open-air museum, complete with huge waterwheels, settling tanks, horse-drawn wagons and steam locomotives. Indoor displays explain the history of clay in Cornwall over two centuries, and a working pottery shows how the raw material can be used. Visitors can also see a modern working clay pit from a viewing area.

The quayside at Looe is lined with working fishing boats

CORNISH CASTLES TO DRAKE'S DEVON

Criss-crossed by rivers, east Cornwall and south Devon are full of spectacular scenery. Splendid castles and historic houses recall a glorious heritage of noble families. Much of the prosperity of the inland area was founded on tin mining, while the port of Plymouth has witnessed many momentous events in English history.

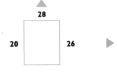

SELECTED PLACES TO VISIT

🏛 ANTONY HOUSE
Map ref 4156

Antony House at Torpoint is an early 18th-century building, with a central block of silver-grey Pentewan stone and wings of red brick joined to the house by colonnades. Antony Woodland Gardens, bordering the Lynher estuary, contain lovely shrubs, rhododendrons, camellias and magnolias.

🏛 BOSCASTLE
Map ref 0990

Boscastle Pottery specialises in Mochaware which can be seen being hand-thrown and painted. The Museum of Witchcraft is the place to learn about the practice of witchcraft, past and present, in Devon and Cornwall.

The 13th-century keep and stone defences of Launceston Castle

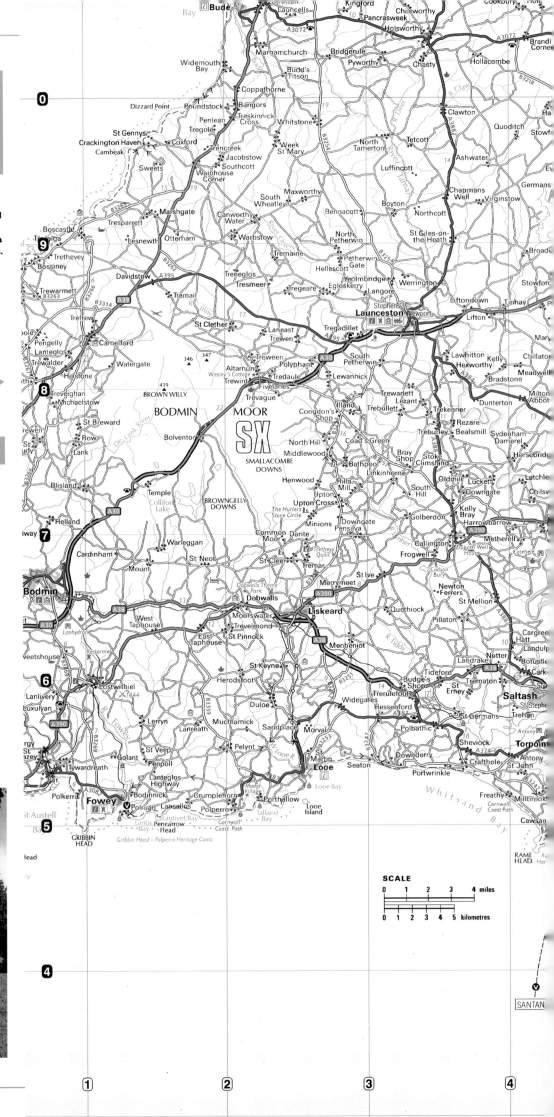

SCALE

0   1   2   3   4 miles

0 1 2 3 4 5 kilometres

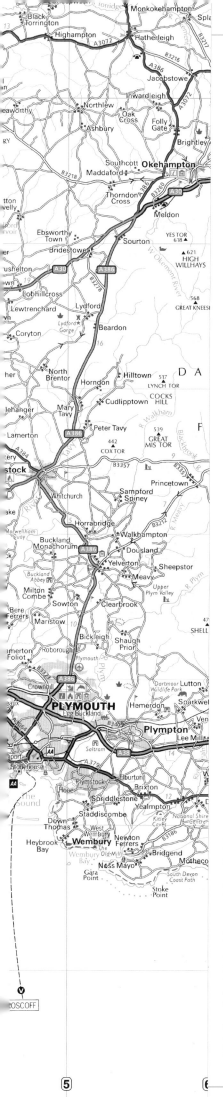

🏛 BUCKLAND ABBEY
Map ref 4866

Buckland Abbey was converted from a Cistercian monastery into a Tudor mansion by Sir Richard Grenville. In 1581 it was sold to Sir Francis Drake, who made it his home. Now owned by the National Trust, it is run by Plymouth City Council as a Drake and Naval Museum, with Drake's famous drum its prize exhibit.

🏛🌿 COTEHELE
Map ref 4268

Cotehele House, a National Trust property, is of medieval origin and is built of grey granite. The house contains original medieval armour, furniture and tapestry. In the grounds are a working watermill and the 15th-century Chapel on the Cliff, built by Sir Richard Edgcumbe after his escape from supporters of Richard III.

On the river can be found the Shamrock, the only surviving Tamar barge, now part of a small shipping museum on the quay.

🏛♟ CREMYLL
Map ref 4553

Cremyll is the 800-acre Mount Edgcumbe Country Park, featuring formal gardens with temples. The restored Tudor mansion house was once the home of the Earl of Mount Edgcumbe.

★ 🏠 DOBWALLS
Map ref 2166

Dobwalls Theme Park combines five adventure play areas with a miniature forest railway in the American railroad style, and has a collection of wildlife paintings and cameos by natural history artist Archibald Thorburn (1860-1935).

🏛🗙🚂 LAUNCESTON
Map ref 3384

Originally the seat of Robert of Mortain, half-brother of William the Conqueror, Launceston Castle now consists of the 13th-century keep and stone defences. Close to the keep is Lawrence House, an elegant Georgian building containing a local history museum.

Launceston's Steam Railway uses 100-year-old locomotives to haul the carriages along the 2ft wide track. Stationary engines are also demonstrated. A car and motorcycle museum contains early machine tools and items of mechanical and scientific interest.

At Trethorne Leisure Farm children can feed and touch a variety of farm animals.

🗙 ★ LYDFORD
Map ref 5084

Lydford Gorge extends for a mile of the River Lyd, in a deep wooded ravine. Here the water swirls through spectacular whirlpools and down waterfalls, the highest being the 90ft White Lady waterfall.

The nearby 12th-century keep was used as the stannary court and prison until they moved to Princetown in the last century.

🏨 🌿 MORWELLHAM QUAY
Map ref 4570

The story of this port, recorded as early as the 12th century, is told at the Quay Centre and Open Air Museum. Until the canal was built the quay was the nearest navigable point to Tavistock. Visitors can take a riverside tramway underground to a copper mine.

🏛🏠🗙 OKEHAMPTON
Map ref 5895

Okehampton Castle was one of Devon's largest and most important. Built in the 11th century, it was home to the Courtenays, Earls of Devon, until it was dismantled in the 16th century when the earl was beheaded for treason. Remains of the Norman keep and motte can still be seen, together with the 14th-century hall and chapel.

An old three-storey mill houses the Okehampton and District Museum of Dartmoor Life.

🏛🏠🗙🌿 PLYMOUTH
Map ref 4755

Plymouth has grown from three separate towns to become the biggest city in the south west, and has long been a major naval port. Since the construction of the new road toll bridge, Plymouth has been linked to Cornwall by two bridges.

Of the two, more interesting is the much smaller bridge built by Isambard Kingdom Brunel and opened by Prince Albert in 1859.

The Merchant's House Museum, a fine example of a 16th-century town house, is devoted to Plymouth's history. At the new Plymouth Dome Visitor Centre more examples of local history in 1620 are on view at Prysten House, a medieval priest's house which is reputed to be the oldest domestic building in the city.

In the City Museum and Art Gallery are collections of Plymouth porcelain, paintings, drawings and silver. Sections are also devoted to local history and archaeology and to natural history.

The names of the Pilgrim Fathers are listed at Island House close to the Mayflower Stone which marks the point of their departure for America.

🚂 PLYM VALLEY RAILWAY STEAM CENTRE
Map ref 5257

To see what is claimed to be the largest steam engine in the northern hemisphere, a Beyer Garratt No 4112 'Springbok', a visit to the Plym Valley Railway Steam Centre is a must. Also on display are various items of rolling stock, steam engines, two diesel cranes and a working diesel shunter.

🏛 SALTRAM HOUSE
Map ref 5155

Saltram House is a George II mansion with its original contents. Portraits by Sir Joshua Reynolds hang throughout the house, and an orangery adorns the garden.

🏛🌿 TAVISTOCK
Map ref 4774

Now an agricultural centre, Tavistock has variously been a medieval stannary town, a focus for the wool trade and a centre for

Steep slate cliffs surround the tiny, romantic harbour at Boscastle

copper mining. Ruins of a 10th-century Benedictine abbey can still be found by the River Tavy.

A statue of Sir Francis Drake stands in Plymouth Road.

★ WESLEY'S COTTAGE
Map ref 2180

Wesley's Cottage at Trewint is named after the founder of Methodism, John Wesley, who stayed at this 18th-century cottage on his visits to preach in Cornwall.

🏠 YELVERTON
Map ref 5268

Yelverton's unusual Paperweight Centre houses the Broughton Collection of more than 800 antique and modern glass paperweights.

DARTMOOR

Anyone who climbs one of the less accessible tors may search in vain for signs of another human being, and sense the isolation at the heart of Dartmoor

It is impossible to study a map of Dartmoor without becoming aware that here the normal trend from wilderness to domesticated usage has been reversed. Testimony to man's long occupation of the moor is everywhere – rarely is the physical evidence on which to base a view of history as clear as it is on Dartmoor. Bronze Age man found its climate more congenial than that of the

Dartmoor's fast-flowing rivers attract the dipper (Cinchus cinchus)

apparently more fertile valleys which fringe the moor, and it continued to be occupied for many centuries before, in the Middle Ages, the majority of the habitations were slowly abandoned.

Some 95,000 acres comprise the National Park (set up in 1951) and they contain the bulk of the remaining wild country in southern Britain.

The imagination of many writers has been fired when, as frequently happens, misty rain shrouds the moor and every shape is distorted into fantastical forms. Conan Doyle's powerful evocation of its barrenness, and of quaking bogs and violent death in *The Hound of the Baskervilles* catches the sense of desolation with great accuracy.

A Harsh Landscape
The quality of all landscape is governed by its underlying rocks, and granite is at the heart of Dartmoor – or rather, it is very often the exposed face of the area. Most estimates suggest that the volcanic surge which formed Land's End,

Carnmenellis, St Austell, Bodmin and Dartmoor occurred about 280 million years ago. The weatherbeaten tors which are such a distinctive feature of Dartmoor were probably created from a particularly hard form of the molten granite which thrust through softer rocks at that time. The remarkable shapes into which these great blocks have been sculpted can be seen at many places on the moor but perhaps most easily at Haytor Rocks and Round Tor. The erosion has been achieved by a combination of wind, rain and frost, while at the eastern or lowland edge of the moor the deep valleys of the Bovey, Dart and Teign demonstrate how the action of rivers can affect a landscape.

The Power of Water
The main rivers of Dartmoor radiate out from a relatively small area of peat bog in the wild northern section of the moor. Differing geological conditions lead them to acquire a variety of characteristics which contribute much to the range of scenery.

In a steep valley formed by the River West Okement above

Meldon, the newest of Dartmoor's reservoirs, is the tiny relict wood of dwarf oaks at Black Tor copse. The Taw rises near the famous letterbox at Cranmere Pool, established some 150 years ago and now a rather select goal for dedicated walkers. Like the Okement, it heads north through wild country, before leaving the moor at Sticklepath where, for a century and a half from 1814, it powered the waterwheels of the tool-making foundries belonging to the Finch family.

The Teign and the East Dart also have their headwaters near Cranmere Pool. The Teign turns east, quickly establishing itself as it runs through softer, more wooded country and settlements. Soon it runs past the foot of the bluff on which stands the dramatically sited Castle Drogo, then enters a 6-mile long stretch of valley containing hanging woodland of oak and beech, lovely at all times but magnificent in autumn. The Bovey follows a scarcely less pleasant path, its valley filled with oak and hazel and the songs of a great variety of birds.

The East and West Dart flow south-east passing the popular tourist spots like Postbridge and Two Bridges before joining at the beauty spot Dartmeet. From here the narrow gorge provides a home for a number of species of trees, from birch and alder to oak, holly and beech. Coppiced stands add variety to the scenery which gradually shades into moorland. Salmon and brown

trout breed here and most of Dartmoor's larger mammals, including the otter, are resident. Woodland species of birds are present throughout the year, hunted by their usual predators – jays, magpies and sparrowhawks.

Higher up in the West Dart is the remarkable ancient relict oakwood, Wistman's Wood. Stunted trees, seeming to grow out of gravel chippings, thrust between lichen-covered granite boulders on a slope, misshapen branches festooned by trailing ferns and mosses. Not easily reached, Wistman's is considered by many to symbolise the spirit of Dartmoor.

The Lyd is, for much of its length, the least remarkable of the rivers mentioned, but, as it leaves the moor, it produces a dramatic farewell, plunging into a narrow ravine south of Lydford. Oak, sycamore and a rich variety of flowers flourish in the humid conditions and the river fashions a series of waterfalls, including the 100ft White Lady, and the 'boiling' pot-holes like the Devil's Cauldron.

Agriculture and Wildlife
The wildlife of Dartmoor is not confined to the rivers although the archetypal water bird, the dipper, has been adopted as the emblem of the Devon Trust for

Right: *Combestone Tor, south of Dartmeet, shows typical Dartmoor scenery*
Below: *The ancient twisted oaks of Wistman's Wood, now a National Nature Reserve*

Nature Conservation. Buzzard, raven and curlew still fly over the wilder areas of the moor where pipits and skylark breed in numbers. The introduction of reservoirs at the end of the 19th century was not universally welcomed but, at well established sites like Burrator, large numbers of wildfowl now add enjoyable variety to the list of birds to be seen on the moor.

The ponies – symbol of the National Park since its foundation in 1951 – were probably introduced some 1500 years ago. Living wild as they do, they have been the subject of some controversy over recent years, often from well-meaning visitors concerned at their apparent lack of condition.

Red deer were present when Dartmoor was first a Royal Forest and later a chase. Unlike the deer of Exmoor they were deliberately hunted to extinction by farmers in the 18th century and have never returned. A more vital source of meat during hard winter months, the rabbit has flourished since its introduction by the Normans.

Plant life is limited on the high moors where cotton grass and heather dominate.

Sphagnum moss adds an intense greenness to the boggy areas; sundew and bog asphodel can be found here. Lower down, farmers are fighting a constant battle against the steady erosion of grazing land by bracken. Conifer plantations have affected the appearance of the moor in recent years, including those at Bellever Wood and Fernworthy Forest which were originally established by the Duchy of Cornwall to provide employment.

Settlement and Management

Mention of the planting of conifers leads naturally to the role of man over the centuries. Dartmoor has a remarkable number of prehistoric remains including hut circles, enclosures and standing stones. The National Trust, which maintains some 3,500 acres on the moor, protects more than 100 hut circles – the majority dating back to the Bronze Age.

The most famous of the moorland settlements is Grimspound with the remains of 24 dwellings inside a crumbling stone wall. Some of the tiny fields on Dartmoor

The ponies were probably introduced to Dartmoor about 1,500 years ago

probably date from the Bronze Age. This was the period of considerable industrial activity and farms were established across the moor to provide crops for the mining communities. Vernacular buildings such as the characteristic longhouse, survive in several settlements on and at the edges of the moor. The woollen industry flourished for centuries and small tucking mills for fulling were common beside streams.

Surface workings and later mine shafts, remains of blowing houses, engine houses with tall, rather sad, plant-hung chimneys, are all reminders of industries which survived until the last century. Water Authorities and the Forestry Commission have wrought considerable changes to the face of the moor since then while large areas of land are controlled by the Ministry of Defence.

The wild and desolate beauty of Dartmoor has many contrasts, with mountains, moors, streams and remote villages. Closer to the coast are the larger towns which rely on sailing and fishing for their livelihood, such as Dartmouth – an important harbour since Roman times

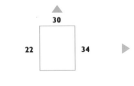

```
        ▲
        30
   ◄  22 │ 34  ►
        ▼
```

TOUR

EASTERN DARTMOOR
64 MILES

The tour begins in the county town of Devon, Exeter, leaving by the B3212 towards the Dartmoor National Park. The first village inside the park is Dunsford, with its thatched cottages and a parish church containing a striking monument to Sir Thomas Fulford.

At the crossroads with the A382 lies Moretonhampstead, formerly a market town. Granite is the main local building material, used here for the 15th-century church and the almshouses in Cross Street.

An outstanding example of Dartmoor's clapper bridges is found at Postbridge, next on the route. The village grew up in the late 18th century where the first turnpike road crossed the East Dart River on its way across Dartmoor.

The tour continues south west, turning sharp left onto the B3357 towards Poundsgate and Ashburton, passing Corndon Tor.

Ashburton, once the hub of the tin and wool trades, now relies largely on tourism. A stannary town, where ore was assayed and taxed before sale, it used water power from the River Ashburn for its fulling mills.

After Ashburton, the route turns north west deeper into the moor, with Buckland in the Moor the next village. A row of thatched cottages sits beside a deep gorge; the main village is on the hill. From Buckland Beacon, rising to 1,280ft, are spectacular views across the moor to the sea. The medieval church has an unusual clock: the letters 'my dear mother' replace the normal digits.

Continuing along the B3387, the next village was immortalised by Uncle Tom Cobley travelling to the fair at Widecombe in the Moor. The 16th-century Church House was originally a brewhouse. The

Stepcote Hill, once the medieval main road into Exeter from the west

sexton's cottage is now the National Trust information centre. A memorial inside St Pancras Church records the day in 1638 when lightning struck, killing four.

The road winds on into Haytor Vale, with the Rippon, Saddle and Haytor rocks rising up to 900ft.

At Bovey Tracey the Dartmoor National Park has an interpretation centre and offices in a lovely Georgian house called Parke. The grounds contain the Parke Rare Breeds Farm: a private collection of animals, including horses, cattle, pigs, sheep and poultry, which aims to preserve genetically pure stock.

After Bovey Tracey, the route turns south east to join the main A38 trunk road back to Exeter.

SELECTED PLACES TO VISIT

BRADLEY MANOR
Map ref 8470

Bradley Manor is a medieval house with its own chapel surrounded by woodland in the valley of the River Lemon.

BRIXHAM
Map ref 9255

Brixham's fishing history features largely in the Museum, which incorporates the National Museum of H M Coastguard. Although the town is still a busy working port, there are many holiday attractions around the Dart estuary.

BUCKFASTLEIGH
Map ref 7466

Built in Saxon times, Buckfast Abbey fell into disrepair following its dissolution in 1539. Benedictine monks have bought the site and restored it as an active monastery.

Buckfast Butterfly Farm has tropical gardens where butterflies and moths fly freely. Steam enthusiasts will enjoy the Dart Valley Railway.

DARTMOUTH
Map ref 8751

Home of the Britannia Royal Naval College, Dartmouth owes its prosperity to the sea. Protected by Dartmouth Castle, the town has depended on its import and export trade.

The Butterwalk Museum includes more than 150 ship models among its nautical exhibits. The Newcomen Memorial Engine commemorates Dartmouth's famous son, Thomas Newcomen.

EXETER
Map ref 9292

Most of Exeter's outstanding buildings date from after the Conquest, such as the Cathedral with its two Norman towers.

Rougemont Castle was built by William the Conqueror in 1068, and extended in 1774. The City Council still meets in the 14th-century Guildhall, and the city's medieval walls are in an excellent state of preservation. The Norman crypt of St Nicholas Priory has been conserved, together with its 15th-century kitchen.

Among the highlights of the Maritime Museum is the oldest working steam dredger. The Rougemont House Museum features costumes and lace, while the Royal Albert Museum includes exhibitions of art, natural history and local history.

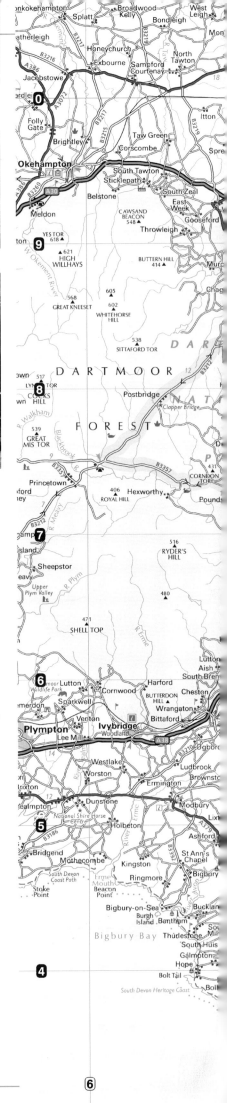

EXMOUTH
Map ref 0080

Exmouth has two miles of sandy beach and an excellent promenade. It was badly damaged in the last war but some interesting historic buildings survived.

Most unusual is A Là Ronde, a 16-sided house built in 1795.

The Country Life Museum concentrates on working exhibits.

KINGSBRIDGE
Map ref 7344

The Cookworthy Museum of Rural Life is named after the founder of the English china clay industry.

The Kingsbridge Miniature Railway carries passengers on a half-mile trip.

OVERBECKS
Map ref 7237

The six-acre garden of Overbecks contains rare plants, shrubs and trees. The Edwardian house has displays on toys, dolls, natural history and shipbuilding.

PAIGNTON
Map ref 8960

In Paignton's Zoological and Botanical Gardens, 1,200 animals live in spacious surroundings.

The Paignton and Dartmouth Railway runs from Paignton to Kingswear.

POWDERHAM
Map ref 9684

Powderham Castle, built in 1390, contains fine furniture, paintings and china. The parkland has a herd of deer and a heronry.

TOPSHAM
Map ref 9788

The entire town is designated as a conservation area. In the Strand is the Museum, whose collections centre on Topsham's history.

TORQUAY
Map ref 9164

Torquay has been a popular resort for 200 years, but Kent's Cavern shows that some 500,000 years ago prehistoric man and animals also found it congenial. Finds from the caves are displayed in Torquay Museum.

Torre Abbey – a 12th-century foundation – is now used as a museum and art gallery. Another local attraction is Aqualand.

TOTNES
Map ref 8060

Totnes Castle's superb Norman motte and bailey tower over the town. Among its fine Tudor houses are Bowden House – home of the British Photographic Museum – the Guildhall, and the Totnes Elizabethan Museum in Fore Street.

UGBROOKE
Map ref 8778

Ugbrooke, the ancestral home of the Lords Clifford of Chudleigh, is noted for its antique embroideries.

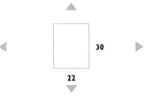

BUDE, BARNSTAPLE AND BIDEFORD

A coast of spectacular scenery stretches from the edge of Cornwall at Bude along to Devon's Hartland Point, Bideford and Combe Martin, with sheer drops, zigzag cliffs and stretches of sand dunes. The quietness of ancient market towns contrasts with the bustle of popular seaside resorts and fishing ports like Ilfracombe and Westward Ho!

```
        ▲
    ┌───────┐
◄   │       │   ►
    │  30   │
    └───────┘
       22
        ▼
```

SELECTED PLACES TO VISIT

🏛 APPLEDORE
Map ref 4630
In the fishing village of Appledore is the North Devon Maritime Museum which includes displays of steam and motor coasters, as well as a full-sized reconstruction of a local kitchen at the turn of the century.

♣ 🏛 ARLINGTON COURT
Map ref 6140
The National Trust now cares for the house, built in 1820 for the Chichester family. Sir Francis Chichester, the world-famous yachtsman, was born in the neighbouring village of Shirwell.

The house contains an intriguing medley of small *objets d'art*, including model ships, shells, pewter and furniture. In the stables is a museum of horse-drawn vehicles. Visitors can take carriage rides around the grounds.

📷🏛 BARNSTAPLE
Map ref 5533
There has been a settlement here since Saxon times, although only the mound of the Norman castle remains. In medieval times wool and pottery played an important role in the town's economy, as did trade with ocean-going ships. Today Barnstaple is still a thriving centre of local agriculture, with a twice-weekly vegetable market and a weekly cattle market.

St Anne's Chapel Museum and Old Grammar School Museum are found in a 14th-century chapel. A 17th-century schoolroom has been restored with the original school furniture, and the crypt houses a museum devoted to the history of schooling. The new Museum of North Devon was opened in 1989.

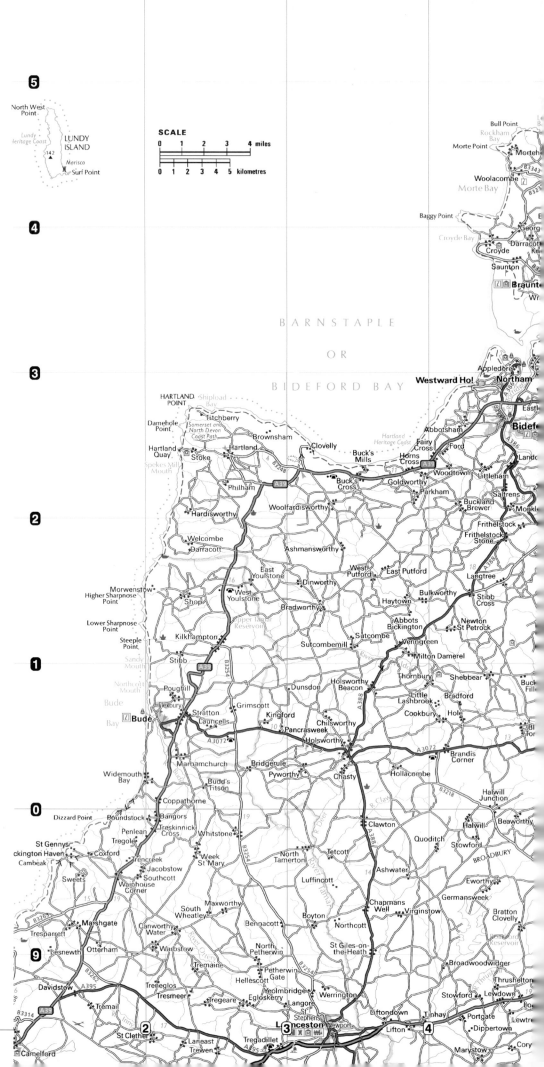

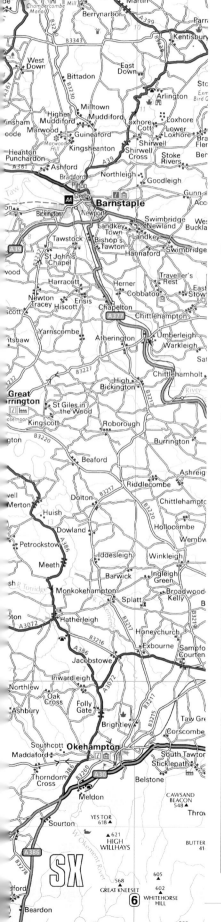

BIDEFORD
Map ref 4426

At Bideford, a magnificent 24-arched bridge spans the River Torridge. The town was an international port in Elizabethan and later times, but tourism is now more important than trade. Day trips sail to Lundy from Bideford.

A statue of Charles Kingsley on the quay at the west end of the bridge commemorates the author of *Westward Ho!* The adventure story was written in nearby Northdown House and gave its name to the neighbouring resort.

BRAUNTON
Map ref 4836

An important village since the Middle Ages, Braunton has a fine parish church dedicated to St Brannoc, whose bones are said to be buried underneath its altar. Next door is Church House with a museum on the ground floor.

To the west lie the extensive sand dunes of Braunton Burrows, a nature reserve.

BUDE
Map ref 2006

Bude, on Cornwall's Atlantic coast, has beautiful sands and is noted for its surfing. However, the sea shows another, more cruel, face in the Bude-Stratton Historical and Folk Museum, with its exhibition of numerous ships wrecked off the coast. The development of the town and its canal is traced using photographs.

Ilfracombe, whose port was important as long ago as the 14th century

CHAMBERCOMBE MANOR
Map ref 5346

One of England's oldest houses is Chambercombe Manor, dating from 1066, with Tudor additions. As well as a chapel built in 1086, a priest hole and an ancient wishing well, the house boasts a haunted room.

CHITTLEHAMPTON
Map ref 6325

The parish church is a remarkable example of local architecture, with a superb decorated west tower.

Two miles outside the village is the Cobbaton Combat Collection, featuring British and Canadian vehicles from World War II, together with other equipment and military documents.

COMBE MARTIN
Map ref 5846

Once a silver–lead mining village, Combe Martin now prospers as a delightful tourist centre.

The Bodstone Barton Working Farm and Country Park, set in an area of outstanding natural beauty, is a dairy farm dating from the 17th century. Both traditional and modern methods are used, and children will enjoy tractor and horse and cart rides, as well as the natural wildlife.

Animals such as monkeys, otters and birds of prey can also be enjoyed at the Combe Martin Wildlife Park and Monkey Sanctuary. There are nature walks through the 15-acre garden, and a large indoor model railway.

Combe Martin Motor Cycle Collection displays a fascinating collection of British motorcycles.

CROYDE
Map ref 4439

The small village of Croyde contains Gem Rock and Shell Museum, showing semi-precious stones and shells from around the world.

GREAT TORRINGTON
Map ref 4919

The ancient market town offers extensive views of the Devon countryside. Its history is recorded in the Town Hall Museum. The area was immortalised by Henry Williamson in his book, *Tarka the Otter*.

At the Dartington Crystal works, visitors can see craftsmen make beautiful lead crystal glassware.

HARTLAND
Map ref 2624

More examples of shipwrecks and smuggling can be found in the Hartland Quay Museum, which also features coastal trade, natural history and local geology.

Docton Mill is still working, more than 700 years after its construction in 1249, surrounded by seven acres of garden and woodlands.

HELE MILL
Map ref 5347

Hele Mill is a fully restored 16th-century watermill, producing wheatflakes and wholemeal flour. On show are an 18ft waterwheel and various items of mill machinery.

ILFRACOMBE
Map ref 5147

A large market town, resort and fishing port, Ilfracombe offers superb views towards both Wales and Lundy from Capstone Point.

Ilfracombe has a large museum of local exhibits, including old workshops and a brass-rubbing centre.

MARWOOD HILL
Map ref 5437

Marwood Hill Gardens have been created during the last 20 years around a fine modern house. The 20 acres contain lakes and a bog garden, as well as rare trees and shrubs.

ROSEMOOR
Map ref 5018

The Royal Horticultural Society's lovely garden at Rosemoor was begun in 1959, with a new garden area under development. In a wooded valley of five acres, it has a wide variety of ornamental shrubs.

TAPELEY PARK
Map ref 4729

Home of the Christie family of Glyndebourne, Tapeley Park has a beautiful Italian garden with rare plants and woodland walks.

WATERMOUTH CASTLE
Map ref 5548

Watermouth Castle offers demonstrations of mechanical music, a model railway, displays of cider making, a smugglers' dungeon and a cycle museum, as well as attractive gardens.

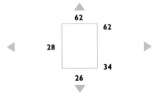

TRADITION AND SERENITY

The hills and rivers of Exmoor and its surrounding countryside, dotted with picturesque hamlets and villages, have a tranquillity still unspoilt despite the obvious attractions to visitors. In many places, traditional crafts and industries are still practised, and the welcome of the busier market towns and coastal resorts is as warm as ever.

```
        62
   62        62
28 ◄    □    ► 28
        34
        26
```

TOUR

EXMOOR AND BRENDON HILLS
77 MILES

The tour begins in the bustling holiday resort of Minehead, following the A39 south east.

Dunster's main street is dominated at one end by the folly tower built as a landmark for shipping, and the other by Dunster Castle. The 11th-century castle has been extended, notably by Anthony Salvin a century ago, and is now owned by the National Trust. Its 17th-century staircase and plaster ceilings are particularly fine, and the terraced garden contains many rare shrubs. Also in the care of

Watersmeet, where the Farley and Hoaroak Waters join the River Lyn

the Trust is the 18th-century Water Mill.

The road continues south east, but at Carhampton the tour turns towards the coast, for a splendid view west along Blue Anchor Bay. Crossing the route of the West Somerset Railway, on the itinerary next is Watchet, a flourishing port since the Middle Ages. In Saxon and Norman times, Watchet had a royal mint, and during the 19th century it was an important centre for the export of iron ore mined in the Brendon Hills. The Museum in the Market House explains the eventful history of the town since prehistoric times.

Turning inland, the route passes through Washford, with its railway museum. Beside the River Washford are the remains of Cleeve Abbey, founded by the Cistercians in the 12th century.

After joining the B3188, Monksilver is the next village, with pretty thatched cottages. In the valley is Combe Sydenham Hall, the Elizabethan manor house which was the home of Elizabetha Sydenham, second wife of Sir Francis Drake. There are waymarked walks in its extensive deer park, and a trout farm.

Just after Elworthy, the route turns right at the crossroads on to the B3224, which follows the whaleback ridge of the Brendon Hills to Wheddon Cross. The area was rich in iron ore and commercial production reached its peak in the last century, when the West Somerset Mineral Railway was built to transport the ore to the South Wales steel works. Today there is little sign of this industrial past.

A detour to the right after the hamlet of Wheddon Cross leads up to the highest point of Exmoor, Dunkery Hill, with superb views from its summit, 1,700ft above sea level, across and beyond the moor. Dunkery Beacon is part of the

national network of beacons lit to mark royal or historical events.

A few miles after Luckwell Bridge, the route turns left on to a minor road to Winsford, where no fewer than seven bridges cross the River Exe. An unusual medieval packhorse bridge consisting of massive stone slabs is found at Tarr Steps, reached through Liscombe across Winsford Hill.

After retracing the path, the tour follows the high ridge of Winsford Hill, surrounded by heather, bracken and gorse, until reaching Simonsbath – at 1,100ft the highest village on Exmoor.

From the heart of the moor, the B3223 heads north towards the coast, passing the National Trust's information centre in a 19th-century fishing lodge at Watersmeet.

The hilltop town of Lynton is linked to the fishing village of Lynmouth by a cliff railway. In 1952 a great flood swept through Lynmouth, killing 32 people. The Lyn and Exmoor Museum in Lynton records that tragic night, together with many happier moments of the history of Exmoor.

Much of the 1,500 acres of dramatic countryside around Countisbury is owned by the National Trust. The tour continues on the A39, making a short diversion into Oare, the setting for *Lorna Doone*, written by R D Blackmore whose grandfather was rector here.

Further east down a sharp incline is picturesque Porlock, from where a detour leads to Porlock Weir's little harbour. Back on the A39, the route passes close to Allerford with its double-arched packhorse bridge, and Selworthy, a picture-book hamlet.

Before returning to Minehead, a short diversion to Luccombe is worthwhile, to see another pretty Exmoor church and village.

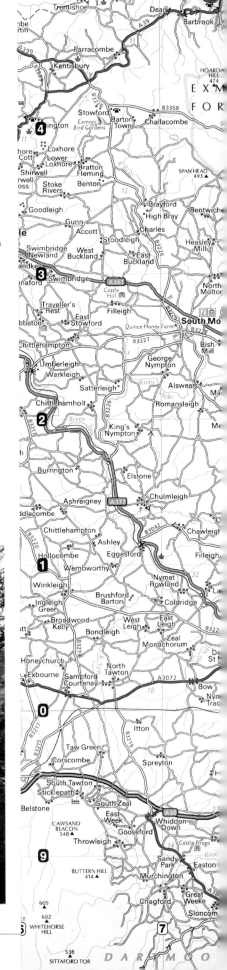

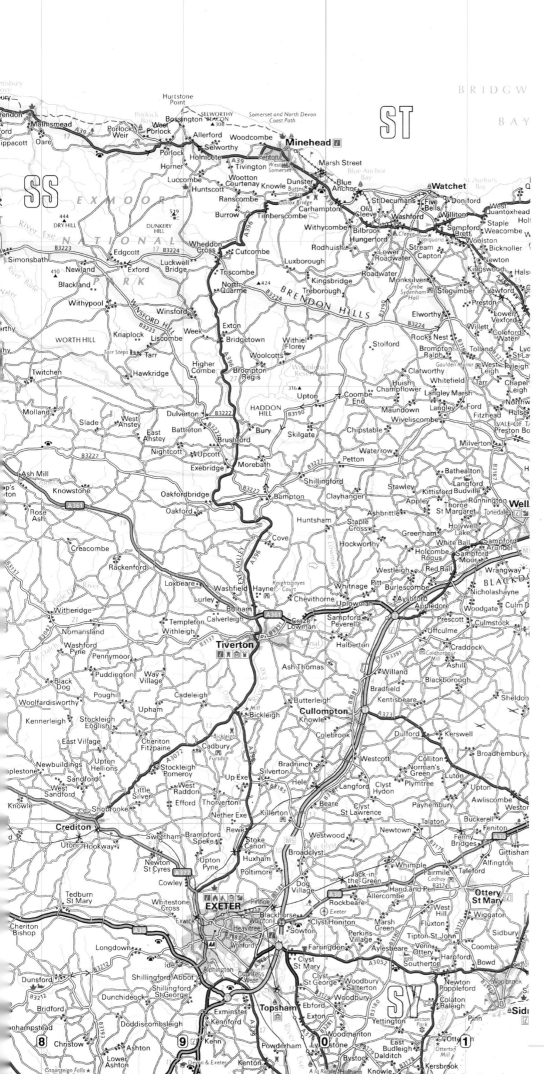

SELECTED PLACES TO VISIT

✗ ★ BICKLEIGH

Map ref 9407

Bickleigh Castle, standing in moated gardens steeped in history, has an 11th-century chapel, an Elizabethan bedroom and a Stuart farmhouse. An exhibition in the town shows the castle's connection with the *Mary Rose* and other aspects of Tudor maritime history.

At Devonshire's Centre in Bickleigh Mill are many different types of craft workshops. The mill itself is in working order. The heritage farm takes a step back in time, with rare breeds of animals reared by traditional methods, and oxen and shire horses working the land.

FURSDON HOUSE

Map ref 9204

Home of the Fursdons since 1259, the house contains a fascinating collection of family furniture, portraits and costumes.

KNIGHTSHAYES COURT

Map ref 9515

Knightshayes Court is a lovely 19th-century house on the east side of the Exe valley, north of Tiverton, with a garden featuring specimen trees and rare shrubs.

MINEHEAD

Map ref 9746

Minehead is a bustling holiday resort. The West Somerset Railway has been revived, and steam and diesel trains run on the 20-mile track to Bishops Lydeard.

The oldest part, Quay Town, is lined with fishermen's cottages.

★ QUINCE HONEY FARM

Map ref 7126

A remarkable exhibition is on show at Quince Honey Farm, the largest wild bee farm in the world. The bees are visible behind glass in their natural habitats, working undisturbed in their colony.

SOUTH MOLTON

Map ref 7125

The Museum in the Georgian Guildhall shows the variety and prosperity of South Molton's history as a centre for the wool and cider industries.

TIVERTON

Map ref 9512

Originally built in 1106, Tiverton Castle has an important collection of arms and armour from the Civil War, when it fell to General Fairfax. As well as the Campbell clock collection, it features a new world tapestry exhibition.

The market town's museum recalls the history of the lace-making industry together with agricultural machinery and relics of the Great Western Railway.

The Grand Western Canal runs trips by horse-drawn barges.

EXMOOR

Unlike Dartmoor, the land of Exmoor rises steeply from the surrounding country, giving an impression of height and a feeling of space and light

Henry Williamson called Exmoor 'the high country of the winds' and Edward Thomas referred to the 'high beacons of Exmoor', yet the highest point, Dunkery Beacon, is only 1,705ft – considerably less than much of Dartmoor. However, the land rises steeply from the surrounding country, giving an impression of greater height. Exmoor does not just attract lovers of wild country – indeed the majority of visitors probably gravitate towards spots like Selworthy, Watersmeet or the Doone Valley. For others, the less frequented valleys with their hidden streams, or the picturesque towns, are the main attraction of this small, remarkably varied, National Park.

Pressure of the Plough

Of all the parks, Exmoor has proved the most vulnerable to the changes that have occurred since it was established in 1954. Post-war agricultural policies encouraged farmers to increase productivity. Government grants were available and Exmoor farmers began to plough up stretches of moorland.

By the 1970s, more and more land was being 'improved' and the situation was causing growing concern among conservationists. From representing a third of the total acreage in 1954, the heather moorland had fallen to about a quarter. A public enquiry was set up and an agreement was reached to stop all reclamation of all moorland within specified areas. Grants would be paid in return for an agreement *not* to plough up land. This negative approach to conservation penalised bodies like the National Trust, by now, following its acquisition of the Holnicote estate, a major landowner on Exmoor. Dedicated to conservation, it was not feasible for the Trust to claim it was considering ploughing up moorland and so

Above right: A stretch of typical Exmoor heather moorland
Above: Rough grassland in the valley near Brendon
Right: Large areas of Exmoor have been reclaimed for agriculture

it did not qualify for compensatory grants.

There is a historical precedent for the reclamation of moorland for agricultural use on Exmoor. The old Royal Forest had not been much used by royalty and, following an Enclosure Act of 1818, it was bought by John Knight, a successful Shropshire ironmaster. He and his family settled at Simonsbath and, by some estimates, reclaimed 15,000 acres of moorland. The Knights developed Simonsbath from a tiny hamlet, built farms and metalled many of the roads across the moor. They laid out the pretty patchwork system of small fields enclosed by high banks and finished with beech hedging which is now accepted as 'traditional' Exmoor.

Chasing Protection

Red deer, the chosen symbol of the Park are, undoubtedly, one of the glories of Exmoor. Here – unlike Dartmoor – the hunting of deer has long been a favoured pursuit of local farmers. In recent years pressure has been applied for hunting to be banned.

Meanwhile, the subjects of the dispute remain hidden in the deep combes for much of the year. Sometimes, usually in the morning or evening, groups of hinds or stags may be seen feeding on the hills. In the autumn the stags become more visible, 'belling' their defiant challenge to competitors. More conspicuous, because they roam the uplands throughout the year, are the ponies. The Exmoor is the only genuinely wild species of pony left in Britain and is rightly protected.

Exmoor is easily accessible from north coast resorts although many visitors probably never venture inland. For others, the exploration of Doone country – R D Blackmore's fictional but plausible landscape – is an essential part of an Exmoor holiday. Hardier visitors will tackle the centre of the moor, from the Chains to Dunkery Beacon a sharp contrast to the gentle, pastoral landscape on the east of the Park.

Flora and Fauna

Exmoor consists mainly of soft sandstones and other sedimentary rocks which, when broken down, produce fertile soils, easily adapted for

The Doone Valley, in the northern part of the Park

agricultural use. The plateau is tilted towards the south and east, explaining why two major rivers, the Barle and the Exe, head for the English, and not the Bristol Channel. Those rivers which head north do so by weight of water created by the high rainfall of the area. The deep, steep-sided, wooded combes which dissect the northern coast bear tribute to the ability of water to influence landscape over a period of many centuries.

The northern and southern moors are a mixture of heathers, bilberry, gorse, grass and bracken. Although a pleasing plant, with a diversity of colour through the seasons, bracken is developing into a new threat to the heather moors. Since the early 1980s, EEC agricultural policy on 'less favoured areas' has given priority to the production of sheep at the expense of beef cattle. Apart from the threat this poses to the local 'Red Ruby' breed of Devon cattle, sheep do not eat the young bracken shoots, and the plant is steadily encroaching onto the upland moors.

Sphagnum mosses, bog asphodel and butterwort are among the plants to be found on the bogs. Purple moor grass grows in abundance on the central peaty uplands, with deer grass and common and hares tail cotton grass. Buzzards wheel in easy spirals over the moor and, in total contrast, it is sometimes possible to see the hurtling aerobatics of the smallest falcon, the merlin. The handsomely plumaged trio of stonechat, whinchat and wheatear breed on the moorland as do several species of game bird, including the black grouse. Razorbill and guillemot breed on the cliffs of the north coast.

Rivers and Combes
Most of the tiny streams, the precursers of Exmoor's great rivers, form in boggy areas like the Chains. Both the Barle and the Exe follow relatively straightforward courses south-east as they leave the area of their headwaters. Beyond Withypool the Barle begins a series of sinuous turns through deepening, heavily wooded valleys. The impressive structure of the old clapper bridge at Tarr Steps is a great attraction. As it leaves the

moor, the river slips almost shyly past lively Dulverton.

The Exe spends some time on relatively open moorland before entering a wooded valley to the south of Winsford. At Coppleham it turns south and, shadowed by the A396, makes its way through exceptionally attractive wooded scenery, leaving the Park above Exbridge.

Both the Exe and the Barle are fine salmon and trout rivers, as are several of the short rivers which head towards the Bristol Channel, thrusting, eager to reach the sea. Only the East Lyn takes a less direct course, approaching its destination at Lynmouth by flowing parallel with the coast and through the beauty-spot of Watersmeet.

Rising on the Chains near Pinkworthy Pond – another of the Knights' creations, but now fitting perfectly into the bleak landscape – the West Lyn flows through the uncompromising

Right: The chosen symbol of the National Park . . .
Below: . . . a red deer stag sporting a full set of antlers

moorland, gathering water and strength for its final burst downhill into Lynton and Lynmouth. That strength was demonstrated on one tragic night in August 1952, when, swollen by hours of rain, a wall of water some 50ft high tore down the valley, devastating everything in its path. Thirteen people died and some of the scars of that night are still visible.

Walking towards Doone country – a combination of Badgworthy and Hoccombe Combes – it is difficult to contemplate such destruction. This is typical 'combe' country, heavily wooded along the valley, the river shining between the trees, and a combination of bell heather and gorse covering the uplands.

It is the contrasts between its component parts which distinguish Exmoor. Fish and chips and cream teas, coaches grinding up Porlock Hill, solitary walkers skirting patches of bog, picture-book towns with thatched cob cottages and souvenir shops, remote communities clinging to a disappearing lifestyle. Trace the history of man's uneasy alliance with nature in the coppiced trees in ancient Horner's Wood and sense the watchful deer. Timeless, ultimately – if we remain vigilant – untamed Exmoor.

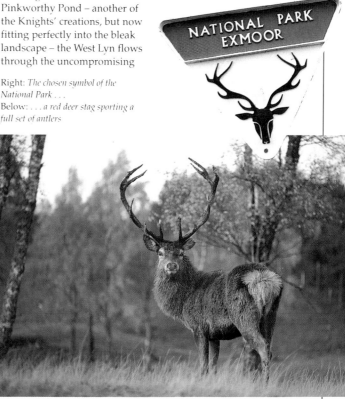

CIDER, LACE AND WOOL

Lyme Bay and its hinterland bring together the riches of east Devon, west Dorset and the southern part of Somerset. Textiles are important to the region's economy, with lace making in Honiton, wool for Axminster carpets, and glove making in Yeovil and Honiton. In many cases, sheep still graze within the cider apple orchards, for whose produce the region is justly famous.

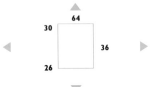

SELECTED PLACES TO VISIT

✿ ★ ABBOTSBURY
Map ref 5785

One of England's largest tithe barns can be found in Abbotsbury. It was built in the 15th century by the same order of Benedictine monks that created the Abbotsbury Swannery.

The mild mediterranean type of climate proves an ideal environment for the exotic and rare plants in Abbotsbury's 20 acres of Sub-Tropical Gardens.

☑ AXMINSTER
Map ref 2998

Axminster is where visitors can see the famous pure wool carpets being made. The museum in the old police station preserves the town's history.

✿ BARRINGTON
Map ref 3918

Barrington Court is a 16th-century Ham Hill stone house owned by the National Trust whose rooms display period and reproduction furniture. The walled gardens were laid out by Gertrude Jekyll in the 1920s, and the estate trail extends over 200 acres.

⚓ BEER
Map ref 2289

Beer has the most westerly white cliffs of the English Channel coastline – its chalk has been quarried for use in buildings such as Exeter Cathedral. The Quarry Caves, which date from Roman times, are open to the public and contain a museum.

Back in the open air are the Pecorama Pleasure Gardens, with a steam and diesel operated passenger-carrying train. Inside the gardens is a children's corner, putting green and aviary, while the main house has an exhibition of model railways.

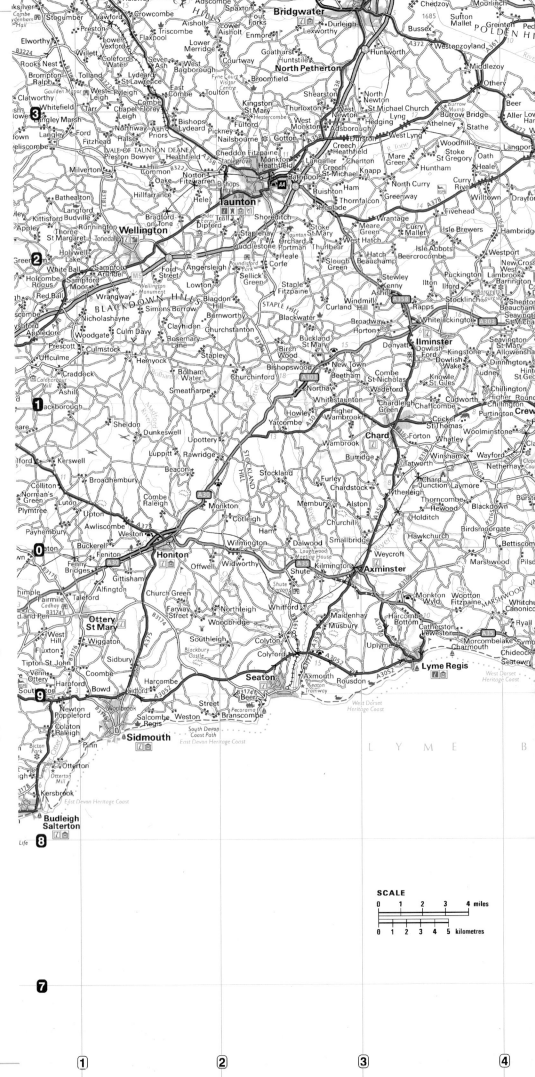

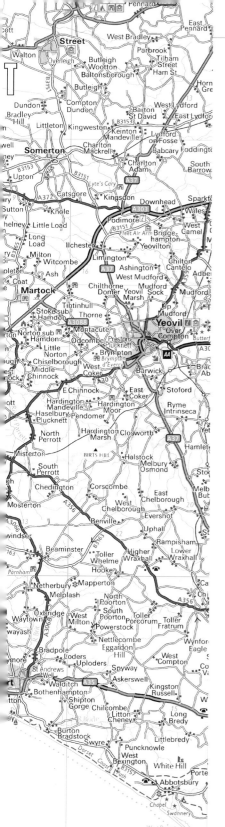

✿ BICTON PARK
Map ref 0785

Fifty acres of lovely gardens at Bicton Park, East Budleigh, include an Italian garden laid out in 1735 and the James Countryside Collection of agricultural implements. The site includes a theme hall and adventure playground.

☑🏛 BRIDPORT
Map ref 4692

Still England's main producer of cord and twines, Bridport has a museum which explains the history of this important local industry.

🏛 BRYMPTON D'EVERCY
Map ref 5115

The Tudor mansion of Brympton d'Evercy has extensive gardens and a vineyard. As well as the I Zingari Cricket Club collection, the house contains the Priest House Country Life Museum, including a distillery.

☑🏛 BUDLEIGH SALTERTON
Map ref 0682

The town's red sandstone cliffs give magnificent views over Lyme Bay. The Fairlynch Arts Centre and Museum contains some shady history in its smugglers' cellar.

★🏛 CIDER FARM
Map ref 1722

At Bradford-on-Tone traditional cider-making can be seen with its museum, press room and orchards and the results tasted at Sheppy's.

✿ CLAPTON COURT
Map ref 4106

Clapton Court Gardens is one of the most beautiful in the county, with rare plants and shrubs in 10 acres of formal and woodland settings.

🏛 COLDHARBOUR MILL
Map ref 0612

The Coldharbour Mill Working Wool Museum in an 18th-century mill at Uffculme produces knitting wool and woven cloth. The museum explains the history of the Devon wool textiles industry.

🚩 FARWAY
Map ref 1895

In a beautiful farm setting with views over the Coly Valley, Farway Countryside Park has a collection of rare breeds and other farm animals. Nature trails explore the 100-acre site and there are adventure playgrounds and animal rides.

🏛☑ FLEET AIR ARM MUSEUM
Map ref 5523

Yeovilton is well known as the home of the Fleet Air Arm Museum. The collections of more than 50 historic aircraft, together with ship and aircraft models, on show under cover, explain the development of aviation at sea since 1908. Special exhibitions concentrate on topics such as the Falklands conflict and Concorde 002 forms part of a display on passenger supersonic flight.

Coldharbour Mill, at Uffculme on the River Culm, is now a working wool museum

★✿ FYNE COURT
Map ref 2232

North of Taunton, at Broomfield, is Fyne Court, headquarters of the Somerset Trust for Nature Conservation and visitor centre for the Quantocks.

☑🏛 HONITON
Map ref 1600

Superb displays of antique and modern Honiton lace can be found in Allhallows Museum and during the summer months demonstrations of the craft take place.

☑🏛 LYME REGIS
Map ref 3492

Basking in royal patronage since Edward I sheltered in its harbour during his wars against the French, Lyme Regis has long been popular.

Local history and geology feature in the Philpot Museum, together with exhibitions of lovely old lace. Visitors can also see a team of modern embroiderers at work on The New World Tapestry, which depicts English attempts to colonise America.

✿ MAPPERTON GARDENS
Map ref 5099

These delightful terraced hillside gardens are set around a 16th- to 17th-century manor house and offer good views and walks.

🏛 MONTACUTE
Map ref 4916

Now a National Trust property, Montacute House is a beautiful late 16th-century mansion, built of Ham Hill stone. It has many Renaissance features, including contemporary plasterwork, chimneypieces and heraldic glass. In the gracious Long Gallery, Elizabethan and Jacobean portraits are on view.

★ OTTERTON MILL
Map ref 0785

Otterton Mill was mentioned in the Domesday Book and is still making wholemeal flour by water power. Other crafts can be seen in practice.

🏛 PARNHAM
Map ref 4700

Parnham is an imposing Tudor manor house with 14 acres of restored formal gardens. Parnham is now the home and workshop of John Makepeace, well-known designer and maker of furniture.

☑🏛 SIDMOUTH
Map ref 1287

As a child, Queen Victoria stayed in this then fashionable resort, now rich in Regency and early Victorian buildings. One of these elegant houses contains the local museum.

A fascinating collection can be found in the vintage Toy and Train Museum in Fields Department Store.

☑✕🏛🚩 TAUNTON
Map ref 2324

Somerset's county town, Taunton has many splendid medieval and Tudor buildings. The restored Norman castle houses both the Somerset County Museum and Somerset Military Museum. The castle acquired some notoriety as the scene of Judge Jeffreys' Bloody Assizes in 1685.

Another fine example of Gertrude Jekyll's landscape work can be seen at Hestercombe Gardens.

☑🏛 YEOVIL
Map ref 5515

Glove making has been a significant local industry for 300 years, as has quarrying for the golden Ham Hill limestone. The manufacture of helicopters now contributes to the town's prosperity. The history of the area can be traced in the refurbished Museum of South Somerset.

THE KINGDOM OF WESSEX

Although the area is rich in ancient history, the golden age of the kingdom of Wessex came in Saxon times, when it formed the centre of King Alfred's power.

Today Wessex is best known as the setting for Thomas Hardy's novels, which capture so vividly a 19th-century rural community on the brink of change.

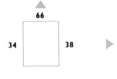

At Watercombe, the tour turns right onto the A352, and right again to Lulworth Cove. This beauty spot was once the haunt of smugglers.

The B3071 leads inland to Wool, leaving the Army firing ranges and the Purbeck Hills in the distance. By the 17th-century bridge over the River Frome is Woolbridge Manor, home of the Turberville family, immortalised in Hardy's *Tess of the D'Urbervilles*.

North from Wool the tour passes the Tank Museum at Bovington Camp. There is a special assault course for children.

While based at Bovington Camp, T E Lawrence, best known as Lawrence of Arabia, bought a cottage at Clouds Hill, now preserved by the National Trust.

From Tolpuddle six agricultural labourers who formed a trade union in 1833 were transported to Australia but, following public outcry, were later pardoned and returned to England. A century

Dorchester's statue of local author Thomas Hardy, born 3 miles away

TOUR

DORSET COAST AND COUNTRY
55 MILES

From Weymouth, the A353 hugs the coast before turning inland towards Preston's 15th-century church, and Osmington's thatched stone cottages. Above Osmington village is the huge White Horse, carved into an acre of the chalk hillside. It is generally thought to have been created in the early 1800s.

later, the Trades Union Congress built six cottages as the Tolpuddle Martyrs Memorial Museum.

On the A35 to the west is Athelhampton, where the Saxon king Athelstan had a palace. The present Athelhampton House was built for Sir William Martyn, lord mayor of London, in 1493. The house is complemented by the gardens, laid out 100 years ago.

Puddletown, with its well-preserved 15th-century church, sits astride a crossroads. The Athelhampton Chantry contains the tombs of the Martyn family and wonderful alabaster effigies.

Take the B3142, closely following the course of the River Piddle.

To the west lies Cerne Abbas, with its huge nude giant carved in the hillside, probably in Roman times. The village itself has a ruined 10th-century Benedictine abbey. Until the railway passed it by, Cerne Abbas was a centre for leather making and brewing.

Due south on the A352 is Dorchester, the county town. It has been a settlement since Roman times, but little survives of its pre-17th century history. The novelist Thomas Hardy spent most of his life in Dorchester.

Three miles east of the town near Higher Bockhampton is Hardy's Cottage, the author's birthplace.

The award-winning County Museum contains exhibitions on prehistoric and Roman history, rural crafts and natural history, as well as a reconstruction of Hardy's study.

Dorchester has many places of interest, including the Dinosaur Museum and the Military Museum, recording 300 years of regimental history. The Tutankhamun Exhibition re-creates the discovery of the Egyptian king's tomb, and the Old Crown Court houses a memorial to the Tolpuddle Martyrs, who received their sentence there.

To the south-west lies Maiden Castle, a series of enormous earthworks forming a hillfort occupied long before the Roman invasion in AD43.

The tour returns to Weymouth by the A354.

SELECTED PLACES TO VISIT

★ BUTTERFLY FARM
Map ref 5916

Set in the grounds of Compton House is Worldwide Butterflies and Lullingstone Silk Farms. A superb collection of free-flying butterflies, active breeding and hatching areas. The process of English-reared silk is shown.

KINGSTON LACY
Map ref 9701

A 17th-century house designed by Sir Roger Pratt, containing paintings by Raphael, Titian, Tintoretto, Rubens, Van Dyke, Velasquez and Murillo. The beautiful park has a herd of Red Devon cattle.

POOLE
Map ref 0190

Poole has flourished as a port and market town since the 13th century, as the exhibits in the Guildhall Museum and the Maritime Museum demonstrate. The Royal National Lifeboat Institution's Museum shows the importance of lifeboats to the maritime community.

Scalpen's Court is a medieval merchant's house with a fascinating display of household equipment.

PORTLAND
Map ref 6874

Joined to Weymouth by an isthmus is the Isle of Portland, famous for its

stone. Portland Castle, part of a chain of 16th-century forts, has been well preserved. Beside the 19th-century Pennsylvania Castle is Avice's Cottage, housing the Portland Museum.

REGIMENTAL BADGES
Map ref 0128
Visible from the A30 London–Salisbury Road, carved on the slopes of Fovant Down, is a unique series of regimental badges, started by the London Rifle Brigade.

⬚⬚⬚ SHAFTESBURY
Map ref 8623
An ancient settlement on a hill, Shaftesbury has seen its importance dwindle. The foundations of the Abbey, established by King Alfred for his daughter, have been thoroughly excavated. King Alfred's Kitchen is the town's only surviving timber-framed building.

At the top of steeply cobbled Guild Hill is the Town Museum, featuring the buttons for which Shaftesbury was once known.

⬚⬚⬚ SHERBORNE
Map ref 6316
Sherborne is renowned for its medieval buildings. Its Abbey was built in AD705, although most of the present structure dates from the 15th century. Parts of the 12th-century Old Castle remain.

❋ STOURHEAD
Map ref 7734
Stourhead Gardens were laid out between 1741 and 1780 with lakes, classical temples and exotic trees. At the edge of the estate King Alfred's Tower, a 160ft folly, offers extensive views.

⬚ ❋ STUDLAND BAY
Map ref 0382
Studland has three miles of fine sandy beaches, backed by nature reserves.

⬚ SWANAGE
Map ref 0278
The Tithe Barn Museum and Art Gallery shows how Swanage's economy once depended on Purbeck stone and marble.

⬚⬚ WEYMOUTH
Map ref 6778
Weymouth was popular with King George III, as his bathing machine in the town's Museum testifies.

Also overlooking the bay are the 350 acres of Lodmoor Country Park, including a Sealife Centre, Tropical Bird Park, Shire Horse Centre and Model Railways.

On Custom House Quay is the Diving Museum and Shipwreck Centre.

⬚⬚ WIMBORNE MINSTER
Map ref 0199
Sole local survivor of the dissolution, Wimborne's Minster has a 12th-century tower. Also a Saxon chest, a 14th-century astronomical clock and early books.

A THOUSAND YEARS OF ROYAL CONNECTIONS

Alfred, most powerful of the Saxon kings, chose Winchester as his capital. William the Conqueror chose the New Forest as his favourite hunting ground. One of the three surviving manuscripts of Magna Carta, signed by King John at Runnymede, is treasured in Salisbury Cathedral.

Today, this booming area has to preserve the best of the past against the pressures of an energy-hungry world, eager to exploit the rich reserves of oil and gas that lie beneath its soil and its sea.

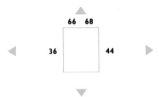

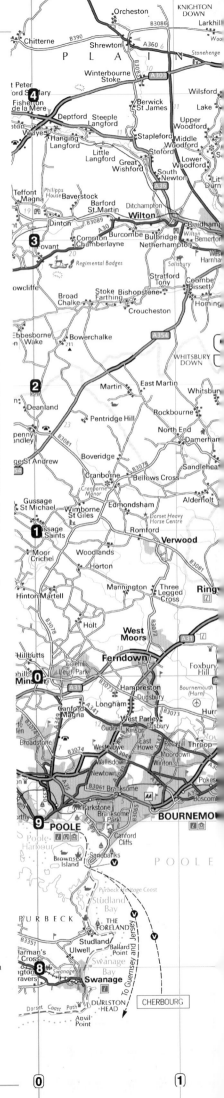

Park Pale Boundary Bank at Lyndhurst in the New Forest

TOUR

THE NEW FOREST
61 MILES

The tour begins at Lyndhurst, recognised as the capital of the New Forest with the residence of the Lord Warden of the Forest now used as the meeting place for the Court of Verderers, governors of the forest since ancient times.

A short distance along the B3056 is Beaulieu, home of the Montagus since the 14th century. The Palace House and Gardens are open to the public. The 13th-century Abbey's exhibition of monastic life and the National Motor Museum with 200 exhibits depicting the history of motoring, contrast the past and present.

Slightly off the main route is Buckler's Hard. In the 18th century this was a naval shipyard, and Nelson's *Agamemnon* was launched from the slipway. The Maritime Museum tells the story of the village.

From Beaulieu the B3054 heads towards Lymington through an area of the forest which was settled by the Romans. This is a busy port, known for yachting, and the River Lymington is sheltered by the Isle of Wight which gives the town two high tides. A car ferry connects the island with the town.

Leaving Lymington, the tour passes through Milford-on-Sea, Barton-on-Sea and New Milton, where a visit to the Sammy Miller Museum provides a fascinating insight into the history of motorcycling.

Christchurch is the next stop. On the edge of the New Forest its long open river front gives an air of tranquillity. Next to the ancient Priory Church is the Red House Museum, featuring the social and natural history of the area. It has an attractive garden with Victorian roses and herb garden.

Heading north on the B3347, the journey follows closely the course of the River Avon, the boundary between Hampshire and Dorset.

Ringwood is a medieval market town, where the Duke of Monmouth sheltered after the battle of Sedgemoor. The market town of Fordingbridge lies north of Ringwood along the A338. Its principal feature is the 15th-century bridge over the River Avon.

Next the tour meanders through some pleasant open areas of the forest, past picnic and parking areas, and through the Boldrewood ornamental drive. Drivers should enjoy the views, but with caution, for the deer and ponies can wander across the road without warning. At Boldrewood there is a Deer Sanctuary with a 19th-century plantation and aboretum and special viewing platforms from which to watch the herds of deer.

The road into Brockenhurst leads through the Rhinefield ornamental drive.

The tour returns via the A337 to Lyndhurst, where the clock of St Michael's Church is considered to be a national horological treasure. In the churchyard is the grave of Mrs Reginald Hargreaves, born Alice Liddell and immortalised as Alice by Lewis Carroll.

SELECTED PLACES TO VISIT

🏛 AMPFIELD
Map ref 4023

Hillier Gardens and Arboretum have one of the largest collections of shrubs and trees in the world. All continents are represented among the 36,000 plants on this 160-acre site.

🏛 BOURNEMOUTH
Map ref 0890

Bournemouth, a popular seaside resort, has many parks and gardens and the deep fissures in the cliffs provide interesting views.

The Big Four Railway Museum and Model Centre contains more than a thousand items of railway memorabilia.

Russell Coates Art Gallery and Museum contains paintings, silver and gold ware, oriental objects and items which belonged to Napoleon and Sir Henry Irving.

The Casa Magni Shelley Museum – named after the poet's Italian home – include notebooks, letters and poems among other exhibits.

⚔ CALSHOT
Map ref 4802

Calshot Castle is one of a number commissioned by Henry VIII as a defence against invasion by the French. The fort survives complete and has been refurbished by English Heritage.

🏛 MOTTISFONT
Map ref 3227

Mottisfont Abbey mansion was converted from a medieval monastery. Of special interest is the

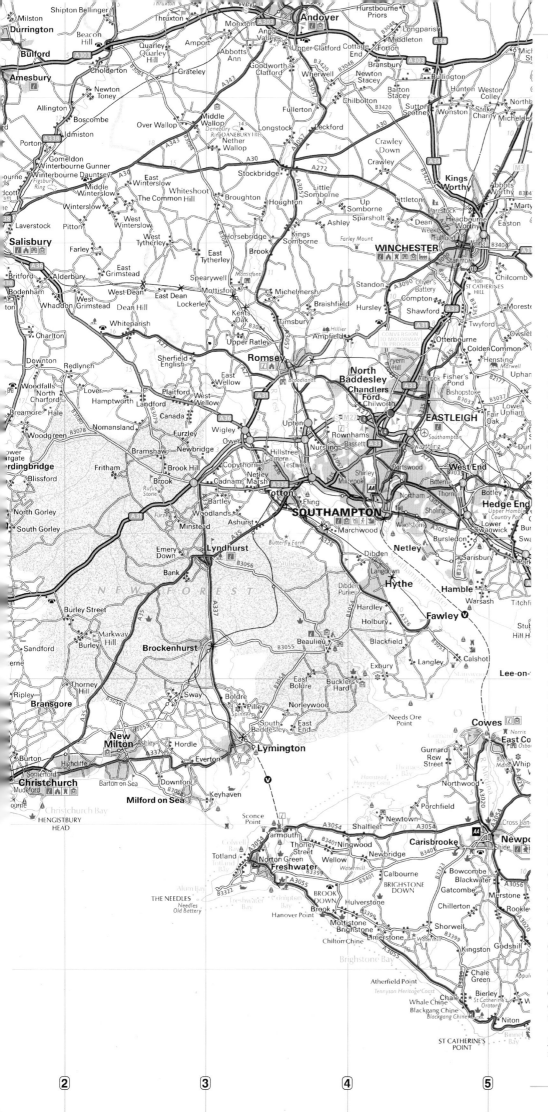

Rex Whistler painting in the drawing room. Its romantic gardens feature a superb collection of species roses.

★ OLD SARUM
Map ref 1332

Two miles to the north of Salisbury, Old Sarum was probably an Iron Age camp, and later Roman Sorbiodunum. Here the foundations of a Norman castle and cathedral city can be seen. A small museum explains the history.

ROMSEY
Map ref 3521

Romsey Abbey, founded in 907, is the burial place of Lord Mountbatten. At nearby Broadlands, the family home, an exhibition traces the lives of Lord and Lady Mountbatten.

SALISBURY
Map ref 1429

Salisbury Cathedral's 404ft spire is the tallest in England, and the nave 198ft high. In the north transept is the oldest clock in England, made in 1386 from wrought iron. It has no dial and only the hour was struck. Among the library's treasures is a manuscript copy of Magna Carta.

Mompesson House in Cathedral Close, now a National Trust property, was built in 1701.

The Salisbury and South Wiltshire Museum contains a nationally important collection of prehistoric remains, among other exhibits.

SOUTHAMPTON
Map ref 4211

Best known for its maritime importance, Southampton has much to remind visitors of its historic past.

Bargate Guildhall Museum, the medieval north gate of the city, is used for short-term displays on special themes. The Maritime Museum is housed in a 600-year-old wool warehouse, while the Tudor House Museum appropriately uses a half-timbered house of the period.

God's Tower House, a 12th-century fortified building, is a museum of archaeology from the Bronze Age to medieval times.

WINCHESTER
Map ref 4829

Winchester was the capital for early English kings and remained a royal city even when London became the national capital. Its famous cathedral was begun in 1079 for William the Conqueror on the site of an old Saxon minster.

The Great Hall is all that remains of Henry III's castle. The legendary Round Table of King Arthur hangs on the west wall of this fine medieval hall. Queen Eleanor's Garden, a recreation of a 13th-century pleasure garden, is reached through the hall.

The museums of the Royal Green Jackets and the Royal Hussars record the city's military heritage.

NEW FOREST

The New Forest represents such a broad spectrum of habitat that each visitor must make the choice as to what represents the 'real' forest

The New Forest is unique, for it includes the largest stretch of lowland heath and woodland left in Western Europe; it has played a prominent role in the history of England; and it is now a popular tourist playground, while continuing to provide a haven for an extraordinary variety of wildlife.

Yet it cannot be denied that many visitors, entering the New Forest for the first time at Cadnam and following the fast dual-carriageway of the A31 to Ringwood, may feel intense disappointment. Scrubby, barren heath is dotted with clumps of trees, largely conifers – can this be the great hunting forest of broadleaved trees and deer grazing in dappled clearings? The answer is yes, since 'forest' in the medieval sense was applied to any area

on which deer were hunted; and no, since that romantic view of the great forests never existed outside fiction!

The Royal Forest

No study of the New Forest, however brief, can ignore its role in the history of England. There is evidence of mesolithic man's occupation of the heathland and neolithic man probably began the process of creating the forest as it is now, by clearing areas of woodland for crop plantation. The thin soil was then worked to exhaustion and the early farmers moved on. As the land recovered, grazing stock were introduced. Where better soils were found, settlements would be established.

After Cnut had 'received all the kingdom of England' he took steps to bind the country together and, in 1018, he issued a number of laws, based on Anglo-Saxon concepts, which included specific mention of the forests. William the Conqueror, a lover of the hunt, imposed strict Forest Laws and extended the size of the New Forest which acquired its name during his reign, in about 1079. William's son, the unpopular William II (Rufus the Red), was killed in mysterious circumstances while hunting in the forest in 1100.

Left: The rich yellow flowers of bog asphodel, common on wet upland heath
Below: The Forest is noted for its badgers, usually seen only at dusk

Royal forests were profitable places in medieval times – judicial fines, rents from assarts (clearings made for agricultural usage), and the sale of timber: all contributing revenue. The Normans believed implicitly in imposing order and the original

A fallow deer fawn; this is the commonest species in the Forest

punishments for breaking the law were extremely harsh. Although they were not often imposed, there is evidence to suggest that the New Forest was considered to be particularly valuable and that it was the subject of heavier than usual fines, rigorously enforced.

Commoner and Verderer

Those rights the commoner did possess were fiercely protected. He could graze his stock on the heathland and if he grazed pigs he qualified for the additional rights of mast and pannage. The rights of turbary – the cutting of peat and turves for fuel – were almost more valuable. Though not a right, he could cut gorse and take dead wood – but if he cut a branch, he was guilty of waste and could be punished.

Over the centuries the rights of commoners have been eroded everywhere but in the New Forest, where commoner and verderer combined in their defence. The verderers have probably existed since the forest was created, but records of their court, the swainmote, go back only to the 14th century. At that time the Verderers' Hall was added to

the royal hunting lodge sited in Lyndhurst.

The verderers' original duties were to protect the royal game and sit in judgement on law-breakers. Over the centuries the function and power of the verderers has changed; they can now find themselves acting for the public against the Crown's present representative, the Forestry Commission. In fact, the Commission is responsible for the many excellent trails, nature walks and drives.

A Rich Harvest

The royal interest in hunting continued through the time of the Stuarts to George III – and the New Forest remained commercially important. Between the 17th and 19th centuries it supplied large quantities of timber to the navy.

The Deer Removal Act of 1851 saw a huge cull of deer – 6,000 fallow deer alone – and another heavy cull took place during World War II. The deer have continued to thrive, but at levels which the forest can support, and there was a pronounced regeneration of trees following the earlier cull. It has been estimated that, in the course of the two World Wars, some 750,000 tons of timber was removed from the forest.

Heathlands, Woodland and Wildlife

The New Forest is a comparatively flat, low lying area of sand, gravel and clay. Within the forest is the largest remaining area of dry and wet heathland in Britain.

The dry northern heaths are covered in heather, dwarf and common gorse, and bristle bent. The troublesome bracken is increasing its acreage here and in the wetter areas of heathland where cross-leaved heath predominates over heather. Bog asphodel, bog myrtle, several species of sundew and various grasses grow in the wetter areas. In both dry and wet heathlands there are a number of rare and local plants, including Hampshire purslane, coral-necklace and wild gladiolus.

The woodland is, if possible, even more excitingly diverse than the heaths. There are old, partially enclosed woodlands with a range of native species like beech and both pedunculate and sessile oak. Beneath them grow holly, hawthorn and yew, with alder indicating the wetter areas. The presence of holly in this undercover is virtually confined to the New Forest.

The 'Ancient and Ornamental' woods consist of unenclosed woodland, some of it very old, and much of the beech and oak bearing signs of pollardising – sawing the lower branches off to stop grazing stock eating new branches. In all these woods the overriding impression when walking within them is that here are the true woodlands of old England.

Finally, there are the 'Statutary Inclosures', commercially managed woods. The Boldrewood and Rhinefield Walks and Ornamental Drives, laid out by the Forestry Commission, permit the visitor to study all these types of woodland.

The fallow deer remains the commonest species in the forest. Unpopular with the royal huntsmen of the Middle Ages because they considered it drove out the other species, it has survived the savage cull of 1851 – allegedly carried out to protect the local people from the temptation to poach – and a second major cull in the 1940s. Some hundreds of roe, and a few red and sika deer are also present. Badger, fox, stoat and weasel live in the forest and the New Forest pony can be a hazard to motorists on many of the roads through the forest.

Given the range of habitat available to them, it is hardly surprising that a great number of bird species have been recorded in the forest. Threatened species like the red-backed shrike, hobby and Dartford warbler all breed on the heathland as does the nightjar. Honey buzzard, hen harrier and merlin are seasonal visitors. The combination of deciduous and coniferous trees ensures a broad spectrum of

woodland species throughout the year while the wetter areas afford the opportunity to study several species of wader.

In 1709 Daniel Defoe outlined a scheme to re-populate the forest, which he later described as 'undoubtedly good, and capable of improvement' – how times change, as 20th-century man struggles to preserve the unique character of the New Forest against improvers!

Below: *Heather in bloom on the lowland heath at Burley*
Right: *An area of spruce plantation within the Forest*

A WORLD OF DIFFERENCE

A short sea journey separates this diamond-shaped island – rich in history and spectacular views – from the mainland. Tourism has been vital to the island's economy since Victorian times, and its varied architectural legacy is delightful.

38 44

SELECTED PLACES TO VISIT

🏛 APPULDURCOMBE
Map ref 5480

At Wroxall are the remains of Appuldurcombe House, built by Sir Robert Worsley in 1710 on the site of a manor house which began as a priory. The gardens which were landscaped by Capability Brown are still beautiful.

🏛 ARRETON
Map ref 5386

Part of the south wing of Haseley Manor dates from the 14th century and 20 rooms are furnished in period style with tableaux. Demonstrations of the potter's craft take place in the studio. Craftsmen in wool, leather, clay, wood, metal and stone are seen at work in the Arreton Craft Village.

Arreton Manor, a 17th-century house, contains the National Wireless Museum.

🏛 BEMBRIDGE
Map ref 6488

In the Maritime Museum is a fascinating collection of salvage and shipwreck items, early diving equipment and ship models. One display records the discovery of H M Submarine *Swordfish*.

✶ BEMBRIDGE WINDMILL
Map ref 6387

Bembridge also has the island's only remaining windmill, built in the 17th century. The four forts off shore are the relics of Victorian defences.

★ BLACKGANG CHINE
Map ref 4876

An exhibition at the Blackgang Sawmill illustrating woodland skills has been added to the Blackgang Chine complex, which includes the Fantasy Theme Park, Fairy Castle, Nursery Rhyme Land, Dinosaur Park and the maritime and history exhibits of St Catherine's Quay.

🏛🐾 BRADING
Map ref 6087

The Osborn-Smith Wax Museum is set in the ancient rectory mansion, partly dating from 1066. Its chamber of horrors with instruments of torture will send shivers up the spine. Its neighbour is the Osborn-Smith Animal World collection of preserved animals, birds and reptiles. The Lilliput Doll and Toy Museum has more than 1,000 exhibits, and a dolls' hospital.

Morton Manor, originally 13th-century but rebuilt in 1680, features 18th- and 19th-century furniture. The splendid terraced gardens include ornamental ponds, a sunken garden and a maze, and there is a wine making museum and vineyard.

✶🌿 CARISBROOKE
Map ref 4888

The old capital of the island houses the Isle of Wight Museum in a 12th-century Norman castle. Its ramparts offer some of the most splendid views of the island. A well 161ft deep, now operated by donkeys, was once worked by prisoners. King Charles I and his children, Henry and Elizabeth, were Carisbrooke Castle's most famous prisoners.

🏛📷✶ COWES
Map ref 4995

Cowes is the yachting capital, especially during Cowes week in August.

Norris Castle, built by Henry VIII, is the home of the Royal Yacht Squadron. Its 22 brass guns are ever ready to start races and fire royal salutes. Among the Maritime Museum's exhibits is the Duke of Edinburgh's *Flying Fifteen*, designed by Uffa Fox.

⚑ FLAMINGO PARK
Map ref 6191

Many hundreds of tame waterfowl which will feed from the hand can be seen at the Flamingo Park water gardens. There is also a tropical house where exotic species fly.

FRESHWATER
Map ref 3487

When Alfred Tennyson bought Faringdon – now an hotel – the area became popular with artists and intellectuals of the time. Since then hotels and roads have been built around the old village. On nearby Tennyson Down a monument commemorates the poet, who walked along here every day.

🏛 GODSHILL
Map ref 5281

A picturesque village with thatched cottages and a 15th-century church, Godshill has a tourist centre in a former blacksmith's forge. Its garden, shaped like the island, has aviaries and a herb garden. The Natural History Centre includes a tropical aquarium, as well as displays of shells, fossils, precious and semi-precious stones and minerals. Replicas of the Crown Jewels and examples of the Princess of Wales's jewellery are on show.

🚂 ISLE OF WIGHT STEAM RAILWAY
Map ref 5589

The Isle of Wight Steam Railway at Havenstreet runs for 1¼ miles. Locomotives in operation, dating from the 1870s, run in Southern Railway livery.

🏛🚗 NEWPORT
Map ref 4989

At the head of the River Medina, Newport is now the capital of the island. Several mosaics and well-preserved baths can be seen at an excavated Roman villa, built around 200 and discovered in 1926.

At Wootton's Butterfly World and

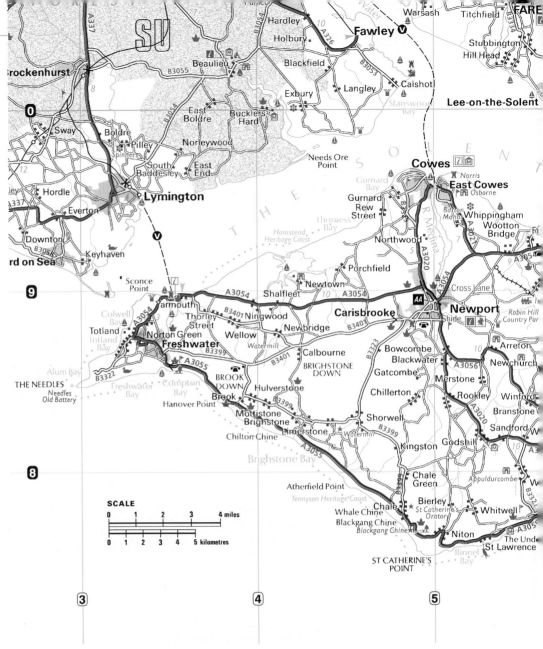

SCALE

0   1   2   3   4 miles

0 1 2 3 4 5 kilometres

makes full use of the natural surroundings.

 ROBIN HILL COUNTRY PARK
Map ref 5287

At Robin Hill Adventure and Zoological Park more than 100 species of wildlife live in 88 acres of woodland and down. A walk-through enclosure, colonies of monkeys, water gardens and a tropical jungle house are other attractions. For the active there are grass sledges, a commando-style assault course and a nature trail.

RYDE
Map ref 5992

Ryde pier – $^1/_2$ mile long – was built in 1813, and the electric railway which links Ryde to Shanklin was built in 1880. This electric train was one of the first in the world.

SANDOWN
Map ref 5984

The Museum of Isle of Wight Geology is housed in Sandown library. Maps and models interpret some of the 5,000 fossils which have been found all over the island. In

the Isle of Wight Zoo on the seafront are rare and endangered animals, birds and reptiles.

SHANKLIN
Map ref 5881

Shanklin Chine is a natural deep winding gorge, home of rare flora and fauna and has a spectacular 45ft waterfall. A Heritage Centre depicts life in Victorian Shanklin.

THE NEEDLES AND ALUM BAY
Map ref 2984

The lookout position of the Needles Old Battery is a former Palmerston Port built to deter French invasion. On the parade ground at the Old Battery two original gun barrels, weighing 12 tons, are on view, and in the powder magazine an exhibition explains the history of the headland.

Spectacular views of the Needles Rock and Lighthouse can be appreciated from the modern chairlift at the Needles Pleasure Park in Alum Bay; the multi-coloured sandstone cliffs of Alum Bay were formed about 50 million years ago.

A second fort, a short distance inland, has been restored and the

Golden Hill Fort and Craft Centre now houses a military museum and centre for some 30 different crafts.

VENTNOR
Map ref 5677

The Botanic Gardens provide a colourful setting for plants from around the world. Hidden underground in the gardens is the Museum of the History of Smuggling.

In walk-through aviaries and around the ornamental lake, exotic birds can be seen at the Tropical Bird Park in nearby St Lawrence.

YARMOUTH
Map ref 3589

Yarmouth Castle was built in the mid-16th century using the latest technology in military engineering. An exhibition of coastal defences is now housed in the Gunners' Lodgings.

At Sconce Point to the east is Fort Victoria Country Park. Built in the 19th century to protect the western approaches to Portsmouth, the fort has an aquarium of marine life.

Nunwell House, Brading, whose lovely rooms include one used by Charles I

Fountain World, hundreds of butterflies fly in exotic surroundings, while fountains play in Italian and Japanese gardens.

NUNWELL HOUSE
Map ref 5987

The remains of a Roman villa with pavements can be seen at Yarbridge.

Nunwell House is an impressive country house in a beautiful garden setting. Five centuries of island history can be seen in its collection of family militaria and the Home Guard Museum.

OSBORNE HOUSE
Map ref 5195

Osborne House in East Cowes, where Queen Victoria died in 1901, was the monarch's favourite holiday home. Designed in the style of an Italian villa by Prince Albert and Thomas Cubitt, the state and private apartments are furnished as they were in her time. The Swiss Chalet, a play house for the royal children, contains the Queen's writing table and porcelain collection. Planted in the extensive grounds are every kind of English tree. Prince Albert personally supervised the landscaping which

The largely rural area of peace and tranquillity to the north, between the Meon Valley and the South Downs, contrasts sharply with the coastal cities of Portsmouth, with its great naval traditions and Chichester, with its bias towards the arts.

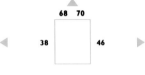

68 70

◄ 38 46 ►

SELECTED PLACES TO VISIT

🏛 ALTON
Map ref 7139

A curved high street leads to Alton's small market square. The Curtis Museum, named after the 18th-century botanist William Curtis, contains the Roman Cup of Selborne, the Alton Buckle and displays of Victorian dolls and the local beer brewing industry. Opposite the museum is the Allen Gallery with English and oriental china from the 14th century and a collection of silver, which includes the famous Tichborne spoons made in 1592.

🏛 BOHUNT MANOR
Map ref 8331

Bohunt Manor, owned by the World Wide Fund for Nature, is a pleasant woodland park with a water garden, lakeside walk, roses and herbaceous borders. More than 40 species of ornamental ducks, geese, cranes and waterfowl can be seen. Unusual trees and shrubs include a Judas tree, a handkerchief tree and one of the tallest tulip trees in the south.

The Hollycombe Steam Collection's steam-driven equipment includes a 2ft-gauge railway running through woodland to give spectacular views of the South Downs.

🏛🏛 CHICHESTER
Map ref 8604

Chichester is both the county town of West Sussex and a cathedral city. The Cathedral houses the shrine to St Richard of Chichester who died in 1253. With its romanesque stone carvings, paintings by Sutherland and Fiebusch, window by Chagall, tapestry by Piper and monuments by Flaxman, there is a wealth of beauty to be absorbed.

The District and Guildhall Museums have displays of local history and archaeological finds. The Pallant House Gallery is a restored Queen Anne town house

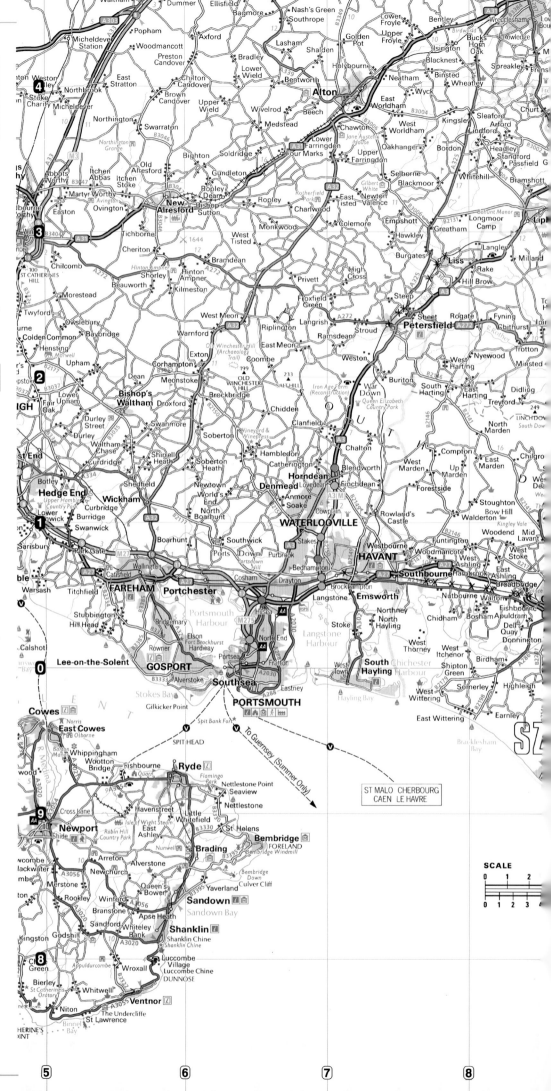

Nelson's flagship, HMS Victory, *now rests at Portsmouth's Naval Base*

containing period furniture, paintings, drawings, prints and sculpture, a collection of Bow porcelain and 18th-century English drinking glasses and enamels.

🏛 FAREHAM
Map ref 5806

Fareham Museum, opened in 1990 in Westbury Manor, an elegant Georgian building in the town centre, features topics as varied as the strawberry industry, cinemas, monasteries and shops, highlighted by life-size sculpted human figures.

🏛 FISHBOURNE
Map ref 8305

The remains of the north wing of Fishbourne's Roman palace were discovered in 1960. The palace has numerous 1st-century mosaic pavements, a replica Roman dining-room, display of Roman farming methods and a garden restored to its original design.

🏛 GOODWOOD
Map ref 8811

Goodwood House, built in the late 18th century, has superb collections of tapestries, furniture, paintings and porcelain. The International Dressage Centre hosts major equestrian events and nearby is the 'Glorious Goodwood' racecourse.

🏛 GOSPORT
Map ref 6199

In Gosport the naval history of this part of the coast can be found in the

Royal Navy Submarine Museum. The attractions here include guided tours through HMS *Alliance* and *Holland I*, the Royal Navy's first submarine, salvaged after 69 years.

🏛 HAVANT
Map ref 7106

Havant and Hayling Island lie between and to the north of Chichester Harbour, designated as an area of Outstanding Natural Beauty, and Langstone Harbour, Havant's medieval port. The port has picturesque waterside inns and the Langstone Mill.

Havant Museum is known for the Vokes Collection of firearms, which includes Buffalo Bill's Winchester rifle. It also has a new local history gallery.

The Sir George Staunton Country Park is a 19th-century country estate with an ornamental farm, where visitors can see and feed rare breeds of domestic animals.

★ IRON AGE FARM
Map ref 7118

On the A3, south of Petersfield is the Butser Ancient Farm reconstruction of an Iron Age farmstead complete with its animals, crops and buildings.

🏛 JANE AUSTEN'S HOUSE
Map ref 7037

The modest 17th-century home of Jane Austen is now a museum in Chawton's main street. Jane Austen spent 12 years here, where most of her major novels were completed. Visitors can picnic in the garden when the house is open.

🦌 MARWELL
Map ref 5022

Marwell Zoological Park is one of the largest zoos in Britain covering over 100 acres. A breeding centre for endangered species, the zoo enables such animals to be reintroduced to their natural habitats. Marwell's animals include big cats such as Asian lions, Siberian tigers, snow leopards and cheetahs, as well as giraffes, monkeys, camels and rhinoceroses.

🚂 NEW ALRESFORD
Map ref 5832

New Alresford Station is the home of the Mid-Hants Railway Watercress Line, where 10 miles of track takes restored steam trains to Alton. At Ropley station a visit to the engine sheds will reveal how enthusiasts spend many hours restoring steam locomotives.

🏛 ★ PORTSMOUTH AND SOUTHSEA
Map ref 6400

Portsmouth and Southsea form an 'island' rich in naval history. In the Portsmouth Naval Base is Nelson's famous flagship, HMS *Victory*. Nearby is the first iron-hulled armoured warship, HMS *Warrior*, berthed at a special jetty. Henry VIII's flagship, the *Mary Rose*, is one of the best known exhibits since it was recovered from the mud in the Solent in 1982.

The Royal Naval Museum alongside HMS *Victory* contains displays from the ship and also tells of the Navy in the present day.

Outside the Naval Base is the D-Day Museum, built to record the 40th anniversary of the Normandy landings. The 83-metre Overlord Embroidery – a present-day Bayeux Tapestry – records the planning and the invasion known as Operation Overlord.

In Eastney Barracks is the Royal Marines Museum.

Other places of interest include Charles Dickens' Birthplace and Museum, and the City Museum and Art Gallery. Portsmouth also has the Cumberland House Natural Science Museum and Butterfly House containing a pair of Boulton and Watt beam engines and reciprocal pumps.

In other parts of the area can be seen forts built at different periods of history. Fort Widley and Spitbank Fort were built in the 1860s against the threat of French invasion. Southsea Castle and Museum, originally built by Henry VIII as part of the coastal defences, now show aspects of local naval history and archaeology.

🌲 QUEEN ELIZABETH COUNTRY PARK
Map ref 7218

To the south of Petersfield the Queen Elizabeth Country Park offers walks, picnic areas and practical demonstrations of forest and agricultural activities.

Close enough to London to attract the commuter, the lovely towns and villages of Surrey and West Sussex have strongly resisted attempts to change. Wooded hills and commons, rivers and valleys make up one of the most attractive landscapes of southern England, from the downlands in the north to the busy but still elegant coastal resorts of Hove, Worthing and Bognor Regis.

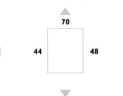

70

44   48

SELECTED PLACES TO VISIT

ARUNDEL
Map ref 0107

Set at the foot of a hill, Arundel is dominated by its famous castle. Founded in Saxon times and much extended after the Conquest, the castle withstood several sieges before being ruined during the Civil War. It was not until the late 18th century that the 10th Duke of Norfolk embarked on a complete restoration. A century later the 15th Duke added two towers.

The Baron's Hall, library and state rooms contain much superb period furniture. Portraits by Van Dyck, Gainsborough and Reynolds grace the castle walls, together with portraits of earls of Arundel and dukes of Norfolk, the ancestral owners.

At one end of the Anglican parish church is the Fitzalan Chapel, where Roman Catholic services are held. The chapel reflects the family's Catholic heritage.

The fascinating Arundel Toy and Military Museum features a private collection displayed in a Georgian cottage in the town centre.

The 55 acres of Arundel's Wildfowl Trust provide a sanctuary and breeding ground for more than 1,000 swans, ducks and geese. Alongside the reed beds and ponds are hides from which many wild birds can be observed. Many others will feed from visitors' hands.

BOGNOR REGIS
Map ref 9399

Bognor achieved its greatest accolade in 1928 with King George V's request, after convalescing in the resort, that Regis should be added to its title. Sandy beaches and municipal investment in leisure and arts facilities help to keep Bognor Regis a popular holiday destination.

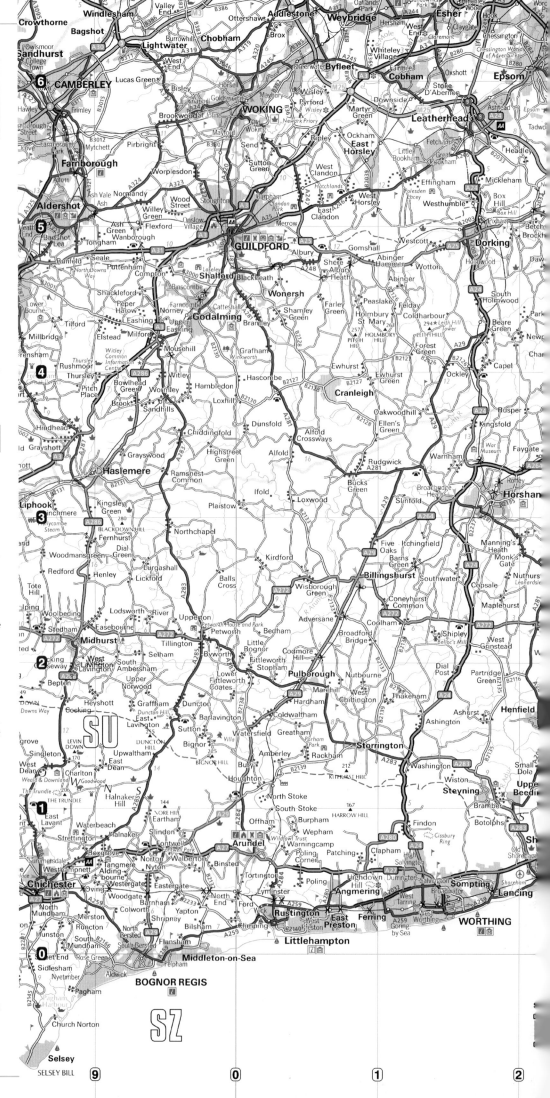

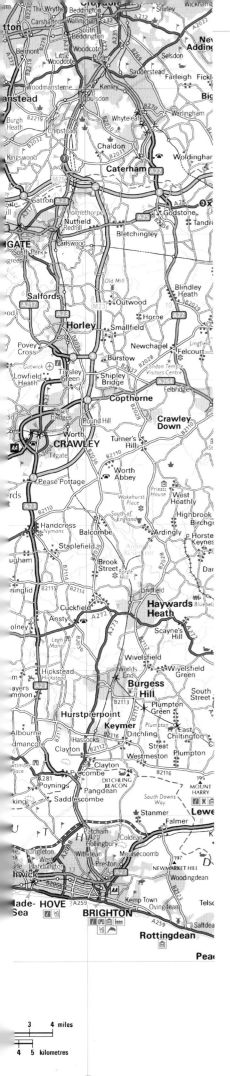

⚘ BOX HILL
Map ref 2051

Few early medieval market towns enjoy such a splendid setting as Dorking, surrounded by Box Hill and the North Downs. Like much of the common land in this part of Surrey, Box Hill is owned by the National Trust. A designated country park of some 800 acres of woods and chalk downland, it offers wonderful views to the South Downs.

🏛️🖼️🏨♨️ BRIGHTON
Map ref 3105

The most fashionable of 19th-century resorts, Brighton today has much to offer. The old town of Brighton around The Lanes is a warren of antique shops, jewellers and restaurants.

The Royal Pavilion in Brighton is now re-opening so visitors can once again enjoy the superb structure created by John Nash and its fantastic internal decorations. Close by are the Museum and Art Gallery, containing old Masters, porcelain, pottery, history, archaeology, and a display of 20th-century art.

The Booth Museum of Natural History features birds, butterflies and the bones of a local dinosaur!

⊕ GATWICK
Map ref 2741

Public viewing galleries enable visitors to watch arrivals and departures from Gatwick Airport, now one of the busiest in Europe and second only to Heathrow in the United Kingdom.

⚲ GATWICK ZOO
Map ref 2341

At Gatwick Zoo, at Charlwood near Crawley, hundreds of animals and birds live in naturalised settings. A windmill is being restored on the 10-acre site, and there is a monkey island with spider and squirrel monkeys.

🏛️📷🖼️ GUILDFORD
Map ref 9949

Important since Saxon times, Guildford was a crossing point on the River Wey for medieval pilgrims travelling from Winchester to Canterbury.

All that remains of the 12th-century castle is the keep, 60ft high, giving a fine view over the town, and the castle ditch is now a flower garden.

The seat of the University of Surrey, Guildford has a thriving cultural life. As well as the world-famous Yvonne Arnaud Theatre, set on the banks of the Wey, an open-air theatre performs in the castle grounds during the summer. Guildford House Gallery, built in 1660, puts on art exhibitions and the Museum in Quarry Street displays local history, archaeology and needlework.

Guildford's cathedral, constructed in simplified Gothic style on a hill outside the town, was started in 1936, but not finished until 1961.

🏛️ HORSHAM
Map ref 1730

Despite large-scale development of the centre, many of the Tudor buildings around Horsham's Carfax remain. The Museum is in the Causeway, where most of the houses date from the 16th and 17th centuries. It has an extensive collection of agricultural implements, as well as replicas of a saddlery, a wheelwright's shop and a blacksmith's, plus displays of toys, costumes and archaeology. Its timber-framed house is surrounded by a walled garden.

🏠 LEGH MANOR
Map ref 2822

Legh Manor at Ansty is an excellent example of the 16th-century timber-framed houses in this area. It is surrounded by a five-acre garden laid out by Gertrude Jekyll.

★ LEITH HILL TOWER
Map ref 1343

Spectacular views can be had from the top of the 18th-century Leith Hill Tower, 1,029ft above sea level on the highest point in south-east England.

❉ LEONARDSLEE GARDENS
Map ref 2225

Near Lower Beeding is Leonardslee Gardens, featuring camellias and specimen trees on the banks of a series of 15th-century hammer ponds amid spectacular views.

🏠 LOSELEY HOUSE
Map ref 9747

An Elizabethan mansion containing contemporary furniture, fine panelling and tapestries, and home to Loseley dairy products.

To the east is 18th-century Clandon Park, which houses the museum of the Queens Royal Surrey regiment. At neighbouring East Clandon is Hatchlands, famous for its Robert Adam interiors.

❉ NYMANS GARDEN
Map ref 2629

Nymans Garden near Handcross has an outstanding worldwide collection of rare trees, shrubs and plants. The magnificent grounds contain a walled garden, sunken garden, pinetum and laurel walk.

🏠 PARHAM PARK
Map ref 0615

Near Storrington is Parham Park, a 16th-century mansion. The Great Hall and Long Gallery are of splendid proportions and the house features needlework, paintings and beautiful furniture.

🏠 PETWORTH
Map ref 9722

Petworth House, built in the 17th century by the Duke of Somerset, stands in a walled park of 2,000 acres. Among its treasures are the Carved Room, considered the finest example of Grinling Gibbons' artistry and paintings (including works by Rembrandt, Holbein, Van Dyck and Reynolds).

The town contains lovely timber-framed houses.

🏠 POLESDEN LACEY
Map ref 1352

National Trust property, Polesden Lacey is the Regency villa where George VI and Queen Elizabeth spent part of their honeymoon.

Brighton's Palace Pier, from which the Victorian Volks Railway runs

❉ REIGATE
Map ref 2550

The 18th-century windmill on Reigate Heath has been converted into a church, linked with St Mary Magdalene's in the town centre.

❉ WAKEHURST PLACE
Map ref 3331

Administered by Kew's Royal Botanic Gardens for the National Trust, Wakehurst features many rare and exotic specimens of trees and shrubs within its water gardens, winter garden, rock walk and the Loder Valley Nature Reserve.

❉ WINKWORTH
Map ref 9942

Winkworth Arboretum covers nearly 100 acres with azaleas and bluebells.

🏛️📷 WORTHING
Map ref 1403

Not only a pleasant resort but also a thriving town, Worthing boasts an excellent Museum and Art Gallery.

3 4 miles

4 5 kilometres

AROUND THE ASHDOWN FOREST

Ashdown Forest, with its acres of wild heathland, moor and woodland, is one of the few parts of England never touched by the plough. Criss-crossed by minor roads and streams and dotted with hamlets, the forest is home to sheep and deer.

To the north of the forest are the elegant Kentish towns of Tunbridge Wells and Sevenoaks; to the south are charming Sussex villages like Alfriston and the beautiful county town of Lewes.

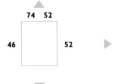

SELECTED PLACES TO VISIT

🏛 ALFRISTON
Map ref 5102

This pretty and ancient village is dominated by St Andrews' 14th-century church, often called the 'cathedral of the South Downs'.

Alfriston Clergy House (also dating from the 14th century) was the first building to be acquired by the National Trust and is open throughout the year.

⛱ 🏖 BEACHY HEAD
Map ref 5895

Some of the best views over the Channel can be obtained from Beachy Head, 536ft above the sea. The lighthouse on the rocks below was constructed in 1902.

🏛 CHARTWELL
Map ref 4551

South of Westerham is Chartwell, home to Churchill from 1924. The house is redolent with atmosphere and, as well as documents, maps and other memorabilia, Chartwell has a museum of gifts Churchill received during his career, and his many uniforms.

🐘 DRUSILLA'S ZOO
Map ref 5204

Always a favourite with children the zoo contains many breeding animals and birds, as well as a railway, adventure playground and restaurant.

📷📷🏖 EASTBOURNE
Map ref 6299

This elegant resort gained its reputation in the 19th century, when the magnificent pier was built. Eastbourne now has facilities for every taste – from the Congress Theatre for ballet, concerts and variety shows to Treasure Island: an

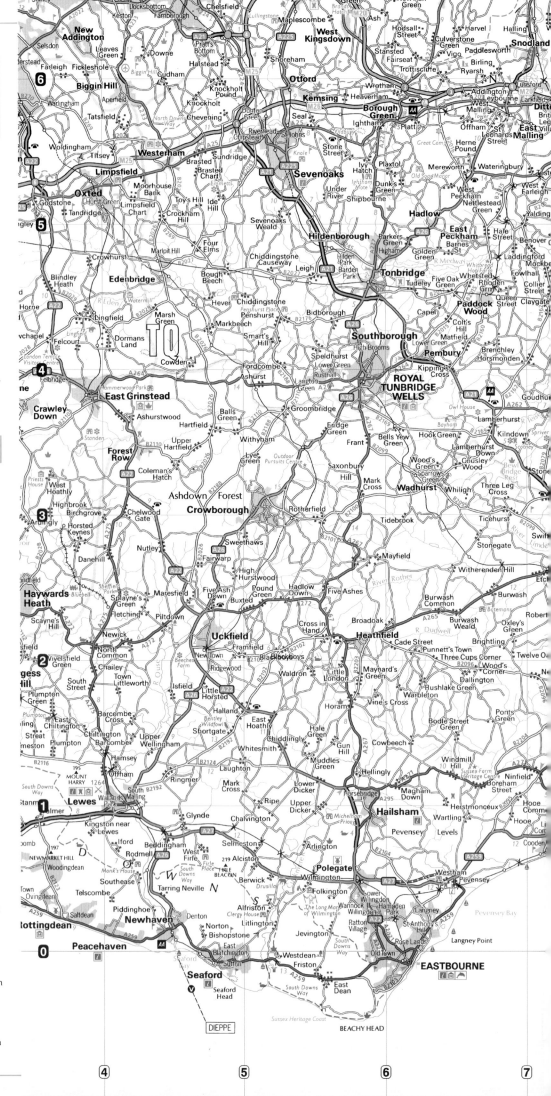

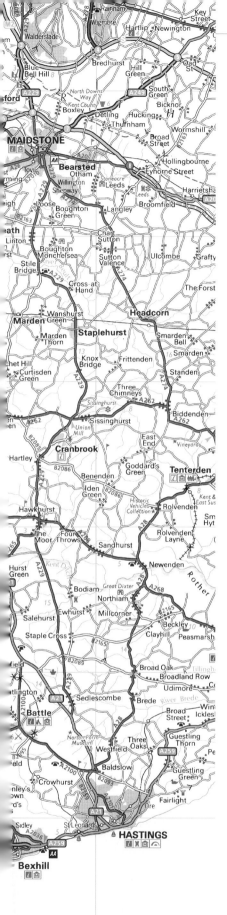

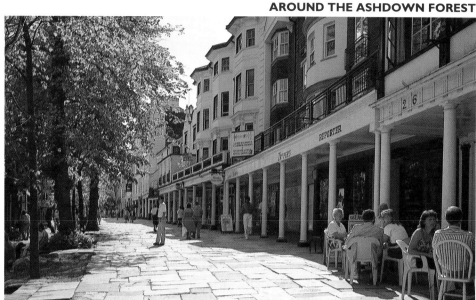

The Pantiles at Tunbridge Wells – a pretty, paved arcade dating from 1687

outdoor playground with paddling pools, galleon, swings and slides.

The Redoubt, built in 1806 to ward off a possible Napoleonic attack, now includes a museum of coastal defence, aquarium and the Blue Temple Grotto. The Wish Tower is is a martello tower, one of 74 constructed along the south coast as a protection against invasion by Napoleon. It is now open as a museum, and in the grounds stands the first permanent Lifeboat Museum, opened in 1937 in the former lifeboat station.

EAST GRINSTEAD
Map ref 3938
Although the town has expanded since its heyday as a medieval market town, the High Street retains most of its original buildings. Outstanding is Sackville College, a Jacobean almshouse set in lovely gardens. The medieval Dorset Arms is still in business, flanked by timber-framed cottages.

EMMETT'S GARDEN
Map ref 4753
In the village of Brasted is Emmett's Garden, a five-acre hillside shrub garden, currently being restored by the National Trust.

FOREST ROW
Map ref 4334
Forest Row is a bustling village on the edge of the Ashdown Forest. Forest golf course is one of the finest in southern England.

The forest itself – immortalised by A A Milne who lived in nearby Hartfield – covers 14,000 acres and consists mainly of heathland.

IGHTHAM
Map ref 5954
Ightham Mote (a National Trust property) is a beautiful medieval moated manor house. Notable features include the Jacobean fireplace and frieze, Palladian window and Chinese wallpaper in the drawing room.

KNOLE
Map ref 5354
The stately home of Knole was begun in 1456 by the Archbishop of Canterbury. Later it became home to the Sackvilles, and is now managed by the National Trust. Glorious parkland with herds of deer surround what is one of the largest houses in England.

LEWES
Map ref 4110
The county town of East Sussex has from early times held an important strategic position. Lewes Castle dates from before the Norman Conquest, and unusually has two keeps. It was acquired for the nation by the Sussex Archaeology Society in 1922. Only the front wall remains of the original Norman entrance; the Barbican was built in the 14th century.

In Barbican House, a timber-framed building, the Sussex Archaeological Society maintains a museum with remains from prehistoric, Roman and Saxon times. Another museum run by the Society is the House of Anne of Cleves in Southover High Street, containing furniture, tapestries and Sussex arts and crafts.

While Lewes has many ancient churches, St Anne's is the only one to have survived almost unaltered. Dating from the end of the 12th century, it has a barrel-shaped Norman font.

PENSHURST
Map ref 5344
Penshurst Place, birthplace of Sir Philip Sidney in 1554, is one of the country's outstanding medieval manor houses. The huge Barons' Hall dates from 1341 and the state rooms are richly furnished. A toy museum and adventure playground appeal to children.

PEVENSEY
Map ref 6504
Pevensey Castle has guarded the coastline since Roman times. Some 800 years later the Normans built a smaller fortress within the Roman walls, creating a castle within a castle. Now mostly ruined, it is cared for by the Ancient Monument Commission.

SHEFFIELD PARK AND THE BLUEBELL LINE
Map ref 4124
The Bluebell Railway boasts the largest collection of locomotives and carriages in the south of England dating from between 1865 and 1958. Steam trains run all year round between Horsted Keynes and Sheffield Park station.

Opposite is Sheffield Park Garden, a 100-acre garden with five lakes, laid out by Capability Brown and maintained by the National Trust.

TUNBRIDGE WELLS
Map ref 5839
Tunbridge Wells owes its birth to the discovery of the springs in 1606. By the end of the century the town was a flourishing spa, fashionable with royalty and dandies. Visitors to the elegant shops in the Pantiles may still taste the medicinal water.

WESTERHAM
Map ref 4454
Two famous sons are commemorated with statues in this pretty village – General James Wolfe and Sir Winston Churchill.

Quebec House, childhood home of General James Wolfe, is now a National Trust property. Four rooms are open, and the Tudor stable block houses an exhibition about the battle of Quebec.

Squerryes Court is a 17th-century manor house with beautiful grounds.

WESTHAM
Map ref 6304
Just west of Pevensey is St Mary's Church in Westham, one of the most outstanding in Sussex. Started in the 11th century, the massive structure was completed four centuries later.

WILMINGTON
Map ref 5404
An agricultural museum is housed in the remains of Wilmington Priory. The Long Man of Wilmington can be seen from here.

SUSSEX DOWNS

Anyone who walks even a few yards along the line of the ancient ridgeway can hardly fail to experience a sense of timelessness

The South Downs Way runs the length of the Sussex Downs, following the line of an ancient ridgeway. Yet, in geological terms, this is an area of very recent development. It is only 10,000 years since the ending of the last Ice Age, when much of the downland landscape was formed by the erosion of the chalk by vast amounts of meltwater. To the traveller approaching from the north the Downs present a steep, initially hostile face, hardly justifying Gilbert White's description 'that chain of majestic mountains'. Once on the Downs, a marvellous view opens out with the land sloping gently away towards the coastal plain and the sea. Included in the landscape are downland, woodland, farmland, settlements, dry valleys, slow-moving rivers and, at the eastern end, rightly famous cliffs. Beyond lie the string of seaside resorts, which, with the towns on the north side of the Downs, are carefully omitted from the Area of Outstanding Natural Beauty!

The Mutton Factory
However natural they may appear, the Sussex Downs are almost exclusively a man-made landscape. The earliest clearances of land were introduced by neolithic man and continued with increased efficiency by Bronze and Iron Age man. The normal pattern of early farming was for forest to be cleared and for crops to be sown. Once the soil was exhausted, grazing animals were introduced and land was later abandoned as the farmers moved on to new areas of forest. In most instances – the New Forest is a good example – the abandoned land quite quickly reverted to heath and woodland, but the thin soil of the eastern Downs was never allowed to recover.

When the Romans arrived crops were still being grown on the Downs but, as farming methods became more sophisticated, it was to the fertile Wealden soils that men turned for their arable needs. On the windswept downland a development was taking place, which was to last until the middle of this century. The grazing of sheep became the major use of the area by the late Middle Ages and it has been estimated that 400,000 ewes were grazing here in the 18th century. Numbers fell back later, influenced by factors like the need for crops at the time of the Napoleonic Wars, and again in 1914.

Even so, there were still relatively large flocks roaming the Downs east of the River Adur up to the outbreak of World War II. For the last 40 years increasingly intensive arable farming has changed the face of the Downs, and only 5% of the important chalk turf survives. Barley, wheat and, in recent years, the eye-catching yellow of oilseed rape, are the most common crops.

The upsurge of interest in conservation has led to suggestions that sheep – preferably the indigenous Southdown – should be re-introduced to the area. More sheep roaming the Downs would add variety and counter the problem of neglect by cropping and controlling the resultant scrub. This rather romantic concept does have some virtue, even if sheep are as artificial a means of controlling the landscape as is the plough. Furthermore, farmers use the land in a way which ensures their continued profitability. EEC policy in the 1980s did tend to encourage sheepmeat production in some 'less favoured areas' – perhaps future incentives might result in the Downs once more being termed 'the mutton factory'.

A Scarred Landscape
Other activities by man have left the downland surface covered with visual clues – not all of which we have succeeded in deciphering – in the form of man-made structures. Once farming was established, neolithic man tended to move on to other occupations, such as prospecting and mining for flint. At several sites there are the remains of mining activity. Those at Cissbury Ring are the most extensive. The earliest remains are the Stone Age earthen long barrows, a form of burial mound, and causewayed enclosures, which may have been meeting and market places for dispersed tribes. Field systems, steps or banks on the hillside fields, were thought to confirm that men were once primarily hill dwellers, but photographic evidence has demonstrated that field systems also existed in the valleys. Bronze Age tumuli or round barrows constitute the largest group of reminders of the past but Iron Age hillforts like Cissbury Ring are the most visible. Built about 250-300BC, and covering 60 acres, Cissbury is an immensely impressive link with a relatively recent past we can barely comprehend.

Woodlands and Butterflies
A link we can comprehend is the ancient downland turf, a relic of the time when the Downs were unimproved. What little remains on the steep escarpments is rich in chalk-loving flowers and butterflies. Another rare survival is the remarkable yew wood at Kingley Vale. In this chalk valley in the south-west corner of the Downs stands a marvellous tangle of great old trees, welded together to form multiple trunks, growing out of bare chalk. Already their successors are growing, as straight as the old yews are gnarled, with oak, ash and whitebeam for company on the slopes. Beside the wood – almost a forest – there are many other species, mixed with scrub and, higher up the slope, the open downland. There is a remarkable range of habitats

SUSSEX DOWNS

The flat heaths of Iping and Ambersham Commons where dry and wet heathlands support a very different range of species with an emphasis on invertebrates – 100 species of spider have been recorded here. Research has suggested that heathers have been established on the sites for approximately 8,000 years. The commons lie close to the A272 as, further east, does The Mens, just inside the boundary of the Downs area. The fascination of this wood is that it has not been intensively managed for a century and all the stages of the development of a wood can be studied here. Beech is the major species, but a mix of Wealden clays results in a range of species and a varied structure to the seven woods which form the reserve. Managed by the Sussex Trust for Nature Conservation, the wood is home to the white admiral butterfly – which adorns their insignia – and to that most beautiful of insects, the purple emperor butterfly. Standing in the woods one has the strong feeling that this is how the old native woodland must have been.

Exploration and Exploitation

At the opposite end of the Sussex Downs is Cuckmere Haven. It includes some of the most spectacular chalk coastline in the country. The downland is full of plants, including rare species of orchids, and the cliffs mark the southernmost breeding range of the fulmar.

The Sussex Downs face many external pressures which may have an influence on the landscape. Potentially the most damaging is from visitors. Much improved travel facilities – particularly by road – have led to greatly increased visitor numbers, more and more of whom are attracted to the Downs rather than – as was once the case concentrating within the resorts.

There is a welter of other problems – demands on land for housing, applications for the extraction of mineral, oil and gas. Stand on the hill beside the Adur and look toward Lancing College – see how many new roads can alter the shape of the landscape. But climb the Downs and tread the old sheepwalks; listen to the lark and you will sense that the prophets of doom are wrong – the Downs will survive.

Opposite page: A male Adonis blue; the females are usually brown

Top: View of the Devil's Dyke and the village of Fulking from the South Downs Way

Above: The silver-spotted skipper, found only on the North and South Downs and the Chilterns

Left: A dark green fritillary butterfly, one of a group named after the similarly spotted flower

within the reserve and just to list the number of species it supports would fill a page. Among the butterflies there are four blue, five fritillaries, five skippers and the white admiral; eleven species of orchid boost the numbers of the flower population; mammals, reptiles, birds and insects – all are well represented. And from the top of the Downs, a view to delight the eye.

FROM OAST TO COAST

Centuries of prosperity from natural resources are visible in the unspoilt villages and grand houses of the Weald. Its iron-rich soil, which once supported both a booming iron-foundry industry and the sheep which attracted an international woollen trade, now nourishes the hops for local oasthouses. Shipbuilding on the Medway and fishing on the Channel coast harvest the riches of the sea.

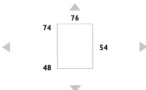

TOUR

WEALDEN TOWNS AND VILLAGES
75 MILES

Leaving Royal Tunbridge Wells on the A267, the route soon turns left onto the B2169 towards Lamberhurst. In the Teise valley lie the impressive ruins of Bayham Abbey, where parts of the medieval church and gatehouse remain.

North east of Lamberhurst is the half-timbered smugglers' haunt, Owl House, surrounded by 13 acres of gardens and lakes. Just south of Lamberhurst is the romantic landscaped garden created 150 years ago around the ruins of 14th-century Scotney Castle.

After Stonecrouch, the itinerary turns left onto the B2079, passing Bedgebury National Pinetum, 150 acres of the Forestry Commission's superb specimen conifers. A wonderful collection of historical keyboard instruments, all in playing order, is found at Finchcocks, a Georgian house near Goudhurst.

Turning right at Iden Green, the B2085 leads to Cranbrook, an important centre of the medieval weaving industry. The town's Union Mill, at 72ft, is the second highest windmill in England.

A major highlight is Sissinghurst Castle, rescued from dereliction in 1930 by writer Vita Sackville-West and her husband Sir Harold Nicolson. Together they created the Elizabethan-style garden, with its famous White Garden, planted entirely with species bearing white flowers or silver leaves. Parts of the house are open, including the 16th-century tower used by Vita Sackville-West as a study.

The charming village of Biddenden has the Baby Carriage Collection: a unique museum of 400 perambulators from the 18th century to the present, displayed in an oasthouse adjoining a moated manor house. Nearby are

Biddenden Vineyards, where the wine-making process can be seen and its products savoured.

Tenterden's high street, lined with Elizabethan and Georgian houses, is a visible record of centuries of prosperity, detailed in the local museum. For the visitor with time to spare, a trip on the Kent and East Sussex steam railway will invoke images of a bygone age.

A different type of transport can be seen at the C M Booth Collection of Historic Vehicles at Rolvenden. Outstanding are the unique collection of Morgan three-wheel cars and the only known Humber tri-car from 1904.

Further south on the A28 lies Northam, famous for the 15th-century half-timbered manor house, Great Dixter, with its delightful gardens.

A right turn will lead to picturesque Bodiam Castle, built in 1385 against a French invasion which never materialised. The imposing moated castle looks complete from the outside, despite being uninhabited since the 17th century, but the interior can be explored by visitors.

Continuing west to the A21, the Robertsbridge Aeronautical Museum displays engines and other aircraft components from World War I. At Hurst Green, the route turns left on to the A265, towards Burwash. Most renowned of Burwash's old ironmasters' houses is Bateman's, a 17th-century building where Rudyard Kipling lived. His rooms and cluttered study have been left unchanged, and his 1928 Rolls Royce is on show.

The old village of Heathfield has a plaque commemorating the death of 15th-century rebel leader Jack Cade, while the Gibraltar Tower honours General George Elliot who defended the Rock in the 1779-83 siege.

The harbour at Rye, on the Rother

Finally, the tour takes the A267 north back to Tunbridge Wells, through the attractive Sussex villages of Cross in Hand, Five Ashes and Mayfield.

SELECTED PLACES TO VISIT

BATTLE
Map ref 7415

Scene of the victory of William over King Harold II in 1066, Battle is a peaceful town today. Just ruins remain of the church built by the Conqueror. A diorama of the battle and a reproduction of the Bayeux Tapestry in the Historical Society's Museum tell the story. The museum contains a collection on the Sussex iron industry.

In the High Street, Buckleys Museum of Shops has an unusual exhibition of grocers, chemists, drapers and sweetshops.

BEXHILL
Map ref 7407

With its five-mile sea frontage, Bexhill has been a popular resort for 100 years, and the De La Warr Pavilion acknowledges the local peer who developed its tourist potential. The Museum of Costume and Social History contains costumes, toys and household appliances.

CHATHAM
Map ref 7567

Many famous ships, including Nelson's *Victory*, were built in Chatham dockyard, established by Henry VIII and now a working museum.

The only surviving Napoleonic fortress in the country, Fort Amherst is currently undergoing extensive restoration, and a visitors' centre has been opened.

FROM OAST TO COAST

⬛✕🖼️⌂ HASTINGS
Map ref 8209

Although the battle which bears its name actually took place six miles inland, the magnificent embroidery commemorating 900 years of history since 1066 is displayed in Hastings Town Hall. Excavations have uncovered much of the structure of the Conqueror's ruined cliff-top castle.

The Fishermen's Museum exhibits the *Enterprise*, last of Hastings' sailing luggers, while the Museum of Local History records archaeology and the history of the fishing industry and the Cinque Ports, of which Hastings was one.

✕❋ LEEDS CASTLE
Map ref 8353

In recent years the meeting place of heads of state, the ninth-century castle stands on two islands in the middle of a lake. Leeds Castle was converted from a stronghold to a palace by Henry VIII.

🖼️🖼️ MAIDSTONE
Map ref 7555

Kent's county town and centre of the hop-growing industry, Maidstone combines the splendour of the 14th-century Archbishop's Palace with factories and modern civic architecture.

The Maidstone Museum and Art Gallery has collections of paintings, furniture and industrial artefacts. It also houses the Museum of the Queen's Own Royal West Kent regiment.

Close to the River Medway, the role of agriculture in the county's economic development is traced in the Cobtree Museum of Kent life.

🖼️✕🖼️ ROCHESTER
Map ref 7468

Rochester is the second oldest see in England after Canterbury, although the present Cathedral dates only from the 11th century.

From the four-storeyed Norman keep – the tallest in England and the sole survivor of Rochester Castle's demolition in 1610 – are extensive views across the city.

The Guildhall Museum features local history.

🖼️🏛️🖼️ RYE
Map ref 9220

Also a Cinque Port, Rye's harbour silted up in the 16th century, and it came to rely on smuggling.

Ypres Tower, a 13th-century fort later used as a prison, now houses a museum covering the Cinque Ports, shipbuilding and smuggling and the pottery industry which still flourishes.

The walled garden, hall and ground floor of Lamb House, home to American novelist Henry James, are open twice a week during the summer.

🏛️ SAILING BARGE MUSEUM
Map ref 9164

More maritime history is preserved in the Dolphin Yard Sailing Barge Museum at Sittingbourne.

With its miles of coastline, fortified by castles and martello towers, Kent has variously repelled and welcomed contact with Europe for hundreds of years. Pilgrims have flocked to Canterbury for almost a millenium. Kent already has three major ferry ports in Dover, Folkestone and Ramsgate, and the imminent completion of the Channel Tunnel can only enhance those links.

78

52

SELECTED PLACES TO VISIT

BRAMBLES
Map ref 1764

Twenty acres of woodland form Brambles Wildlife Park, where deer, foxes and owls may be seen. As well as rare breeds of farm animals, the park features a frog and toad garden and fish ponds.

BROADSTAIRS
Map ref 3967

Bleak House, where Charles Dickens planned the novel of the same name and wrote *David Copperfield*, is now a museum, including not only mementoes of the author, but items smuggled or salvaged from wrecks on the Goodwin Sands.

Dickens' possessions are also found in the Dickens House Museum, model for Betsy Trotwood's house in *David Copperfield*.

The Crampton Tower Museum has exhibits connected with Thomas Russell Crampton, the Victorian engineer, and local railways.

CANTERBURY
Map ref 1457

Canterbury Cathedral, founded by St Augustine in 597, is the mother church of the Anglican communion. The crypt is the oldest remaining part, dating from 1100. The cathedral is the last resting place of King Henry IV and Edward the Black Prince, as well as of Thomas à Becket, murdered in 1170 within its walls.

The ruins of St Augustine's Abbey stand on the site first consecrated by a Norman round church. A museum explains its history.

The Royal Museum contains Anglo-Saxon jewellery, porcelain and glass. In the same building, the Art Gallery includes work by local artist Thomas Sidney Cooper, RA, and the Buffs Regimental Museum.

Canterbury Heritage, set in a 14th-century hospice beside the

The ornate 19th-century Royal Museum and Art Gallery in Canterbury's High Street

River Stour starts with the Roman town and continues to the present day: among the reconstructions are a medieval street and the city during the Civil War.

Modern-day visitors can join the pilgrims of Chaucer's *Canterbury Tales* in the shell of St Margaret's Church for an audio-visual experience which transports them from London's Tabard Inn to the shrine of Thomas à Becket.

Canterbury's most famous literary son was Christopher Marlowe, contemporary of Shakespeare and author of *Dr Faustus* and the *Jew of Malta*, among others. A statue stands in Dane John Gardens, and the city's theatre is named after him.

Three miles outside Canterbury is Blean Bird Park.

DEAL
Map ref 3752
Built by Henry VIII against possible French invasion, Deal Castle still has cannons on the battlements. A museum of prehistoric, Roman and Saxon items tells the history of the town, a story continued in the local library's splendid Deal Archaeological Collection.

A Maritime and Local History Museum preserves seafaring traditions. The Time-Ball Tower is a unique museum of maritime communications in a 19th-century semaphore tower.

DOVER
Map ref 3141
A busy port, Dover has been in the forefront of British history for more than two centuries.

The Roman Painted House. dating from the 2nd century AD, has the best preserved and oldest Roman wall paintings in northern Europe and an almost complete underfloor heating system.

High on the white cliffs, Dover Castle is a Norman castle with keep built on a site fortified in prehistoric times. For 1900 years a Roman lighthouse or pharos has stood beside the castle.

★ DYMCHURCH
Map ref 1029
During the summer, you can visit Dymchurch's Martello Tower, one of a series of round towers built to defend against Napoleonic invasion.

FAVERSHAM
Map ref 0161
More than 50 listed buildings bear witness to the importance of Faversham since medieval times. The Fleur de Lis Heritage Centre vividly presents the town's history in what was originally a 16th-century coaching inn. Finds from the Roman and Anglo-Saxon settlements are preserved in Maison Dieu at Ospringe.

FOLKESTONE
Map ref 2336
As well as being an important ferry port, Folkestone is now the site for the entrance of the Channel Tunnel. The Eurotunnel Exhibition Centre explains the massive project through model layouts, a full-size section of a proposed train and a viewing tower.

The history of the area is recorded in Folkestone's museum.

GODINTON PARK
Map ref 9844
Godinton Park, west of Ashford, is a mainly Jacobean house with fine carving and panelling, furniture and portraits. The formal 18th-century gardens feature topiary work.

HERNE BAY
Map ref 1768
Boasting the second longest pier in England, Herne Bay has been a popular resort since Victorian times.

★ MARGATE
Map ref 3571
Margate, where the bathing machine was invented, is still popular with holidaymakers.

The Tudor House in King Street houses a museum of local history.

The 14th-century chapel of nearby Salmestone Grange contains beautiful 20th-century windows by Australian artist John Trinick.

NEW ROMNEY
Map ref 0624
The world's smallest public railway, the Romney, Hythe and Dymchurch Railway has locomotives of one-third normal size. It runs from Hythe to Dungeness lighthouse through Dymchurch and New Romney, where there is a large indoor railway exhibition.

RAMSGATE
Map ref 3865
Ramsgate's sandy beaches have made it an attractive resort for more than 150 years. Some of that history is captured in the town's museum.

RECULVER
Map ref 2269
At Reculver, east of Herne Bay, are the ruined walls of the 3rd-century Roman shore fort. The 7th-century Anglo-Saxon church with 12th-century Norman extensions including two huge towers, remains.

SANDWICH
Map ref 3358
An original Cinque Port cut off from the sea by silt, Sandwich is surrounded by two miles of ramparts which follow the line of the old town walls.

Just outside Sandwich are the ruins of the Roman fort Rutupiae, the main landing place for Caesar's troops. It was later fortified as the main fort of the Saxon shore and the massive walls still survive. A museum explains its history.

WALMER CASTLE
Map ref 3749
Close by the town of Deal, Walmer Castle was also built by Henry VIII. Since the 1700s the castle has been the official residence of the Lord Warden of the Cinque Ports.

WHITSTABLE
Map ref 1066
Oysters have long been the principal industry of this town. The `castle' park and greenhouses are open to the public.

ACROSS THE LANDSKER

Artist Graham Sutherland's evocative phrase encapsulates the Pembrokeshire which inspired him, just as it inspired St David to found his monastery here 14 centuries ago. The majestic and dangerous coastline, wild Prescelly Hills, and valley settlements are steeped in beauty and history.

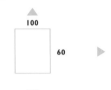

TOUR

ST DAVID'S, FISHGUARD AND PRESCELLY HILLS (MYNYDD PRESELI)
64 MILES

A scenic journey lies ahead, as the first 16 miles of the tour, from Havordfordwest to St David's, traverse 17 hills. Travelling north west on the A487, shortly before Newgale is the magnificent tower of Roch Castle, perched on a high rock.

The road meets the coast at Newgale, with its 2-mile stretch of sand and huge pebble beach, where an invisible line, the 'Landsker', separates the northern Welsh-speaking half of Dyfed from the English-speaking southern half.

The National Trust owns 1,309 acres of unspoilt coastline and 2,150 acres of commons from west of Newgale beach to St David's Head, all within the Pembrokeshire Coast National Park.

There is a National Trust shop at Solva, a picturesque fishing village where yachtsmen enjoy the safe harbour. In a disused Chapel is Solva Nectarium, where butterflies and moths from around the world are bred and can be seen at close quarters.

St David's, in size a village but a city by virtue of its cathedral, was founded by Wales's patron saint in the 6th century. The present Cathedral, almost hidden in a precinct down a long flight of steps, has Norman arches and a nave with a 15th-century carved oak roof. St David's bones are said to lie in Holy Trinity Chapel.

Across the trout steam immediately in front of the cathedral are the extensive remains of the 13th-century Bishop's Palace, with its open arcade and banqueting hall featuring a well-preserved rose window.

A mile to the north west is the lovely beach of Whitesand Bay, which is also popular for bathing and surfboarding. From here are excellent views of Ramsey Island

and the seven dangerous rocks, known as the Bishop and his Clerks. Despite its remoteness, this headland appears on the oldest known map of the world, dating from the 2nd century BC.

The highest cliffs in south Wales run along this stretch of coast; this tour proceeds parallel to the coast, still on the A487. Passing through the hilltop village of Mathry, there are superb views over fertile fields towards the Prescelly Hills.

The road meets the coast again at Goodwick, sheltering behind the great breakwater which protects Fishguard harbour – departure point for ferries to Ireland. The old town of Fishguard is a mile away, overlooking the harbour. From here the road turns sharply down to the Lower Town, where the River Gwaun emerges into the sea. The little harbour with its old pier is popular with yachts.

The A487 climbs steeply at first and then more gradually, up to Dinas, where the church now standing has replaced one engulfed by the sea. Extensive views over Newport Bay can be seen as the road descends into Newport, with its sandy estuary. Although a small town nowadays, Newport was capital of the Norman barony of Cemaes and has had a charter since 1240. Newport Castle, seat of the lords of Cemaes, was restored from ruins in the 19th century and is now a private residence.

The tour soon turns west onto the B4329, through the wild uplands of the Prescelly Hills. To the right is the great cromlech of Pentre Ifan, a burial chamber which is one of Wales's finest prehistoric monuments. Further along on the left soars the summit of Foel Cwm-

Cerwym, 1,760ft above sea level, giving views to the Wicklow Mountains in Ireland and to Dunkery Beacon, the highest point on Exmoor. To the right is Foel Eryr, `hill of the eagles', where the River Gwaun has its source. The hills, from which the famous bluestones were carried for Stonehenge, are rich in prehistoric remains.

A few miles before Haverfordwest is Scolton Manor Museum and Country Park, a Georgian mansion set in 60 acres of parkland. A fine display of the history and natural history of Pembrokeshire is found in the hall and stables, and a nature trail runs through the park. The tour then returns to Haverfordwest.

SELECTED PLACES TO VISIT

✕ ⓗ ★ CAREW
Map ref 0404

In the upper reaches of Milford Haven lies the village of Carew. Its ruined castle was first constructed by Gerald de Windsor, founder of Pembroke Castle.

Overlooking the road opposite the inn stands a 9th-century 14ft high Celtic cross, featuring characteristically intricate decoration.

ⓘ ✕ ⓖ HAVERFORDWEST
Map ref 9515

Pembrokeshire was swallowed up into the larger county of Dyfed in 1974, but local people still keep their old loyalties and nowhere more so than in Haverfordwest, Pembrokeshire's former county

Pembrokeshire's Point St John, looking towards Ramsey Island

ACROSS THE LANDSKER

town. The prosperous town has many Regency and early Victorian houses and warehouses serving as a reminder of its days as a busy port.

Towering over the market town is the Castle, built in the 12th century but deserted after the Civil War. A prison until 1820, it now houses the Museum, including military items connected with the Pembroke Yeomanry, an Art Gallery and Record Office.

Within the grounds of Picton Castle is the Graham Sutherland Art Gallery. Oil paintings, watercolours, lithographs and etchings are on display, donated by the artist who was inspired by what he described as the 'excellent strangeness' of the Pembrokeshire landscape.

🐾 MANOR HOUSE WILDLIFE AND LEISURE PARK
Map ref 0801

At St Florence is the Manor House Wildlife and Leisure Park. Set in 12 acres of wooded grounds, the wildlife includes exotic birds, reptiles and fish, as well as a pets corner and children's playground.

🏰✕🏛 PEMBROKE
Map ref 9901

On a natural fortress of limestone stands Pembroke Castle, built in the 12th century by the English and never captured by the Welsh. Birthplace of Henry VII in 1457, the castle withstood many attacks until defeated by Cromwell after a lengthy siege. It remains the second largest castle in south Wales after Caerphilly, with a splendid 12th-century round keep.

The Castle Hill Museum concentrates on preserving everyday objects used in the past three centuries. An unusual collection of Romany artefacts is found in the National Museum of Gypsy Caravans.

To the north is Pembroke Dock, home of the Royal Navy Dockyards from 1814 to 1926. As well as many naval vessels, the first royal yacht, the *Victoria and Albert*, was built here.

✕🏰🏛 TENBY
Map ref 1300

The pretty seaside town of Tenby, birthplace of artist Augustus John, has had a turbulent history since Roman times. In a ferocious attack by the Welsh in 1150, both town and Norman castle were razed to the ground. The castle was rebuilt by the Earl of Pembroke and Tenby flourished during the Tudor period, thanks to the wool industry. A disastrous siege by Cromwell started a decline from which Tenby recovered in the last century, with its development as a seaside resort and the coming of the railway. The ruins of the castle contain the Tenby Museum, and the Tudor Merchant's House on Quay Hill has early frescos.

From Tenby boat trips run to Caldey Island, home of monks since the 6th century, and noted for its seabird colonies.

PEMBROKESHIRE

The enchantment of Pembrokeshire derives from its range of habitats and, in particular, its coastline – encompassing some of the finest scenery in Britain

Welsh writers were describing Pembrokeshire as 'The Land of Magic and Enchantment' as early as the 11th century. Incorporating the smallest National Park (225 square miles), this is still a land full of diverse pleasures.

The truism that the character of a landscape is defined by its geological formation is given an added emphasis in Pembrokeshire. St David's peninsula is formed from some of the earliest rocks to be found on earth and the northern part of the area is dominated by hard volcanic rocks. In the south, there are deposits of old red sandstone, coal and limestone – softer and producing more fertile soils when broken down. All these formations lie roughly north-west to south-east on a flattish plateau which stands about 200ft above the sea.

Culture in Retreat

There is a clear separation between the English-speaking region known as 'Little England beyond Wales' south of Newgale in the west and Amroth in the east, and the Welsh-speaking peoples of St David's peninsula and the Preseli Hills.

To find out how the social demarcation arose it is necessary to look at the arrival of the conquering Normans in the 11th century. Using Pembroke as their base they concentrated on holding the fertile lands of the south. Starting with Pembroke in 1090, they built many castles in the 11th and 12th centuries, including Carew, Haverfordwest, Tenby and the still magnificent structure of Manorbier. As in other parts of Wales, the Welsh retreated, with their customs and language intact, to the north.

Long before the Normans, the land was settled by Stone Age cave dwellers, followed by neolithic farmers and Bronze Age traders in metal.

The Pembrokeshire Coast Path as it passes Moylgrove, near Cardigan

Pembrokeshire is full of reminders of the early settlers, including the famous burial sites at Pentre Ifan and Coetan Arthur near Whitesand Bay. Popular with summer visitors, Whitesand is traditionally believed to be the place from which St Patrick sailed for Ireland. Inland, the tiny cathedral of St David's is a further reminder of the great influence religion had on the area from the Dark to the early Middle Ages. It is still possible to find fine examples of Celtic religious art in Pembrokeshire.

A Trading History

Pembrokeshire had been colonised from the sea and, after the Normans brought a degree of stability to the region, the people of Pembrokeshire developed trading links with many countries. There were frequent raids on the castles by the Welsh at the time of both Llywelyn ap Gruffydd and Owain Glyndwr.

The second civil war saw another period of unrest, with several battles fought in and around Pembrokeshire, while Pembroke Castle held out against Cromwell for seven weeks in 1648. However, this part of ancient Dyfed has enjoyed comparative calm since the Normans arrived. Today, much of Pembrokeshire gives an impression of relative prosperity, its mainstays being farming and tourism, with the

major industrial activity at Milford Haven Refinery.

The natural harbour of Milford Haven was formed as the sea rose at the end of the last Ice Age and drowned the river valley. Defoe considered the harbour to be 'one of the greatest and best inlets of water in Britain' and Nelson went further, classing it with Trincomalee in Ceylon (Sri Lanka) as the best in the world. Surprisingly, it was not until the advent of the supertankers of the 1950s and 60s that it was developed as a major port, but it is now the largest in Britain, with several refineries and a terminal. The spectacle of the lights and the flames from the refineries against the night sky is immensely dramatic.

Preservation and Recreation

By and large, Pembrokeshire has retained its rural character and the National Park Authority appears to face fewer major conservation problems than elsewhere. Inevitably there are threats of erosion by the sea or oil pollution from tankers, while the presence of Ministry of Defence firing ranges results in restricted public access to the superb range of limestone cliffs lying between St Govan's and Linney Head. Perhaps proposed changes to the structure of NATO will lead the Ministry to give up the land but, in the meantime, the authority and

Above left: Small colonies of grey seals can be seen off the coast

Above right: The fine dolmen Carreg Sampson at Mathry, near Abercastle, dates from 3,000BC

the army have worked hard to achieve an amicable relationship.

The ideal way to absorb the beauty of Pembroke's scenery is to walk the long-distance coastal path which follows, with only occasional diversions, 170 miles of coast from St Dogmaels to Amroth.

For the naturalist, the coast of Pembroke has always had a special attraction. The great sweep of Cardigan Bay is winter home to a large flock of common scoter; the islands of the Skomer complex rank among the best in the world for their seabird populations. Much the largest concentration of the Atlantic grey seal breeds off the coast of Pembroke, while maritime plants flourish on the cliffs and heaths.

The cliffs from Linney Head to Stackpole are both geologically important, and provide spectacular nesting sites for yet more seabirds. Here, the presence of the army, and the consequent restriction of public access, has probably helped to protect the birds. After this, the softer sandstone country of the final part of the walk may seem positively tame, but it has great charm and historic interest.

Magnificent, Mysterious Lands
The combination of historical
and scientific importance can
lead the visitor to concentrate
on the coast and miss the many
other habitats. In purely

Left: *The steep cliffs of St David's
Head soon give way to heathland and
grassland*
Below: *Stack Rocks, due south of the
village of Warren. Countless seabirds
nest here*

geographical terms, Mynydd
Preseli is neither a true mountain range, nor even a major
moorland habitat. But, though
fields may encroach onto the
moorland, the Prescelly Hills
retain a brooding presence
which, certainly in winter, can
seem distinctly menacing. West
of the hills there are areas of
lowland heath.

The estuaries of the two
Cleddau rivers and their
various tributaries have a
lovely, timeless air. Waders feed
undisturbed on the tidal
mudflats, and many of the
small communities perched
above the river banks or hidden
in deep woods, seem
untouched by change.

Most of the woods in
Pembrokeshire show the
influence of man, but they
attract many woodland birds,
and are rich in deciduous trees
– oak, ash, hazel and beech
predominate. There are a
number of freshwater lakes,
like Bosherston, with an
abundance of plant, insect and
animal life.

For the tourist much else
remains. The touching sight of
the tiny 13th-century St
Govan's Chapel, wedged in a
cleft in the cliffs. Remote Dale,
the Marloes peninsula,
picturesque Broad Haven, the
charm of Tenby and St David's
– less than 40 miles apart, but
representative of the two
cultures lying at the core of
Pembrokeshire.

RIVERS AND CASTLES

Criss-crossed by rivers and fortified with castles, this part of Wales was the scene of conflict between the Welsh and the English, as well as much destruction in the Civil War.

Today its shows a more peaceful face, from the trout-filled River Teifi in the north to the outstanding beauty of Gower, and the sandy estuaries of the Towy and Taf, inspiration of poet Dylan Thomas.

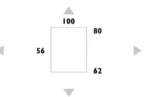

SELECTED PLACES TO VISIT

🏛 ABERGWILI
Map ref 4320

Two miles east of Carmarthen is Abergwili, where the Carmarthen Museum is found inside the Old Bishop's Palace, rebuilt in 1903 after a devastating fire. Displays of cheese and butter making combine with exhibitions on local geology and natural history to paint a comprehensive picture of the area from prehistoric, Roman and medieval times to the present.

ℹ CARDIGAN
Map ref 1846

Scene of the first National Eisteddfod in the 12th century, Cardigan Castle today stands in ruins on a knoll overlooking the estuary of the Teifi. Cardigan was once an important sea port, as can be seen from the warehouses around the old bridge, but today its prosperity comes mainly from market trade and the tourism industry.

The eastern end of the Gower Peninsula looking towards The Mumbles

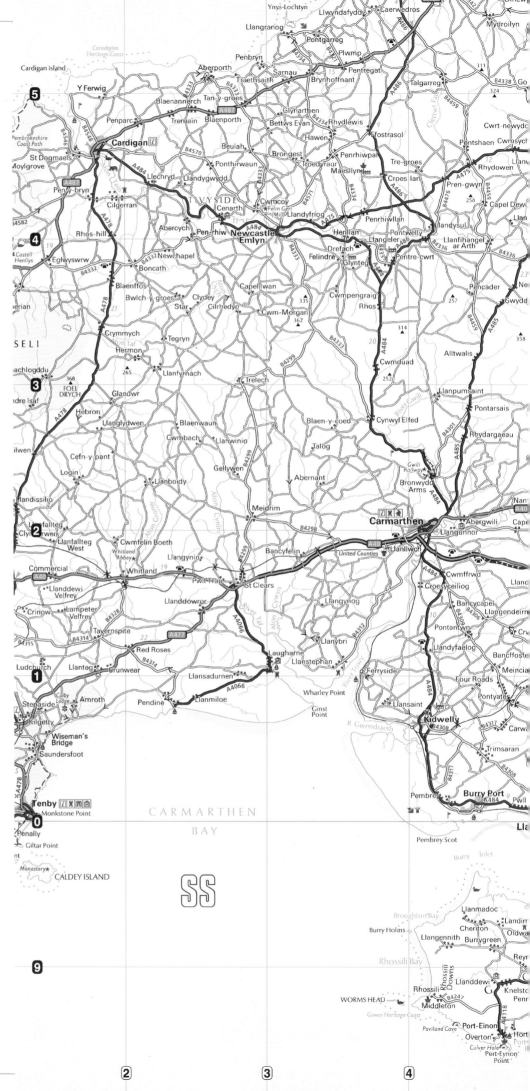

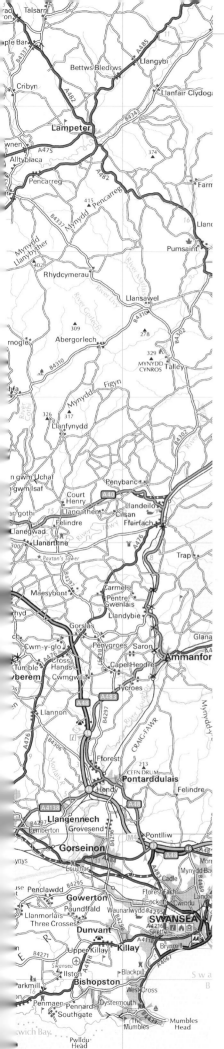

CARMARTHEN
Map ref 4020
County town of Dyfed, Carmarthen still enjoys romantic associations with King Arthur's wizard Merlin.

An amphitheatre seating 5,000 has been excavated, showing the town's importance in Roman times. The remains of the medieval castle are all but hidden by later development. Many statues and memorials to famous people adorn the town, including one to Brinley Richards, composer of *God Bless The Prince Of Wales*.

Carmarthen has five market days; wares sold range from laverbread, the local delicacy of edible seaweed, to Welsh lovespoons.

CILGERRAN
Map ref 1943
Set in a beautiful gorge, Cilgerran village is one long street. Its picturesque little 13th-century castle, standing above the River Teifi, was immortalised in paint by Turner. Cilgerran is well-known for coracles, used on the river by local fishermen since time immemorial.

DREFACH VELINDRE
Map ref 3538
The Museum of the Welsh Woollen Industry, a branch of the National Museum of Wales, is housed within a working mill. The museum's fascinating collection traces the industry's progress since the Middle Ages.

FELIN GERI MILL
Map ref 2942
At Cwmcoy is Felin Geri Mill, one of the last watermills in Britain to use the original means of production to grind stoneground wholemeal flour commercially. The 16th-century mill is open so visitors can see all stages. Water power is also used for the unusual sawmill which has been refurbished. An adventure playground, nature reserve and craft workshops add to the interest of the site.

GOWER
Map ref 6186
Around Swansea Bay at the beginning of the Gower Peninsula is the delightful resort of Mumbles, popular for sunbathing and water sports, and overlooked by Oystermouth Castle.

Gower, first to be designated as an Area of Outstanding Natural Beauty, extends for 16 miles west of Swansea. A walker's paradise, it has a picturesque coast with coves and bays. At Port Eynon Point is the extraordinary Culver Hole, a giant cave partially blocked by masonry.

GWILI RAILWAY
Map ref 4124
Just to the north of Carmarthen is the Gwili Railway, one of Wales's 'great little trains', running up the Towy valley.

KIDWELLY
Map ref 4006
The best preserved of the area's nine Norman castles, Kidwelly Castle

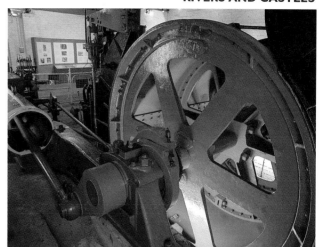
The Kidwelly Industrial Museum, housed in an old tin-plate factory

was untouched by the Civil Wars. The church of St Mary the Virgin, once part of a Benedictine priory, enjoyed similar good fortune, being spared destruction at the dissolution of the monasteries.

More recent history is preserved in the Kidwelly Industrial Museum, housed in the remains of a former tinplate works. As well as original machinery and buildings, there are exhibits on the coal industry.

LAMPETER
Map ref 5748
A university town, market town and administrative centre, Lampeter is sited on a gentle hill beside the River Teifi. It grew up around a Norman castle, the remains of which can be seen in the grounds of St David's College.

The college, founded in the 1820s to train men for the Anglican ministry, was designed on the Oxford principle, with a quadrangle, cloisters and a neo-Gothic chapel. It is open to visitors.

LAUGHARNE
Map ref 3011
A simple wooden cross in Laugharne churchyard marks the grave of Dylan Thomas, who lived and worked in the Boat House which is now a museum dedicated to Wales's greatest poet. Original furniture and family photographs help to tell his story. Laugharne, with its Norman castle, 15th-century church and elegant houses, is still redolent with the atmosphere of *Under Milk Wood*.

LLANSTEPHAN
Map ref 3511
Perched on the summit of a hill stands the impressive shell of Llanstephan Castle, one of the string of nine fortifications put up by the Normans. At the foot of the hill is the village.

NEWCASTLE EMLYN
Map ref 3040
Only a ruined arch remains of the 'new' castle – built in the 13th century – which gave this market town its name. The main street has a market hall with a tower, and the

150-year-old church is built of local slate.

PUMSAINT
Map ref 6540
Dolaucothi Gold Mines offer the rare chance to experience gold mining directly. Visitors borrow miners' helmets and lamps for underground tours, run throughout the summer. Mining machinery from the 1930s is on display in the mine yard. The mines were first exploited by the Romans and last worked in 1938.

SWANSEA
Map ref 6592
In Swansea, industrial development and seaside resort are successfully combined. While the tin and coal industries have declined, the oil terminals have ensured the town's prosperity.

Recently the docks and the surrounding area have been imaginatively revamped as a marina, with a Maritime and Industrial Museum included in the development. The museum houses a complete working woollen mill.

Swansea is a university town, and the university museum, founded in 1835, contains much of interest on local archaeology and natural history. It features a reproduction of a 19th-century Welsh kitchen and displays of local china and pottery.

The Glynn Vivian Art Gallery and Museum houses Swansea china and contemporary British paintings.

TALLEY
Map ref 6332
Remains of the 12th-century Talley Abbey stand next to the 13th-century parish church in a lovely lakeside setting.

WHITLAND ABBEY
Map ref 1916
The sparse ruins of Whitland Abbey are all that remain of the first Cistercian abbey in Wales. A mile to the south is the small market town of Whitland, the place where Hywel the Good and his wise men codified the laws of Wales; an exhibition in the old market square explains.

The Vale of Neath and the Rhondda Valley, once ruled by `king coal', have turned in the 20th century to other industries for continued prosperity.

From the Treorchy Male Voice Choir to operatic baritone Sir Geraint Evans and from composer Joseph Parry to pop star Tom Jones, the valleys have produced many famous musicians.

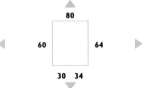

SELECTED PLACES TO VISIT

♛ ABERDARE
Map ref 0002

In Victoria Square is a fine statue of Caradog (Griffith Rhys Jones), the choirmaster who led the South Wales Choral Union to success at the Crystal Palace, London, in 1872 and 1873. Aberdare is equally proud of its poet Alun Lewis.

To the west is the Dare Valley Country Park, where an industry trail demonstrates the history of local coal mining.

★ ⛰ ABERDULAIS FALLS
Map ref 7799

In the wooded gorge of the Vale of Neath are Aberdulais Falls, whose beauty inspired a painting by Turner. Since the 16th century these falls have provided power for industries ranging from copper to tinplate. Nearby the restored Dulais Ironworks tell the story of this important local industry.

ⅰ BARRY
Map ref 1268

A boom port from the end of the 19th century, Barry no longer exports coal but has developed other industries. Today it is also a popular holiday destination, drawing visitors to the enormous funfair on Barry Island and the attractive beaches.

At the Welsh Hawking Centre, more than 200 eagles, owls, hawks, falcons, buzzards and other birds of prey can be seen.

⚔ BRIDGEND
Map ref 9079

Still a busy market town – for all its importance as an industrial centre – Bridgend stands at the confluence of the Rivers Llynfi, Ogmore and Garw. Its strategic importance to the Normans can be seen in the ruins of the 12th-century castle, called the Newcastle, on the hill.

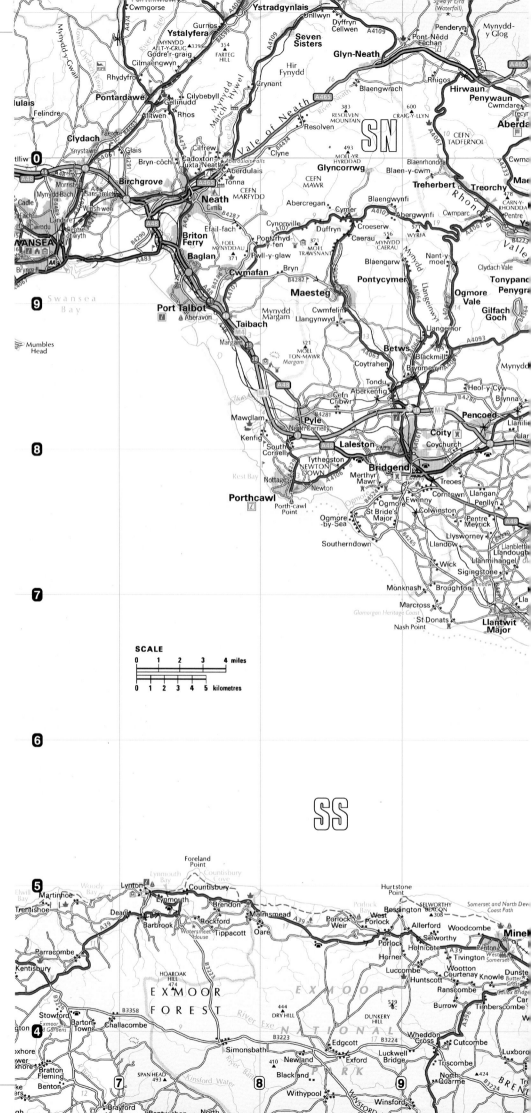

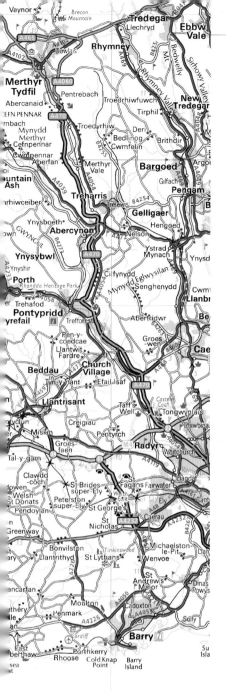

✗ CASTEL COCH
Map ref 1382

Near Tongwynlais is Castel Coch, often described as a fairytale castle. Built on a hillside in red stone in 1260 and restored 100 years ago, the castle is notable for its conical roofs and its splendid interior.

✗ COITY
Map ref 9281

North east of Bridgend is the village of Coity. Of the attractive 12th-century castle parts of the square keep remain, together with the later chapel. The village also has a lovely medieval church, from around 1324, built in cruciform shape and little altered in later years. A particular feature are its gargoyles.

🏛 ▼ CYNONVILLE
Map ref 8395

The Welsh Miners' Museum and Afan Argoed Country Park are at Cynonville. The museum, in a picturesque setting with simulated coal faces, pit gear and other equipment, shows the harsher side of the industry. Walks and trails cross the wooded park and there are picnic sites and a visitors' centre.

♠ EWENNY PRIORY
Map ref 9177

A mighty fortress as well as a religious building Ewenny Priory, south of Bridgend, contains original Norman piers and arches.

🏛 ⚓ ▼ MARGAM
Map ref 8185

The 850 acres of Margam Park transport the visitor back through the centuries, from Roman times and the early Christian era, recalled by ancient milestones and Celtic crosses, to the days when Margam Abbey was one of Wales's major Cistercian buildings. In the abbey

Beautiful 13th-century Castel Coch was restored in the 19th century

are tombs of the Mansel family, who took it over after the dissolution of the monasteries. Thomas Mansel Talbot in the 18th century built the beautiful Orangery, with its graceful architecture.

Within the park are waymarked walks, where many sculptures can be seen, together with a maze, theatre and adventure playground. Fallow deer graze peacefully in the open parkland. From the car park, a road train runs to Margam Castle and a visitor centre.

⊡ 🏛 MERTHYR TYDFIL
Map ref 0506

Iron from Merthyr Tydfil was used to make British cannon in the Napoleonic wars and the tracks for railways worldwide. Wealthy local ironmaster William Crawshay built Cyfarthfa Castle in 1825 in medieval style, surrounded by magnificent gardens. Today the castle houses the town's Museum and Art Gallery.

More local history exhibits can be found in Joseph Parry's Cottage, birthplace of the composer. Items depicting his life and works are also on show, and there is an open-air display with an excavated section of the Glamorganshire canal.

⛰ NEATH
Map ref 7597

Foundations of the Roman fort which once defended this crossing point on the River Neath are still visible. The gatehouse is the only relic of the 12th-century castle around which the town grew up, while the ruins of Neath Abbey, a Cistercian house of similar date, can be seen beside more modern factories. Much of the town's industrial heritage is being preserved.

✗ OGMORE CASTLE
Map ref 8876

Of Ogmore Castle, built on the river, the inner and outer wards and early

12th-century keep survive. The impressive west wall rises to 40 feet.

Closeby is Merthyr Mawr, worth a visit to see its famous thatched cottages, preserved as though in aspic from 200 years ago.

✗ OLD BEAUPRE CASTLE
Map ref 0172

Old Beaupre Castle is a fortified manor house, rebuilt in the 16th century, with a splendid Italianate gatehouse and porch. In the pretty village of St Hilary there are thatched cottages, an inn and a 14th-century church.

⊡ PONTYPRIDD
Map ref 0790

Where the Rivers Taff and Rhondda meet, a picturesque single-arched bridge spans the water. Around the bridge Pontypridd grew up as a market town and a centre for the coal industry.

Pontypridd prides itself on its musical heritage. Sir Geraint Evans and Stuart Burrows, the opera singers, were born here, and 1960s pop heart-throb Tom Jones comes from Treforest. Within Ynysangharad Park are statues of Evan and James James, the father and son team who wrote and composed the Welsh national anthem, *Land Of My Fathers*.

⊡ PORT TALBOT
Map ref 7589

Its sandy beaches and dunes belie the view that Port Talbot's main claim to fame is its steelworks. The western part of Aberavon beach has a promenade and a huge well-equipped leisure complex, while the eastern beach with its high dunes has remained undeveloped.

⊕ 🏛 RHOOSE
Map ref 0666

On the outskirts of Barry is Cardiff Airport, which has an interesting Wales Aircraft Museum. A Viscount airliner and Vulcan bomber are the highlights of a display of more than 30 aircraft, and there are aircraft engines and related items. Children can sit in the cockpit of a Sea Hawk.

⌂ TINKINSWOOD
Map ref 0973

The massive cromlech of Tinkinswood and its huge capstone, weighing more than 40 tons, stand close to the village of St Nicholas' with its typical thatched cottages. This prehistoric chambered tomb is one of the largest and best preserved in Wales.

✗ 🏛 WELSH FOLK MUSEUM
Map ref 1277

The fascinating Welsh Folk Museum at St Fagans concentrates on social history. In its extensive grounds are traditional buildings of the 15th to 19th centuries, transported from different parts of Wales. At this open-air museum, within the walls of the 16th-century St Fagans Castle, demonstrations of many rural crafts take place throughout the year.

AROUND THE SEVERN ESTUARY

On the English side of the Severn estuary the spectacular rocks and gorges of the Mendips contrast with the marshes of the Somerset Levels. On the Welsh side, the magnificent castles and thriving ports reflect the strategic and economic importance of the southern gateway to the principality.

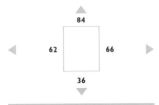

```
        ▲
       84
   ◄  62   66  ►
       36
        ▼
```

TOUR

MENDIP HILLS AND SOMERSET LEVELS
65 MILES

Taking the A370 north from Weston-super-Mare, the tour forks right on to the A371 towards Banwell, whose church contains some beautiful 15th-century Flemish stained glass.

At the crossroads with the B3134 stands the peaceful village of Burrington. Just south is Burrington Combe where, sheltering under one of its great rocks, the hymn writer Revd Augustus Toplady was inspired to write *Rock of Ages*.

The tour follows the line of the Mendip Hills, turning sharply right on to the B3371 to climb through to Cheddar Gorge, where the limestone cliffs split into two sheer walls. Huge stalactites and stalagmites are found in its famous caves and caving expeditions leave daily. Authentic Cheddar cheese is

Glastonbury's Tithe Barn houses the Somerset Rural Life Museum

available from some local farmhouses.

Taking the A371 south east, a detour to the left at Easton leads to Wookey Hole. Unlike the mainly dry caves at Cheddar, Wookey has a large underground lake fed by the River Axe. Inhabited from the Stone Age to Roman times, the cave is said to be haunted by a medieval witch. Close by is a 17th-century mill where fine writing paper is still made by hand. The mill also contains a fairground by night exhibition and vintage penny slot machines.

The cathedral city of Wells, although small, is full of ecclesiastical splendour. The cathedral itself, started in 1180, has magnificent arches, windows and vaulted ceilings. The gateway from the cathedral green to the market place is called Penniless Porch after the beggars who found it a profitable pitch. In the moat surrounding the 13th-century Bishop's Palace is a group of swans who pull the gatehouse bell twice daily to summon food.

A place of pilgrimage from early times, Glastonbury is where Joseph of Arimathea is reputed to have buried the Holy Grail and built the first Christian church in England. The ruins of the later abbey now stand on the site. A winter-flowering thorn in the abbey grounds may be a cutting from Joseph's staff which, according to the legend, took root in the soil. The museum has a superb model of the medieval abbey in which King Arthur and Queen Guinevere are said to have been buried.

Recent local history is recorded in Glastonbury's Somerset Rural Life Museum, with a farmhouse kitchen and displays of cider-making.

In Glastonbury Tribunal's 15th-century courthouse are some of the archaeological finds from the nearby lake village at Meare, inhabited between 300BC and AD100. Meare itself has a 14th-century Fish House, from which fishermen supplied the abbots of Glastonbury.

Rising from the marshy pastures of the Somerset Levels are the Wedmore Hills. At Wedmore the route turns left on to the B3139, across the lowland area which has been drained.

After crossing the motorway and the A38, the road meets the coast at Burnham-on-Sea, a seaside resort with a magnificent view of the bay.

As the road goes north and turns inland, Brent Knoll with its huge Iron Age camp is outlined starkly. At East Brent, the tour joins the A370 to return to Weston-super-Mare, with the Bleadon Hills on the right.

SELECTED PLACES TO VISIT

BRISTOL
Map ref 5873
Among the highlights of this ancient city and port are the splendid City Museum and Art Gallery and the Exploratory Hands-On Science Centre.

The story of local seafaring is told in the Maritime Heritage Centre and the SS *Great Britain* is on display in Great Western Dock. The Bristol Industrial Museum, close by, houses aircraft, engines and railway exhibits.

Bristol's Zoological Gardens have a large collection of animals, including gorillas, okapi and reptiles, and a new World of Water.

In the New Room, the world's oldest Methodist chapel, John Wesley preached his first sermon in 1739. The chapel and the living rooms are preserved in their original form.

CAERLEON
Map ref 3491
The ramparts of the Roman fort of Isca can still be seen, together with the amphitheatre, excavated in 1920 and remains of the Roman baths. Many of the finds are displayed in the Legionary Museum. In the Middle Ages the site became romantically associated with King Arthur's Camelot.

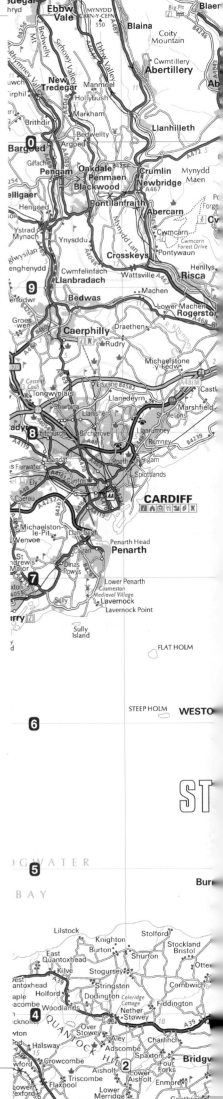

CAERPHILLY
Map ref 1587

Caerphilly owes its reputation both to the famous local cheese and to its 13th-century Castle: a superb example of concentric structure, its ruins stand on a 30-acre site protected by an extensive moat.

CALDICOT
Map ref 4888

Caldicot's restored Norman border castle contains a local history museum and art exhibition. The grounds are a countryside park.

CARDIFF
Map ref 1876

The heart of the Welsh capital is Cardiff's Castle. The Normans built a motte and bailey inside the ruins of the Roman fort and it was extended in later centuries. A major transformation took place in the 19th century to form the now magnificent edifice of which the city is justly proud.

Within Cathays Park stands the National Museum of Wales, with its internationally famous collection of modern paintings and sculpture.

A different light is shed on the past in the Welsh Folk Museum at St Fagans, which concentrates on social history.

CHEPSTOW
Map ref 5393

At the western end of the Severn Bridge, with its Norman Castle towering over the River Wye, Chepstow has an excellent museum covering the history of the area from Roman times onward.

NEWPORT
Map ref 3188

An important port for centuries, Newport belies its name. Its Castle was destroyed during the Civil War and only ruins remain. Relics of the 1839 Chartist riots are found in the town's Museum.

STREET
Map ref 4836

Clarks' shoe factory at Street, founded in 1825, has a museum of shoes from Roman times to the present, as well as engravings, illustrations, fashion plates and machinery from the firm's past.

TINTERN
Map ref 5200

Tintern Abbey was founded in 1131 for monks of the Cistercian order. The beautiful shell of the church was immortalised in paint by Turner and in poetry by Wordsworth.

WESTON-SUPER-MARE
Map ref 3260

Weston-super-Mare's Heritage Centre explains the history of town and country, while the Woodspring Museum, in the workshops of the Edwardian Gaslight Company, includes displays on the Victorian seaside holiday, an old chemist's shop and historic transport.

SALISBURY PLAIN AND THE COTSWOLDS

Man has inhabited this favoured area for thousands of years and the remains of prehistoric worship are everywhere. The Romans left their mark in Cirencester and Bath, and the Saxons founded churches and settlements. The Middle Ages too were a prosperous period, particularly based on wool, and many early markets survive. Bath led the way in 18th-century fashionable society, and the Kennet and Avon Canal brought the benefits of the industrial revolution without its disadvantages. The natural beauty of the hills and valleys has inspired the carving of many white horses which fascinate the visitor.

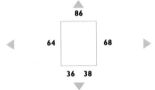

SELECTED PLACES TO VISIT

AVEBURY
Map ref 1069

One of the most important megalithic monuments in Europe, Avebury is a 28-acre site with stone circles enclosed by banks and ditches. The whole compact village comes within the earthworks, and many original standing stones were broken up to build cottages.

Nearby are the West Kennet Long Barrow, a wedge-shaped prehistoric burial place, sealed by sarsen stones, and Silbury Hill, Europe's largest example of a man-made prehistoric mound. Windmill Hill, a 21-acre Neolithic causewayed camp with three concentric ditches, forms the largest earthwork of its type in Britain.

Pottery, bones and other finds from these sites are preserved in the Alexander Keiller Museum. The Wiltshire Folk Life Society's display of the thatcher, cheese-maker, blacksmith, wheelwright, saddler and shepherd is found in the superb Great Barn, dating from 1690.

BARBURY
Map ref 1575

Barbury Castle was an ancient hillfort, set in a commanding position 850ft up on the Marlborough Downs adjacent to the prehistoric route of the Ridgeway Path. Its Country Park offers downland walks with spectacular views of the Vale of the White Horse.

BATH
Map ref 7464

Bath's hot springs first attracted the Romans to build the spa of Aqua Sulis, and the remains of the baths and other archaeological finds can be seen. The excavations of the Roman temple precinct under the Pump Room are also open to view.

In Saxon times King Offa founded an abbey at Bath, where King Edgar was crowned in 973.

Bath's fashionable heyday came in the 18th century, when Beau Nash regulated the bathing and constructed the assembly rooms and theatres. Today Bath is Britain's best-preserved Georgian city.

The Holburne Museum contains a valuable collection of silver, porcelain and old Masters.

BRADFORD-ON-AVON
Map ref 8260

St Laurence is a rare example of a complete Saxon church, which lay undiscovered until the middle of the 19th century.

The town was noted for weaving and many weavers' cottages can still be seen, together with the Hall built by a rich clothier.

CHAVENAGE
Map ref 8695

To the north west of Tetbury is Chavenage, an unspoilt Elizabethan manor house.

CHIPPENHAM
Map ref 9273

In King Alfred's time there was a market place in Chippenham and it continues today. A centre of the cloth industry, Chippenham has many lovely half-timbered Tudor buildings and Georgian houses.

The Yelde Hall Museum in the 15th-century former town hall contains geological, archaeological and photographic exhibits.

CIRENCESTER
Map ref 0201

Second only to London as the largest town in Roman Britain, Cirencester grew up around a 1st-century fort. Many antiquities from the Roman period are on display in the Corinium Museum. Outstanding are the mosaic floors, sculptures and five-letter square palindrome. The museum also contains displays of Cotswold life.

Nothing remains of the royal Saxon city, nor the great Norman abbey, but the parish church contains some rare treasures, including the Boleyn Cup, made for Queen Anne Boleyn.

CLAVERTON MANOR
Map ref 7864

At Claverton Manor, near Bath, is the American Museum, featuring American domestic life and Wild West and Indian collections.

DEVIZES
Map ref 0061

Devizes grew up around a Norman castle, which was ruined in the 16th century and its stones used to build houses. The town was fashionable in the 18th century, as its elegant Georgian buildings show.

The Kennet and Avon Canal, linking London and Bristol, made Devizes an important 19th-century commercial centre. It boasts the longest flight of locks in the country, raising the water level 230ft through 29 locks. In a warehouse by the canal is an exhibition explaining its development.

Devizes Museum has major collections of finds from palaeolithic to Anglo-Saxon times. Local geology, biology and natural history are strongly featured, and the art gallery has a John Piper window.

LACOCK
Map ref 9268

Lacock Abbey and village were given to the National Trust by the Talbot family in 1944. In its narrow winding streets are houses from the 14th to 18th centuries, demonstrating a rich variety of architectural styles. The abbey, founded in 1232, was converted into a country house after 1539. The photographic pioneer William Henry Fox Talbot conducted his experiments here and the museum of historic photographs and equipment at the entrance gate is named after him.

LONGLEAT
Map ref 8143

The first stately home to open to the public commercially, Longleat House is the family seat of the Marquess of Bath. Built in 1580, the house is decorated in ornate Italian style.

In the Safari Park, wild animals roam free.

MALMESBURY
Map ref 9387

Much of Malmesbury's Abbey, founded around AD640, is ruined, but the massive Norman south porch still soars above the town.

The local Museum is named after the Saxon king Athelstan but its collections reflect the later history of the town. The market cross dating from 1490 is over 40ft high with arches, buttresses and battlements.

SHELDON MANOR
Map ref 8874

One of the oldest Plantagenet manor houses, featuring an early oak staircase, Sheldon Manor was built in 1282. The chapel is 15th-century, and the gardens feature old-fashioned roses and ancient yews.

STONEHENGE
Map ref 1243

This atmospheric and world-famous prehistoric monument has an outer ring and inner horseshoe of sarsen stones, with bluestones set up inside and outside the horseshoe and a central altar stone. On the longest day of the year, the monument's axis points towards sunrise.

TETBURY
Map ref 8993

A typical quiet Cotswold market town, Tetbury has a splendid 17th-century market hall. Within the Old Court House is the Police Bygones Museum, containing uniforms, batons and items used by the Gloucestershire Constabulary.

Built in stages, 3,000 to 5,000 years ago, Stonehenge is world famous

★ WHITE HORSE
Map ref 9050

The White Horse on Bratton Down is the oldest in Wiltshire, dating from 1778 and reputed to have been remodelled on a Saxon carving of King Alfred's horse.

Westbury's wool and cloth industry was important in medieval times, later replaced by leatherwork and glove-making.

Although the industrial revolution and 20th-century technological advances have vastly expanded the former market towns of Newbury, Swindon, Didcot and Basingstoke, most rural parts of north Hampshire, Berkshire and south Oxfordshire have resisted the pressures of over-development. Hillforts, barrows, abbeys and castles tell the story of a favoured countryside long colonised by man, yet still retaining its colour and mystery.

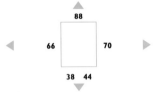

SELECTED PLACES TO VISIT

🎫🏛 ABINGDON
Map ref 4997

Site of a long-ruined early Saxon abbey, Abingdon has some medieval and early Elizabethan buildings as well as the surviving gateway of the later Saxon abbey, built in 955.

Abingdon Museum is the Town Hall, an elegant 17th-century building erected by Christopher Kempster, one of Wren's master masons. Its collections range from local industry such as clothmaking and the MG car company to archaeology and local history.

🎫🏛 ANDOVER
Map ref 3645

Originally a Saxon town, Andover has expanded rapidly in recent years. The nearby hillfort of Danebury was much older, and the story of the settlement, based on recent extensive excavations, is told in the new Museum of the Iron Age. The Andover Museum and Art Gallery has an aquarium featuring local fish from the River Test.

🏚 BASILDON HOUSE
Map ref 6178

A classical 18th-century house, Basildon Park is found in a beautiful setting overlooking the Thames Valley. The focal point of the interior is an unusual Octagon Room, and the house has a decorative Shell Room, as well as important pictures and furniture.

🏚 BASING HOUSE
Map ref 6653

At Old Basing are the ruins of Basing House, once the largest private house in Tudor England but

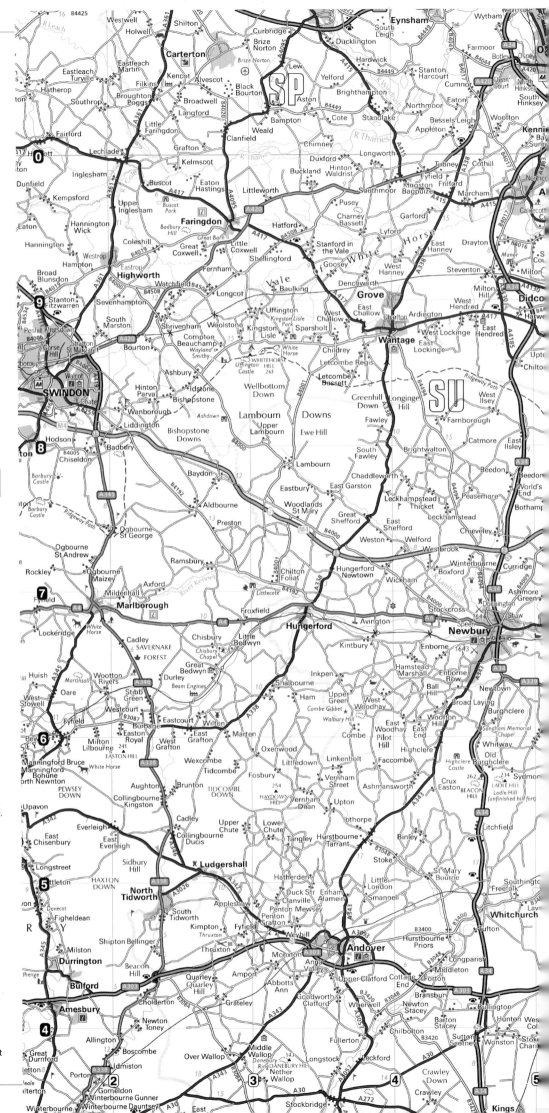

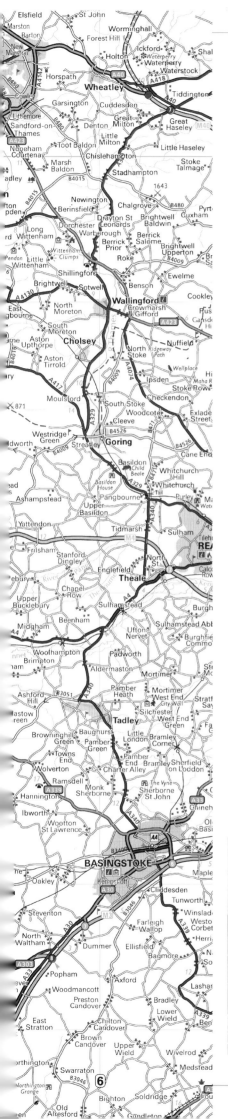

destroyed in the Civil War. The site was occupied in the Iron Age, and an exhibition sets out its complex history.

BASINGSTOKE
Map ref 6352
In the expanding modern town of Basingstoke, with its skyscraper office blocks and new housing estates, the Willis Museum and Art Gallery has a major display on the archaeology of Hampshire, featuring flint tools and the tusk of a woolly mammoth. There are also collections of clocks, toys and embroidery and a fascinating display on the natural history of north Hampshire.

CHILD BEALE
Map ref 6278
At Lower Basildon, ornamental pheasants, peacocks, flamingoes, highland cattle and rare sheep wander around the Child Beale Wildlife Trust's Church Farm. Visitors can walk beside the river or take a boat trip, and there are craftwork and information centres as well as paddling pools, an adventure playground and a miniature railway.

DIDCOT
Map ref 5190
Didcot owes its prosperity chiefly to the coming of the railway. Appropriately, the Railway Centre by the town's Parkway Station has the largest collection of rolling stock from the old Great Western Railway company. It includes 20 steam locomotives, a diesel railcar and much passenger and freight rolling stock, in a GWR engine shed. A typical Victorian station has been reconstructed with original track.

DONNINGTON CASTLE
Map ref 4668
Donnington Castle was one of the casualties of the Civil War, and only two of its round towers and the gateway remain.

FINKLEY DOWN FARM AND COUNTRY PARK
Map ref 3746
At Finkley Down Farm and Country Park near Andover, farm animals

The silk mill at Whitchurch survives as a working factory

are kept in a natural environment. Children enjoy the pets' corner and adventure playground.

HIGHCLERE
Map ref 4459
Highclere Castle, ancestral home of the Earl of Carnarvon, was built in sumptuous Victorian style. The fifth Earl was famous for his association with the discovery of Tutankhamun's tomb, which is said to have brought a curse causing his death for disturbing the king's rest. The castle contains some of his Egyptian finds, as well as portraits by Van Dyck and old Masters.

NEWBURY
Map ref 4666
An ancient town, Newbury grew rich from cloth in Tudor times, and many fine buildings remain from this period. The Newbury District Museum, housed in 17th- and 18th-century buildings beside the wharf, explains the history of the Kennet and Avon canal. Other displays feature the unusual local pastime of ballooning and Civil War battles.

SAVERNAKE FOREST
Map ref 2265
Today only a small portion remains of the vast forest in which Saxon kings hunted, but with careful management it is a haven for deer, wild birds and many rare species of plants. In the 18th century, Capability Brown planted the Grand Avenue and Eight Walks of magnificent oaks and beeches.

SILCHESTER
Map ref 6262
The Roman city of Calleva Atrebatum was built on the site of a Celtic settlement, with the walls following its octagonal shape. The best preserved stretch of wall is near Silchester's medieval church of St Mary. The site has been fully excavated and houses, temples, a forum and an amphitheatre un-covered. In the village of Silchester is the Calleva Museum, which gives a graphic display of the Roman town, but the principal remains are preserved in Reading Museum.

SWINDON
Map ref 1484
Before the coming of the Great Western Railway in 1842, Swindon

was a small market town. Even its rapid growth in that period was out paced by further expansion to meet industrial development after World War II. More recently still Swindon has spearheaded the revolution in the high-tech computer industry.

The Great Western Railway Museum is housed in a Victorian Gothic building and exhibits include famous locomotives and models, prints and other items on the history of the GWR. Next door, the Railway Village Museum has been refurbished as a typical Victorian railway foreman's home.

The Museum and Art Gallery has one of the best collections of 20th-century British painting outside London, and also features local archaeology and history. The Richard Jeffries Museum at Coate, birthplace of the nature writer, contains manuscript and first editions of works by Jeffries.

THE VYNE
Map ref 6356
The Vyne at Sherborne St John is a lovely Tudor mansion house, extensively altered in 1654, when John Webb built onto it the earliest classical portico to an English country house. The Tudor chapel contains Renaissance glass, and the house has a Palladian staircase.

UFFINGTON
Map ref 3089
The prehistoric fort, Uffington Castle is set on the highest point of the Berkshire Downs, 856ft up on White Horse Hill. Below it, cut in the chalk, is the horse which gives the area its name.

WANTAGE
Map ref 3988
The history of the Vale of the White Horse and the town of Wantage is recorded in the Vale and Downland Museum. Wantage was the birthplace of King Alfred.

WATERSHIP DOWN
Map ref 5256
Just south of Kingsclere is Watership Down, immortalised by Richard Adams in his novel of the same name. Footpaths cross this beauty spot although the rabbits tend to stay well underground.

WAYLAND'S SMITHY
Map ref 2786
At Wayland's Smithy – a megalithic long barrow – travellers were said to be able to get their horses shod by the smith of Scandinavian legend, who could forge invincible swords and shields.

WHITCHURCH
Map ref 4648
A Georgian coaching town, Whitchurch today is mainly visited for its Silk Mill, where the early 19th-century wheel which has drawn power for the mill for 150 years still drives the original machinery to produce silk by traditional methods.

THE PROSPEROUS HOME COUNTIES

A web-like network of roads converging on London covers this part of the Home Counties. From the Roman settlement of St Albans in the north, passing William the Conqueror's royal castle at Windsor, to the medieval bishopric of Farnham in the south, the area has been home to the country's leaders for thousands of years. Today, many noble and historic buildings jostle with the settlements of a booming population, drawn inexorably towards the wealth and power of the capital.

```
        92
88    ┌─────┐
      │      │  74
68    └─────┘
      44  46
```

SELECTED PLACES TO VISIT

ALDERSHOT
Map ref 8650

Within the military town of Aldershot are three museums. The Airborne Forces Museum has briefing models for World War II operations and its post-War display includes exhibits from the Falklands conflict.

In Buller Barracks is the Royal Corps of Transport Museum.

Aldershot Military Museum in Queen's Avenue tells the story of the British army since 1854.

BERKHAMSTED
Map ref 9907

Little remains of Berkhamsted Castle today except the motte and bailey and an unusual double moat.

The small town has many attractive buildings dating from the Tudor and Jacobean periods.

CHALFONT ST GILES
Map ref 9893

The Chiltern Open Air Museum, set in Newland Park, records 500 years of rural life.

In the village is the 16th-century cottage in which poet John Milton wrote *Paradise Lost* and began *Paradise Regained*. There are many rare books, including first editions.

CHESSINGTON
Map ref 1863

Chessington World of Adventures is a popular leisure park, with features such as the Runaway Mine Train, Dragon River Flume and Safari Skyway Monorail, together with a circus academy and children's clown town. The zoological gardens are open all year round.

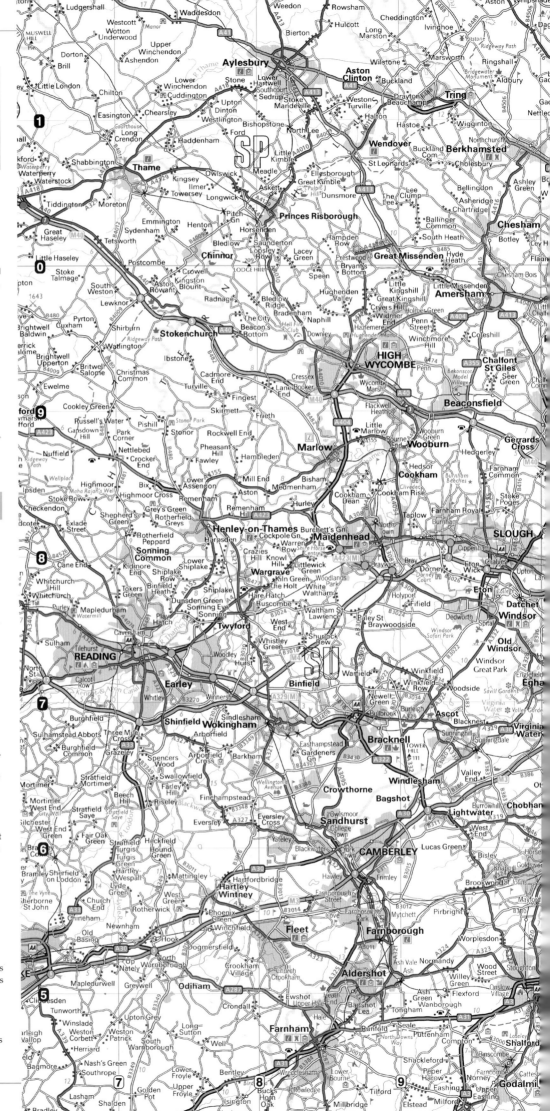

Stratfield Saye, the country seat of the Duke of Wellington

⌂ CLIVEDEN
Map ref 9185

Once the home of Lady Nancy Astor, Cliveden is now owned by the National Trust and let as an hotel. The present house, built in 1851, is set on cliffs 200ft above the Thames surrounded by extensive gardens and woodland.

⬚✕⌂ FARNHAM
Map ref 8446

The ruined keep is all that now remains of Farnham's 12th-century castle, inhabited for centuries by the bishops of Winchester. Farnham town, birthplace and home of travel writer William Cobbett, is noted for its Georgian houses.

⬚ HENLEY-ON-THAMES
Map ref 7682

A mile-long stretch of the River Thames at Henley is where the Royal Regatta is held each July.

⬚✕⌂ READING
Map ref 7173

The county town of Berkshire, Reading has both an industrial and rural heritage.

Blake's Lock Museum contains reconstructions and relics of the commercial and industrial life of the town.

The Museum of Rural Life, part of the University of Reading, has a fascinating collection of agricultural, craft and domestic items.

Roman history is well represented in Reading's main museum, with a wealth of exhibits from nearby Silchester.

✽ ROYAL NATIONAL ROSE SOCIETY
Map ref 1304

Lovers of roses will find seventh heaven in the Gardens of the Rose in Chiswellgreen owned by the Royal National Rose Society, with more than 30,000 plants displayed in 1,650 varieties.

⬚✕⌂✕⌂ ST ALBANS
Map ref 1407

The splendours of Verulamium – the only British city to be given the status of a *municipium*, which made its inhabitants Roman citizens – can be seen in the Verulamium Museum. Within the site is the only Roman theatre open to view in Britain.

The huge cathedral which houses St Alban's shrine dates from the 11th century and contains fine medieval paintings.

The Clock Tower – one of only two medieval clock towers in the country – is a good example of an early 15th-century curfew tower giving extensive views over the city. The Museum of St Albans records the city since Roman times.

✽ SAVILL GARDENS
Map ref 9771

Twenty acres of Windsor Great Park form the Savill Gardens, with formal areas of roses and herbaceous borders, trees and shrubs giving year-round colour.

★ SHIRE HORSE CENTRE
Map ref 8580

The Courage Shire Horse Centre in Maidenhead is a working stable where up to 12 of the brewery's shire horses can be seen being fed, groomed and harnessed.

⌂ STRATFIELD SAYE
Map ref 6961

Presented to the victorious Duke of Wellington by a grateful nation, this 17th-century mansion contains paintings, prints and mementoes. The Duke's huge funeral carriage forms part of the display, while his famous horse, Copenhagen, is buried in the grounds.

⌂ THORPE PARK
Map ref 0367

Thorpe Park near Chertsey has become a highly successful theme park, based on a maritime theme. Land trains and waterbuses provide free transport around the fun-filled complex. A less energetic feature is the Craft Centre, where pottery making, spinning, wood and wax carving and corn dolly making are demonstrated.

✽ VALLEY GARDENS
Map ref 9769

The Valley Gardens adjoin the lake of Virginia Water, delighting the eye with rhododendrons, camellias and magnolias and other species.

⬚✕⌂ WINDSOR
Map ref 9576

Windsor Castle – the world's largest inhabited castle – was founded by William the Conqueror and extended and improved by most subsequent sovereigns. It is surrounded by Windsor Great Park, covering some 1,800 acres.

The lower ward contains the 230ft long St George's Chapel where the Knights of the Order of the Garter are invested by HM The Queen. Many royal or noble people are buried here, including Kings Henry VI, Henry VIII, Charles I, George VI and Jane Seymour.

The state apartments are in the upper ward showing just a small part of the fabulous art treasures owned by the Queen.

In the middle ward is the huge Round Tower. From the top, 230ft up, are superb views of 12 counties, the River Thames, and the famous playing fields of Eton College.

Queen Mary's Dolls House, given to the queen in 1924, is a perfect fully working palace in miniature.

One of the best military museums in the country is found at Combermere Barracks. The Household Cavalry Museum displays uniforms, armour, weapons and horse furniture of the last four centuries.

The royal theme continues with Madame Tussaud's Royalty and Empire exhibition at Windsor and Eton Central Station.

⌂ WINDSOR SAFARI PARK
Map ref 9475

Visitors can drive through wild animal reserves to see lions, elephants, giraffe and many other creatures. Among the other attractions are a walk-through Tropical World and the well known killer whale and dolphin shows.

LONDON

No other capital in the world has the number of parks, gardens and squares which lighten the centre of London, nor the woods and heathland which ventilate its outer reaches

Engravings. Above: London Bridge in the 17th century
Below: Wren's contribution to the London skyline

In a Royal Commission Report of 1928, Sir Mortimer Wheeler made a typical trenchant comment, asserting that there was no valid reason for supposing that London existed before AD43. No research since that has produced evidence to challenge that conclusion and so credit for the creation of London must go to the Roman general Aulus Plautius who swept across south-east Britain in that year. Almost certainly he built a bridge while waiting for the Emperor Claudius to arrive and once the crossing was established London appears to have developed with quite remarkable speed. Within a few years merchants had established themselves and London was, in the words of Tacitus, 'a great trading centre'

Power and Prosperity

In AD60 London experienced the first of many disasters which were to affect it in the succeeding centuries, when Boudicca and her Iceni tribesmen destroyed it. London was soon rebuilt, probably becoming the administrative centre of the province in the early part of the second century. The Romans withdrew in 410 and London gained its first bishop in 604.

London grew in importance and prosperity for almost 100 years and became, under William the Conqueror, the capital of England. But it was a capital with two centres – Westminster, where political power would eventually reside, and the City where the merchants were all-powerful. Linking the two was the Strand, home of the wealthy and linking the two sides of the river was London Bridge; in 1209 the stone bridge destined to survive until the 19th century was completed.

It was during the 13th century that executive power began to be concentrated in London, firstly by the establishment of three great offices of State, the Exchequer, the Chancery and the Privy Seal, and later by the Inns of Court. In the 16th century the population increased rapidly, expanding beyond the walls of the City against the expressed wishes of Queen Elizabeth I. The Great Fire of 1666 destroyed over 13,000 houses in the city, but gave to the world the masterpieces of Christopher Wren. Soon the villages to the north and west of London were absorbed and, for the first time, the area south of the Thames began to be developed.

Times of Change

As the Victorian – and, co-incidentally, the railway – era began, London entered the unprecedented period of growth which would lead, in some 70 years, to a four-fold increase in population.

By the outbreak of war in 1914 London was still the financial centre of the world and was steadily expanding in size. However, changes were occurring – the Empire was under threat, and trade, although not yet declining was, in many instances, stagnant.

Rebuilding the Future

From the moment the first bomb fell on August 27th, 1940, to the end of the war, more than a fifth of the City was destroyed. Yet the people emerged stronger than ever. Before long, new office blocks and high rise flats were being built to replace poor housing stock. Much of the building of

Once rare, the black redstart colonised London after World War Two

the 1950s and 60s has been the subject of fierce criticism and indeed has been pulled down, but the abiding impression was one of renewed vitality. The City of London regained its position in the financial world, new buildings on the South Bank dedicated to the arts highlighted a period of revival which was to draw many members of the international arts circuit to London.

Treasures of the city

Buckingham Palace. This, the Queen's residence, was built in 1703 by the Duke of Buckingham, as Buckingham House. George III bought it in 1762 and it was remodelled for George IV in 1825 and renamed Buckingham Palace. The Royal Family live in the north wing.

Houses of Parliament. Turned over to the state institutions during the reign of Henry VIII, a fire destroyed most of the palace in 1834. Today's building, designed by Charles Barry, covers eight acres. At the north end is the clock tower which contains Big Ben – the $13^1/_2$-ton hour bell.

Kensington Palace. Birthplace of Queen Victoria and now the residence of a number of the members of the Royal Family, Kensington Palace's state apartments display pictures and furniture, and there is a section on the Great Exhibition.

The London Dungeon. This award-winning museum leads the visitor through the seamy side of life in past centuries. Methods of torture and death, medical practices and black magic are represented.

The London Planetarium. Here, the beauty of the night skies is represented and explained by a projection on to the inside of the Planetarium's dome, together with a fascinating commentary.

London Zoo. Opened to the public in 1847, the collection of animals currently numbers around 8,000. It includes rare and endangered species from around the world. There is also a children's zoo.

The eye-catching Lloyds building, designed by Richard Rogers

Above: *One of the Docklands Light Railway's driverless trains*
Right: *Tower Bridge, seen from the William Curtis Ecological Park*

Madame Tussaud's. This famous wax world collection was founded in Paris in 1770. The collection includes historical figures, film stars, sportsmen, royalty and, in the Chamber of Horrors, reconstructions of historic crimes.

Museums and Art Galleries. London has a fabulous range of museums and art galleries; far too numerous to list here. Among the best and most popular are the National Gallery and the National Portrait Gallery in Trafalgar; the British Museum, the Tate Gallery; the museums complex in South Kensington, which includes the Victoria and Albert Museum, the Natural History Museum, the Science Museum and the Geological Museum. Some of the lesser museums are excellent value, including the Jewish Museum, the National Postal Museum and, in the Barbican Complex, the Museum of London.

Parks and Gardens. London is much blessed in the number of its parks – gardens and other open spaces. The inner parkland includes Hyde Park, St James's Park and Regent's Park.

Royal Mews. These are the home of the state coaches, including the gold state coach made in 1762 and used for every coronation since. The Irish state coach, driving carriages and royal sleighs can also be seen.

St Paul's Cathedral. The largest and most famous church in the city, St Paul's was built by Sir Christopher Wren after the Great Fire of London in 1666.

Tower Bridge. Nearly a century old, much of the original machinery can still be seen in the south tower. The covered walkway, at 142ft, gives a panoramic view of the Thames.

Tower of London. One of the most outstanding examples of Norman military architecture in Europe, the Tower of London houses the Royal Armouries. Other features include the Crown Jewels and the tower ravens.

OUTER LONDON

Within 20 miles of London are tranquil countryside, single-track roads with passing places and villages with ducks still swimming on the ponds. This is the Hertfordshire of Ebenezer Howard's new town of Welwyn Garden City, of modern Hatfield with its old town and historic house, and of Hertford, which preserves its castle and its cottages. Even Essex's bustling new town of Harlow is set in a sea of green fields and ancient villages.

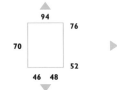

SELECTED PLACES TO VISIT

AYOT ST LAWRENCE
Map ref 1915
Shaw's Corner was home to writer George Bernard Shaw and his wife for 46 years. The downstairs rooms have been preserved by the National Trust as they were in his lifetime. The kitchen and pantry have recently also been opened to visitors.

BRAND'S HATCH
Map ref 5764
Set in a natural amphitheatre, the world-famous motor racing circuit has hosted many Grand Prix since it was established in the early 1920s.

COBHAM
Map ref 6769
Owletts is a modest red brick house built in the time of Charles II. Its

Hertford Castle

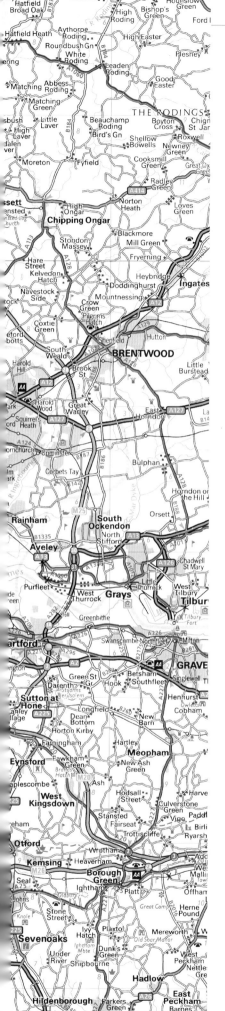

contemporary staircase and plasterwork ceiling remain. The property, with its small pleasure and kitchen gardens, is administered by the National Trust.

▼ CHESSINGTON WORLD OF ADVENTURES
Map ref 1962

Set in 65 acres of lovely countryside, Chessington has more than 100 attractions arranged in themed areas. The zoo can be viewed from the Safari Skyway monorail and there is also an international circus.

🏛 EPPING FOREST
Map ref 4096

Now covering about 5,600 acres, Epping Forest was more than 10 times that size in the days when Saxon, Norman and Tudor kings hunted there. The forest is noted for its hornbeam trees.

The Epping Forest Museum is housed in the Queen Elizabeth Hunting Lodge, Chingford.

▦ EYNSFORD
Map ref 5465

Once the residence of a Norman knight, Eynsford Castle now consists only of a rectangular stone hall, 30ft high curtain wall and ditch, set in a pretty little village.

▦ HAM HOUSE
Map ref 1773

This lovely house was built in 1610, and redecorated in the fashionable style of the 1670s. There is a restored 17th-century garden.

▦ HAMPTON COURT PALACE
Map ref 1568

Begun by Cardinal Wolsey in the 16th century and expanded by various monarchs, the palace offers handsome gardens and parkland. Special attractions include the orangery, vine and maze.

▥▦ HARLOW
Map ref 4711

Harlow has grown enormously as a new town and its museum explores local history from Roman to modern times. Passmore House is an early Georgian building, set in gardens from which part of the medieval moat of the earlier house is visible.

Specialised transport in the last two centuries is the theme of the Mark Hall Cycle Museum. Displays trace the history of the bicycle from 1819 to the present day. Outside are three walled period gardens, a Tudor herb garden and cottage garden.

▦ HATFIELD
Map ref 2308

Historic home of the Marquess of Salisbury, Hatfield House was built by Robert Cecil, first earl of Salisbury, in 1611 and has remained in the Cecil family since then. The great hall and other rooms are full of important pictures, furniture, tapestries and armour. As well as a national collection of model soldiers, there is a special exhibition of classic and vintage cars.

Within the extensive park and gardens stands the Old Palace – the surviving wing of the Royal Palace in which Queen Elizabeth I spent much of her childhood.

★ HAYES HILL FARM
Map ref 3804

Always popular with children is Hayes Hill Farm, where farmyard animals live in natural surroundings and craftsmen practise their traditional skills. The main feature of the farm is the restored Tudor barn.

▥▦▦ HERTFORD
Map ref 3212

The picturesque small county town of Hertford stands at the confluence of three rivers, the Lea, Beane and Mimram. The present castle dates mainly from the 15th century and is now used as the offices of the town council. Band concerts take place in the grounds, which contain an interesting example of a medieval ice room.

The town is an unusual mixture of old and new buildings. The Castle Hall strikes a somewhat jarring modern note, while the County Hall is more Scandinavian in style.

▦ KENWOOD
Map ref 2686

A beautiful part of Hamstead Heath is the wooded grounds of Kenwood, laid out in the 18th century. The grounds, house and contents were bequeathed to the nation in 1927 and include a fine collection of paintings and an exhibition of 18th-century shoebuckles and jewellery.

❋ KEW
Map ref 1876

Now covering 300 acres, the gardens at Kew are world-famous. The west of the gardens are largely woodland and arboretum, while the formal gardens are in the eastern half. There are also notable architectural features in the Palm House and the 163ft-high Chinese Pagoda.

Queen Elizabeth Hunting Lodge, Chingford, built for Henry VII

▦ LULLINGSTONE
Map ref 5264

To experience the comforts of life in Roman Britain, Lullingstone is the place to visit. Its remains are so well preserved that the layout of the villa, built during the first century and occupied until the fifth, can clearly be seen. It has been completely excavated and roofed over and the outstanding mosaic floors are on display. There is also an example of an early Christian chapel, rare in a private Roman dwelling.

Lullingstone Castle is a mainly 18th-century house with a splendid 15th-century gate tower. The great hall, library, staircase and state rooms are open to the public. The attractive grounds include a herb garden and the church of St Botolph.

🏛 MOSQUITO AIRCRAFT MUSEUM
Map ref 1803

The nearby town of Hatfield was the birthplace of the De Havilland aircraft and 18 of the company's planes, including three Mosquitoes, a Vampire, Venom and Horsa, can be seen at the Mosquito Aircraft Museum in London Colney. The collection also contains photographs, aero engines and memorabilia.

▦▦ TILBURY
Map ref 6476

Tilbury Fort was the scene of Queen Elizabeth I's review of the army mustered to oppose the Spanish Armada. Tilbury is now an important trading port.

The Thurrock Riverside Museum tells the story of the people associated with the River Thames.

▦ WALTHAM ABBEY
Map ref 3800

Among the ruins of Waltham Abbey still stands the Abbey Gatehouse, with separate entrances for pedestrians and carriages. The Norman abbey church contains a museum.

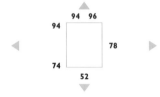

ESSEX: TOWN AND COUNTRY

In the south, along the banks of the Thames from Purfleet to Canvey Island, is the industrialised face of Essex with docks, oil terminals and factories. Further north are the picturesque villages of The Rodings, clustered near the country town of Chelmsford. Nearer to the Suffolk border are the wool towns, villages and windmills which hark back to past prosperity.

```
        94  96
    94  ┌──────┐
    ◄   │      │   ►
        │   78 │
    74  └──────┘
          52
           ▼
```

SELECTED PLACES TO VISIT

BISHOP'S STORTFORD
Map ref 4821
Bishop's Stortford, a busy market town, has an unusual museum: the Rhodes Memorial Museum and Commonwealth Centre. In an early 19th-century house it has displays illustrating the life and work of Cecil Rhodes in Africa.

CASTLE HEDINGHAM
Map ref 7835
The village is dominated by the great Norman keep of Hedingham Castle (100ft high) built in the 12th century by the De Veres, earls of Oxford. The banqueting Hall, minstrels' gallery and other parts of the castle have been well preserved.

Trips on an old-fashioned steam train can be enjoyed at the Colne Valley Railway. The original buildings of the Colne Valley and Halstead railway have been rebuilt on the site and there are seven steam locomotives. Other items of rolling stock are preserved in the museum. The site covers five wooded acres beside the river.

CHELMSFORD
Map ref 7007
The county town of Essex, Chelmsford is a thriving area of commerce and light industry. Something of its quieter, more rural past is captured in the displays of social history in the Chelmsford and Essex Museum, through archaeological finds, coins, costumes and paintings. The traditions of the Essex regiment also feature in a separate museum in the same building.

COGGESHALL
Map ref 8522
This delightful village owed its prosperity to wool and lace-making, as can be seen in the many beautiful

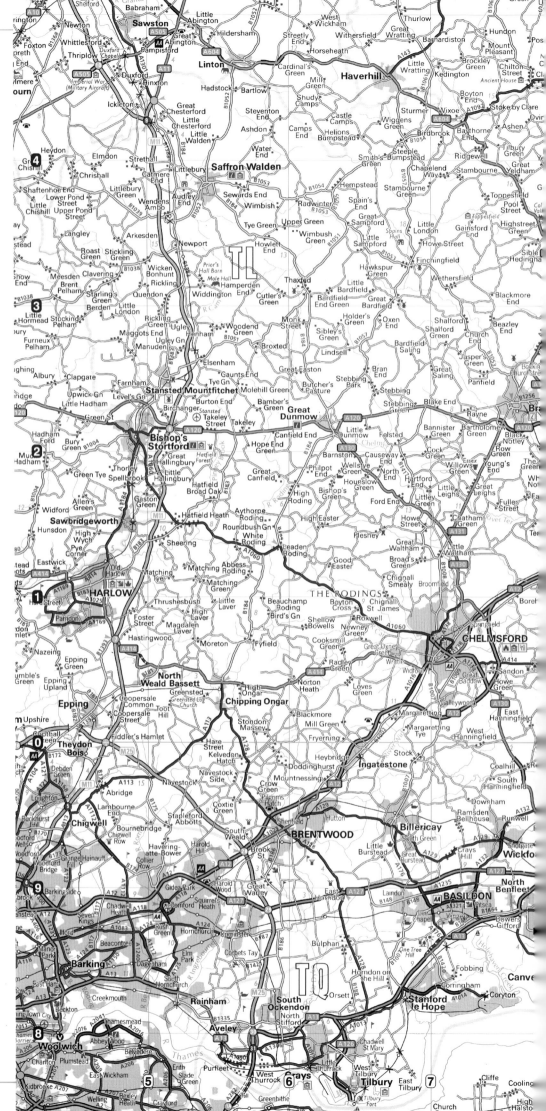

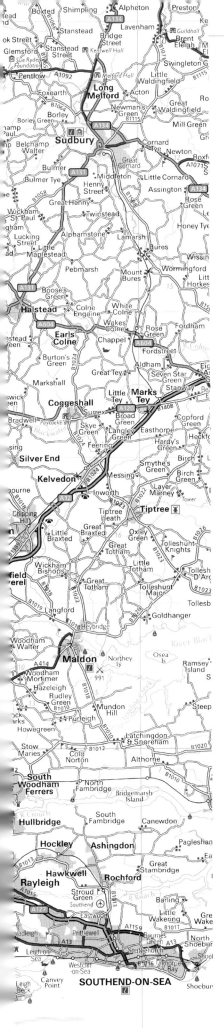

houses built for local merchants. Perhaps the best known is Paycocke's, a wool merchant's house dating from about 1500, now cared for by the National Trust. Its rich panelling and wood carving are especially fine and the house features a display of local lace.

Coggeshall Grange Barn is the oldest surviving timber-framed barn in Europe, dating from around 1140. Originally part of the Cistercian monastery of Coggeshall, it was restored recently and is also managed by the National Trust.

★ GREENSTED-JUXTA-ONGAR
Map ref 5303

Ongar is an Anglo-Saxon word meaning grazing land. The church at Greensted is the only surviving Saxon church with a nave wall built of logs. Made of oak, the logs were split into sections and set upright in an oak sill. The church is thought to have been founded around 1013. The body of King Edmund rested here on its way to Bury St Edmunds.

⚔ HADLEIGH
Map ref 8185

The ruins of Hadleigh Castle inspired John Constable for one of his famous landscape paintings. The castle, founded in 1231 and rebuilt by Edward III in the 14th century, has walls of Kentish rag. Two of the original towers survived the landslide which destroyed much of the structure, and they give views to the River Thames.

♦ HATFIELD FOREST
Map ref 5420

Hatfield Forest, near Bishop's Stortford, consists of more than 1,000 acres of ancient woodland, once part of the royal forests of Essex. For those with time to spare, the chases and rides make excellent walks, and the two lakes offer good coarse fishing.

★ LAYER MARNEY
Map ref 9217

Near Tiptree, Layer Marney Tower at the entrance to Lord Marney's mansion is a splendid 16th-century red brick edifice. The west wing of the main building contains architectural detail of the same type, while a long gallery of two storeys forms the south side.

⚓✕ MALDON
Map ref 8507

The beautiful old town of Maldon stands on the hill where, in 991, Brythnoth's Saxons desperately tried to resist the Viking invasion across the causeway from Northey Island. The story of the three-day battle is told in the stirring Anglo-Saxon epic poem, *The Battle of Maldon*.

The National Trust now owns the bird reserve on Northey Island in the Blackwater estuary. This is a Grade 1 site for overwintering birds and for saltmarsh plants. To visit, permits must be obtained 24 hours in advance. Access is limited as the island is cut off at high tide.

Today Maldon is important for sailing and fishing. The 13th-century church of All Saints attracts visitors to its unique triangular tower.

🏖 SOUTHEND-ON-SEA
Map ref 8886

One of the biggest seaside resorts in the country, Southend suffered a major disaster in June 1986 when its mile-long pier - the longest in Britain - was rammed by a ship. A lengthy programme of work is in progress to restore the pier to its former glory.

🏛 SPAINS HALL
Map ref 6734

The gardens of Spains Hall, near Finchingfield, are particularly attractive. A highlight of the flower garden is a large 17th-century Cedar of Lebanon. Within the house is much 18th- and 19th-century furniture and other *objets d'art*.

🏚 STANSTED MOUNTFITCHET
Map ref 5125

Stansted Mountfitchet has an excellently preserved windmill, with its machinery and other equipment intact. The imposing red brick structure is 65ft high.

🏚 THAXTED
Map ref 6131

This beautiful village with medieval church and timbered guildhall has many old houses and cottages. Thaxted also boasts a fine tower mill, dating from 1804, with five floors. Most of the original machinery survives and the sails and fantail have been re-erected. The first two floors are devoted to a museum of rural life.

🏛 UPMINSTER
Map ref 5686

A major exhibition of more than 2,000 examples of old agricultural and domestic implements and craft tools can be seen in the Tithe Barn Agricultural & Folk Museum at Upminster.

Paycocke's House at Coggeshall is a fine example of a medieval merchant's house

FROM BOUDICCA TO JOHN CONSTABLE

The eastern edge of Essex is dominated by the university town of Colchester, home of the Iceni tribe and their queen Boudicca and scene of many battles against the Roman invaders. Not far to the north, some 1,800 years later, the countryside around East Bergholt and Flatford Mill was to inspire many of the paintings of John Constable, arguably England's finest landscape artist.

98

◄ 76 ►

54 ▼

SELECTED PLACES TO VISIT

🄜 CLACTON-ON-SEA
Map ref 1715

Clacton is a traditional Victorian seaside resort complete with promenade, pier, pavilion, scenic railways and municipal gardens.

Bourne Mill, Colchester; a converted Dutch-gabled fishing lodge of 1591

🄜🄐🄧🄐🄜 COLCHESTER
Map ref 9925

Colchester, dating back to the Iron Age, claims to be the oldest recorded town in England. It was the first settled by the Romans, then captured by Boudicca (Boadicea), queen of the Iceni. Eventually the Romans retook the city and rebuilt the settlement, which became one of the most important Roman centres in Britain.

After the Romans left, Colchester was invaded by the Anglo-Saxons, the Danes and finally the Normans, who built the massive castle of which only the keep now survives. The castle was constructed on the vaults of the Roman temple of Claudius and it now houses an important collection of antiquities.

In 1989, Colchester celebrated the 800th anniversary of King Richard's royal charter.

The town was beseiged by Cromwell's army during the Civil War, and the two Royalist commanders were executed for their defiance.

During the Middle Ages, weaving was the chief trade. Now Colchester is famous for its oysters.

It is perhaps not unreasonable that a town of Colchester's history should boast as many as five museums. As well as the Castle museum, there is the Natural History Museum in All Saints Church – a building dating back to the 15th century with a flint tower.

Also in an ecclesiastical setting is the Social History Museum in Holy Trinity Church.

Hollytrees Museum has a collection of toys and costumes in a lovely Georgian house and Tymperleys Clock Museum contains a collection of locally made clocks.

🐘 COLCHESTER ZOO
Map ref 9522
Colchester Zoo can be found in the 40-acre park of Stanway Hall. The zoo is home to a large collection of mammals, and includes a reptile house, aquarium and birdland. A miniature railway runs along the side of the lake.

🏛🎨 DEDHAM
Map ref 0533
Famed for its connections with artists John Constable and Sir Alfred Munnings, Dedham is an attractive village. The church tower features in many of Constable's paintings.

In Castle House, home of Sir

Alfred Munnings, many of his paintings, sketches and drawings are on display.

In the Art and Craft Centre – converted from a church – is a toy museum.

✳ ELMSTEAD MARKET
Map ref 0624
Beth Chatto Gardens, begun fewer than 30 years ago, is unusual in contrasting different types of garden. The shade garden has flowering plants and plants with fine foliage, while the dry garden, in full sun and gravelly soil, features plants adapted to drought. A wet environment is provided by the five large pools, well stocked with fish, which are surrounded by plants preferring boggy conditions. There are also nurseries which include more than 1,000 differing species of plant.

🏛 FELIXSTOWE
Map ref 3035
A popular family resort, with a wide range of facilities, Felixtowe is also a continental ferry port, with sailings to Zeebrugge. The Q Tower on South Hill, a martello tower built in 1810 as a defence against the expected invasion by Napoleon, is open during the summer.

⭐ FLATFORD MILL
Map ref 0733
Just upstream from Flatford Mill is the Bridge Cottage, immortalised in a number of Constable's paintings,

The heavily decorated exterior of the 15th-century Ancient House, Ipswich

which now houses a display about the artist. The peace and beauty of the landscape which inspired the artist in the early 19th century have survived the attention of sightseers.

A display of prints of Constable's work and photographs, and tools used by the craftsmen of his day can be found in Granary Bygones, which also contains a collection of vintage bicycles.

🏛 HADLEIGH
Map ref 8187
Hadleigh, to the west of Ipswich, has a long high street with attractive examples of local architectural styles. In Wolves Wood – managed by the Royal Society for the Protection of Birds – a variety of woodland birds can be seen by walkers along the signposted paths.

🏛 HARWICH
Map ref 2531
A busy port for more than a millenium, Harwich today is an important car ferry port to the Hook of Holland and Scandinavia. Its narrow cobbled streets add to the seafaring atmosphere.

🏛🎨🏛 IPSWICH
Map ref 1644
The county town of Suffolk and a major commercial and shopping centre, Ipswich is particularly rich in medieval churches.

Christchurch Mansion, an extensive Tudor town house, has an outstanding collection of decorative art, including china and glass. The adjoining Wolsey Art Gallery has a display of paintings by famous local artists. Gainsborough (who lived in Ipswich) and Constable are well represented, together with other Suffolk artists.

The Ancient House in the Butter Market has Britain's finest example of pargeting, a form of decorative plasterwork. In Ipswich Museum are replicas of the major Saxon treasures and a Roman villa.

⭐ MISTLEY
Map ref 1231
Only two great lodges survive of the ambitious plan by Richard Rigby (Paymaster General in 1762) to build a spa town in Mistley and Manningtree. The lodges were the work of Robert Adam, who was also responsible for the twin square porticoed towers which are the sole relics of a church.

⭐ ROSE GREEN
Map ref 9744
St James's Chapel at Rose Green is a small thatched flint and stone chapel, built in the 13th century, once attached to a nearby castle.

🏛 WALTON ON THE NAZE
Map ref 2622
The Naze is a promontory jutting out into the North Sea, with a tower to warn sailors of the rocky coastline. The town itself is popular for bathing and sea fishing, while the salt-marshes behind offer wonderful scope for birdwatchers.

MOUNTAINS AND WATERFALLS

The majestic landscape of the Brecon Beacons and the Black Mountain, clear rivers and sparkling waterfalls make this one of Wales's most visually stunning areas. Castles perched on limestone crags, spa resorts and bustling market towns provide a continuity between past and present.

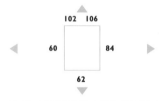

TOUR

BRECON BEACONS, VALE OF NEATH AND FFOREST FAWR
67 MILES

From Brecon, the tour takes the A470 south-west into the Brecon Beacons. Within the 520 square miles of national park, largely formed of old red sandstone rock, is spectacular scenery. The name of these towering flat-topped mountains, with their sheer rockfaces, moorlands, lakes, waterfalls and caves, came from the network of beacons used to warn of danger and to celebrate national events.

At Libanus a side road to the right leads to the Brecon Beacons National Park Mountain Centre, a useful source of information on local geology, flora and fauna and possible start point for exploration on foot.

The A470 climbs on, with superb views to the left of the twin summits of Pen-y-Fan at 2,907ft and Corn Du at 2,863ft. The National Trust manages more than 8,000 acres of the main part of the Brecon Beacons range, including Pen-y-Fan, its highest peak, generously given by the appropriately named Sir Brian Mountain, chairman of the Eagle Star insurance company.

If time permits (and the ascent takes only about 1¹/₂ hours), the mountain can be climbed by the 'easy' route, starting at the Storey Arms centre and walking up a gently winding path. The effort is rewarded at the summit by magnificent views of the Malvern Hills, the Bristol Channel, and north and south Wales. In contrast, the northern side of the mountain is not so hospitable, with sheer precipices looking dizzily down to the valley of the River Taff.

At the fork of the road, the tour bears right on to the A4059 towards Hirwaun, where it turns right on to the A465 for Glyn-Neath and the Vale of Neath.

After a short distance on the right is the hamlet of Pont-Nêdd Féchan, at the beginning of the Vale of Neath, where the Rivers Nedd and Mellte meet in spectacular ravines and waterfalls, only accessible on foot. At Glyn-Neath opencast coal workings mark the end of the coal-mining area stretching to the south-west and the transition to limestone.

The road follows the deeply wooded gorge of the River Neath to Aberdulais (see page 62). Here the tour takes a sharp turn northwards on to the A4109, following the valley of the River Dulais, where at Crynant the Cefn Coed archaeological museum explains how the power of the waterfalls has provided energy for coal and mineral workings.

At Dyffryn Cellwen the tour turns left on to the A4221 and along to Abercraf, passing the Henrhyd Falls on a by-road to the right, and then takes the A4067 north-east into the Fforest Fawr. Two miles north of Abercraf, near Glyntawe, are the Dan-yr-Ogof caves, famous for their coloured stalactites and stalagmites and underground lakes, in a splendid setting reminiscent of Cheddar Gorge.

The Fforest Fawr (the Great Forest) derives its name from the medieval term for a royal hunting ground, and has always been moorland rather than a wooded forest. Here the Lords of Brecon hunted for game.

The road runs in the shadow of Fan Gilorych, which rises to 2,382ft, passing the Cray reservoir on the left and down into Sennybridge, meeting the valley of the River Usk at the southernmost point of Mynydd Eppynt.

At Sennybridge the tour joins the main A40 back to Brecon.

SELECTED PLACES TO VISIT

BRECON
Map ref 0428
Set in the picturesque Usk valley with the magnificent Brecon

This beautiful waterfall is on the River Mellte in the southern Brecon Beacons

Beacons to the south, Brecon has been settled since Iron Age times.

The present town grew up around the Norman castle, now ruined and with little remaining of its former glory. Close by is the cathedral, also built in Norman times. Formerly an abbey church, it was elevated to the status of cathedral only in 1923.

A quietly prosperous market town, Brecon has an important museum containing many items of folk life, such as Welsh lovespoons and costumes, a reconstructed Welsh kitchen, and a prehistoric boat.

Brecon is a military town too, and many objects relating to the history of the South Wales Borders and Monmouthshire regiments (now merged into the Royal Regiment of Wales) are displayed in the 24th Regiment Museum in the old barracks. Among the mementoes proudly on show are 16 of the 23 Victoria Crosses, won for exceptional bravery, weapons, photographs and a special exhibition on the Zulu War.

BRECON MOUNTAIN RAILWAY
Map ref 0509
The Brecon Mountain Railway starts at Pant Station north of Merthyr Tydfil and continues through the beautiful scenery of the Brecon Beacons National Park, as far as the Taf Fechan. The train is pulled by a vintage steam locomotive, and more are on display in the workshops at Pant Station.

BUILTH WELLS
Map ref 0350
Set at an important junction of many roads in the valley of the River Wye, Builth Wells became a fashionable spa town in the early 19th century. Now it is the permanent headquarters of the Royal Welsh Show, held each summer, and a centre for ponytrekking, fishing and canoeing.

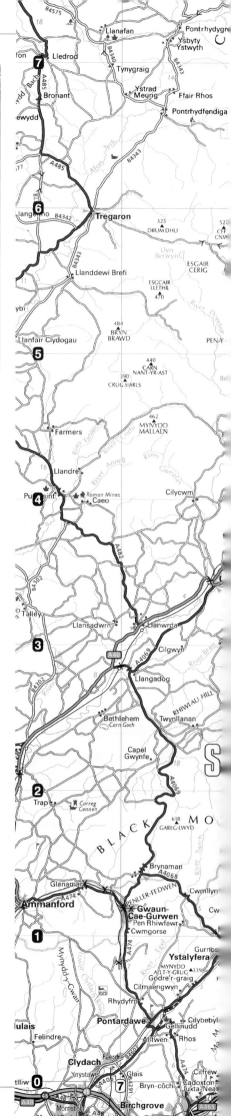

✕ ⛵ CARREG CENNEN
Map ref 6719

On the peak of a limestone crag, soaring to 300ft above the Cennen valley, with the Black Mountain as its backdrop, the small but striking castle of Carreg Cennen, near the village of Trapp, was considered impregnable until its capture by Owain Glyndwr. On the south side is a passage which bores through the solid rock for 150ft. A torch is advisable for visitors wanting to reach the wishing well.

⚘ GARWNANT
Map ref 0013

To the south of the Brecon Beacons, 5 miles north of Merthy Tydfil, the Garwnant Forest Centre is housed in converted farm buildings. It offers a wealth of information about the facilities, with trails leading into the wooded valleys. There is also a children's adventure play area.

⊞⊠ LLANDOVERY
Map ref 7634

Set between the Rivers Towy and Bran, surrounded by smaller streams and at the junction of several roads, Llandovery was a major centre for cattle droving at the end of the 18th century, when herds of black cattle were driven from the Welsh hills to English cattle markets. The town still has an important cattle market today.

However, only fragments remain of the Norman castle which was captured by the Welsh. At the north end of the town is Llanfair Church, where Wales's famous hymnwriter Williams Williams is buried.

⊞⊞ LLANDRINDOD WELLS
Map ref 0561

Wales's main spa town, Llandrindod Wells was particularly popular at the turn of the century, when visitors were attracted to travel by train to take its restorative waters. Today visitors continue to find its excellent conference facilities, drama festival and Victorian festival, a reason to make the journey, as well as to taste the springs.

The town Museum contains exhibits excavated from the Roman Camp at Castell Collen to the north. A Victorian spa gallery with 19th-century chemists' equipment and costumes gives a flavour of life 100 years ago.

TRESCASTLE
Map ref 8829

From Trescastle, with its ruined 12th-century castle and large motte and bailey, a mountain road runs past the Usk reservoir and into the Black Mountain, climbing close to its 2,632ft peak.

⚘ Y GAER
Map ref 0029

The Romans built a fort, Y Gaer, near Battle village, where huge grassy ramparts and remains of walls and gates still conjure up the scale of the fortification.

BRECON BEACONS

The majestic Brecon Beacons, towering above the valley of the River Usk, give their name to the surrounding 519 square miles of National Park

The Brecon Beacons National Park is spread over parts of Dyfed, Gwent, Mid-Glamorgan and Powys. Set up in 1957, it is the youngest of the National Parks and differs from the others in one important respect. In most of the Parks, but the Peak District in particular, the fight had been to bring about accessibility to large areas of land, privately owned and effectively barred to the public. In complete contrast, the Brecons contained a great deal of common land – some 35 per cent – and the designation was intended to protect land and ensure that free access would continue to be available. For over a century people had used the Brecons as an escape from the mills and mines of the South Wales valleys.

Ironically, within a few years, industry in the valleys was in decline, but the demand for a place to `get away from it all' has, if anything, increased in the last 20 years. Both Cardiff and Swansea are less than 30 miles from the Park and visitors from the Midlands can travel down the M5, M50 and A40 through Abergavenny into the Park. From London and the south-east the M4 runs direct to Newport and the nearest point of the Park, at Pontypool, is then just 10 miles from junction 26.

If the National Parks were analysed and ranked in order of the problems they face, the Brecons would almost certainly emerge at the bottom of the list. That is not to understate the problems the Park does face, but the military presence is very limited, there are few `honeypots' to worry the purist, and little sign that developers and planners are seriously challenging the natural scenery of this Park.

A Distinctive Beauty

Daniel Defoe must have approached the mountains of the Brecon Beacons from the north to have described them as `horrid and frightful'. But Defoe was rarely at ease in wild country – it was not until much later that writers began to appreciate its special beauty.

It is perfectly possible to travel the length of the Brecon Beacons National Park from Abergavenny to Llandovery, along the A40, without leaving the gentle valleys. Sugar Loaf and Table Mountain rise to the right of the road early on, Bryn can be seen on the left behind Talybont, but the classic Beacons – Cribin, Corn Du and Pen-y-Fan, the highest peak south of the Snowdon range – are all 5 miles south of the Brecon by-pass.

Only the A470 passes near them. Even after leaving the valley of the Usk, the A40 stays

The dark, brooding range of the Black Mountains lies to the west of the Brecon Beacons

in river valleys, curtained from `horrid and frightful' sights by trees.

Ancient Flora

Had Defoe come to the Brecons from the south, he would have found a very different landscape of long, gradually sloping moorland: grassland dominated by purple moor-grass, mat-grass and fescues. The moorland ends with dramatic suddenness where the action of grit-filled Ice Age glaciers has carved sheer cliffs from the surface of the old red sandstone. On the cliff edges grow plants which are survivals of an older, pre-Ice Age flora: purple saxifrage and globe flower. Far below the peaks, trapped in the U-shaped valleys or *cwms*, lie small, dark,

Above: *The spectacular cave system of Dan-yr-Ogof, created by the Tawe*
Right: *A narrow boat 'locking' up the Monmouthshire and Brecon Canal*

The Mighty Contrasts

The classic mountains of the centre are flanked by two ranges. To the west lies the Black Mountain, remarkably remote, brooding and full of myth and mystery and not to be confused with the Black Mountains which run north from the valley of the Usk to Hay-on-Wye. Crossed only by the A479, they form the eastern edge of the Park. The main plant cover is heather, with bilberry and crowberry;

running close to the northern boundary of the Park, before leaving it at Abergavenny. From Brecon, the river has another companion, the Monmouthshire and Brecon Canal, one of those rare creations of man which enhance the scenery and are a joy in any season. Lovers of wildfowl will appreciate another man-made feature, Talybont Reservoir, with its huge winter flocks of duck.

Purely on grounds of height

A lesser horseshoe bat – inhabitant of the cave system of Craig-y-Ciliau

corrie lakes – though now a reservoir, Llyn-y-Fan Fach is a classic example.

At the very southernmost part of the Brecons, the sandstone gives way to a narrow band of limestone and millstone grit which effectively forms the boundary of the Park. Beyond it lie the industrial valleys of South Wales to which so many people moved in the 19th century. Derelict farm buildings dotted about within the National Park are mute testimony to that migration.

Waterfalls and Wildlife

The presence of the limestone adds greatly to the variety of the Brecons' scenery. In many places boisterous waterfalls tumble over layers of millstone grit, while spectacular cave formations have been carved out of the limestone by rivers which run off the peaty high moorland to create the famous valleys to the south. The valley of Taf Fawr and the waterfalls of the Hepste and the Mellte are always a particular delight.

Several of the cave systems are dangerous and require permits, but the Dan-yr-Ogof show caverns on the River Tawe are perfectly safe for visitors. Just to the east is the NCC reserve of Ogof Ffynon Ddu, containing one of the largest cave systems in Britain (permit required). Above it the `grikes' – narrow slits in the limestone – contain rare plants like mountain everlasting, lily-of-the-valley and mountain melick. Heather and bilberry cover the moor where common upland birds like wheatear and ring ouzel breed. Ogof Ffynon Ddu is one of several upland areas where it is possible to see the low level, fast flight of a hunting merlin.

bracken is becoming a problem on some sites such as the slopes of the Sugar Loaf mountain. In complete contrast, just below Talgarth, and on the northern edge of the Brecons, is the lovely mixed woodland of Pwyll-y-Wrach. A clear, fast stream runs through the wood which is alive with flowers in both spring and summer.

South of the Black Mountains, near Crickhowell, there is a famous outcrop of limestone, Craig-y-Ciliau. Here five rare whitebeams – small-leaved lime and beech trees, considerably further west than their normal range – are among the fascinating variety of trees, plants, birds and mammals taking advantage of a number of habitats; limestone crags, heath, stream, bog and a cave system used by lesser horseshoe bats.

The Usk is the major river, rising in the north-west and then, in company with the A40,

and wildness, the Brecon Beacons have acted as a barrier, between the Welsh and the English, and between North and South Wales, limiting the spread of industrialisation although this was due, in part, to the coal seams halting where the millstone grit began. Sheep farming was always the industry of the mountains and there are still many times more sheep than people living in the Brecon Beacons.

Man has, inevitably, left evidence of his occupation throughout the Brecons.

Barrows, stone circles, hill forts – all have been located. Near Brecon is the Roman fort of Y Gaer and the Normans left a number of castles, none more impressive than Carreg Cennen. In total contrast is the tranquil Augustinian Priory at Llanthony where it is still possible to see, as did Giraldus in the 12th century `the tops of the mountains touching the heavens'.

The globe flower is one of the Beacons' throwbacks to pre-Ice Age flora

THE MARCHES

A belligerent past, recalled by many castles and fortifications, saw this border country contested bitterly between the Welsh and the invading Romans, and later between the Welsh and the English.

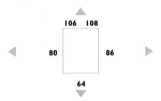

106 108

80   86

64

TOUR

FORTIFICATIONS ALONG THE WELSH BORDERS
64 MILES

Starting in England, at Ross-on-Wye, the tour travels west along the A40/A49, turning left on to the B4521 after Peterstow. It crosses into Wales just before Skenfrith.

Skenfrith Castle formed the easternmost point and the smallest of the trilateral border defences erected to keep out the Welsh from this north-east corner of Monmouthshire. Set on the river, the 13th-century round keep within a walled circuit was built by Hubert de Burgh. The village church houses the 15th-century embroidery known as the Skenfrith Cope.

Turning right on to the B4347, the next stopping place on the tour is Grosmont, northern point of the trilateral defences. Grosmont Castle, rebuilt on a mound in the 13th century by Hubert de Burgh, is surrounded by a deep ditch. The town was burned by Owain Glyndwr, who was defeated here by Henry of Monmouth, later Henry V.

At Pontrilas the tour joins the A465, turning south west towards Abergavenny. To the right are the magnificent Black Mountains of Gwent, with peaks rising to 2,660ft. Passing the ancient hamlet of Llanvihangel Crucorney, at the foot of the 1,601ft high 'holy mountain' of Skirrid-Fawr, the route leads into Abergavenny.

Set in a bowl surrounded by three mighty peaks, Abergavenny has been a strategic crossing point for centuries and was fortified by the Romans. The Normans built a castle as yet another defence in the constant battles against the Welsh. The remains of the castle are used for the district museum.

The B4233 heads due east to Llantilio-Crossenny, where the church stands among prehistoric earthworks. On the other side of the road is the moated enclosure of Hen-Gwrt, a rectangular medieval manor house.

A short diversion leads to the third – and finest – of Hubert de Burgh's trilateral defences, White Castle.

Continuing east, the tour reaches Monmouth, county town of old Monmouthshire and now part of Gwent. Henry V was born in the since-ruined Norman castle, but the beautiful bridge, built in 1260, still spans the River Monnow.

Crossing into England, the tour takes the A466 and B4231 to Clearwell, where exhibits of local mining and geology are on display in the Clearwell Caves Ancient Iron Mines. Eight large caverns can be visited, and there are vintage engines on show.

This is the edge of the Forest of Dean, which covers some 27,000 acres and contains around 20 million trees. Mining for coal and quarrying for stone have long been important local industries. Turning north on the B4228, the road passes Coleford, with its rows of terraced miners' cottages.

There are many trails through the forest, and one of the most spectacular starts from Symonds Yat (400ft high) overlooking the magnificent gorge of the Wye Valley. The Herefordshire Rural Heritage Museum at Symonds Yat houses a large collection of historic farm machinery.

The final castle of the tour is found on the B4228 at Goodrich, hewn between the 12th and 14th centuries from the sandstone on which its stands. The Wye Valley Open Farm houses rare breeds of domestic animals. Continue north for the return to Ross-on-Wye.

SELECTED PLACES TO VISIT

🏛 BERRINGTON HALL
Map ref 5164
Berrington Hall, to the north of Leominster, is an elegant late 18th-century house, landscaped by Capability Brown. Inside are beautiful ceilings and fine furniture.

🏛 BLAENAVON
Map ref 2509
The Big Pit Mining Museum is in a mine worked until 1980. Visitors with safety helmets and lamps can descend to 300ft to experience what life was like for South Wales miners. On the surface are the pithead baths and changing rooms and an exhibition of the history of Big Pit.

🏛 BURTON COURT
Map ref 4357
This mainly Georgian house has a 14th-century timber-roofed great hall. It contains collections of European and Oriental costumes, ship models and a working model fairground.

🏛 CROFT CASTLE
Map ref 4566
Croft castle has walls and corner towers dating from the 14th century. The interior is mainly 18th century. A fine avenue of 350-year-old Spanish chestnuts graces the

The ancient and attractive town of Ross-on-Wye

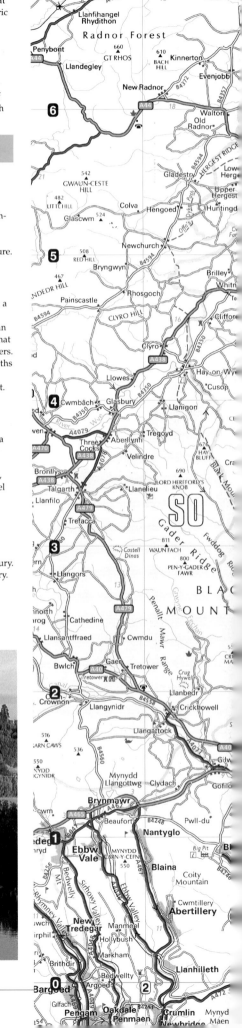

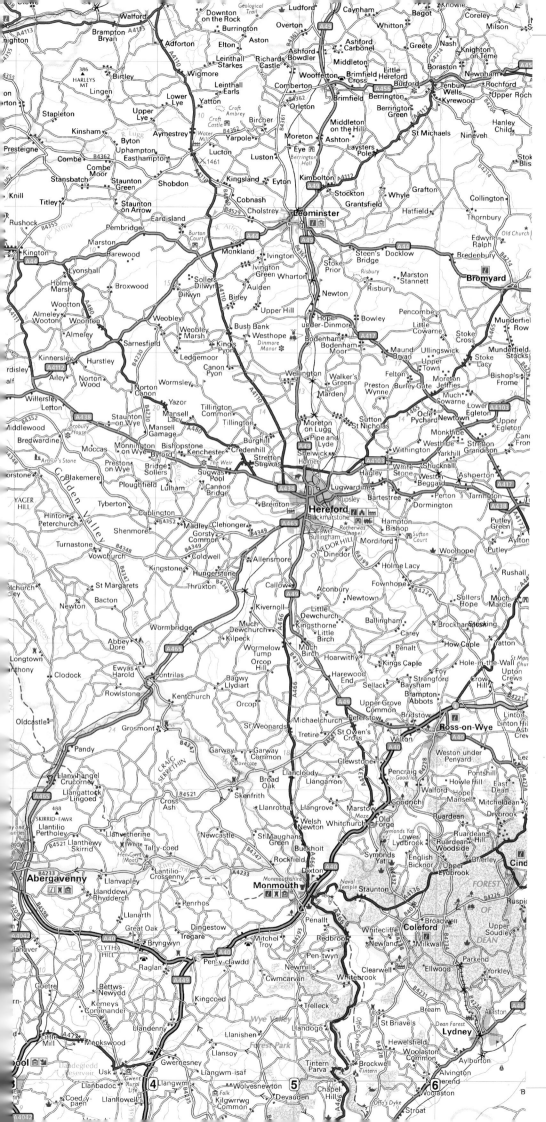

gardens, and a footpath leads to
Croft Ambrey, an Iron Age fort.

❋ DINMORE MANOR
Map ref 4950

Between Hereford and Leominster
is Dinmore Manor, a chapel of the
Knights of St John of Jerusalem,
with cloisters and music room
dating back to the 12th century.

⬚ HAY-ON-WYE
Map ref 2343

Hay-on-Wye is a paradise for
bookworms, with more second-
hand bookshops to the square inch
than in any other town or village. It
is set high above the river, with the
Black Mountains as a backdrop.

⬚⬚⬚⬚⬚⬚ HEREFORD
Map ref 5139

The history of the cathedral city,
once the Saxon capital of West
Mercia, is preserved and explained
in the Museum and Art Gallery.

A branch museum in Churchill
Gardens features a Victorian
nursery, pantry and parlour, and the
Brian Hatton Art Gallery is devoted
to works by this local artist.

The superb cathedral, on a 7th-
century consecrated site but dating
back to Norman times, contains the
Mappa Mundi, a map of the world
drawn about 1300.

Hereford is famous for cider, and
the Cider Museum and King Offa
Cider Brandy Distillery trace the
history of cider making.

The St John & Coningsby
Museum has armour and other
items associated with the Knights of
St John for whom the 13th-century
chapel and hall were built. The Old
House, a Jacobean town house, is
furnished in 17th-century style.

❋ HERGEST CROFT
Map ref 2756

Hergest Croft Gardens lie on the
route of the Offa's Dyke Path and
on the edge of Hergest Ridge. They
are a blaze of colour.

⬚⬚ LEOMINSTER
Map ref 4959

An old wool town, Leominster is
also renowned for cider and cattle.
The folk museum reflects these
agricultural interests and also
features archaeological objects,
historic maps and costumes.

⬚ ROSS-ON-WYE
Map ref 6024

This lovely market town benefited
greatly from the philanthropy of
John Kyrle, a 17th-century resident
whose influence can be seen in
many public buildings and works.
He laid out The Prospect, a public
garden, and gave the town its water
supply.

✕ ⬚⬚ TRETOWER
Map ref 1821

Tretower Court, home of the family
of famous poet Henry Vaughan, is a
fortified manor house dating from
the 15th century. Nearby are the
ruins of Tretower Castle, a Norman
defence with a circular keep.

LAND OF THE LOWER SEVERN

The fertile Vale of Evesham, the medieval abbeys and manor houses and the magnificent cathedrals of Gloucester and Worcester make this one of the most peaceful and attractive corners of England, although the battlefields from the Wars of the Roses and the Civil War remind the visitor that it was not always so. Elgar and Holst were just two of the many musicians and artists to find inspiration here.

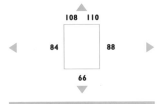

```
        108  110
    84            88
          66
```

TOUR

WESTERN COTSWOLDS, VALE OF EVESHAM AND TEWKESBURY
43 MILES

Leaving Cheltenham on the B4632 through Prestbury, the tour passes the beauty spot of Cleeve Hill on its way to Winchcombe.

The little town of Winchcombe was once capital of Anglo-Saxon Mercia. The ruins of the abbey here, built in 797, have been excavated. Sudeley Castle, birthplace of Queen Katherine Parr, the wife who surivived Henry VIII, houses works by Turner, Constable, Rubens and Van Dyck, as well as antique furniture and tapestries.

The town's Folk Museum has a display of police uniforms and equipment, and the Railway Museum contains fascinating memorabilia.

Seventeen cloister arches feature in the excavated remains of Hailes Abbey, built in 1246.

At Toddington station near Didbrook, the Gloucestershire and Warwickshire Steam Railway runs a round trip of 6 miles to Winchcombe.

Slightly off the B4632 is Stanway House, a Jacobean manor built of limestone with a gatehouse and tithe barn. The tour rejoins the road just north of Stanton, and meets the A44 at the beautiful Cotswold village of Broadway, famed for its antique shops. The Broadway Tower Country Park features a folly tower built in 1799. From its observation room are

The gateway of Jacobean Stanway House in Gloucestershire

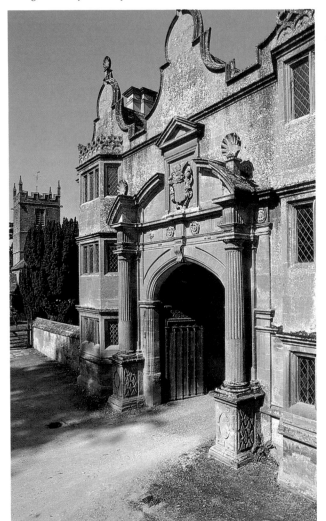

magnificent views over 12 counties.

The tour continues north, forking left on to the B4035 along the fertile Vale of Evesham. In the centre of Bretforton is The Fleece Inn, owned by the National Trust. This medieval half-timbered farmhouse, licensed in 1848, remains largely unaltered.

Evesham is the next major town, a centre of the Vale's fruit-growing industry. Its ruined 14th-century abbey stands close to the river. The Almonry Museum is in a 14th-century stone and half-timbered building, connected with the abbey, and tells the story of the Vale.

The tour travels south and west on the A435 passing pretty villages such as Conderton where pottery is hand-made, and Beckford where silk is hand-printed.

Tewkesbury is an attractive town of medieval black-and-white houses and inns. The Lancastrians were defeated here in 1471 during the Wars of the Roses, and a model of the battle can be seen in Tewkesbury Museum.

The tour turns left on to the A4019 at Coombe Hill for the journey back to Cheltenham.

SELECTED PLACES TO VISIT

CHELTENHAM
Map ref 9523
Fashionable spa and centre for music and the arts, Cheltenham abounds in elegant Regency houses. Arguably its most beautiful building is the Pittville Pump Room, a masterpiece of 19th-century classical revival. The Pump Room also houses the Museum and Gallery of Fashion, with displays depicting the town's history.

Cheltenham's Art Gallery and Museum has a superb collection of paintings from the 16th century onwards, and furniture and metal-work made by followers of William Morris. Material on the social history and archaeology of the Cotswolds is found in the museum.

In the Regency house where the composer of *The Planets* was born in 1874 is the Gustav Holst Museum.

GLOUCESTER
Map ref 8418
The Roman fortified settlement of Glevum guarded the route into Wales. The county town and cathedral city of Gloucester is now a commercial centre.

The cathedral is a Norman foundation. Its highlight is a magnificent medieval stained glass window, 72ft by 38ft.

Gloucester's many fascinating museums feature Roman mosaics and sculpture, antique furniture and barometers, a freshwater aquarium, wheelwright's shop and a Double Gloucester dairy, to name but a few.

GREAT MALVERN
Map ref 7846
The 9-mile range of the Malvern Hills makes a perfect backdrop to this former spa town. The museum

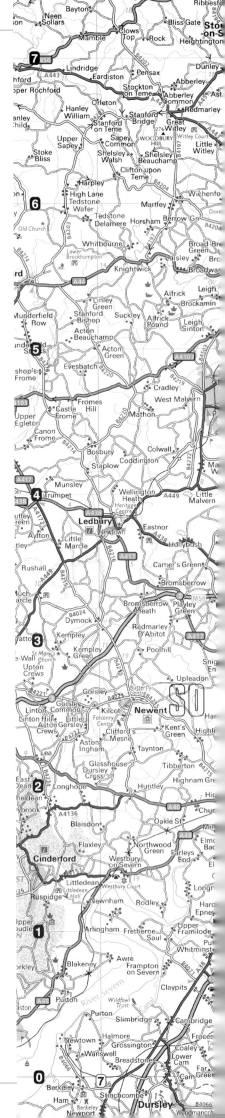

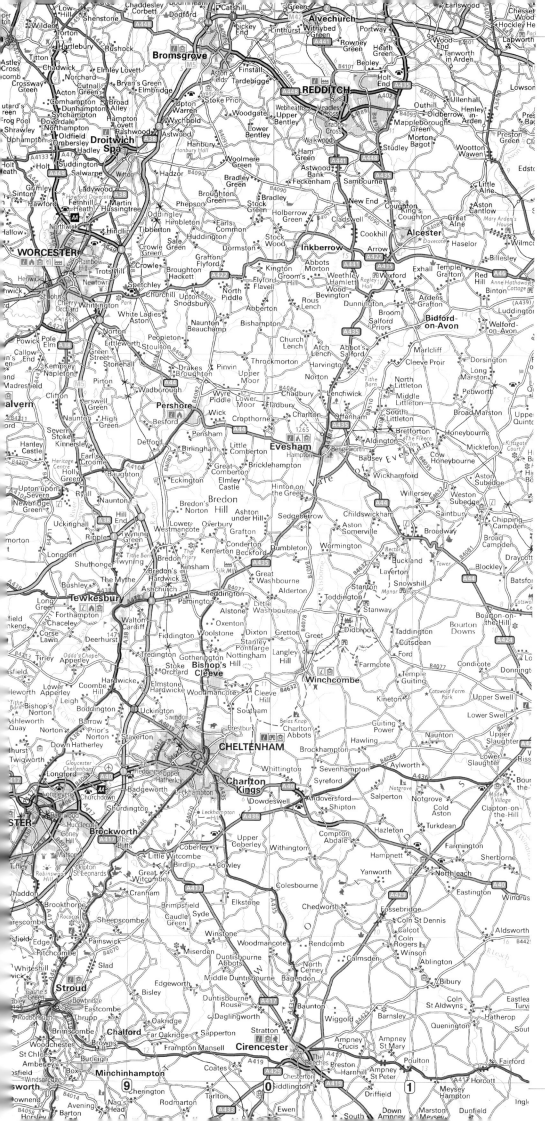

– in one of the two buildings which survive from the Benedictine monastery – covers the town's history, from water cure to the silicon chip.

🏛 LITTLEDEAN HALL
Map ref 6714

Littledean Hall stands on the remains of an 11th-century Saxon hall.

The site is of great archaeological significance as the Roman temple discovered here in 1984 has proved to be the largest building of its type yet found in Britain.

🏛🏛 PERSHORE
Map ref 9445

The market town of Pershore stands beside a six-arched bridge, built in the 14th century over the River Avon. Only part of Pershore Abbey survived the dissolution, but its Norman lantern tower and intricately carved vaulting are outstanding.

🏛🏛 REDDITCH
Map ref 0565

The Forge Mill Museum in Redditch is the only remaining water-driven needle-scouring mill, demonstrating the history of needlemaking and the fishing tackle industry.

🏛🏛 STROUD
Map ref 8505

The history of this old wool town is recorded in the Stroud District Museum. The exhibits cover geology, local crafts and industrial archaeology.

❀ WESTBURY COURT
Map ref 7214

Westbury Court Garden is a formal Dutch water garden, laid out at the end of the 17th century, and recently restored.

⚐ WILDFOWL TRUST
Map ref 7305

Close to the Severn estuary at Slimbridge is the Wildfowl Trust established by Sir Peter Scott. Here the world's largest collection of swans, ducks and geese can be studied and other wildfowl can be viewed. Nature trails, permanent exhibitions and a tropical house all explain the Trust's conservation work.

🏛🏛🏛🏛 WORCESTER
Map ref 8555

County town of Hereford and Worcester, this ancient city has a magnificent Norman cathedral containing the tomb of King John. It boasts the finest collection of Worcester china in the world in the Dyson Perrins Museum.

The City Museum and Art Gallery houses collections on local regiments, natural history, geology and fine art. The Tudor House Museum features domestic and local history.

Charles II had his headquarters at the Commandery during the Battle of Worcester in 1651, and the museum contains Civil War relics.

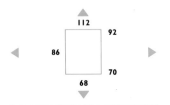

STATESMEN, SCHOLARS AND THE BARD

This area is rich in historical associations. Here lived great statesmen like Churchill and his ancestor the Duke of Marlborough; here lived Oxford scholars who have added to human knowledge over many centuries; and here lived William Shakespeare, the finest English playwright of any age.

```
        112
    ◄    [  86  92  ]    ►
         68    70
        ▼
```

TOUR

BLENHEIM PALACE AND THE CENTRAL COTSWOLDS
65 MILES

The tour begins in Oxford, heading north on the A34. In the simple village churchyard of Bladon, to the south of Blenheim Park, is the grave of Sir Winston Churchill, beside that of his parents, Lord and Lady Randolph Churchill.

Blenheim Palace was built by Vanbrugh to recognise the victory of the first Duke of Marlborough over the French. The magnificent 2,000-acre park was landscaped by Capability Brown. The gilded staterooms contain fine paintings, furniture and tapestries, and the bedroom where Sir Winston was born in 1874 forms part of the Churchill Exhibition.

Woodstock town has many lovely stone houses. The Oxfordshire County Museum features a changing programme of selected treasures.

At a crossroads take the B4437 left towards Chipping Norton, passing through Charlbury. Before Blenheim Palace was built, nearby Cornbury House was the largest house in Oxfordshire.

The road climbs through the Cotswold scenery and at its highest point of 700ft meets Chipping Norton. 'Chipping' meant 'market'; the town's position at the junction of many roads was ideal. Many superb examples of 17th-century Cotswold stone buildings remain, including delightful almshouses and the Guildhall.

From Chipping Norton the tour joins the A44, turning left at the crossroads on to the A437 and into Gloucestershire. Stow-on-the-Wold is also set high up at a major crossroads. Once a bustling centre for wool, Stow has many elegant Cotswold town houses. In the market square are the medieval town stocks.

Taking the A429 south and west, the route comes to Bourton-on-the-

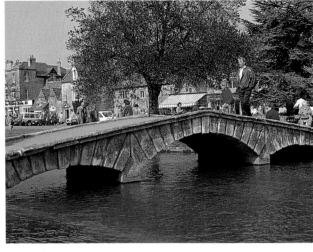

One of the many bridges across the River Windrush in the Cotswold village of Bourton-on-the-Water

Water, where the River Windrush is crossed by many bridges.

Behind the Old New Inn is the fascinating Model Village, built in Cotswold stone to one-ninth of the scale of the actual village. In the Old Mill is the Village Life Exhibition, showing a complete Edwardian village shop with bedroom, bathroom and kitchen. The exhibition also features a blacksmith's forge.

Within the four acres of Birdland Zoo Gardens are some 1,200 species of foreign and exotic birds. Folly Farm is a conservation centre for many rare and endangered species of fowl. The Cotswolds Motor Museum in an old barley mill has cars, motorcycles and a large collection of old advertising signs.

By way of Little Rissington and Westcote, the tour returns to Oxfordshire on the A424 and travels south to hilly Burford. One of the most beautiful Cotswold towns, Burford is rich in medieval houses and has an ancient church. Among the 16th-century buildings is Tolsey House, where the 13th-century charters of the town and its silver maces are preserved. Just south of Burford is the 200-acre Cotswold Wildlife Park.

Taking the A40 towards Oxford, the tour soon turns left on to the B4047, passing the romantic ruins of 15th-century Minster Lovell Hall. The busy market town of Witney is famous for blankets; the old Blanket Hall has an unusual one-handed clock. The church's magnificent spire is visible for miles around. At one end of the wide main street is the unique Butter Cross, built in 1683, with a gabled roof crowned by a clock-turret and sundial, and resting on 13 Cotswold stone pillars.

Leaving Witney, the tour takes the A40 back to Oxford.

SELECTED PLACES TO VISIT

🏠 ANNE HATHAWAY'S COTTAGE
Map ref 1755

Anne Hathaway's Cottage, early home of Shakespeare's wife is a substantial Tudor thatched farmhouse at Shottery. The house now shows many aspects of English life in 16th-century.

🏛🅿 BANBURY
Map ref 4540

Banbury's original cross – of nursery rhyme fame – was destroyed by Puritans and replaced in Victorian times. The museum preserves the chequered history of this market town.

🌳 BATSFORD ARBORETUM
Map ref 1833

At Moreton-in-Marsh is the privately owned Batsford Aboretum, with many rare trees in its large collection. Nearby is the Cotswold Falconry Centre where the emphasis is on breeding and conservation. Eagles, hawks, owls and falcons may be seen.

🏛🅿🏨 OXFORD
Map ref 5206

The city of 'dreaming spires', Oxford has been a seat of learning since the 11th century. The historic colleges, many of which can be visited, and other beautiful buildings add to the pervasive atmosphere of scholarly tradition. The Museum of Oxford has permanent displays which explain the city's archaeology and history.

The Ashmolean Museum of Art and Archaeology houses many treasures, including the fine jewel made in the 9th century for King Alfred. Among its exhibits are archaeological finds from Britain, Europe, Egypt and the Near East. Art is represented by many famous oil paintings, as well as ceramics, silver, porcelain, sculpture and pottery from around the world.

The Museum of the History of Science contains the finest collection of early astronomical, mathematical and optical instruments in the world.

🏛🅿 ROYAL LEAMINGTON SPA
Map ref 3265

Leamington Spa prospered as taking the waters became a fashionable pastime in the late 18th century, and acquired its royal prefix after Queen Victoria's visit in 1838. Many of its fine Georgian and

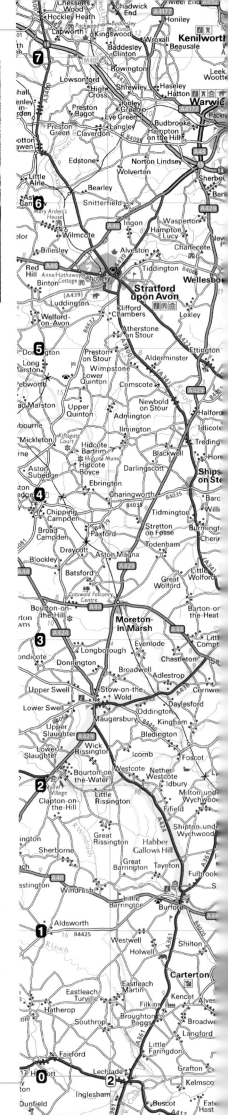

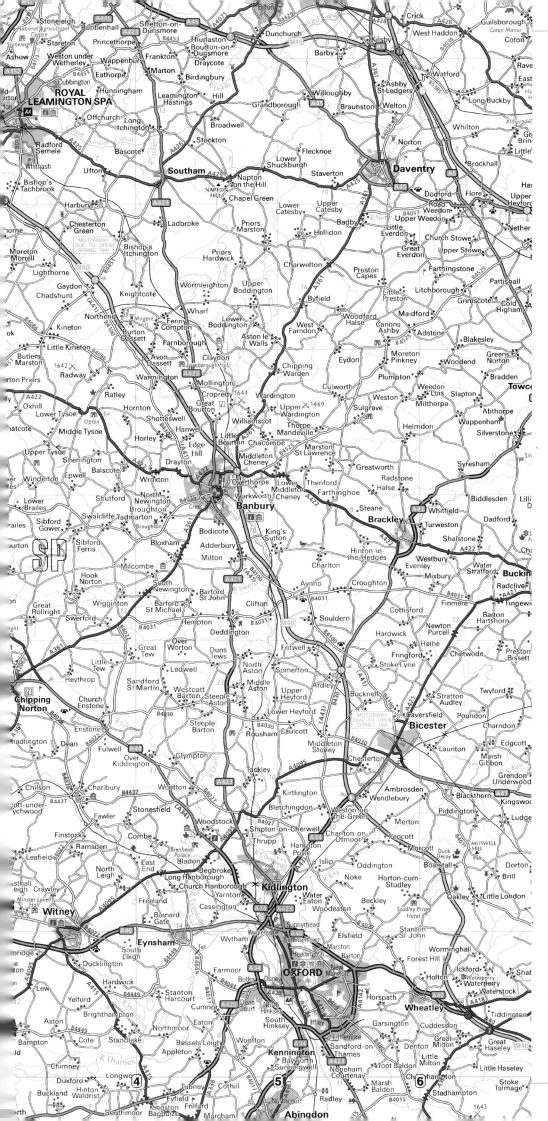

Regency houses rival those of Bath. The Art Gallery and Museum have collections of Dutch and Flemish paintings, 20th-century English watercolours, pottery and porcelain.

STRATFORD-UPON-AVON
Map ref 2154

The Shakespearean connection has made this busy market town one of Britain's most popular tourist destinations.

Shakespeare's birthplace is a half-timbered building, including numerous exhibits of the era of the playwright who was born on 23 April 1564. New Place preserves in an Elizabethan knot garden the foundations of Shakespeare's last home.

There is much else to see in Stratford, such as the Motor Museum with its vintage cars and motorcycles, and the Teddy Bear Museum which will delight children of all ages.

WARWICK
Map ref 2665

Warwick Castle, with its staterooms, great hall, dungeon and torture chamber, is the most-visited stately home in Great Britain. Its outstanding 14th-century buildings include Guy's Tower (128ft high), Caesar's Tower and the Clock Tower. Within the extensive grounds are a Victorian rose garden, river island, peacock gardens and woodland walks.

Lord Leycester Hospital is a group of 14th-century buildings converted into a home for old soldiers in 1571 and still serving that purpose. The chapel, great hall and the Guildhall which contain the museum of the Queen's Own Hussars, can all be visited. In a half-timbered Elizabethan building, Oken's House, is the Warwick Doll Museum.

The Castle Mill, Warwick – as seen from the mill garden in Mill Street

The willow warbler arrives early in April and is found in woodlands

CHILTERNS

Wooded in the west, but mostly windswept and bare near Ivinghoe in the east, the Chiltern Hills extend in a majestic line from Goring in the Thames Valley to a point near Hitchin

Three hundred and nine square miles of the Chiltern Hills were designated as an Area of Outstanding Natural Beauty (AONB) in 1964.

The Chilterns run north-east from the Thames at Goring Gap to Hitchin in Hertfordshire. All the major towns in the area – Henley, High Wycombe, Amersham, Chesham, Berkhamsted, Tring, Dunstable and Luton – are omitted, which results in some very strangely shaped boundary lines, resembling the pieces of a jigsaw.

Current estimates suggest that a staggering 8.5 million people live within 25 miles of the Chilterns – half a million within 2 miles – and the area is well served by both public and private transport. The provision of rail, underground and bus services have historically tended to be better to the north of London and the road system has been further improved in recent years. The Chilterns now have the mixed blessing of one motorway (the M40) running through them, with the M1 to the north-east negotiating its way through what might be termed the Luton/Dunstable `gap' and

Junction 18 of the M25 100yds or so from the boundary. Small wonder that this major recreational area is under unremitting pressure from visitors – it probably enjoys less respite, in what would normally be considered off-peak times, than other Areas of Outstanding Natural Beauty or National Parks.

Planned Management

The list of problems arising from this pressure is long and not difficult to envisage. Tourist attractions become grossly overused; constant attention is needed to combat footpath erosion and damage to often sensitive downland habitats; the continuing demand for housing in the south-east – the *average* increase in housing planned by the four counties which border the AONB is in excess of 40 per cent by the year 2001 – produces increasing pressure for land for roads, shops and parking facilities.

Not as immediately obvious is the need to study how changing agricultural practices may be affecting the landscape. Once grazing (particularly by sheep) stops on any downland site, there is a reversion to

scrub while the problem of the removal of hedges is one that has received wide coverage nationally. The glory of the Chilterns are their magnificent woodlands, but they require careful management if their quality is to be maintained and an overall plan (subsequently updated) was produced in 1971 by the Chilterns Standing Committee.

Within the Chilterns AONB lie four counties, Bedfordshire, Buckinghamshire, Hertfordshire and Oxfordshire, and eleven District Councils, and opportunities for policy disagreements must have been considerable. To add to this, many bodies like the Countryside Commission, the Forestry Commission, the National Trust, Country Landowners Association, National Farmers Union and others were closely involved in various aspects of management. In some other areas legitimate conflicts of interests have led to difficulties. In the Chilterns there has been a high level of agreement, with the Standing Committee, formed in 1967, having produced a sensible outline of general policies, a document called *A Plan of the Chilterns,*

which remains the framework within which the various bodies work.

Beech Woodlands

The Chilterns form part of the chalk ridge which runs in a north-easterly direction from the Dorset Heaths to the North Norfolk coast, with two fingers radiating out from Hampshire, one to create the South Downs ridge, the other the North Downs. The Chilterns follow the classic pattern with a steep, north facing scarp, broken by five gaps, at Goring, Princes Risborough, Wendover, Tring, and Dunstable. Of the rivers which created these gaps, only the Thames remains but man has made good use of the others as convenient land routes including the Roman roads, Akeman Street at Tring (the modern A41) and Watling Street (A5) at Dunstable.

To the south, the land falls gently away to the London Basin. For much of their length, the Chilterns are covered by magnificent beech woods, nurtured by a clay-with-flints oil, but in the northern section, the trees are replaced by open downland, typified by Dunstable Downs. Much of the finest woodland has National Nature Reserve status.

Beechwoods are renowned for their autumn colour – Burnham Beeches is almost synonymous with chocolate box pictures of russet and gold leaved trees – but they have a great appeal in most seasons of the year. The spread of their foliage, and the carpeting effect of their leaves, limits the number of plants which grow beneath a beechwood canopy but does not deter the seeds of bluebells which annually lighten great tracts of wooded Chiltern slopes. Bird's nest orchid, several species of helleborines, Solomon's seal and small shrubs like the evergreen spurge laurel grow

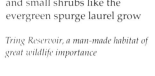

Tring Reservoir, a man-made habitat of great wildlife importance

The florets of broad-leaved helliborine, a woodland species often pollinated by wasps

in the chalk woods with some rarities, including the appropriately named ghost orchid, in the protected areas. More open sites attract a richer variety of trees including oak, silver birch and sycamore with box in several places. Plants like dog's mercury, bugle, hairy violet, wood anemone and wood-sorrel are likely to be found at these sites.

Although not matching the oak, it has been estimated that beech can sustain around 200 different invertebrates, ensuring that each year the songs of migrants like chiffchaff and willow warbler will be heard in the woods from quite early in spring. Resident birds include tits, chaffinches, robins, woodpigeon, with the manic call of the green woodpecker always liable to disturb quiet moments. In years when there is a good supply of beechmast the numbers of resident birds will increase during the autumn, supplemented by other species.

Scrubland and Wetland
A good example of scrub habitat can be found at Coombe Hill, one of the highest points in the Chilterns. Heather and gorse dot the summit, with wayfaring tree and juniper – a common colonizer on Chiltern scrub. Dunstable Downs is a good example of open downland, giving an air of spaciousness comparable to that on the very similar Sussex Downs – it is also sometimes as crowded!

For a complete contrast in habitats it is possible to visit the National Nature Reserve at Tring Reservoirs. A wetland habitat in a predominately chalkland area is certain to attract a large and varied `clientele' and Tring is no exception. Plants, invertebrates, birds and mammals all find

Above: *Autumn beeches on the National Trust's 4,000 acre Ashridge Estate, Hertfordshire*
Right: *Hairy violet, which thrives in the Chilterns' mixed woodland*

welcome shelter here in an invaluable habitat provided by the efforts of man.

An Historic Route
The Ridgeway Path keeps close company with the northern boundary of the area, from Ivinghoe Beacon to Goring, before crossing the Thames and entering the neighbouring North Wessex AONB on its way to Avebury. Planned by the Countryside Commission, the Path is based on a much longer, prehistoric way which probably ran from Hunstanton in Norfolk to near Lyme Regis in Dorset – effectively following the natural chalk ridge all the way.

Like Tring, the Ridgeway is a reminder of the important part man has played over the centuries in creating the landscape of Britain – there are many other visible examples in the Chilterns area. Grim's Ditch is a simple bank and ditch system, probably Iron Age in origin and quite possibly a boundary. Sections occur at a

number of places on the south side of the scarp. Bronze Age round barrows, hill forts from the Iron Age, the Icknield Way and the Roman mounds at Thornborough are early examples of man's occupation. From the time of the Normans onwards there are many reminders, including sites of deserted villages which date mostly from medieval times.

Some of the finest houses in England lie on or near the Chilterns, ranging from grand mansions like Cliveden above the Thames near Maidenhead, to smaller houses like Disraeli's home, Hughenden Manor at High Wycombe. Not that the

vernacular architecture suffers by comparison. Delightful villages with many brick-and-flint cottages attract visitors and London commuters, who invariably – no unique problem this – push up prices beyond the range of locals. There can be no denying that this has often affected the `balance' of the villages and it has become fashionable to criticise incomers. However, many newcomers have used their energies and enthusiasm to bring fresh impetus to their adopted villages, including – if it is not a contradiction – actively promoting the need for conservation!

Good communication links from the Grand Union Canal, trunk roads and, more recently, the M1 motorway, have encouraged the development of industries like footwear and car-making alongside the more traditional agriculture. Britain's biggest experiment in new town planning is taking place at Milton Keynes. Museums and mansions store a wealth of artistic treasures and fascinating history.

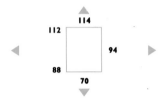

```
        114
   112  [ ]  94
        88
        70
```

SELECTED PLACES TO VISIT

ALTHORP HALL
Map ref 6865

Althorp Hall, home of the Spencer family since 1508, has attracted especial interest since Lady Diana Spencer became the Princess of Wales. The Elizabethan house was entirely restored in 1983, and has paintings by Van Dyck, Reynolds, Gainsborough and Rubens, as well as rare furniture and porcelain.

AYLESBURY
Map ref 8214

Buckinghamshire's county town since the 16th century, Aylesbury has kept some of the atmosphere of its past, despite major developments in the last 20 years. The County Museum occupies a group of Georgian buildings, opposite two 15th-century houses.

BEDFORD
Map ref 0450

County town, trading place and a centre of the automobile industry, Bedford also has a place in religious history. The Bunyan Museum is found in the meeting house built in 1850 on the site where John Bunyan had preached. The museum contains a world-famous collection of more than 400 editions of his works.

The Cecil Higgins Art Gallery and Museum has outstanding collections of English drawings and watercolours, prints, modern sculpture, ceramics and glass. The Bedford Museum specialises in local and natural history.

CHICHELEY HALL
Map ref 9145

This unspoilt Georgian hall has fine panelling, a Palladian hall and a remarkable hidden library. A naval museum containing memorabilia of

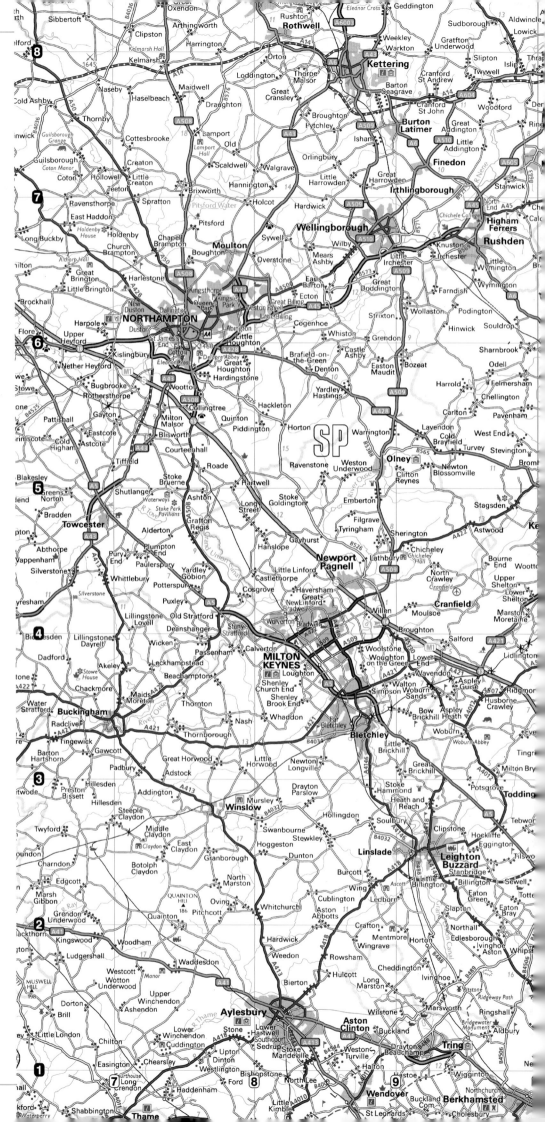

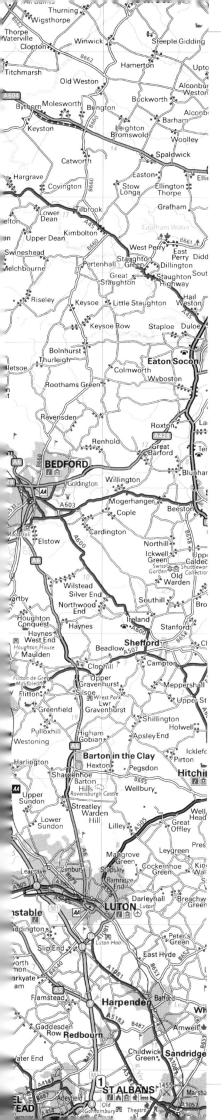

Admiral Beatty has been created in the house.

⌂▐ DELAPRE ABBEY
Map ref 7659

Delapre Abbey was rebuilt in the 17th century on the site of a Cluniac nunnery and now contains the archives of the Northamptonshire Record Office. It has a particularly beautiful walled garden.

⌂ DUNSTABLE
Map ref 0222

Henry I established a priory in Dunstable in 1131, where four centuries later the momentous divorce proceedings between Henry VIII and Catherine of Aragon were heard. The priory paid the price at the dissolution of the monasteries, with only the nave spared for destruction, which today is the parish church.

⌂⌂ KETTERING
Map ref 8778

Kettering is a centre for the footwear industry. It has an Art Gallery named after the famous artist Alfred East, who was a native of the town, and gave it many of its paintings. The gallery features changing exhibitions of craft and photography.

Wicksteed Park has a large free playground and a variety of other amusements.

⌂ LEIGHTON BUZZARD AND LINSLADE
Map ref 9225

Once two separate towns divided by the River Ouse, Leighton Buzzard and Linslade are now one entity.

Leighton Buzzard, mentioned in the Domesday Book, still has medieval thatched cottages and a pentagonal Market Cross dating from around 1400. Linslade, beside the Grand Union Canal, has more industry.

At Pages Park station is a narrow gauge railway, built to carry sand but closed down in 1967. A voluntary railway society now operates a passenger service over 3¹/₂ miles.

⌂⌂⊕ LUTON
Map ref 0921

Luton is an important centre for the automobile industry, superseding the straw-hat industry for which the town was famous from the 17th century. The airport has brought additional prosperity.

The Luton Museum and Art Gallery has collections on the social and natural history of the town.

⌂ LUTON HOO
Map ref 1119

The artistic glory of the town of Luton is found in the Wernher Collection at nearby Luton Hoo, a mansion designed by Robert Adam and landscaped by Capability Brown. Its treasures include Russian Fabergé jewellery, paintings by Rembrandt and other Dutch Masters, tapestries and porcelain.

⌂⌂ MILTON KEYNES
Map ref 8239

Once a small village, Milton Keynes has become a major new city incorporating the towns of Bletchley, Stony Stratford and Wolverton and 13 nearby villages. The controversial development has produced one of the largest covered shopping malls in Europe, as well as innovative office buildings and leisure centres. Many of the houses have been designed with solar-powered heating and imaginative methods of energy conservation.

⌂⌂ NORTHAMPTON
Map ref 7661

Famous for its boot and shoe industry, the county town of Northampton was an Anglo-Saxon settlement. The Central Museum and Art Gallery's collection of footwear includes Queen Victoria's wedding shoes and ballet pumps worn by Nijinsky and Dame Margot Fonteyn. Its archaeological exhibits range from the Iron Age to medieval pottery.

The Hunsbury Hill Industrial Museum displays an old steam roller, railway engines and wagons.

At Brixworth is one of the finest Anglo-saxon churches in the country, with most of its original 7th-century features intact. The

Footbridge over the Ouse in Bedford. The river is an attractive feature

Anglo-Saxon tower of Earls Barton's Norman church is another example of pre-Conquest architecture.

⌂ OLNEY
Map ref 8953

The Cowper and Newton Museum commemorates poet and hymnwriter William Cowper, who lived in the house from 1768 to 1786, and his friend John Newton, curate of Olney and author of *Amazing Grace* and other famous hymns.

✿ STOKE PARK PAVILIONS
Map ref 7548

The main house of Stoke Park was burnt down in 1886, but its twin 17th-century pavilions – thought to have been built by Inigo Jones – survive amid extensive gardens.

⌂ TRING
Map ref 9512

Beneath the Chiltern Hills, the small town of Tring has a Zoological Museum which is a branch of London's Natural History Museum. Founded by Baron Rothschild, a famous collector, who bequeathed his extensive collection of insects, the museum also features mounted specimens of mammals and birds and shells.

⌂ WATERWAYS MUSEUM
Map ref 7449

The Canal Museum at Stoke Bruerne on the Grand Union Canal records over 200 years of the colourful history of the country's waterways, together with rural life and crafts. Based in an old corn mill beside a flight of locks, the museum has some fascinating examples of working narrowboats.

⌂ WHIPSNADE
Map ref 0117

Britain's first open-air zoo, Whipsnade has rare and endangered species among the 2,000 animals and birds living in the park, observed from the safety of a car or from the zoo's road train. Sealions and other water mammals are also on display.

FROM THE CAM TO THE OUSE

The great rivers of the Cam and the Ouse have made this region attractive for settlers. Roman towns sprang up at the natural crossing points, and the fertile soil encouraged cultivation. Scholars have been drawn to Cambridge for centuries, while prosperous modern towns have grown around the market towns and villages.

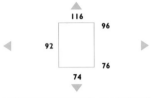

TOUR

ANGLESEY ABBEY, NEWMARKET AND SAFFRON WALDEN
55 MILES

The tour leaves Cambridge on the A1303 eastwards, turning left onto the B1102 just after the junction with the A45.

Near the village of Lode is Anglesey Abbey, built around 1600 on a medieval site. In its 100-acre garden, laid out this century, are majestic trees and sculptures, while the house contains paintings and *objets d'art* from around the world.

Shortly after Lode is Swaffham Prior, standing on one of Cambridgeshire's few hills. Within its churchyard are two churches; St Mary's, built in the 12th century with an octagonal tower reminiscent of Ely Cathedral's, is now the parish church, and 13th-century St Cyriac's used as a community centre.

The church at Burwell also has an octagonal tower. Only a dried-up moat remains of the 12th-century castle, and Burwell today is mainly characterised by 17th- and 18th-century pink and white buildings, and a post mill.

Newmarket, synonymous with horse racing since 1605, houses both the Jockey Club and Tattersalls. The development of the sport is brought to life in the National Horse Racing Museum, next to the Jockey Club in the High Street. Nell Gwynne's cottage is in Palace Street, having escaped the fire which in 1683 destroyed most of the town. Beside Newmarket Heath is the National Stud.

The tour turns south on the B1061 through fertile fenland to Balsham. The village marks one end of the 3-mile-long Fleam Dyke, a huge 7th-century earthwork erected to protect East Anglia from invasion.

On the B1052 are Linton Zoological Gardens.

Continuing south into Essex, the tour reaches Saffron Walden, a centre for the wool trade, gaining its name from the yellow dye also used as a medicine.

South of the town is Mole Hall Wildlife Park. The park features birds and animals, together with a new butterfly and insect pavilion.

The Jacobean elegance of Audley End House comes into view across the bridge over the River Cam, built by Robert Adam. Constructed in the 17th century for Thomas Howard, Earl of Suffolk the house also has many features created by Adam, together with a magnificent entrance hall and staircase. This splendour is matched by the grounds.

From Audley End the B1383 runs north, passing through Great Chesterford where the Romans once had a military post. Join the A1301 and then take a left turn on to the A505 which leads past Duxford Chapel – a 14th-century travellers' hospice – to Duxford Airfield, the former Battle of Britain fighter station. More than 120 historic aircraft are on display.

Turning back to Duxford Chapel the tour goes left towards Whittlesford. In Trumpington church is the second oldest brass in the country, dated 1289, in memory of Sir Roger de Trumpington. Neighbouring Grantchester was immortalised by Rupert Brooke in the poem, *The Old Vicarage, Grantchester*, which encapsulated the serenity of the village before World War I.

SELECTED PLACES TO VISIT

❋ ✕ ASTON END
Map ref 2924
To the east of Stevenage are Benington Lordship Gardens, 7 acres of terraces overlooking lakes and parkland on the site of a Norman castle, of which the keep and moat can still be seen.

▣❋▥▣ CAMBRIDGE
Map ref 4359
On the banks of the Cam, Cambridge was a Roman and Saxon town before its world-renowned university was founded in the early 13th century. Many of the university's 30 colleges line the east bank of the river, and most of these beautiful buildings can be visited. King's College has a permanent exhibition on the history of its famous chapel.

The Fitzwilliam Museum is a treasure-house of art and archaeology, containing Egyptian, Greek and Roman antiquities, illuminated manuscripts, and paintings by Titian, Rembrandt, Gainsborough, Hogarth and Turner.

The Scott Polar Research Institute preserves material from Arctic and Antarctic exhibitions, while the Cambridge and County Folk Museum covers local history. One of Britain's earliest surviving Saxon churches, St Bene't's, is the oldest building in the city.

▥▣ HITCHIN
Map ref 1829
The rich variety of buildings from the 17th to the 19th centuries shows

Trinity College, Cambridge, is famed for its beautiful library by Wren

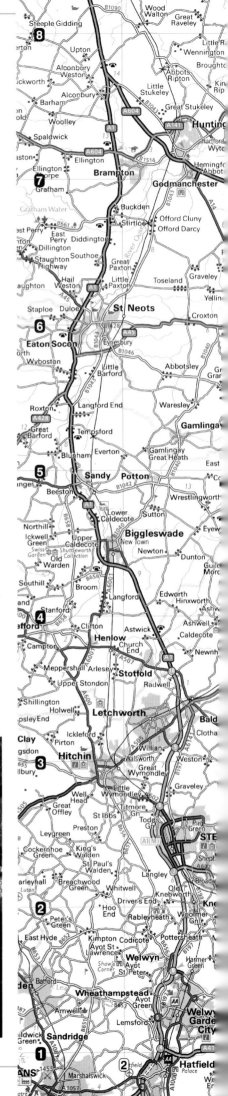

how Hitchin prospered from its wool industry. Within its Museum and Art Gallery are watercolours by local artist Samuel Lucas Snr, as well as displays of local and natural history and costumes. The building houses the regimental museum of the Hertfordshire Yeomanry.

HUNTINGDON AND GODMANCHESTER
Map ref 2470

Huntingdon is the birthplace of the Lord Protector, Oliver Cromwell. The grammar school which he – and diarist Samuel Pepys – attended is now the Cromwell Museum. Formerly the county town of old Huntingdonshire, it has been an important settlement on the Great Ouse since Roman times.

Across the river lies Godmanchester, also a Roman settlement, with which Huntingdon is now amalgamated. Between the two is a 17th-century raised causeway. Beside the river stands Island Hall, a mid 18th-century mansion.

LETCHWORTH
Map ref 1834

The story of this pioneering town is told in the First Garden City Heritage Museum, which contains the original offices of the architects who conceived and developed Letchworth as Britain's first garden city.

OLD KNEBWORTH
Map ref 2321

Knebworth House, family home of the Lyttons since 1490, was transformed in Gothic style in 1843. Among its splendours are the state drawing room and Jacobean banqueting hall, and a fascinating exhibition on the 1877 Delhi Durbar and the family's Indian connections.

SHUTTLEWORTH COLLECTION
Map ref 1544

West of Biggleswade at Old Warden is the Shuttleworth Collection of historic aeroplanes, from the 1909 Bleriot to the 1941 Spitfire. Also, motorcars and carriages.

STEVENAGE
Map ref 2525

The old town with its 17th-century cottages and medieval church still thrives, but Stevenage today is a well-planned and booming new town. The story of its development is told in the Museum in the undercroft of St George's church.

ST IVES
Map ref 3273

Perhaps the prettiest part of this picturesque town is its narrow bridge of six arches with a rare bridge chapel, dating from 1415. The history of St Ives can be traced in the Norris Museum.

HISTORIC EAST ANGLIA

Delightful villages, elegant mansions and important historical sites make this a fascinating area to visit. Many places seem untouched by the 20th century and offer a glimpse of traditional English rural life.

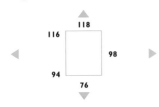

TOUR

PICTURESQUE TOWNS AND VILLAGES ALONG THE ESSEX/SUFFOLK BORDERS
69 MILES

Leaving Bury St Edmunds on the A134, the tour forks left at Cross Green on to the A1141. The first major village is one of the most picturesque in East Anglia. Lavenham has been conserved as an example of a prosperous medieval Suffolk wool town, without the intrusion of telegraph poles or double yellow lines.

Its cathedral-like church was endowed by wool merchants in thanksgiving for the end of the Wars of the Roses in 1485. The Priory is a medieval timber-framed building, erected for Benedictine Monks. Perhaps the most beautiful of Lavenham's Tudor buildings is the 16th-century Guildhall, now owned by the National Trust. Dominating the 13th-century market place, it houses a display of coopers' tools and an exhibition of 700 years of the woollen cloth trade.

A winding road leads to Melford Hall, a turreted Tudor mansion with pepperpot towers, little changed since 1578 and retaining the original panelled banqueting hall where Queen Elizabeth I was entertained. The house later acquired an 18th-century drawing room, a Regency library and a Victorian bedroom, and has a Beatrix Potter display.

The grounds of the hall contains an octagonal Tudor pavilion overlooking the village green. Long Melford itself is an attractive village, and the timber-framed and galleried 16th-century Bull Inn is reputed to be haunted.

Just to the north is Kentwell Hall, a red-brick Tudor manor, surrounded by a moat. Over the last 20 years the house has been restored and its once-fine gardens recreated. Still a family home, it has a 15th-century moat house and brick-paved Tudor-rose maze. In the gardens rare breeds of domestic farm animals roam among timber-framed farm buildings.

The Ancient House Museum, Clare – originally a priest's house

The tour continues south into Sudbury, birthplace of Thomas Gainsborough, portrait and landscape painter, in 1727. The weaving industry of this thriving market town dates back to the 13th century, and rows of weavers' cottages can still be seen. Gainsborough's House contains 18th-century furniture and china, together with works by the artist and his contemporaries.

Turning off the A131 on to the B1058, the route reaches Castle Hedingham (see also page 76). The village is dominated by the Norman keep of Hedingham Castle, 100ft high, built in the 12th century by the earls of Oxford.

A dog-leg across the junction with the A604 leads to Wethersfield, where the church, dating mainly from the 13th and 14th century, has a 15th-century nave and clerestory and includes fragments of medieval stained glass.

A right turn leads to Finchingfield, with delightful greens, medieval cottages and Georgian houses. Beside a footbridge stands the old workhouse, with its four-stack chimney. Through the arch of the timbered 15th-century Guildhall, with its small museum, is the church of St John the Baptist, with a Norman tower.

One mile north-west is Spains Hall, a 16th-century red brick and stone house.

Continuing north, the next village is Hempstead, birthplace of highwayman and robber Dick Turpin. A benefactor of mankind is also connected with Hempstead, for the church has a memorial to William Harvey, the 17th-century scientist who discovered the circulation of the blood, and lies buried here.

Steeple Bumpstead stands at a junction of country roads. Outside its church is a wall monument to Sir Henry Bendyshe, who died in 1717. The Guildhall, which dates from 1592, is a charming half-timbered building.

The next stretch of the journey along the A1092 travels through many beautiful villages and towns with examples of pargeting, the ornamental plaster coating on buildings which is typical of the region.

Stoke by Clare once had a Benedictine priory, but only a few remains survive. The neighbouring village of Clare has a 15th-century priest's house demonstrating magnificent pargetry. Now the Ancient House Museum of local history, it includes photographs, domestic tools, costumes and local crafts, and archaeological items from Roman times.

Clare had a Norman castle and remains can still be seen on its 100ft-high Saxon motte. Clare Priory – converted into a house in 1604 – is again being used by Augustinian friars.

At Cavendish, ancestral village of the dukes of Devonshire, thatched cottages nestle beside the green beneath St Mary's church.

The 16th-century Old Rectory is headquarters of the Sue Ryder Foundation and houses a museum which explains the history of the charity, set up by Lady Ryder, to care for the sick and disabled. The gardens and chapel are open to the public.

Nether Hall, a 15th-century manor house with an adjacent museum, is surrounded by its own vineyards.

The tour turns left through Glemsford to join the B1066, and continues north. Shortly before Bury St Edmunds, a turning to the left leads to Horringer and nearby Ickworth. Started around 1794, Ickworth's extraordinary elliptical Rotunda is 100ft high with two curved corridors which were designed to be painting and sculpture galleries. It has magnificent staterooms with Regency furniture and silver. The park of the house, landscaped by Capability Brown, contains an old walled garden and summerhouse, formal garden and several miles of waymarked woodland walks.

The return to Bury St Edmunds is via the A143.

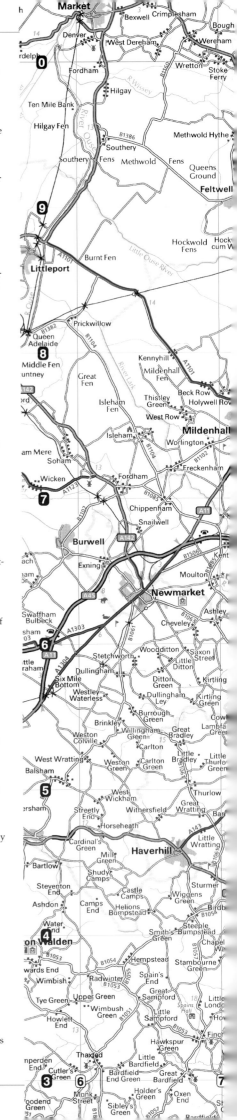

★ ANGLO-SAXON VILLAGE RECONSTRUCTION
Map ref 7972

North west of Bury St Edmunds, at West Stow, is this fascinating reconstruction of a pagan Anglo-Saxon settlement, destroyed during a sand storm. Five buildings have been reconstructed on the site of an excavated settlement from AD500, built using the same techniques, tools and building materials as were used in the original farming village.

BURY ST EDMUNDS
Map ref 8465

The town was named after King Edmund, the murdered Saxon king canonised after miracles were attributed to him. His body was interred here 33 years after his death, in the monastery built in 630 which was granted abbey status in 1032. To mark the 1100th anniversary of St Edmund's death, extensions to the cathedral church of St James's south of the Norman gate were completed in 1970.

Moyses Hall Museum is found in a rare 12th-century house. Among its exhibits are the death mask of William Corder and other relics of the Maria Marten Red Barn murder of 1828. Timepieces from the 16th century onwards are contained in the Gershom Parkington Collection, housed in a Queen Anne building, Angel Corner.

One of the town's most elegant buildings in Market Cross was originally designed by Robert Adam as a playhouse. The upper floor is now used as an art gallery. The Theatre Royal, built in 1819, is a rare example of a late Georgian playhouse with a fine pit, boxes and gallery. In the care of the National Trust, it is still a working theatre.

GRIMES GRAVES
Map ref 8290

These neolithic flint mines, some 4,000 years old, are an intricate network of more than 300 pits and shafts. This is the largest known group of flint mines in Britain. Each shaft provided about eight tons of flint. One pit, 30ft deep, and its seven galleries are open to the public.

STOWMARKET
Map ref 0758

An extensive open-air Museum of East Anglian Life in the centre of Stowmarket brings the past alive with working exhibits and demonstrations. There are reconstructed buildings including a watermill and a smithy.

THETFORD
Map ref 8684

Thetford's Ancient House Museum features displays on local history and Breckland natural history in an early Tudor timber-framed building. Extensive remains of the 12th-century monastery are found at Thetford Priory.

SONGS, SHIPS AND SEA

The East Anglian coast – where villages have vanished under the sea's pounding; where reedy marshes are home to rare and native birds; where estuaries cut their way inland to ancient boatbuilding harbours; where the stunning Sutton Hoo Anglo-Saxon ship burial was discovered, 1,300 years after being placed under a burial mound; and where the great 20th-century composer Sir Benjamin Britten created a world-famous musical centre in an old maltings – retains its mystery, even to those who know it well.

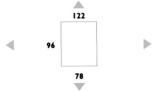

SELECTED PLACES TO VISIT

☐☐ ALDEBURGH
Map ref 4656

This quiet unspoilt resort has been made famous by the festival started in 1948 by composer Benjamin Britten and tenor Peter Pears, which has developed into a year-round programme of music, divided between Aldeburgh and Snape Maltings concert hall. The Aldeburgh Festival takes place in June, and the Maltings Proms in August.

Aldeburgh grew up on the site of the medieval fishing and shipbuilding centre of Slaughden, a town which was destroyed by the sea. It has a long, steeply shelving shingle beach with fishing boats. The Moot Hall, centre of the town in Tudor times, is now only yards from the sea, which has worn away the shoreline. The Moot Hall Museum contains old maps and prints, as well as other objects of local interest.

★ BRUISYARD WINERY AND VINEYARD
Map ref 3364

Set in a 10-acre site, the Bruisyard Winery and Vineyard produces the estate-bottled Bruisyard St Peter English wine. It also has one of the

The Moot Hall, once the town hall and centre of Aldeburgh, is now by the sea!

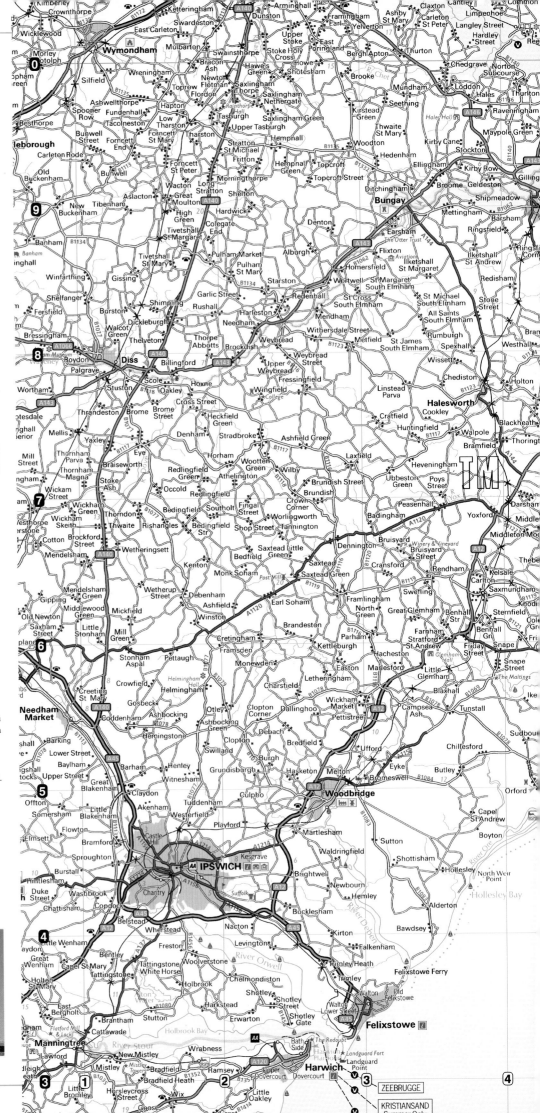

largest ornamental herb gardens in East Anglia, growing herbs for culinary and medicinal purposes and for pot-pourri.

☒ BUNGAY
Map ref 3491

At the centre of this market town stood Bungay Castle, although now only twin towers and massive flint walls are all that remain of the Norman edifice. Most buildings date from the 18th century, as a great fire in 1688 destroyed the town and melted the bells of St Mary's church.

The museum is housed in the district council offices. The displays concentrate on local history, including coins, pictures and photographs.

⬚ CARLTON COLVILLE
Map ref 5290

At Carlton Colville is the East Anglia Transport Museum, where working vehicles reconstruct a street scene from the 1930s. Visitors can ride on trams, trolley bus and a narrow-gauge railway, and see steam, motor and electric vehicles.

⬚ DUNWICH
Map ref 4771

The former major seaport of Dunwich, with its monastic houses, hospitals, three of its nine churches and 400 houses, was engulfed by the sea in January 1326. Today only a small village and a few ruins survive 700 more years of coastal erosion. At Orford the Dunwich Underwater Exploration exhibition shows the progress of underwater exploration of the site of the submerged settlement.

South of the village is Dunwich Common, which has extensive views of the sea, the marshy nature reserve and Sizewell nuclear power station.

⬚ FLIXTON
Map ref 3286

At Flixton Norfolk and Suffolk Aviation Museum preserves a collection of 16 historic aircraft, together with models, paintings and flying relics from the days of the Wright Brothers to the present.

❀ HELMINGHAM HALL
Map ref 1857

Helmingham Hall is a Tudor house with moated gardens which have changed little since Elizabethan times. Its two drawbridges are raised every night. The walled garden contains many rare roses, herbaceous borders and a fine kitchen garden. These are set within an ancient deer park containing a herd of more than 500 red and fallow deer, as well as highland cattle, which can be seen from safari rides.

🐾 KESSINGLAND
Map ref 5285

The Suffolk Wildlife and Rare Breeds Park at Kessingland covers 70 acres of woodland. The richly varied collection of animals includes lions, tigers, leopards, monkeys, zebras and chimpanzees. The park is well suited to families, with East Anglia's longest miniature railway and children's play area.

⬚⬚ LOWESTOFT
Map ref 5594

Lowestoft successfully combines its tradition of fishing and commercial port with popularity as a holiday resort. The south beach is particularly fine for bathing and amusements, while the north beach has cliffs and sand dunes. Ness Point is the most easterly point of Britain.

In 1801, some 23 years before the formation of the Royal National Lifeboat Institution, Lowestoft founded a lifeboat station. The Maritime Museum traces the seafaring history of the town, with models of fishing and commercial ships, a lifeboat display and fishing tools and shipwright's gear.

☒ ORFORD
Map ref 4250

Orford Castle has a remarkable 90ft high 18-sided keep with views across the River Alde to Orford Ness. It was built by Henry II around 1165 for coastal defence.

OULTON BROAD
Map ref 5093

Yacht, dinghy and motorboat sailing and racing take place on this lovely stretch of inland water. The Norfolk Broads now have the status of a National Park.

☒ POST MILL
Map ref 2465

Saxtead Green has a traditional Suffolk post mill in perfect working order. The 18th-century mill has a three-storey roundhouse, four patent sails, two pairs of stones and a fantail. A mill has stood on this site since the 13th century.

⬚⬚ SOUTHWOLD
Map ref 5275

Like Bungay, Southwold experienced a disastrous fire in the 17th century. The town was built around nine greens and has many period houses and cottages. Visible

The harbour at Lowestoft, now site of both the leisure and fishing industries

for miles around is the white lighthouse, built 100 years ago.

A Saxon fishing port, Southwold's prosperity began to diminish in the Middle Ages as the harbour silted up. Today it thrives mainly as a centre for visitors, attracted by its Dutch cottages, old ship's figureheads, and maritime history. The author George Orwell lived here during the 1930s.

In the museum, housed in a typical Dutch gabled cottage, is a panorama of the famous Battle of Sole Bay, fought off the town in 1672, when the Duke of York (who later became James II) resisted an onslaught by the Dutch fleet. There are also exhibits on the old Sothwold railway, and local history and archaeology.

★ THE OTTER TRUST
Map ref 3288

South west of Bungay at Earsham is the Otter Trust, where the world's largest collection of otters can be seen in natural enclosures on the banks of the River Waveney.

⬚ THE SIZEWELL INFORMATION CENTRE
Map ref 4862

The Sizewell Information Centre at Leiston gives details about all aspects of the electricity supply industry.

⬚☒ WOODBRIDGE
Map ref 2649

Boatbuilding and sail making have been the main crafts of this busy town, standing at the head of the Deben estuary. On the quayside are many old buildings, including the magnificent 18th-century weather-boarded Tide Mill, which has been restored to working order.

Just outside the town is the site of the Sutton Hoo ship burial. Excavations in 1939 revealed the important remains of a Saxon ship and a vast treasure hoard, much now in the British Museum. The local museum has a special exhibition which explains the excavations and the finds, as well as other illustrations of the maritime history of Woodbridge.

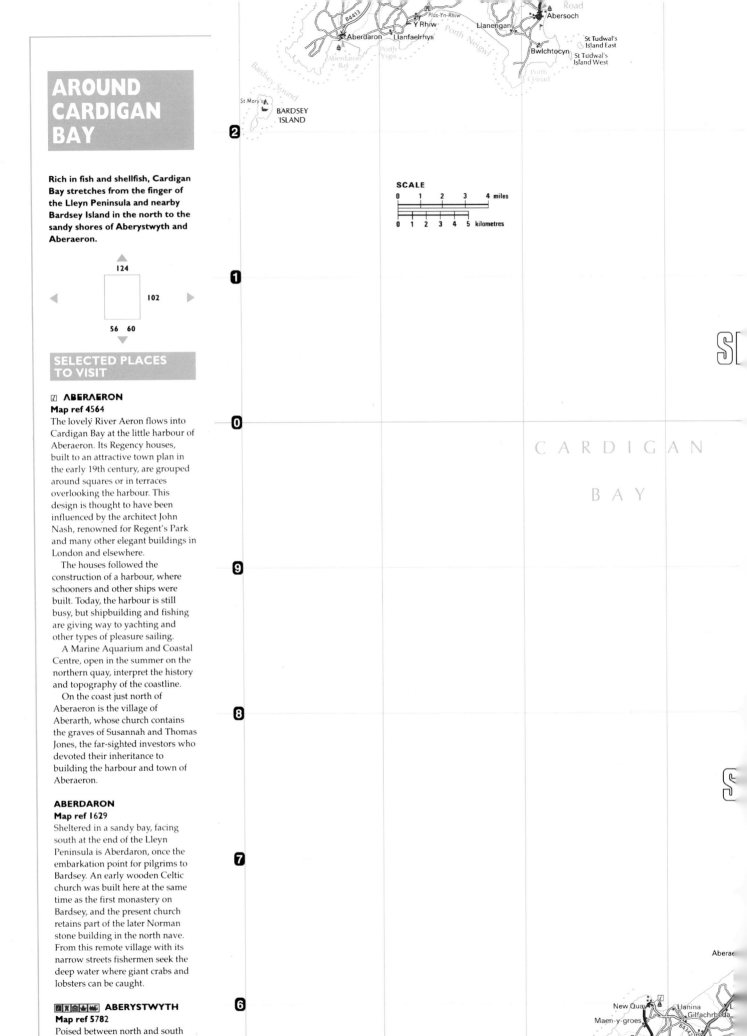

AROUND CARDIGAN BAY

Rich in fish and shellfish, Cardigan Bay stretches from the finger of the Lleyn Peninsula and nearby Bardsey Island in the north to the sandy shores of Aberystwyth and Aberaeron.

124

◄ 102 ►

56 60

SELECTED PLACES TO VISIT

ⓩ ABERAERON
Map ref 4564

The lovely River Aeron flows into Cardigan Bay at the little harbour of Aberaeron. Its Regency houses, built to an attractive town plan in the early 19th century, are grouped around squares or in terraces overlooking the harbour. This design is thought to have been influenced by the architect John Nash, renowned for Regent's Park and many other elegant buildings in London and elsewhere.

The houses followed the construction of a harbour, where schooners and other ships were built. Today, the harbour is still busy, but shipbuilding and fishing are giving way to yachting and other types of pleasure sailing.

A Marine Aquarium and Coastal Centre, open in the summer on the northern quay, interpret the history and topography of the coastline.

On the coast just north of Aberaeron is the village of Aberarth, whose church contains the graves of Susannah and Thomas Jones, the far-sighted investors who devoted their inheritance to building the harbour and town of Aberaeron.

ABERDARON
Map ref 1629

Sheltered in a sandy bay, facing south at the end of the Lleyn Peninsula is Aberdaron, once the embarkation point for pilgrims to Bardsey. An early wooden Celtic church was built here at the same time as the first monastery on Bardsey, and the present church retains part of the later Norman stone building in the north nave. From this remote village with its narrow streets fishermen seek the deep water where giant crabs and lobsters can be caught.

ⓩⓧⓘⓐⓦ ABERYSTWYTH
Map ref 5782

Poised between north and south Wales, Aberystwyth is an elegant coastal resort and university town.

SCALE

0 1 2 3 4 miles

0 1 2 3 4 5 kilometres

CARDIGAN

BAY

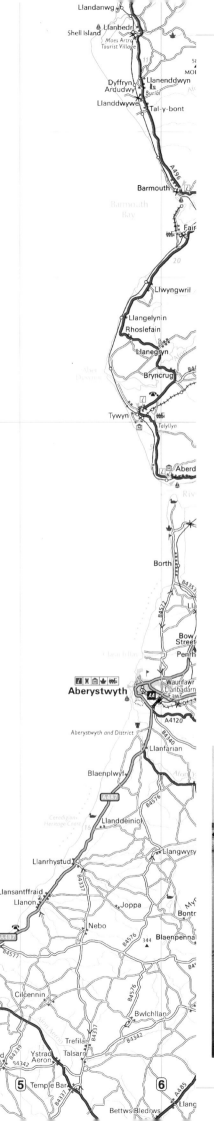

The castle built by Edward I, captured by Owain Glyndwr and recaptured by Prince Henry in 1408, fell into decay after surrendering to the Parliamentary army in 1646 during the Civil War. Its precincts are laid out as public gardens.

The curving bay with its shingle beach and Victorian buildings is a popular destination for holiday makers. The beach is overlooked by the 485ft-high Constitution Hill, which can be climbed on foot by a cliff path or by funicular railway. The journey is worth the effort, for a camera obscura on its summit is able to project some 60 miles of landscape, including the Snowdonia mountains.

The University of Wales started life in a neo-Gothic hotel on the Promenade, built at huge expense by Thomas Savin as part of an ambitious plan to attract tourists to the town with cheap rail travel. The venture failed and the hotel sold by its bankrupt owner to become the first constituent college of the University of Wales. Today the university has moved to a purpose-built campus on the hill overlooking the town. Prince Charles spent a term here, familiarising himself with the rudiments of the essential second language for a Prince of Wales.

The site is dominated by the imposing Edwardian building of the National Library of Wales, one of Britain's six copyright libraries. As well as storing a huge collection of books in all languages, it specialises in Welsh and Celtic literature. The library contains well over two million printed books and more than 35,000 manuscripts, as well as musical publications, prints, drawings and old deeds. Exhibitions of pictures and changing displays of the library's treasures are on show.

The important part played by religion and the chapel in Welsh culture and social history is traced in Yr Hen Gapel. The museum's permanent exhibition and

temporary displays reflect the traditions of both rural and industrial Wales.

South of Aberystwyth's town centre is Pen Dinas, a shapely hill on which once stood a prehistoric double fort, one of the largest in west Wales.

♠ ⌂ BARDSEY ISLAND
Map ref 1322

Access to and from the island is extremely difficult, thanks to the vicious tide-race in the 2-mile sound that separates it from the mainland. Bardsey Island, whose name is thought to be a corruption of 'Bards Eyre' (island of bards), is known in Welsh as Ynys Enlli, or 'isle of the eddies', reflecting the force of the boiling waves which pound its shores.

Bardsey Island has long been a holy place, and 20,000 saints are reputed to lie buried there. Such was the veneration in which it was held that, in the Middle Ages, two pilgrimages to Bardsey were considered equivalent in merit to one to Rome.

In AD516 St Cadfan founded the Abbey of St Mary, succeeded by a medieval monastery, of which a ruined 13th-century tower is the only relic. Today the island has only five inhabitants, who farm its hilly slopes and preserve its religious traditions.

♠ DYFFRYN ARDUDWY
Map ref 5724

The name describes both the village and the area between the ridge and the sea, where the large empty plateau is dotted with ancient stones. Behind the school at Dyffryn Ardudwy are two prehistoric burial chambers. The coastline here is mainly sand dunes.

★ MAES ARTRO TOURIST VILLAGE
Map ref 5729

The Maes Artro village is a wartime RAF camp imaginatively converted to include displays of old farm

AROUND CARDIGAN BAY

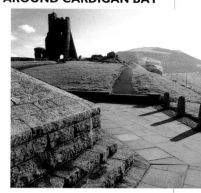

The ruins of Aberystwyth's much fought over medieval castle, perched on the headland

implements, a village of yesteryear, and playground and nature trails in lovely wooded grounds. An original air raid shelter has been restored, as well as a spitfire.

☑ NEW QUAY
Map ref 3859

One of the prettiest seaside villages on Cardigan Bay, with a tiny harbour and sandy beach, New Quay is set on a hillside. New Quay Head is a bluff 300ft above the port, looking down on its fishing boats and yachts.

☑ ⌂ ⚙ TYWYN
Map ref 5701

At Tywyn at Wharf Station is the famous Talyllyn Railway, the oldest 2ft 3in narrow-gauge railway in the world, built in 1865. Saved from closure by a voluntary preservation society, the railway now run steam trains on the $7^{1}/_{4}$ mile track through the hills from Tywyn to Nant Gwernol. Forest walks and waterfalls add to the attractions here.

The station also houses a museum which features changing exhibitions.

The little harbour at Aberaeron overlooked by Regency houses

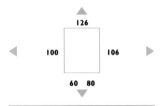

WOOL AND WATER

Some of the most spectacular scenery in Wales is to be found in the flooded valleys of the Elan to the south of the region and the peaks of Cader and Aran in the north. The traditional industry of wool continues, but mining for lead and silver is only a memory.

```
        ▲
       126
 ◄  100    106  ►
     60  80
        ▼
```

TOUR

ELAN VALLEY RESERVOIRS AND DEVIL'S BRIDGE
57 MILES

From Llanidloes the tour takes the B4518 scenic route south, climbing steeply and then descending towards Pant-y-dwr, the hamlet of St Harmon and Rhayader.

Rhayader is an important junction on the River Wye, and the gateway to the reservoirs of the Elan Valley. Here the tour continues on the B4518, through Llansantffraed Cwmdeuddwr with its ancient inn set above the Wye, towards Elan Village.

The group of majestic reservoirs in the Elan Valley was built to provide Birmingham with water. First started in 1892 and completed in 1907, the dams were formally opened by King Edward VII in 1904. The dams were faced with fine stonework, which adds to their beauty. (The Claerwen dam to the west, constructed after World War II, is faced in concrete.)

About three miles from Rhayader, before reaching Cuban Coch, a call to the Visitor Centre close to Elan Village will explain the history of the construction of the dams through a fascinating slide show and exhibition. As well as displays of paintings by local artists, the centre has a superb bronze sculpture commemorating the poet Shelley, who lived in the valley for a time.

The first dam on the tour is the 500-acre Cuban Coch, magnificently set in a narrow part of the valley, surrounded by crags and wooded hillsides. The scene is particularly spectacular after rain.

Skirting along the north side of the reservoir, the route turns right to travel northwards, along the eastern side of Garreg-Ddu reservoir. A submerged causeway runs across the lake.

The road crosses the River Elan at the head of Garreg-Ddu to hug the southern side of Pen-y-Garreg reservoir. It moves away from the edge of the water as it passes through the hamlet of Hirnant, with

the 200-acre reservoir of Craig-Goch, the highest of the dams, on the right.

Crossing the river again, the tour turns left on to the dramatic mountain road across wild open moorland, with the peak of Geifas rising to 1,873ft to the south. The first point of habitation is not for some 9 miles, at the scattered village of Cwmystwyth, where the old lead mines are all now closed.

The road joins the B4574 towards Devil's Bridge, passing picnic sites and forest and nature trails. Hidden in a deep wooded gorge are the Mynach Falls, a series of awe-inspiring waterfalls, with three bridges piled one on top of the other. The village name is derived from the legend which says that the bottom bridge was thrown across the River Rheidol by the Devil; other stories allege that the monks of Strata Florida laid it across during the Middle Ages.

From Devil's Bridge the narrow-gauge Rheidol Railway runs on its 12-mile trip to the coast at Aberystwyth.

Continuing up the Rheidol valley, the tour reaches Ponterwyd, turning left to visit the mid 19th-century Llywernog Silver Lead Mine. The mine has been turned into an open-air museum, with a miners' trail walk, underground drift mine and working machinery. Among the exhibits are the last Cornish roll crusher in Wales, many waterwheels and other equipment. A giant 50ft-diameter overshot waterwheel dating from 1865 is being restored and reconstructed.

Three miles west of Ponterwyd is the Bwlch Nant-Yr-Arian Forest Visitor Centre, run by the Forestry Commission, with much information about the region.

From Ponterwyd the A44 leads eastwards across the ridge of Plynlimon Fawr to Llangurig, following the course of the Wye valley. To the left are the conifers of the Hafren Forest; to the right the Forestry Commission's massive plantations.

Llangurig, some 900ft above sea level, is in the centre of the sheep farming area, although its fortunes were once more closely linked with the lead mining industry. At the junction, the tour takes the A470 for the descent into Llanidloes.

SELECTED PLACES TO VISIT

🏛 CENTRE FOR ALTERNATIVE TECHNOLOGY
Map ref 7504

The contrast between 19th- and late 20th-century technology could scarcely be greater than at Machynlleth. Here, in an old slate quarry overlooking the Snowdonia National Park, a permanent working exhibition demonstrates technologies designed to improve the environment, such as solar power, wind and water, and organic gardening.

☑ ★ DOLGELLAU
Map ref 7217

A centre of the woollen weaving industry in the 18th and 19th centuries, Dolgellau was involved in mineral working in the middle of the last century but is now a market town and administrative centre. Above it looms Cader Idris, at 2,927ft one of the highest peaks in Wales, lying between the valleys of the Mawddach and Dysynni. Away to the north west is the still higher peak of Aran Mawddwy, at 2,969ft. A Nature Information Centre to the west of Dolgellau is run by the Snowdonia National Park.

⚓ FAIRBOURNE
Map ref 6213

At the mouth of Barmouth Bay are Fairbourne Railway and Butterfly Safari. The narrow-gauge steam railway, restored in 1985, passes through breathtaking scenery on its way to Porth Penrhyn terminus, and stops can be made to enjoy some of the superb beaches. At Gorsaf Newydd terminus there are locomotive sheds and engineering works.

LLANBADARN FAWR
Map ref 6281

Close to Aberystwyth is Llanbadarn Fawr, where St Padarn established a Christian settlement in the 6th century. By the 11th century, Llanbadarn had a library larger than Canterbury and York and a scriptorium where illuminated manuscripts were copied.

The dam of the Elan Valley's Pen-y-Garreg Reservoir

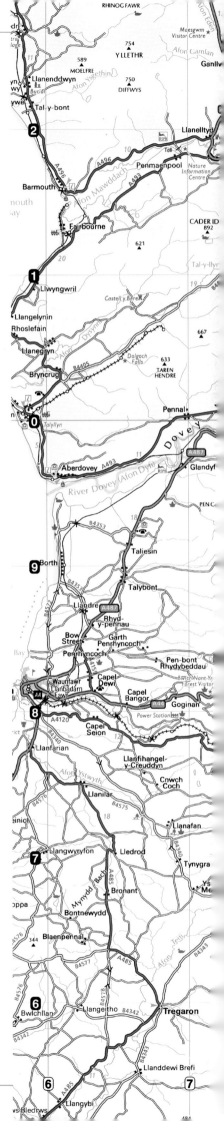

WOOL AND WATER

On St Padarn's Day, 15 April, 1988, a transformation of the south transept of Llanbadarn Fawr's church was unveiled by the Archbishop of Wales. A stained glass window now illustrates themes from the saint's life, and three rooms explain his work and the medieval and modern history of the village. The centre of the transept has become a new chapel with a granite altar, flanked by two ancient Celtic crosses which stood in the churchyard until 1916.

☑ ⌂ LLANIDLOES
Map ref 9584
Standing at the junction of the Severn and Clywedog rivers, Llanidloes has been an important centre for the mining industry and the wool trade. The town has mid Wales's only surviving example of a 16th-century timbered market hall, with open arches to accommodate the stalls and a plaque recording the fact that John Wesley preached here. The upper floor houses a museum of local history.

⌂ ☑ RAILWAY MUSEUM
Map ref 7507
Railways feature strongly in this part of Wales, and the Railway Museum at Corris preserves relics of the light industrial railway which brought slates from the local quarries to the main line at Machynlleth from 1890 to 1948, and other railway memorabilia. Some old wagons are on show and half-a-mile of track has been reinstated. The railway does not carry passengers.

⌂ TALIESIN
Map ref 6693
Taliesin is the reputed birthplace of the 6th-century Welsh bard Taliesin, but the chamber in which he is supposed to be buried has been dated as thousands of years older. At nearby Tre'r-ddol is a chapel which has been turned into a museum commemorating the religious revival of 1859.

A locomotive steaming along Fairbourne's carefully restored narrow-gauge railway

SHROPSHIRE HILLS

The Shropshire Hills incorporate four hill ranges, running roughly parallel to each other but consisting of totally different rock formations, and possessing very different characteristics

The Shropshire Hills were designated an Area of Outstanding Natural Beauty in 1958. Within their 330 square miles are several distinctive upland areas demonstrating varying landscape characteristics. Farming is now very much the major industry, following the eclipse of quarrying and mining during the course of this century. Traditionally known for sheep and beef cattle breeding, cereals have played an increasing role here in recent years.

This region of small villages – many no more than hamlets – has two expanding towns, Shrewsbury and Telford, a short way from the designated area. In recent years Shrewsbury, the county town, has developed considerably, spreading far beyond the natural boundaries imposed by the sweep of the Severn around an old town. The growth of Telford has not proceeded at the rate originally envisaged, but there have been improvements to the road system, including the completion of the M54 link from the M6 to the town. Other roads have been upgraded with the result that traffic from the West Midlands towns now has easier access to the Shropshire Hills.

The Tourist Industry

For many years Shropshire has adopted a relaxed approach to tourism, making few efforts to compete with neighbouring counties. The result has been a wonderful bonus for those who,

The raven is ideally suited to the harsh moorland which covers the Long Mynd

having stumbled across it, have virtually had much of Shropshire to themselves – particularly the more westerly parts of the designated area. It seems likely that this situation may change as the 1990s proceed, for there are now plans to expand tourism as a means of bringing revenue to the county's rural areas. Inevitably, this will create problems, not least the possibility that the improved roads and delightful small hamlets will attract commuters to the county.

Professional incomers, working away from the area, coupled to an ageing local population and limited opportunities for young people – this is an increasingly common scenario in many parts of

Bog pimpernel is found in the boggy moorland areas of the Hills

Britain. The situation will need to be monitored if future tourists are not to find beautifully manicured villages in remote valleys with no-one available to operate the petrol pump at the local garage!

Other problems in the Shropshire Hills are almost all related to the dangers faced by various habitats. Broadleaved woods have declined through lack of management while some commercial afforestation has been ineptly planned, producing unsightly blocks of conifers which do not enhance the traditional scenery of open hilltops framed by an expanse of sky. The need to designate the Clun plateau as an Environmentally Sensitive Area was influenced by modern patterns of agriculture. This area of small fields surrounded by hedges, with oakwoods and gentle pastureland spreading out over rounded hills, presents a delightful picture of traditional farming. But it has experienced all too familiar pressures – hedges and trees rooted up, rough pasture improved and herb-rich meadows lost.

Sandstone and Limestone

At the eastern edge of the area are the highest hills, Brown Clee and Titterstone Clee (1,772 ft and 1,750 ft respectively). These are sandstone formations, capped by basalt. The whole area is mainly moorland, with fine views in all directions from the top of Brown Clee, whose lower slopes have a mixture of native hardwoods and planted conifers. To the south is the prominent ridge of Clee Hill, another moorland area.

Between Corve Dale and Ape Dale lies Wenlock Edge, perhaps the most famous of the Shropshire escarpments, running for 15 miles from Much Wenlock to Craven Arms. The edge of this steep limestone ridge has been softened by its heavily wooded profile. Conifer plantations have altered the profile in places, but oak and ash have survived in some strength, and the Edge attracts a very wide range of plant, bird and animal species. On the west of the scarp, at Edge Wood, the visitor can see the effects of management practices on woodland and obtain an idea of the variety of both flora and fauna such a wood can support. Further along the escarpment, the National Trust has constructed a path through a patch of ash woodland suitable for wheelchair users.

The Bleak Moorlands
The great pre-Cambrian ridge of the Long Mynd is covered with moorland. Hard, bleak country, owned by the National Trust, it rises steeply from the fertile valley of Church Stretton, broken by a series of `batches' or ravines, the best known of which is Carding Mill Valley. The moorland of the plateau, reminiscent of Dartmoor, is criss-crossed by unfenced roads permitting the motorist to explore the area. The area was grazed by sheep for centuries and is now managed as a grouse moor, ensuring that the heather is not driven back by bracken. The streams which created the valleys rise in boggy areas where *Sphagnum* mosses, bog pimpernel and bog violet grow. Caddis flies, mayflies and stonefly larvae live in the pure water of the streams, providing food for dippers. Other

moorland birds found here include buzzard, raven, ring ouzel and wheatear. Tormentil and heath bedstraw are among acid-loving plants which thrive on the Long Mynd.

The Stiperstones and Beyond
To the north-west along the narrow roads from Church Stretton, are the Stiperstones, where the presence of strangely shaped rocks have ensured a tradition of legend. These remarkable outcrops are created from quartzite and reach their highest point at the Devil's Chair, a comfortless spot on fine days and menacing when low clouds gather round it. The Stiperstones Ridge has been designated a national nature reserve because of the importance of its high moorland habitat.

Lying to the west of the Stiperstones are the deserted sites of lead mines – operated from Roman times until this century. Although being reclaimed by nature, they, and their spoil tips simply add to the bleakness. By contrast, in the aptly named Hope Valley, regeneration of the old oak woodland is being encouraged by the removal of conifers.

North of the Stiperstones Ridge, at the very edge of the Shropshire Hills area, is the

remarkable Earl's Hill. Only the Malvern Hills and parts of Anglesey are older than this steep-sided hill rising abruptly out of the Shropshire plain, surrounded by good farming land. Part grass, part scrub, with wooded outcrops almost to the summit, Earl's Hill is home to a remarkably varied wildlife. Some species can only survive on specialised sites or are confined to specific parts of the country and the scree slopes here are home to rock stonecrop and navelwort. Bracken and bramble are colonizing the scrub with ash and a variety of flowers, supplying a fascinating insight into natural regeneration. Birdlife is well varied, enhanced by the presence of a stream.

Commanding Views
Visually the most dramatic hill in the whole area is the Wrekin, a typically volcanic formation, with immense views from its summit, almost certainly the headquarters of the Cornovil tribe, who controlled the area before the arrival of the Romans.

After the Romans came centuries of wars between Celtic chiefs and the Mercians. The Normans imposed their rule, building great castles

The dark, bleak country of the Long Mynd – a pre-Cambrian ridge

along the restless border. From them sprang the Marcher Lords who were to control the borders until the Civil War. From the 17th century on there began a settled period, as the great families concentrated on running their estates. Later, the industrial revolution can be said to have begun in the east of the county, at Ironbridge and Coalbrookdale, but then it moved on, leaving only memories: typical, somehow, of timeless Shropshire.

The Stiperstones, south-west of Shrewsbury, reach their peak at 1,700ft

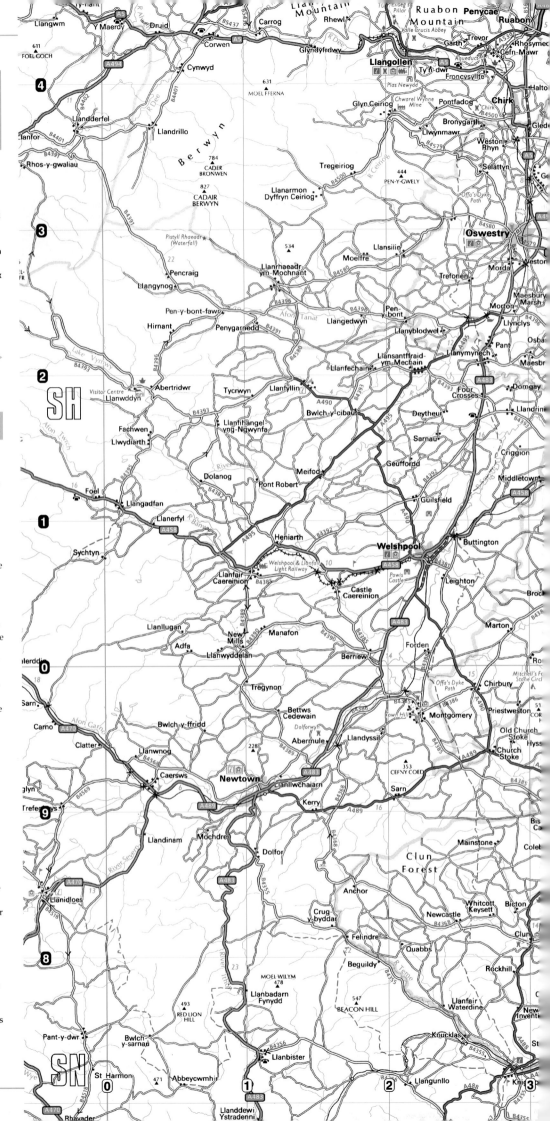

THE WELSH-ENGLISH BORDERS

The bloody history of conflict between the Welsh and the English has left a legacy of castles and fortifications. Offa's Dyke, 142 miles long and completed in the late 8th century by the Mercian king, marked the frontier between the Welsh and the Anglo-Saxons. Remains of the massive earthwork are particularly well preserved in this part of mid Wales.

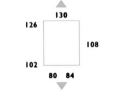

SELECTED PLACES TO VISIT

✗ CHIRK
Map ref 2538

Just on the Welsh side of the border, commanding fine views over the surrounding countryside, is Chirk Castle, a Marcher fortress completed in 1310, now in the care of the National Trust. The elegant staterooms have elaborate plasterwork and superb Adam-style furniture, tapestries and portraits.

⛏ CHWAREL WYNNE MINE
Map ref 2138

The Chwarel Wynne Mine is a slate mine, museum and education centre on a lovely 12-acre site at Glyn Ceiriog. The history of the industry is explained by a video film and guides take visitors on a tour of the underground workings, while the museum contains many relics of the slate industry.

✗ ⊞ CLUN
Map ref 3082

In his poem, *A Shropshire Lad*, published in 1896, A E Housman wrote:

> Clunton and Clunbury,
> Clungunford and Clun
> Are the quietest places
> Under the sun.

For centuries, however, Clun experienced fighting and dispute, being claimed by both Welsh and English. Between 1195 and 1400 the Welsh attacked the castle and burned the town no fewer than four times.

Clun stands close to Offa's Dyke and Clun Castle was built by the Normans to defend the Welsh border. The Clun Town Trust Museum is housed in the Georgian town hall, original court house to Clun Castle. It contains flint tools, maps of earthworks and other relics of the early Bronze Age settlement as well as items of local domestic history.

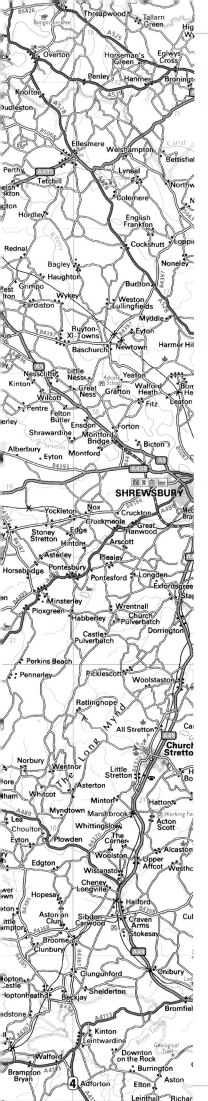

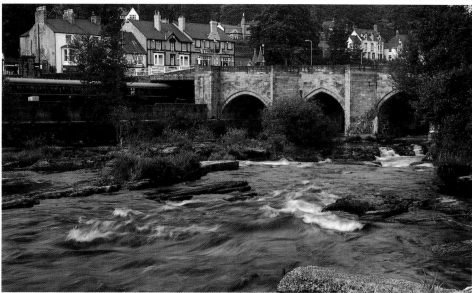

✓☓☷ LLANGOLLEN
Map ref 2342

Home of the international Eisteddfod, Llangollen welcomes dancers and singers from around the world for a week each July. The festival takes place beneath the hill of Dinas Bran, with the remains of its pre-Norman castle, said to have contained the Holy Grail.

About a mile to the west is Valle Crucis Abbey, founded in 1201 for Cistercian monks by Madog ap Grufydd, prince of Powys. The buildings which remain date mainly from the 13th century.

Aspects of Llangollen's more recent past can be seen at the Canal Museum and Passenger Boat Trip Centre. Visitors can travel in a horse- drawn passenger boat along the beautiful Vale of Llangollen.

Rail travel is the theme at the old Great Western Railway Station. The station has been restored and locomotives and rolling stock are on display. Passenger trains run on the 3¹/₂-mile round trip between Llangollen and Berwyn Station.

★ ♠ LLANWYDDYN
Map ref 0318

On the southern edge of the 4-mile-long Lake Vyrnwy is the Llanwyddyn which replaced the village drowned in 1883, when the upper reaches of the river were dammed to provide Liverpool with a new reservoir. The stone-faced dam is in a beautiful setting among the hills, and Vyrnwy is now a bird sanctuary. A visitor centre in an old chapel provides information.

☓ ☐ ☀ MONTGOMERY
Map ref 2296

Montgomery is more English than Welsh in architectural style, with half-timbered Elizabethan and Jacobean houses, Georgian red brick buildings and an 18th-century town hall. Behind its cobbled market square is the castle hill, with the restored ruins of the 13th-century castle. At the time of the Civil War, the castle was occupied by the philosopher, diplomat and writer Lord Herbert of Charbury, brother of the mystical poet George Herbert.

✓☐ NEWTOWN
Map ref 1192

Enterprise and activity have characterised Newtown, market town and centre of the 19th-century woollen trade. In 1859 the world's first mail-order firm was established in the Royal Welsh Warehouse next to the railway station, marketing Welsh flannel products. Newtown today attracts manufacturers like Laura Ashley.

Newtown was the birthplace of Robert Owen, founder of the Co-operative movement. He is buried in the old churchyard near the bridge over the River Severn. In Broad Street is a Robert Owen Museum. Commercial Street has a small textile museum.

A glimpse of the history of retailing can be seen at No 24 High Street. Here the branch of stationers W H Smith has been completely restored as it was in 1927. On the first floor is a museum, with photographs, and memorabilia dating back 200 years.

☐☐ OSWESTRY
Map ref 2830

Remains of the massive Iron Age hill fort, covering 68 acres, can still be seen.

Scene of many battles over the centuries and devastating fires in the 16th century, Oswestry today is visibly a 19th-century market town. The Montgomery Canal which helped to bring it prosperity is being restored.

The Military Museum at West Felton has displays from armies around the world during the last four centuries. The town's Cycle Museum has exhibits ranging from penny farthings to cycles of the 1930s.

☷ PLAS NEWYDD
Map ref 2242

Plas Newydd was the home of the 'Ladies of Llangollen', Lady Eleanor Butler and Sarah Ponsonby, from 1780 to 1831. This ornate house

The old Dee bridge, Llangollen

contains many household and personal items.

☷ POWIS CASTLE
Map ref 2207

Just to the south of Welshpool is Powis Castle, home of the Herbert family from 1587 until l952, when it was given to the National Trust. It contains Wales's finest country house collection, and includes a museum acknowledging connections with Clive of India. The gardens are of great horticultural and historical importance.

☷ STOKESAY
Map ref 4382

Some 10 miles east of Clun is Stokesay Castle, oldest surviving example of a 13th-century fortified manor house, with a quaint Elizabethan gatehouse.

☐☐ WELSHPOOL
Map ref 2307

Half-timbered and Georgian houses also feature in the main street of this market town, and the church has a medieval timbered roof.

☷ WELSHPOOL AND LLANFAIR LIGHT RAILWAY
Map ref 1206

Along the 8-mile track between Welshpool and Llanfair Caereinion runs the Welshpool and Llanfair Light Railway. Built in the early 20th century, the line was saved by enthusiasts in 1956 who restored the track and reopened the line through to Welshpool in 1981.

☐ WESTON RHYN
Map ref 2835

The Tyn-y-Rhos Hall Museum of Victoriana is found in a small manor house furnished in late 19th-century style. The hall is now home to an Orthodox monastic community, who offer guided tours.

☓ WHITTINGTON
Map ref 3232

To the north-east of Oswestry are the remains of Whittington Castle.

HISTORIC SHROPSHIRE

Just a dozen or more miles west of industrial Wolverhampton lie the beautiful valley of the Severn, the Wyre Forest, the Clee Hills and Wenlock Edge. Traditional black-and-white timbered villages stand little changed by the last 400 years, contrasting with the area's Victorian industrial heritage, also proudly preserved.

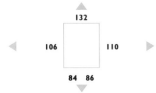

TOUR

IRONBRIDGE GORGE, BRIDGNORTH, BEWDLEY AND CLEE HILL
67 MILES

The tour leaves Ludlow on the A49, turning almost immediately north on to the B4365, following the River Corve, which winds through Corve Dale with its lovely 15th- and 16th-century manor farms. To the right are the twin hills of Titterstone Clee and Brown Clee; to the left the limestone ridge of Wenlock Edge.

At Munslow Aston is a 14th-century manor, The White House, with an agricultural museum. The tour passes through Munslow village, with its characteristic black-and-white houses and Norman church.

Outstanding among the local architecture is Shipton Hall, built in 1587. The Elizabethan house was later enlarged and its interior modernised in the 1760s by Thomas Pritchard, juxtaposing original Tudor panelling with rococo plasterwork. In the grounds is a medieval dovecote, together with Georgian stables, also built by Pritchard. The parish church dates from Saxon times, and there is a working pottery.

The lovely market town of Much Wenlock, granted its first charter in 1468, also features many black-and-white houses. Its priory, founded in the 7th century, was destroyed by the Danes and rebuilt by Lady Godiva. The remains still show interesting carvings in the chapter house and south transept, and the nave aisle has splendid arches. An interpretation of the history of both town and priory is found in Much Wenlock Museum, housed in the old market hall.

At Ironbridge is the magnificent award-winning open-air museum which brings together much of the area's industrial heritage. The first iron bridge in the world, built by Abraham Darby in 1778, spans the narrow gorge of the River Severn.

It was the initiative that brought the Industrial Revolution to this part of Shropshire, and the unique museum combines a large number of sites over 6 square miles representing different crafts and industries.

To take just a few examples, the Blist Hill Open Air Museum on a 42-acre woodland site has recreated a Victorian village revealing how people lived and worked. The Coalbrookdale Museum and Furnace Site shows the blast furnace where Abraham Darby perfected the technique of smelting iron ore using coke, crucial to the construction of the Iron Bridge. Original buildings and workshop tell the story of the Coalport China Company from the late 18th century to 1926. The Jackfield Tile Museum, recently opened, is a museum of 19th-century tiles created on the site of the Craven Dunnill factory, once one of the world's largest ceramic tile producers.

Through Broseley the tour makes for Bridgnorth, an ancient market town with a wealth of historic features. Bridgnorth is at two levels, with the Low Town and High Town connected by a short funicular railway and flights of steep steps as well as by a winding road. The tower of Bridgnorth Castle defies gravity, leaning at an angle of 17 degrees – greater than that of the Tower of Pisa. The town hall was erected in 1652, to replace the hall burnt down in the Civil War, and has interesting stained glass windows.

Although the tour will shortly be heading for Bewdley, it makes a detour here to see the Midland Motor Museum, 1½ miles south of Bridgnorth on the A458 Stourbridge road. More than 100 sports and racing cars dating from 1920 to 1980 have been preserved and restored in the converted stables of Stanmore Hall, surrounded by parkland.

Mortorcar is not the only means of transport from Bridgnorth to Bewdley. The Severn Valley Railway – a leading standard gauge steam railway with one of the largest collections of locomotives and rolling stock in Britain – runs steam train services on the 16-mile journey along the picturesque Severn valley from Bridgnorth to Bewdley and on to Kidderminster.

The ruins of Much Wenlock Priory, founded in the 7th century

Resuming the tour, the B4363 road between Bridgnorth and Bewdley passes old manors such as Kinlet Hall and farmhouses as it heads towards the Wyre Forest, forking left at Kinlet on to the B4194 towards Bewdley.

Bewdley Museum is found in a row of 18th-century butchers' shops known as The Shambles. The displays and demonstrations explain the crafts and industries of the area, including charcoal burning, basket making, coopering (barrel making), rope making and clay pipe making. The museum's sawyard and brass foundry are often in operation, and there is a working waterwheel.

On the eastern side of Bewdley towards Kidderminster, is the West Midlands Safari and Leisure Park, a 200-acre site where a wide variety of animals live in conditions close to their natural habitats. A train ride leads to an amusement area.

Turning west, the tour retraces its steps through Bewdley on the B4190, joining the A4117 which will lead back to Ludlow. The road passes beside the Wyre Forest, known for its birch trees, and the market town of Cleobury Mortimer, with its half-timbered houses. One of Shropshire's most famous sights is to the north, where Titterstone Clee Hill, 1,749ft high, is crowned by a prehistoric hill fort. Four miles more lead back to Ludlow.

SELECTED PLACES TO VISIT

CAER CARADOC
Map ref 479S
Near the small market town is the 1,506ft-high oval summit of Caer Caradoc. In a cave halfway down the western slope of the hill is the cave where Caractacus, the British chieftain, made his final unsuccessful stand against the invading Romans in AD50.

DUDMASTON HALL
Map ref 7588
This 17th-century house set in extensive parkland features Dutch flower paintings, modern pictures, watercolours and modern sculpture.

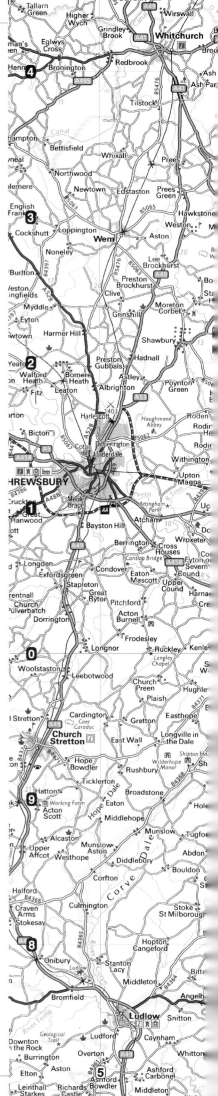

☐ ☒ ☐ LUDLOW
Map ref 5274

Ludlow Castle, with its impressive red sandstone keep, is one of the country's most important monuments. Built in 1085 and developed and rebuilt by Norman, Plantagenet and Lancastrian kings, it now includes the tower, great hall and chamber.

Displays in Ludlow Museum tell the story of the foundation of the planned Norman town, and its development from capital of the Welsh Marches to Victorian market town.

The parish church of St Laurence dominates the town like a cathedral. In the churchyard are the ashes of poet A E Housman (1859-1936). Nearby are ancient inns and the Reader's House, a privately owned medieval building with Tudor and Jacobean additions.

☐ ☒ ☐ ☐ SHREWSBURY
Map ref 4913

County town of Shropshire, Shrewsbury has many half-timbered black-and-white houses, such as Rowley's House Museum, where nine galleries include Roman remains from Wroxeter, costumes, art and local history. The lovely Georgian building of Clive House, in which Lord Clive lived, is now a museum housing fine collections of Shropshire porcelain and ceramics.

Shrewsbury's castle, founded in 1083 and much altered since, reopened in 1985 as the Shropshire Regimental Museum. Among its fascinating exhibits is a lock of Napoleon's hair.

☐ WORKING FARM MUSEUM
Map ref 4589

Acton Scott Working Farm Museum, at the centre of a 1,200-acre estate, demonstrates agricultural practice before the advent of electricity and the petrol engine. Work is done by hand or by heavy horses and visitors can participate in some of the tasks. Traditional crafts and skills are demonstrated, including cider making and steam-powered threshing of home-grown corn.

Fish Street, one of Shrewsbury's many attractive side streets that reward exploration

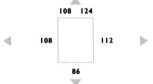

RURAL AND INDUSTRIAL HERITAGE

Traditional rural crafts exist alongside the more modern developments of the Industrial Revolution. Both can be seen in the museums of the area, with the history of mechanised transportation figuring greatly in the museums of Birmingham.

```
        108  124
            ▲
◀   108        112   ▶
            ▼
         86
```

SELECTED PLACES TO VISIT

BIRMINGHAM
Map ref 0688

Aston Hall, a Jacobean mansion, is noted for its panelled long gallery, balustraded staircase, plaster friezes and ceiling.

Sarehole Mill at Hall Green is an 18th-century water-powered mill, now restored to working order. Displays illustrate different aspects of milling and blade-grinding.

The Railway Museum at Tyseley features not only steam engines, specialist coaches and goods trains but also a railway restaurant and vintage buffet car. At Wythall the Midland Bus and Transport Museum has a large collection of buses and coaches and visitors can see restoration in progress.

The 15-acre Botanical Gardens contain plants from the tropics and rainforests and rare trees and alpine plants in different glasshouses. Among the gardens are aviaries.

In the City Museum and Art Gallery are paintings from the 14th century to the present, including an important collection of pre-Raphaelite work. The museum features prehistoric, Greek, Egyptian and Roman antiquities and the Pinto Collection of Wooden bygones.

The Museum of Science and Industry records developments since the Industrial Revolution with working exhibits.

BROMSGROVE
Map ref 9471

The Avoncroft Museum of Buildings has brought together historic buildings which would have been destroyed if they had not been dismantled, transported to the museum and re-erected.

They include a working windmill, cockpit, barn, 1946 prefab, fully equipped nail and chain making workshop, 15th- and 16th-century timber-framed houses, and a Georgian ice house and earth closet.

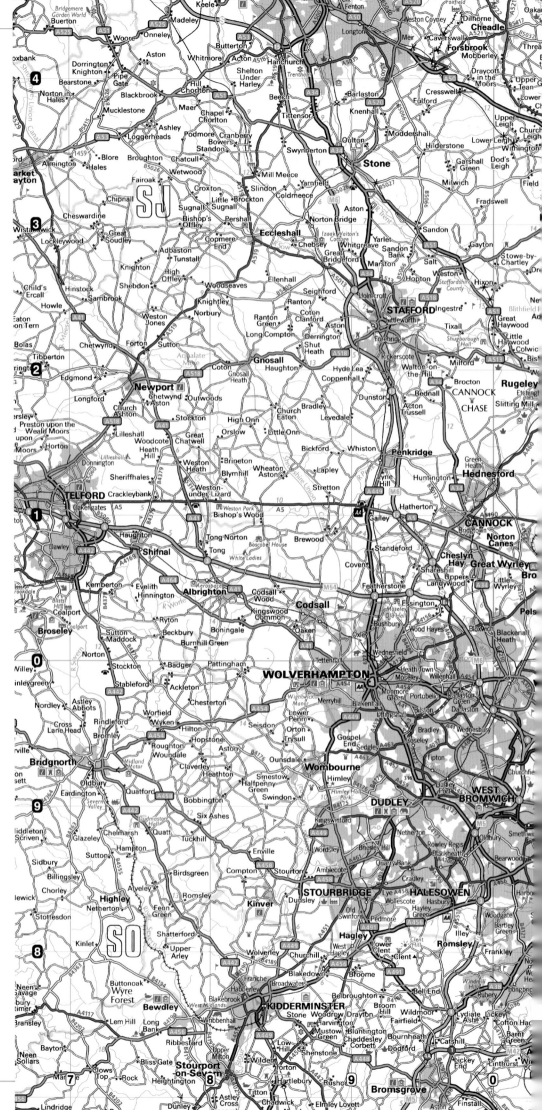

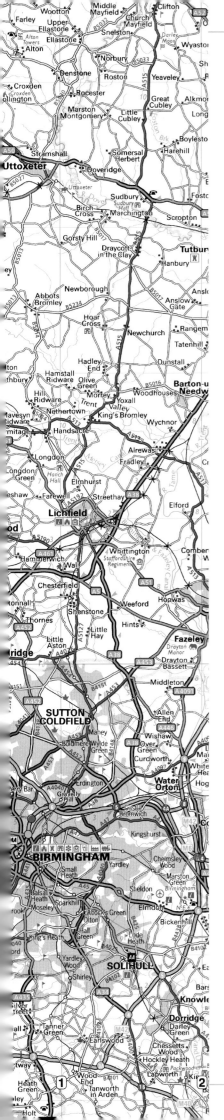

The 14th-century roof from Guesten Hall, Worcester, is the latest addition.

The Bromsgrove Museum displays local industries and crafts.

☗ CANNOCK CHASE
Map ref 9817

Three thousand acres of woods and heathlands make up the Cannock Chase Country Park. The Chase is a remnant of a vast oak forest and hunting ground which covered much of Staffordshire in Norman times and has numerous walks, trails and picnic sites.

⊞⊠⊞⊞ DUDLEY
Map ref 9490

The Black Country Museum has re-erected historic local buildings to form a village. The open-air museum includes a chainmaker's house and workshop, chemist's shop, pub, chapel and canal boat dock, with narrowboats on display.

Dudley Zoo, set in the ruins of the medieval castle, is home to more than 1,000 mammals, birds and reptiles.

The Dudley Canal Boat Trust runs electric narrowboat tours through the caverns and tunnels created under Dudley Castle Hill during the limestone quarrying era.

The Dudley Museum and Art Gallery includes the Brooke Robinson collection of fine and decorative art and a geological gallery.

⊞ HAGLEY
Map ref 9282

Hagley Hall, completed in 1760, features fine Italian plasterwork and an exhibition of 18th-century furniture and paintings. In the grounds are an Ionic temple, rotunda and Gothic ruins.

KINGS NORTON
Map ref 0579

At Kings Norton the Patrick Collection traces the history of the motorcar from the beginning of this century to the present day.

⊞⊞⊞ LICHFIELD
Map ref 1209

With its three sandstone spires, Lichfield Cathedral is unique in England. The original cathedral was consecrated in 700, but the present building was not completed until the early 14th century.

Hanch Hall, dating from the 13th century, has collections of needlework, antique dolls, teapots and 17th-century parchments.

Lichfield Heritage Exhibition and Treasury trace the history of Lichfield through its people. It depicts the Civil War, the siege of Lichfield Cathedral and displays some fine silver.

Samuel Johnson's birthplace is now a museum devoted to the life and works of the great lexicographer and his friends.

⊞ NATIONAL MOTORCYCLE MUSEUM
Map ref 2183

The National Motorcycle Museum

at Bickenhill, near Solihull, has 550 British machines dating from 1898. All are immaculately restored.

⊞ SHUGBOROUGH HALL
Map ref 9922

Staffordshire's County Museum is housed in the servant's quarters of Shugborough Hall, the ancestral home of the earls of Lichfield, where the fifth Earl, Patrick Lichfield, still lives. There are collections of 18th-century ceramics, French furniture, paintings and silver. The brewhouse, butler's pantry and kitchens have been restored. In the 900-acre grounds are a farm with rare animal breeds and a working corn mill.

⊞⊞⊠ STAFFORD
Map ref 9224

Stafford Castle and Trail overlooks this county town. Recent excavations have revealed a medieval borough.

The Art Gallery concentrates on the work of British craftsmen, while the William Salt Library preserves books, documents, engravings and drawings of Staffordshire history in an 18th-century town house.

Within the 16th-century Ancient High House, believed to be England's largest timber-framed town house – is a collection of costumes, furniture and paintings.

⊞⊞ STOURBRIDGE
Map ref 8684

Stourbridge is famous for crystal, and its manufacturers offer guided tours to see glass hand made, cut and polished in the traditional way.

Stourbridge Navigation Trust Bonded Warehouse has been restored as a community centre and craft workshop.

⊞ SUDBURY HALL
Map ref 1532

Sudbury Hall is a richly decorated Charles II house, with ornate plasterwork by Pettifer and Bradbury and paintings by Laguerre. The carvings on the staircase are by Grinling Gibbons.

⊞⊞ SUTTON COLDFIELD
Map ref 1395

This medieval market town has become a dormitory for Birmingham. Its 2,400-acre park is one of Britain's best examples of natural park. Through it runs the ancient Roman Ryknild Street. Several 16th-century stone houses can still be seen around the town.

The DMNS Model Railway includes scale models of New Street Station, Birmingham and other city centre buildings. The garden railway also features a model of Rugeley Power Station (by appointment only on weekends and bank holidays).

UTTOXETER
Map ref 0934

The Uttoxeter Heritage Centre, in 17th-century timber-framed cottages which have been restored, shows the town's development through an Edwardian shop window.

⊞ WEST BROMWICH
Map ref 0090

The Manor House is listed in the Domesday Book. The Great Hall, built in 1920, has been preserved in the original style.

The Oak House, with its collection of 16th- and 17th-century English oak furniture, is a timber-framed Tudor yeoman's house with panelled rooms and a lantern tower.

⊞⊞ WOLVERHAMPTON
Map ref 9397

Wolverhampton's Central Art Gallery features English watercolours and oil paintings, but also modern paintings, prints and sculptures, and oriental art and weapons.

At Bantock House Museum are 18th-century English enamels, and 18th- and 19th-century Midland japanned wares.

Birmingham, heart of the canal network, has more miles of waterway than Venice

IT'S NOT ALL GREY

The landscape and history quickly take the visitor away from the mining and industrial version normally associated with this part of the country. The green open spaces which surround the cities of Coventry and Leicester have many surprises to offer.

134 138

110   114

88 92

SELECTED PLACES TO VISIT

🏛 ARBURY HALL
Map ref 3589

Arbury Hall, an Elizabethan country house, altered in the 18th century, is a fine example of Gothic revival architecture. The stable block, with its doorway by Wren, houses a cycle museum.

🏛🏰 ASHBY-DE-LA-ZOUCH
Map ref 3516

The ruins of Ashby-de-la-Zouch Castle, once a Norman manor house, include parts of the tower and walls, great hall and private chambers, the kitchen and chapel.

🏛🏛 BURTON UPON TRENT
Map ref 2424

The Bass Museum of Brewing has a reconstructed 1920s Edwardian bar and a Chairman's Gallery explaining brewing and malting. Outside, exhibits include delivery vehicles and the famous Bass Shire Horses.

🏛🏛🏛 COVENTRY
Map ref 3378

Coventry Cathedral, designed by Sir Basil Spence to replace the cathedral destroyed in World War II, is an outstanding example of modern art, with its engraved screen, Sutherland tapestry and baptistry windows. The visitor centre shows the history of the city and its cathedral.

St Mary's Guildhall is a medieval hall with old council chamber, armoury and crypt. Mary Queen of Scots was held prisoner here.

The partial reconstruction of Lunt Roman Fort shows the massive circular timber enclosure, ramparts, the eastern gate and the granary.

Coventry's museums include a Toy Museum, the Herbert Art Gallery and Museum, the Museum of British Road Transport and the Midland Air Museum.

A statue of Coventry's famous naked lady, Lady Godiva, stands in Broadgate and 'Peeping Tom' is commemorated by three statues.

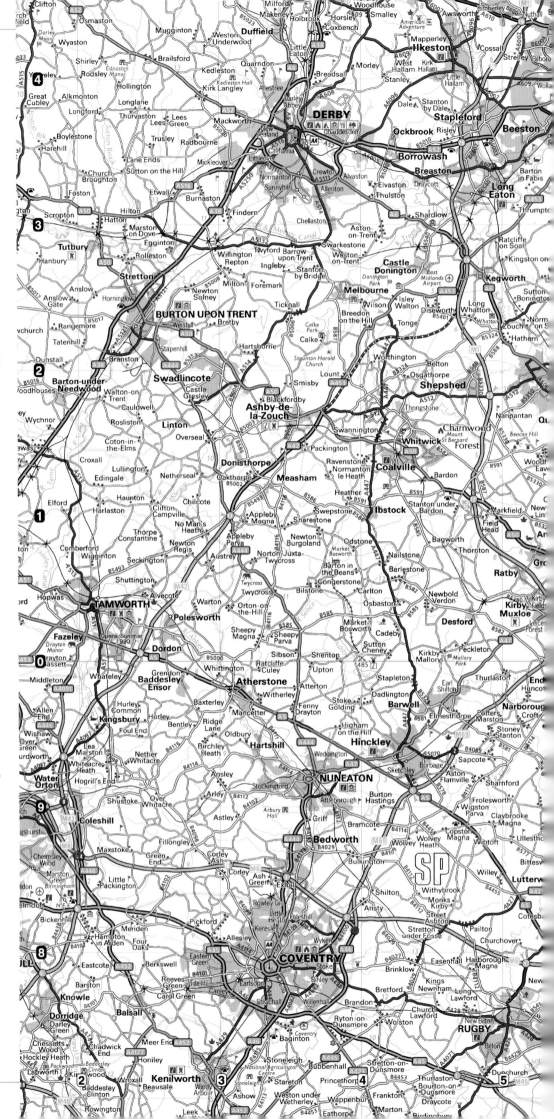

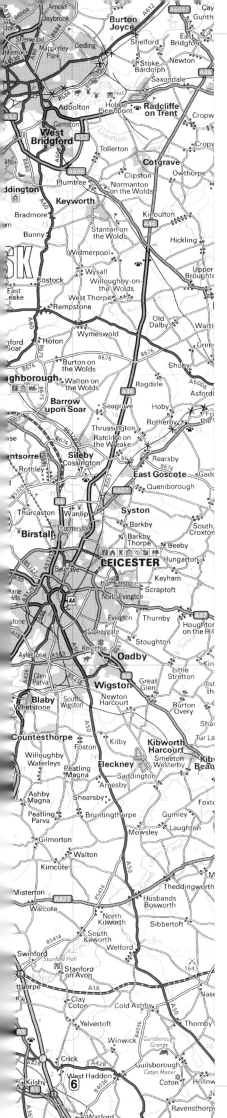

▪ DONINGTON PARK
Map ref 4326

The Donington collection of Grand Prix racing cars is the largest on display to the public. The exhibition adjoins the Donington Park racing circuit and features the Speedway Hall of Fame.

✈ EAST MIDLANDS AIRPORT
Map ref 4625

At East Midlands Aeropark there are a number of aviation-linked recreational facilities and exhibits. A viewing mound enables visitors to watch planes take off and land.

⊞⊠ KENILWORTH
Map ref 2873

Kenilworth Castle was a stronghold for the kings of England during the 11th and 12th centuries. Today the remains of the keep, much of the banqueting hall added by John of Gaunt in the 14th century, and a 16th-century gatehouse still survive. An exhibition about Elizabeth I can be seen in the barn.

In the Abbey Barn, built of Norman stonework from the Abbey ruins, tiles, gargoyles, farm and tannery tools are displayed.

⊞⊠⊠⊠⊠⊠⊠ LEICESTER
Map ref 5804

The parish church of St Martin became the City's Cathedral in the early 20th century, the bishopric having lapsed in the 8th century. The medieval building was almost completely rebuilt externally in the 19th century. The spire is over 220ft high.

The Guildhall is a 14th-century medieval hall of Corpus Christi Gild, used as a town hall from the late 15th century until 1876.

The Museum and Art Gallery includes 20th-century German art, as well as displays of 18th- to 20th-century English paintings and drawings, ceramics, silver, Egyptology, geology and natural history.

Remains of the Roman Baths and Jewry Wall can be seen at the Jewry Wall Museum, with exhibits on the archaeology and history of Leicestershire before 1485.

A Museum of Costume is housed in the late medieval building of Wygston's House where drapers' and shoe shops of the 1920s have been reconstructed. At Newarke House Museum the displays include local history and crafts from 1485, toys and games, clocks and mechanical instruments, a 19th-century street scene and an early 20th-century shop. The William Carey Museum, housed in the 19th-century Central Baptist Church, recalls missionary work in India through letters, photographs and mementoes.

Belgrave Hall, a Queen Anne country house with rock and water gardens, is now a museum with period furniture.

Leicester's Museum of Technology has original beam engines, a steam shovel, a section on the history of machine knitting and collections of horse-drawn vehicles, cycles and motorcycles. British Gas's John Doran Museum, in part of the old gasworks, includes displays on the production, distribution and uses of gas.

The Museum of the Royal Leicestershire regiment is found in a 15th-century gatehouse.

⊞⊠ LOUGHBOROUGH
Map ref 5319

Loughborough is famous for its bell casting, and the Bellfoundry Museum records the evolution of the craft. A carillon of 47 bells cast as a World War I memorial can be seen in the 150ft bell tower in Queens Park.

The 25-acre Whatton Gardens include formal areas and wilderness. Unusual plants grow beside roses, azaleas and rhododendrons and rock pools.

The Great Central Railway is a privately operated steam railway between Loughborough Central and Rothley, also calling at Quorn and Woodhouse stations. A museum and locomotive depot can be found at Loughborough.

⊞ MELBOURNE
Map ref 3925

Melbourne Hall has been variously the home of Prime Minister Lord Melbourne and Lady Caroline Lamb. It possesses one of the most famous formal gardens in Britain.

Spence's modern Coventry Cathedral, with the old cathedral spire behind

⊞⊠ NUNEATON
Map ref 3693

The Nuneaton Library holds a collection of photographs, letters, first editions and biographies of George Eliot.

⊠ RUDDINGTON
Map ref 5533

Ruddington Village Museum is split between two sites in the village centre. At the Hermitage, the oldest house in the village, displays of postcards, documents and photographs show village and family histories. One room is devoted to excavations on the site of the old mother church of Flawford. A reconstruction of the local fish and chip shop, chemist, cobbler, ironmonger and Edwardian schoolroom can be found in St Peter's Rooms, part of the 19th-century school.

Ruddington Framework Knitters' Museum is a unique complex of early 19th-century framework knitters' buildings, including a restored workshop with working equipment and workers' cottages.

⊞⊠⊠ TAMWORTH
Map ref 2104

Tamworth Castle Museum, a Norman castle with 15th-century banqueting hall and Jacobean state apartments, houses a local history collection and includes coins from the local Saxon mint.

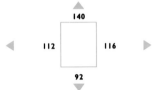
Rutland, once the smallest county in England but now swallowed up in Leicestershire, is well worth visiting and has a history worth discovering. In the past, visiting peers of the realm paid a toll in the form of decorated horseshoes, which can still be seen at Oakham Castle.

```
          140
      ◀  112    116  ▶
           92
```

SELECTED PLACES TO VISIT

⌂ BEDE HOUSE
Map ref 8897
The 13th-century house at Lyddington, formerly the home of the Bishops of Lincoln, was converted to almshouses in 1602 by Lord Burghley.

⌂ BELTON
Map ref 9339
Belton House, built between 1684 and 1688, is set in 1,000 acres of rolling parkland, including 19th-century formal gardens with an orangery. Brownlow family silver, Grinling Gibbons carvings, paintings, porcelain and tapestries can be found among the displays.

⌂ BELVOIR
Map ref 8234
Belvoir Castle has been the home of the dukes of Rutland since the 16th century. The present castle was rebuilt in the early 19th century in medieval style. It now houses the Museum of the 17th/21st Lancers and armoury and notable *objets d'art*.

⌂ ☇ ⚘ BURGHLEY
Map ref 0406
Burghley, built by William Cecil in the 16th century, has famous painted ceilings and silver fireplaces. It contains a large number of Italian Old Masters, beautiful tapestries, china and historic relics. The park, used for Burghley Horse Trials, was laid out by Capability Brown.

⌂ DEENE PARK
Map ref 9592
Deene Park has been in the same family since Sir Robert Brudenell acquired the house in the early 16th century. One of his better known descendants was the Seventh Earl of Cardigan, who led the charge of the Light Brigade.

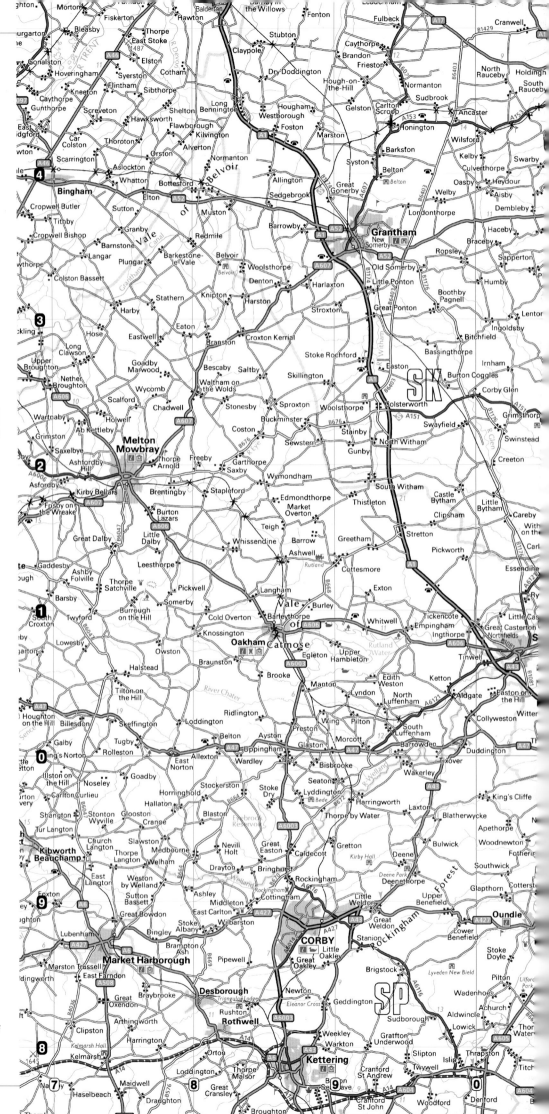

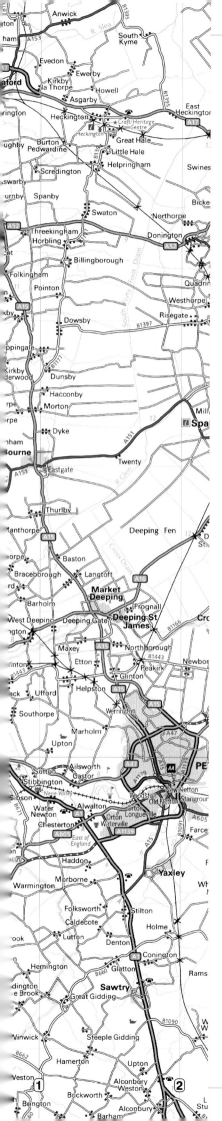

★ ELEANOR CROSS
Map ref 8983

The cross at Geddington is one of nine erected by Edward I to mark the resting places of the coffin of his Queen, Eleanor of Castile, on its journey from Harby to London.

⬚⬚ GRANTHAM
Map ref 9236

St Wulfram's Church has the sixth highest spire, at 282½ft, of any parish church in England.

Grantham House dates from the 14th century, and was extensively restored in the 16th to 18th centuries (by appointment only on Wednesdays).

The Grantham Museum includes displays illustrating the archaeology, natural and local history of the area.

⬚ GRIMSTHORPE
Map ref 0423

Grimsthorpe Castle developed from a medieval tower into a quadrangular Tudor house in the mid-16th century, with the later addition of a baroque north front and 19th-century façade on the west front. The house contains a fine collection of paintings and furniture.

⬚ KIRBY HALL
Map ref 9393

Kirby Hall is a fine example of an Elizabethan mansion built from stone with a variety of architectural detail. Additions to the house in the 17th century are ascribed to Inigo Jones. The gardens were remodelled by Sir Christopher Hatton.

⬚ LYVEDEN NEW BIELD
Map ref 9786

Lyveden New Bield is the shell of an uncompleted Renaissance building designed in the shape of the cross by Sir Thomas Tresham.

⬚⬚ MARKET HARBOROUGH
Map ref 7387

The 14th-century steeple of St Dionysius's church is made from Rutland limestone, while the rest of the building was rebuilt from Northampton ironstone in the 1470s. The timber-framed Old Grammar School, dates from the mid-17th century.

The Harborough Museum includes the Symington collection of corsetry and displays on the town.

⬚⬚ MELTON MOWBRAY
Map ref 7518

The Church of St Mary was called by Pevsner 'the stateliest and most impressive of all the churches in Leicestershire'.

The Melton Carnegie Museum has displays on Stilton cheese and Melton pies among the exhibits of local life past and present.

⬚ NENE VALLEY RAILWAY
Map ref 1098

A standard-gauge steam railway, runs for 7 miles from Wansford Station, Stibbington, through the Nene Park to Orton Mere and Peterborough.

⬚⬚⬚ OAKHAM
Map ref 8608

The Norman banqueting hall is almost all that remains of Oakham Castle, a late 12th-century manor house.

Rutland County Museum has exhibits relating to the varied history and way of life in Rutland.

⬚ OUNDLE
Map ref 0388

Victorian and Edwardian costumes are displayed at Southwick Hall, a 14th-century manor house with Elizabethan and Georgian additions.

Late 19th-century machinery for water and electricity supply is a feature at Ashton Mill where antique farm machinery can be found alongside a fish museum.

⬚ ROCKINGHAM
Map ref 8692

Rockingham Castle, an Elizabethan family house built within the walls of an earlier Norman keep, dominates the village from the top of the hill. The Castle has a particularly fine collection of Rockingham China.

⬚ RUTLAND RAILWAY
Map ref 8914

At the Iron Ore Mines siding the Rutland Railway Museum has a collection of industrial steam and diesel locomotives and many wagons and coaches representing the past activities of the local ironstone quarries and other mines.

⬚ RUTLAND WATER
Map ref 9008

Rutland Water, with its 27-mile long shoreline covering 3,100 acres, is the largest man-made lake in western Europe. With landscaped picnic areas, adventure playgrounds, trout fishing, sailing, cruises, canoeing, windsurfing, Barnsdale drought garden and arboretum, there is a wide range of opportunities.

⬚⬚ STAMFORD
Map ref 0307

The Stamford Museum includes finds from the recent excavation of the castle, and has some original clothes of famous fat man Daniel Lambert together with those of the midget General Tom Thumb.

Browne's Hospital is an ancient almshouse founded by wool merchant William Browne in the 15th century. There is fine medieval stained glass and an exhibition of almshouse life.

A complete Victorian steam brewery with original equipment is kept in a timber-framed medieval building at the Stamford Steam Brewery Museum.

⬚ TRIANGULAR LODGE
Map ref 8483

At Rushton the Triangular Lodge was built to symbolise the Holy Trinity by Sir Thomas Tresham in the late 16th century. This unusual building has three sides, with three floors, trefoil windows and three gables on each side.

Market Harborough's open market, below the Old Grammar School

Two cathedrals dominate the Fen landscape, Ely and Peterborough, and Boston's famous stump has been a landmark for centuries. The fertile soil, reclaimed with such difficulty from the marshes, has brought prosperity with flowers, fruit and vegetables.

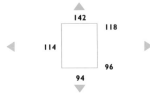

142
118
114
94
96

SELECTED PLACES TO VISIT

ℹ BOSTON
Map ref 3343

From as far away as Halton Holegate, 15 miles distant, the remarkable landmark of Boston Stump can be seen. This is the 272ft-high steeple of St Botolph's 14th-century church which has long guided travellers across the Fens and sailors in The Wash. On a clear day, from the top of the Stump, Lincoln can be seen, 28 miles to the north west.

The church contains a memorial to John Cotton, the minister who led the band of Puritans who sailed for America in 1630 and founded the city of the same name there.

The American connection is taken up in Fydell House, which contains an American Room. It stands next to the 15th-century Guildhall, in which the Pilgrim Fathers were imprisoned after their first attempt to escape to religious freedom, now used as a museum.

A major port in medieval times, Boston now is a centre for international trade.

Peterborough's fine, substantially Norman, cathedral

116

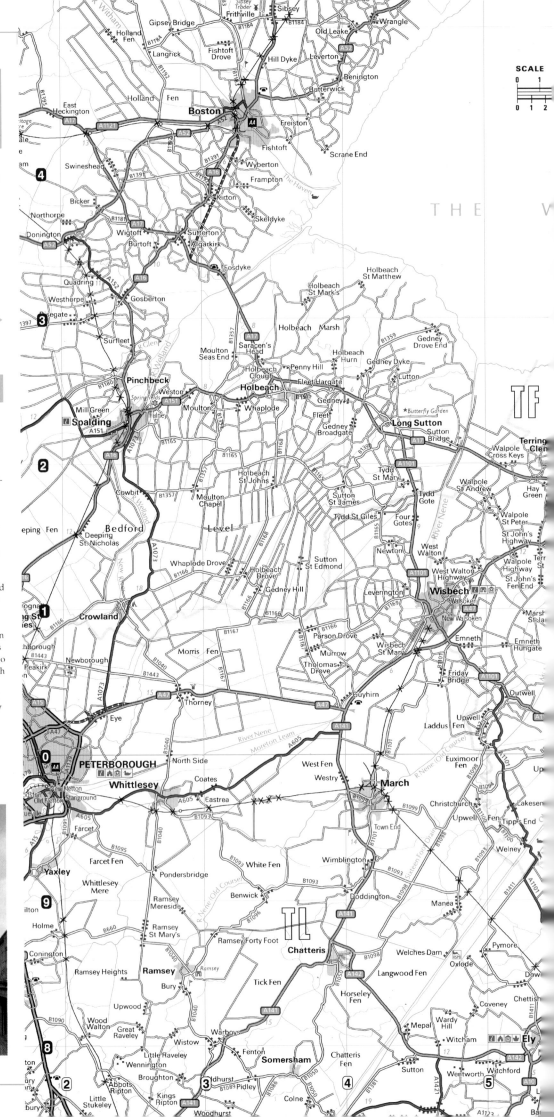

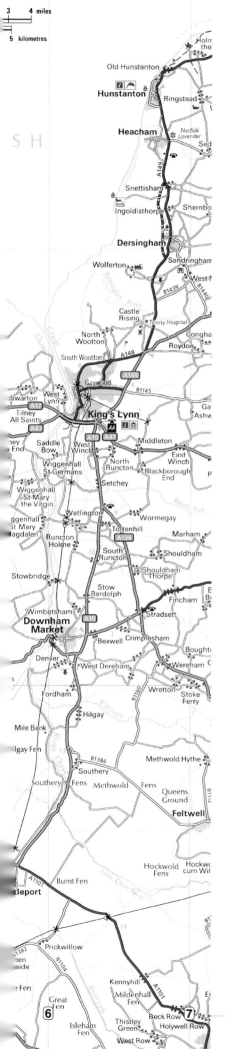

★ BUTTERFLY GARDEN
Map ref 4424

Long Sutton has one of the country's largest indoor tropical gardens, Butterfly Garden, where exotic butterflies fly freely and scorpions and tarantulas roam in an insectarium. Outdoors are butterfly and bee gardens, designed to attract native species, and wildflower meadows.

⬛⬛⬛ ELY
Map ref 5581

Until the marshes around Ely were drained in the 17th century, the city stood on an island surrounded by miles of swamp and fen. This was the country from which Hereward the Wake led the resistance to William the Conqueror until 1071.

A focal point of the Fens, the octagonal tower of Ely Cathedral can be seen for miles across the flat landscape. St Etheldreda founded an abbey here in 670, and the Norman cathedral was built on the site in 1083.

Ely now has a Stained Glass Museum, set up to preserve stained glass from redundant churches and other buildings. The art of designing and making stained glass windows is explained and the museum also features modern stained glass.

HOLBEACH
Map ref 3425

The Church of All Saints in Holbeach is totally unaltered since its construction in 1380, giving a unique picture of the change in architectural styles between the Decorated and Perpendicular.

Holbeach is a quiet market town.

MARCH
Map ref 4298

March owes its origins to a religious settlement. The 15th-century church of St Wendreda honours the Saxon gentlewoman who first established a religious community here. The church has a superb hammerbeam roof with more than 100 carved wooden angels, saints and martyrs.

A touch of humour can be seen with the inclusion of a carving of the devil.

⬛⬛⬛⬛ PETERBOROUGH
Map ref 2099

For almost 6,000 years Peterborough has been the scene of human endeavour, shown by the discovery of the site of a thatched hut dating from around 3700BC. Today Peterborough is a development area.

The Roman legions marched to Peterborough and founded a mighty 27-acre fortress now long ruined and buried. A monastery, built in 656, had to be replaced in the 10th century following a raid by Vikings. Destroyed by fire in 1116, this early abbey formed the site for the magnificent cathedral built between 1118 and 1258. Catherine of Aragon and Mary Queen of Scots – whose body was later removed by her son James I to Westminster Abbey – were buried here.

Peterborough has glorious medieval and Tudor buildings, standing cheek-by-jowl with modern tower blocks and factories. The Great Gate on Cathedral Square is Norman, and next to it is the chancel of St Thomas of Canterbury's 14th-century chapel. The parish church of St John the Baptist dates from 1402.

Longthorpe Tower displays some of the best examples of English medieval wall paintings.

The City Museum and Art Gallery features an unusual collection of straw marquetry and carved bonework made by French soldiers imprisoned during the Napoleonic Wars.

⬛ RAMSEY
Map ref 2985

Ramsey was the site of a Benedictine abbey, founded in 969 and dissolved in 1539. A house, now a school, was built on the spot around 1600, and incorporates the abbey's 13th-century Lady Chapel. The highly decorated remains of the 15th-century gatehouse are now owned by the National Trust.

⬛ SPALDING
Map ref 2522

Famous for tulips and daffodils, Spalding holds an annual May flower parade. The flower-growing fields stretch for 10,000 acres.

Spalding is a market town set on the River Welland, spanned by seven bridges. Its 13th-century church of St Mary and St Nicholas has unusual double aisles.

❋ SPRINGFIELDS
Map ref 2724

To the east of Spalding are Springfields Gardens, where more than a million bulbs and over 200,000 plants provide a glorious display in 25 acres of lawns, glasshouses and flowerbeds.

WHITTLESEY
Map ref 2697

Until a major drainage scheme of 1851 removed the water from the 1,900-acre Whittlesey Mere, the frozen lake in winter provided a faster and easier means of travel – by means of skates – than was possible in warmer weather.

Today Whittlesey is an industrial and market town.

⬛⬛⬛ WISBECH
Map ref 4609

Set on the banks of the River Nene, surrounded by bulb fields, orchards and fruit fields, Wisbech is a prosperous market town.

Along the Brinks – two rows of houses set beside the river – are superb Georgian buildings, including Peckover House, which is owned by the National Trust. This elegant town house on the North Brink, built in 1722, has fine plaster and wood rococo decoration, and a 2-acre Victorian garden. Octavia Hill, founder of the National Trust, was born in a house on the South Brink.

The Wisbech and Fenland Museum in the town centre was established in 1781.

The riverside walk along the Great Ouse in Ely

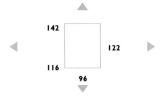

SAINTS AND SAND-DUNES

In Walsingham, this part of Norfolk has one of England's holiest shrines, and the region has many ancient and medieval churches. The sand dunes and salt-marshes of the north coast provide sanctuary for many rare species of seabirds in protected nature reserves.

```
        ▲
       142
◄  ┌─────────┐  ►
116│         │122
   └─────────┘
       96
        ▼
```

TOUR

NORTH WEST NORFOLK
74 MILES

From King's Lynn, the tour takes the busy A47 south-west, turning left after Narborough towards West Acre and Castle Acre. These villages, mentioned in the Domesday Book, grew up where the ancient Peddars' Way cross the River Nar.

William de Warenne, son-in-law of the Conqueror, built a huge castle here, together with a priory for the monks he brought over from Normandy. Little remains of the castle except the earthworks, part of the keep and 13th-century bailey, but the priory's atmospheric ruins still preserve the church and its arcaded west front, monastic buildings, the prior's lodging and later 16th-century gatehouse.

The tour joins the A1065, turning north towards the coast. It passes through a number of villages named after saints, as this part of Norfolk was a place of pilgrimage. Near East Raynham is Raynham Hall, home of the 18th-century politician known as 'Turnip' Townshend, because of his advocacy of turnip growing as part of crop rotation.

Fakenham, at a crossroads, is a charming market town with a 15th-century church and Georgian buildings. Continuing north, the route passes through East Barsham, from where Henry VIII made a pilgrimage to the shrine of Our Lady of Walsingham, a few miles away. At Houghton St Giles, the slipper chapel where pilgrims removed their shoes before under-taking the final part of their journey barefoot is still a revered spot.

The shrine at Walsingham was founded in 1601 by Lady Richeldis de Faverches, following a vision, and added to by Augustinians and Franciscans. After his later quarrel with the Pope, Henry VIII had the shrine destroyed, but pilgrims still come to pay their devotions here at a new shrine built in the 1930s.

From religion the tour next turns

its attention to lighter pursuits. The longest 10¹/₄in gauge railway in Britain runs on the 4-mile track between Walsingham and Wells.

Wells-next-the-Sea is a slight misnomer, for today the little town is separated from the sea by a mile of sand dunes. The old-fashioned port, with its coasters and shrimp and whelk fishing boats, is set on an estuary.

The north Norfolk coast has 10 miles of nature reserves of dunes and salt-marshes, popular with birdwatchers and botanists, managed by the Nature Conservancy Council. Following the A149, the tour soon reaches Holkham, where Lady Ann's Drive gives access to the marshes and mudflats.

Inland is Holkham Hall, an 18th-century Palladian mansion, home to Coke of Norfolk and the earls of Leicester. It has a magnificent marble hall and a superb collection of paintings by Rubens, Van Dyck, Poussin, Claude and Gainsborough.

Further west along the A149 lies Brancaster Staithe, from where a boat service sails to Scolt Head Island. A bird sanctuary and nature study area, the island, like the neighbouring mainland, is made up of sand dunes and salt-marshes which stretches for 3¹/₂ miles from Brancaster Harbour to Burnham Harbour.

The tour turns southwards at Old Hunstanton, and comes to Hunstanton, East Anglia's only west-facing resort. Hunstanton also has miles of sandy beaches and distinctive striped cliffs, made of layers of carr stone, red chalk and white chalk.

Blakeney Point, a nature reserve east of Wells-next-the-Sea

At Heacham, the village sign and a memorial in the church commemorate the Red Indian princess, Pocahontas, who married John Rolfe of Heacham Hall in 1614 in Virginia. The fields around Heacham are full of lavender, harvested from July to mid-August. Caley Mill is the home of the National Collection of Lavenders, where the methods of harvesting and distillation of lavender water are explained.

Sandringham is not a village, but consists entirely of the 7,000-acre royal estate and country park, with its magnificent red brick house, open to the public except when any member of the Royal Family is in residence.

Queen Victoria bought the house in 1862 for the Prince of Wales, and it contains portraits of British and European royal families. An exhibition of sculpture, china, ornaments and furniture is found in the house, and there is a museum of motorcars and dolls. The country park is a blaze of rhododendrons in the summer, and footpaths lead through the delightful woodland.

From the A149, a right turn leads to Wolferton, where a unique museum has been created as a labour of love by a former railwayman and his wife. Wolferton Station, once the arrival point for kings, queens and emperors visiting the royal estate of Sandringham, fell into disrepair as road transport superseded rail. The superb reception rooms were saved from

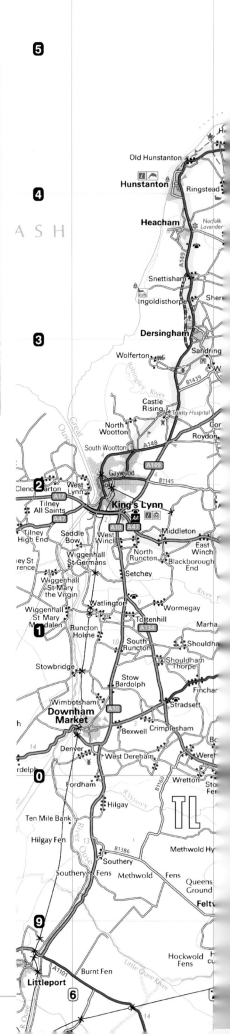

demolition when the station closed in 1966 and restored as a museum of Edwardian social life by Mr and Mrs Eric Walker. The fine exhibits include Queen Victoria's travelling bed.

To the east of Castle Rising church are the lovely 17th-century almshouses of Trinity Hospital. The Castle itself is now ruined, but it is possible to climb the steep flights of stone stairs inside the fine 50ft keep to look down into the shell of the Great Hall. The castle was built in 1150 by the Earl of Arundel, and is reached by a 13th-century bridge across a ditch.

From here the tour returns to King's Lynn on the A148.

SELECTED PLACES TO VISIT

⌂ COCKLEY CLEY
Map ref 7904

South of Swaffham is a full-scale reconstruction, as it is thought to have been at the time of Queen Boudicca, of an Iceni encampment on its original site. In a nearby 15th-century forge cottage is a museum of local history from prehistoric times to the present. The village also boasts an early Saxon church, dating from around 630.

KING'S LYNN
Map ref 6318

The king who elevated Bishop's Lynn to regal status in 1539 was Henry VIII, but the town has royal connections at least 300 years before, when King John left the town just before his death, and lost his treasure in the Wash. Charters from those days are still to be seen in one of the town's two guildhalls.

The Lynn Museum throws light on many aspects of the town's archaeology, geology and natural history. It has a particularly interesting collection of medieval pilgrims' badges. The Museum of Social History is an elegant 18th-century house housing displays of costume, ceramics, glass, toys and domestic items.

⌂ NORFOLK RURAL LIFE MUSEUM
Map ref 9716

Close by Gressenhall in an old workhouse, is found the Norfolk Rural Life Museum, telling the story of 200 years of village life and agriculture through reconstructed workshops and large displays.

⚑ NORTH ELMHAM
Map ref 9922

The ruins of an early 11th-century Saxon cathedral lie beside the ruins of a 14th-century manor house in a moated enclosure.

⌂ THURSFORD COLLECTION
Map ref 9835

Fairground organs, barrel organs, engines and ploughing engines are among the exhibits at this exciting museum. There is also a children's play area and a steam railway.

NORFOLK BROADS

More than 30 large and very beautiful sheets of water between Norwich, Lowestoft and Sea Palling, together with rivers, lakes and canals, provide some 200 miles of water for cruising and sailing

n a book compiled with the motorist in mind, the Broads present something of a problem, as the area is most easily seen from a boat! For the visitor with limited time, however, the area can be explored by car, sometimes taking in places less populated than those which can be seen from the water.

The Broads contain about 30 lakes, almost all shallow and fringed by willow and alder car or reed and saw-sedge. Most are little more than large pools, excavated as man dug for peat in the early Middle Ages and flooded as the sea level rose during the 14th century. Surprisingly, this detail of history was not confirmed until research was carried out during the 1950s. Linked by some 200 miles of rivers, streams and dykes, the Broads are among the busiest navigable waterways in Europe.

A Threatened Environment

When the National Parks were set up, in the early 1950s, there was strong support for the inclusion of the Broads but, to the surprise of many, the area was not designated. Lacking the protection offered by National Park status, suffering from unforeseen changes in agricultural practice, the

Left: *Horsey Mere, connected to Hickling Broad, is a haven for wildlife*
Below: *Hickling, the largest of the Broads, is the centre of a National Reserve*

Broads faced a number of problems, among them erosion of the river and lake banks and high rates of pollution.

Less busy now than during the 1960s and 70s, the Broads continue to attract many tourists who hire boats from various centres, setting off to cruise the rivers and lakes, displaying a wide variation of competence in seamanship. Some estimates suggest that erosion of the banks by the wash from pleasure boats has been at the rate of nine to ten feet every ten years.

Pollution takes two forms, that created by motor boats, and the less obvious, but ultimately more destructive, pollution caused by the overuse of chemicals. Extensive use of phosphates and nitrates in farming led to heavy concentrations leeching into the waters of the Broads. This encouraged plant and fish growth but it also led to a rapid increase in the amount of algae in the water. The build-up of algae, first on the surface then, as it died, as a sort of carpet on the bed of the broads, resulted in the disruption of the food chain. As a result several of the broads are now unable to

support life and are, effectively, dead.

Affording Protection

The unchecked growth of the tourist industry led, as elsewhere, to problems with unsightly developments. The decline of thatching, once a major industry, permitted the re-colonization of fen areas by scrub, depriving several species of their natural habitat. Further pressure on wildlife habitat came from the draining of grazing marshland and its conversion into grain producing land. The threatened loss of the important Halvergate Marsh highlighted this problem, and drew attention to the overall need to protect habitats, with emphasis on the requirements of the high ratio of rare species found in the area.

In 1978 a Broads Authority was set up in an attempt to counter all these problems. Lacking proper funding and sufficient powers the Authority still did a good job in laying the foundations for improvements. Nonetheless, there was considerable relief in conservation circles when the roads effectively became a recognised national asset with the passing of the

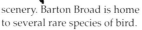

1988 Broads Act. A new Broads Authority came into being a year later and, although not quite a National Park, the Broads now have the opportunity to begin combating problems.

The Main Waterways

The defined area lies along five main rivers, in outline rather like some bizarre starfish! The rivers themselves are connected by artificial cuttings called dykes or fleets. The north-east arm of the Broads extends to the coast and incorporated two of the best known Broads – Horsey Mere and Hickling Broad – both linked to the River Thurne. This is flat country, often windy, and therefore attracts many sailing boats.

The most northerly arm of the Broads follows the River Ant through Barton Broad and on to join the River Bure near St Benet's Abbey. The Ant is perhaps the least used of the rivers, yet it contains some delightful, typical, Broads scenery. Barton Broad is home to several rare species of bird.

The Bure is navigable, though pursuing a very windy course, from Coltishall, through Wroxham and past Great and Little Hoveton Broads. Wroxham is the tourist map of the area; the banks of the river lined with boatyards. The Bure skirts Ranworth Broad and

Above: The beautiful swallowtail butterfly can be seen in summer at Horsey Mere
Below: An avocet feeding at Breydon Water – a large inland estuary

Marshes before gathering in the Ant and the Thurne and turning south. At Acle it turns east with a final change of direction at Great Yarmouth, heading south, behind the town, to join Breydon Water. The ruler-straight A47 runs through the centre of the Broads area, below the Bure. Here the landscape is flat, cattle-grazing marshland, drained by man and still possessing old windpumps, sometimes open to visitors.

Breydon Water is a very large inland estuary which attracts a variety of wildfowl and waders to its mudflats. Brent, pink-footed, white-fronted and bean geese use the estuary to rest and feed. Avocet are regular visitors and spoonbill, increasingly seen on the Norfolk coast, add a slightly flamboyant touch to many a winter's day. Like the Bure, both the River Yare and the Waveney empty into Breydon Water.

At its western limit, the Norfolk Broads area touches the Norwich ring road, following the Yare east past Reedham and on to Breydon. The Yare is the broadest of rivers, navigable by sea-going ships as far as Norwich. Above Reedham it is joined by the Chet, which leads through a combination of wooded country and marsh.

The Waveney, which for much of its course forms the boundary between Norfolk and Suffolk, enters the area at Bungay and heads east through Beccles towards Lowestoft before veering north past the overused Oulton Broad.

A small group of Broads lies between the Thurne and Yare sections of the area; comprising Filby, Rollesby and Ormesby Broads, they are possibly the least spoilt of the Broads. Unlike many of the others which have no direct access by

road, they are crossed by the A149, which divides Rollesby and Ormesby, and the A1064 crossing the Filby Broad.

A Unique Wildlife

Man may reasonably claim much of the responsibility for the creation of the Broads, but it is the use wildlife has made of the various habitats that makes it of such international significance. To appreciate the variety and importance of these habitats it is necessary to look no further than Hickling Broad. One of the largest stretches of open water in southern England, Hickling has reed and sedgebeds, grazing marshes with draining ditches, pools, meadows and woodland.

Frogbit grows in the water, with reeds and bulrush at the margins. Near the edges and on the marshes grow a staggering variety of plants - water violet, marsh sowthistle, milk parsley, purple loosestrife, hemp agrimony, marsh pea, various orchids and several rushes are but a selection. Hickling is not a freshwater site and several of the plants found here are normally associated only with the coast, including marsh mallow with its lovely sugar pink flowers – a reminder that the sweets were once made from its roots.

The shy, slow-stepping bittern breeds here, as does the bearded tit; marsh and Montagu's harrier breed though not on a regular basis. Gadwell, shoveler, pochard, garganey with, in winter, teal, wigeon, pintail, goldeneye and scaup are among the duck species. Black tern and osprey in summer and autumn, great grey shrike and hen harrier in winter regularly add to the pleasures afforded bird watchers. There are many moths, including the migrant great brocade, but the great attraction for most visitors is the colony of the spectacular swallowtail butterfly.

The need to protect this marvellous lowland area is surely not in doubt. Already the Authority has taken some enterprising steps – involving educating the public, sponsoring research into more efficient boat design and, crucially, into defeating the spread of algae. With renewed consciousness of the problems, and increased goodwill, the chances of saving the Broads are probably higher than for a very long time.

This part of Norfolk is dominated by the fine city of Norwich which is steeped in history, and the massive waterways of the Broads. The coastline from Great Yarmouth to Sheringham offers excellent beaches.

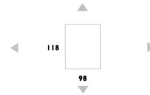

▲

118

◄ ▶

98

▼

SELECTED PLACES TO VISIT

🏛 BEESTON HALL
Map ref 3422

Beeston Hall, north-east of Wroxham, is an 18th-century mansion in a flintfaced gothic style with neo-classical interiors. The Hall has been associated with the Preston family since 1640.

🏛 BLICKLING
Map ref 1828

Blickling Hall is a Jacobean red brick mansion set in grounds with an early 19th-century orangery, mile-long lake and parkland. Inside can be seen a number of rooms in greatly contrasting styles, from the gilded State Bedroom, to the Peter-the-Great Room in a light neo-classical style, and a Jacobean Long Gallery, all containing fine pieces of furniture, tapestries and pictures.

Earlier owners of the estate were the Boleyn family, whose most famous daughter was Henry VIII's wife, Anne Boleyn. Legend tells how, on the anniversary of her beheading, her ghost returns with head in lap.

♣ 🏛 BROADLAND CONSERVATION CENTRE
Map ref 3515

The Broadland Conservation Centre, along a short nature trail leading to Ranworth Inner Broad, has displays on the history and preservation of the Broads. The birdlife can be seen in its natural habitat from a floating gallery.

🏛 CAISTER
Map ref 5313

The remains of Caister's Roman port can be seen close to the ruins of the 15th-century moated castle. The castle was built by Sir John Fastolf, and includes a 98ft-high round tower and gatehouse. In the 15th and 16th centuries Caister Castle was home to the Paston family; the *Paston Letters* reveal the domestic life of that era. Part of the grounds contain a veteran and vintage car museum.

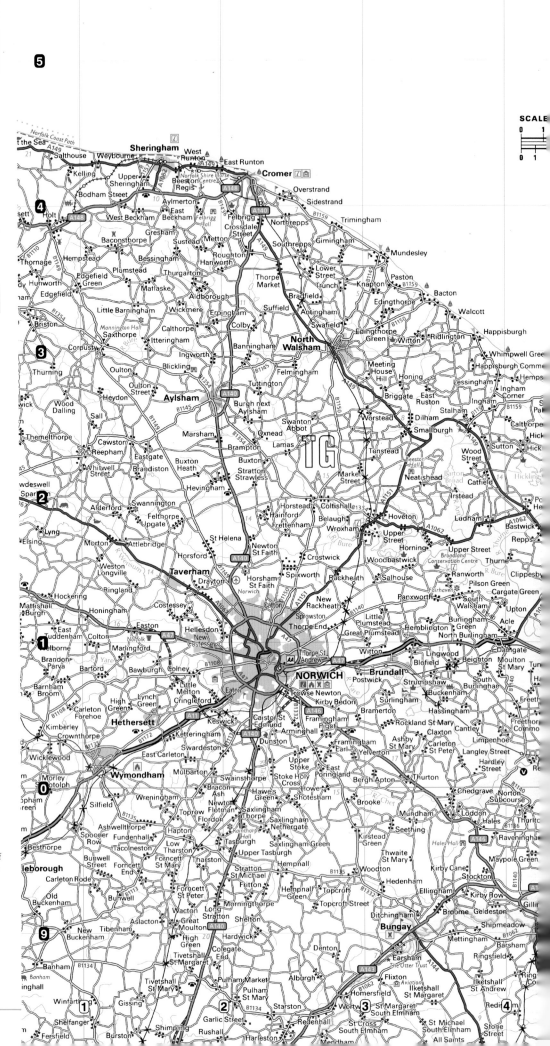

Dressed for action – an RNLI lifeboat man in the museum at Cromer

CROMER
Map ref 2243

Cromer's St Peter and St Paul's Church tower at 160ft is the tallest in Norfolk. Two miles inland was a Roman camp near Beacon Hill, Norfolk's highest point. Three fishermen's cottages form the Cromer Museum, one furnished in a Victorian period setting. A Lifeboat Museum is housed in the No 2 Boathouse at the end of The Gangway with displays and pictures on Cromer Lifeboats and the RNLI.

Two miles east of Cromer at Overstrand is The Pleasaunce, partly designed by Lutyens, with gardens laid out by Gertrude Jekyll.

GREAT YARMOUTH
Map ref 5307

A thriving port for more than 1,000 years, the town is also a premier seaside resort with its Pleasure Beach, two waxwork museums, Merrivale Model Village and the Venetian Waterways.

The old part of the town is linked to the mainland by the Haven Bridge. To the south of the bridge is the waterfront with Tudor, Georgian and Victorian buildings. At South Quay is Elizabeth House, a museum of 19th-century domestic life. Among narrow alleys of The Rows are the 17th-century Old Merchants' and the 13th-century Tolhouse - reputed to be the oldest civic building in Britain - now a museum of local history.

The Maritime Museum for East Anglia includes the history of herring fishing, the wherry, lifesaving and the oil and gas industry. Hundreds of butterflies fly freely with tropical birds and plants at the Butterfly Farm and Tropical Gardens. Towards the end of the spit is the 144-ft Nelson's Monument erected in 1819.

MUNDESLEY
Map ref 3136

Stow Mill to the south of Mundesley is a tower mill built in 1827 which is being restored to working order.

NORFOLK SHIRE HORSE CENTRE
Map ref 1743

At West Runton the Norfolk Shire Horse Centre, Shire and Suffolk horses give working demonstrations. Mountain and moorland ponies and domestic animals are also kept, and horse-drawn wagons and machinery are on display.

NORWICH
Map ref 2308

Originally settled by the Saxons, Norwich has a fascinating history, through Norman times and the development of the medieval cloth industry and into the 20th century. Although the new blends in with the old, its streets retain much of their earlier character.

Much of the medieval city wall can still be seen around the centre, together with some of the gates which gave access to the city.

The centre is dominated by Norwich Castle, now a splendid museum. Built in 1075, it has been the military and political focal point for the area. It has served as the county gaol and at one time was the Sheriff of Norfolk's residence. As a museum it is well known for its Rotunda, ecology gallery, and collections of natural history and regional archaeology. The castle's many art galleries give a picture of life through the eyes of artists of the Norwich School. Visitors can join tours to see the battlements, for a magnificent view of the city and surrounding countryside, and to explore the dungeons.

The city boasts three other important museums. Stranger's Hall, a medieval merchant's house, was turned into a Folk Museum at the beginning of the century and now includes the development of domestic life. A collection of local trade signs can also be seen. The Bridewell Museum, originally an ancient merchant house and later a prison, features exhibits on the social and industrial development of the city. The smallest museum of St Peter Hungate is a 15th-century church situated in the cobbled Elm Hill. This fine church has a hammer-beam roof and examples of Norwich painted glass. The museum is a brass rubbing centre and includes exhibits relating to church art.

Norwich Cathedral is considered one of the finest examples of ecclesiastical architecture in England. The building was started in 1090 but was not finished and consecrated until 1278. It remains one of the country's best preserved and most beautiful cathedrals.

Beside the Norman cathedral there are some 30 medieval churches to be found today in the city centre. One of the most impressive of these is the largest parish church in Norwich, St Peter Mancroft, which overlooks the attractive market place.

ORMESBY ST MICHAEL
Map ref 4714

The Broadland Tractor Museum at Ormesby St Michael has a fine collection of tractors and unusual agricultural machinery.

SOMERLEYTON
Map ref 4897

Somerleyton House, rebuilt in the mid-19th century, is an interesting blend of architectural styles, including neo-Jacobean, Italian and Palladian. Stone brought from France has been creatively combined with red brick. The Hall contains tapestries, paintings and carvings by the sculptor Grinling Gibbons. In the 12 acres of gardens are a children's farm, an aviary, a miniature railway and a magnificent yew maze.

THRIGBY HALL
Map ref 4713

Thrigby Hall Wildlife Gardens feature a varied selection of Asian wildlife and a lake with ornamental wildfowl, set in a 250-year-old landscaped garden.

WROXHAM
Map ref 2918

The Barton House Railway at Wroxham is a 3in-gauge miniature steam railway and 7in-gauge riverside railway with full size accessories. For a display of rural crafts a visit to Wroxham Barns will provide an interesting insight into the manufacture of a wide range of items. The workshops are housed in a collection of 18th-century barns set in 7 acres of parkland.

Great Yarmouth, a busy sea port and resort rolled into one

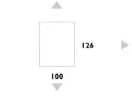
Around Caernarfon Bay lie the Isle of Anglesey and the Lleyn Peninsula. Many monks and pilgrims passed this way to the sacred sites such as Holy Island and Bardsey Island. Cromlechs and other relics show a still older religious culture here.

▲

◄ | 126 | ►

100
▼

TOUR

LLEYN PENINSULA
72 MILES

Leaving Porthmadog, the tour takes the A487 through Tremadog – birthplace of Lawrence of Arabia – and Penmorfa, where a tablet in the church commemorates Sir John Owen, Royalist leader in the Civil War.

The route continues through Pant-glas and Nasareth to Llanllyfni, where it turns left to pass the Old Welsh Country Life Museum towards the A499.

At the junction is Clynnog-fawr, a pretty whitewashed village with a church dedicated to St Beuno, standing on the site of a Christian foundation dating from 606. Inside the church is the chest of Beuno, an ancient oak strong-box. The saint's original cell, once a place of pilgrimage, is now a chapel on the south side of the church, and a holy well named after him stands outside the village, beside a cromlech.

To the left on the A499 is the peak of Y Gyrn-Ddu, rising to 1,713ft; ahead is the village of Llanaelhaearn, 300ft above sea level, and the triple peaks of The Rivals (Yr Eifl, literally `the forks'), falling steeply to the sea. On the most easterly peak is Tre'r Ceiri, known as the Town of the Giants, one of the most important prehistoric hut circle clusters in Wales, where a hoard of gold is said to have been stored. Parts of the surrounding walls still rise to 15ft.

Here the tour turns right on to the B4417, continuing around the coast of the peninsula. Today Nefyn and neighbouring Morfa Nefyn are popular holiday resorts, with sandy beaches, bathing and sea-fishing.

Sheltered in a sandy bay, facing south, is Aberdaron, once the embarkation point for pilgrims making the dangerous journey to the holy island of Bardsey, described in detail on page 101.

A wooden Celtic church was built here at the same time as the first monastery on Bardsey, and the present church retains part of the later Norman stone building in the north nave.

The tour follows the line of the coast, near Porth Neigwl (Hell's Mouth Bay) where, surrounded by perpendicular cliffs, powerful currents have destroyed many ships.

On this unclassified road is Plas-Yn-Rhiw, a small manor house, part medieval with Tudor and Georgian additions. Its ornamental gardens with flowering trees and shrubs, include sub-tropical specimens.

Abersoch lies on the more peaceful bay known as St Tudwal's Road, after the 6th-century Breton saint, who is said to have founded a chapel on one of the two offshore islands which bear his name. Abersoch is popular with holidaymakers for its sandy beaches, yachting and fishing.

At Abersoch the tour rejoins the A499 to drive north to Llanbedrog. Close by is the Ffynnon Arian or Silve Spring, claimed to be a holy healing well.

The next stop is at the well-known resort of Pwllheli. Once a port and shipbuilding centre, Pwllheli declined in industrial importance as its harbour silted up. Since 1890 it has prospered on tourism, thanks to the 5-mile sweep of the south beach, and the popular holiday camp to the north. Pwllheli is also a market town.

From Pwllheli the tour continues along the shore, taking the A497. Shortly on the left is Penarth Fawr, part of an early 15th-century house. The hall, buttery and screen have been preserved.

Llanystumdwy (`the church at the end of the river') is the village where Liberal Prime Minister and great orator Lloyd George lived. He lies buried here beside the River Dwyfor, from which he took the title `Earl of Dwyfor'.

Born in Manchester, Lloyd George moved here as an infant after the death of his father. The Lloyd George Memorial Museum outlines the statesman's life and includes freedom caskets and other memorabilia. His boyhood cottage home, Highgate, is also open to the public.

Criccieth, an attractive resort where Lloyd George practised as a solicitor and lived in adult life, has a long promenade and wide beach. Only a few 16th- and 17th-century houses remain of the old borough, founded in 1284. A castle, built here before the Norman conquest, was strengthened by Edward I with two baileys and a notable gatehouse. From the ruins there are magnificent views over Snowdonia. From Criccieth, the tour returns to Porthmadog.

Caernarfon's massive castle, overlooking the Menai Strait

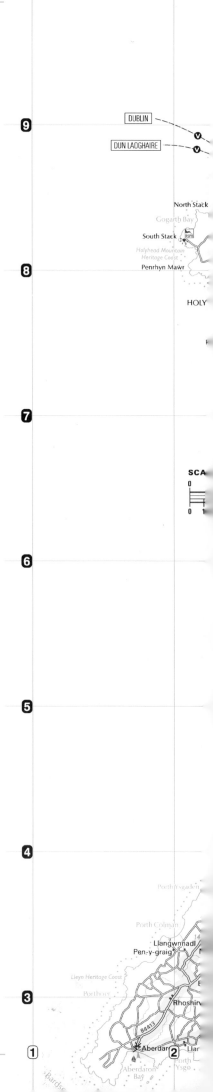

⬚✕⬚ CAERNARFON
Map ref 4863

Caernarfon lies in the shadow of its great castle, where the present Prince of Wales was invested in 1969. It was started by Edward I in 1283 and completed in 1328, and Edward II, first Prince of Wales, was born here. It has polygonal angle towers, a notable Eagle Tower and extensive town walls.

Remains of Segontium Roman Fort and a museum can be found half-a-mile from the town centre.

🏛 DIN LLIGWY
Map ref 4986

The remains of a 4th-century village, with two circular and seven rectangular buildings encircled by a pentagonal stone wall.

⬚ HOLYHEAD
Map ref 2483

Ferries still sail from Holyhead to Ireland on a route followed by travellers for centuries. Almost joined to Holy Island, it has been an important religious centre since pre-Roman times.

⬚⬚✕★ LLANBERIS
Map ref 5660

Dolbadarn Castle is a native Welsh stronghold with a 13th-century three-storeyed round tower.

The famous Snowdon Mountain Railway, first opened in 1896, climbs more than $4^1/_2$ miles from Llanberis to the summit of Snowdon.

The Lake Railway takes a 4-mile journey to and from Gilfach Ddu, beside the Welsh Slate Museum and the centre of Padarn Country park. The line was formerly used to carry slate from the quarries to Port Dinorwic. The museum was created when the extensive Dinorwic Quarry closed in 1969.

⬚⬚ MENAI BRIDGE
Map ref 5573

The remarkable 1,000ft-long bridge which joins Anglesey to the mainland was completed by Telford in 1826. By the shores of the Menai Strait is the Tegfryn Art Gallery, exhibiting paintings by local artists.

On the island side is the village with the longest name in Wales, generally known by the abbreviation Llanfair PG.

⬚⬚ PORTHMADOG
Map ref 5638

The town grew up around the harbour, built in 1821. The story of the reclamation of the land from the sea is told in a 1,300ft square mural in Porthmadog Pottery, which is situated in an old flour mill of 1862.

The historic Ffestiniog narrow-gauge railway originally carried slate from the mines at Blaeunau Ffestiniog to Porthmadog harbour. The line, closed in 1946, has now been reopened by enthusiasts. There is a railway museum in the harbour station.

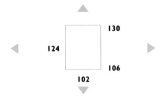

LAND OF THE EAGLE

The Welsh call Snowdonia `Eyri', Land of the Eagle, and the image is apt for one of the most dramatic and beautiful mountain ranges in Britain. Rivers, streams and lakes, both natural and man-made, add to the grandeur of the remote landscape. Welsh is still widely spoken.

```
         ▲
      ┌──────┐   130
◄  124 │      │   ►
      └──────┘   106
         102
         ▼
```

TOUR

BLAENAU FFESTINIOG, BALA AND LLYN BRENIG
76 MILES

The tour travels through some of the most breathtaking scenery of the Snowdonia National Park. Leaving Betws-y-coed on the A470, it travels south-west through the Gwydyr Forest, with the 2,860ft peak of Moel-Siabod looming to the right.

Dolwyddelan is the only settlement in the valley, and as soon as the road leaves the former quarrying village it begins to climb. High on a crag is Dolwyddelan Castle, a Welsh-built castle erected in 1170 to guard the upper valleys.

The road climbs on up into the moorland of the Crimea Pass, and steeply descends to Blaenau Ffestiniog, former slate quarrying centre. At the Llechwedd Slate Caverns an underground tramway leads into parts of the mine where Victorian mining conditions have been recreated. Visitors can explore the Deep Mine.

The Gloddfa Ganol Slate Mine is the largest slate mine in the world. Here the extensive underground workings can be explored and slate splitting can be seen. There are quarrymen's cottages to view and a museum, and conducted tours by Land Rover around the site.

In 1963 The Queen opened the Ffestiniog Pumped Storage Scheme, the first hydro-electric pumped storage station built for the Central Electricity Generating Board. A short detour on to the A496 leads to the power station, where guided tours are available of this example of modern technology set against the spectacular background of the old slate quarries. In the information centre are a cinema and an exhibition about the scheme.

The tour continues south on the A470 to Ffestiniog, at the head of the valley. Here the historic narrow-gauge steam railway which originally carried slate to the harbour at Porthmadog has been

reopened for passengers. South of Ffestiniog is the stunning 300ft waterfall of Rhaeadr Cynfal.

Turning east, the tour takes the B4391 towards Bala, between the peaks. To the north, Arenig Fach at 2,264ft is the highest point of the wide Migneint Moor, while Arenig Fawr to the south is even higher, at 2,799ft. This is the head of the Tryweryn valley, drowned to create the long reservoir of Llyn Celyn, which supplies Liverpool. The route follows the A4212 around the reservoir to Bala.

Bala stands at the north-eastern corner of the largest natural lake in Wales, Llyn Tegid (Bala Lake), 4 1/2 miles long and nearly 1 mile wide. A narrow-gauge railway runs along the southern side of the lake to Llanuwchllyn. One of the early centres of Methodism, Bala has a statue commemorating Thomas

Charles, who founded the British and Foreign Bible Society and the Sunday School movement. A centre for sailing and fishing, it is said that a rare white-scaled salmon inhabits the lake.

From Bala the tour moves outside the national park, travelling north-east on the A494 through remote hill country, to join the A5 at Druid. On the left is Foel Goch, rising to 2,005ft. At Cerrigydrudion the route turns off to the village, with its early 18th-century almshouses, north through heather moorlands and spruce forests towards Brenig reservoir.

The 1,800-acre estate is owned by Welsh Water plc, and the 920 acres of the reservoir supply water to north east Wales. Brenig has a major fly fishery, which hosted the world championships in 1990. It is a water sports centre. A wide variety of wildlife can be observed, with buzzards, ravens, cormorants and even the occasional peregrine or merlin visiting the nature reserve, and rare plants grow. An archaeological trail leads past Bronze Age burial mounds and medieval farmhouses, hidden in the remote countryside. The Llyn Brenig Visitor Centre includes a bilingual Welsh/English exhibition on the local geology, archaeology and natural history.

Joining the A543, the tour

descends towards Pentrefoelas, with the 3-mile-long Alwen reservoir lying open to the left among the slopes of the Mynydd Hiraethog. At Pentrefoelas the journey turns north-west to Llanrwst, market town for the farms of the Conwy valley. The bridge that spans the River Conwy is said to have been built by architect Inigo Jones in 1636. On the opposite bank is the privately owned Tudor mansion of Gwydir Castle, with its former chapel, Gwydyr Uchaf, also attributed to Inigo Jones. It has a rare example of a Welsh painted roof of the period.

The tour returns to Betws-y-coed on the B5106.

Blaenau Ffestiniog against a backdrop of slag heaps

SELECTED PLACES TO VISIT

🚻📷🅿️♿ BETWS-Y-COED
Map ref 8055

In a deeply wooded valley, where three rivers meet, lies the beauty spot of Betws-y-coed.

At the Conwy Valley Railway Museum two large buildings display items connected with local narrow- and standard-gauge railways. In the grounds are model railway layouts and a steam-hauled miniature railway.

🏛 BODRHYDDRAN HALL
Map ref 0478

To the east of Rhuddlan is this mainly 17th-century manor house set in lovely grounds. It contains many notable paintings, and collections of furniture and armour.

🚻🐘♿ COLWYN BAY
Map ref 8479

At the Welsh Mountain Zoo and Flagstaff Gardens at Colwyn Bay, animals live in natural settings.

🚻❌♿ CONWY
Map ref 7778

Edward I's magnificent fortress still dominates the town. The 15ft-thick walls of Conwy Castle were built in the shape of a Welsh harp. Telford spanned the Conwy with an iron

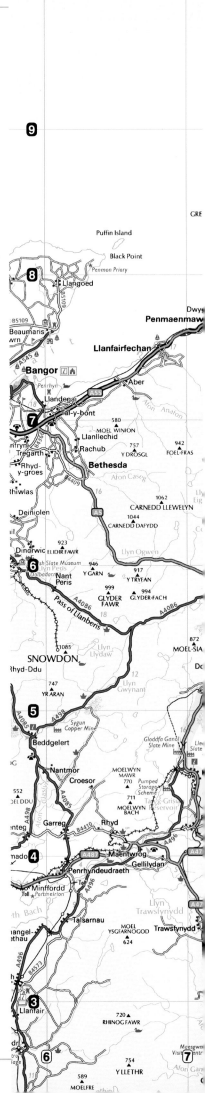

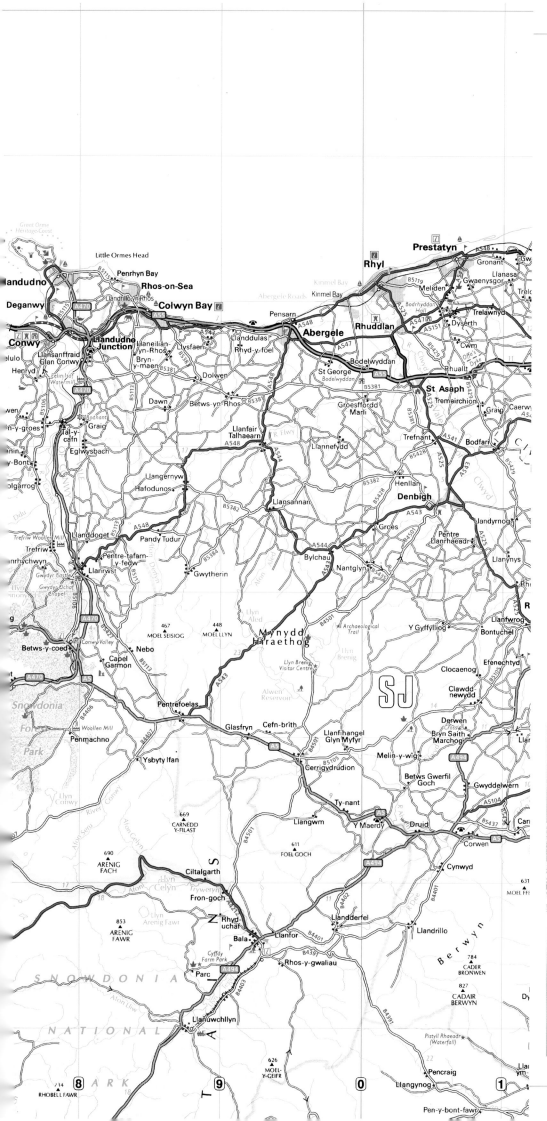

LAND OF THE EAGLE

suspension bridge, and Robert Stephenson built a tubular bridge in 1822. A road bridge was constructed in 1958.

Aberconwy house dates from the 14th century and now has the Conwy exhibition of the borough from Roman times.

✗ DENBIGH
Map ref 0466
African explorer H M Stanley was born in this market town in 1841.

Denbigh Castle stands 467ft up on a hilltop. Parts of the town's medieval walls remain, and Leicester's Folly, a ruined church.

✗ PENRHYN CASTLE
Map ref 6172
The huge neo-Norman structure of Penrhyn Castle dates from the 19th century. As well as fine panelling and plasterwork, it has a natural history collection featuring species native to Snowdonia and two museums.

★ PORTMEIRION
Map ref 5937
Created by Sir Clough Williams-Ellis, this Italianate village is a remarkable example of architectural imagination built on the shores of Cardigan Bay.

✗ RHUDDLAN
Map ref 0278
Another of Edward I's massive fortresses, Rhuddlan Castle was built to a diamond plan with two gatehouses and six round towers.

↳ SNOWDON
Map ref 6254
The focal point of the Snowdonia range, Snowdon at 3,560ft is the highest and most beautiful summit in Wales, approached by numerous walks and climbs, as well as by the Llanberis mountain railway.

The Swallow Falls, 2 miles from Betws-y-coed, are deservedly popular

SNOWDONIA

Snowdonia National Park includes the highest land in England and Wales, with the highest mountain, bleak moorland and, on its western edges, some beautiful coastal scenery

A redshank in typical pose in the boggy area of the Migneint

overing an area of 840 square miles – in reality much larger than Snowdonia itself – the Snowdonia National Park was one of three designated in 1951. Both Blaenau Ffestiniog and Dinorwic have, sensibly, been excluded from the Park – being major victims of the scars left by the slate mining industry.

No view for or against nuclear power is needed to criticise the power station at Trawsfynydd – by any criteria this is an ugly building of the sort which should never be allowed to disfigure a National Park. By contrast there is, above Dinorwic, an excellent example of how man can minimise the effects of necessary interference

with landscape. Here, an electricity generating station has been sited in the largest man-made cavern in the world, leaving few external signs. Not a cheap solution, but demonstrating what can be achieved by an imaginative approach.

The problem of over-visiting is common to all our National Parks and seems to have defied all attempts at resolution, no matter how imaginative. Inevitably, Snowdon is the attraction of the Park, sometimes scathingly referred to as `the highest slum in Britain'. It may be the tallest mountain outside Scotland but, unlike many Scottish `Munros' (peaks over 3,000ft), Snowdon

is all too accessible and the paradox facing officials is that any attempt at controlling entrance to the Park runs counter to a basic tenet of the outdoor movement – the `right to roam'.

A Changing Landscape

The most popular approach to Snowdonia is along the A5 from Llangollen, entering the Park just beyond Pentrefoelas. Ahead lies the upland plateau, the centre of the Park, with Snowdonia's peaks rising above it. Between the mountain ranges – Carneddau, Arennig, Aran, Cader Idris and Rhinog – but unseen from the road, thread valleys where fledgling rivers rise. To the west of the

plateau lies rich agricultural land and, near to the coast, dunes and marshes.

A lesson not absorbed by many modern conservationists is that Nature is singularly adept at re-colonizing sites – a small quarry near the Dinorwic site referred to earlier, had been reclaimed within a very few years. So it was after the Ice Age, as arctic plants began to appear, followed, as the temperature increased, by others. Birch and pine were succeeded by sessile oak and so the process has continued, subject to variations created by such factors as soil types, the

A view of the Park near Cader Idris, its second major mountain range

shape of the land and the amount of rainfall.

Parts of Snowdonia still remain important sites for arctic plants, while boggy areas have developed on sites like Migneint, as bleak as any area in England or Scotland. Heather has all but disappeared over much of the Park since this was a great sheep grazing area with little grouse shooting, but, lower down, old oakwoods have survived in the sheltered valleys.

It is difficult to imagine, but Yr Wyddfa – Snowdon – was once at the bottom of a valley. Immense forces drove the layers of rock upwards and slowly all but the hardest were attacked and worn down. Finally, the glaciers of the Ice Age moved through the valleys, creating the classic U-shaped upland formations.

Unique Habitats

The list of arctic-alpine plants to be found in the Snowdon range includes the Snowdon lily. It grows nowhere else in Britain and, in other parts of the world, occurs in a different habitat. Mountain avens, moss campion, alpine meadow-rue, arctic mouse-ear, mountain sorrel are just some of the plants which are restricted to a few sites here or in other upland areas.

Although comparisons are always difficult, Cader Idris, the second major mountain range within the National Park, has strong claims to be considered superior to Snowdon. It can be circled by car, and approached via Llynnau Cregennen, two beautiful lakes with outstanding views over Cardigan Bay towards the Lleyn Peninsula. Like all mountain climbs, none of the routes to the top should be underestimated but when the 2,930ft summit is reached, the views are magnificent. More lakes, Llyn y Gadair to the north-west, Llyn Cau to the south-east, can be seen far below – the bowl in which Llyn Cau lies is a fine example of a cwm. More arctic-alpines grow on Cader, including a number of ferns. The boggy areas are home to plants like sundew and common butterwort, while the lower slopes contain a mixture of mat-grass, heather and sheep's fescue.

The Hunter and the Hunted

The great upland plateau of Migneint contains a high percentage of bog habitat which can be studied in comfort from a car driving along the B4407. Close by the road, the Afon Conwy begins to assert itself, swollen by waters squeezed from the sodden peat. Migneint has always been called `the swampy place', and anyone parking a car and wandering off the road will soon learn why. The boggy areas contain few plants, but curlew, lapwing and redshank live on them together with the beautiful

golden plover. Merlin, short-eared owl and hen harrier are the main birds of prey while the red kite is a not uncommon visitor although it does not breed in Snowdonia.

One of the best of the heather moors, though remarkably remote, considering it is only a few miles behind Harlech, is to be found surrounding Rhinog. Red grouse and wheatear breed among the heather with, higher up, raven and ring ouzel.

The woodlands, particularly where the soil is less acidic and has permitted a range of trees to grow, attract summer visitors like wood warbler and redstart. All three woodpeckers, sparrowhawk and tawny owl are likely to be resident, with dipper and grey wagtail living beside the streams at the bottom of the valleys.

A fine example of an old oak woodland site in the National Park is Coed Dinorwic. Now part of the Padarn Country Park, it has not been grazed for years and ground cover plants are well established under the smallish oaks. Pied flycatcher feed on the abundant caterpillars of the mottled umber moth and, although unlikely to be seen, the polecat is known to hunt in the reserve. A more varied wood is Coedydd Maentwrog, containing sessile oak, alder, birch, rowan and sycamore. The flowering plants grow through the ground cover of ferns, lichens and mosses. Grassy clearings, heathland and a marshy area at the top of the wood complete a pleasing range of habitats, each with its own specialized plant and bird life.

Legendary Beaches

The coastal scenery offers a complete contrast to the bleakness of the moors and mountains. From Traeth Bach to the estuary of the Dyfi there are miles of beaches overlooking wide sweeping bays and backed by wonderful views inland towards areas like Rhinog and Cader Idris. The range of habitats, sandy shores and dunes, marshy land and sheltered waters, ensure that both waders and wildfowl are usually present in some variety.

Bleak though much of the

Above: *The Park emblem combines the Welshness and the mountainous nature of the area*
Left: *Mountain avens, one of the artic alpines found on the Snowdon range*
Below left: *A golden plover sporting its dark-bellied summer plumage*

region may be, man has lived here for many thousands of years, and the stone circles, burial chambers and standing stones which dot the area are all reminders of early man. There are still some traces of Roman occupation, but it was in the period of the early Middle Ages when the Welsh princes were battling with the English kings that Snowdonia assumed great importance. Here the Welsh had their impenetrable strongholds, hedged around by Edward I's fine, inconsequential, castles. Here, too, the legends of monsters and of King Arthur who, men said, slept with his warriors, awaiting the call to return and save the land.

Perhaps only the once and future king could find an equitable solution to the problems of over-crowding in this wonderful, rugged land of Snowdonia to which so many, having once tasted its special appeal, return again and again.

Llyn Gwynant, one of the many beautiful lakes to be found in Snowdonia

DEESIDE AND MERSEYSIDE

Coal and iron and the deep channel of the Mersey made this region one of Britain's most prosperous in the 19th century. There are many relics, however, of the medieval past, with castles telling of the endless conflicts between the Welsh and the English, and shops and houses reflecting earlier prosperity.

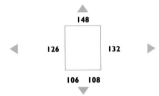

SELECTED PLACES TO VISIT

🅿🅿🏛 BIRKENHEAD
Map ref 3388

Birkenhead Priory on the Wirral Peninsula existed long before any town was formed; the priory was founded in 1150, but was neglected after the dissolution. It was not until the steam ferry service began in 1817 that the town and port started to expand. A new interpretation centre traces the site's history.

The Williamson Art Gallery and Museum has a major collection of English watercolours and paintings of the Liverpool school. The museum has a local history and maritime theme.

🏛 ★ BWLCHGWYN
Map ref 2553

The Geological and Folk Museum of North Wales is found in the old silica quarry at Bwlchgwyn, some 5 miles north-west of Wrexham. It contains an exhibition of the region's geology. In a rock garden, large specimens of indigenous rock types can be seen, and a geological trail leads the visitor.

🅿🅰✗🏛🅿 CHESTER
Map ref 4165

The Roman camp of Deva on the River Dee was established here in 79 and much of the Roman wall survives, together with a large Roman amphitheatre. The Grosvenor Museum houses a major collection of Roman antiquities, as well as coins from Chester's medieval mint, natural history and art.

The county town of Chester has been a cathedral city since 1541, although a church stood on the cathedral site before the 9th century. A unique feature is the city's medieval Rows, where galleries form a separate upper level of shops reached by narrow flights of steps leading from the shops at pavement level.

At the Chester Visitor Centre 2,000 years of the city's history are

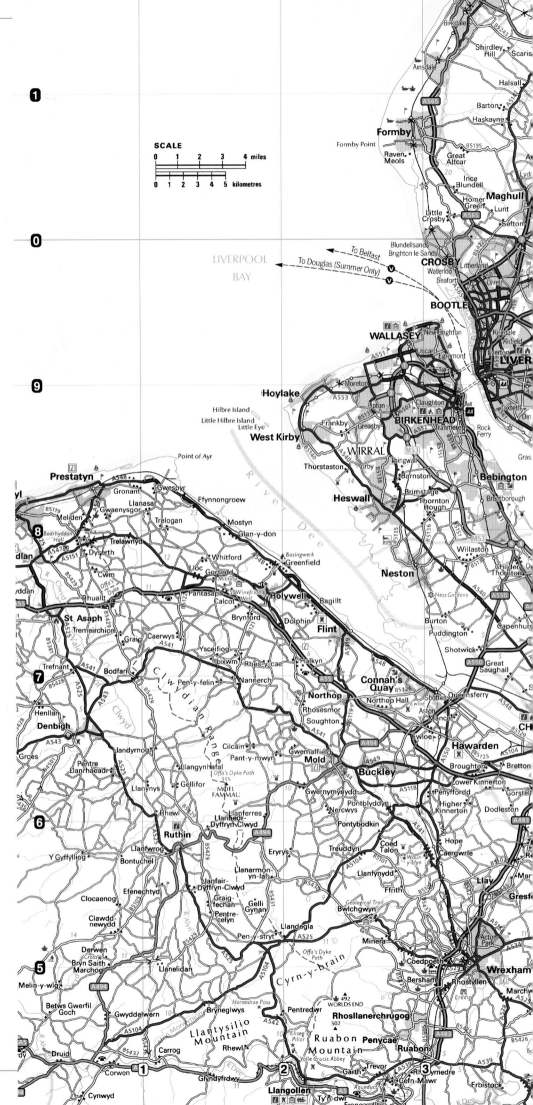

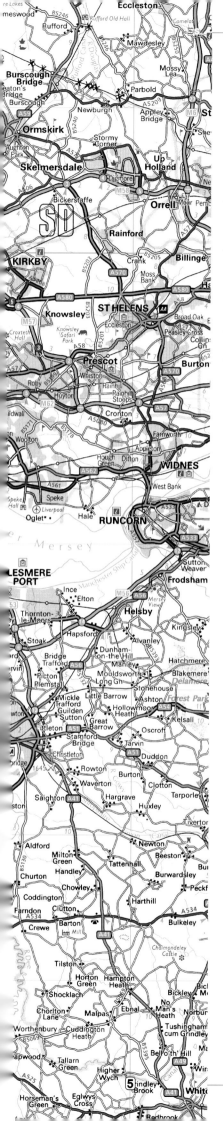

Liverpool's Clayton Square, a smart new shopping precinct

explained. The Chester Heritage Centre in St Michael's church interprets the city's history and architectural heritage.

CHESTER ZOO
Map ref 4271
Chester Zoo is one of Europe's finest, with 3,500 animals in 110 acres of enclosures and landscaped gardens. There is an aquarium, tropical house and waterbus rides.

ELLESMERE PORT
Map ref 3978
Ellesmere Port owes its importance to its situation on the Mersey at the junction of the Shropshire Union and Manchester Ship canals; cargoes were transferred from sea-going vessels to smaller boats for transport through the inland waterways. The docks are now a Boat Museum. Exhibitions on canals, horses and the town, a blacksmith's forge, dockers' cottages and restored warehouses and workshops all recreate a picture of the town in its industrial heyday.

ERDDIG
Map ref 3348
South of Wrexham is Erddig, a late 17th-century house with 18th-century additions, managed by the National Trust. Outbuildings include kitchen, laundry, bakehouse, stables, sawmill, smithy and joiner's shop. The large walled garden has been restored to its 18th-century formal design. At weekends a visitor centre is open.

EWLOE
Map ref 2867
Hidden in woods is Ewloe Castle, a Welsh fortress built in 1257. One hundred years previously, Henry II had been defeated nearby by the sons of Owain Gwynedd.

FLINT
Map ref 2374
Flint Castle was the first of a chain of castles built by Edward I. Ruined in the Civil Wars, the castle has a circular detached keep which was originally surrounded by a moat.

HARWARDEN
Map ref 3365
Set on a steep hill, Hawarden was the home of Gladstone, four times British prime minister, who married local heiress Catherine Glynne. The castle was built in 1752 on the site of a 13th-century castle ruined in the Civil Wars.

KNOWSLEY
Map ref 4695
At Knowsley Safari Park, near Prescot, lions, tigers, elephants and monkeys can be seen in drive-through reserves.

LIVERPOOL
Map ref 3593
Liverpool began as a fishing village in the 13th century, and grew from the 18th century to become Europe's greatest Atlantic seaport.

The Merseyside Maritime Museum at Albert Dock is a large museum in restored 19th-century docklands. The Albert Warehouse contains displays about the port of Liverpool. As well as floating craft, there are outdoor exhibits and demonstrations of maritime crafts.

The Liverpool Museum was formed in 1851 when the 13th Earl of Derby left his large natural history collections to the city. Since then these have grown, ranging from land transport to ceramics, and antiquities and ethnology to displays of clocks and space technology. The new natural history gallery has already won four awards. Inside the domed auditorium of the Planetarium special effects recreate the changing night sky and take visitors through space and time to explore the

universe. The Museum of Labour History traces the importance of the trade union and working class movement to the city.

The Walker Art Gallery has an outstanding collection of European paintings, sculpture and drawings from 1300 to the present day, while the Sudley Art Gallery has the Emma Holt bequest of 19th-century British paintings and sculpture.

Two cathedrals, one Anglican and one Roman Catholic, have been built during this century.

NESS GARDENS
Map ref 3175
Ness Gardens are the University of Liverpool's Botanic Gardens. Sweeping lawns and specimen trees and shrubs are complemented by rock, heather, rose and water gardens.

ST WINIFRED'S WELL
Map ref 1876
A holy spring is said to have appeared here when St Winifred was beheaded for spurning Prince Caradoc's advances and has been a place of pilgrimage for centuries.

SPEKE HALL
Map ref 4383
A splendid Elizabethan manor house around a courtyard, Speke Hall is one of the most famous half-timbered houses in the country. The Tudor Great Hall contrasts with small Victorian panelled rooms and the house has fine examples of William Morris wallpaper.

WREXHAM
Map ref 3449
Wrexham was the centre of the north Wales coalfield, on which the local iron and steel industries were based. Bersham Industrial Heritage Centre in a Victorian school building explains the history of ironworking in the area. Demonstrations of smithing show the uses to which the iron was put.

SALT, COTTON AND POTTERY

From Stoke-on-Trent in the south to Manchester in the north, inland waterways like the Manchester Ship canal, the many railway lines passing through Crewe and modern motorways have provided vital communication links for the region's booming textile, salt mining, pottery and engineering industries.

This prosperity has left a glorious legacy of superb museums, libraries and art galleries.

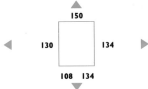

SELECTED PLACES TO VISIT

BOLTON
Map ref 7309

Cloth making in Bolton originates with wool making in the 12th century, but it was during the 18th century that Richard Arkwright made the waterframe, Samuel Crompton the spinning mule and James Hargraves the spinning jenny which revolutionalised the textile industry. The Tonge More Textile Museum includes these famous machines among its historic collections.

BRAMALL HALL
Map ref 8884

Bramall Hall, set in landscaped Bramhall Park, is considered one of England's finest black-and-white houses. Dating from the 14th century, the house has medieval wall-paintings, period furniture and portraits of the Davenport family who lived here for 500 years.

CHATTERLEY WHITFIELD MINING MUSEUM
Map ref 8854

At Chatterley Whitfield Mining Museum, 3 miles north of Stoke-on-Trent, there are guided underground tours of the mine. The museum also includes pit ponies, steam winding engines and working steam locomotives.

CREWE
Map ref 6956

Crewe owes its reputation to the railway. Between 1840 and 1858 four separate lines were built through Crewe, connecting it to Chester, Manchester, Stoke-on-Trent and Shrewsbury, and a locomotive works was established in 1843. By the 1930s a quarter of the population was employed by the railways.

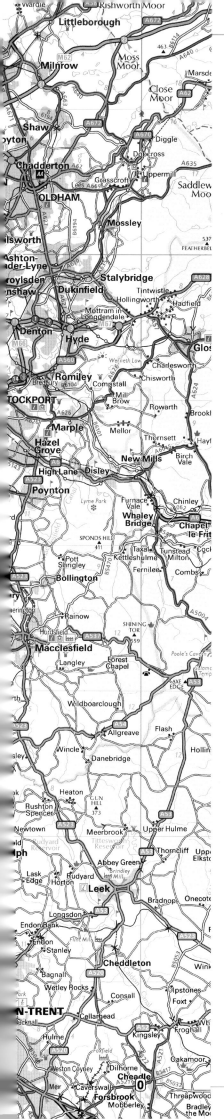

⚑ DARESBURY
Map ref 5482

Norton Priory at Daresbury near Runcorn, has seen the largest excavation of any monastic site in Britain. The priory's remains include a 12th-century undercroft, a Norman doorway and a statue of St Christopher. The finds have been used to create a large and comprehensive exhibition about medieval monastic life in Britain.

⬚ LITTLE MORETON HALL
Map ref 8459

South of Congleton is Little Moreton Hall, a superb example of a timber-framed moated manor house. Started in the 15th century, it has a long wainscoted gallery, chapel, great hall and knot garden, and is owned by the National Trust.

▦▦▦ MANCHESTER
Map ref 8599

The university city of Manchester has a wealth of museums, art galleries and libraries.

The City Art Gallery has an unrivalled display of treasures set in a classical building dating from 1829. The Whitworth Art Gallery, part of the university, has one of the best collections of English watercolours.

The Manchester Museum, also part of the university, is well-known for Egyptian antiquities, as well as more than eight million specimens of rocks, minerals, fossils, coins and ethnic craftsmanship.

Little Moreton Hall, a picture-book example of timber framing

In the Greater Manchester Museum of Science and Industry is a superb collection of steam and internal combustion engines, printing and textile machinery, railway locomotives and rolling stock.

More than 60 buses and other vehicles from the Manchester area are featured in the Museum of Transport.

The John Rylands University Library is world-famous, with numerous early manuscripts and rare editions of the Bible included in its huge collections.

NANTWICH
Map ref 6553

The Domesday Book records eight salt pits at Nantwich, and salt mining brought prosperity until the mid-19th century.

Set on the River Weaver, Nantwich saw its communications greatly increased as the Birmingham and Liverpool Junction canal brought connections with Chester and the Black Country, and a railway line through the town opened from Crewe to Shrewsbury.

St Mary's Church, one of only two town centre buildings to survive the devastating fire of 1583, has one of Britain's finest stone pulpits.

Nantwich's best-known building, Churche's Mansion, a half-timbered house constructed in 1577, survived the 1583 fire because it was outside the old town.

▦▦▦ SALFORD
Map ref 8298

Salford Museum and Art Gallery combines the industrial and artistic elements of the town's history. The glory of the art gallery is a large collection of paintings and drawings by L S Lowry, the well-known local artist.

In the unusual setting of a listed Georgian building is the Salford Mining Museum.

Local social history is the theme of Ordsall Hall Museum, in a half-timbered house with a wing built of brick in 1639.

▦▦▦▦ STOKE-ON-TRENT
Map ref 8847

Pottery has been made in this part of north Staffordshire since long before the Romans came. The five towns of Arnold Bennett's novels amalgamated with the sixth in 1910 to form Stoke-on-Trent. One of the country's largest and finest collections of ceramics, with a particular emphasis on Staffordshire porcelain and pottery, is found in the City Museum and Art Gallery.

At the Gladstone Pottery Museum, a Victorian pottery has been preserved, complete with giant bottle ovens, workshops and old warehouses. Craftsmen and women demonstrate the traditional skills.

At the Wedgwood Visitor Centre the old skills are demonstrated and a museum has a comprehensive collection of ceramics since 1750. The art gallery contains paintings by Reynolds, Stubbs and Romney. The Sir Henry Doulton gallery at the Doulton factory contains some 300 pottery figures.

Ford Green Hall is a 16th-century timber-framed farmhouse, furnished with items from the 15th to the 19th centuries.

⚑ VALE ROYAL ABBEY
Map ref 6470

Vale Royal Abbey is a stately home built around the monastery of 1277, which survives the abbey of the same date. James I was one of a number of royal visitors.

WARRINGTON
Map ref 5789

At the gateway from Cheshire to Lancashire, Warrington has played a strategic role since Roman times. Its town museum traces the past from the ancient Britons to the present. At the Peninsula Barracks is the museum of the South Lancashire regiment.

▦ WIGAN
Map ref 5705

Probably Wigan's most famous attribute is its pier, immortalised in George Orwell's novel. Today the restored pier, at the heart of the town's canal basin, has five renovated warehouses, an educational centre and an exhibition on turn-of-the-century Wigan. Linked to it by a waterbus is Trencherfield, an old textile mill with the world's largest working mill engine and a pier replica.

CAVES, CRAGS AND SPAS

The High or Dark Peak, the northern half of the magnificent Peak District National Park, is austere, with peat moorlands rising to 2,000ft cut by deep water-filled valleys.

The southern or White Peak is limestone, with its typical caves, underground springs and woody crags.

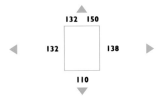

TOUR

PEAK DISTRICT
43 MILES

Many of the villages keep up the centuries-old tradition of dressing their holy wells with flowers on one Sunday each year, reproducing a biblical theme or scene in thousands of petals, leaves, mosses and cones.

The tour begins at Buxton, travelling north on the A6. Although Buxton itself stands at 1,007ft, even higher hills surround it, such as Hob Tor at 1,644ft, to the west. The route forks right on to the A623 into the Peak District National Park, and at Sparrowpit takes a left fork on towards Castleton.

Above the large village of Castleton, set at the western entrance to the Hope Valley, soars the ruined keep of Peveril Castle, built by Henry II and described in the novel *Peveril of the Peak*, written by Sir Walter Scott.

The nearest cave to the village is one of the area's most spectacular, Peak Cavern, linked to the castle by a hidden passage. A half-mile walk, lit by electric light, takes the visitor to impressive natural rock chambers. In the grand entrance chamber ropes have been made for more than 500 years.

A mile-long underground boat trip along canals made by 19th-century lead miners open out into Speedwell Cavern, under the Winnats Ravine. The cavern is floodlit, and visitors can see – and hear – water ceaselessly falling into the Bottomless Pit.

The tour continues into Hathersage, reputed birthplace of Robin Hood's partner, Little John. At the highest point of this small town is the 14th-century church of St Michael, featuring a fine collection of memorial brasses dating back to 1459.

From here the tour takes the B6001, passing Eyam Moor with its prehistoric circle of 16 stones, called Wet Withins. Eyam village, high on the moor, is famous for the courageous action of its inhabitants during the 1665-66 Plague. Led by their rector, William Mompesson, the villagers isolated themselves to prevent the plague spreading elsewhere. More than 80 per cent of the inhabitants died, but the disease was contained. A number of houses dating from that time survive, and a chair in the 13th-century church commemorates the grim event. In the churchyard is a rare Anglo-Saxon cross with its cross-head remaining. A commemorative service takes place on the last Sunday of August.

From Eyam the tour joins the A623 to Stoney Middleton, set amid towering limestone crags and quarries. In front of the unusual octagonal church are two wells which are dressed each year in August.

At the crossroads the tour turns right, picking up the B6001, southwards to Bakewell. Sheltered in the Wye valley surrounded by wooded hills, this small market town has many warm brownstone buildings dating from the 17th and 18th centuries. The `well' refers to the warm springs which come to the surface here, and in which visitors can swim at the 17th-century Bath House at a constant temperature of 15°C.

A beautiful arched packhorse bridge, dating from the 13th century, spans the River Wye, and Bakewell's medieval church has an 8th-century sculptured cross and other Anglo-Saxon stone fragments. The Old House with its original wattle and daub interior walls and an open-timbered chamber, is now a museum.

Two miles south-east of Bakewell is Haddon Hall, considered to be the most complete and authentic example of a medieval manorial home. The banqueting hall, long gallery and chapel with frescos have been well preserved, and the garden is noted for its roses.

Retracing the A6, following the Wye valley, the tour meets Ashford, a little village with three bridges across the river. Close by are the quarries from which Ashford marble was extracted, and to the south is the Magpie lead mine.

The route takes the B6465 north through the rocky moorlands of the High Peak, past the Iron Age fort of Fin Cop to the north-west, and turns towards Tideswell, with its dominant 14th-century church, the 'Cathedral of the Peak', which has one of the earliest Perpendicular towers in England.

At Millers Dale two sets of late 19th-century industrial lime kilns stand beside the Monsal Trail, one to the east and one to the west. From here the tour continues on the A6 back to Buxton.

The Corkscrew roller-coaster, probably Alton Towers' most famous ride

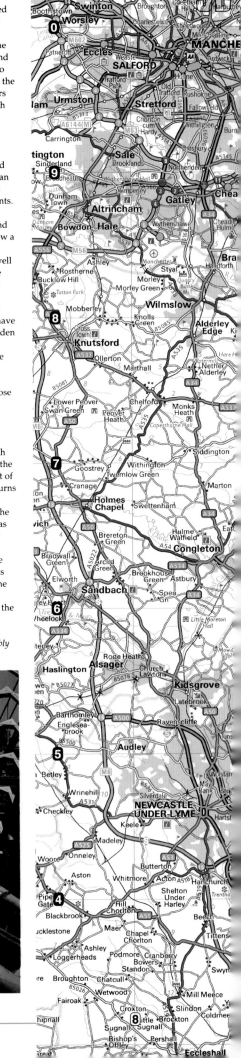

CAVES, CRAGS AND SPAS

SELECTED PLACES TO VISIT

ALTON TOWERS
Map ref 0643

This outstanding leisure park has more than 125 rides and attractions grouped into five themed areas.

ARBOR LOW STONE CIRCLE
Map ref 1563

Derbyshire's most ancient monument is the prehistoric henge Arbor Low, 1,200ft up on Middleton Moor. More than 40 huge slabs of limestone lie in a circle, surrounded by a bank and ditch.

★ BUXTON
Map ref 0674

One of England's oldest spas, Buxton waters were enjoyed by the Romans, but it was the 5th Duke of Devonshire who in 1780 started to establish the town as a rival to Bath. The Crescent opposite the town's hot springs is the most outstanding example of its Regency architecture. The nine springs produce a pale blue water which, unlike most spa water, is palatable to drink.

Housed in The Cresent is Buxton's Micrarium, where remote-controlled microscopes enable visitors to view in detail hundreds of specimens.

One hundred acres of woodland make up Buxton's Country Park. Panoramic views can be seen from Solomon's Temple, and Poole's Cavern is an awesome sight. The cave has a Roman exhibition and displays of archaeological finds.

DINTING RAILWAY
Map ref 0394

To the west of Glossop is Dinting Railway Centre, usually in steam between March and October. Special steam weekends take place at bank holidays.

FOXFIELD
Map ref 9745

West of Cheadle is the Foxfield Steam Railway, which takes a five-mile round trip from Blythe Bridge through rural Staffordshire.

✱ HARE HILL
Map ref 8876

Four miles north west of Macclesfield, Hare Hill features rhododendrons and azaleas and a lovely walled garden with pergola.

HOWDEN MOORS
Map ref 1690

The reservoirs of the Upper Derwent – Ladybower, Derwent and Howden – are a spectacular sight within the High Peak hills.

MACCLESFIELD
Map ref 9573

An old silk-manufacturing town, where black-and-white timbered houses stand in steep streets, Macclesfield has an excellent museum on the edge of West Park. Among its collection of paintings are works by Charles Tunnicliffe, the well-known bird artist.

135

PEAK DISTRICT

The popularity of the Peak District, as a haven for those wishing to escape the cities of the industrial north, provided the inspiration behind the creation of all our National Parks

Historically it is very appropriate that the Peak District should have been the first National Park to be designated in 1951. It was over the bleak, inhospitable moorland of Kinder Scout that men had physically fought in support of their claim to the right of public access. Throughout the early years of the century, more and more young people had sought an escape in the Peak District by spending their weekends hiking on the moors. The problem was that much of the best moorland was either privately owned and managed for game bird shooting, or controlled by the water authorities and trespassing was forcefully discouraged.

The curlew, seen here with young, is a typical moorland bird of the Dark Peak

The Right of Public Access
A number of factors combined to bring matters to a head on 24th April 1932 with the Mass Trespass on Kinder Scout, following which six ramblers were arrested and five received prison sentences. It has been estimated that, at the time, half the population of England lived within 60 miles of Buxton. Good public transport was available and rambling was increasingly popular. The rise of the Labour Party, heightened political awareness – assisted by improved opportunities for adult education – and the

frustrations of increased unemployment, all led to a more militant stance by the working class with protest rallies and calls for unrestricted public access to the moors.

A Legislative Partnership
By itself, the mass trespass – in reality involving relatively few people and only the first of several similar demonstrations – might have had little effect, but the prison sentences, and the growing involvement of middle-class supporters like Professor Joad led to the matter receiving wider publicity. No government action was taken until 1939 when the weak Access to the Mountains Act reached the Statute Book.

Immediately after the war, the Dower report laid out clear, sensible guidelines for the creation of National Parks. That report, and another by Sir Arthur Hobhouse, provided the framework on which the 1949 National Parks and Access to the Countryside Act was based. Two years later the Peak Park was designated and 10 more followed in the next six years.

The Peak District National Park is the only one run by an independent board, with a separate staff – roughly what Dower had recommended. It has pioneered many ideas, from the first ranger service, to the introduction, at Losehill Hall, of the first residential centre where public and professionals alike can study a wide range of conservation subjects. Many of the authority's innovative moves have been adopted by similar bodies at home and abroad.

Before all this could be considered the staff had to resolve the problem of access – the `right to roam'. In Britain, unlike many other countries, the term `National Park' is not synonymous with public ownership – in 1951 the bulk of the moorland was in private hands and so it remains. However, as a result of access agreements made between the National Park Board and some

owners, the public now have the right, subject only to certain byelaws and restrictions during the shooting season, to walk unhindered over 76 square miles of moorland. On Good Friday, 1954, at a ceremony in Edale, the first of the agreements was formally confirmed – not, with hindsight, a great advance, but a staging post in the continuing struggle for rights of access.

White and Dark Peaks
Not surprisingly, the major problem facing the Peak District is over-visiting for, in addition to the nearby industrial towns, this is the nearest National Park to London. It has confronted the situation with a number of ingenious solutions including closing off the Goyt and Upper Derwent valleys to cars at busy periods and providing alternative transport. Modern industry, particularly fluorspar mining, is another major problem with its constant threat to the landscape.

One of the great pleasures awaiting every first time visitor to the Peak District National Park is the realization that it is really two parks in one. Furthermore, the motorist will find that both are more accessible than some other Parks and that it is possible, if not desirable, to distill a little of the flavour of both in just one day!

At the heart of the Park is the limestone area known as the White Peak, extending roughly from the River Hamps in the west to the Derwent in the east. Surrounding this, in a U-shape, is the area of the Dark Peak, formed by a sandstone rock known as millstone grit. In a band between the two lies an area of fertile dales carved out of shale by the action of several rivers, including the Derwent and the Wye.

The contrast between the landscapes and the character of the White and Dark Peaks is very pronounced. The White Peak, as its name seems to

Above: *The Park's millstone symbol recalls both the local grit and old Peakland industry*
Left: *Over Owler Tor is a superb viewpoint for the deep cut of Derwent Dale*

imply, is a softer, more rounded landscape, with lovely, green dales through which flow the Dove, the Hamps, the Manifold and the Wye. On the 1,000ft plateau at the centre of the White Peak, there is a distinctive pattern of white stone walls enclosing small fields. Here the dales are dry, deserted by the water which created them, yet filled with a wonderful array of lime-loving plants.

Although a great colonizer of shallow limestone soils, ash rarely remains the dominant tree, but in the Peak District some of the most attractive woods are composed almost entirely of ash with hawthorn and hazel enhancing the ground cover. Yew flourishes here and some important sites contain small-leaved lime, including one beside the Manifold at Ilam. Giant bellflower, yellow archangel, star-of-Bethlehem, sanicle and dog's mercury may be found in the woodlands.

The A515 is a valuable road for anyone wishing to explore the White Peak area, since it passes most of the main beauty spots – Dovedale, the Manifold and Hamps valleys, Tissington and the fascinating, evocative stone circle at Arbor Low. The whole of the White Peak area has been exceptionally well signposted as part of the Park's policy on visitor control. The impression given is of relative freedom of access – in reality, there is less than in the Dark Peak because of the demands of farming.

A hint of the grandeur of the Dark Peak can be obtained by taking the A57 up Snake Pass. On the left of the road is the lowering bulk of the Kinder

Massif, to the right Hope Woodlands and then Bleaklow Moor. On the slopes of the plateau of the Dark Peak, there is heather moor while the top is a desert of peat. And `desert' is no idle description, for the peat is slowly dying, the plants which normally build up blanket bog having been killed, probably by pollution. There is some plant life – Kinder and Bleaklow have cloudberry, crowberry and bilberry interspersed with deeply eroded hags, or gullies, of peat. Red grouse, curlew and dunlin are typical moorland birds who breed on the high moors.

In the early part of this century the Dark Peak came to represent, for many men and women, an ideal challenge offering them a transitory freedom from everyday working life, coupled with the opportunity to test themselves in a very different environment to that in which they lived. For others, the less dominating scenery of the White Peak offered a sort of balm, a reminder that life had a gentler, more contemplative side. And, for many – not only in the North – no choice was, or could be, made between the two parts of their beloved Peak District.

Yellow archangel is found in the woodlands of the White Peak

Nottingham, Derby and Sheffield are the focal points, but within the forests and crags of this varied landscape are historic houses, villages and small towns. This is D H Lawrence country; a contrast between industrial power and untamed nature.

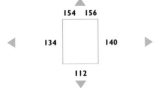

```
        154  156
    134          140
        112
```

BOLSOVER
Map ref 4771
Originally Norman, Bolsover Castle, on a wooded hill, was rebuilt in 1613. Richly carved fireplaces and allegorical frescos adorn the buildings, and there is an unusual 170ft-long indoor riding school.

CHATSWORTH
Map ref 2671
One of the richest collections of fine and decorative art is found in Chatsworth, 17th-century home of the Duke and Duchess of Devonshire. The superb gardens were laid out by Capability Brown. Varied breeds of farm livestock can be seen, with an explanation of the farms' management.

CHESTERFIELD
Map ref 3871
Chesterfield is known for the remarkable crooked spire of its 11th-century church. Other aspects of the town's history are displayed in the Peacock Information and Heritage Centre in a medieval timber-framed building thought to have been the guildhall.

CLUMBER PARK
Map ref 6375
Owned by the National Trust, Clumber Park has 3,800 acres of 18th-century parkland. The house was demolished in 1938, but a fine Gothic chapel was built in 1886-89. The superb 80-acre lake has a foot ferry, bridge and temples.

CONISBROUGH
Map ref 4798
Conisbrough Castle's 90ft-high white circular 12th-century keep with six buttresses is the oldest surviving example of its type in England.

CRESWELL
Map ref 5474
The Creswell Crags Visitor Centre explains the archaeological significance of this limestone gorge, once the home of Stone Age Man.

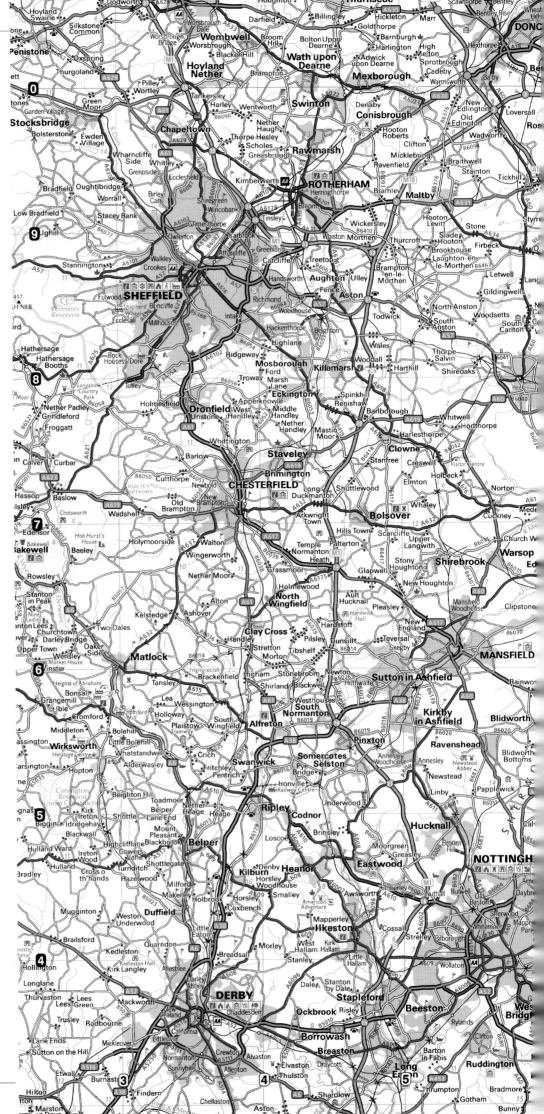

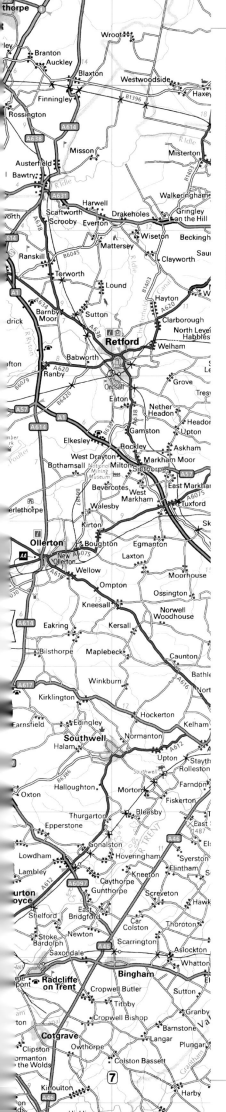

Roman lead workings and caves can be explored at High Tor, above Matlock

⬛ CROMFORD MILL
Map ref 3057

Cromford Mill is the site of the world's first successful water-powered cotton-spinning mill.

⬛ DERBY
Map ref 3637

Derby's history as a centre of silk, railways and Rolls Royce engines is captured in the Industrial Museum, housed in an early 18th-century silk mill and adjoining flour mill. The Royal Crown Derby Porcelain Co Museum recalls the local china and pottery industry.

In the City Museum and Art Gallery is a room devoted to Bonnie Prince Charlie's 1745 rebellion, as well as exhibitions of antiquities, costumes, coins and medals, among its large collections. Pickford's House Museum, built in 1770, features Derby's social history.

⬛ EASTWOOD
Map ref 4746

Birthplace of D H Lawrence in 1885, Eastwood has restored the author's house as a museum not only of his life but of working-class life in Victorian times. The 'Sons and Lovers' cottage where his family lived from 1887 to 1891 has been furnished as described.

⬛ HEIGHTS OF ABRAHAM
Map ref 2859

A spa in Victorian times, Matlock is a popular resort on the Derwent. From the heights of Abraham – reached by cable-car from Matlock – are extensive views of the Derwent Valley. Nestus lead mine is easy to tour, and at the Great Masson Cavern there are guided tours underground. At Temple Mine, old lead and fluorspar workings have been reconstructed as in the 1920s and 30s. The history of the Derbyshire lead industry is explained in the Peak District Mining Museum, and the museum contains Britain's only early 19th-century water pressure pumping engine.

⬛ KEDLESTON HALL
Map ref 3140

Kedleston Hall, built by Robert Adam in the mid-17th century, has a unique marble hall, superb staterooms and the Marquis of Curzon's Indian Museum containing silver and ivories.

⬛ LONGSHAW
Map ref 2679

Longshaw Estate, owned by the National Trust, offers dramatic views and varied walks within 1,600 acres of open moorland, woodland and farms in the Peak National Park. Stone for the Derwent and Howden dams was quaried here, and millstones can be seen in quarries on the estate.

⬛ MIDLAND RAILWAY CENTRE
Map ref 4152

The Midland Railway Centre operates a regular steam train passenger service for some 3 miles between Butterley Station and Ironville. A 57-acre museum site depicts the history of the Midland Railway.

⬛ NEWSTEAD ABBEY
Map ref 5454

The original 12th-century priory was rebuilt as a country mansion by the Byron family in the 16th and 17th centuries. Poet Lord Byron lived here, his manuscripts and first editions are preserved.

⬛ NOTTINGHAM
Map ref 3957

An ancient city, Nottingham achieved great prosperity from its lace making, hosiery, tobacco and cycle making industries. The university city is rich in museums and historic buildings.

Nottingham Castle had a turbulent history, but now houses the City Museum and Art Gallery, with works by Nottingham-born artists R P Bonington and Thomas and Paul Sandby as the highlights of the art collection. The splendid exhibitions reflect all aspects of the city's history, and there is an excellent Regimental Museum.

In Wollaton Hall, a lovely Elizabethan mansion, is the Natural History Museum, with a wide range of displays of birds, mammals, minerals and fossils. The park is home to herds of fallow and red deer.

Various museums cover the importance of Nottingham's hosiery and lace industries, including the Museum of Costume and Textiles, the Lace Hall and the Industrial Museum.

The remains of Sherwood Forest, legendary home of Robin Hood, lie to the north east.

⬛ RIBER CASTLE
Map ref 3159

The 19th-century Riber Castle is the centre of a wildlife park, 853ft-high on Riber Hill. Concerned with preserving rare animals and endangered European species, there is a comprehensive collection of lynx.

CITY AND COUNTRYSIDE

⬛ SHEFFIELD
Map ref 3587

Knife blades have been made in Sheffield for more than 700 years, based on local iron ore. The development of the city as an industrial centre over the past 400 years is the theme of Sheffield's Industrial Museum, with displays, and demonstrations by craftsmen.

In the late 18th/early 19th-century crucible steel and scythe works of Abbeydale Industrial Hamlet, are water wheels, a worker's cottage, manager's house and museum, showing manufacture of steel from raw materials to finished product.

The City Museum features geology, natural sciences and archaeology of the region, as well as the typical cutlery, ceramics and plate trades of Sheffield. Social history is the theme of Bishop's House, a restored 15th-century building.

⬛ THE AMERICAN ADVENTURE
Map ref 4444

Near Ilkeston is The American Adventure, a major leisure park with 100 rides and attractions on a Wild West theme, with a play area for young children.

⬛ TRAMWAY MUSEUM
Map ref 3555

Vintage electric, horse-drawn and steam tramcars from around the world are found in the National Tramway Museum at Crich. A mile-long tramway offers rides with lovely views over the Derwent valley. A street with a tramway has been reconstructed and there are workshops and a power station.

⬛ WHITTINGTON
Map ref 3874

Two miles to the north of Chesterfield is Revolution House a 14th-century manor house where the revolution of 1688, which brought William and Mary to the throne, was plotted.

⬛ WIRKSWORTH
Map ref 2855

Wirksworth is a small town set 500ft above sea level in a bowl in the hills above the River Derwent. Inspired by a Civic Trust project, the town has been regenerated from the decline of the lead mining industry, with a Heritage Centre to recreate pride in local history. Three floors typify Wirksworth past, present and future, and workshops demonstrate the crafts of cabinet makers, silversmiths and blacksmiths.

Wirksworth's National Stone Centre interprets the history of stone from prehistoric times to the present day.

At Middleton the Top Engine House has an old beam engine, built in 1829 to haul wagons on the Cromford and High Peak railway.

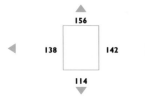

TREASURES OF EASTERN ENGLAND

The glories of Lincoln Cathedral and Southwell Minster and the memorabilia of the Wesleys at Epworth remind visitors of the spiritual dimensions, while the castles and historic houses of the region speak of more temporal activities. There is much to savour in this part of Eastern England.

156

◀ 138   142 ▶

114

SELECTED PLACES TO VISIT

BILLINGHAY
Map ref 1455

To the north-east of Sleaford, the Billinghay Vicarage Museum, housed in a 17th-century `mud and stud' cottage, includes a display of old village photographs. Three rooms are furnished to reflect different periods of its history.

🏛 DODDINGTON
Map ref 8970

Doddington Hall, five miles south-west of Lincoln, is a romantic mansion, built in brick and stone by Robert Smythson in 1600, with a Tudor gatehouse and walled rose garden. Inside its elegant Georgian rooms are fine collections of period furniture, porcelain, textiles and pictures.

🏛 EPWORTH
Map ref 7705

Epworth is known internationally as the home of the Wesleys, being the birthplace of John Wesley, founder of Methodism, and of his brother Charles, the prolific hymnwriter. The places to see are the parish church of St Andrews where Samuel Wesley was rector and is buried, the Wesley memorial church, the Old Rectory where John and Charles were born and the Market Cross from which John preached when he was not permitted to use the church.

🏛 GAINSBOROUGH
Map ref 8492

The 15th-century Old Hall has had a varied history, used as a linen factory, theatre, tavern, tenements and a soup kitchen. Today it has a complete medieval kitchen, great hall, wings and tower with displays on medieval life in Lincolnshire, the restoration of the building and Richard III, who stayed there in 1483.

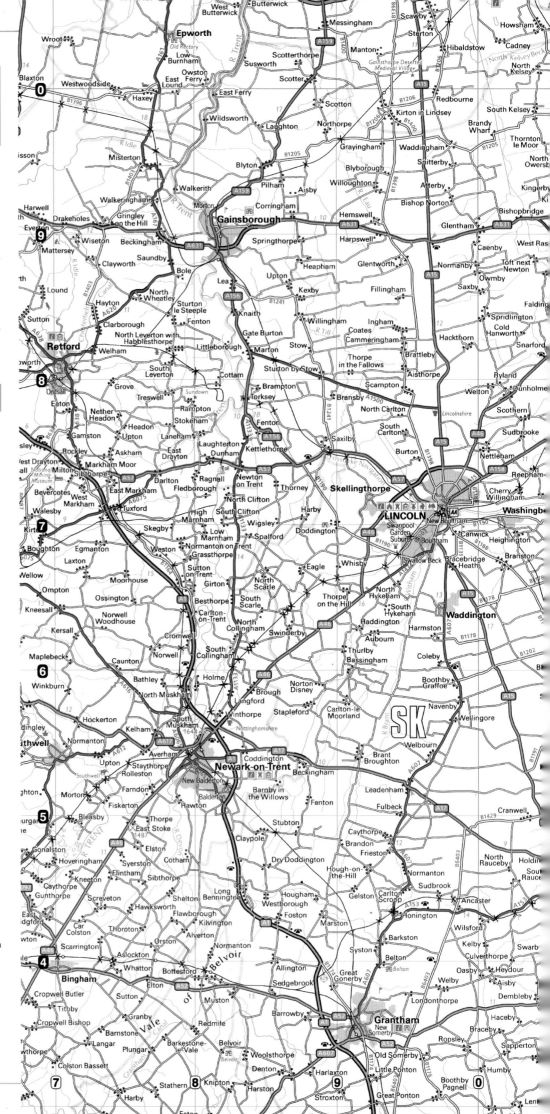

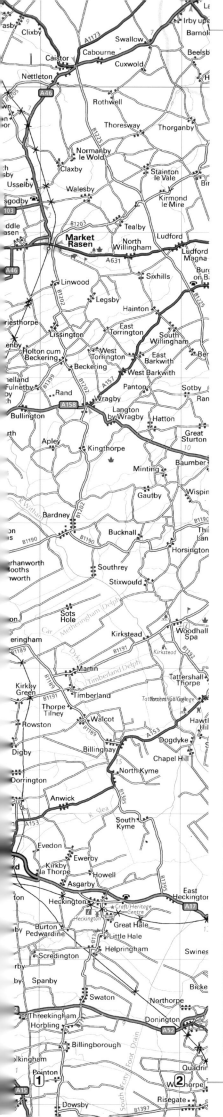

✦ ★ ☑ HECKINGTON
Map ref 1442

At Heckington Windmill, the only surviving eight-sail windmill in Britain in full working order, stoneground flour can be bought.

The Pearoom opposite has a craft shop, craft gallery, heritage gallery and 19 workshops for resident craftspeople.

HEMSWELL
Map ref 9291

A Canberra bomber, two jets and a Sycamore helicopter are displayed outside at the Bomber County Aviation Museum. Also on view are uniforms and weapons.

☑☐☒☐☒☐☒ LINCOLN
Map ref 9772

Lincoln Cathedral, one of the finest Gothic buildings in the country, dominates the city. The triple towers of this 365ft-high cathedral, built on a 200ft-high limestone plateau, can be seen for many miles, especially when it is floodlight. The present building, noted for the ornamental carvings in the Angel Choir, was completed in 1280 following the destruction of the earlier Norman cathedral by an earthquake.

The City and County Museum is housed in a former 13th-century friary. The exhibits include the best preserved of the surviving copies of the Magna Carta.

Lincoln Castle, built by William the Conqueror in 1068 on the site of a Roman camp, retains a complete curtain wall, Norman bailey and two mottes. The castle walls have three towers, including an observatory tower and a walkway. From 1787 to 1878 the castle was also the county gaol. The Courts of Assize, now the Crown Courts, were built in the grounds in 1826.

The open timber-framed roof of Lincoln's Guildhall is decorated with carved bosses from the 15th and 16th centuries. A display of civic regalia, including Richard II and Henry VII swords, can be viewed. Nearby, St Mary's Guildhall, a fine Grade I listed 12th-century building, now restored, has a Norman arch entrance and a great hall on the upper floor. Beneath the building the old Roman road is visible.

The upper room of the Jews' Court, another 12th-century building, was once used as a synagogue for the Jewish community. The building is now occupied by the Society for Lincolnshire History and Archaeology.

The Museum of Lincolnshire Life has been created to give a picture of the country's domestic, commercial and military life.

More than 1,000 toys can be seen at The Incredibly Fantastic Old Toy Show in an old church hall in Westgate.

An exhibition of cycles dating from 1818 at the National Cycle Museum shows the evolution of the cycle and its accessories.

☒ NATIONAL MINING MUSEUM
Map ref 7073

A modern colliery is next to the National Mining Museum at Lound Hall, Haughton. The museum exhibits tools, headgear, lamps, electrical equipment, coal-face machinery and locomotives. On Sundays the engines are usually in steam.

☑☒☐ NEWARK-ON-TRENT
Map ref 8054

The ruins of Newark Castle, built by Alexander, bishop of Lincoln, are well preserved. The north gateway, which dates from 1170, is the largest of any castle in England. King John died at the castle in 1216.

On display in the Georgian town hall is the Newark Civic Plate Collection.

Local history is the theme of Newark Museum, which also covers archaeology, natural history and art. The Millgate Museum of Social and Folk Life shows the home and working life from Victorian time to the 1950s.

Newark Air Museum's exhibition hall has a flight simulator among its equipment and aviation memorabilia. On show are 30 airframes ranging from the Vulcan bomber to the Zurowski homebuilt helicopter.

In the Vina Cooke Museum of Dolls and Bygone Childhood is a large collection of Victorian and Edwardian dolls. Character dolls of the Royal family and television and film stars hand-made by Vina Cooke are displayed in a 17th-century house.

NORTH HYKEHAM
Map ref 9465

The Lincolnshire Vintage Vehicle Society maintains an interesting collection of restored commercial and private vehicles including a Leyland Lion Bus, a 1947 Leyland Merryweather Fire Engine and a 1908 horse-drawn hearse at its North Hykeham premises.

☑☐ RETFORD
Map ref 7182

Retford's Bassetlaw Museum includes displays of bygones and decorative arts with its local history and archaeolgy exhibits.

♣ SOUTHWELL
Map ref 6956

Southwell Minster is a beautiful Norman church, particularly famous for its intricate stone carvings of different types of foliage, known as the Leaves of Southwell, in the chapter house.

↘ SUTTON-CUM-LOUND
Map ref 6985

The Wetlands Waterfowl Reserve and Exotic Bird Park is home to many species of wild birds, plants and trees, covering 32 acres.

Lincoln Cathedral is one of the largest churches in England

PEACEFUL LINCOLNSHIRE

Between the Wash and the Humber, the fenland of south Lincolnshire and the wolds of the north form a quiet oasis inland from the North Sea. A region of small farming villages and market towns, it has an important heritage coast around Skegness.

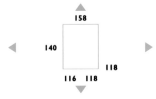

```
        158
         ▲
140  ◄  [ ]  ►   118
         ▼
     116  118
```

SELECTED PLACES TO VISIT

🏛✶ ALFORD
Map ref 4576

Alford Folk Museum, housed in a thatched Tudor manor, features local history and archaeology displays.

The Alford five-sailed, six-storeyed windmill is a working tower mill originally built in 1813.

To the north west are the Claythorpe Watermill, built in 1720 and now fully restored, and Wildfowl Gardens, where rare species can be seen.

✶ BOLINGBROKE
Map ref 3465

Bolingbroke Castle was occupied by John of Gaunt in the 14th century and was the birthplace in 1366 of his son, who became Henry IV. The castle was destroyed after the Civil War but recent excavations have revealed remains of the gatehouse, towers and curtain wall.

✶ BURGH LE MARSH
Map ref 5165

The well preserved five-sailed brick-tower mill, built in 1833, is in full working order although, unusually, the sails turn clockwise.

The Lincolnshire Railway Museum is housed in the former Great Northern Railway goods depot at Burgh le Marsh Station Yard.

The recently excavated ruins of Bolingbroke Castle

142

One of the several Spitfires housed in the old RAF station at Coningsby

CONINGSBY
Map ref 2457

The Battle of Britain Memorial Flight, consisting of the only flying Lancaster bomber in Europe, two Hurricanes and five Spitfires, is housed in a hangar together with other contemporary memorabilia.

EAST KIRKBY
Map ref 3363

The Lincolnshire Aviation Heritage Centre is based on a partially renovated wartime bomber airfield. The site includes the control tower and displays of aircraft and artefacts portraying the history of flying.

GIBRALTAR POINT
Map ref 5557

With 1,500 acres of sand dunes, salt-marsh, sandy and muddy shores, the Gibraltar Point National Nature Reserve with its interpretative visitor centre gives plenty of scope to those wishing to study the flora and fauna in their natural habitat.

GREAT STEEPING
Map ref 4364

The Northcote Heavy Horse Centre at Great Steeping features rare breeds of farm animals, dalmation carriage dogs and a collection of horse-drawn vehicles as well as shire horses.

GUNBY HALL
Map ref 4767

Gunby Hall, now in the care of the National Trust, was built for William Massingberd in 1700, incorporating contemporary wainscoting and a fine oak staircase. It contains some interesting English furniture and portraits by Reynolds. Outside the house are a walled kitchen garden, herbaceous borders and sweeping lawns.

HORNCASTLE
Map ref 2669

Horncastle is one of the principal market towns serving this agricultural area. The walls of its old Roman town of Banovallum have been partially preserved, and relics of the Civil War, can be seen in St Mary's church.

LEGBOURNE
Map ref 3585

The Legbourne Railway Museum, includes a fully equipped signal box. The museum houses Lincolnshire railway relics, steam locomotive nameplates and signs.

LOUTH
Map ref 3287

The Louth Naturalists, Antiquarian and Literary Society Museum has a fine collection of moths and butterflies. Sketches by 19th-century local artist Bennett Hubbard are shown also.

The Church of St James claims that its crocketed spire is the tallest, at 295ft, of any on a parish church in England. The body of the church, completed in 1441, is a fine example of late Gothic Perpendicular.

MABLETHORPE
Map ref 5185

Mablethorpe is a quiet holiday resort. Its Animal Gardens emphasise the county's wildlife through the ages with displays on the natural dunes and in the gardens.

Among the more than 4,500 items on display at Ye Olde Curiosity Museum are glass lampshades, irons, kettles, cleaners, bed warmers and dolly pegs.

MARKBY
Map ref 4878

St Peter's Church at Markby, with medieval work and boxed pews, is the only example of a thatched church in the county.

MAWTHORPE MUSEUM
Map ref 4574

Two miles south of Alford is Mawthorpe Museum with its working model of a fairground and a large working fairground organ. Steam engines, oil engines, carts, wagons, tractors and agricultural machinery are on display.

SIBSEY
Map ref 3552

Sibsey Trader Mill remains one of the few six-sailed corn mills in the country; built on the typical Lincolnshire lines of brick tower with tarred exterior and whitewashed inner walls.

SKEGNESS
Map ref 5664

The tropical house at this popular resort's Natureland Marine Zoo and Seal Sanctuary includes such fascinating creatures as giant African snails, crocodiles and scorpions. Elsewhere at the zoo there are tropical fish, aviaries, a walk-through tropical butterfly house and a seal hospital.

The 19th-century farm buildings which make up Church Farm Museum house the Bernard Best collection of agricultural machinery. The farmhouse has been furnished in the way a tenant farmer would have lived at the beginning of the century. To complete the picture a late 18th-century timber-framed thatched cottage and a 19th-century barn have been re-erected on the site.

STICKFORD
Map ref 3561

A private collection of military motorcycles, heavy vehicles, weapons, uniforms and medals is the basis for the Allied Forces Military Museum at Stickford.

TATTERSHALL
Map ref 2357

Tattershall Castle, a moated castle built in 1440 by Ralph Cromwell, was rescued from dereliction early this century. The castle is a fine example of early brick building. The tower was added to the original medieval castle. A model of the castle as it was in 1693 is on view in the guardhouse.

The Collegiate Church of the Holy Trinity could be mistaken for a cathedral by its size. Its medieval brasses and the glass in the East Window are well known.

One mile west of Tattershall is the only known land drainage pumping station worked by steam. The Dogdyke pumping station still has some of its original equipment, including a beam engine by Bradley and Craven.

WOODHALL SPA
Map ref 1962

Housed in an original Victorian galvanised iron bungalow, the Woodhall Spa Cottage Museum tells the story of the growth and development of this Victorian spa town.

LINCOLNSHIRE WOLDS

Tennyson summed up the Wolds perfectly. 'Calm and deep peace' was his description and, though the landscape has changed, it is still possible to find those qualities on the old ridgeway tracks

The Lincolnshire Wolds cover an area of 216 square miles of chalk hills in the counties of Humberside and Lincolnshire. They were designated as an Area of Outstanding Natural Beauty (AONB) in February 1973.

Left: *A typical farmland bird, the dunnock is easily distinguished by its grey plumage*

Part of the chalk belt which stretches from Dorset through East Anglia is broken by the Wash, and then continues through Lincolnshire to Yorkshire. Evidence for the belief that the belt was once continuous can be found at Red Hill on the Wolds. This has a cliff of red chalk, and the nearest example of red chalk occurs at Hunstanton, where the Dorset belt enters the Wash.

Rich Green Landscape

The Wolds present the classic chalk profile. Rounded, not very high – 550ft maximum – they run north-west to south-east for some 40 miles from the Humber towards the Wash. The western scarp is steep, overlooking green fields which lie on the good soil of the Lincolnshire Clay Vale. Because of the flat land around them, the views over the Vale and the Midlands plain are surprisingly extensive. To the east the slopes are gentle; running down to the field and dyke system that stretches to the sea, 10 miles away. Few places in Britain provide better growing and grazing land. The north of the area comprises a high plateau and ridges, while further south

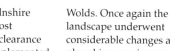

the scarp is cut by deep, winding valleys. To the south of the Wolds lies rich, peaty, fen land.

Verse of Change

The Wolds themselves have been increasingly converted from their traditional grazing use, with small hedged fields, to conform to the demands of intensive – usually arable – farming. The new scheme consists of neat, regular fields with grassland confined to the steeper, less accessible slopes. One recurring problem in rural areas is that more intensive farming frequently provides less employment. The decline in military establishments, particularly RAF, has had, and will continue to have in the 1990s, an adverse effect on rural employment. Alongside this has to be set the problem of commuter villages, serving the various towns which border the AONB.

Although both County Councils have made specific provisions to protect the AONB, there has not been much formal liaison between them, and tourism has not been actively promoted. There are signs that this is now changing, with both the Viking Way long-distance footpath and the Lincolnshire connections of the Victorian poet laureate, Lord Tennyson, receiving attention from tourist departments. Born in Somersby in 1809, Tennyson fell in love with Rosa Baring of nearby Harrington Hall, and it seems likely that the formal garden of this lovely mellow brick house provided the inspiration for *Maud's* garden. The increased demand by corporate bodies for the provision of days out in traditional country pursuits, walking, hunting and shooting, would appear to be another possible growth area.

By comparison with some AONBs, the Wolds face relatively few problems other than those already mentioned –

so affected the Lincolnshire landscape. They almost certainly started the clearance of the forests, and implemented a form of grazing.

The Romans built forts at Caister and Horncastle – the unclassified road known as High Street is their link road. A glance at the village place names will confirm that the Danes were heavy settlers in the Wolds during the late 9th and early 10th centuries.

The reclamation of the marshes began in medieval times and by the 14th century, Lincolnshire appears to have been quite densely populated with villages, or perhaps more accurately, hamlets, occurring every mile or so on the Wolds. The Black Death changed the situation and the population was cut by more than a third. Over most of Britain the population gradually recovered, as did the villages, but in Lincolnshire a great number of settlements were deserted and disappeared

Wolds. Once again the landscape underwent considerable changes as ploughing was increased. Finally came post-World War II developments in agriculture and various changes brought about by EC agricultural policy.

The Importance of Management

Today, the few remaining grassland areas and abandoned chalk pits are an important habitat for chalk-loving flowers and insects. In some areas scrub woodland may become established, with ash, beech, oak and the ubiquitous sycamore all present. Occasionally there are managed areas of woodland in which oak, ash and hazel are still coppiced to preserve their traditional appearance. The hedges of the Wolds mainly consist of hawthorn, blackthorn, holly and elder, which many might consider the true make-up of Britain's hedgerows.

For those wishing to see what the old Wold downland looked like, one of the best spots is a former quarry site on the side of Red Hill, south-west of Louth. Re-colonized by grass, this is, in summer, a mass of lime-loving flowers, including kidney vetch, yellow-wort and bee and pyramid orchid. Later in the year, basil-thyme and gentian appear amidst the grass. A second part of the site, beyond the cliff of red chalk mentioned earlier, provides a good insight into the results of not grazing a site. The grassland soon deteriorates to scrub unless managed, raising, in turn, the question, how 'natural' is a natural landscape?

One example of a species which proved unable to cope with the changing patterns of farming, and the loss of its grassland habitat, is the stone curlew. At one time its range extended to the Wolds, but in recent years it has been restricted to the chalklands of Norfolk and southern England. This sort of example of the marked impact of intensive cultivation was particularly noticeable in both Norfolk and Lincolnshire from the early years of this century.

One interesting result of the concern expressed at the time was the formation in these areas of some of the earliest nature reserves and conservation trusts.

Above: *Abundant on limestone grassland, kidney vetch can be seen on the side of Red Hill*
Left: *This peaceful scene was once the site of the Battle of Winceby, fought in 1643*

agricultural change and development pressures.

Cultivated Change

Prehistoric barrows are found all along the ridge of the Wolds and New Stone Age farmers probably created the Bluestone Heath Road some 4,000 years ago. This is a typical ridgeway route, avoiding what would have been marshy, heavily forested land below, and giving fine views and warnings of danger in all directions. These early farmers probably began the unbroken pattern of agricultural change which has

during the next few centuries. Many such villages could be identified as humps beneath the grass which covered the Wolds as sheep grazing became the staple industry of the area until the 20th century. A typical example of a lost village can be seen from near the southern end of the Bluestone Heath Road. The village of Calceby was probably founded by the Danes and certainly occurs in *Domesday* book. As with many similar settlements, it survived for some 200 years after the Black Death, gradually fading away during the 17th century.

The later parliamentary enclosures are commemorated in the narrow, straight roads, with wide grass verges, fringed by cowparsley, which are almost the trademark of the

THE INDEPENDENT ISLE OF MAN

The island, in the middle of the Irish Sea, is an independent sovereign country under the British crown, part of the British Isles, but not of the United Kingdom. It has seen human settlement since Iron Age times. The Vikings who settled here from the 9th century brought a strong tradition of democratic government which has survived to modern times.

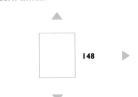

148

From Laxey, electric trains run to the summit of Snaefell

TOUR

THE ISLE OF MAN TOURIST TROPHY CIRCUIT
38 MILES

The tour follows the route taken each June by the motorcycle riders in the TT Races. With individual riders reaching 150mph and lap speeds in excess of 100mph, the roads are closed to the public during the races. This tour can be taken at a more leisurely pace.

Douglas, where the tour begins, is the island's capital and seat of government. The Tynwald, the Manx Parliament, meets in the House of Keys on Prospect Hill. The Manx Museum includes displays of local archaeology, history, natural history, folk life and the arts.

The journey proceeds down Bray Hill to a right-angled bend at Quarterdeck, heading west, on the A1, through the sharp downhill bends of Union Mills and Ballagarey leading to the Crosby crossroads.

To the north of the road is the ruined and roofless St Trinian's Chapel. Built in the 14th century on the site of a keill – the earliest known Christian churches – it once belonged to St Ninian's Priory at Whithorn in Galloway.

The tour continues along the A1 to St John's and Rynwald Hill. On each 5 July (Tynwald Day) the church of St John sees the gathering of the Members of the House of Keys and the Legislative Council for the Tynwald Court. The Vikings who colonised the island continued their custom of establishing a *Thing* – the annual assembly of their communities to make laws and settle disputes. Tynwald Hill was the site of these assemblies, its name modified from the Icelandic *Thingvöllr* (assembly held in an open space).

From St John's the tour turns north along the A4 over Ballig Bridge, up Creg Willey's Hill, and along an undulating straight section across open country to Kirkmichael. This peaceful resort has a parish church with a fine collection of runic and other Celtic crosses. To the north is Bishops Court, home of the Bishops of Sodor and Man.

The route continues to the picturesque village of Ballaugh, near the site of an excavated Viking burial. To the right of the road is Cashtal Lajer, a circular Iron Age homestead 120ft in diameter. Next on the left is Curraghs Wildlife Park, forming part of the Ballaugh Curraghs 211-acre nature reserve. In the park are many varieties of birds and animals in natural settings.

From Ballaugh the tour heads towards Ramsey, the second largest town on the island, round the Quarry Bends and along the Sulby Straight towards Ramsey Bay. A visit to Ramsey by Queen Victoria and Prince Albert in 1847 is commemorated by the Albert Tower. The Grove Rural Life Museum is found in a Victorian house, with early agricultural implements displayed in outbuildings.

Leaving Ramsey, the tour sweeps round the hairpin to begin the climb towards Snaefell. From the 2,034ft summit, reached on foot or by mountain railway, the views are spectacular. It is said that six kingdoms can be seen – the Island itself, Scotland, England, Wales, Ireland and, above, the Kingdom of Heaven.

Highest point on the mountain road is The Bungalow, a stopping point for the Snaefell Railway as well as a vantage point for the TT races. Here Murray's Museum features 150 motorcycles and bicycles, and motoring and motorcycling memorabilia.

The final leg of the tour takes the A18 south back to Douglas through sweeping bends and an acute hairpin at Governor's Bridge.

SELECTED PLACES TO VISIT

CASTLETOWN
Map ref 2466

Overlooking Castletown's small tidal harbour is Castle Rushen, one of the finest medieval fortresses in the British Isles, with a Norman keep. The castle has been used as a fortress, barracks, prison, lunatic asylum and courts. Until the mid-19th century it was the seat of Government for the island.

Also overlooking the harbour is the Nautical Museum with exhibits dating from the 17th century. Of major interest is the clipper *Peggy*, walled up and forgotten in the boat cellar for 100 years until discovered in 1935 and restored.

CREGNEISH
Map ref 1867

The village, which is the property of the Manx Museum and National Trust, is 450ft above sea level and looks out over the Spanish Head, Calf of Man, a bird sanctuary and the open sea. An open-air Folk Museum features traditional Manx cottages, some thatched, including a crofter-fisherman's home, farmstead, weaver's house and turner's shop.

Spinning demonstrations are given on certain days and sometimes a blacksmith can be seen at work.

★ DERBYHAVEN
Map ref 2866

This small fishing village stands where the Langness peninsula joins

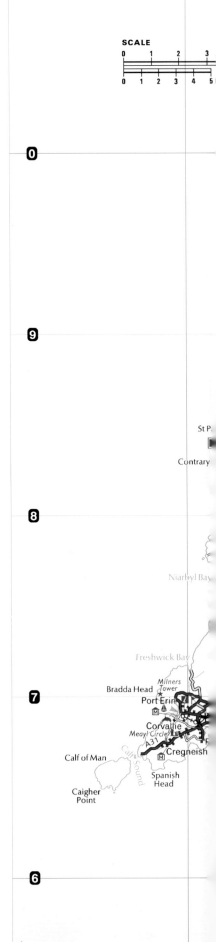

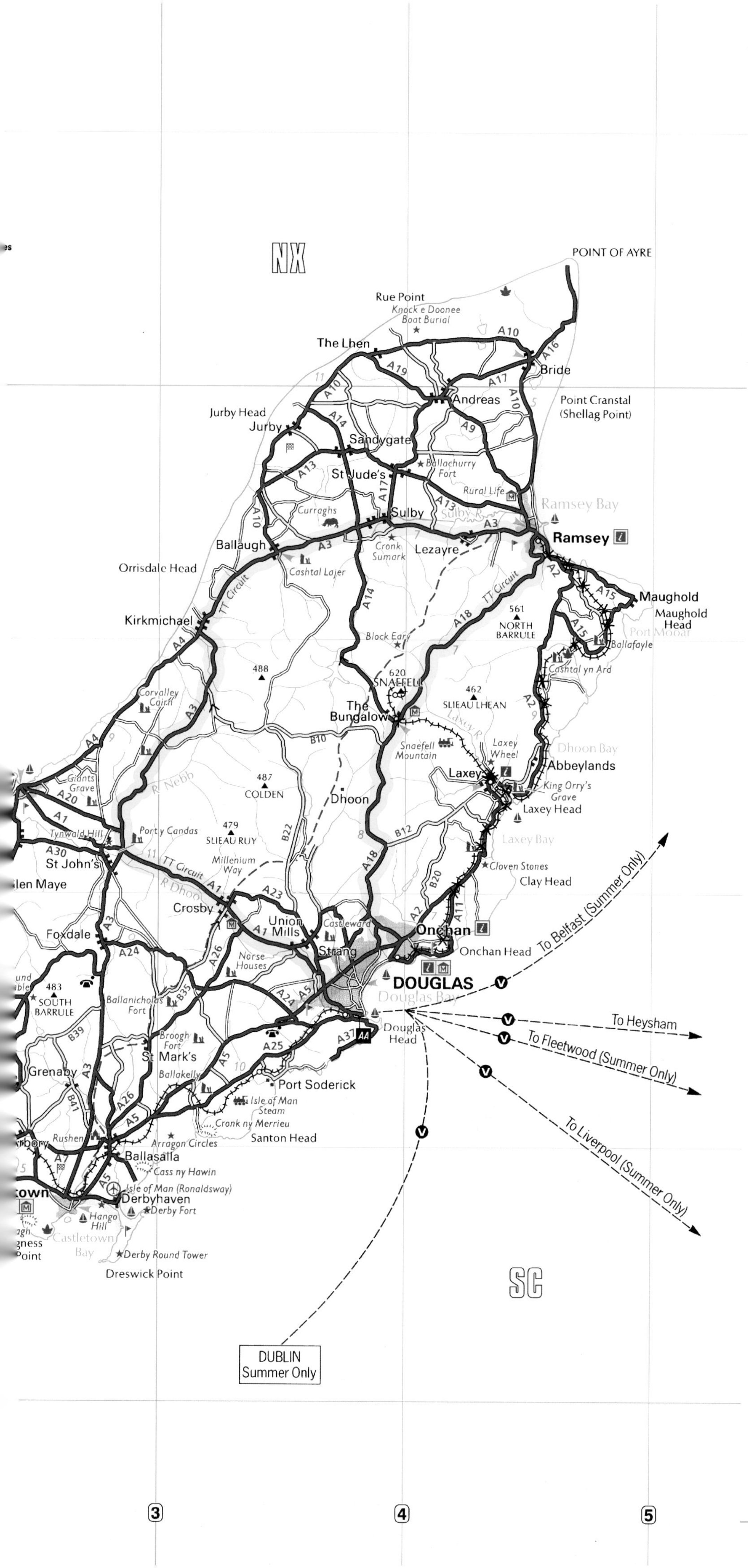

The map labels (geographic text on the map):

POINT OF AYRE
NX
Rue Point
Knock e Doonee
Boat Burial
The Lhen
A10
A16
A19
Bride
A17
Andreas
A10
Jurby Head
Jurby
A14
A9
Point Cranstal
(Shellag Point)
Sandygate
A13
St Jude's
Ballachurry
Fort
A17
A13
Sulby
Rural Life
Sulby R.
Ramsey Bay
Curraghs
A3
Ballaugh
Lezayre
A3
Ramsey
Orrisdale Head
Cronk
Sumark
A2
Cashtal Lajer
TT Circuit
Maughold
A15
Kirkmichael
A18
TT Circuit
561
Maughold
Head
A4
A14
NORTH
BARRULE
A15
Port Mooar
Block Eary
Ballafayle
488
620
SNAEFELL
Cashtal yn Ard
Corvalley
Cairn
A4
The
Bungalow
462
SLIEAU LHEAN
A29
Dhoon Bay
A4
B10
Laxey
Wheel
Abbeylands
487
COLDEN
Snaefell
Mountain
Laxey
King Orry's
Grave
Giants
Grave
R. Nebb
Dhoon
B22
Laxey Head
A20
479
SLIEAU RUY
Cloven Stones
Tynwald Hill
Port y Candas
Millenium
Way
B12
B20
Clay Head
A1
A30
St John's
R. Dhoo
TT Circuit
A1
len Maye
Crosby
A23
A18
To Belfast (Summer Only)
Foxdale
A1
Union
Mills
Castleward
A2
A11
A24
A26
Norse
Houses
Strang
Onchan
Onchan Head
To Heysham
483
SOUTH
BARRULE
Ballanicholas
Fort
B35
A2
A5
DOUGLAS
Douglas Bay
To Fleetwood (Summer Only)
Brooegh
Fort
Douglas
Head
To Liverpool (Summer Only)
B39
St Mark's
Ballakelly
A3
A25
AA
Grenaby
A26
A5
Port Soderick
B41
Isle of Man
Steam
A5
Cronk ny Merriu
Rushen
Arragon Circles
Santon Head
Ballasalla
A7
Cass ny Hawin
Isle of Man (Ronaldsway)
own
Derbyhaven
Derby Fort
Hango
Hill
Castletown
Bay
Derby Round Tower
ness
Point
Dreswick Point
SC
DUBLIN
Summer Only

THE INDEPENDENT ISLE OF MAN

the mainland. On the peninsula, which is a bird sanctuary, are the Derby Round Tower, a look-out tower, and Derby Fort, a 16th-century circular stone fort. Close by are the ruins of a 12th-century chapel on the site of a Celtic keill. In the late 17th century the sands between the peninsula and the mainland were the scene of the forerunner of the Epsom Derby horse races.

★ 🏭 LAXEY
Map ref 4384
This tidal harbour town, once a busy fishing port, boasts the largest water-wheel in the world. The *Lady Isabella*, named after the wife of the island's Lieutenant Governor in 1854, is 72¹/₂ft across and was used to keep the nearby lead mines free from water. Although the mines have closed, the wheel is still a showpiece for visitors. From Laxey electric trains run to the summit of Snaefell.

📖 ONCHAN HEAD
Map ref 4377
At the north end of Douglas Bay, Onchan Head provides some spectacular views. On a clear day the Cumberland Hills in England can be seen.

The parish register at Onchan records the marriage of the Captain of the *Bounty*, William Bligh RN.

📖 🏛 ✕ PEEL
Map ref 2484
The round tower of Peel Castle, on St Patrick's Isle, dates from the 10th century, while the castle itself was built in the 15th century to replace a timber fort and to protect the cathedral of St German's. The round fort at the northern end of the Isle dates from the 16th century. The Church of St Patrick on the Isle is also believed to be 10th-century.

The beautiful ruined cathedral of St German, built within the curtain wall of Peel Castle in the 13th century, remains the Cathedral of Sodor and Man.

📖 🏛 PORT ERIN
Map ref 1969
The village is screened by low hills: Bradda Hill to the north and Mull Hill to the south. On the south side of the bay are the Marine Biological Station and Aquarium.

Port Erin and Port St Mary, to the south-east, share a parish church known as Kirk Christ Rushen, which was created some 700 years ago close to the site of an ancient Celtic church.

⛪ RUSHEN
Map ref 2771
The remains of the Abbey of St Mary of Rushen can be seen near the village of Ballasalla. Built almost entirely of local limestone, parts of the old priory buildings survive. Close by is the 14th-century Monks Bridge, the oldest on the Island, across the Silver Burn.

LANCASHIRE BY SEA

West of the A6 and M6 is an unspoilt Lancashire, little known except for its huge, highly popular seaside resorts. The wide sand-dunes and reclaimed marshes stretch for miles against the background of Morecambe Bay and the far-off Lake District peaks.

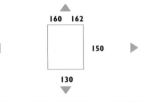

SELECTED PLACES TO VISIT

BLACKPOOL
Map ref 3136

With its world-famous Golden Mile of sand, its 6-mile promenade and spectacular illuminations, dominated by the 518ft tower, Blackpool is deservedly a magnet to holidaymakers and conference goers. In 1735 the first inn opened to cater for the first seekers after sun and sand and the arrival of the railway in 1846 brought industrial workers from all over Lancashire for the Wakes Week holidays.

Today several million visitors come each year to enjoy the funfair and amusements, to climb the tower and see its aquarium, piers, Winter Gardens and Zoological Gardens, where more than 500 large and small mammals and birds can be seen.

The Grundy Art Gallery, established in 1911, houses a permanent collection of paintings by 19th- and 20th-century artists.

One of the locomotives that can be seen at Carnforth's Steamtown Museum

SCALE

0 1 2 3 4 miles

0 1 2 3 4 5 kilometres

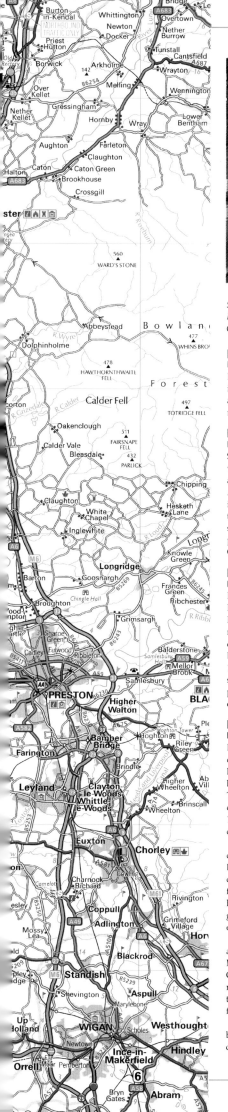

St George's Quay, Lancaster, on the River Lune, is overlooked by the Custom House – now a museum

◪ CARNFORTH
Map ref 4971

Housed in the old LMS engine shed is the Steamtown Railway Museum, a collection of locomotives used on main lines and industrial railways.

◪◪ CHORLEY
Map ref 5817

Set in some 99 acres of park and woodland is the richly plastered and timbered Renaissance house of Astley Hall. Its beautiful furnishings include a 17th-century tapestry in the drawing room illustrating the story of the Golden Fleece. Wooden panel portraits of Drake and Columbus adorn the great hall.

◪◪ FLEETWOOD
Map ref 3448

Fleetwood took its name from Sir Peter Hesketh-Fleetwood of Rossall Hall, who founded a town and market inland away from the dockyards and fish wharves. Despite the coming of the railway in 1840, Fleetwood never achieved the status of Liverpool as a shipping port, but it still has an important deep-sea fishing industry.

◪◪◪◪ LANCASTER
Map ref 4762

Lancaster was the site of a Roman camp by the river, and excavations have revealed a 2nd-century church beneath an Anglo-Saxon church. The present priory and parish church of St Mary's dates from the 14th century and has outstanding carved medieval choir stalls.

Parts of the keep of the Norman castle can still be seen on Castle Hill. The Shire Hall, adjoining the castle, contains a display of shields from 1129 onwards. The dungeons, hanging corner and drop room are a grim reminder of the brutalities of early prisons.

Lancaster was an important port, as is shown in the Maritime Museum, housed in the former Custom House built in 1764. The museum has displays on maritime trade, the Lancaster Canal and the fishing industry of Morecambe Bay.

The City Museum, in a Georgian building in the market square, has collections of archaeological and social history, together with a regimental museum.

★ LEISURE LAKES
Map ref 4217

The hinterland of Southport is below high tide level and large sums have been spent to pump the water away so the land can be cultivated. At Martin Mere more than 1,500 swans, geese and ducks from around the world and three flocks of flamingos take advantage of the 20-acre lake and 300-acre refuge. Birds can be viewed from comfortable hides, and visually handicapped visitors can follow a nature trail with taped commentaries. There are tarmaced paths and free wheelchairs for the disabled. A Norwegian log visitor centre has an exhibition gallery and education complex.

◪ LYTHAM ST ANNE'S
Map ref 3426

The railway also came to the small Regency towns of Lytham and St Anne's in 1846, bringing visitors to the 6¹/₂ miles of sandy beaches and dunes. Today the resort is particularly popular with golfers, for its championship golf courses, especially Royal Lytham St Anne's which has hosted the British Open tournament.

Lytham St Anne's retains much of its 19th-century charm. A windmill has stood on the village green for 800 years and half-timbered buildings mingle with peaceful parks and gardens. Among the attractions of the coast are bathing, sailing and water-skiing.

◪◪ MORECAMBE AND HEYSHAM
Map ref 4364

Morecambe and Heysham together form a lively seaside resort with vast stretches of sand. A large leisure complex provides varied entertainment, including dolphin and sealion shows at Marineland, alligators and examples of tropical and freshwater and marine fish.

The setting of the towns is magnificent, with superb sunsets across Morecambe Bay and views to the highest Lake District hills.

◪◪ PRESTON
Map ref 5429

Preston, an inland seaport on the River Ribble, was the birthplace in

LANCASHIRE BY SEA

1732 of Richard Arkwright, who set up his cotton spinning machine in Stonygate. It was also the birthplace of the Temperance Movement, when Joseph Livesey and his friends coined the word teetotal and opened the first temperance hotel.

Preston's history as a borough goes back more than 600 years, and a church has stood on the site of the present parish church for more than 1,200 years. Cromwell decisively defeated the Royalist forces at the Battle of Preston in 1648.

Cotton brought Preston its greatest prosperity and in the Harris Museum and Art Gallery an exhibition tells the story. Among the fine collections in this neo-classical building is material relating to Francis Thompson, the religious poet born at Preston in 1859 and best known for *The Hound of Heaven*. Within its extensive collections the art gallery has paintings by Stanley Spencer, Augustus John, Pissarro, Munnings and Dame Laura Knight, works by the Devis family and the Houghton bequest of ceramics.

◪ RUFFORD OLD HALL
Map ref 4616

One of Lancashire's finest 15th-century buildings, Rufford Old Hall is remarkable for the ornate hammer-beam roof and screen in the Great Hall. Here and in the Carolean Wing are fine collections of 17th-century oak furniture, arms and armour from the 16th-century and tapestries. This National Trust property also has a rare example of a movable screen.

◪◪◪◪ SOUTHPORT
Map ref 3317

The gracious resort of Southport enjoys a wide expanse of sands and an artificial boating lake. The Botanic Gardens Museum has a rare early dug-out canoe from nearby Martin Mere, together with a display on the local shrimping industry and local and natural history. Other exhibits include a reconstructed display of the Ainsdale National Nature Reserve, Victorian parlour and doll collection. The Atkinson Art Gallery specialises in 19th- and 20th-century oil paintings, watercolours, drawings and prints, and 20th-century sculpture.

Steamport Transport Museum is possibly the largest centre of its type in north-west England. One thousand feet of standard-gauge track connect it to the British Rail system, and former BR locomotives and industrial engines are on display. The collection is not restricted to rail, but includes local buses, tramcars, traction engines and other vehicles.

On a 5-acre site Southport Zoo has duck and flamingo pools, aquarium, reptile house, champanzee enclosure and alligator beach among its attractions.

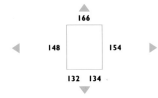
Throughout Lancashire and neighbouring Yorkshire are examples of the cotton making, wool spinning and cloth making industries on which this area grew prosperous. The spirit of the ordinary people who made this possible is plain to see in Rochdale's Pioneers Museum, where the Co-operative movement began, and in numerous restored mills and factories.

```
        166
   148       154
        132  134
```

SELECTED PLACES TO VISIT

BLACKBURN
Map ref 6727

While Blackburn's principal industry has been cotton, other textiles too are manufactured here. James Hargreaves, inventor of the spinning jenny, was born here, and models of his machine and Crompton's mule can be seen in the Lewis Museum of Textile Machinery. The museum has a series of period rooms portraying the development of the textile industry since the 18th century.

Blackburn's Museum and Art Gallery has excellent art collections, and the museum's exhibits range from fine books and manuscripts to militaria and ceramics.

BROWSHOLME HALL
Map ref 6846

To the north west of Clitheroe on the edge of the lonely Forest of Bowland is Browsholme Hall, home of the Parker family since 1507. The Tudor house has Elizabethan, Queen Anne and Regency features, and interesting portraits, furniture, panelling and antiquities.

BURNLEY
Map ref 8433

The noisy atmosphere of a Victorian weaving factory can be experienced at the Queen Street Mill. This weaving museum is Britain's sole surviving working steam-powered mill. Staff work 300 Lancashire looms, producing thousands of yard of cloth each year.

BURY
Map ref 8011

A bronze statue of Sir Robert Peel MP, born in Bury and founder of the modern police force stands proudly in the market place. Bury is a cotton town whose story unfolds in the Museum.

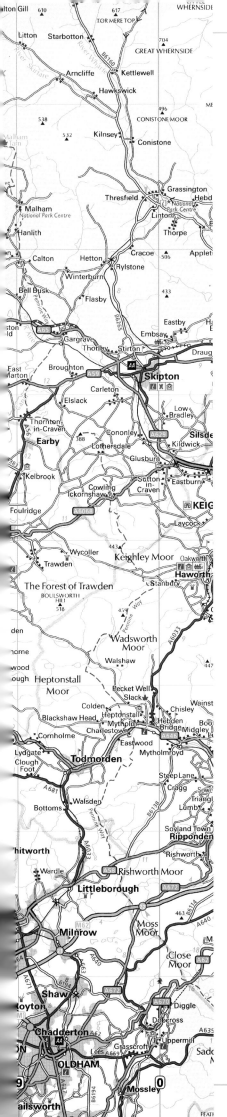

The Bury Art Gallery and Museum houses the Wrigley collection of 19th-century British paintings donated by the children of Thomas Wrigley, local papermaker, pamphleteer and philanthropist.

The delights of the Upper Irwell Valley can be discovered on the 8¹/₂ miles of railway track between Bury and Rawtenstall. The first section between Bury and Ramsbottom was opened in 1987; the remaining 4 miles from Ramsbottom to Rawtenstall is expected to open in 1991. The Bury Transport Museum at Bury station is the centre of a growing collection of historic vehicles.

▣✕◩ CLITHEROE
Map ref 7441

Witches used to gather at Malkin Tower, almost 2,000ft up on Pendle Hill outside Clitheroe, to light their fires and cast their spells. From the more peaceful summit today can be seen Whalley Abbey, York Minster and the Irish Sea.

On a limestone rock at the end of Clitheroe's main street is Clitheroe Castle, one of the oldest structures in Lancashire. Close by is Castle House, which houses the museum with its important collection of carboniferous fossils. The upper floor is devoted to geology, and the ground floor to local history and archaeology. A special feature is the recently restored Hacking Ferry boat.

▣ GAWTHORPE HALL
Map ref 8134

Gawthorpe Hall, built around 1600, was the home of the Shuttleworth family until 1972, when the National Trust assumed the responsibility. It was restored in the 1850s by Sir Charles Barry, whose designs have recently been recreated in the principal rooms. The Kay-Shuttleworth collections of embroidery, lace and costumes are on the first floor.

▣ HEBDEN BRIDGE
Map ref 9927

Connected to Heptonstall by a very steep road, Hebden Bridge grew up as a weaving town. In a restored three-storey former textile warehouse is the Automobilia Motor Museum, with its collection of Austin and Morris cars, motorcycles and memorabilia.

★ NATIONAL PARK CENTRE
Map ref 9063

The 4,000-acre Malham Tarn estate, owned by the National Trust, is part of the Yorkshire Dales national park and an internationally important nature reserve. There is public access to the south shore of the Tarn and walks to Malham Cove and Gordale Scar.

▣◩ ROCHDALE
Map ref 8914

At 31 Toad Street, Rochdale, is one of Britain's most unusual museums. The Rochdale Pioneers Museum is housed in the original shop opened

The remains of Clitheroe Castle's Norman keep

by the Rochdale Equitable Pioneers Society on 21 December 1844. That action, more than 150 years ago, was the start of the Co-operative ('Co-op') movement, which since has spread worldwide. In the shop are period furniture and equipment, while the back room tells the story of the movement from the pioneers to the centenary of the society in 1944. Documents and photographs are also exhibited.

▣ SAMLESBURY HALL
Map ref 6331

To the west of Blackburn is Samlesbury Hall, a restored half-timbered 14th-century manor house administered by the Samlesbury Hall Trust.

▣✕◩ SKIPTON
Map ref 9951

Skipton Castle is one of the best-preserved medieval castles in England. It has massive round towers and a conduit court.

In Skipton's town hall is the Craven Museum, with its well-known collection of folk life and lead mining exhibits.

▨ TEXTILES MUSEUM
Map ref 7822

At Helmshore is a water-powered fulling mill dating from 1789. Now an industrial museum, it houses early textile machinery.

▣ TOWNELEY HALL
Map ref 8631

Charles Towneley, of the Towneley family whose connection with nearby Burnley goes back to the 13th century, was a great connoisseur whose collection of Greek and Roman sculptures is in the British Museum.

Towneley Hall, beside the River Calder, now houses the Art Gallery and Museum.

★ TURTON TOWER
Map ref 7316

Turton Tower is an historic house incorporating a 15th-century peel tower and Elizabethan half-timbered buildings. It features arms and armour, period furniture and a museum of local history.

▣ WHALLEY
Map ref 7437

In Whalley churchyard are three Saxon crosses and part of another is found in the church. Six gravestones remain from the 13th century. St Mary's church has Norman stones, a 13th-century nave, aisles and chancel. It contains a wealth of historic carvings and examples of local craftsmanship from the medieval period onwards. Burne-Jones designed its stained-glass window showing the Good Shepherd.

Of Whalley Abbey only ruins remain, showing where the walls, gateways, porter's lodge and stables stood. The remains are in beautiful gardens stretching to the river.

YORKSHIRE DALES

What makes the Yorkshire Dales so attractive is the sense of balance. The landscape, based on limestone, has pleasing variations but the overall effect is consistent

The Yorkshire Dales were designated a National Park in 1954 – the third largest in size after the Lake District and Snowdonia, covering 680 square miles. 'Dale' is the Norse word for valley and the Dales consist of a number of valleys of varying size and character. The best known, and most visited, are Swaledale, Wensleydale, Wharfedale and Ribblesdale but several others have fervent champions, including Arkengarthdale, Garsdale, Dent, Littondale and Malham.

The landscape of the Yorkshire Dales has a pleasing degree of harmony, greens and greys predominating in its colour scheme. The vernacular architecture fits and enhances the landscape as do the contributions of those who, over the centuries, have invaded the area. There is a paradox here; in an area noted for its apparent insularity and reluctance to absorb change, the influences of the past are more pronounced than in many other parts of Britain where they have been absorbed, adapted, even discarded.

Historic Settlements
There are signs of Neolithic and Bronze Age settlements and of Iron Age farmers – indeed at Semer Water in Wensleydale all three occur on a site uncovered in 1937. During the Iron Age the Celtic Brigantes arrived in northern Britain, settling in the Dales, trading in horses and farming – the first Dalesmen. The Romans defeated them some time in the 1st century AD and, to maintain control, built forts linked by a road system which still survives.

The Anglo-Saxons arrived in the 4th century and colonized the hillsides of Wensleydale and Swaledale, where the remains of their field systems can still be seen outside many villages. They were joined, first by the Danes, and then, in the 9th and 10th centuries, by the Norse Vikings. Settling in the upper levels of the western dales the Norsemen had a great influence on the language and culture of the area.

Norman influence can be traced throughout the Dales, most visibly at Richmond, where the castle stands so dramatically on its cliff, symbolically guarding the entrance to Swaledale. Perhaps the very appearance of the castle ensured relatively peaceful conditions, permitting the great monasteries to make the next major contribution to the landscape of the Dales over the following centuries.

Cultivated Beauty
Hauntingly beautiful ruins of abbeys like Fountains, Jervaulx and Bolton are tangible reminders of monastic influence, but it was the working of the vast estates they owned in the uplands which laid the foundations of today's scenery. Using lay-brothers and local labour the monks cleared the land, introduced sheep farming, extended the framework of the road system laid down by the Romans and, in the 13th century, began the practice of enclosing the land with drystone walls. The prosperity of medieval England was founded on wool and the Dales provided a high percentage of that wealth.

The Dissolution of the Monasteries led to two rebellions – the Pilgrimage of Grace and the Rising of the North – but many profited from dispersal of the lands. Within a hundred years or so, landlords and tenants alike were building sturdy yeoman's houses and farms, invariably of local stone and creating that sense of harmony to which reference has already been made. The general level of prosperity in each of the principal building periods – the second coinciding with the passion for Georgian architecture – was not sufficiently high to encourage experimental or unsuitable work. Vernacular housing built for the local industries that developed in the 18th and 19th centuries conformed to the overall style of Dales architecture and even Georgian building incorporated local characteristics.

During the late 18th and early 19th centuries came a series of Enclosure Acts which were to establish the landscape in the pattern of small, dry-stone walled fields it retains today. In the Dales, even more than in the Peak District, the blending of man-made features with the natural scenery produces a wonderfully pleasing landscape.

Harmony in Contrast
Nor should it be assumed that the overall effect of this harmony leads to blandness; a brief study of some of the individual Dales will reveal their varying character.

Swaledale, the most northerly of the Dales, lies on millstone grit and has an uncompromising beauty, softening as it approaches Reeth and richly wooded from there to Richmond. Both

Right: The ruins of Jervaulx Abbey lie in a wooded park at East Witton
Below: The poisonous globeflower, like a large buttercup, grows in gullies and pastures

Above: *The austere beauty of Gunnerside, whose meadows are dotted with lonely barns*

Right: *The Yorkshire Dales National Park's emblem is a Swaledale ram*

Wensleydale, the largest of the dales, and Wharfedale, are formed from Yoredale beds, and combine scars with pasture. Wensleydale's early scenery, above Hawes, can be spectacular, though not harsh; it then settles into a more pastoral mood, as the River Ure flows past a series of lively villages. Wharfedale is the most varied of the Dales, lushly wooded and remarkably beautiful at Bolton, spectacular at Kilnsey Crag, sparklingly pretty above Hubberholme where the river tumbles over shallow pavements as if pleased to escape from the bleak moorlands above. In Ribblesdale, all the rocks that form the Dales combine in bleak, hard mountain and moorland country. This is the least populated Dale but much visited, often by those wishing only to photograph the famous Ribble Head viaduct.

All limestone country is noted for the variety of its plants and the Dales are no exception, possessing many specialized species. Where woods occur, along the rivers, there is a different, but no less varied flora. Ash is the major tree species here and on the open, grazed areas, which are home to a marvellous variety of scrub trees and bushes. Some relict wood survives and, at Malham Tarn, there is a wetland site of unequalled quality.

Exploration and Extraction

All National Parks face the paradox that increased public mobility has encouraged flying visits at the expense of more leisurely exploration – Ribble Head is a good example. The Dales authority has negotiated access to hundreds of acres of moorland for those who love walking, and some of the best walking country along the entire length of the Pennine Way footpath can be found in the Yorkshire Dales, but it has to be conceded that many tourists prefer to stay close to the car parks or picnic places.

One problem confronting the Yorkshire Dales National Park is the large-scale removal of its very fabric – limestone. There are several active quarries within the boundary of the Park, most licenced before 1954 and therefore not subject to the planning controls any new application would face. Apart from the visual impact these large sites have on the landscape, they create problems of noise, dust and traffic.

Against this, quarrying and other forms of mineral extraction have long been traditional in the area, and many Dales dwellers resent attempts to interfere with local industry. The obvious alternative, tourism, may inject fresh money to the Dales, but it invariably brings new problems, frequently interfering with the very patterns of life many tourists come specifically to see in National Parks. In attempting both to develop tourism and control it, the National Park authorities have to pursue a delicate balance between, for example, the demands of vocal and articulate outside conservationists – frequently with access to press and broadcasting resources – and those who live in the area and may have a firmer appreciation of local requirements.

This is most certainly not a problem restricted to the National Parks, but the achieving of a balance satisfactory to the majority of pressure groups – and we all qualify for inclusion in that catch-all title in some form – is the only way to secure areas as outstandingly beautiful as the Yorkshire Dales.

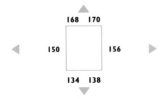

YORKSHIRE, RURAL AND URBAN

The tour guides the visitor through the southern part of the Yorkshire Dales National Park, but there is much else to see in this part of Yorkshire, dominated by major cities, yet full of charming villages and small towns.

```
        168  170
   ◄  150       156  ►
        134  138
```

TOUR

FOUNTAINS ABBEY, NIDDERDALE AND WHARFEDALE
75 MILES

Travelling east from Harrogate on the A6055, the tour rapidly reaches Knaresborough, set on a hill overlooking the River Nidd. The keep, two baileys and gatehouses of the Norman castle can be seen on the hillside.

From Knaresborough the tour turns north-west on the B6165. Ripley is full of reminders of the Ingilby family, long connected with the area. Ripley Castle, home of the Ingilbys since 1350, was rebuilt in the 18th century, but a small tower block remains of the original castle where Cromwell spent the night after the battle of Marston Moor.

The tour continues north on the A61 to Ripon, incorporated in AD886. Its lovely cathedral stands on the site where a monastery was founded in 657. Ripon has a Prison and Police Museum, in the cells of the strangely named Liberty Gaol.

Just outside Ripon is the village of Studley Roger, home of the Aislabie family. After the South Sea Bubble disaster, local MP John Aislabie had to resign as chancellor of the exchequer, and he occupied his enforced retirement by developing his estates at Studley Royal. The remains of Fountains Abbey became

the focal point of the 18th-century landscaped garden at Studley Royal.

A turning south off the B6265 leads to Brimham Rocks; the strange and fantastic rock formations stand on heather moorland overlooking Nidderdale at a height of 950ft.

At the next crossroads the tour turns right towards Pateley Bridge, running along the eastern bank of the Nidd through Glasshouses. Pateley Bridge, surrounded by green hills, has a fascinating collection of more than 5,000 items of dales history in the Nidderdale Museum.

The tour climbs steeply west on the B6265 through an area mined for lead from Roman times to the early 20th century. On Greenhow Hill, 1,400ft above sea level, are two of the oldest mines, the Jack Ass and Sam Oon levels.

Just down the hill are the Stump Cross Caverns, discovered in 1860: a succession of spectacular caverns, reached by an illuminated sloping tunnel. There is a guided tour.

From Greenhow Hill the tour travels south across high moorland and descends to Blubberhouses, where it joins the A59. At Bolton Abbey, on the River Wharfe, the romantic ruins of the 12th-century Augustinian priory in a riverside setting were captured in Landseer's famous painting, *Bolton Abbey in the Olden Times*.

At the east end of the ruins are the 57 stepping stones, used to cross the Wharfe before the footbridge was built. Less than a mile from the priory is the famous Strid, a narrow chasm through which the River Wharfe rushes with great speed.

Using the B6160 to cut through to the A65, the tour goes south to Ilkley, a former spa town on both sides of the Wharfe, crossed by three bridges. On the site of the Roman fort stands Manor House Museum and Art Gallery. The Elizabethan house shows an exposed piece of Roman wall and Roman antiquities, and has typical farmhouse furniture from the 17th and 18th centuries.

From Ilkley the A65 follows the Wharfe to Otley, birthplace of furniture-maker Thomas Chippendale. Otley Museum has objects related to local history since prehistoric times.

The A659 leads to Harewood House, home of the Earl and

Countess of Harewood. Designed in 1759, the house contains Chippendale furniture, paintings and porcelain. The Bird Garden in 4½ acres has over 150 species.

The tour returns to Harrogate on the A61.

SELECTED PLACES TO VISIT

🚉🏛️🅰️ BRADFORD
Map ref 1734

Bradford Industrial Museum in a former spinning mill features galleries of machinery, a transport shed with locomotives and trams and a mill-owner's house. Bradford also has the National Museum of Photography, Film and Television and the award-winning Colour Museum.

Cartwright Hall in Lister Park has excellent collections of paintings and sculpture. Bolling Hall is a 15th-century manor house with a rare Chippendale bed and a ghost room.

🏛️📷 HALIFAX
Map ref 0826

A cloth town since the 15th century, Halifax has many lovely buildings. Piece Hall, a unique 18th-century cloth hall, has been restored and converted to house museums, galleries and shops. Bankfield Museum has one of the finest collections of costume and textiles from all periods and all parts of the world.

More than 100 machines are on show in Calderdale Industrial Museum including textile machinery, and machines to work leather, make cork linings and wrap toffees. Street scenes with authentic sounds and smells recreate Halifax of the 1850s.

✳️ HARLOW CAR
Map ref 2855

West of Harrogate are Harlow Car Gardens, 68 acres of ornamental and woodland gardens, and the trial grounds of the Northern Horticultural Society.

🏛️📷 HARROGATE
Map ref 3055

The elegant spa town of Harrogate, 400ft above sea level, is popular as a holiday and conference centre. It is still possible to take the waters in the Royal Pump Room Museum, a domed building erected over the main sulphur spring in 1842. Low Harrogate is full of Victorian and Edwardian buildings, and the Valley Gardens extend from the Pump Room Museum to Harlow Moor. High Harrogate contains Georgian-style houses.

🏛️📷🏠 HAWORTH
Map ref 0536

The parsonage where the Brontes lived is now a museum to the literary family, furnished as it was in their day, with displays of their

Harewood, north of Leeds, is one of England's most palatial houses

YORKSHIRE, RURAL AND URBAN

Brimham Rocks – blocks of eroded dark millstone grit south-west of Ripon

personal treasures, books, manuscripts and pictures.

HUDDERSFIELD
Map ref 1416

Huddersfield has an excellent art gallery with works by Henry Moore, Lowry, Turner, Constable and Gainsborough, among many famous artists. The Tolson Memorial Museum in Ravensknowle Park has collections of archaeology, folk life, horse-drawn vehicles and toys.

KIRKSTALL ABBEY
Map ref 2635

Kirkstall Abbey is the most complete 12th-century Cistercian abbey in Britain. There is a folk museum in the gatehouse.

LEEDS
Map ref 3033

Authorised by an Act of Parliament in 1758, Middleton Railway is the world's oldest railway. The first to succeed with steam locomotives, it now has a collection of preserved industrial steam and diesel engines.

MONK BRETTON
Map ref 3706

East of Barnsley is Monk Bretton Priory, a 12th-century Cluniac foundation. Much of the church and claustral buildings remain.

TEMPLE NEWSAM
Map ref 3633

Temple Newsam is a Tudor and Jacobean house, set in 900 acres of parkland. Among its treasures are Chippendale furniture, medieval silver and gold, ceramics and paintings. Rare breeds of animals are preserved in its home farm.

WAKEFIELD
Map ref 3421

Wakefield's Art Gallery features 20th-century paintings and sculptures, with particular emphasis on Barbara Hepworth and Henry Moore, both born locally. The museum includes Charles Waterton's 19th-century collection of exotic birds and animals.

YORK MINSTER TO THE HUMBER BRIDGE

The spectacular Humber toll bridge, 4,626ft long, opened in 1981 to link Humberside and Yorkshire. The rolling hills and farmland to the north contrast with industrialised towns closer to the river. The area abounds in magnificent houses and churches, the most outstanding being York Minster, second only in importance to Canterbury Cathedral.

```
        170  172
         △
   ◀  154    158  ▶
        138
         ▽
```

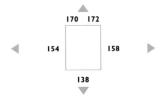

TOUR

VALE OF YORK, CASTLE HOWARD AND THE YORKSHIRE WOLDS
62 MILES

The tour strikes north from York on the B1363, heading through the eastern edge of the Vale of York. Once part of the ancient Forest of Galtres where the Normans hunted, it was cleared from the time of Charles I and its woodland history only survives in its placenames.

Sutton-on-the-Forest lies within the demesne of Sutton Park, home of the Sheffield family for almost 700 years. The present house is early Georgian, and the gardens are a particular feature, with a lily canal, woodland walks and nature trail.

At Stillington the tour turns right towards Sheriff Hutton. In the church is a small alabaster monument to Edward, Prince of Wales, son of Richard 'Crookback', who later became Richard III. The prince, who died in 1493 aged just 10, is buried there. Only the 14th-century keep remains of the Norman castle, where Edward IV's daughter and the Earl of Warwick were imprisoned. Sheriff Hutton Park, a Grade I historic house dating from 1616 and set in 170 acres, was originally King James I's hunting lodge.

As the tour continues east, on the left are the low rolling Howardian Hills. The most magnificent of the many fine houses tucked away in the hills is Castle Howard itself, set in 1,000 acres of parkland. Vanbrugh built the house in the 18th century for Charles Howard, 3rd Earl of Carlisle, and it is still occupied by the Howard family. Within the palatial building are collections of porcelain, paintings and furniture. The 18th-century stable court houses Britain's largest

private collection of 18th- to 20th-century costumes. The superb garden features Vanbrugh's Temple of the Four Winds and Hawksmoor's great Mausoleum.

The twin towns of Malton and Norton, originally the Roman fort of Derventio, lie on opposite banks of the River Derwent. Malton Museum features extensive collections of excavated Roman objects and items of prehistoric and medieval interest. Malton is a busy agricultural centre. Eden Camp, a former prisoner-of-war camp, near Old Malton to the north east, is now a museum of life during World War II.

The tour takes the B1248 south-east from Norton through the chalk ridges of the Yorkshire Wolds. After North Grimston the road forks, with the tour taking the left fork to climb through Duggelby to Sledmere.

Capability Brown created a 2,000-acre park for Sledmere House, a lovely Georgian manor. Its 100ft-long library is justly famous, and the house features contemporary furniture, as well as paintings and porcelain. The village has many monuments erected by the Sykes family of Sledmere House, and a huge 60ft-high war memorial.

From Sledmere the route follows the B1251 towards Fridaythorpe, where it crosses the Wolds Way long-distance footpath, and joins the A166 to travel west to Stamford Bridge, scene of the famous battle in 1066. Here King Harold defeated the Danes on 25 September, before marching south to meet defeat by the forces of William of Normandy at Hastings on 14 October.

York Minster, the largest Gothic cathedral in Europe, from Bootham Bar

As the A166 approaches York, it passes the Yorkshire Museum of Farming at Murton, where displays tell the story of 200 years of local agriculture. From here the tour returns to York.

SELECTED PLACES TO VISIT

BARTON-UPON-HUMBER
Map ref 0221
The Barton Clay Pits Project has exhibitions on natural history and recreational opportunities in the clay pits.

❀ BURNBY
Map ref 8247
Burnby Hall Gardens contain superb examples of waterlilies and rare plants from around the world, and a museum houses Major Stewart's extensive collection of ethnic exhibits.

⌂ CARLTON
Map ref 6523
Carlton Towers, Yorkshire home of the Duke of Norfolk, is still a family home. The Victorian Gothic house contains china, silver, carvings and stained glass, together with family uniforms and coronation robes.

🖼 DONCASTER
Map ref 5703
Extensive displays on archaeology, natural history and local history are found in Doncaster's Museum and Art Gallery.

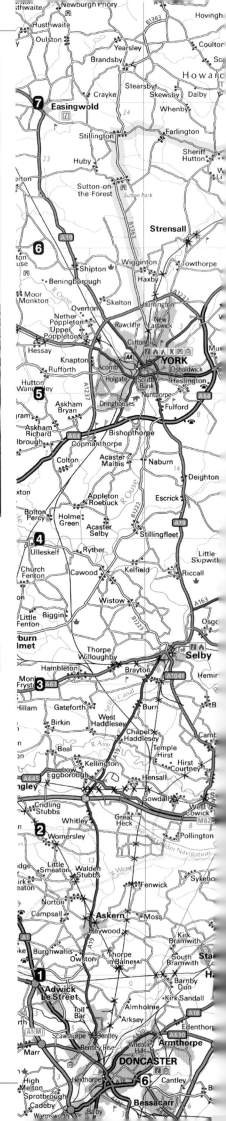

HOWDEN
Map ref 7428
The choir and chapter house of the medieval minster church of Howden are ruined, but the fine nave and tower remain.

NORMANBY
Map ref 8916
To the north of Scunthorpe is Normanby Hall, a Regency mansion decorated and furnished in period style. In the 350 acres of parkland there are deer herds and wildfowl, nature trails, craft workshops and a farming museum.

POCKLINGTON
Map ref 8149
Pocklington has a magnificent medieval church. Close by is Penny Arcadia, an unusual museum of coin-operated amusement machines, with audio-visual presentation and guided tours.

SELBY
Map ref 6133
Selby Abbey is probably the most outstanding example of a monastic abbey used as a parish church in the north of England.

SCUNTHORPE
Map ref 9111
The Regional Museum for South Humberside features displays on local history, particularly ironworking, archaeology and natural science.

YORK
Map ref 6152
The fascinating Roman, Viking, medieval and industrial history of York is well documented in its many museums. The Yorkshire Museum has extensive collections from all periods, and in its gardens are the ruins of St Mary's Abbey. The popular Castle Museum has reconstructed streets and period rooms, an Edwardian park, costume and jewellery, arms and armour, working watermill and Childsplay Gallery.

Jorvik Viking Centre has a recreation of Viking York, complete with sights, sounds and smells. In the Friargate Wax Museum, more than 60 lifesize figures in period costume are set in reconstructed historical scenes.

The National Railway Museum has a superb collection illustrating the history and development of British railway engineering from the earliest horse-drawn vehicles to the present. Rail Riders World at York Station has one of the biggest model railway layouts in the country.

York Minster had undergone extensive remedial work to its central tower shortly before lightning caused a disastrous fire in 1984. Four years of painstaking work were needed to repair the storm damage. The minster's undercroft contains a museum.

The eastern coast between Bridlington and Cleethorpes is one of Britain's least-known treasures. Excellent museums and galleries capture the atmosphere of the area's traditions of fishing and farming. The new Humber Bridge enables the visitor to cross the Humber quickly and easily and gives spectacular views.

```
        172
  156  [   ]
        140 142
```

SELECTED PLACES TO VISIT

▲▥▣ BEVERLEY
Map ref 0339

The town, once twice the size of Hull, is dominated by Beverley Minster with its delicate tracery of stonework. Outstanding features of this Gothic church are the 14th-century Percy Tomb and some fine wood carvings.

The mainly 18th-century Guildhall has 16th-century furniture in the magistrates' room and Georgian court room, which is still in use. The plasterwork ceiling of the court room includes as a motif a Figure of Justice without the blindfold.

The 600-year-old building of Beverley Friary, with its medieval and Tudor wall paintings, is also used as a youth hostel.

Beverley's main council office, The Hall, substantially dates from the 18th century. There are some original stucco ceilings and in the Chinese Room is hand-painted wallpaper (not open).

The Art Gallery has a display of the works of local artist Fred Elwell, supplemented by a series of exhibitions of paintings and other

The unusual twin towers of Beverley's 13th-century Minster

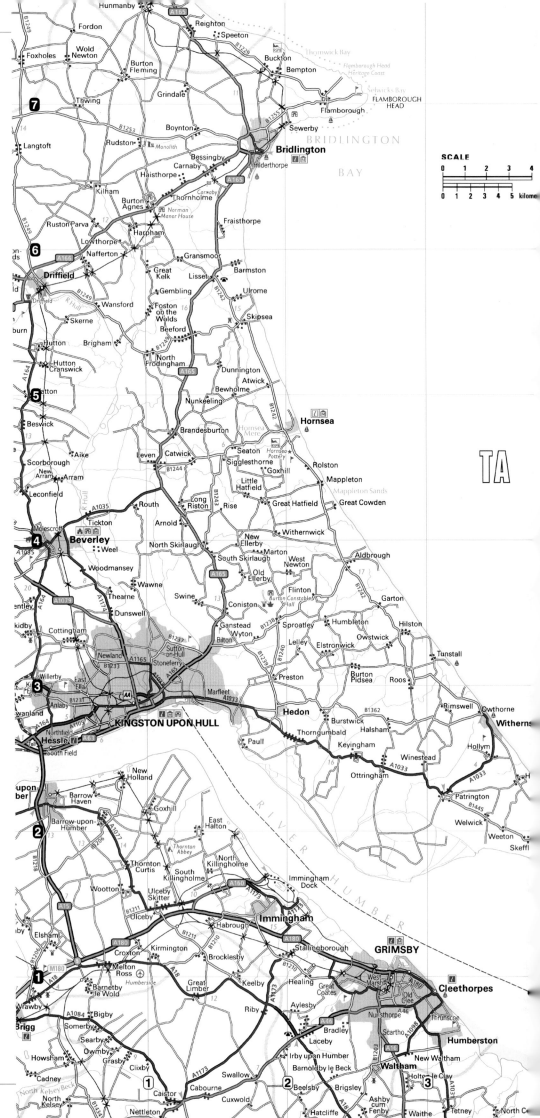

crafts. Beverley Heritage Centre depicts the history of the town.

The Museum of Army Transport is not confined to land vehicles, but also includes transport used by the army on the sea and in the air. There are two large exhibition halls, and the huge Blackburn Beverley aircraft.

🖼📷 BRIDLINGTON
Map ref 1866
The Bayle Museum, housed in a 14th-century Augustinian monastic gatehouse, includes a shoemaker's workshop and Victorian kitchen together with items of local history and early agricultural tools.

A history of the harbour in photographs and models can be seen at the Harbour History Room and Aquarium. Also exhibited is a North Sea aquarium and a diorama on fishing techniques.

🏛 BURTON AGNES
Map ref 1063
Burton Agnes Hall is a fine example of a late Elizabethan house well known for its collection of modern French paintings and fine china, decorated ceilings and overmantels and exquisite furniture.

🏛♣🍷 BURTON CONSTABLE HALL
Map ref 1835
One and a half miles north of Sproatley is the red brick Burton Constable Hall, which contains a fascinating collection of 18th-century scientific instruments. The house is 16th-century with 18th-century state rooms by Adam, Lightoller and others. The surrounding 200 acres of parkland were laid out by Capability Brown.

🖼 CLEETHORPES
Map ref 3109
Cleethorpes is a particularly popular resort with its 3 miles of sandy beaches. Jungleland and the Mini-Beasts Zoo by the boating lake has a fascinating and educational spider display room, indoor tropical garden and a wild flower garden.

FLAMBOROUGH HEAD
Map ref 2571
In the 10th century Flamborough Head was the scene of the successful invasion of England by the Vikings. Today these spectacular chalk cliffs have been colonised by thousands of seabirds and there is a heritage centre.

GREAT DRIFFIELD
Map ref 0357
Cruckley Animal Farm, a working family farm, is home to many rare breeds among its cows, sheep and pigs. A hatchery, children's paddock and waterfowl lake are included.

🖼📷 GRIMSBY
Map ref 2710
An important deep-sea fishing port, Grimsby received its charter in 1202, making it England's oldest chartered town. A 1907 non-conformist chapel is the home for the Welholme Galleries, which display Napoleonic and 19th-century ship models, marine paintings and the Hallgarth collection of Lincolnshire photographs, social and local history.

🖼📷 HORNSEA
Map ref 1947
A landscaped park is the setting for the famous Hornsea Pottery factory, together with other attractions. These include the World of Wings conservation centre for birds of prey, a showroom of Peter Black's car collection, butterfly farm, model village and children's playground and fort. The manufacture of pottery can be viewed from a newly created gallery walk.

The Hornsea Museum, also known as The North Holderness Museum of Village Life, is housed in a former farmhouse. The award-winning small museum features village life through a Victorian kitchen, parlour, bedroom and dairy decorated in the style of a typical farmhouse and through farm implements and tools of local craftsmen.

IMMINGHAM
Map ref 1714
The effect of the Grand Central Railway and the creation of the deep-water port on the development of Immingham are demonstrated in the museum. The displays make full use of archive material, artefacts and photographs from the railway. There are also galleries devoted to local history and archaeology.

🖼📷🖼 KINGSTON UPON HULL
Map ref 0928
Britain's third largest port, a university town and industrial centre, Hull is rich in museums and galleries, each with its own speciality.

In the High Street is Wilberforce House, the early 17th-century mansion where anti-slavery campaigner William Wilberforce was born. Exhibits on the evils of slavery are on display, together with period furniture, silver and costumes.

Exhibits in the Town Docks Museum focus on the importance of fish and fishing, with special displays concentrating on trawling and whaling.

The 1½ mile-long Humber Bridge

The Ferens Art Gallery includes superb collections of Old Masters, 19th-century marine paintings, and contemporary works.

Humberside archaeology is featured at the Hull and East Riding Museum, including the Iron Age Hasholme boat and chariot burials, and a splendid display of Romano-British mosaics. At Streetlife in the Hull Museum of Transport, are horse-drawn vehicles and turn-of-the-century motor vehicles including the rare Ryde Pier and Kitson trams.

Maister House, rebuilt in 1744 and now in the care of the National Trust, has a fine example of a staircase hall designed in the Palladian manner, and ironwork by Robert Bakewell.

🏛 NORMAN MANOR HOUSE
Map ref 1263
Burton Agnes Manor House is a rare example of a Norman house. Although altered and encased in brick during the 17th and 18th centuries, the Norman piers and groined roof of a lower chamber remain.

🏛 SEWERBY
Map ref 2068
To the north of Bridlington is the Model Village of Portminian at Sewerby. The model village, laid out on a 1-acre site, has been created to represent a rural seaside community, with more than 200 stone-faced buildings and many hand-made model figures.

Sewerby Hall Park and Zoo includes an aviary, old English walled garden, art gallery and museum and a display devoted to Amy Johnson, the English pioneer airwoman who flew solo from London to Australia in 1930.

⚲ THORNTON ABBEY
Map ref 1218
Thornton Abbey, founded in 1139 by the Augustinian order, has a splendid 14th-century crenellated gatehouse approached across a 120ft-long bridge over a dry moat. The ruins of the abbey church and octagonal chapter house are open, and there is a small exhibition.

PEACEFUL LAKES AND RUGGED FELLS

The western boundary of the Lake District National Park comes close to the coast of Cumbria. The beauty of the peaceful lakes and rugged fells contrasts sharply with important ship-building and industrial towns on the coast, such as Barrow-in-Furness and Sellafield's nuclear reprocessing plant. The coastline has historic castles and sandy beaches to appeal to the visitor.

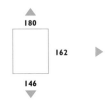

180

162

146

TOUR

BORROWDALE, BUTTERMERE AND WHINLATTER PASS
40 MILES

From Keswick, the tour takes the B5289 between the eastern side of Derwent Water and the Borrowdale Fells. At the southern end of the lake, just before Grange, is the magnificent sight of the Lodore Falls. Shortly after the right turn to Grange is the famous Bowder Stone, a huge glacial rock.

Negotiating the narrow road at Rosthwaite, the tour curves round the valley into the little hamlet of Seatoller, where an information centre is run by the Lake District National Park in a converted barn. The road climbs up sharply beside a deep chasm across the Honister Pass, and then begins the descent towards Buttermere.

The three lakes which follow in quick succession – Buttermere, Crummock Water and Loweswater – are all under the protection of the National Trust. The Trust's activity to increase native hardwoods around the lake can be seen, mainly in the form of planted oaks. The road follows Buttermere's eastern shore, while on the far side of the lake can be seen the peaks of High Stile (2,644ft), High Crag and Red Pike.

Where Buttermere meets Crummock Water lies the little hamlet of Buttermere. The road hugs the lake, overlooked by the massive splendour of Grasmoor Fell at 2,792ft.

The tour turns left for a sharp descent towards Loweswater, rather than following the B5289 through Lorton Vale to Cockermouth. Loweswater village is reached after the road crosses a stream. After another climb, the tour turns right

Windsurfers on Coniston Water, which lies south of Coniston itself

at a T-junction on to the A5086, travelling north-east to Cockermouth.

Cockermouth was the birthplace of poet William Wordsworth in 1770, and the house where he was born, now owned by the National Trust, contains some of the poet's possessions. The walled garden in which Wordsworth played as a child can still be enjoyed.

Cockermouth had a castle back in the 12th century, but the existing castle dates mostly from the 13th and 14th centuries. Slighted after the Civil War, it was partially rebuilt in the 19th century. It is open to the public during the Cockermouth festival in August.

A Doll and Toy Museum in the Market Place has a collection of costume dolls and toys.

The B5289 climbs slowly out of Cockermouth, passing under the A66 with the outline of the high fells on the horizon. Taking the turn for High Lorton, the tour climbs up to the Whinlatter Pass, some 1,043ft above sea level. A Roman road once ran across the pass, and in 1761 the turnpike road from Kendal to Cockermouth opened to run the same way.

Just before the road enters Thornthwaite Forest, a lovely view of Bassenthwaite Lake to the north can be seen. This is Forestry Commission land, and a visitor centre here has displays about the area.

Shortly after Braithwaite, the route rejoins the A66 to Keswick.

SELECTED PLACES TO VISIT

BARROW-IN-FURNESS
Map ref 2068
While Barrow is mainly an industrial town, building ships and nuclear submarines, it was once mainly known for powerful 12th-century Furness Abbey, a Cistercian foundation in the Glen of Deadley Nightshade to the north east. Furness Museum features finds from late Stone Age sites, as well as models of Vickers ships.

CONISHEAD PRIORY
Map ref 3176
On the shores of Morecambe Bay is Conishead Priory, a 19th-century Gothic mansion built on the site of a 12th-century priory.

CONISTON
Map ref 3097
The Old Man of Coniston, 2,635ft high, towers over this grey slate village beside Coniston Water. The steam yacht *Gondola* has been plying up and down the lake in stately fashion since she was first launched in 1859. The Ruskin Museum contains letters, sketchbooks and personal items of the writer and critic who lived nearby and is buried in Coniston churchyard.

KESWICK
Map ref 2625
Keswick stands beneath the huge smooth fell of Skiddaw, 3,053ft high, on the banks of the River Greta, overlooking the beautiful expanse of Derwent Water.

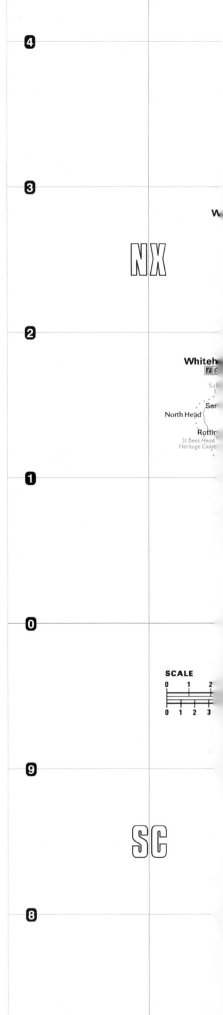

NX

Whiteh

Sal

Sar

North Head

Rottin

St Bees Head
Heritage Coast

SC

SCALE

0   1   2

0   1   2   3

9

PEACEFUL LAKES AND RUGGED FELLS

The beauty of the scenery made Keswick a mecca for poets and painters at the beginning of the 19th century. Coleridge came to live in Greta Hall in 1800, and Southey followed in 1803. Charles Lamb, Scott, Tennyson and R L Stevenson were all frequent visitors, as also were William and Dorothy Wordsworth, who were living in nearby Grasmere.

Keswick's Museum and Art Gallery is rich in literary associations. Manuscripts and memorabilia of Hugh Walpole, Robert Southey and Wordsworth are on display. The museum has a large geological collection, and a scale model of the Lake District.

✿ LINGHOLM
Map ref 2424
On the western side of Derwent Water are Lingholm Gardens. Here, both formal and woodland gardens can be enjoyed.

MILLOM
Map ref 1780
The main hall of Millom Folk Museum is devoted to a display on the Hodbarrow Iron Ore Mines, Millon Iron Worls and agriculture. Behind the mine is the domestic display, including a reconstructed miner's cottage.

MIREHOUSE
Map ref 2328
Close by Bassenthwaite Lake is Mirehouse, a 17th-century manor house containing manuscripts and portraits of Bacon, Tennyson and Carlyle.

MUNCASTER CASTLE
Map ref 1196
At the foot of Eskdale is Muncaster Castle, a 13th-century castle with a fine collection of 16th- and 17th-century furnishings. In the lovely grounds is an aviary which specialises in owls.

MUNCASTER MILL
Map ref 0997
Ravenglass is an 18th-century mill where all the milling equipment is water powered and where stoneground flour is made for sale.

RAVENGLASS & ESKDALE RAILWAY
Map ref 0797
A 15in narrow-gauge railway established in 1875 to carry iron ore, this is now a passenger line running 7 miles from Ravenglass to Eskdale.

ULVERSTON
Map ref 2777
One of Ulverston's most famous sons was Stan Laurel, and a private house in Upper Brook Street claims to contain the world's largest collection of Laurel and Hardy memorabilia.

Within this busy market town is Cumbria Crystal's factory, specialising in traditionally crafted glassware based on 18th-century designs.

THE LAKES: PRESERVING THE BALANCE

This section of the Lake District National Park contains two of its most famous lakes – Windermere and Ullswater – and numerous remote and imposing peaks.

A delicate balance has to be maintained between preserving unspoilt scenery which inspired Wordsworth and other writers and artists, while catering for the many modern visitors also eager to appreciate its beauty.

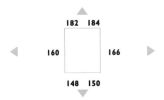

◀ 160   182 184   166 ▶
148 150

TOUR

SHAP FELL, ULLSWATER AND WINDERMERE
62 MILES

The tour begins from Kendal, heading north on the A6. This has been the main route from England to Scotland for centuries.

The road climbs steadily, giving views across to the High Street range in the far west and the Shap fells ahead. The fells form the eastern boundary of the Lake District National Park. Three north-south routes converge here, the A6 trunk road, the M6 motorway, and between them the London to Glasgow railway line.

From the windswept heights of Shap fells, the road descends towards Shap village, passing the granite quarries on the left. Shap, which stands at 872ft, was an important coaching centre, and Bonnie Prince Charlie spent a night here during the 1745 rebellion. A brief detour to the left leads to Shap Abbey, founded in 1189 and dissolved in 1540.

The tour continues north on the A6 to Penrith, Saxon capital of Cumbria. The southern approach to the town passes near two ancient earthworks, King Arthur's Round Table, possibly dating from 1,000BC, and Mayburgh, a circular mound of even earlier date.

Penrith suffered in the border wars, when the warning beacon on Beacon Hill to the north of the town was frequently lit. Last used for defensive purposes in 1745, the beacon is now confined to marking national and royal celebrations. An exhibition on the history of Penrith and the Eden Valley is found in the former Robinson's School, together with displays of archaeological finds, including Roman pottery.

The tour leaves Penrith on the A66, passing the 14th-century defensive tower which is all that remains of Penrith Castle, and quickly forks left on to the A592 towards Ullswater. Dalemain House is on the right. This lovely house, originally a medieval pele tower, was enlarged in Tudor times and given a Georgian façade in 1745. The resulting diversity of styles includes a 15th-century fireplace, Tudor plasterwork, Chinese wallpaper and Queen Anne furniture.

The tour bypasses the ancient village of Dacre with its wealth of Anglo-Saxon history to follow the western shore of Ullswater, arguably the most beautiful of all the area's lakes. Through Watermillock and past the Outward Bound school, the road is joined by the A5091 from the right just where the dramatic waterfall of Aira Force falls 70ft.

From the road the peak of Place Fell, 2,156ft up, can be seen beyond the head of the lake. Next comes the hamlet of Patterdale, surrounded on three sides by high peaks. Here the A592 starts its ascent towards Kirkstone Pass which, at 1,489ft, is the highest road in the Lake District. The tour branches off right from the A592 into Ambleside.

Ambleside has been a tourist destination since the 19th century, although it was a strategic crossing point from Roman times. Bridge House, a tiny 16th-century building, contains a National Trust information centre. St Mary's church, designed by Gilbert Scott with a 180ft spire and completed in 1854, has a bible and lectern donated by Wordsworth's widow Mary, and a memorial window in the Wordsworth chapel.

Joining the A591, the tour travels south-east towards Windermere, along the northern edge of the lake, to the National Park visitor centre at Brock Hole. Surrounded by 32 acres of gardens and woodland, the centre has a permanent exhibition on Living Lakeland, audio-visual shows, launch trips on the lake and special events.

Windermere town grew rapidly after the railway arrived in 1847, bringing many visitors to the largest lake in England. The Steamboat Museum has a unique collection of Victorian and Edwardian steamboats and other

A view of Helm Cray, which rises up above Grasmere

historic motor and sailing boats which plied up and down, many of which are still afloat and in working order in a wet dock.

The tour returns to Kendal via the A591 and A684.

SELECTED PLACES TO VISIT

★ 🚤 CARTMEL PRIORY GATEHOUSE
Map ref 3778

Once part of Cartmel Priory, the medieval church of St Mary and St Michael escaped destruction during the dissolution of the monasteries because St Michael's chapel in the priory's south aisle was claimed as a parish church. Apart from the church, all that is left of the 14th-century Augustinian priory is the Gatehouse, now owned by the National Trust.

🚹 GRANGE-OVER-SANDS
Map ref 4277

Grange-over-Sands stands just outside the southern boundary of the National Park. It is possible, with guidance, to walk across the sands of Morecambe Bay to Morecambe, 8 miles away. This route was used as the main road from Lancaster before the railway.

🚹 🏛 ♣ 🅿 GRASMERE
Map ref 3407

The Wordsworth family came to Grasmere in 1799, and lie buried in the village churchyard. Poet William Wordsworth spent his most creative years at Dove Cottage and the house has been preserved as recorded in the journals of his sister Dorothy. The Wordsworth Museum is adjacent.

🏛 🚹 HAWKSHEAD
Map ref 3597

In the office of William Heelis, solicitor husband of Beatrix Potter, the National Trust has created an exhibition of her life as author, artist, farmer and protector of the Lake District, together with original drawings and illustrations.

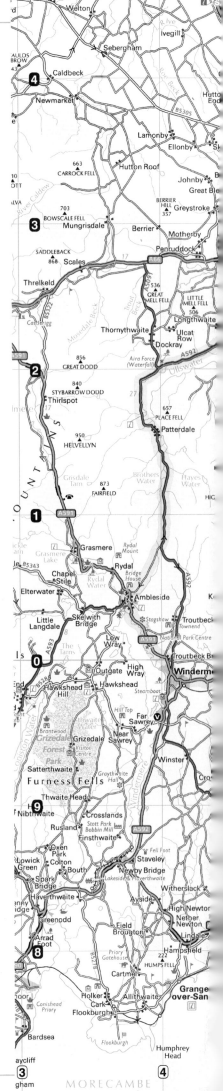

MORECAMBE

THE LAKES: PRESERVING THE BALANCE

⌂ HILL TOP
Map ref 3796

Beatrix Potter used the small 17th-century farmhouse of Hill Top at Near Sawrey as a retreat and source of inspiration for many of her Peter Rabbit books. She bequeathed it, like the rest of her estate, to the National Trust.

⌂🏛 HOLKER
Map ref 3677

A variety of activities are available within the 122 acres of deer park at Holker Hall, including a motor museum, baby animal farm, craft and countryside museum and exhibition of Victorian and Edwardian kitchens.

⊠✗🏛 KENDAL
Map ref 5393

A town founded on wool, Kendal is nicknamed the 'auld grey town' because of the grey limestone used for many of its buildings.

Kendal Museum specialises in natural history and archaeology, while the Abbot Hall Museum of Lakeland Life and Industry (housed in Abbot Hall's stable block) captures social and working life. Abbot Hall features Gillow furniture and other *objets d'art*, and modern galleries display fine and decorative arts.

⌣ LEIGHTON HALL
Map ref 4976

This neo-Gothic mansion was built around 1800. Home of the Gillow family, it contains good early Gillow furniture. Birds of prey give regular flying displays, weather permitting.

✗ SIZERGH CASTLE
Map ref 4987

South of Kendal is Sizergh Castle, home of the Strickland family for more than 700 years. It has an impressive 14th-century pele tower, and was extended in Tudor times. The interior features some of the finest Elizabethan carved overmantels in England. The castle, in the care of the National Trust, is surrounded by beautiful and interesting gardens.

A quiet back lane leading to the market place in Kendal

LAKE DISTRICT

Walking is by far the best way to explore this wonderfully varied area. Most of the mountains are easily accessible and from almost any height the lakes acquire a new perspective

The 250ft-deep glacial lake, Wast Water, overlooked by Scafell and Great Gable

Not only the largest but the most spectacular of the National Parks, the Lake District was designated in 1951. It covers 880 square miles of 'the wildest, most barren and frightful (country) . . . in England'. That was Defoe's description, nor was he alone in his dread of an area now suffering from a surfeit of visitors.

In fairness, it was almost 100 years after the death of Defoe, in 1731, before writers began to express appreciation of natural beauty.

In 1835 Wordsworth published arguably the best guide book to the Lakes – his *Guide through the District of the Lakes* – in which he highlighted the problem popularity might bring to such a relatively compact area. It was a problem that would grow in a way he could never have contemplated even though he, and Ruskin, were later to fulminate against railway extensions here and in the Peak District. Today, the car brings the great northern cities, Liverpool and Manchester, to within less than two hours of the Lake District and even London is no more than five hours away.

Education for Conservation

The contradictions between the needs of tourism and conservation meet head-on in the Lake District. Many attempts have been made to reconcile them but few of the increasingly draconian solutions proposed in some quarters in recent years have appeared to be either workable or acceptable!

The plain fact is that unlimited public access to sensitive environments like the Lakes will lead, if uncontrolled, to its destruction. Equally, issuing tickets, restricting access, even imposing charges for entry, runs utterly counter to all that the 'freedom to roam' movement holds dear. Levying holidaymakers would require a deal of administration if it were to be collected efficiently; the danger is that those with most to gain from a few days in this lovely countryside would be discouraged. Worse, it might increase the numbers of day visitors, already the cause of much of the problem.

Inevitably, the car has been cast as the villain but, for an increasing number of people, it is the tool by which they can discover the countryside. At times the conservation movement seems reluctant to accept that the car is with us for the foreseeable future – the trick will be in learning how to live with it. Nor is it entirely disingenuous to point out that people are responsible for the wholesale wearing down of paths; for the turning of some Lakeland 'honeypots' into places resembling Trafalgar Square on New Year's Eve; for driving power boats dangerously up and down Windermere; for the disgraceful – sometimes fatal to livestock – litter problem affecting the National Parks.

The importance of informing and educating must be highlighted – educating people to understand and protect their heritage; persuading them to follow waymarked paths away from tourist traps on their own voyages of discovery. The National Park authority and other bodies – notably the Forestry Commission, the National Trust and the Regional Tourist Board – are showing the way by providing information centres and distributing literature.

Programmes for the education of children are vital and the very numbers of families joining the major conservation bodies is an indication of how much people want to be involved. Progress may be slow, paths may continue to be eroded for the foreseeable future but the alternative – barring entry, frustrating and effectively disenfranchising people – is no solution.

Contrasting Views

The Lake District covers a wide range of scenery and habitat including coastal dunes, marshes, rivers, waterfalls, lakes, oak woodland, conifer forests, moorland, scree and above it all, the mountains, including the highest in England. Almost as varied are the geological formations of the area. In the north are the softish rocks of the Skiddaw Slates, producing rounded mountains and gentle fells. South of this are the harder volcanic Borrowdale rocks, from which are formed the more jagged central peaks. Below Ambleside, Silurian slates and mudstones have created the lower hills and well-farmed slopes through which visitors from the south approach the Lake District. Around all this there is a band of carboniferous limestone with its distinctive scenery and flora and fauna.

Most of the mountains are accessible to anyone of average fitness, assuming one of the easy routes to the top is chosen – and that suitable clothing is worn. For visitors with disabilities and others who are restricted to the use of the car there are roads beside several of the lakes, while the views from the roads over the main passes are invariably dramatic.

Water's Edge and Woodland

The lakes themselves are full of variety, some teeming with life, others, glacial lakes like Wast Water, exhausted, almost lifeless. The lakes that remain full of nutrients are invariably associated with several habitats, ensuring that they are home to a wide range of species.

The edges are often marshy, colonized by water-loving plants like skull-cap and gipsywort and attracting many birds from heron to snipe. Spreading upwards from the shore are the old oak woods, containing the richest variety of wildlife. The red squirrel has not yet been challenged by the grey in the Lakes, while roe deer, most delicate and charming creatures, are often seen early in the morning or in car headlights late at night close to the rough roads bordering the lakes. Common woodland species of birds include tits, jay, great spotted woodpecker and, in summer, pied flycatcher and redstart with sparrowhawk

Top: *The peregrine falcon, found in the uplands, can dive at a speed of up to 180 miles per hour*
Above: *The goldeneye, belonging to the sea duck group, can easily be seen at Coniston*

preying on the smaller species.

A good place to enjoy lakeside woodland is the beautiful Friar's Crag Nature Walk at Derwent Water, part of which is accessible to wheelchair users. The road on the east side of Coniston, past Ruskin's home Brantwood, never strays far from the water's edge as it passes through a series of splendid woods. There are parking places and the chance to see ducks like goldeneye and the two saw-bills, goosander and merganser, without leaving the car.

Higher up the fells the woodland becomes mixed, attracting different species of birds and, on the acid soil, plants like wood sorrel and foxglove. Naturally, the uplands are less appealing to wildlife though mountain parsley grows freely on the rocks and drystone walls together with several ferns. Tormentil, very much a plant of the National Parks, is usually present, its yellow flowers providing a welcome touch of colour from spring to autumn.

Sundew, butterwort and heath bedstraw grow in the boggy areas, with rushes, cotton grass and the aromatic bog-myrtle. The acid waters of the tarns attract colonies of localized plants like bogbean and there are, on some of the high crags, a few pockets of alpine plants. Several birds of prey breed on the uplands, including buzzard and peregrine falcon. In some places bracken is becoming a problem and good management of the uplands is very much a priority of the National Trust, the biggest landowner in the Lake District.

An Unforgettable Landscape

Land management is nothing new in the Lake District and, as elsewhere, much of what seems to be a natural landscape owes its present form to the work of generations of man. Man, in fact, has been associated with the Lake District for at least 5,000 years. In that time he has hunted, produced tools, felled the forest, developed settlements, constructed stone circles and hill-forts, grown crops and raised sheep. Wave after wave of incomers have brought new cultures and new ideas, and all have been absorbed. Man has evolved

and so has this beautiful landscape – and it will continue to do so.

Wordsworth said of the Lakes that they were for every man with 'an eye to perceive and a heart to enjoy'. In 1902 the National Trust made an appeal on behalf of Brandelhow Woods. Accompanying one subscription was this: 'I am a working man and cannot afford more than 2 shillings but I once saw Derwent Water and can never forget it'. Wordsworth could not have expressed it better!

FELLS AND FALLS

Where Cumbria joins Yorkshire, the scenery changes from the slate of the Lake District to the limestone of the Yorkshire Dales. This remote area is perhaps better known to the hillwalker than to the motorised tourist, yet amply repays a visit with spectacular scenery of fells and waterfalls.

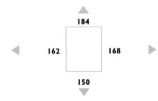

184

162   168

150

TOUR

THE NORTH YORKSHIRE AND CUMBRIA BORDER DALES
71 MILES

The tour sets out south from Sedbergh in the Yorkshire Dales National Park. The National Park Centre in Main Street is a useful initial port of call.

Taking the C road through Millthrop, the next village is Dent, on the River Dee, in Dentdale. Dent was an important textile centre for many years, particularly for the knitting of worsted stockings. A fountain commemorates Adam Sedgwick, born in Dent and a distinguished professor of geology at Cambridge University in the early 19th century.

After retracing the route out of Dent, the tour climbs south-west towards Kirkby Lonsdale, passing the peak of Calf Top (1,998ft) on the right, with the even higher summit of Crag Hill (2,251ft) to the east.

Kirkby Lonsdale is a typical Pennine town, built of yellow limestone, with cobbled streets and 18th-century houses. The market town for the Lune Valley, Kirkby Lonsdale stands on a high bank overlooking the river. The 12th-century church of St Mary was built on the site of a Saxon church, and some Norman archways survive. Writer and critic John Ruskin considered the view from the Brow 'one of the loveliest scenes in England, therefore in the world'; after such praise, to name this part of the town Ruskin's View was the least the townsfolk could do.

From Kirkby Lonsdale the tour takes the A65 south-east to Ingleton, once an important staging-post on the Leeds-Kendal packhorse way and on the busy Keighley-Kendal turnpike. The town has seen much industry, from wool, tanning and quarrying to coal mining. The railway brought many visitors in the 19th century to see the magnificent waterfalls and to climb to the 2,373ft-high peak of Ingleborough Mountain.

On the tour, the best view of Ingleborough Hill is from Chapel le Dale, set in the valley gouged out by a glacier some two million years ago. On the summit are the remains of an Iron Age settlement. On its north side is Alum Pot, one of the region's most famous potholes, while Gaping Gill, opposite, has the highest waterfall in England.

Up ahead is the viaduct of the Settle-Carlisle railway, itself currently under threat of closure. On the right is Langstrothdale Chase, the game reserve of the noble family of Percy. The tour continues through lonely moorland, which passes close to Dodd Fell on its way to Hawes.

At 800ft, Hawes is the highest market town in Yorkshire and the second highest in England. It is noted for Wensleydale cheese, a traditional industry revived in the 1930s by local entrepreneur Kit Calvert.

In Hawes is the second National Park Centre encountered on the tour, containing information about the Yorkshire Dales and an interpretive display on local farming. The Upper Dales Folk Museum in Station Yard has collections on folk life, trades and occupations of the Upper Dales. The displays feature sheep and hay farming, peat cuttings, hand knitting and cheese making.

Hardraw Force, a spectacular waterfall 2 miles to the north, has an amphitheatre in the ravine where 19th-century brass band and choral competitions were held. It is possible to walk right behind the waterfall.

The tour continues north, climbing steeply up over the fells across Buttertubs Pass, a bleak and exposed highway, into Swaledale. To the left, walkers on the Pennine Way cross the heather-clad summit of Great Shunner Fell, at 2,339ft. The tiny village of Keld, high above a wooded gorge, stands among hills formerly worked for lead, surrounded by spectacular waterfalls.

Following the B6270, the tour crosses Birk Dale, finally descending into Kirkby Stephen. As in other Westmorland towns and villages, wool was spun in the open-air gallery of the house opposite the church. There are some lovely Georgian houses in the town, including Winton Hall, built in 1726. The tour heads back to Sedbergh on the beautiful but lonely A683, across fells giving superb views of the Pennines.

SELECTED PLACES TO VISIT

✳ ACORN BANK
Map ref 6228

Between Temple Sowerby – sometimes known as the queen of Westmorland villages – and Newbiggin lies the 18th-century red sandstone house of Acorn Bank, let to the Sue Ryder Foundation.

The churchyard and vicarage of Kirkby Lonsdale's Norman church – St Mary's

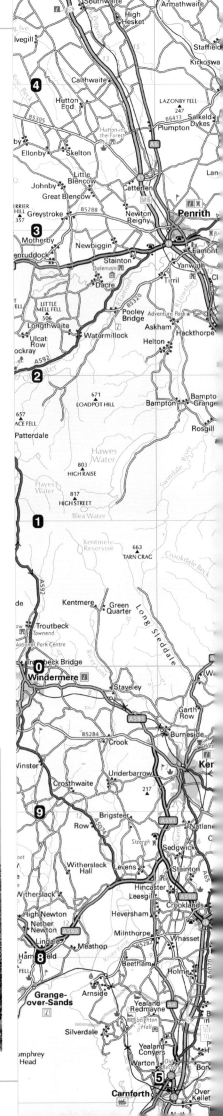

FELLS AND FALLS

Its 2½ acre garden is in the care of the National Trust. Under fine oaks grow a vast display of daffodils, while inside the garden walls are two orchards with fruit trees, surrounded by mixed borders with shrubs, herbaceous plants and roses. Its famous herb garden has the largest collection of culinary and medicinal plants in the north.

✔ ❧ APPLEBY-IN-WESTMORLAND
Map ref 6820

Set in the Eden Valley, and the county town of Westmorland until it became part of the larger county of Cumbria in 1974, Appleby still retains the longer version of its name. Nine hundred years ago, it was transferred from Scotland to England.

Lady Anne Clifford's tomb is in St Lawrence's church. Its organ, formerly in Carlisle Cathedral, is the third oldest in the country.

✗ ✔ BROUGH
Map ref 7914

The A66 through Brough follows the route of the old Roman road. Strategically placed, Brough was a coaching town.

The remains of Brough Castle, built on the site of the Roman fort of Verterae, can still be seen. St Michael's medieval church has a 17th-century stone pulpit.

✗ CONSERVATION CENTRE
Map ref 6819

Appleby Castle, built in 12th-century motte and bailey style, was restored in 1653, by Lady Anne Clifford. The grounds of the castle have been turned into a Conservation Centre, where the Rare Breeds Survival Trust supports a collection of waterfowl, pheasant, poultry and owls. Within the Norman keep are Roman armour and insignia, among many artefacts.

⌘ KILLHOPE WHEEL
Map ref 8243

North west of Cowshill in County Durham is the Killhope Wheel Lead Mining Centre, where the emphasis is on encouraging visitors to experience panning for lead and see working machinery. The lead mine and crushing mill buildings have been restored as they were in the late 19th century.

✔ ★ SEDBERGH
Map ref 6693

Part of Yorkshire until local government reorganisation in 1974, Sedbergh is now in Cumbria. A market town, it is also home to a famous public school, founded in 1525, of whose pupils Professor Adam Sedgwick is arguably the most distinguished. The Howgill fells which surround Sedbergh are formed of the same rock as those of the southern Lake District.

There is a National Park Centre here which provides information about the Dales.

DALE AND RAIL

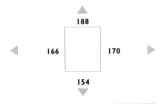

Here the Yorkshire Dales National Park runs over the border into County Durham. Bare crags, once rich in lead, contrast with lush river valleys. Darlington and Shildon experienced the pioneering days of the railway, as first coal and then passengers travelled to Stockton's harbour.

```
        ▲
       188

◄  166      170  ►

       154
        ▼
```

TOUR

BARNARD CASTLE, WITH ARKENGARTHDALE, WENSLEYDALE AND SWALEDALE
54 MILES

The tour leaves Richmond on the B6274, heading north on the A66 out of Yorkshire and into County Durham. At Greta Bridge the River Greta flows through a wooded glen to join the larger River Tees. The lovely view of the bridge of 1776 was painted by John Cotman, while Turner painted the *Meeting of the Waters* in the grounds of Rokeby Park.

On a cliff above the River Tees is Barnard Castle, a 12th-century castle with a circular three-storeyed keep whose ruins cover 6½ acres. The surviving Round Tower, dating from the 14th century, is said to have inspired Sir Walter Scott as he wrote the novel *Rokeby* at nearby Rokeby Park. The town which grew up around the castle has many fine buildings.

West of the town is the imposing French-style chateau of the Bowes Museum, built in 1869 to house John Bowes' superb collections of paintings and decorative arts. Among the exhibits are internationally important paintings, English and French furniture from the 16th to the 19th centuries, porcelain, silver, carvings and sculptures. There are galleries of music and costume and a children's room. The museum also features regional archaeology and bygones.

From Barnard Castle the tour turns south on the B6277, passing the picturesque remains of Egglestone Abbey, where the greater part of the 13th-century nave and chancel still stands beside the River Tees.

The lonely road south towards Arkengarthdale climbs through moorland before descending to a crossroads, with the mighty peak of Great Pinseat (1,913ft) ahead. As lead mining country from Roman times, the hills are scarred with entrance holes and passageways.

The industry reached its peak during the 19th century, but collapsed in the 1880s, causing severe depopulation as families moved to the Lancashire cotton towns and the United States for economic survival.

Today the area is a popular touring destination for visitors to the Yorkshire Dales National Park, and an information centre near Reeth explains how the heritage of the region is being conserved. Reeth stands on the hillside where Arkengarthdale joins Swaledale, and its Folk Museum illustrates local life and traditions.

The tour turns south towards Grinton, a riverside village whose name derives from a Saxon word meaning green enclosure. Its imposing church was the centre of worship for a parish stretching to the Cumbrian border, and contains remains of the original Norman structure in the nave and font.

Continuing south, the tour comes upon Castle Bolton, built in the late 14th century and deserted by the Scrope family in 1678. Mary Queen of Scots was imprisoned here from 1568 to 1569 by Lord Scrope, Warden of the Western Marches, to whom she had surrendered at Carlisle. The imposing castle, which still dominates this part of the valley, contains tapestries and arms.

The route passes through Carperby, where the Wensleydale breed of sheep was developed in the 1830s. Nearby are the stones of an early Bronze Age stone circle, and the National Park Centre, with its interpretative display, guides and other local information. It meets the A684 by Aysgarth Falls, where the River Ure plunges spectacularly down a series of cataracts. The falls nearest the 70ft-high bridge are known as High Force, and a footpath leads to Middle Force and Lower Force. Near the bridge is Yore Mill, now the Yorkshire Carriage Museum, containing more than 60 horse-drawn vehicles.

From Aysgarth the tour takes the A684 through Wensleydale to Wensley, once a market town and capital of the valley but now a small village. Its 14th-century market charter passed to nearby Leyburn after Wensley was decimated by the plague in 1563. The lovely medieval

High above the Tees at Barnard Castle are the remains of the castle

church stands on the site of an earlier religious building, from which Saxon relics have been set into the north aisle. The church includes a carved screen from Easby Abbey.

Leyburn's most famous viewpoint is from the Shawl, a mile-long terrace shaded by larches from which there are superb views along Wensleydale to Castle Bolton to the west and Middleham Castle to the south. The name derives from a legend that Mary Queen of Scots dropped her shawl in this hillside town while attempting to escape from Castle Bolton.

From Leyburn the tour turns north on to the A6108, at first surrounded by heathery slopes and then between wooded hills and the River Swale, for a scenic journey to Richmond.

SELECTED PLACES TO VISIT

DARLINGTON
Map ref 2914

The first fare-paying passenger steam trains ran from Darlington to Stockton-on-Tees in 1825, and a Railway Centre and Museum has been created at North Road station, still in use. Exhibits include a railway coach of about 1845 and steam locomotives, among which is Stephenson's *Locomotion No 1*.

Darlington Museum preserves other aspects of the town's history, and has an observation beehive on show during the summer.

EASBY ABBEY
Map ref 1800

Just to the south east of Richmond is Easby Abbey, built on the banks of the River Swale in 1155. The gatehouse is little altered since the 14th century, and the remains include a great refectory and church.

RABY
Map ref 1322

Set in 200 acres of deer park, Raby Castle is mainly 14th-century, with later alterations. The 600-year-old kitchen can still be seen, and there are carriages on display in the coach house.

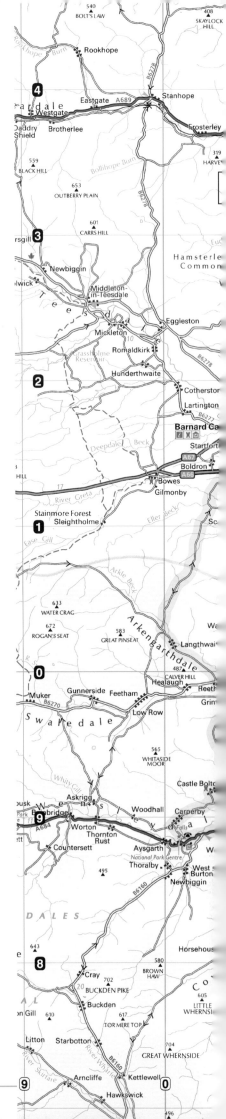

RICHMOND
Map ref 1702

Richmond Castle, founded upon sheer rocks overlooking the River Swale in 1071 to withstand the Saxons, never had its fortifications put to the test, so that much of its fabric has survived. From its splendid 100ft high 12th-century keep are magnificent views across the North York Moors and Swaledale. Two of the towers are left on the massive curtain wall.

The market town grew up around the castle. It has an unusual medieval church with shops built into the walls. Since 1973 the church has housed the Green Howards Regimental Museum, tracing 300 years of regimental history through uniforms, weapons, medals and silver. This award-winning museum also has a special Victoria Cross exhibition.

Other aspects of history are recorded in the Richmondshire Museum, which features lead mining, agriculture, transport (including a railway station model), costume and needlecraft. A highlight of the displays is the set of James Herriot's veterinary surgery from the BBC television series.

Richmond's Georgian Theatre Royal, built in 1788, is the oldest theatre in Britain still in its original form and in use as a live theatre. Its Museum contains the oldest complete set of painted scenery in the country, together with playbills and photographs.

SHILDON
Map ref 2226

The Timothy Hackworth Museum commemorates the work of the railway pioneer who built Sans Pareil, one of the first engines to be made. A replica of the locomotive stands outside the museum in Hackworth's cottage. The line built by Stephenson to transport coal to Stockton rapidly developed into an early passenger route.

WITTON LE WEAR
Map ref 1432

At the upper end of Witton le Wear is a peel tower, part of a medieval manor, while around the River Wear is a nature reserve. On the opposite bank to the village is Witton Castle, with a 14th-century keep.

Stephenson's Locomotion No 1, displayed in the Darlington Railway Museum

FROM JAMES HERRIOT TO JAMES COOK

While the Yorkshire Dales are familiar from James Herriot's popular vet stories, less well-known is the countryside around Middlesbrough which inspired explorer James Cook.

Durham Cathedral is probably the supreme example of man's response to the natural beauty of the region, which contains so many other magnificent churches.

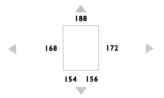

TOUR

THE CLEVELAND AND HAMBLETON HILLS
70 MILES

Leaving Thirsk on the A170, the tour soon zigzags up the 1 in 4 gradient to Sutton Bank. A North York Moors National Park information centre explains the natural history of the area.

Turning sharply right, the tour passes the famous White Horse, created in 1857 by Kilburn village schoolmaster John Hodgson and his pupils. The huge horse, 314ft long and 228ft high, is visible from the A1 and the London-Edinburgh railway line.

Kilburn is known for its woodcarving, a craft popularised locally by Robert Thompson (1876-1955). Furniture bearing his church mouse symbol can be found in buildings around the country, including York Minster and Westminster Abbey.

The tour passes the turning to Shandy Hall, a medieval house where Laurence Sterne wrote *Tristram Shandy* and *A Sentimental Journey,* and which is now a museum. At the Coxwold crossroads, a short detour leads south to Newburgh Priory. Originally built in 1145, the priory has been a private home since 1538.

Coxwold has a church with an octagonal tower and a Breeches Bible dating from 1601. Sterne served as vicar here and his remains lie in the churchyard.

The tour runs along the southern boundary of the National Park to Byland Abbey, where ruins of the church and monastic buildings from the late 12th and early 13th centuries can be seen.

Turning right at Wass, the tour climbs to Ampleforth. Sheltered below the Hambleton Hills' wooded slopes is its college, founded in 1802.

At Oswaldkirk the tour joins the A170 at Sproxton to travel north to Helmsley. A settlement in Roman times, Helmsley is recorded in the *Domesday* Book as a market town. Helmsley Castle was besieged and slighted during the Civil War. The D-shaped keep and spectacular earthwork defences dominate the town.

To the south west is Duncombe Park, ancestral home of the earls of Feversham, built by Vanbrugh in the early 18th century. The house was opened to the public by the present Lord Feversham at Easter 1990. A pleasant terrace walk leads through the grounds to Helmsley Castle.

From Helmsley a detour left off the B1257 shows Rievaulx Abbey to full advantage. The ruined abbey, founded in 1132 for Cistercian monks, stands in the lovely valley of the Rye. Its soaring Gothic arches are outstanding. Rievaulx Terrace, now in the care of the National Trust, is reached from a side road in the village. The $^1/_2$-mile long grass-

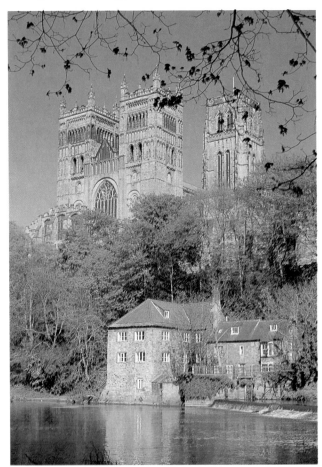

covered terrace and adjoining woodlands give vistas over the abbey and the Rye Valley. Thomas Duncombe built the walk and the mock Ionic and Tuscan temples at each end in 1758. In the basement is an exhibition of 18th-century English landscape design.

The road now travels north through pasture-land and hillfarms, passing on the right Spout House, formerly the Sun Inn, a 16th-century cruck house which has been restored. It crosses the Cleveland Hills at Chop Gate (pronounced Yat), a name thought to derive from the fact that pedlars used the path or gap regularly. The tour briefly ventures north of the National Park boundary to visit Stokesley, a busy little market town below the northern edge of the moors, where the River Leven runs beside the main street.

Following the A172 towards the south-west, shortly after its junction with the A19, the tour passes Mount Grace Priory. The most important Carthusian ruin in England, the 14th-century priory is owned by the National Trust and cared for by English Heritage. The monks lived in cells, one of which has been reconstructed and furnished.

Shortly after, the tour turns right on to the A684 to Northallerton. The area was occupied by the Roman 6th legion, and Anglo-Saxon carved stone fragments in the imposing parish church, the nave of which is early Norman, speak of a pre-Conquest religious settlement.

The tour returns to Thirsk via the A168.

Durham's 12th-century cathedral stands high above the River Wear

SELECTED PLACES TO VISIT

★ CAPTAIN COOK MUSEUM
Map ref 5810

The schoolroom, at Great Ayton, where explorer Captain James Cook was educated is now a museum. On Easby Moor is a 60ft obelisk erected to his memory.

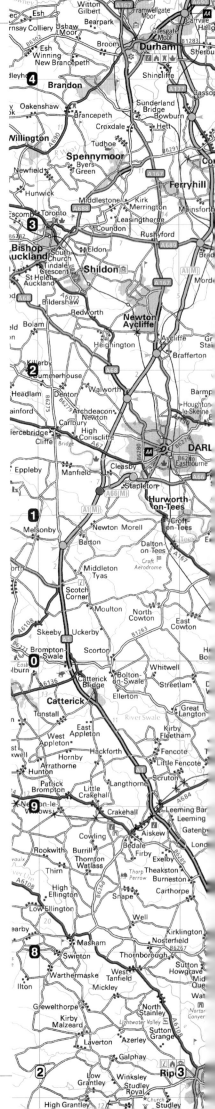

FROM JAMES HERRIOT TO JAMES COOK

▣▲✈▣ DURHAM
Map ref 2742

The monks of Lindisfarne founded an abbey in Durham in AD995 and the magnificent cathedral was built on its site between 1093 and 1133. The Norman castle was created as a defence against the Scots soon after the Conquest. It was not until 1832 that the university was established, as the third English university after Oxford and Cambridge.

In the lofty cathedral lie the remains of the Venerable Bede, St Cuthbert and St Oswald, and relics of the saints are displayed in its Treasury Museum.

Durham's Oriental Museum, part of the university, has artefacts of many periods and countries ranging from ancient Egypt to Japan. The Durham Light Infantry Museum presents the history of the regiment.

▣▣ HARTLEPOOL
Map ref 5134

A medieval port, Hartlepool exported much Durham coal in the 19th century. The Maritime Museum traces the history of the town, the Gray Art Gallery and Museum features local exhibits.

▣ MARTON
Map ref 5216

The birthplace of Captain Cook is now a museum illustrating his voyages of discovery.

▣▲▣ MIDDLESBROUGH
Map ref 5020

County town of Cleveland and now the administrative centre of Teeside, Middlesbrough became prosperous during the Industrial Revolution. The Dorman Museum illustrates the social and industrial history of Middlesbrough and features displays of local pottery.

▣ 🐎 REDCAR
Map ref 6125

Redcar's golden sands attract many holidaymakers, as well as thoroughbreds exercising for the races held at the course in the town centre. A lifeboat museum on the sea front houses the *Zetland*, the oldest surviving lifeboat in the world.

▣▣ STOCKTON-ON-TEES
Map ref 4417

A market town since medieval times and a port since the 18th century, Stockton grew rapidly when the railway came in 1825. Preston Hall Museum depicts Victorian social history with a reconstructed street and working blacksmiths and farriers.

▣ 🐎 THIRSK
Map ref 4282

A busy market town, Thirsk was the inspiration for James Herriot's fictional Darrowby, centre of his stories about a Yorkshire vet. Settled in pre-Roman times, Thirsk was mentioned in the *Domesday* Book.

COAST, CLIFFS AND CASCADES

Long before early man first created settlements on the moors, the sea was eroding the coastline. Whether on the shore or inland, the scenery is spectacular, with deep ravines cutting through the moors, waterfalls cascading down the rocks and the onslaught of the sea constantly bombarding the coast.

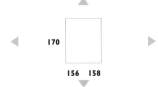

TOUR

WHITBY AND THE NORTH YORKSHIRE MOORS
64 MILES

The tour sets out from Scarborough on the A165 coast road, joining the A171 at Burniston. On the right is the wide expanse of the North Sea, scene of so many shipwrecks and brave deeds by lifeboatmen. The coast is extremely prone to erosion, and the main road runs some way inland, avoiding the crumbling cliffs.

The North York Moors National Park extends from Pickering and Scarborough in the south to just beyond Staithes in the north, where North Yorkshire is divided from Cleveland.

Many standing stones and circles can be found within the man-made forest, as the A171 climbs past Harwood Dale. The tour takes an unclassified road, descending steeply through Fylingthorpe to Robin Hood's Bay. The picturesque village can only be approached on foot; cars must be parked above. Houses cluster together on the steep hillside. One has been turned into an exhibition centre, while the Smuggling Experience helps visitors to picture the excitement of fishing history, as well as its dangerous side. The old coroner's court is now a folk museum.

Another steep road leads north from the car park, to rejoin the A171 to Whitby. The tradition of Christianity in Whitby goes back more than 1,300 years. The first abbey was founded in AD657 by St Hilda, and the Synod of Whitby which established the method of calculating the date of Easter was held here in AD663. The early abbey and its Norman replacement have both been destroyed, and the gaunt ruins on the headland above the town are 13th-century.

Whitby is a picturesque port at the mouth of the River Esk

The 199 steps of Church Stairs towards the abbey lead to St Mary's parish church, with its Norman tower. Bram Stoker used its graveyard as the setting for the opening of *Dracula*.

Whitby is both a fishing port and seaside resort. While apprenticed to a grocer at Staithes, further up the coast, James – later Captain – Cook was first drawn to a seafaring career. The original grocer's shop by Staithes harbour has long since been washed away, and it was from Whitby that Cook sailed in the *Endeavour* in 1768 via Cape Horn to Tahiti and the Australian coast. His house in Grape Lane is now a museum, and Whitby Museum also contains material about Cook among its fascinating exhibits.

There is a strong tradition of sea rescue in the town; Whitby lifeboatmen have won more gold medals from the RNLI than any other crew in the country. The Lifeboat Museum tells the moving story of their gallantry.

From Whitby, the tour turns inland, along Esk Dale to Grosmont, terminus of the North York Moors Railway. The route turns away from the railway in a loop back to the A169 and then crosses and recrosses the railway line by Goathland station. At Goathland a short walk leads to the splendid sight of Mallyan Spout, a waterfall descending 70ft.

The tour continues south, passing the eerie Fylingdales early warning radar domes on the left before reaching Saltersgate Inn. This was a stopping point for weary drivers leading packhorses laden with sea salt and salted fish inland from the coast. A viewpoint above the dramatic Hole of Horcum looks both over the Bridestones Nature

Reserve and prehistoric remains towards the coast and also inland to the ravine separating Levisham from Lockton and the railway making its way down Newton Dale to Pickering.

As the tour approaches Pickering, the ruined 12th-century castle can be seen to the right. Above the main street of the market town stands the medieval parish church which has important 15th-century frescos of biblical scenes. Beside Pickering Beck is the Beck Isle Museum of Rural Life, which recreates the Victorian era through a grocer's shop, printer's workshop, children's room, costume room and kitchen.

A detour to the south of Pickering on the A169 leads to Kirby Misperton. Flamingo Land is a one-price family funpark based around an 18th-century house and 375-acre zoo. More than 1,000 animals, 50 rides and eight international shows are included, and there are many undercover attractions.

Returning to Pickering, the tour follows the southern boundary of the National Park along the A170 back towards the coast. Thornton Dale has 17th-century almshouses, village stocks and market cross, and a short walk reveals delightful thatched cottages and Edwardian houses along the beck.

Ebberston Hall, just before Ebberston village, was built in 1718 by Colen Campbell. Its single-storey interior features carved wood friezes and contemporary furniture, together with family portraits. The surrounding deer park includes a waterfall and canal, with black swans and waterfowl. To the north of the road are many ancient earthworks, as the tour makes its way back to Scarborough.

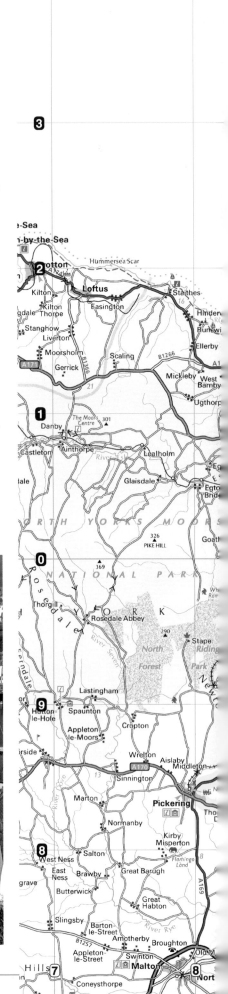

SCALE

0 1 2 3   4 miles

0 1 2 3 4 5 kilometres

North Yorkshire and Cleveland
Heritage Coast

dsborough

Overdale Wyke

rthe

Sandsend

Sandsend Wyke

ley

Whitby

wholm

Saltwick Bay

Ruswarp

Briggswath

Stainsacre

slaby

Sneaton

High Hawsker

eights

Ugglebarnby

Iburndale

Ness Point or
North Cheek

smont

Robin Hood's Bay

Fylingthorpe

Robin Hood's
Bay

Old Peak or
South Cheek

292

A171

Staintondale

Hayburn Wyke

Harwood Dale

O   R   S

Cloughton Wyke

Cloughton

Burniston

Cromer Point

Bridestones
(Rock formations)

Bickley

Silpho

Broxa

Cleveland Way

Langdale
End

Hackness

Suffield

Staindale

ckton

239

Scalby

North   Riding   Forest   Park

River Derwent

Falsgrave

Scarborough

Bee Dale

Sea Cut

Oliver's Mount

TA

West
Ayton

East
Ayton

A170

AA A165

Cayton Bay

Sawdon

Hutton
Buscel

Irton

Osgodby

the Wyke

Ebberston

Ruston

Wykeham

Seamer

Eastfield

B1261

Cayton

A170

Snainton

Brompton

Lebberston

A1039

Filey Brigg

Allerston

Gristhorpe

Filey

Hertford

The   Ca

Muston

Yedingham

Folkton

Willerby

Staxton

Flixton

Filey Bay

B1258

Sherburn

Ganton

Knapton

East Heslerton

Potter
Brompton

Hunmanby

A165

West
Heslerton

A64

Fordon

Reighton

Wold
Newton

Speeton

Thorpe
Bassett

Wintringham

Foxholes

B1229

Buckton

ngton

Woids Way

9

Butterwick

0

Weaverthorpe

Thwing

Burton
Fleming

1

Grindale

2

Bempton

Helperthorpe

COAST, CLIFFS AND CASCADES

By Thornton Beck, in Thornton Dale; one of Yorkshire's prettiest villages

SELECTED PLACES TO VISIT

⑦ FILEY
Map ref 1281

Filey has superb beaches as well as the natural pier of Filey Brigg with views of Scarborough Castle and Flamborough Head. Filey Folk Museum captures the history of the town.

⑦ ✕ 🏛 🐘 🎒 SCARBOROUGH
Map ref 0488

Early Iron Age people were the first to settle here, and the Romans used the defensive headland as a signal station. A Viking raider named Skardi gave his name to the town in AD966, while substantial ruins survive of the Norman castle built on the headland in 1136.

Scarborough has been a fishing port since the 13th century, and its popularity as a spa dates from 1620. During the 19th century the railway brought many visitors.

The Rotunda Museum is an unusual example of an early purpose-built museum. Its changing exhibitions feature local history and archaeology. A frieze showing a geological section of the coast can be viewed. A good head for heights is also required to take full advantage of the Bygone and Maritime Scarborough Exhibition and Lighthouse Tower. Viewing the specimens and exhibits in the museum is less taxing.

Scarborough Art Gallery, in a 19th-century Italian-style villa in The Crescent, has a splendid collection of British portraits and narrative paintings. The former home of the literary Sitwell family, Wood End, also in The Crescent, is now a museum of natural history.

Another literary connection is that of local playwright Alan Ayckbourn, who premieres his plays at the Theatre in the Round before they transfer to London.

Watersplash World, a water theme park, and Marvels Leisure and Amusement Park provide thrills and spills.

NORTH YORK MOORS

Wide, uninterrupted expanses of heather moorland, secluded farming dales and a dramatic coastline are just a few of the ingredients which make up the North York Moors

Designated in 1952, the North York Moors National Park covers an area of 533 square miles. In form it is a high plateau covered with a vast carpet of moorland, a carpet that can be breath-takingly coloured in autumn. The combination of these wonderful, isolated moors with beautiful, hidden dales and a spectacular coastline make this one of the most delightfully varied of all the National Parks. Furthermore, it is, together with Northumberland, the least touristy of the parks; its moors are frequently home only to sheep, pheasants and grouse.

Unlike Northumberland with its artificial boundaries, North Yorks is a physical entity – the boundaries are natural, the overall character somehow defined by them. The Clevedon Hills lie to the north, with the sea to the east, the Tabular Hills to the south and the Hambledon Hills forming a barrier to the west. Beyond the boundaries the view north is over the Eskdale Valley to the Cheviots, south to the Vale of York and the Yorkshire Wolds and, to the west, the Pennines.

Valuable Assets

Some years ago, in the face of opposition from the Parks authority, permission was granted to extract potash from Boulby (within the area of the National Park) on the grounds that it was the only site where this important fertilizer is found in Britain. Many felt this might be treated as a precedent which could be extended to affect other National Parks. In the event, an application for a second site was turned down, and the ruling has not been used elsewhere. The North York Moors National Park faces fewer pressures than several of the other Parks, with tourism, though growing, markedly less intrusive than in areas like the Lake District. Of course, the area will increase in popularity, and the authority will need to make provision to combat the obvious problems such an increase will bring. Little can be done about the oldest problem of all, erosion of the magnificent coastline, with estimated losses of up to 3ft a year occurring in places. Improved agricultural techniques and EC policy has resulted in the loss of some of the moorland – the current value of a well managed grouse moor tends to preclude conversion to arable or other use.

Moorland and Birdlife

Moorland still accounts for about 40% of the acreage of the Park and, wherever heather is managed for red grouse, a varied and exciting wildlife occurs. Bilberry is mixed with heather on the drier slopes while cross-leaved heath grows with mar-grass and rushes on the wetter areas.

Bogs have developed in poorly drained areas in both the valleys and on the high moors and here the plants will invariably include, in addition to *Sphagnum* mosses, various cottongrasses, bog myrtle and bog rosemary and a number of plants which are confined to northern sites such as lesser twayblade.

The haunting cry of the curlew is a common sound on the moors, while the beautiful golden plover, shepherding her bewitching chicks across a moorland road in spring, is an

On the drier moorland slopes bilberry is mixed with the heather

unforgettable sight. The moors are a stronghold of the shyest of our birds of prey, the dashing, low-flying merlin.

The North York Moors Authority is responsible for Levisham Moor, which could almost be termed the archetypal upland moor. The enormous, curving valley of the Hole of Horcum is surrounded by heather moorland into which bracken has encroached. All the plants listed above occur in the reserve, with fascinating rarities including some arctic-alpine plants on the southern limit of their range.

In the lower valleys primrose and bluebell grow on the woodland floor with meadowsweet along the edges of the small streams. Alder and willow flourish here, giving way to oak and a whole range of other trees in the main wooded areas. It is possible to identify small-leaved lime, beech, field maple – at the northern limit of its natural range – and guelder rose among the oak, with some Scots pine.

As the wood gives way to moorland, so birch and rowan take over. The common woodland birds are present – tits, chaffinch, nuthatch and woodpecker among them.

Vale and Dale

Levisham lies on the limestone that creates the comparatively gentle landscape of the Hambleton and Tabular Hills. The high central plateau is

Old Ralph's Cross on Westerdale Moor – the basis for the National Park's symbol

The mysterious, huge hollow in Levisham Moor, known as the Hole of Horcum

mainly sandstone while the sea cliffs are of various formations, mainly laid down in the Jurassic period.

From the centre of the moorland a number of small rivers flow south to join the River Derwent on the Vale of Pickering. Few can immediately name these rivers – the Seth, the Hodge Beck, the Dove, the Severan and the Pickering Beck – yet they have carved a series of lovely, winding, dales whose very names read like poetry to anyone who knows them. They are Bilsdale, Bransdale, Farnsdale, Rosedale and Newtondale and all have claims to be the 'best'.

Farndale is the most famous because of its marvellous spring display of daffodils, although it is equally lovely at other seasons. Bilsdale is the most accessible, with a main road, the B2157, running through it. Bransdale belongs to the National Trust and, partly because there is no through road, it has preserved a very real sense of what life was like 30 or 40 years ago – for much of the year this is far more of a hidden valley than, say, the Doone Valley on Exmoor. Rosedale shows the influence of man, and woman, with reminders of a Cistercian nunnery in the name of the hamlet halfway along its 7-mile length, and some signs of the iron extracting industry which was begun in the medieval

period and continued until the 20th century. Newtondale is probably seen in more relaxed fashion and possibly by more visitors than the others since the wonderfully picturesque North York Moors Railway runs along it on its way to Goathland and Grosmont.

Grosmont is in Esk Dale and the River Esk attracts a series of becks and small rivers which, flowing north to join it, have created a number of short dales, Baysdale, Westerdale, Danby Dale, Great Fryup Dale and Glaisdale – collectively, perhaps the best kept secret of all in this rather secretive National Park.

A Rich Coastline
The Esk enters the sea at Whitby, a town of immense attraction which need not have been omitted from the National Park. The coastline of this whole area, from above Staithes to below Cloughton, has some quite remarkable geological features and areas of wildlife importance. At the landslip of Beast Cliff and the wave-cut platform at Robin Hood's Bay, they combine, for both are nationally famous for the richness of their plant and bird life.

Ancient Landmarks
The symbol of the National Park is a stone cross, based on Ralph's Cross on Westerdale Moor. These medieval waymarks – there are more than 30 of them – are just one reminder of man's long occupancy of the area. The first

The trilling cry of the curlew is often heard over the moors during its courtship flight

settlers and hunters probably arrived at the end of the Neolithic period and operated in a warm, heavily forested landscape. Bronze Age man left burial mounds on many of the ridges and the most tangible reminder of the Roman occupancy is on Wheeldale Moor, where Wade's Causeway is one of the best preserved of their roads.

The Danes left a different legacy, the place names which persist here and across Yorkshire in the Dales. The Normans built castles and encouraged the monasteries. The Cistercians may have chosen difficult, remote places to site their abbeys, but they were usually places of great beauty. Few rival Rievaulx in its setting or the quality of its buildings.

The monks introduced sheep farming, which became the

staple industry of medieval times, supported by a range of quarrying and mining activities such as those at Roseland mentioned above. Stone was used in building, from the abbeys to the present Houses of Parliament, and in the vernacular buildings of the area. Limestone, alum shale, ironstone and Whitby jet were all exploited. Defoe, who devoted little time to describing rural Yorkshire, made mention of its minerals, including alum and jet.

Most of the industries have gone now, but the sheep remain, roaming the moors and dales. Grouse whirr away before the approach of man, still working the land from small, old settlements. There may be pressures for change but, on the North York Moors, the pace of change is refreshingly slow.

SOUTHERN- MOST SCOTLAND

The Mull of Galloway lies at the southernmost tip of Scotland, where the sandy beaches and rich agricultural region enjoy a mild climate influenced by the Gulf Stream. Prehistoric man, drawn to this favoured area, has left many traces of occupation.

The cradle of Christianity in Scotland in the 4th century, the region experienced the bitter side of religion with the persecution of the Covenanters 1,300 years later.

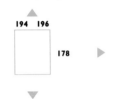

SELECTED PLACES TO VISIT

🦆 ✕ AILSA CRAIG
Map ref 0299
Ten miles offshore from Girvan lies Ailsa Criag, a volcanic island rising more than 1,000ft out of the sea. It is a nesting ground for thousands of seabirds, including gannets and puffins, and the source of granite used to make the stones for the game of curling.

✱ ARDWELL HOUSE
Map ref 1145
On the rocky west coast of Luce Bay at Ardwell is a remarkably well-preserved broch, a type of prehistoric circular stone tower more usually found in the north of Scotland. It has the unusual feature of entrances on both seaward and landward sides. The walls are 13ft thick and the interior is 30ft in diameter.

The gardens and grounds of Ardwell House, with flowering shrubs and woodland walks, are open to the public.

BALLANTRAE
Map ref 0783
The dramatic coast road south from Girvan leads through Kennedy's Pass to Ballantrae, now a thriving centre for agriculture but formerly a smugglers' haunt and fishing port. The imposing ruins of 13th-century Ardstinchar Castle stand at the mouth of the river.

✱ BARGANY GARDENS
Map ref 2400
Bargany's lovely gardens are open to the public. There are woodland walks which display snowdrops, daffodils and bluebells in spring. Ornamental trees and fine azaleas and rhododendrons surround the lilypond. Visitors can buy plants from the gardens.

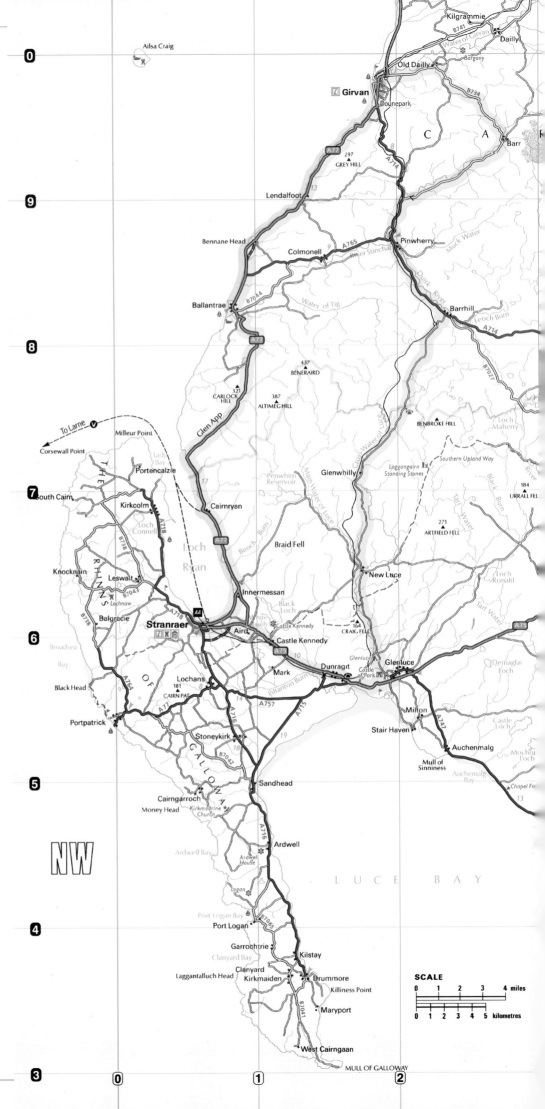

BARSALLOCH FORT
Map ref 3442

Excavations at Barsalloch Fort, west of Monreith, have revealed occupation more than 6,000 years ago by fishermen and food gatherers. This Iron Age fort, enclosed by a horseshoe-shaped ditch 12ft deep and 33ft wide, is poised on the edge of a bluff some 60ft above the shore.

CAIRNRYAN
Map ref 0568

The modern port of Cairnryan, half-way down the east side of Loch Ryan, was created during World War II in preparation for the D-Day invasion and is now used for freight traffic. Lochryan House, built in 1701 in a Dutch style, is largely unspoilt.

CARSCREUGH
Map ref 2361

To the north east of the village of Glenluce are the ruins of Carscreugh Castle, built in 1680.

CASTLE KENNEDY
Map ref 1161

The ivy-clad ruins of Castle Kennedy, destroyed by fire in 1716, still stand between White Loch and Black Loch, surrounded by superb 17th-century gardens which are noted for their flowering shrubs.

CHAPEL FINIAN
Map ref 2749

The remains of this small Norman chapel, or oratory, lie on the coast 5 miles north west of Port William. It is said to have been founded by a blind Irish princess who landed here, bathed her face in the water and had her sight restored.

GLENLUCE ABBEY
Map ref 1858

The remains of Glenluce Abbey stand to the north west of the village on a wooded site, founded in 1190 as a Cistercian house. The south aisle and transept of the abbey church remain and the fine 15th-century vaulted chapter house is almost intact.

LOGAN GARDENS
Map ref 0943

To the north of the small fishing village of Port Logan are Logan Gardens, an outstation of the Edinburgh Royal Botanic Gardens, where rare shrubs, tropical plants, tree-ferns and plants from the warm temperate regions of the southern hemisphere flourish in a walled garden.

MULL OF GALLOWAY
Map ref 1531

On a clear day both Ireland and the Isle of Man can be seen from the Mull, its rocky headland rising 210ft above sea level, at the southernmost point of Scotland. On the top of the Mull stands a 60ft lighthouse built in 1830, and 128 steps lead down to the fog-horn on a railed terrace from which the views are spectacular.

NEWTON STEWART
Map ref 4065

Newton Stewart is a busy market town and educational centre on the River Cree. Visitors can see mohair rugs and scarves being made at the woollen mills. The granite Cree Bridge, built in 1813 to replace one swept away in floods, links the town to Minnigaff. To the south east is Bargaly Glen which is associated with John Buchan's novel, *The Thirty-Nine Steps*.

A recently opened museum in York Road tells the history of the town and The Machers district from prehistoric times. Its displays include a reconstructed forge, kitchens, laundry and schoolroom.

OLD DAILLY
Map ref 2399

In the valley to the northeast of Girvan lies the hamlet of Old Dailly by the ruins of a 14th-century kirk, surrounded by graves of Covenanters. The nearby ford across the Water of Girvan is believed to date from prehistoric times. Further upstream is new Dailly with its growing population.

Close to the Daillys are several occupied castles, including the 16th-century Killochan Castle, a stronghold of the Cathcarts of Carleton, and those of Penkill, Dalquharran and Kilkerran.

ST NINIAN'S CAVE
Map ref 4136

A short moorland walk to the west coast leads to St Ninian's Cave, used by the missionary as a retreat. Crosses on the walls were probably carved by his followers.

STRANRAER
Map ref 0661

Formerly a royal and municipal burgh at the head of the natural harbour of Loch Ryan, Stranraer is a busy seaport for ferries to Northern Ireland and the Isle of Man and an agricultural centre.

The Mull of Galloway, complete with its 60ft lighthouse

The 16th-century castle of St John, headquarters for Graham of Claverhouse during his campaigns of religious persecution, when many Covenanters were held in its dungeon, was used as a town gaol in the 18th and 19th centuries.

WHITHORN
Map ref 4440

Whithorn is one of the oldest Christian centres in Britain and the earliest in Scotland. St Ninian established a monastery and church here, and his shrine later became a place of pilgrimage, visited by Robert Bruce, James IV and Mary Queen of Scots, before such pilgrimages were made illegal in 1581.

Guided tours and a viewing platform show the excavations of the site in progress. Finds include early Christian graves, buildings and sculptured stones. A Viking house has been reconstructed.

The ruins of the adjacent 12th-century Whithorn Priory, erected partly on the foundations originally used by St Ninian, are scant, although the Norman doorway to the nave is recognisable. Early Christian monuments include the 5th-century Latinus stone.

WIGTOWN
Map ref 4355

This medieval town has two crosses, one dating from 1748 with a sundial and the other commemorating the battle of Waterloo. The ancient church, dedicated to St Machutus, lies in ruins adjacent to the parish church which was constructed in 1853. In the churchyard is a 10th-century interlaced cross-shaft, while above the town stands a monument to the Covenanters who were martyred for their beliefs.

North of the Solway Firth lies an area of remote lochs, gentle hills and dense coniferous forests. With places to visit ranging from early Christian monuments to a 20th-century power station, there is much to interest the visitor to this area.

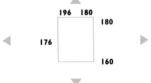

SELECTED PLACES TO VISIT

★ BRUCE'S STONE
Map ref 5577

Bruce's Stone is a memorial to the Battle of Glentrool (1307) at which Robert Bruce defeated a larger English force by rolling boulders down on them. Appropriately, a large granite boulder was placed in position in 1929 to commemorate the event.

⌖ CAIRN HOLY CHAMBERED CAIRNS
Map ref 5253

Close to Ravenshall Point are Cairn Holy Chambered Cairns, survivors of a larger group, dating from the Neolithic period. The bigger of the two remaining cairns is remarkably fine and taken together they represent the best of the Clyde group of cairns. When excavated in 1949 the two tombs produced a number of valuable finds including a flint knife and Beaker pottery.

⚔ CARDONESS CASTLE
Map ref 5855

Overlooking the Water of Fleet is the old McCulloch stronghold of Cardoness Castle, which dates from the 15th century. A tower house, it was acknowledged by an English spy to be very strong. The tower has been unoccupied since the end of the 17th century.

⚔ CARSLUITH CASTLE
Map ref 4854

On the coast are the ruins of 16th-century Carsluith Castle with its well preserved four-storeyed tower. Few details are known of its history, although it belonged to the Church in the Middle Ages.

CRUGGLETON
Map ref 4745

The hamlet of Cruggleton overlooking its bay, has a part Norman church with a rather fine 12th-century chancel arch, doors and windows. Cruggleton Castle today is an interesting ruin in an

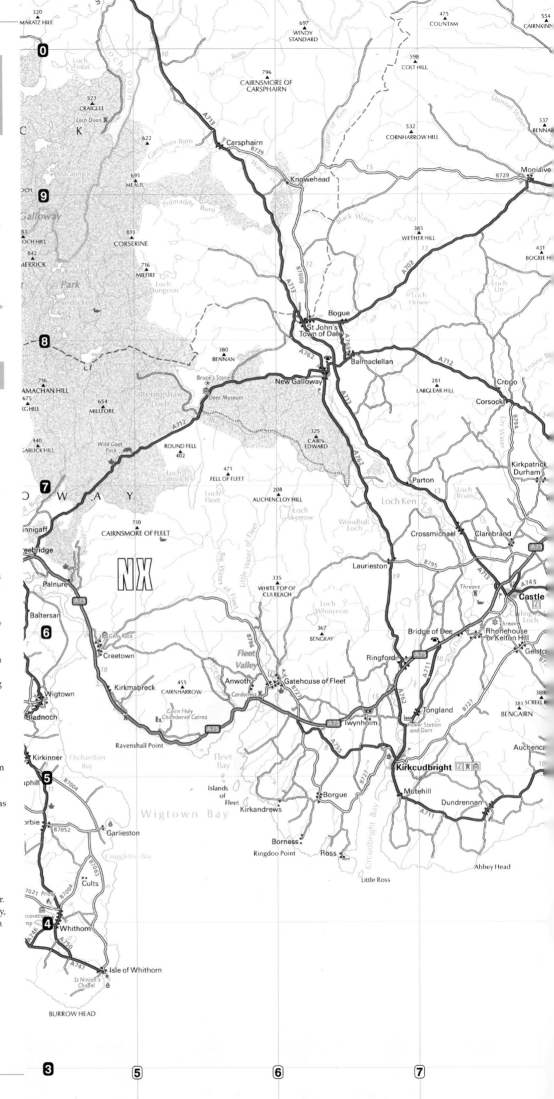

area which maintains a pleasing remoteness – which belies its former reputation as a stronghold.

🏛 DUNDRENNAN ABBEY
Map ref 7546

Dundrennan Abbey was founded in the late 12th century by Cistercian monks and is a daughter-house of Rievaulx Abbey. Although much reduced the abbey remains a marvellous example of medieval workmanship.

Alan, the last of the lords of Galloway is buried here – a multilated effigy of a knight in the north transept may represent him – and the abbey was probably endowed by the lords of Galloway. Mary, Queen of Scots spent her last night on Scottish soil at Dundrennan on 15th May 1568. She sailed from nearby Port Mary, seeking shelter in England, where she was imprisoned and eventually executed.

🏛 GALLOWAY DEER MUSEUM
Map ref 5576

Galloway Deer Museum has been established in a converted farm near to Clatteringshaws Loch. In addition to detailed features on deer and other wildlife, there is information on the geology and history of the Galloway area. The museum is part of the 250 square mile Galloway Forest Park owned by the Forestry Commission.

GARLIESTON
Map ref 4746

Garlieston is a little port, founded by the then future 7th Earl of Galloway, Lord Garlies, in the 18th century. Galloway House (not open) was built by the 6th Earl in 1740 and enlarged in the 19th century by William Burn – who was best known for his development of Scottish Baronial. Sir Robert Lorimer decorated the hall but, although involved in garden design in Fife, he did not have a hand in the lovely gardens here. Covering 30 acres Galloway House Gardens feature snowdrops and daffodils, rhododendrons and azaleas. There is a walled garden and a camellia house.

☑ 🌿 GATEHOUSE OF FLEET
Map ref 6056

Gatehouse is a planned town, laid out, as so many of its type were, in the 18th century and intended to be a centre for cotton manufacturing. Standing on the Water of Fleet, near where it enters Fleet Bay, it had good transport potential and initially developed until there were six cotton mills, a brewery and a tannery. Within about a hundred years trade had declined and the town lost its impetus. Several buildings survive, including Cally House – now a hotel – and one of the mill buildings, restored as a visitor centre.

In an inn at Gatehouse Burns is said to have written the words of *Scots Wha Hae*.

Above: *This granite boulder, Bruce's Stone, marks a victory over the English*

Below: *The Isle of Whithorn is now a busy holiday resort*

🏛 GEM ROCK MUSEUM
Map ref 4759

The Gem Rock Museum at Creetown has been assembled by the owners of the museum while travelling around the world. The collections of minerals and gemstones are displayed in three large exhibition halls and includes a gemstone workshop. The village itself, a rather charming place, features in Sir Walter Scott's *Guy Mannering* as Porton Ferry.

★ ISLE OF WHITHORN
Map ref 4736

The Isle of Whithorn was once an island but is now a rather busy holiday resort, popular with the yachting community. There is a small, charming 14th-century chapel dedicated to St Ninian and almost certainly used by pilgrims travelling to Whithorn.

☑ ✕ 🏛 KIRKCUDBRIGHT
Map ref 6852

Kirkcudbright was a great place for artists in the late 19th century and Broughton House was the home of E A Hornel. It now houses an exhibition of his paintings. The Stewartry Museum reflects the influence of artists on the community, but covers a much wider spectrum in its many fascinating displays.

The town is the capital of old Stewartry – the term means that the area was Crown property, administered by a steward, not a sheriff – and has some very pleasing features, including the

Mercat Cross of 1610 and a fine toll booth.

🏛 POWER STATION AND DAM
Map ref 6854

The South of Scotland Electricity Board has devised a tour of the Galloway hydro-electricity scheme at Tongland, which includes a video presentation and a visit to the power station and dam. When the salmon are returning to spawn, the fish ladder at the dam is popular.

All that remains of Dundrennan Abbey, founded over 800 years ago

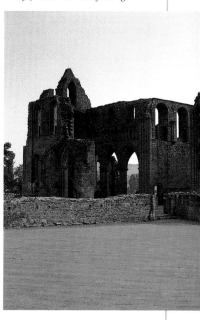

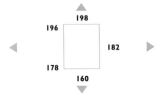
Called 'The Queen of the South' by Sir Walter Scott, Dumfries is the hub of this gentle Lowland area, with roads radiating in all directions, making this a good centre from which the visitor may explore the oddly named village of St John's Town of Dalry, and impressive Drumlanrig Castle.

```
        ▲
       198
  196  ┌───┐
  ◄    │   │   182   ►
       └───┘
  178
       160
        ▼
```

TOUR

SOLWAY FIRTH, LOCH KEN AND NITHSDALE
83 MILES

Well known ballads and little known country, this farming area of Dumfries and Galloway possesses a variety of interests.

The tour leaves Dumfries by the A710, travelling south parallel to the Solway Firth.

Sweetheart Abbey takes its name from Lady Devorguilla, wife of John Balliol, founder of the Oxford college. After the death of her husband she had his heart embalmed and, when she died, it was buried with her in the abbey church which she had endowed in 1273. This Cistercian abbey lacks a roof, but much of the attractive sandstone building remains intact.

First mentioned in 1559, the corn mill at New Abbey was, almost certainly, built by the monks of the abbey. The present white painted mill probably dates from the late 18th century. It has a pitch-back wheel, not often found in small mills.

Just south of the charming hamlet of Kirkbean are Arbigland Gardens with an ancient broadwalk leading to a woodland garden. The gardens have been developed over three centuries.

A short detour leads past Sandyhills to Rockcliffe, both small resorts developed as a result of the Victorian passion for sea bathing. It is possible to walk along the rough coastline from Rockcliffe to Kippford, a scattered village with a tradition of smuggling but now a fine high-tide anchorage for sailing craft. The path between the villages, the Jubilee Path, is owned by the National Trust for Scotland and there are superb views from it over the nearby headlands to the distant hills of Galloway. Between the villages is the Mark of Mote, a 100ft-high granite outcrop concealing between its two peaks a Dark Age hill-top settlement. In the 1970s excavations uncovered artefacts suggesting that the site was an important centre for highly skilled metal working by Celtic craftsmen. Just offshore is Rough Island, a 20-acre bird sanctuary also owned by the NTS and accessible at low tide.

At the mouth of the River Urr is Dalbeattie which was, until the arrival of the railways, the main point of sea-borne trade for the area. The town exported local granite around the world – much of the Thames Embankment in London is built with material from Dalbeattie. Crossing the River Urr, the tour continues west on the A745 through Castle Douglas. Standing on an island in the River Dee near Castle Douglas is Threave Castle, a bleak, four-storey ruin built in the 14th century. The Threave estate was given to the National Trust for Scotland with the object of protecting wildfowl and there is access to the Threave Wildfowl Refuge on the banks of the Dee from November to March. A mile west of Castle Douglas is Threave Garden, renowned for its springtime displays of daffodils (over 200 species) and flowering shrubs. Since 1960 it has been a teaching garden and, although containing much formal planting, a place where many visitors find ideas and inspiration for their own gardens.

Retrace the route and turn north-west by the A713. Halfway along Loch Ken is the tiny estate village of Parton with a delightful terrace of cottages facing the road. Remain on the eastern shore of Loch Ken to reach St John's Town of Dalry. Its name is said to derive from the old tradition that John the Baptist rested in the village during his supposed travels through Britain. Set on a steep hill, the houses along its main street demonstrate a wide range of architectural styles.

From St John's, the route lies north-east through bleak moorland and rough pastureland. For a time, the switchback road is accompanied by Blackmark Burn and later by Castlefairn Water which joins two other streams near Moniaive. This pretty village of whitewashed houses was originally two separate communities.

Three miles to the east is the attractive Maxwelton House, set round three sides of a courtyard. Birthplace of Annie Laurie, who rejected William Douglas and was immortalized in his love song.

Further north, among lowland hills in the pleasant valley of the Nith is Thornhill, a small town with strong memories of the Covenanters. Just past the attractive village of Carronbridge the route makes a detour to Drumlanrig Castle, a remarkable multi-turreted castle built in pink sandstone. Approached over a fine bridge across the Nith and set in beautiful woodland – so well landscaped as to appear natural – the house is a breathtaking paradox. The front is a riot of windows, balustrades and towers in a Baroque style, while the rest is very simple. Inside are outstanding collections of paintings and furniture.

The route now heads south passing Ellisland Farm. Robert Burns leased this farm beside the Nith for three years composing, among other poems, *Tam O'Shanter*. It is open to the public and contains Burns memorabilia. Stay on the A76 for the return to Dumfries.

The entrance to a mineshaft in the lead mining area of Wanlockhead

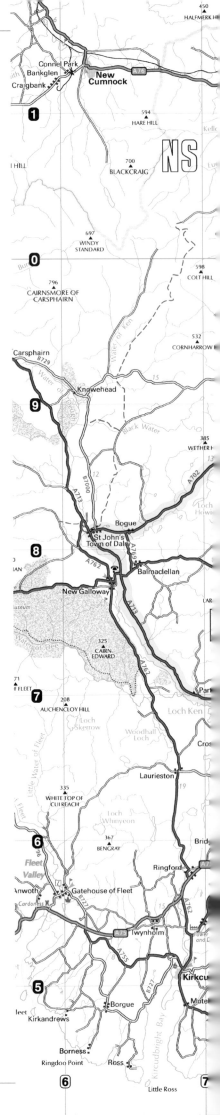

THE HINTERLAND OF DUMFRIES

✠ CAERLAVEROCK CASTLE
Map ref 0265

Overlooking the marshes are the ruins of the 13th-century Caerlaverock Castle. Frequently under siege during the Border wars it was reduced to ruins in 1640. Built of sandstone, it has a romantic appearance.

CAERLAVEROCK NATIONAL NATURE RESERVE
Map ref 0365

Caerlaverock is one of the largest remaining salt-marshes in Britain, of particular importance as the winter home of the entire Spitsbergen population of barnacle geese, many other wildfowl and the most northerly breeding site of the natterjack toad. Visitors are well catered for.

⌂ DRUMCOLTRAN TOWER
Map ref 8668

Drumcoltran Tower is a 16th-century, three storeyed, tower house.

DUMFRIES
Map ref 9776

The largest town in the south-west of Scotland, Dumfries stands beside the River Nith at the centre of a largely agricultural area. It has a long and significant history, for it was here, in 1306, that Robert Bruce killed Edward I's representative and precipitated the Wars of Independence. Over the centuries Dumfries has acquired a number of attractive sandstone buildings and is justifiably known as the Queen of the South.

⚘ MABIE FOREST
Map ref 9571

Throughout the coastal area of Dumfries and Galloway there are a series of fine viewpoints overlooking the Solway Firth and few surpass those at Mabie. From picnic places provided by the Forestry Commission, the walks spread out over a hillside. Developed from old woodland surrounding Mabie House the woods contain an unusual number of species.

⌂ ORCHARDTON TOWER
Map ref 8155

At Palnackie, Orchardton Tower is an unusual 15th-century circular tower built by John Cairns.

WANLOCKHEAD
Map ref 8613

Lead mining was carried on in the Lowther Hills from Roman times until the 1950s. At Wanlockhead a blacksmith's forge has been well restored and forms the visitor centre for a fascinating museum.

In addition there is an outdoor trail. At Lochnell visitors are taken into the mine and guided along a narrow passage where a vein of lead can still be seen.

CARLISLE TO HAWICK

Dissected by the two fast roads which converge on the M6 above Carlisle, this part of the Borders and west along the Solway Firth forms an area which remains unexplored by many tourists. Historically the area is very well served with medieval priories at Lanercost and Wetheral and the remarkable stone cross at Ruthwell.

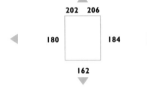

	202	206	
180			184
	162		

SELECTED PLACES TO VISIT

ANNAN
Map ref 2065

Many of Annan's red stone buildings are a product of the Victorian era when the growth of fishing first attracted anglers to the River Annan.

CARLISLE
Map ref 4056

Always strategically valuable, Carlisle's long history dates from prehistoric times. Agricola founded a settlement here in AD78 and his fort was replaced by the town of Luguvalium as the importance of Hadrian's Wall grew in the following century. The Normans began the building of the castle and the priory church, which became the cathedral in 1133.

The Castle was fortified by William Rufus in 1092, the keep and defensive walls were added in the 12th century. The unusually low, wide battlements were introduced following the development of heavy artillery in the 16th century. In the 19th century much of the castle was demolished but the inner and outer

Lanercost Priory, founded in 1166, suffered much during the Border Wars

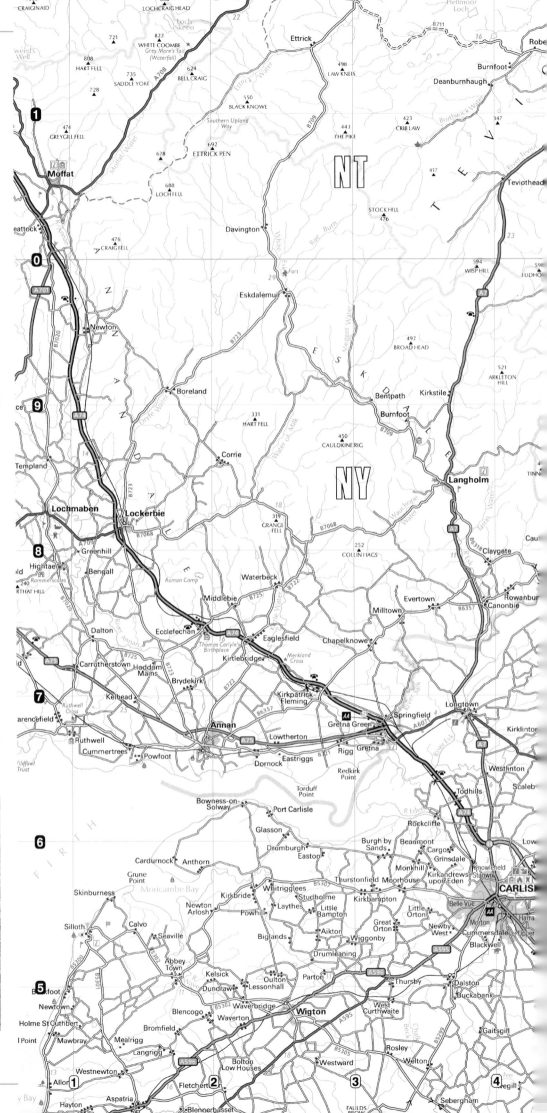

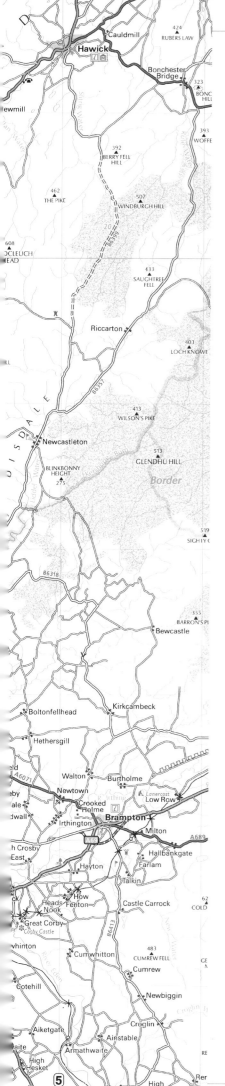

gatehouses survive with the curtain walls enclosing the inner and outer baileys, and the keep.

Carlisle Cathedral is the second smallest in England. The central part of the chancel and, in particular, the east window rank among the finest surviving Decorated architecture in England. Forty-six superbly carved choir stalls, dating from the early 1400s, add to the glories of a cathedral which, although much changed over the centuries, has retained the essential character of a medieval building.

◪ THOMAS CARLYLE'S BIRTHPLACE
Map ref 1974

Thomas Carlyle was born at Ecclefechan in 1795. He left the area at the age of fourteen, to go to Edinburgh University, but stipulated in his will that he should be buried in the village. The family house was built by his father and uncle, both master masons, and is typical of the artisan's house of the period. Restored to its 19th-century appearance it contains manuscript letters and personal belongings.

✳ CORBY CASTLE
Map ref 4753

Corby Castle incorporates a pele tower, and has been owned by the Howard family since the 17th century. The gardens, laid out in the 18th century, run along the river for about a mile. They are at their best in spring and early summer.

◪ CRAIGLEUCH
Map ref 3487

A baronial mansion here houses the Craigleuch Collection, which consists of ancient artefacts made from wood, jade, ivory and coral plus hundreds of rare tribal sculptures and prehistoric stone pipes carved as animals and birds.

▣ GRETNA GREEN
Map ref 3367

Gretna has a long and dramatic history – it was destroyed during the Border wars of the 14th century but tends to be remembered for its traffic in instant marriages. Partly for its proximity to the Border, the Old Blacksmith's Shop became the centre for these weddings, performed by an 'anvil priest' assisted by two witnesses. In 1940 an Act of Parliament finally stopped 'anvil marriages'.

★ GREY MARE'S TAIL
Map ref 1815

The Grey Mare's Tail is a spectacular waterfall created by the 200ft plunge of the Tail Burn from its 'hanging' valley to join Moffat Water. The falls are named after Tam O'Shanter's mare in Burns's poem. Sir Walter Scott was a regular visitor to the area – he describes the falls in *Marmion*.

▣▣ HAWICK
Map ref 5115

The prosperity of Hawick is firmly based on sheep – it has a thriving

The Grey Mare's Tail waterfall, created by the Tail Burn

market and woollen mills feature in its buildings. In a fine parkland setting by the River Teviot is Wilton Lodge, containing a museum concentrating on the history and trade of the Borders, but including subjects as varied as natural history and rugby.

⚔ HERMITAGE CASTLE
Map ref 4996

This was formerly a stronghold of the Douglas clan, dating mainly from the 14th century. It has been well restored and has attractive gardens.

⚔ HIGHTAE'S CASTLE AND HIGHTAE LOCHS
Map ref 0777

The reed and woodland fringed Castle and Hightae Lochs provide a valuable wetland habitat for large numbers of greylag geese and a few pink-footed geese.

◪ LANERCOST PRIORY
Map ref 5564

The priory at Lanercost, in the lovely wooded valley of the River Irthing, was founded in about 1166. Given its proximity to Hadrian's Wall, it was inevitable that the priory would suffer during the Border wars. In 1296 the claustral buildings were burnt out, and in 1346 the land and buildings were wasted by King David II. In 1306 the mortally ill Edward I stayed at Lanercost for six months, at great cost to the resources of the community.

⚑ NEWCASTLETON
Map ref 4787

Newcastleton, in the Border valley of Liddesdale, featured in Sir Walter Scott's historical novel *Guy Mannering*. The village consists of a large central square and two smaller squares linked by a main street. It is a model village, re-established in 1793 by the Duke of Buccleuch on

the site of Copshaw Holme – a village probably destroyed by Cromwell's troops. The Duke leased the cottages to local craftsmen.

⚑ POWFOOT
Map ref 1565

Powfoot owes its beginnings to the 18th-century interest in sea-bathing, and is today the site of a challenging golf course. The views across the Solway Firth to the hills of the Lake District are simply magnificent.

★ RUTHWELL CROSS
Map ref 1068

In farming country close to the Solway Firth a parish church houses one of the great treasures of the 7th century, the Ruthwell Cross. The splendid 18ft-high carved stone cross is now set in a specially built apse in the church. Two of the four faces show scenes from the life of Christ; the others show scroll work, and parts of an ancient poem, *The Dream of the Rood*, in Runic characters. Broken up in the 18th century, it was restored by a 19th-century minister.

◪ RUTHWELL MUSEUM
Map ref 1067

Dr Henry Duncan, in addition to his duties as parish minister, founded the first savings bank in the world – the Duncan Savings Bank Museum is now housed in a cottage beside the original bank.

★ WETHERAL PRIORY GATEHOUSE
Map ref 4654

A Benedictine priory was founded at Wetheral in 1106-12 but only the 15th-century three-storey crenellated gatehouse has survived, serving as the vicarage for the parish church.

HADRIAN'S WALL AND HEXHAM

Here is the historic heart of Northumberland; the wall the Romans built to divide Scotland from England. In majestic sweeps it traverses the Northumbrian fells, beginning just west of Newcastle and leading to Carlisle; a joy to those interested in history, archaeology or, simply, magnificent scenery. In contrast, Hexham will bring the traveller sharply back to the present!

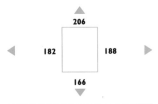

```
          ▲
        206
  ◀  182     188  ▶
        166
          ▼
```

TOUR

HADRIAN'S WALL AND THE SOUTH TYNE VALLEY
62 MILES

The tour starts at Hexham – with its almost medieval feel – heading

bridge abutments which carried Hadrian's Wall across the river.

The straight but deeply undulating B6318 – one of General Wade's military roads – enters the Northumberland National Park (see page 186) between Chester's Fort and the Temple of Mithras at Carrawburgh. Not yet fully excavated, the fort (Brocolitia) lies beneath grass earthworks. The Mithraeum was discovered by a farmer in 1949 and excavated in the early 1950s. It is unusually well preserved, having been embedded in a peat bog. The interior details on the site are copies, but the originals are in the Museum of Antiquities, Newcastle.

Housesteads Roman Fort is the most visited of all the sites along Hadrian's Wall, and the reasons are not difficult to find. Vercovicium is dramatically situated on the exposed whinstone ridge, giving outstanding views. The 5-acre fort site, not yet fully excavated, has the only known Roman hospital in Britain. A civil settlement outside the walls and a series of field systems reflect the changing patterns of agricultural practice over a period of at least 2,000 years. The National Trust, who own the site, and English Heritage, provide a fine visitor centre and museum respectively.

north following the course of the River North Tyne, to Chester's Fort and Museum on Hadrian's Wall, across the lovely 18th-century five-arched bridge at Chollerford. Seemingly a rather disjointed site set in parkland beside the Tyne, Chester's repays careful study and a good place to start is the museum. Purpose-built by Norman Shaw for the Clayton family – who owned and developed the site – it is now maintained as an example of museum layout of the early 20th century.

Within the walls of a fort (Cilurnum) lie the remains of the commanding officer's house and bath-house, barrack blocks and headquarters building. Outside the walls is the remarkably well preserved communal bath-house and a large civil settlement. A short distance away are the remains of the

A mile or so on from Housesteads, south of the road, is Chesterholm (Vindolanda), a partially excavated fort and large civil settlement close to the old frontier along the Stanegate, a road built by Agricola.

Also on Stanegate, off the tour near Gilsland, is Carvoran Roman Army Museum. The unexcavated fort, once home to the only archer company on Hadrian's Wall, stands beside a museum devoted to describing the Roman army.

At Greenfield the tour turns east to Haltwhistle, a small grey stone town, lying beside the River South Tyne. Effectively by-passed by the A69, Haltwhistle is worth visiting for its exceptional Early English church.

After Haltwhistle the direction is south, along minor roads to the

A689 and on to Alston. Alston, in Cumbria, claims to be the highest market town in England. Lead mining has long been a local industry, and the town developed in the 19th century when the mining company built some good housing for the miners. With its steep, cobbled, main street the town has a rather old-fashioned air. The South Tynedale Railway starts at the station, running through a beautiful Pennine valley for about 1½ miles before returning to Alston.

From Alston the tour joins the A686 heading north-east to Langley, through superb moorland scenery, now designated as an Area of Outstanding Natural Beauty (the North Pennines AONB). North of the road is Allen Banks (NT), 194 acres of lovely, mature deciduous wood clothing the valley of the River Allen. Originally laid out as the pleasure gardens of Ridley Hall, they contain 14 miles of riverside paths, a tarn and fine views towards Hadrian's Wall.

SELECTED PLACES TO VISIT

▦ BLACK MIDDENS BASTLE HOUSE
Map ref 7890
Owned by English Heritage, this is a classic example of a

Hadrian's Wall, which originally ran for 73½ miles with ditches either side

Northumbrian bastle – a defensive farmhouse with accommodation for animals at ground level and an outside staircase to the first floor living room.

▲ BLANCHLAND
Map ref 9650
Blanchland village is indivisibly bound to the abbey and its buildings, several having uses never contemplated by the Premonstratensian Canons who built them. Entrance to the square is beyond the large, 15th-century abbey gatehouse. The square may have been the outer courtyard of the abbey and the hotel was the abbey guest house, its garden the cloister. Much of the present village was

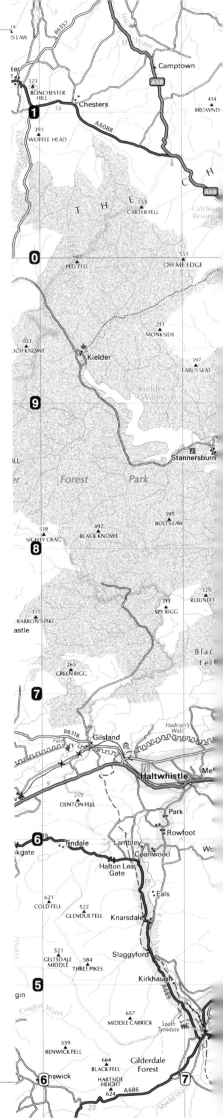

HADRIAN'S WALL AND HEXHAM

built by trustees of the Crowe estate in the 18th century to accommodate lead mine workers.

⛏ CRAGSIDE
Map ref 0603

Cragside House is dramatically perched on rock above a wooded gorge built by Norman Shaw for William Armstrong, inventor, arms manufacturer and philanthropist. There is a huge drawing room, lit by a curved glass roof and the library has stained glass by William Morris. Cragside was the first house in the world to be lit by electricity generated by water-power. Full of Victoriana and heavily Teutonic, it is almost a definitive statement of the taste and character of a 19th-century self-made man.

Lord Armstrong transformed the grounds into a Country Park by planting millions of trees, diverting streams, creating lakes, terraces and a waterfall. An insight into his other achievements can be gained by visiting the Armstrong Energy Centre in the old stable block, below the house and overlooking one of the lakes.

🏛🏠 HEXHAM
Map ref 9265

Hexham is a bustling shopping and market town on the banks of the River Tyne, serving a wide area of Northumberland. The turbulent past of Hexham is not reflected in its finest building, the 12th-century abbey which stands beside the market place. Part of the church is even older, the apse and crypt surviving from the church built by St Wilfred in AD678. The abbey possesses several Anglo-Saxon items but the medieval furnishings are outstanding, particularly the misericords and the night stairs used by monks on their way to night time services – said to be haunted, they are the best preserved of any in Britain. The Augustinians adopted the abbey as a priory church in 1113, altering it considerably; it underwent further, inappropriate, alterations in Victorian times. Hexham has various fine buildings including the 12th-century Priory Gate, the 14th-century Manor Office, the early 15th-century Moot Hall and the 17th-century Grammar School.

⛏ WALLINGTON
Map ref 0385

Wallington House was built around the remains of a 17th-century castle, with its delicate 18th-century plasterwork on the ceilings and interesting 19th-century murals in the central hall.

Capability Brown attended school at the estate village of Cambo and it would be nice to think that he worked on the garden at Wallington, but the only formal evidence is of his plans for the setting of the ornamental lake at Rothley on the estate. The gardens, with their woods and walks, wall garden and conservatory contrast with the surrounding moorland.

NORTHUMBERLAND

The remote Northumberland National Park is a place of wild, untamed beauty which can be explored in comparative peace, often only sharing the area with birds and animals

Northumberland has a marvellous coastline, yet its National Park, set up in 1956, is entirely land-locked. At the time, it appeared that the greatest threat to conservation in the area was to the Cheviots and the moors north of Hadrian's Wall. The problems identified in 1956 have not gone away – the Ministry of Defence still uses large tracts of the Park for military training and Forestry Commission plantations disfigure the landscape – but the Park authority has ensured that they have not become worse. Also, the coastal scenery remains under less threat and is now protected by both Heritage Coast and Area of Outstanding Natural Beauty status. Organisations like the National Trust and the Nature Conservancy Council are actively involved and there is now a Coast Management Plan.

An imaginative selection of boundaries was involved in setting up the Northumberland National Park, since it was

Peel Crags are typical of the exposed rocks found in Northumberland

necessary to link two distinct areas. The result does have a rather artificial appearance – unlike, say, North Yorkshire, where boundaries are naturally defined by the land mass.

Undiscovered Beauty
No one has fully explained why the Northumberland National Park remains stubbornly undiscovered. The suggestion is often made that, somehow, knowledge of the bloody history of the area affects visitors, making them feel ill at ease. No other Park has so few settlements within its boundaries – perhaps it is

Left: *The siskin, associated with conifers, can be found in Northumberland's forests*
Below: *Northumberland's grouse moors provide a perfect home for the short-eared owl*

simply too difficult to reach from the major centres of population. Certainly, the motorist will discover that no road directly links the north and south of the Park, but this is not a unique situation. Whatever the reason, even the Tyneside towns seem not to have that affinity with the countryside that the towns of South Yorkshire or South Wales share with the Peak District and the Brecons respectively.

The Dividing Line
The southern limit of the Park extends to just below Hadrian's Wall to secure the bleak, windswept commons lying immediately to the north of the Wall. The wildest of the Park's scenery, it shades into Wark Forest, one of nine Forestry Commission Plantations comprising the Border Forest. Since 1926 the Commission has planted 145,000 acres of Scots pine, Norway spruce and Japanese larch to create this, the largest man-made forest in western Europe.

North of Wark Forest the boundary of the Park is nipped in to a narrow waist along the winding valley of the River North Tyne which only begins to widen as it leaves the Park, near Bellingham. Across the Tyne lie more commons, then Redesdale and the only major road, the A68 – slicing the Park almost exactly in half.

Beyond the A68 the Park

widens out, extending from Carter Bar on the Scottish border to the Simonside hills east of Otterburn. An area of heather moorland, it is here, between Redesdale and Upper Coquetdale, that the Ministry of Defence maintains a major presence. Clearly, Parliament is the proper forum for discussion over the balance to be struck between the requirements of defence and conservation. However it is over 30 years since Parliament *specifically* set aside this area for the enjoyment of the public – still denied access to large tracts.

Hills and Dales
The Coquet is one of the loveliest rivers in England and Upper Coquetdale runs almost the width of the Park. The river rises under the grass-covered ridges of the Cheviot Hills which form the western flank of the Park. Breamish Valley comes closest to being the `honeypot' of the Park; from Ingram a road runs almost due west into the heart of this increasingly rugged valley.

Geologically, the Cheviots are the centre of the region, a centre of lava and granite, ringed by soft sandstone, on which the lowland farms have developed. A further ring consists of hard rocks, driven upwards to form ridges, inner surfaces worn into steep slopes and crags, outer sloping away in typical glacier patterns. This pattern is repeated, the outer farmed area broken by outcrops of sandstone and the remarkable feature of hard dolerite rocks known as the Great Whin Sill.

Because there is such a diversity of habitat in the Park, the wildlife is correspondingly varied. Conservationists – and most flowering plants – may have an in-built aversion to large coniferous forests, but birds and animals do not, and roe deer have become common in areas like Wark Forest. Badger, fox and red squirrel have joined the roe deer in colonising the forest, while birds like goldcrest, crossbill and siskin are always at home in conifers; the siskin has prospered and greatly extended its range since the Forestry Commission began its work.

Native woodland, mostly confined to valley sites and principally comprised of sessile oak, provide a habitat for a more varied wildlife. Heath bedstraw and tormentil grow under the oak while birch is invading the moorland in places, growing over heather and *Sphagnum* mosses.

A Seasonal Habitat

Loughs are fairly common; they may contain lime-rich waters or, on the high ground, be surrounded by acid bogs. When in open land they attract many wildfowl – in winter, goldeneye join regulars like teal and wigeon and it is not uncommon to see migrating pink-footed, greylag and bean geese, while whooper swans also use the loughs to rest and feed. Lime-rich sites naturally attract many plants and slowly silt up, extending and altering the range of habitat still further. Acid bogs form on high land, including the Cheviots – plants will include heather, cloudberry, bilberry and cottongrass.

The grouse moors support well-managed heather stands and are home to typical moorland birdlife – dunlin, golden plover, short-eared owl and the curlew, symbol of the Park. The crags hold perhaps the richest plant variety of all, partly because the ubiquitous sheep cannot graze the vegetation, but mainly because the rocks are so varied. Both the Whin Sill and the sandstone crags have several specialised plants.

A Peaceful Existence

Northumberland has more obvious signs of 20th-century man's occupancy than any other National Park, but earlier men left some impressive traces – the large Iron Age hill-fort on Yeavering Bell and Hadrian's Wall are obvious examples. The Romans left many other reminders of their occupation but, unusually, the Normans did not. There are motte and bailey mounds in one or two places but otherwise the area seems to have been left to local overlords. Throughout the early Middle Ages skirmishes were a regular part of Border life, with the many full-scale wars between England and Scotland invariably affecting the region. The pele house,

Right: Recognised by its slender, square stems, hedge bedstraw grows on roadside banks
Below: The Cheviot Hills, near Yeavering, show their typical smooth-topped conical shape

and the smaller bastle house, formed the basic defence against the Scottish raiders from the 13th century onwards. Then, as now, farming was the major industry, although the habit of dividing farms equally among sons on a father's death, led to uneconomic units being created.

Farming is still the largest employer but tourism is increasing in importance, although the relative remoteness of the Park will probably mean that it will never be over-visited. Those who love this part of Northumberland for the sense of isolation, even of slight menace on the empty hills, will not complain if this remains the undiscovered National Park.

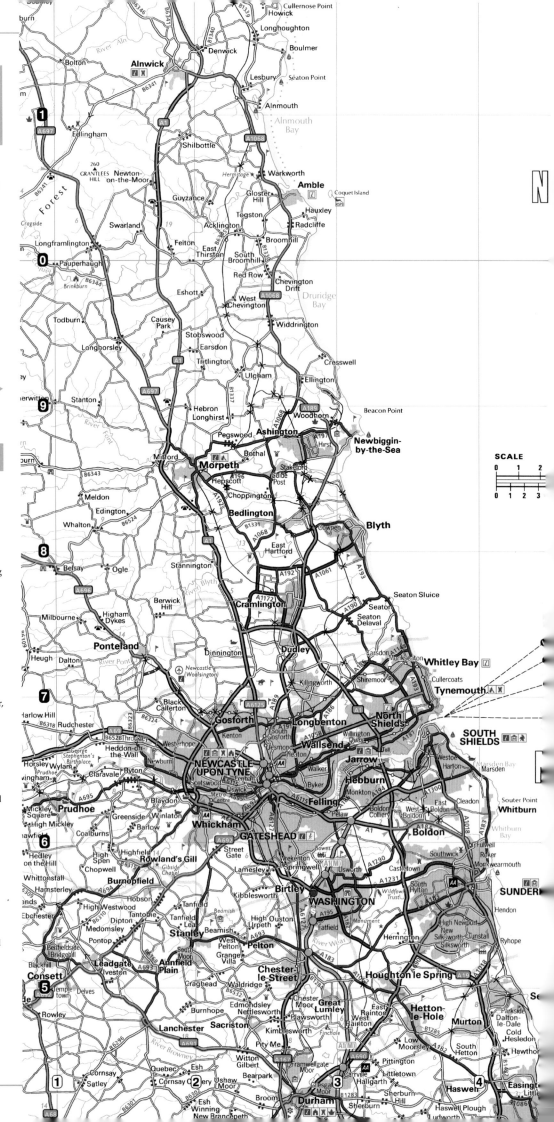

NEWCASTLE AND TYNESIDE

The revitalised city and industrial centre of Newcastle-upon-Tyne is fast becoming recognised as the major focus for arts and recreation in northern England, with its art galleries, museums, theatres and other places of learning and entertainment.

The city was birthplace of the railway pioneer, George Stephenson, whose innovation originally made this area of coastline accessible. The resorts are as popular today as then.

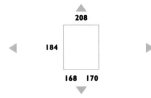

208
184
168 170

SELECTED PLACES TO VISIT

ALNMOUTH
Map ref 2510

The seaport of Alnmouth on the River Aln was transformed in 1806 when a severe storm changed the course of the river, taking it away from the harbour which had been the centre of a thriving shipbuilding industry.

Alnmouth had also been a notable grain port – some of the 18th-century granary buildings are now houses. After this cataclysm, Alnmouth developed into a peaceful resort and now attracts boating enthusiasts, golfers and summer visitors, offering miles of golden sands, with a hinterland of high dunes and saltings by the river, popular with birdwatchers.

ALNWICK
Map ref 1815

Alnwick Castle, an imposing medieval building was extensively restored by Anthony Salvin in the 19th century and lavishly decorated in the classical style of the Italian Renaissance for the 4th Duke of Northumberland. The keep and some other parts of the building date back to the 12th century, and since 1309 it has been in the possession of that great Northumberland dynasty, the Percys. The staterooms contain paintings by Van Dyck, Titian, Tintoretto, Canaletto, and many other artists, and there is a splendid collection of Meissen china. Stone figures on the battlements were intended to deter attackers – Alnwick has been the scene of many a Border skirmish. The castle's grounds, Hulne Park, were partly laid out by the celebrated Northumbrian, Capability Brown.

SCALE
0   1   2
0   1   2   3

⌂ BELSAY
Map ref 1079
Now in the care of English Heritage, the 14th-century castle, or tower-house, adjoins an early 17th-century house with an 18th-century ruined wing. The imposing 18th-century Belsay Hall is an important neo-Classical house designed by Sir Charles Monk. He used stone from the estate quarry to create Belsay's wild and lovely quarry garden, and there are formal terraces, winter garden, rose garden and a wooded park.

⌂ BRINKBURN PRIORY
Map ref 1299
A 12th-century priory, Brinkburn was subject to Border raids, and has largely disappeared. The church – a pleasing mixture of Norman and Early English styles – survives and is occasionally used. In the last century it was substantially restored by the industrialist, Lord Armstrong, builder of Cragside (see page 185).

★ GIBSIDE CHAPEL
Map ref 1658
A Palladian building of honey-coloured sandstone, designed by James Paine as a mausoleum for the Bowes family, ancestors of Queen Elizabeth the Queen Mother. The chapel took 42 years to build, with a 7-year break, and was completed in 1812. The National Trust restored the building in 1965 and acquired it, with its avenue of Turkey oaks, in 1974.

LANCHESTER
Map ref 1647
The Roman Fort of Longovicium, after which Lanchester was named, occupies a 6-acre site ½ mile south-west of the present village. The fort was built in AD122 to guard a section of Dere Street, the Roman road linking Hadrian's Wall with York. Until the 18th century the road was in good repair; then stone was pilfered from it for building, and now little remains. The village is large and pleasant; it has a grand church, dating from Norman times, largely reinforced by stones from the Roman fort!

⌂ MARSDEN BAY
Map ref 3966
The limestone stacks of Marsden Rocks provide shelter and an excellent breeding site for a large colony of seabirds; the National Trust protects the rocks and 2½ miles of coastline. Marsden Bay is surrounded by high limestone cliffland; at its foot is the Grotto, a natural cave hollowed out of the cliff by the tides which has been a public house since 1828 – reached by steps or by a lift.

⌂ MORPETH CHANTRY BAGPIPE MUSEUM
Map ref 2086
A medieval chantry houses this museum which has one of the largest bagpipe collections in the

Above: *Newcastle's 'Coathanger' suspension bridge*

Below: *The exposed magnesian limestone sea stacks of Marsden Rocks*

world. It traces the history of the bagpipes and their music, including the Northumbrian pipes, which have a particularly sweet and haunting sound.

⌂ NEWCASTLE-UPON-TYNE
Map ref 2566
Transformed in the first half of the 19th century this is one of the finest and most elegant town centres in the country. Northumberland's capital is once again being revitalized; the town has its own Underground system and one of the largest modern indoor shopping complexes in Europe.

The oldest part of Newcastle, the Quayside, once its commercial heart, is likely to become so again under a somewhat different guise. The restored 18th-century monastery of Blackfriars will tell the visitor much about Newcastle's history – it houses a museum and information centre. In a former almshouse and Holy Jesus Hospital is the John George Joicey Museum. An audio-visual presentation traces the history of the Tyne Flood of 1771 and the Great Fire of 1854, as well as a regimental collection of the 15th/19th Kings Royal Hussars. One of the finest natural history collections can be found in the Hancock Museum. Nearby, the Museum of Antiquities is the museum for Hadrian's Wall.

★ GEORGE STEPHENSON'S BIRTHPLACE
Map ref 1266
George Stephenson, the railway pioneer, was born in this small

cottage near Wylan, now protected by the National Trust.

⌂ TYNEMOUTH
Map ref 3669
The ruins of Tynemouth Castle and the priory within its walls stand on the headland at the mouth of the River Tyne. The ancient Northumbrian kings are buried here, and monastic buildings have occupied the spot since the 6th century.

WALLSEND
Map ref 2966
Beside the Roman fort of Segedunum, which marked the eastern end of Hadrian's Wall, a Heritage Centre tells the history of Wallsend from Roman times.

⌂ ★ WARKWORTH
Map ref 2505
The market town of Warkworth is on a loop of the River Coquet overlooked by its castle which is managed by English Heritage. Warkworth was a Percy castle which underwent restoration by Salvin, and the keep is now in good condition, though much of the castle is in ruins.

The Hermitage, a small 14th-century chapel and sacristy is a mile up-river from the castle.

⌂ WASHINGTON
Map ref 2957
An early 17th-century house, Washington Old Hall was the home of George Washington's ancestors. Managed by the National Trust the house has been restored.

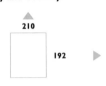

ISLES OF THE SOUTH WEST

In the south-west corner of the Highlands are the most southerly islands of the Hebrides. Islay offers the finest whisky, superb climbing and walking can be found in the Paps of Jura and a sense of peace is the gift of the gardens and ruins of Colonsay and Oronsay.

▲
210

◄   192   ►

▼

SELECTED PLACES TO VISIT

COLONSAY, ORONSAY AND ISLAY

There is access between the islands of Colonsay and Oronsay only for 3 hours around low tide when it is possible to reach Oronsay on foot or by post-bus. The Strand, the narrow strait separating them, divides two very different islands.

Colonsay and Oronsay lie on very old Torridonian sandstone with grits, mudstones and flags and the raised beaches found here and on Islay and Jura are among the best in Britain. Seals breed on many of the islets which surround the islands while peregrine falcon and golden eagle find the rabbit population a valuable food source. Most visitors will wish to see the wild goats, said to be the descendants of those that swam ashore from Armada ships wrecked in these waters in 1588. There are colonies of these black-fleeced, long horned goats on both islands.

COLONSAY

Under the protection of the MacPhies for centuries, Colonsay did not suffer the forced evictions that left many Hebridean islands run-down, melancholy places. Three generations of the Strathcona family have devoted time and money to improving facilities and developing the gardens of Colonsay House.

The influence of the Gulf Stream is quite marked on Colonsay with its sub-tropical gardens and rich pasture land, fringed by *machair*. The island is full of evidence that man has found this a congenial spot at least since Stone Age man left flint tools and other remains. There are Pictish forts, standing stones and, discovered under the sands of Kiloran Bay, the remains of a Viking warlord, his ship and horse. Dun Eibhinn, just north of the junction of the island's three roads, gives excellent views over the island while the remains of a small dun at Tobar Fuar serve as a tee on the golf

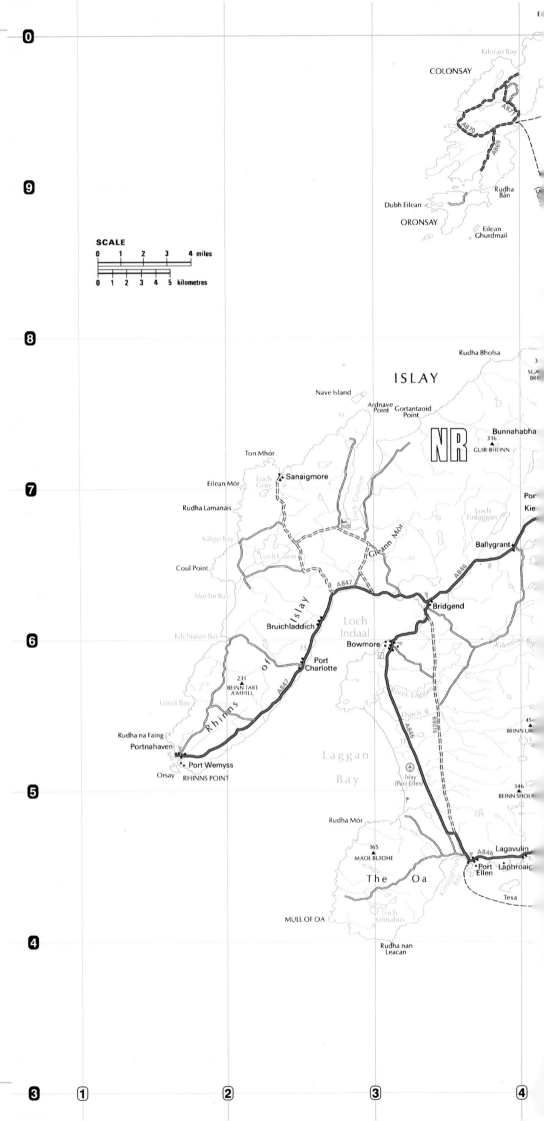

SCALE

0   1   2   3   4 miles

0   1   2   3   4   5 kilometres

course! Fingal's Limpet Hammers, one of the best of the groups of standing stones, can be seen at Lower Kilchattan.

KILORAN
Map ref 3896
Colonsay House, at Kiloran, is early 18th-century with many later additions. Stones from Kiloran Abbey – reputed to have been founded by St Columba, but of which no trace remains – are said to have been used in its construction. With lower than average rainfall, coupled with the warm waters of the Gulf Stream, it is possible to grow many semi-tender trees and shrubs. Rhododendrons flourish in these conditions with azaleas, Chilean fire bush, tender myrtles and several *grevillea* species. A stream and wooded area add to the pleasures of the garden.

ORONSAY
Oronsay is a peaceful place for reflection, possessing tangible evidence of the magnificent work of Celtic craftsmen. Part legend, part fact, the history of early Christian religion seems to flow from the island.

ORONSAY PRIORY
Map ref 3588
This Augustinian priory was founded in the 14th century. The ruins of the priory lie to the north of the church. Most of the buildings are late 14th to early 16th century, the bulk of the work possibly carried out in the 15th century when the priory became a centre for stone carving.

There are several late medieval crosses on the site, the most important being the Oronsay Cross, one of the last works of the Iona school of masons. The shaft is covered with leafy roundels, a characteristic motif, with two little animals on both front and back.

However it is the elongated figure of Christ crucified that confirms this as a masterpiece – suffering that the viewer can almost share. Over 30 grave-slabs complete a memorable collection of decorative stone work.

ISLAY
By contrast with most of the Inner Hebrides, Islay is a hive of activity, its distilleries in great demand for the production of the distinctively flavoured whisky many lovers of *uisgebaugh* consider simply the best malt made. Islay has more diverse scenery and places of interest than Colonsay and Oronsay, ranging from flat boggy lowland to the high hills behind the east coast, including 1,500ft high Beinn Bheigeir; from the cliffs of the Mull of Oa, with its bleak monument to American servicemen drowned when two troopships sank nearby in 1918, to the Rhinns of Islay and its stone circles. There are 5 miles of unspoilt sandy beach at Laggan Bay and a nature reserve at Loch Gruinart.

BALLINABY
Map ref 2366
Two thousand years old and now worn very thin, the 16ft high standing stone is one of the most impressive in the west of Scotland. The stone stands north of Ballinaby farm near the road round Loch Gorm with a second, broken, stone a further 200 yards north.

☑ BOWMORE
Map ref 3159
When Daniel Campbell of Shawfield and Islay wished to move the village of Killarow away from Islay House (just above Bridgend) in 1768, he built the village of Bowmore on the east shore of Loch Indaal. The village is laid out on a grid plan, with a wide main street leading to the circular parish church, a singular, white-painted building entered through a stone-faced rectangular porch and tower.

DUN NOSEBRIDGE
Map ref 3860
Dun Nosebridge, about a mile east of Mulindry, is one of the most striking hill forts in Scotland. Possibly less than 2,000 years old, some of its features set it aside from most Iron Age work. It stands on a grassy ridge, overlooking Loch Indaal.

★ KILDALTON CROSS
Map ref 4750
Extensively restored, the charming, simple, late 12th-century parish church at Kildalton contains a rare treasure – an 8th-century Early Christian cross. Bearing marked similarities to crosses on Iona, this ringed cross has a wealth of detail.

🖼 LOCH GRUINART NATURE RESERVE
Map ref 2867
An RSPB reserve at one of the most important wintering sites for barnacle geese in Britain – up to 18,000 have been observed on Islay, with 4,000 whitefronted geese. Many other wildfowl, waders and several birds of prey, including golden eagle, visit the reserve. Both grouse species nest on the moorland areas.

RHINNS OF ISLAY LIGHTHOUSE
Map ref 1552
The island of Orsay lies just south of the Rhinns. The lighthouse was designed by Robert Stevenson and built in 1824-5. Described as one of 'undoubtedly the three best revolving lights in the world' the light was alternatively stationary and revolving, thus allowing mariners to identify it. The original weights are no longer in place – the Rhinns of Islay lighthouse, like many others, is now automatic.

Kildalton Cross is a fine Celtic cross on the south coast of Islay

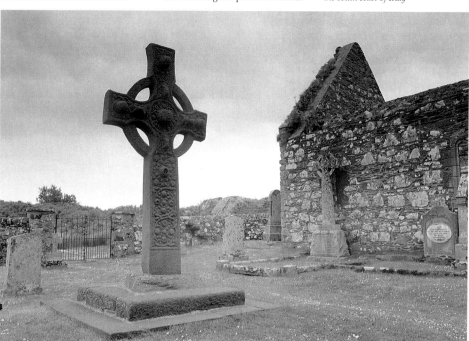

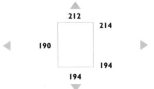

THE LOCHS AND ISLES OF STRATHCLYDE

The area of Strathclyde based around Loch Fyne and the Isle of Bute, is not the easiest part of Scotland to tour, being fragmented by a network of lochs and kyles.

However, patience will be well rewarded and assistance is provided in the form of the A83, which runs down almost the entire western length of Loch Fyne.

```
        212
          ▲
    ◄  190   214  ►
          ▼
        194
        194
```

SELECTED PLACES TO VISIT

ARDRISHAIG
Map ref 8485

On the west shore of Loch Gilp, Ardrishaig marks the southern end of the Crinan Canal which links this grey stone village with the coastal village of Crinan, some 9 miles to the north west. The canal and most of the two villages were built towards the end of the 18th century; the waterway provided safe access to the Clyde, the north-west coast, and, notably, the Hebridean fisheries. Before the canal was built seafarers would negotiate the arduous, and very often, hazardous 120-mile journey around the Mull of Kintyre.

The canal is now essentially a paradise for holiday yachtsmen, rather than commercial users.

❋ CRARAE GLEN
Map ref 9897

A 30-acre site created around a burn in a deep glen beside Loch Fyne, Crarae Glen garden gives fine views over the loch. Conifers and rare species of ornamental and exotic trees and shrubs, including notable collections of rhododendrons, azaleas, sorbus, magnolias, eucryphias and many others flourish here. Begun by his mother and father, the garden was extended by Sir George Campbell in the early 1930s.

★ DUNADD FORT
Map ref 8493

West of the village of Kilmichael Glassary, Dunadd hill-fort straddles a rocky outcrop. It dates from the Iron Age and was inhabited until the 9th century. Dunadd was the capital of Dalriada, the kingdom transferred by the Scots when they migrated here from Antrim, in the north of Ireland, in the 6th century.

Nearby, carvings of a boar and a footprint probably indicate a site where kings were invested with

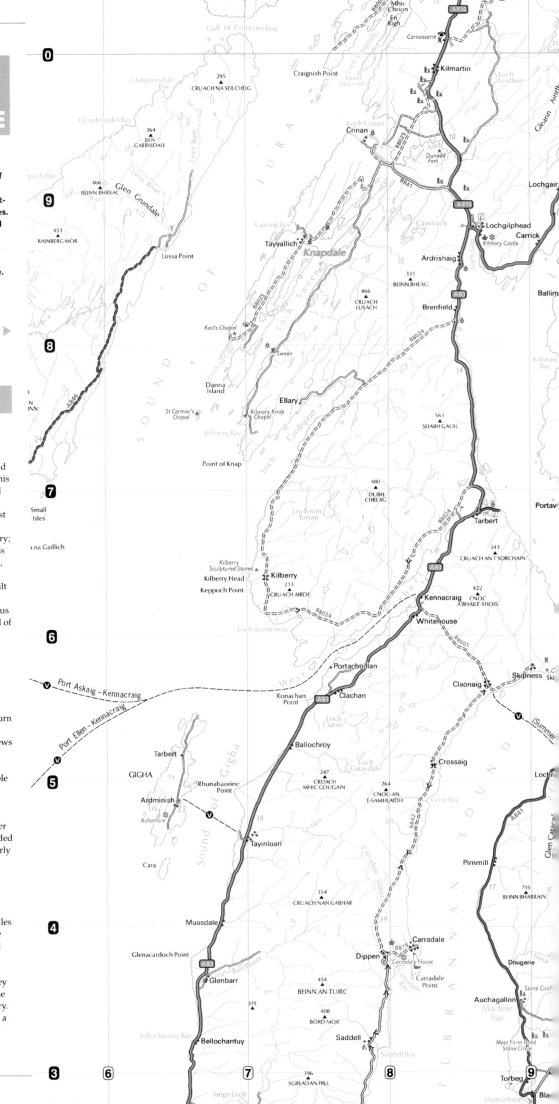

royal power, and evidence of metal-working has been found on the site.

❀ ♣ KILMORY CASTLE
Map ref 8687

South of Lochgilphead are the 18th-century gardens of Kilmory Castle, now under restoration after years of neglect. Many of the fine shrubs and trees have survived and the garden is now returning to something approaching its previous fine state.

★ KILMORY KNAP CHAPEL
Map ref 7074

Loch Sween and Loch Caolisport are divided by a peninsula called the Point of Knap or Knapdale, on which stands the stone built village of Kilmory. The ruined chapel of Kilmory Knap contains a collection of late medieval crosses and grave slabes, with carvings of chiefs and warriors. Outside the chapel is MacMillan's Cross, which has par-ticularly fine and intricate carvings.

☒☒⌂ ROTHESAY
Map ref 0865

The Bute Museum in Stuart Street contains comprehensive displays tracing the local and natural history of the Isle of Bute, including pre-historic flints and pots, a collection of early Christian crosses and more recent bygones such as models of Clyde steamers. The geological survey of the island can be seen and there is a children's touch table.

The beautiful gardens at Crarae Glen beside Strathclyde's Loch Fyne

A splendid red sandstone castle, dating from the 12th to the 16th centuries, Rothesay Castle stands on the edge of the town, overlooking Rothesay Bay. It is the only castle in Scotland to have been built as an almost circular enclosure – a shell-keep – and is remarkably well preserved. The four magnificent projecting drum towers were added in the late 13th century, and in the reign of James IV a gatehouse. The curtain walls are 30ft high, and are surrounded by a moat.

More peaceful interest can be found at Ardencraig gardens where particular attention is paid to introducing rare plants.

⚔ SKIPNESS CASTLE
Map ref 9157

A magnificent 13th-century red sandstone castle, this was originally a hall-house and chapel at opposite ends of a courtyard. Overlooking Skipness Bay, the castle was originally a stronghold held on behalf of the MacDonald chiefs. The MacDonalds forfeited it in the 15th century and it was then granted to the Campbell clan who added a tower house and then abandoned the castle in the late 17th century. Although it has been uninhabited ever since and lacking a roof it remains in good condition.

⚔ SWEEN CASTLE
Map ref 7279

Overlooking Loch Sween, Sween Castle is a quadrangular stone castle, dating from the 12th century

when the area was ruled by the Norse. It was then, captured and largely destroyed in the mid-17th century by Colkitto MacDonald, lieutenant to the Marquis of Montrose.

ⓘ TARBERT
Map ref 8668

Not to be confused with the capital of Harris in the Hebrides, this Tarbert is situated at the head of East Loch Tarbert, on a landlocked bay, a perfect haven for fishing boats and small craft. Tarbert is a busy and attractive resort and a fishing port, once the centre of the Loch Fyne herring industry.

On a hill above the village are the remains of the 15th-century castle, now an ivy-clad ruin, overlooking the harbour. The earliest fortresses on this site were built to repel Viking invaders during their long struggle with the Scots for possession of the strategically sited isthmus upon which Tarbert stands. The name of the village derives from *tarbet* – a narrow strip of land with water on either side over which boats can be drawn.

TAYNISH
Map ref 7383

There is a Nature Conservancy Council reserve on the Taynish peninsula: oakwood ridges interspersed with areas of boggy ground, wet meadowland and heath fringed with mixed woodland. The oakwoods have an undercarr of hazel, holly, rowan, ash and honeysuckle; there is a rich variety of lichens on the trees, with mosses on the boulders lying on the woodland floor. Many species of butterfly are attracted to the open areas where orchids grow among the rushes and grasses. The warm shallow waters around the peninsula have a wide range of seaweeds, sponges and sea-urchins. Both otter and common seal are present on the islets offshore.

TAYVALLICH
Map ref 7484

Tayvallich has its own natural harbour on Loch a' Bhealaich. Once a centre for the lobster and herring industries, Tayvallich is now a tourist centre, offering safe bathing, good walking into the heart of Knapdale, fishing and sailing. To the north of the village is Carsaig Bay with fine views over the Sound to the hills of Jura.

TIGHNABRUAICH VILLAGE
Map ref 9773

On a reach of the Kyles of Bute, this village has a mild climate and sub-tropical plants. Its name is Gaelic for house on the hill and its largely Victorian dwellings are disposed around a wooded hillside with distant views of the Arran mountains. Tighnabruaich is largely a sailing centre with a long pier for steamers to decant and collect visitors.

From a point a mile to the north of the village is a wonderful panoramic view of the Kyles.

ARRAN, SOUTH KINTYRE AND GIGHA

The Isle of Arran offers opportunities to explore the range of hills of which Goat Fell is the highest and most attractive peak to climbers. Less energetic visitors may enjoy a visit to the famous Brodick Castle and Garden. Kintyre has miles of Forestry Commission walks at Carradale, and the small resort of Southend Village at the southern end of the peninsula gives superb views to the North Antrim coast. The little island of Gigha must be visited for its scenery and the lovely garden of Achamore.

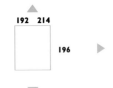

SELECTED PLACES TO VISIT

❋ ACHAMORE GARDEN, ISLE OF GIGHA
Map ref 6447

After buying the little island of Gigha in 1944 in order to create a garden there, Sir James Horlick realised his ambition to grow rare, difficult and unusual plants. He bequeathed his exceptionally fine collection of sub-tropical plants, including azaleas, camellias and tender rhododendrons to the National Trust for Scotland. The Trust has successfully bred from them to supply some of its west coast gardens which have an equally mild moist climate and acid soil. Achamore Garden has shelter belts of evergreen plants, open glades, paths and rides. The damper parts have naturalised candelabra primulas.

Gigha is Gaelic for God's island and this tiny paradise is wonderfully peaceful, with many other features worth exploring, including several prehistoric and archaeological sites and the ruined 13th-century church of Kilchattan.

BLACKWATERFOOT
Map ref 9028

On Drumadoon Bay on the Isle of Arran, the small hamlet of Blackwaterfoot looks over Kilbrennan Sound to Kintyre. Visitors can enjoy fishing, golfing, pony trekking and safe bathing. Robert the Bruce landed here in the early 14th century, and is reputed to have taken refuge in King's Cave, near Blackwaterfoot. Shiskine church, some 2 miles north-east has a carved tombstone.

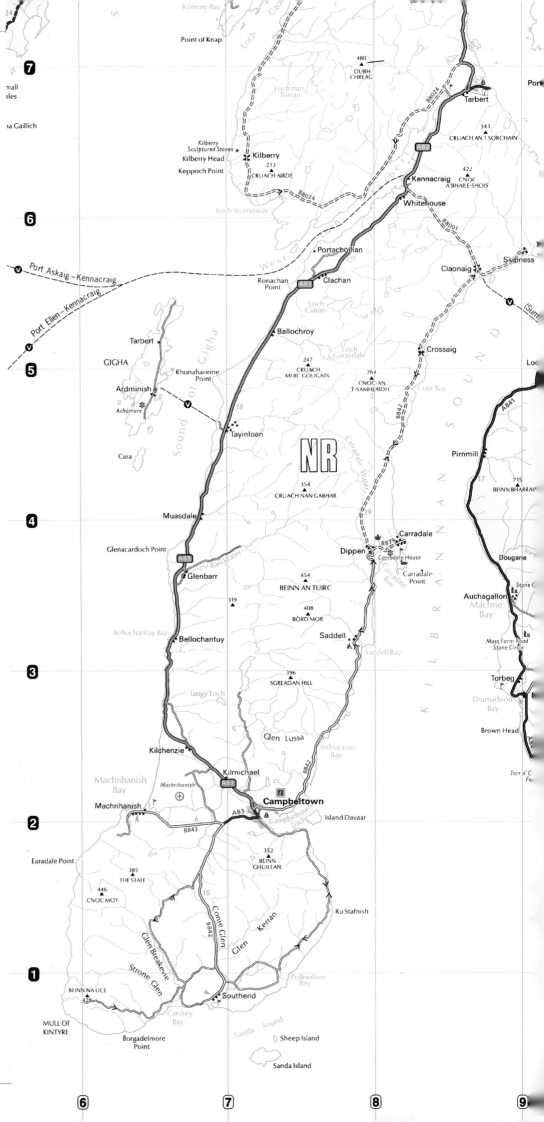

☑ ✗ ☖ ⌂ BRODICK
Map ref 0136

Brodick, the main town of the Isle of Arran, is a busy port. Climbers come to Brodick to ascend the highest peak on Arran, Goat Fell. However, the jewel in Brodick's crown is its castle, with its collections of paintings, furniture, silver and porcelain, and its superb woodland gardens and country park. There has been a castle on the site since the 14th century.

Brodick Castle has a fine 60-acre garden with a splendid rhododendron collection, a Victorian rose garden, and extensive woodlands which harbour red squirrel. The Arran Heritage Museum, near the castle entrance, features many local buildings, including a blacksmith's shop.

☖ CAMPBELTOWN
Map ref 7221

The 7th Earl of Argyll, Archibald Campbell, built a castle in the early 1600s on a small hill overlooking Campbeltown's natural harbour. The Earl encouraged settlers from the Lowlands in order to promote a healthy economy, and in 1700 the town became a royal burgh. It is known that a church existed in the 13th century at Kilkerran on the south side of the bay, and an Early Christian cross can be seen in the cemetery. A striking 14th-century cross, probably from Kilkivan, has been re-sited at one end of Main Street.

The town is an appealing mixture of old and new, with some notable 18th-century buildings, including Castlehill Church, built on the site of the castle, and Town House, which has an unusual octagonal steeple. In 1913 the Wee Picture House opened – one of Scotland's earliest cinemas.

❀ ☙ ⌫ ⚐ CARRADALE
Map ref 8138

The village with its small, well protected harbour faces the Isle of Arran across Kilbrannan Sound. The Forestry Commission owns 16,000 acres near Carradale and provides a small centre with information on the variety of forest walks which the Commission has laid out over the estate.

One of these leads to Carradale Point where there are the vitrefied remains of a large fort, thought to date back to 1500BC.

CNOC MOY
Map ref 6216

Some 4 miles to the south-south-west of Machrihanish is the 1462ft high limestone peak of Cnoc Moy. Its sea-facing slopes are honeycombed with caves containing stalactites.

CORRIE
Map ref 0343

Corrie means circular hollow on a hillside, which aptly describes the site of this lovely little village at the foot of Goat Fell, on the Isle of Arran. A row of white cottages stand overlooking the Firth of Clyde; the remainder of the village hugs the shore. Harold Macmillan's grandfather was born here, in 1813, and it must have looked much the same then as it does today.

GOATFELL
Map ref 9842

Goat Fell, the highest mountain, at 2,866ft, on the Isle of Arran, in the care of the National Trust for Scotland, offers rock climbing and ridge walking, with magnificent views over the Firth of Clyde.

LAMLASH
Map ref 0332

Lamlash, on the Isle of Arran, is protected by Holy Island – 1,000ft high and 2 miles long – lying across the breadth of Lamlash Bay. St Molaise lived in a cave on Holy Island, and it is open to visitors; there are Runic inscriptions inside.

The largest village on Arran, Lamlash is a tourist centre with good fishing, dinghy sailing, bathing, golfing and walking. In addition, underwater enthusiasts dive to the wreck of the brig *Derwent*.

✗ LOCHRANZA
Map ref 9451

A hall-house was built at Lochranza in the 14th century, at the northern

Goat Fell on the Isle of Arran with Brodick Bay in the foreground

end of the Isle of Arran, overlooking the small sea loch at the foot of Glen Chalmadale. Robert the Bruce may have stayed in the original castle when he first came to Scotland, from Ireland, in the early 14th century. The present ruin is largely 17th-century. The village offers safe bathing from a pebble beach, and fishing.

MACHRIHANISH BAY
Map ref 6322

Machrihanish was a coal-working centre for nearly two hundred years, until 1967. Traces may still be found of the light railway which served the collieries, and later carried tourists and other passengers. Today the bay is best known for its 3½ miles of pale golden sand facing the Atlantic – safe for walkers but less so for swimmers as the undertow here is treacherous.

⛟ MOSS FARM ROAD STONE CIRCLE
Map ref 9033

About 1½ miles inland on the south bank of Machrie Bay is the most remarkable concentration of Neolithic and Bronze Age monuments in Scotland. The Moss Farm Road Stone Circle comprise eight principal stone circles and two cairns in the care of the Scottish Development Department, together with other less clearly defined monuments and field systems.

⚑ SOUTHEND VILLAGE
Map ref 6908

This small holiday resort, popular with swimmers and golfers, looks towards the Northern Ireland coast some 15 miles to the south. St Columba is said to have landed here in AD560, and there is a holy well and a ruined chapel dedicated to the saint at Keil Point, a mile to the west.

St Columba's Footsteps are impressions of two right feet in the rock behind the western end of the churchyard.

BALLADS AND VERSE

The Firth of Clyde, south from Ayr, is particularly famous for its connection with Robert Burns, whose work celebrated the lives of local people. Large and small scale industry exist throughout this area, formerly renowned for cloth manufacture and still famous for the blended whisky of local grocer John Walker.

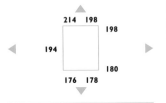

```
        214   198
                   198
    194
                   180
        176   178
```

TOUR

CARRICK COAST, DOON VALLEY AND BURNS' COUNTRY
55 MILES

The tour leaves Ayr by the B7024 south to Alloway, now virtually part of Ayr. The thatched and whitewashed cottage in which Burns was born, 25 January 1759, and spent the first seven years of his life, survives as part of a museum. Next to the ruined Alloway Kirk where Tam O'Shanter interrupted the witches orgy, stands the Land o'Burns Centre with its fine multi-screen audio-visual display. In addition to details of the poet's life, the presentation demonstrates the living conditions of the farming community in which he grew up.

Across the road is a splendid monument to the poet in the form of a Grecian temple, containing other memorabilia, including the wedding ring of Jean Armour, whom he married in 1788.

Beyond the monument turn right to join the A719. Continue southwards to the tiny, silted harbour of Dunure. Here seems a hardly appropriate place for a rather grand scheme to convert it to a sea-port but, in the 19th century, a local estate owner planned to do just that. He ran out of money and the pretty, whitewashed village is now a peaceful place popular with yachtsmen and fishermen.

Dominating the bay to the south lie the grim ruins of Dunure Castle where, in 1570, the 4th Earl of Cassillis is said to have roasted the lay abbot of Crossraguel Abbey, in order to obtain the rich abbey lands.

A few miles further and the tour passes Culzean Castle. Built between 1772-92 by Robert Adam, this masterpiece of Gothic architecture on a superb cliff-top site is owned by the National Trust for Scotland. There are some fine examples of Adam's work, including the magnificent oval

staircase and the circular drawing room with its views across the Firth of Clyde to Ailsa Craig.

The top flat was given to President Eisenhower in recognition of his wartime achievements and there is a display tracing his career.

Adam was also responsible for the Home Farm, built in the grounds of the castle. Adapted in 1971-73 as the visitor centre for what was Scotland's first Country Park, it has a walled garden, a deer park, an aviary, an orangery, and many miles of wonderfully varied footpaths.

The tiny fishing village of Maidens acquired its name from a group of rocks, which lay offshore. Douglas Graham, the inspiration for Burns' Tam O'Shanter lived in Shanter farm, above the village. He was an occasional smuggler of 'Arran water' (whisky), and it was the name of his boat that Burns gave to his hero.

Turnberry has some fine beaches but is best known for one of its two golf courses. The British Championship periodically returns to the Ailsa course. The shoreline and rocky inlets permit dramatic views of Ailsa Craig.

From Turnberry the route returns inland, on the A77 to Kirkoswald. Another member of the cast of *Tam* was Souter Johnnie. John Davidson – the village cobbler, or souter – lived here in a thatched cottage. Tools of Souter Johnnie's trade are featured in an exhibition with Burns relics. Life-sized stone figures of the souter and other characters from the ballad can be seen in the cottage.

Between Kirkoswald and Maybole lie the extensive ruins of Crossraguel Abbey, a 13th-century Cluniac foundation. During the War of Independence most of the original buildings were destroyed but the monastery thrived in the next two centuries. The surprisingly plain church, claustral buildings, and abbot's house survive with part of the four-storey Tower House and castellated gatehouse.

At Maybole the tour turns south-east onto the B7023 and at Crosshill joins the B741. On the road to

The ferry to Arran at Ardrossan

Straiton is the superb Regency Blairquhan House, approached along a 3 mile private drive beside the Water of Girvan.

At Dalmellington the tour makes its final turn back to Ayr, through the Doon Valley.

SELECTED PLACES TO VISIT

ARDROSSAN
Map ref 2342
At first glance a terminal for passenger and cargo ships – ferries leave for Brodick and Douglas on the Isle of Man – Ardrossan soon reveals some good stone houses. Much of the town was laid out by the Earl of Eglinton in the early 19th century. Offshore is the nature reserve of Horse Isle.

AYR
Map ref 3422
At the heart of Burns country lies the popular resort of Ayr. It has 2½ miles of sandy beach overlooking the busy Firth of Clyde. The town is built on either side of the River Ayr and one of the four bridges which now span the river, the 12th-century Auld Brig was immortalized by Burns in *The Brigs of Ayr*. In Ayr, it is almost impossible to escape his influence. However, in the Maclaurin Art Gallery and Rozelle House there is a modern art collection and Henry Moore sculptures. The park has a nature trail and a small military museum.

THE BACHELORS' CLUB
Map ref 4427
In 1780, Robert Burns and a group of friends founded a debating club in this two-storey 17th-century thatched house. A year later he was initiated into Freemasonry here.

The unpretentious but charming house now contains Burns relics and period furnishings which form the basis of a small museum in the care of the National Trust for Scotland.

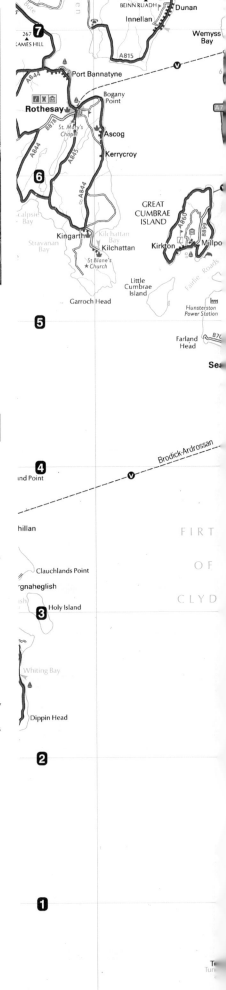

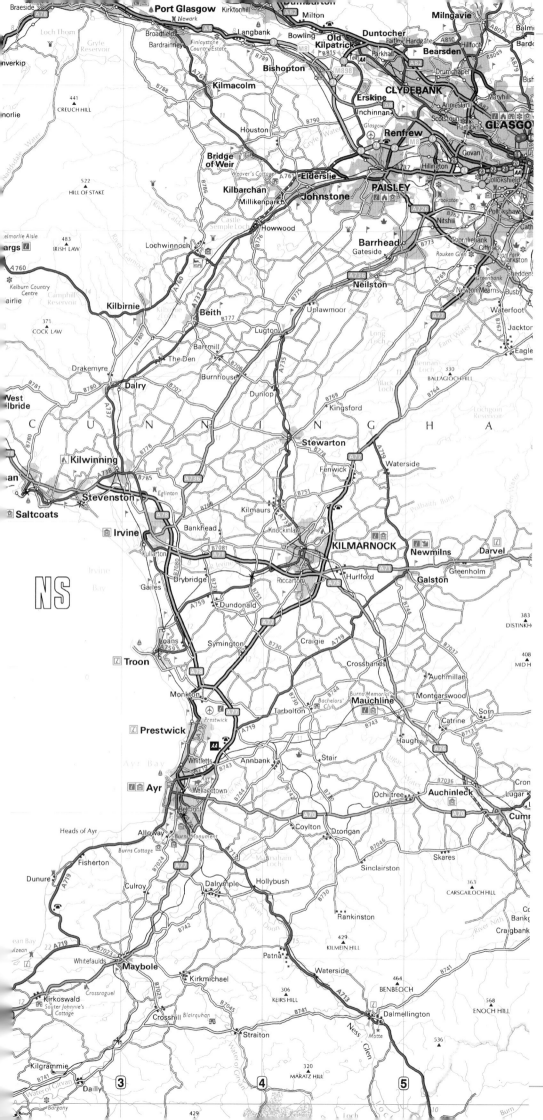

BALLADS AND VERSE

❋ KELBURN COUNTRY CENTRE
Map ref 2256

The historic estate of the earls of Glasgow with beautiful gardens and spectacular scenery. A range of shrubs, including rhododendrons and azaleas, ensures a lengthy display of colour, while the Kel Burn falls through a lovely glen, in a series of waterfalls.

▥▥ KILMARNOCK
Map ref 4438

Dean Castle and Country Park on the outskirts of Kilmarnock, are the fascinating remains of a 14th-century stronghold. The castle was virtually destroyed by fire in the 18th century and was not reconstructed until Edwardian times.

Today, the building houses the varied Howard de Walden collection which includes arms and armour, Brussels tapestries, and a fine display of early keyboard and other instruments. Parts of the palace have been restored to their 13th- and 14th-century state. There is a 200-acre country park and a visitor centre in the restored Dower House.

The Dick Institute, in Elimbank Avenue, is a museum with displays of geology, engineering, archaeology, and local and natural history. There is a newly modernised art gallery with an important collection of paintings.

▨ LARGS
Map ref 2158

Most of the old church of Largs has disappeared, but the north transept survives, containing a fine Renaissance monument of 1636.

▥ WEAVER'S COTTAGE
Map ref 4164

Weaver's Cottage, at Kilbarchen, is an early 18th-century cottage which has been preserved with its looms and weaving equipment.

Demonstrations of weaving can be seen at Weaver's Cottage, Kilbarchen

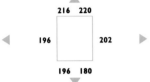

AN INDUSTRIAL HERITAGE

The area immediately around Glasgow is a conurbation of small towns; some new, like Cumbernauld and East Kilbride, Glasgow's first overspill town; others with an ancient history like Hamilton, or Kirkintilloch, which dates from the 12th century.

New Lanark is the site of one of the most exciting ventures in Scotland's industrial history; and the spirit which made this possible is still present in the village.

```
          216  220
  ◀    196        202    ▶
          196  180
              ▼
```

SELECTED PLACES TO VISIT

🏛 AUCHINLECK
Map ref 5121

Set near the Lugar Water, 3 miles west of Auchinleck is Affleck Big House – the local name for a fine house built in 1780 for Lord Auchinleck, the father of Samuel Johnson's biographer and great friend, James Boswell. Partially the work of the Adam brothers, the house was built on the site of two earlier keeps belonging to the Boswell family.

Dr Johnson stayed here and praised the 'elegant modern mansion', and it was from Affleck that he and James Boswell departed for their celebrated tour of the Hebrides.

The Boswell Museum is housed in the old parish church – it contains portraits and mementos of James Boswell and of another of Auchinleck's sons, the pioneer of gas lighting, William Murdoch. Boswell is buried in the family mausoleum beside the church.

⚜ CHATELHERAULT COUNTRY PARK
Map ref 5563

Chatelherault Country Park, on the edge of Glasgow, has an 18th-century Adam hunting lodge, set on a hill in the country park which once belonged to the dukes of Hamilton. The lodge has been cleverly restored to its former ornate splendour.

One of Scotland's newest country parks, Chatelherault offers many woodland and country walks. An interpretive centre illustrates the work of the many employees on the 18th-century Hamilton estate. An ancient breed of white cattle grazes the parkland and there is an adventure playground for younger visitors.

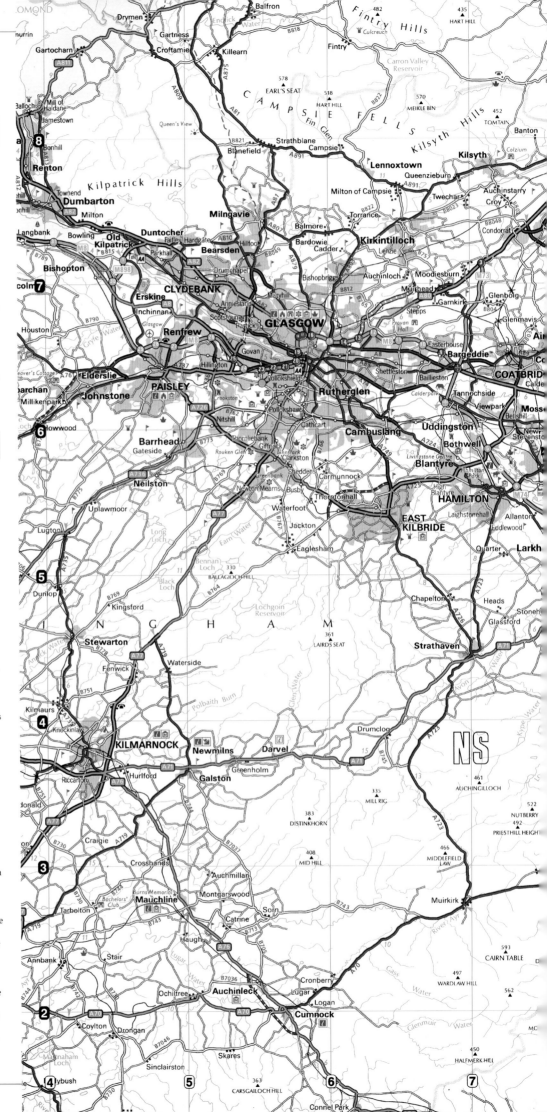

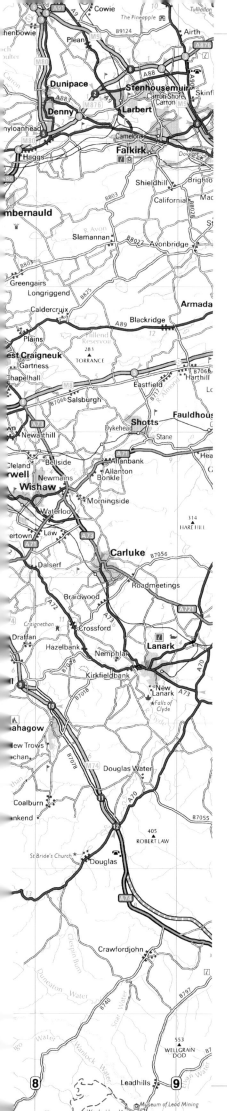

New Lanark's mill buildings and sandstone houses, now restored

COATBRIDGE
Map ref 7363

Coatbridge was the main centre of the Scottish iron and steel industry in the 19th century. The Summerlee Heritage Park, designed around 25 acres of the site of an ironworks, displays the traditional working machinery used in the metal and heavy engineering industries, and illustrates the effect of the Industrial Revolution upon Scottish life.

✗ CRAIGNETHAN CASTLE
Map ref 8247

Craignethan Castle was built in the 16th century on a promontory above the River Nethan by the illegitimate son of the 1st Earl of Arran. The castle was slighted in 1579 and a new laird's house, built in the outer court nearly a century later, is still inhabited; the remainder of the building is in ruins. There is a small museum.

CUMBERNAULD
Map ref 7676

Planned in 1956 to house Glasgow's overspill population, and one of Scotland's first new towns, Cumbernauld boasts that every house has its own garage or parking space, there are no traffic wardens or traffic lights, and its shops, offices and entertainments are all together in one massive complex. Not everyone has been impressed by the result, but the ideas used have been adapted by town planners all over the world.

EAGLESHAM VILLAGE
Map ref 5752

Eaglesham is notable for being Scotland's first village to be listed as a place of special historic and architectural interest. Designed in the late 18th century by the Earl of Eglinton, on the edge of high moorland, the village had been a spinning and weaving centre with a cotton mill on the river, which burned down in 1876. Industry ceased at Eaglesham with the advent of power looms in the industrial towns.

It was here that Rudolf Hess, Hitler's deputy, crashed-landed in 1941.

★ ★ FALLS OF CLYDE
Map ref 8842

Many famous artists have visited and painted the spectacular Falls of Clyde, and they have been admired by poets and authors like Coleridge, Scott and Dickens. Corra Lynn is 90ft high – one of several waterfalls in this Scottish Wildlife Reserve which includes both banks of the River Clyde upstream from New Lanark. There are woodland walks on both sides of the gorge, some skirting the water's edge. The Visitor Centre is just downstream from the lowest fall.

❋ GREENBANK GARDEN
Map ref 5556

Laid out in the 2½-acre grounds of an attractive Georgian house (not open), on the extreme southern perimeter of Glasgow, Greenbank is a demonstration garden, largely designed to help the amateur gardener. Part of the garden is intended for wheelchair users with stone troughs and raised beds placed at the right level for a seated gardener; the large greenhouse and the potting shed are also accessible. The garden is walled, and planted in a series of rooms with imaginative and colourful layouts.

▥ LIVINGSTONE CENTRE
Map ref 6857

Shuttle Row in Blantyre, a block of 18th-century millworkers tenements, now forms the Livingstone Centre: birthplace in 1813 of the explorer David Livingstone, who lived here during his childhood and while studying to be a doctor. The restored buildings now house exhibitions of his travels in Africa and his statue is on the tower of the Livingstone Memorial church.

▨ ★ ▣ MAUCHLINE
Map ref 4827

The village of Mauchline and surrounding countryside have many associations with Robert Burns. The poet courted Jean Armour here; he rented part of the building that is now the Burns House Museum, in Castle Street, his wife's room is open for visitors and four of his daughters are buried in

the churchyard. Opposite the museum is Poosie Nansie's Inn, where the Jolly Beggars met and made merry.

NEW LANARK
Map ref 8842

The Derbyshire mill owner and inventor, Richard Arkwright, and an entrepreneur, David Dale, designed New Lanark in the late 18th and early 19th centuries, once the largest cotton spinning factory in Britain. Robert Owen (Dale's son-in-law) was appointed manager in 1798. He introduced sweeping reforms to improve conditions of work and also set out to demonstrate how a community could be organised happily at home, work, and in education – there was a school for the children and an adult learning centre. Seven-storey textile mill buildings and elegant Georgian sandstone houses have been cleverly restored by the New Lanark Association, after the village fell into disrepair when the mills closed in the 1960s. Two of the buildings have been converted to a Visitor Centre with exhibitions on the social and industrial past of the village. There is a resident population, many of whom are skilled in a variety of crafts.

★ ST BRIDE'S CHURCH
Map ref 8431

St Bride's Church at Douglas, is all that remains of a castle rebuilt by Adam in 1759. Unfortunately colliery workings undermined the building and its foundations were so severely damaged that it had to be demolished. The present building is probably late 14th-century, extensively restored in the mid-19th century.

The interesting octagonal bell tower is 16th-century. However the importance of St Bride's lies in the many medieval grave-effigies and monuments to be found within the choir. The earliest was probably completed by the middle of the 14th century, and there are several others which are of the 15th century.

GLASGOW

A centre of the Industrial Revolution and distinctly Victorian in character, 20th-century Glasgow has shed its mantle of depression and emerged as a cosmopolitan centre of the Arts

The third largest city in Britain, and Scotland's biggest, Glasgow began to develop only three centuries ago. St Mungo built a church on what is now the site of the cathedral in the 6th century and the cathedral itself was built in 1136. Glasgow became a royal burgh in 1454 but by the end of the 17th century it was still largely restricted to the north bank of the Clyde.

The development began with the growth of Port Glasgow as a popular port for goods from the New World. Tobacco became a major trade, to be replaced later by cotton. The proximity of coalfields ensured Glasgow's continued growth and the evolutionary process was maintained during the 19th century as heavy industry and ship-building increased in importance. Immigrants flocked to the city, producing a wonderfully cosmopolitan society, but Glasgow has achieved notoriety as a city of slums. Ironically, the developing Victorian city had many classically inspired buildings by architects of

Above: *Glasgow's Broomielaw Bridge*

Below: *Tolbooth Steeple at Glasgow Cross rises to 126ft*

note, headed by Greek Thomson.

It was not until the second half of the 20th century that Glasgow began slum clearance. Some of the earliest schemes, involving the removal of whole communities to out-of-town sites, appeared to create almost as many difficulties as they solved but gradually the situation has improved. Glasgow has also adapted to the loss of heavy industry, replacing it by light engineering and hi-tech industries. A major new road system has been built, while the underground provides public transport.

The cultural – in the broadest sense – renaissance of Glasgow is one of the most remarkable stories of late 20th-century Britain epitomised by the Burrell Collection. Gathered by Sir William Burrell over a period of 80 years, this treasure-house of a collection deserved a very special setting and Glasgow rose to the challenge. In 1990 Glasgow became European City of Culture and Scottish Opera finally has a permanent home in the converted King's Theatre

in Glasgow. The Mayfest has grown in a few years from being a community project to an international festival. Glasgow has rediscovered its architectural heritage, realising that in Charles Rennie Mackintosh it has a major architect of the 20th century.

In 1988 Glasgow was home to a summer-long Garden Festival – in keeping with its reputation for open spaces. One of the best areas for wildlife is Linn Park while Pollok Country Park has gardens and nature trails. The landscaped grounds of Ross Hall Park contrast with the deep, wooded Rouken Glen Park and its riverside walks.

All this, and much more, has helped Glasgow to throw off the dark mood that afflicted it for so long and move toward a late 20th-century Age of Enlightenment.

Treasures of the City

Botanic Gardens. Established in 1817, but moved to their present site in 1842, the Botanic Gardens are laid out with lawns and beds, sloping down to the River Kibble. A major feature is the quite spectacular glasshouse, the Kibble Palace, 23,000 sq ft of Victorian exotica.

Burrell Collection. Housed in a specially designed gallery by Barry Gasson the Burrell Collection was amassed by Sir William Burrell and gifted to the city in 1944. This extraordinary collection ranges from Ancient Egyptian alabaster and Chinese ceramics to Japanese prints; from Turkish carpets to European medieval art; outstanding collections of stained glass, tapestries, British silver; and paintings and sculptures of the last six centuries.

Glasgow Art Gallery and Museum. Arguably the best civic collection of European painting, the Glasgow Art Gallery and Museum has supplementary displays, including a collection of furniture in the Glasgow style.

Glasgow Cathedral. A very well preserved early Gothic cathedral, Glasgow Cathedral was raised over the shrine of St Mungo with a 13th-century crypt, 14th-century flat timber roof and a fine 15th-century chapter house. The trade guilds defended it during the Reformation, and are commemorated on the choir pews – as are those organisations who contributed to the renovation work of the 1950s.

Haggs Castle. A fascinating experience for children, the museum provides work sheets and quizzes, prompting them to discover the history of Haggs Castle; different ages and styles are depicted in the rooms.

Hunterian Art Gallery. Based on a collection bequeathed in

the 18th century by Dr William Hunter, the Hunterian Art Gallery has added 19th- and 20th-century Scottish paintings and other contemporary British work.

Hunterian Museum. Another legacy of Dr Hunter is the collection of some 30,000 coins and medals housed in the Hunterian Museum in the main building of the university.

Museum of Transport. Steam locomotives, buses and trams and a range of vehicles from

Below: *The city's principal square, George Square, and the Victorian City Chambers*

horse-drawn to those of the present day – a journey of glorious nostalgia.

People's Palace. The lives of ordinary Glasgow people seen through a kaleidoscope of exhibits, featuring the city's trades and industries and campaigning materials. Behind the hall lies the Winter Gardens, a huge remarkable

Victorian conservatory of glass and iron.

Pollok House. Set in Pollok Country Park, the house contains a fine collection of Spanish paintings, including work by El Greco, Goya and Murillo. Some of the furnishings have long been with the house.

Above: *The western façade of Mackintosh's Glasgow School of Art*
Left: *A peaceful view of Queen's Park, named after Mary Queen of Scots*

Provand's Lordship. Provand's Lordship is the oldest house in Glasgow. Built in 1471, it has the plain appearance befitting a cathedral manse. Once the city residence of the Prebend of Provan, a canon of the cathedral, it is now restored, and contains a fine collection of 17th-century Scottish furniture and other exhibits.

Provan Hall. The country residence of the Prebend, Provan Hall stands in Austinlea Park. This 15th-century mansion house has some later work but is substantially unchanged.

Tenement House. A time capsule consisting of a first floor flat and an interpretive display on the ground floor of a Victorian tenement. The typical flat, two rooms, kitchen and bathroom, contains the original box-beds, kitchen range, sink and coal-bunker. The building was completed in 1892.

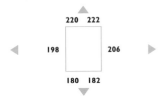

THE LOWLANDS

The magnificent rolling countryside here in the middle of what is known as the Lowlands may seem somewhat of a contradiction in terms; although not mountainous it is certainly not lowland!

```
        220  222
  198  ┌──────┐  206
       │      │
        180  182
```

TOUR

UPPER TWEED VALLEY, TALLA AND MEGGET RESERVOIRS AND TRAQUAIR HOUSE
50 MILES

The tour begins at the tweed-producing town of Peebles. A mile or so west of the town is the great tower house of Neidpath Castle, on its promontory over the Tweed. For centuries the home of the Hays family, later created earls of Tweeddale, it was built in the late 14th-century on a 13th-century site. Cromwell attempted to slight it, but its 12ft thick walls survived, although the interior of the tower was much re-modelled in the late 17th century.

Lovers of the works of Sir Walter Scott will wish to make a detour along an unclassified road shortly after leaving Neidpath to Kirkton Manor. It was here that Scott wrote *The Black Dwarf*.

Back on the B712, the tour passes Stobo with its heavily restored Norman church of St Mungo, on the way to Dawyck Botanic Garden. One of several outstations of the Royal Botanic Garden, Edinburgh, Dawyck was once a semi-wild arboretum but, since the 19th century, has increasingly become a man-made garden. It retains an impressive collection of mature trees, including the Dawyck beech, with many flowering shrubs and spring displays of bulbs.

Just before Drumelzier lie the scant ruins of Tinnis Castle, built in the early 16th century for the Tweedie family. Where the tour joins the A701 another diversion is essential, to visit Broughton and the John Buchan Centre. Here displays commemorate, not only the author of *Greenmantle* and *The Thirty-nine Steps*, but his beloved sister Anna, who wrote under the name of O Douglas.

From Broughton the road leads to Tweedsmuir, travelling close to the twisting River Tweed and descending through glorious, rolling, hill and sheep country. A little beyond Tweedsmuir is the Border Collie and Shepherd Centre where, on a small hill farm, there are sheepdog displays. The tour now turns south-east, around 2,755ft Broad Law, one of the highest of the Lowland Hills, to lonely Talla Reservoir and on, through simply breathtaking scenery to the new Megget Reservoir and the beautiful St Mary's Loch. South of the Loch is Tibbie Shiel's Inn, separating St Mary's from the equally lovely Loch of the Lowes. James Hogg, the Ettrick Shepherd, was a regular at the inn.

Retrace the A708 and continue to the Gordon Arms Hotel where the tour route turns north for Traquair House. Possibly the most romantic of Scotland's great houses, Traquair has been occupied by 20 generations of the Stuart family and probably dates back to the 10th century. No less than 27 Scottish and English kings have stayed in the house.

Outwardly plain and functional but with a fine collection of historic treasures, the house owes its very special atmosphere to its connection with an almost unprecedented number of lost causes – most involving the House of Stuart. The Bear Gates are said to have been closed after the departure of Prince Charles Edward Stuart, on his march into England in 1745, and are not to be opened again until a Stuart once more sits on the throne of Scotland. Visitors can enjoy home-brewed beer and woodland walks.

Continue on the south bank of the Tweed for Kailzie Gardens, 17 acres of garden, ringed by woodland, in a very attractive setting. There are many mature trees, a walk lined with laburnum and underplanted with azaleas, rhododendrons and spring bulbs, and a waterfowl pond. A major attraction is the large walled garden, with shrub and rose beds, a herb garden and several 'secret' gardens.

Remain on the B709 for return to Peebles.

SELECTED PLACES TO VISIT

BATHGATE
Map ref 0169

Cairnpapple Hill, at Bathgate, is exposed and rather cheerless, yet it was used for ritual, ceremony, burials and assembly over a period of some 3,000 years.

This fascinating site contains the remains of burial pits, a henge, standing stones and various cairns. Neolithic, Bronze Age and Iron Age phases have all been identified – among the many fragments gathered on the site was a stone axe chip from the Neolithic factory at Great Langdale in Cumbria.

BIGGAR
Map ref 0437

A small town with a fine, wide, tree-lined main street. The restored church of St Mary was built in 1575 on the site of a 12th-century church. The Gladstone Court Museum features a 19th-century street, with shops, a bank, library and schoolroom. Greenhill Covenanter's House contains relics of the Covenanting period, housed in a 17th-century farmhouse transported stone by stone from Wiston. Moat Park Heritage Centre describes the history and geology of the Upper Clyde and Tweed valleys.

The beautiful scenery around St Mary's Loch, south of Peebles

✠ BLACKNESS
Map ref 0580

Blackness Castle lies on the shores of the Firth of Forth. A sturdy, impressive 15th-century building with 17th-century artillery emplacements, Blackness has been a Covenanters' prison, powder magazine and a youth hostel.

EDINBURGH
Map ref 2573

See page 204.

⌂ HOPETOUN
Map ref 0878

Hopetoun is a house of parts – the core, by Sir William Bruce, was completed in 1703 while the outer sections were the work of William Adam.

After William's death in 1748, his sons John and Robert completed the exterior and decorated the interior. The reception rooms are simply magnificent, containing the finest work carried out by the Adam family in Scotland and much of the pleasure in the house lies in comparing the contrasting architectural styles.

Hopetoun is the home of the Marquis of Linlithgow, and stands in the worthy setting of a beautiful 18th-century park beside the Firth of Forth.

⌂ THE HOUSE OF THE BINNS
Map ref 0478

North-east of Linlithgow is The House of the Binns, a 17th-century house with superb ceilings built for General Tam Dalyell who raised the Royal Scots Greys in 1681.

⌂ LINLITHGOW
Map ref 0177

Linlithgow is dominated by the ruins of its magnificent Royal Palace, built between the 15th and 17th centuries on the site of a 12th-century building. Nearby is the fine medieval parish church of St Michael's with its controversial steeple added in 1964.

⌂ ★ PEEBLES
Map ref 2540

Peebles received a charter according it royal burgh status from King David II in 1367. Like most wool towns it is a pleasant place, nowadays concentrating on being a holiday resort.

The Trinitarians, or Red Friars, settled in Scotland and the nave and west tower of their friary can be seen at Cross Kirk. Close by are the ruins of St Andrew's Church, founded in 1195, which became a collegiate church in the 16th century. The Tweeddale Museum is the place to study the heritage and culture of the area.

★ TORPHICHEN PRECEPTORY
Map ref 9673

Torphichen Preceptory was once the principal Scottish base of the Knights Hospitallers of St John. The site contains some remains of their church, rebuilt in the 18th century, and an exhibition.

EDINBURGH

Visitors to the splendid capital city of Scotland – Edinburgh – will enjoy the contrasts of the Old and New Town with its cultural and historical treasures

Seven hills rise from the low-lying ground on the south of the Firth of Forth with, at their centre, the volcanic rock known as Castle Rock. The site was an obvious one for a fortification and, during the period when the Northumbrian kings ruled this area, Edwin of Northumbria either built or enlarged a fortress on the site, giving his name to the future capital of Scotland. `Edwin's burgh' gained in significance during the reign of Malcolm III when his wife, Queen Margaret, built a chapel on the rock. King David I gave the town royal burgh status, and with it special trading privileges.

Throughout the Middle Ages, Anglo-Scottish relationships remained troubled and Edinburgh finally fell to the Scots in 1341, succeeding Dunfermline and Perth as capital city.

The old town was confined

Right: Edinburgh as it looked in the early 17th century
Below: A panoramic view of the city from Calton Hill

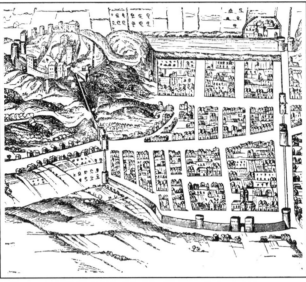

within the boundaries of the defensive King's Wall and could only develop upwards, becoming a series of tall tenemented buildings. Some overspill occurred, but well-founded fear of attack by the English restricted any wholesale expansion.

In 1543 the infant Mary was crowned Queen of Scots, breaking an agreement with Henry VIII. A year later the English fleet arrived in strength off Edinburgh and, though the castle successfully resisted the attack, the town and Holyroodhouse were burnt.

Only when the Hanoverian family was firmly established and the Jacobite threat had receded was Edinburgh able to expand in safety. The designs of a young architect, James Craig, were chosen – he proposed a classical, but recognisably Scottish, scheme and New Town was established. Built on high ground, the regular, grid-like pattern of the streets and fine quality buildings north of Princes Street, contrast with the winding, rather confused

streets and more vernacular houses of Old Town.

New Town was built during that remarkable period known as the Scottish Enlightenment. Primarily Edinburgh-based, the Scottish cultural influence in the 18th and 19th centuries was out of all proportion to its size. The philosopher David Hume, and founder of modern economics, Adam Smith were among the leaders, followed by Burns, the painter Allan Ramsay and, later, Sir Walter Scott. Boswell, Smollett, Thomas Carlyle and others went to England, where their work had considerable effect.

The expansion of Edinburgh has continued and, if Devolution does occur, the Scottish Assembly will be located in the city, joining the Supreme Courts of Justice and the Scottish Office.

Treasures of Old Town

Edinburgh Castle. Sited dramatically on Castle Rock, the castle is a magnificent spectacle. St Margaret's Chapel is 11th-century but parts of the castle are much younger – it was last extensively altered in Victorian times. The Great Hall dates from the reign of James IV and the apartments where the future James VI of Scotland and I of England was born to Mary Queen of Scots, are open to the public. The Scottish Regalia are displayed in the Crown Room.

Gladstone's Land. A restored and furnished 17th-century merchant's house, complete with shop and goods of the period. Architecturally of interest since this six-storeyed tenement retains its arcaded front.

Huntly House. A well-preserved town house of the 16th century, Huntly House has period rooms and workshops. Run by the District Council, it is now the main museum of local history.

John Knox's House. A 15th-century house which contains many relics of the 16th-century preacher who established the Presbyterian Church of Scotland. The house has a magnificent painted ceiling and original floor in the oak room.

Lady Stair's House. An attractive house, dating from 1622, it contains objects associated with three of Scotland's finest writers, Burns, Scott and Stevenson.

Outlook Tower Visitor Centre. There are fine views of the city from the *camera obscura* at the top of the tower – added in 1853 to a 17th-century building.

Palace of Holyroodhouse. David I founded the Abbey of Holyrood and it is from the guesthouse that the royal palace developed. Only the ruined 13th-century nave of the abbey church remains. Several of the older apartments have associations with Mary Queen of Scots, who held court here between 1561 and 1567. Charles II was responsible for much of the newer building. The 17th-century staterooms are open and there are contemporary portraits of many Scottish monarchs in the picture gallery.

The People's Story. Sited in the Canongate Tolbooth, this 16th-century prison now houses a reconstruction of ordinary life in Edinburgh since the late 18th century to the present day.

St Giles Cathedral. Dedicated in 1243 but largely destroyed by the English in 1385, the cathedral was rebuilt and extended over the centuries; at one time it was divided internally into four churches. The showpiece of the cathedral is the Thistle Chapel completed for the Knights of the Most Ancient and Most Noble Order of the Thistle in 1911 by Sir Robert Lorimer. The superb 15th-century crown steeple is supported by four magnificent

Planned by Robert Adam in 1791, Charlotte Square is the height of Georgian elegance

pillars in Norman style. The building was refaced in smooth stone during a controversial restoration in 1829.

Treasures of New Town

Charlotte Square. Robert Adam designed the north side houses and No 7 has been restored in the style of 1800, the year it was built.

National Gallery of Scotland. Some fine Scottish paintings hang with European masters in this splendid gallery.

Royal Botanic Garden. The largest collection of

The pre-Reformation John Knox House is now a museum

rhododendrons in Britain is the backdrop to 70 acres of varied gardens, among them an arboretum, a peat garden and a woodland garden. Most areas are accessible to wheelchair users.

Scott Memorial. The result of a competition won by George Kemp, this remarkable structure contains representations of 64 of Scott's characters. Kemp was drowned before its completion.

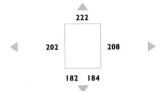

TWEED AND WOOL

An area of wonderful, rolling hills where quiet roads lead to small hamlets and Edinburgh seems an age away – yet can be reached in less than an hour. There are fine houses, romantic castles and scenery which, though very different to that traditionally associated with Scotland, has immense charm and fierce advocates.

```
              ▲
            222
   ◄  202      208  ►
            182  184
              ▼
```

202 · 208 · 222 · 182 · 184

TOUR

THE SCOTT COUNTRY
65 MILES

In the 19th century, woollen mills were built at Hawick and this Border town has since become famous throughout the world for its hosiery and other knitted goods. The town is also a sheep market, selling more than 250,000 sheep each year (see also page 183).

Some 8 miles due north from Hawick is another mill town, Selkirk, where cloth has been woven since the mid-17th century. Selkirk is a good centre for exploring the Borders and there is a ceremony each June, popular with tourists, called the Common Riding, celebrating the way the men of the town defended their beaten king, James IV at the battle of Flodden in 1513, when Selkirk was destroyed by the English.

The town abuts Ettrick Forest, and overlooks the Ettrick Water, a famous salmon and trout stream feeding into the Tweed a couple of miles away.

In the early 18th century Sir Walter Scott was sheriff of the county, and the route goes to the north-east passing his home on the Tweed near Melrose, Abbotsford House. Built, at great expense, for Scott in the 1820s it was purchased for him by his friends when bankruptcy threatened. A whimsical mixture of styles, Abbotsford incorporates fragments from several historic buildings. It contains the author's important armoury collection, his magnificent library and other relics and mementoes.

A short diversion leads to Galashiels immediately to the north of Abbotsford upon the shores of the River Gala, another tributary of the Tweed. The Nether Mill Museum features a display on the town's important woollen industry, including guided tours of the mill, as well as an exhibition tracing the history of Galashiels.

The tour travels west to Melrose and its beautiful ruined Cistercian Abbey, victim of Border battles in the 14th century. Nearby is Priorwood Garden, which was the monks' orchard, and now grows flowers for drying. Melrose has become an important tourist centre and the Motor Museum will be of interest to vintage car enthusiasts.

The road winds south-east from Melrose and then turns north-east to the 12th- and 13th-century ruins of Dryburgh Abbey which, after suffering at the hands of the English in 1322, was rebuilt with financial help from Robert the Bruce.

A little north of Dryburgh is Scott's View, justly famous, with the Tweed making a great loop beneath and the Eildon Hills in the background. Scott's funeral procession halted here for a few moments on the way to his burial at Dryburgh Abbey.

It is well worth making a detour to Mellerstain, a great Georgian house, and a magnificent example of the work of the Adam family. Robert's library, with its decorated ceiling still in its original colours, is generally acknowledged to be the finest of its kind in Scotland.

The next stop along the route is at Greenknowe Tower, a late 16th-century tower-house. At the crossroads turn right and travel south-east to Kelso via the imposing Floors Castle set on a terrace overlooking the Tweed. Floors was developed last century from the original plain 18th-century house – designed by Adam for the Duke of Roxburghe – into a splendid castle resembling a French chateau. Kelso Abbey was founded in the 12th century for monks from Chartres. It is the largest of the Border abbeys.

From Kelso the road winds south-west, passing through Jedburgh, another town that has experienced a number of attacks by the English. One of its best features is the ruin of the Augustinian abbey founded by King David I. Even in its ruined state, Jedburgh priory is a very powerful building, a site of considerable spiritual strength yet, reflected in the Jed Water, also a very lovely place. Worth visiting are Queen Mary's House, a 16th-century fortified house (a bastle-house), now a museum devoted to relics of the Queen, and the hump-backed bridge at the bottom of Canongate.

For the last part of the journey back to Hawick the road runs close to the River Teviot.

SELECTED PLACES TO VISIT

🏛 BOWHILL
Map ref 4227

An outstanding collection of pictures are on display in Bowhill House, which was, for generations, the home of the Scotts of Buccleuch. Among artists represented in the collection are Van Dyke, Canaletto, Reynolds, Gainsborough and Claude Lorraine.

The River Tweed as it flows through Kelso – a good angling centre

To add to the pleasures of the house there is a fabulous collection of French porcelain and furniture.

DUNS
Map ref 7855

Duns is still a pleasant country market town at the foot of Duns Law. Originally on the hill, the town was destroyed in 1545. For an historic town, Duns has a surprising number of well-known buildings that are relatively modern. The parish church and the town hall are both 19th-century, Duns Castle is 20th-century and the Jim Clark Memorial Room commemorates the world champion motor-racing champion, killed in Germany in 1968.

HAILES CASTLE
Map ref 5675

Hailes Castle is where Bothwell brought Mary, Queen of Scots after their escape from rebel nobles at Borthwick. Essentially a 13th- to 15th-century building, Hailes was dismantled during Cromwell's 1650 invasion. The ruins are very attractive – they stand on a rocky outcrop above the River Tyne, surrounded on three sides by trees.

PHANTASSIE DOOCOT
Map ref 6077

Phantassie Doocot in the pretty village of East Hinton has over 500 nesting boxes for pigeons, providing a ready source of pigeon meat – usually at the expense of tenants' crops.

PRESTON MILL
Map ref 5977

The River Tyne flows past the 17th-century Preston Mill, the oldest surviving water-powered meal mill in the country, which last worked commercially in 1957. Built in a gloriously warm sandstone and roofed in red pantiles, Preston is one of the most attractive mills in the country and is maintained in fine working condition by the National Trust for Scotland.

THIRLESTANE CASTLE
Map ref 5347

The many turrets give Thirlestane a fairytale appearance and it has something of a fairytale history. Home of the Maitlands since 1228, the present building is based around a castle of the 1590s. The second, Renaissance work, was carried out in the 1670s by Sir William Bruce, while the final phase, in Scottish baronial style, was added in the 1840s. Thirlestane has the best Baroque plasterwork in Scotland, ironically the work of an Englishman, George Dunsterfield. The old family nurseries now house a wonderful collection of antique dolls and toys.

TRAPRAIN LAW
Map ref 5774

Excavations at Traprain Law earlier this century revealed a Celtic town and a cache of Roman silver – now in the Royal Museum of Scotland.

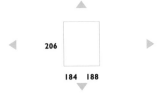

CATTLE, KIPPERS AND CASTLES

Lovely though the countryside is, most visitors to this part of Northumberland have eyes only for the spectacular coastline in all its variety. Whether it is history or natural history, colourful fishing villages or dramatic castles, all are available in a remarkably small area.

◄ 206 ►

184 188

▲ 206

184 188 ▼

TOUR

ENGLAND'S MOST NORTHERLY CORNER
76 MILES

The market town of Berwick-on-Tweed is on the north bank of the River Tweed, which marks the border between Scotland and England; small wonder that, in the past, there has so often been dissension – usually violent – as to which country it belongs. After changing hands 14 times it is now firmly established in Northumberland, and linked to the remainder of the county by three bridges, one of which was designed by Robert Stephenson to carry the railway.

The town's 16th-century grey stone walls are an impressive feature, enclosing narrow winding streets, or gates, and red-roofed stone buildings, mostly built in the Elizabethan and Georgian periods. A major industry is salmon netting; the Tweed is one of the finest salmon rivers in Britain.

The tour travels the B6354 road south-west for about 8 miles to the first of two estate villages, Etal, which boasts the ruins of a 14th-century tower-house and gatehouse, on a promontory above the River Till. The Scots destroyed this castle on their way to the Battle of Flodden.

Etal Manor, an 18th-century house, is the home of the Joicey family, owners of the Etal and Ford estates, who built this attractive village at the same time as the manor.

A couple of miles further on is the second estate village, Ford. James IV of Scotland made its castle his headquarters for a time in 1513. The Delaval family altered the castle when they acquired it in the 18th century, and through marriage it passed to the Waterford family and was eventually purchased by the Joiceys of Etal.

The widowed Marchioness of Waterford remodelled the castle in

Town Gate, one of several gates within Berwick-upon-Tweed's fine walls

the 19th century and rebuilt the village. She was an accomplished artist, and her watercolour murals on the walls of the now disused village school depict scenes from the Old Testament; she used local inhabitants for her models.

Nearby is the restored 19th-century Heatherslaw Mill, which grinds corn and produces wholemeal flour for sale.

From Ford the route curves through the lovely Glendale countryside to Doddington, south of which St Cuthbert's Cave or Cuddy's Crag may be seen.

The route then runs due south to the market town of Wooler, a base for exploring the Cheviot Hills, and the Northumberland National Park. Take the B6348 to Chillingham, criss-crossing the River Till.

Chillingham is probably more famous for its herd of wild white cattle, than for its 14th-century castle overlooking the River Till, in whose 600 acres of medieval parkland the cattle roam. The cattle were trapped in the park when it was walled in 1220, and the breed has remained pure ever since. Above the park is the Iron Age hillfort of Ross Castle.

From Chillingham the route curves to the south-east, through Eglingham and then turns north again on a winding road for some 12 miles to a delightful stretch of coast, beginning with Beadnell, a village believed to date from Saxon times. The 18th-century limekilns

beside the sea were restored by the National Trust, which protects several properties along this coast. Beadnell has a little harbour that, surprisingly on an east coast, faces west!

A mile north is the port and fishing village of Seahouses, popular with holidaymakers, and offering fine bathing. From here it is possible to embark, in good weather, for the Farne Islands, and gain information about the more accessible islands, the Inner Farne and Staple Island.

The next port of call is the village of Bamburgh, famous for the great 12th-century red sandstone keep of its castle. This is spectacularly sited on a tall outcrop of the Whin Sill, the hard seam of dolerite rock which traverses Northumberland, emerging at the coast and, further on, as the Farne Islands.

The castle's dramatic position ensures unequalled views in all directions – to Holy Island and Lindisfarne, the Farnes, south to Dunstanburgh Castle, and inland again to the Cheviots. It is home to the Armstrong family, descendants of the Victorian industrialist Lord Armstrong, who bought and extensively restored the castle.

From Bamburgh the route runs westward passing the small town of Belford with its restored Palladian hall designed by James Paine, and now divided into elegant residential apartments. There is a 14 mile stretch of road, a little inland from the coast, to negotiate back to Berwick, but one notable diversion should be made to Holy Island and

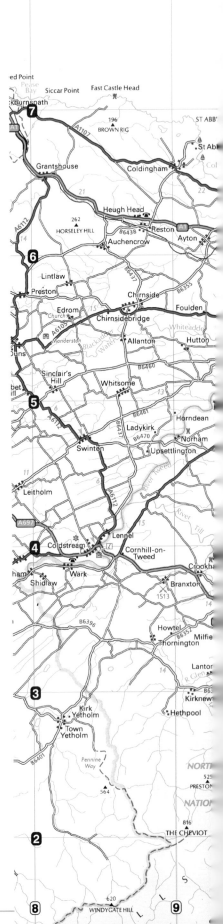

Map

SCALE

0 1 2 3 4 miles

0 1 2 3 4 5 kilometres

NU

...emouth
Burnmouth
Marshall Meadows Bay
...e Barn
1333
A6105
A6461
B6461
Tweedmouth
...st Ord
A698
Berwick-upon-Tweed
Barracks
Town Ramparts
Spittal
Huds Head
North Northumberland Heritage Coast
...urton
...ornton
Scremerston
Cheswick
B6525
Ancroft
Haggerston
Beal
Bowsden
The Lady ...terford Hall
B6353
Lowick
East Kyloe
Fenwick
Buckton
St Cuthbert's Cave
CAUSEWAY FLOODED AT HIGH TIDE
HOLY ISLAND
Holy Island
Lindisfarne Priory
Lindisfarne
Castle Point
Guile Point
North Northumberland Heritage Coast
Staple Sound
FARNE ISLANDS
Inner Sound
Budle Bay
Bamburgh
...nton ...own
Nesbit
Doddington
River Till
B6525
B6349
B6348
Belford
B1342
B1340
B1341
Lucker
Warenford
Seahouses
North Sunderland
Beadnell
Swinhoe
Beadnell Bay
...d
Wooler
Chatton
Newstead
Chathill
Tughall
Ros Castle
Newtown
Chillingham
Ellingham
Preston
High Newton by-the-Sea
Brunton
267
CATERAN HILL
North Charlton
Christon Bank
Embleton
Ilderton
Old Bewick
Falloden
Embleton Bay
New Bewick
Ditchburn
South Charlton
Rock
Dunstanburgh
A697
567
MOOR HILL
Eglingham
Rennington
Stamford
Craster
Howick Hall
...side
Beanley
River Breamish
B6346
B1339
Cullernose Point
Howick
Powburn
B6341
Longhoughton
334
COCHRANE PIKE
...ngram
Branton
Fawdon
Glanton
Denwick
Boulmer
Bolton
Great Ryle
Alnwick

0 1 2 3

the romantic castle of Lindisfarne so beautifully sited and built that it might have been hewn *in situ* from its rock.

A visit to Lindisfarne is very much dependent upon the stages of the tide; the causeway to it disappears under the waves for about 6 hours during each high tide!

SELECTED PLACES TO VISIT

CRASTER
Map ref 2519

Craster is noted for its oak-cured kippers; it has a smokery for herring brought from Scotland's western fisheries. The tiny harbour has hardly changed since it was built at the beginning of this century, though some of the fishermen's cottages now belong to incomers. The 15th-century Craster Tower is 1/2 mile inland.

DUNSTANBURGH CASTLE
Map ref 2623

The 2nd Earl of Lancaster built the splendidly sited Dunstanburgh Castle in the early 14th century; it is virtually impossible to attack from the sea. It was extended by John of Gaunt, and changed hands – and allegiance – two or three times during the Wars of the Roses.

The dramatic ruin covers some 11 acres, the most extensive of all Northumberland's many castle sites, and can be reached by a coastal walk from nearby Craster.

MANDERSTON HOUSE
Map ref 8254

Built for Sir James Miller around an 18th-century house, Manderston has a rather plain exterior, which belies the ostentatious Edwardian interior. The staircase is modelled on that in the Petit Trianon at Versailles and plated in silver. The floors are marble, the wall coverings silk damask and the stuccoed ceilings among the finest to be completed this century. The ballroom is painted in Sir James' racing colours and the stable block is arguably the grandest in Britain – possibly in Europe!

Below stairs, the kitchens and other offices are equally lavish but, if all this grandeur palls, there are splendid formal gardens and lakeside walks.

NORHAM CASTLE
Map ref 9148

A border fortress on the south bank of the Tweed, Norham was begun in the 12th century, and was the scene of many a raid, until it fell to James IV of Scotland on his way to Flodden. It has one of the finest Norman keeps in Britain, with 90ft-high walls.

To mark the start of the salmon fishing season each February, the vicar of Norham village officiates at the lantern-lit Blessing of the Nets ceremony from a coble – a flat-bottomed fishing boat.

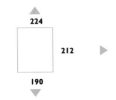

IONA, STAFFA, COLL AND TIREE

Each of these little islands of the Inner Hebrides has a flavour all of its own. Think of the monks of Iona; the music of Fingal's Cave on Staffa; Coll with its crofts, rocks and low hills; and fertile Tiree with its long hours of sunshine.

224

◀ 212 ▶

190

SELECTED PLACES TO VISIT

COLL

Coll looks a most inhospitable place when approached by steamer from Oban. Once the pier at Arinagour is reached that impression is quickly rectified, for the village has made great efforts to appeal to visitors, with neat, flower-decked cottages, colourful shops and a tea room.

The road south-west to Arileod runs through peaty heather moorland, dotted with lochans famous for their fighting trout. Breachacha Castle was visited and dismissed by Dr Johnson in 1773 – he was writing of the smaller version newly completed by the MacLeans, not this grand 15th-century castle at the head of a sea-loch. Built between 1430-50, it was occupied by the Lords of the Isles and the MacLeans. In the 1970s the older castle was restored from ruin, becoming the headquarters of a trust organizing voluntary work overseas for young people.

Take the road north-west towards Arnabost and the view ahead changes. Here there is bright, clean shell-sand, sometimes piled into dunes 100ft high, with cattle grazing the *machair* – sandy, grassy land, rich in minerals derived from wind-blown sand – which invariably attracts a wealth of plant life.

IONA

It is possible that St Columba was very far from being the dove of the Church he is called in Gaelic, for, before he arrived on Iona in AD563, he may have been responsible for causing a war over the disputed ownership of a document.

Whether excommunicated or not, he left Ireland and travelled by coracle to the kingdom of Dalriada where he had kinsmen, and where, with 12 followers, he founded a religious community which came to be known throughout the Christian world. From the 332ft viewpoint of

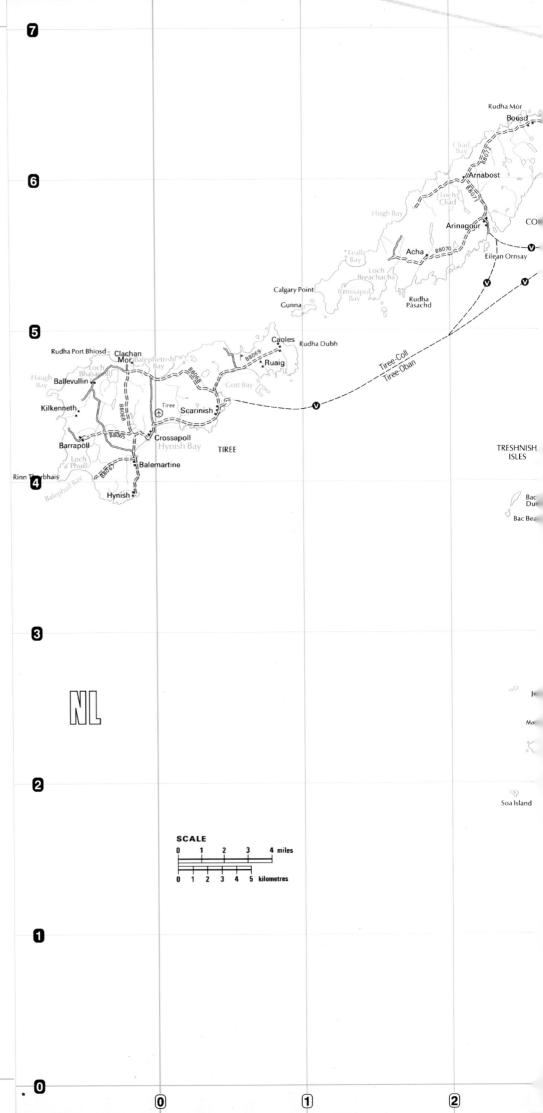

NL

SCALE

| 0 | 1 | 2 | 3 | 4 miles |

| 0 | 1 | 2 | 3 | 4 | 5 kilometres |

Dun I on the north of the island it is possible to see most of the Hebrides and appreciate the beauty of Iona. Samuel Johnson spoke for all who have visited this enchanted Celtic island – 'That man is little to be envied . . . whose piety would not grow warmer among the ruins of Iona'.

♠ ★ THE ABBEY, NUNNERY AND MACLEAN'S CROSS
Map ref 2824
Iona quickly became established as a centre of learning and remained so long after the pre-eminence of the Celtic church waned following the Synod of Whitby in AD663, when the Roman church gained ascendency.

The early monastery was a wooden building, enclosed within an earth bank, parts of which can still be seen to the north west of the present abbey. Among other buildings there was a scriptorium, the significance of which has grown with the modern theory that much of the Book of Kells may have been prepared on Iona before being taken to Ireland.

There is no dispute over the significance of the Iona school of stone carving, represented on the island by several great crosses. The most complete is the late 8th-century St Martin's Cross, some 17ft high.

Norsemen sacked Iona first in AD795, returning twice and murdering every member of the monastic community at St Martyr's Bay in AD806.

A strong community was re-established and both the Benedictine abbey and the Augustinian nunnery were founded around AD1220, with additional building continuing for about 300 years. A great deal of restoration work has been carried out on the abbey during this century. St Matthew's Cross and the restored St John's Cross stand, with St Martin's, near the west end of the abbey's nave. The nunnery is still a ruin, picturesque and surrounded by wild flowers. Fragments of the earliest cross, St Oran's, are in the nunnery. Later, but very fine, is the medieval MacLean's Cross, beside the road to the abbey. Thomas Telford was responsible for the handsome parish church of 1824.

The oldest building on Iona is St Oran's Chapel, a pink granite 11th-century church. Beside it is the early Christian burial ground Reilig Odhrain where, according to tradition, are buried 60 kings: 48 Scottish, eight Norwegian and four Irish.

ISLAND OF MULL
See page 212-3.

STAFFA
Map ref 3335
Staffa was discovered by Sir Joseph Banks in 1772 – that is to say, he was the first to write about it. Banks' curiosity was stimulated by what he learnt from the inhabitants of Mull when forced to shelter in the Sound on his way to Iceland.

In 1829 the sound of waves crashing into the cave so inspired Felix Mendelssohn that a year later, in Rome, he completed the first version of his *Hebrides* or *Fingal's Cave* overture.

◠ FINGAL'S CAVE
Map ref 3335
Fingal's Cave is one of several on Staffa – others are Boat, Clamshell, Goat, Cormorants and MacKinnon's. However the cave of Fionn mac Cumhaill – the legendary Irish giant credited with the creation of Staffa and the Giant's Causeway in Northern Ireland – has always received most attention.

The cave itself is well over 200ft long and 60ft high at its entrance, and is said to have inspired Felix Mendelssohn's *Hebrides Overture*.

The medieval MacLean's Cross on the eastern side of Iona

TIREE
Tiree is so flat – rarely more than 25ft above sea level – and exposed to Atlantic gales that no trees grow on it, yet it is a fertile place, its name meaning 'land of corn'. The pastures are grazed by sheep and cattle; the *machair* is particularly rich in buttercups and daisies.

Balemartine is the prettiest village on the island but Hynish is the most fascinating. Skerryvore is some 12 miles off the coast of Tiree and is constantly washed by the Atlantic, yet it was chosen for the site of a lighthouse, built 1837-42.

Stone was quarried on Mull and carefully shaped at Hynish before being shipped to the rock. The pier, dock, storehouses and barracks for the men engaged on the work have survived, as have the keepers' cottages and a signalling station now containing a museum telling the story of Skerryvore.

A simple, thick stone-walled, thatched croft on Tiree

OBAN AND THE ISLAND OF MULL

Oban is the tourist and trading centre of Argyll, with boat services to the Hebridean Islands.

Misty, mysterious, beautiful Mull is the biggest, and wettest, of the Inner Hebrides. It has a wonderfully varied landscape which can be explored by driving around the often single track roads. Tobermory, the capital, is a rather incongruously colourful town with a fine harbour overlooking the Sound of Mull. Most visitors travel from Oban to Craignure on the island.

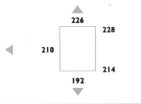

```
          226
              228
210
              214
          192
```

SELECTED PLACES TO VISIT

✿ ARDUAINE GARDENS
Map ref 7911

Pronounced Ardoony, Arduaine Gardens are delightful, in a romantic setting. The garden overlooks Asknish Bay and the view westwards is of the Slate Islands of Luing, Shuna and Seil. It has one of the finest rhododendron collections in Scotland, with a variety of skilfully blended and colourful herbaceous plants which can be seen from a maze of paths. Created in the early 1900s, Arduaine suffered from neglect following World War II and was cared for by a nanny until taken over by the present owners.

✗ CARNASSERIE CASTLE
Map ref 8402

A tower-house entirely the work of one man, John Carswell, Bishop of the Isles (1567–72), who published the first book to be printed in Gaelic. Carnasserie dominates the upper part of the Kilmartin Valley and is an important link between castles and the unprotected mansion houses of later centuries.

The sheltered bay and anchorage of Tobermory on the island of Mull

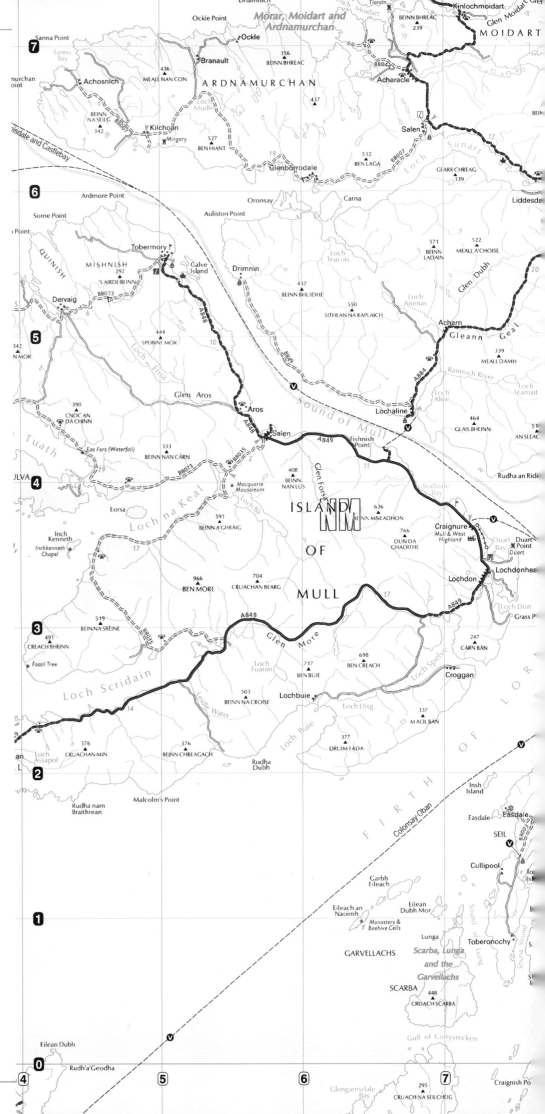

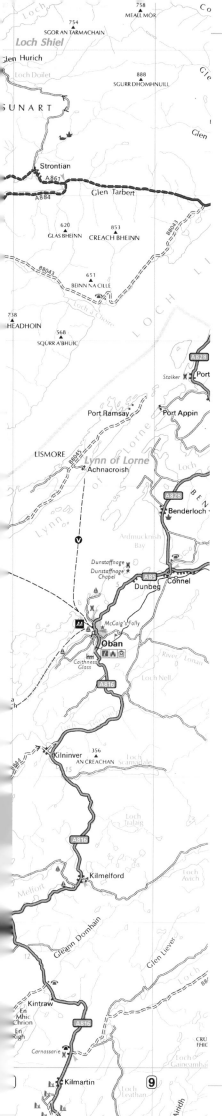

The Gribun Pass, with its steep cliffs and narrow, winding road

DERVAIG
Map ref 4352

South-west of Tobermory is Dervaig, reached along a dramatic road of hairpin bends and glorious views. Arguably the most attractive settlement on the island it is a planned village, built in 1799.

✗ DUART CASTLE
Map ref 7535

Duart is the most prominent sight on the east coast when approaching Mull by boat from Oban. Started in the 13th century, it was the home of the MacLeans until confiscated following the Jacobite rising in 1745. The ruins were bought back by Fitzroy MacLean, a remarkable man who took part in the Charge of the Light Brigade as a young man and who died in 1937 at the age of 101. A family home still, there are displays of MacLean relics.

✗ ★ DUNSTAFFNAGE CASTLE AND CHAPEL
Map ref 8734

The 13th-century Dunstaffnage Castle stands on an ancient site. Following its removal from Dunadd the Stone of Destiny is said to have been kept here until taken to Scone (see page 221). In the 18th century, when owned by the Campbells, the castle was a Hanoverian base. The interior was destroyed by fire in 1810.

The 13th-century chapel was used for the burial of Campbells and contains some beautiful stone work.

❋ EASDALE
Map ref 7417

Parts of the classic Ealing comedy, *Whisky Galore,* were filmed at Easdale on Seil Island close to the old slate quarries. From Dun Mor above Easdale there is a panoramic view of the Slate Islands, while the lovely garden of An Cala, frequently ablaze with colour, contrasts with the bleakness of the abandoned quarries and their flooded pits.

Seil Island is reached by Telford's single arched Clachan Bridge, universally called 'the only bridge over the Atlantic'.

On the island of Easdale the Folk Museum traces the workings of the slate industry.

★ INCH KENNETH
Map ref 4435

The small island of Inch Kenneth, burial ground of the Lords of the Isles, has the remains of a chapel and Celtic crosses.

❋ ➘ LOCH SUNART WOODLANDS
Map ref 8364

Between Strontian and Arriundle there is a nature reserve, part of the Loch Sunart Woodlands. Predominately oak wood, the great interest lies in the mosses and lichens – evidence both of the cleanness of the air and of the humidity. The Strontian Glen Trail leads through the woods to the old lead mines.

★ McCAIG'S FOLLY
Map ref 8530

Overlooking the town of Oban is McCaig's Folly, an unfinished granite structure resembling the Colosseum in Rome. Begun in the 1890s by John McCaig (a local banker), as a means of relieving unemployment in the area, but never finished, the central space has now been laid out as a garden.

★ MACQUARIE MAUSOLEUM
Map ref 5539

Lachlan Macquarie is buried in the Macquarie mausoleum near Loch Ba. Born in poverty on the island of Ulva he became a general, was made Governor of New South Wales, purchased an estate on Mull, and laid out the model village, Salen, in 1809.

✗ MINGARY CASTLE
Map ref 5163

Just outside Kilchoan on the road to Ardnamurchan, this 13th-century castle, now a shell, has a long history of sieges. Mingary is prominently placed on a rock beside the shore, with commanding views. One of the unsuccessful sieges was aided by the Spanish, but the best-known came in 1644 when a fire was lit at the gates to achieve success.

➥ MULL AND WEST HIGHLAND RAILWAY
Map ref 7236

Both steam and diesel trains run on this narrow gauge railway between Craignure and Torosay Castle.

◫▲◲ OBAN
Map ref 8628

When Dr Johnson and James Boswell stayed at Oban in 1773, the village consisted of a few cottages. Its expansion to a town came in the later years of the 19th century, stimulated by the arrival of the railway and the proximity of several attractions – Iona, Fingal's Cave on Staffa and the tidal whirlpool of the Gulf of Corryvreckan.

The pleasant little granite St Columba's Cathedral was designed by Sir Giles Gilbert Scott. Dunollie Castle was almost certainly one of the earliest centres of the kingdom of Dalriada.

✗ STALKER CASTLE
Map ref 9347

Stalker Castle is a privately owned four-storey tower-house standing on a tiny island in Loch Laich, built around 1540 by Sir Alan Stewart James. Ownership changed among the clans until William III took the castle in 1690. It remained habitable until 1800 and was restored in the 1970s.

◲ TOBERMORY
Map ref 5055

The island's capital, Tobermory was originally founded by the British Society for Encouraging Fisheries. It has a sheltered bay and anchorage.

⌂ TOROSAY CASTLE
Map ref 7434

Torosay is a classic example of the Scottish Baronial style so beloved of the Victorians – it has a Landseer painting at the top of the stairs. To supplement the grandeur, there is a magnificent terraced garden.

LOCHS AND GARDENS

North of Glasgow lies an area of picturesque glens and lochs, high mountains and fine country estates. Seemingly little settled and little changed since Victorian times, this area has a tranquility of its own.

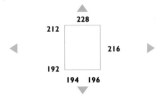

```
        228
  212 ┌──────┐
      │      │ 216
  192 └──────┘
      194  196
```

TOUR

LOCH LOMOND AND INVERARAY
103 MILES

The tour starts at Helensburgh, built as a resort and named for the wife of its designer, Sir James Colquhoun. The television pioneer, John Logie Baird was born in Helensburgh in 1888 – there is a memorial to him in Hermitage Park.

From Helensburgh the route heads for Loch Lomond, the largest loch in Britain and one of the loveliest. The A82 is joined opposite Inchmurrin, largest of the many wooded islands on the lower part of the loch.

accompanied by the West Highland Railway as it makes its way to Ardlui, set among mountains at the head of the loch. North of Ardlui the road climbs through Glen Falloch, a very lovely area of mountain and moorland with clumps of pine on scattered outcrops of rock.

The two major routes to the West Highlands converge at Crianlarich and, with the West Highland Way (Scotland's first long-distance footpath), create an impression that all roads lead to this popular centre for climbers. At Tyndrum the tour route turns west along Glen Lochy with Ben Lui rising to the left.

Beyond Dalmally, on a promontory jutting into Loch Awe, stand the romantic ruins of Kilchurn Castle, built by Sir Colin Campbell of Glenorchy in the 15th century and added to in the following two centuries.

The route follows the east shore of Loch Awe then branches left across moorland and down wooded Glen Aray to Inveraray. The old Royal Burgh was demolished in the 18th century when the 3rd Duke of Argyll was building his castle. Its successor is a striking example of how a planned town can work. Much of the architecture is Georgian and many of the buildings are now whitewashed, reflecting well in the waters of Loch Fyne. The 20th-century Bell Tower is both a war memorial to members of the Campbell family and a fine view-point – it stands 126ft high.

As the route leaves the town it passes a delightful 18th-century bridge over the Shira and then runs alongside the rocky foreshore of the equally delightful Loch Fyne.

At Cairndow on the opposite bank of the loch are the lovely woods of Strone Gardens featuring the tallest tree in Britain. As at Inveraray Castle, conifers grow particularly well at Strone.

The scenery from here, along Glen Kinglas and Glen Croe is rarely less than remarkable and is, at times, breathtaking. At the summit of wild Glen Croe is Rest and be Thankful, described in verse by Wordsworth. Ben Arthur, or the Cobbler, rises on the left of the road as it descends to Arrochar where the route turns down the east shore of the narrow sea-loch, Loch Long. From Garelochhead it follows the edge of Gare Loch, passing through Rhu on the return to Helensburgh.

SELECTED PLACES TO VISIT

✱ ARDANAISEIG HOTEL AND GARDEN
Map ref 0824

The 19th-century woodland Ardanaiseig Garden stands on the shores of Loch Awe. There are impressive displays of rare trees and shrubs including rhododen-drons and azaleas. There is a walled garden with roses and stunning views across the loch and to Ben Cruachan (3,689ft) to the north.

The picturesque village of Luss is part of the estates of the Colquhouns who have owned the land for at least six centuries. Luss was rebuilt in Victorian times.

Between Luss and Tarbet there are fine views of Ben Lomond, the most southerly of Scotland's munros (as all mountains of 3,000ft and over are called). The road runs along a wooded hillside before entering Tarbet, a Victorian resort built around its large hotel. From this point on the road is

Set in parkland east of the town and just above the loch, is the Gothic Inveraray Castle. The interior of the castle is magnificent, remarkably so as it has endured major fires in each of the last two centuries. The painted dining room and the armoury hall are among the best of their kind, with an excellent collection of portraits, tapestries and English and French furniture.

A small museum in the grounds serves as a reminder that Inveraray was a wartime Commando base.

Steamer trips can be taken on Loch Lomond, Britain's largest lake

✱ BENMORE YOUNGER BOTANIC GARDEN
Map ref 1485

Named for the man who gave it to the nation, Benmore is one of the longest established (1820) and best woodland gardens in Britain – the wellingtonia avenue is justly famous for the size of many of its specimens. Monkey puzzle trees flourish here in the moist

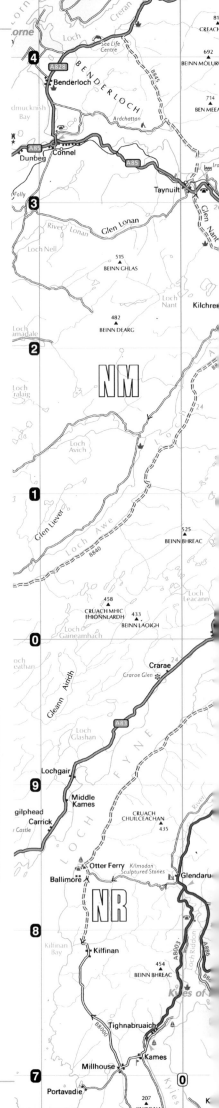

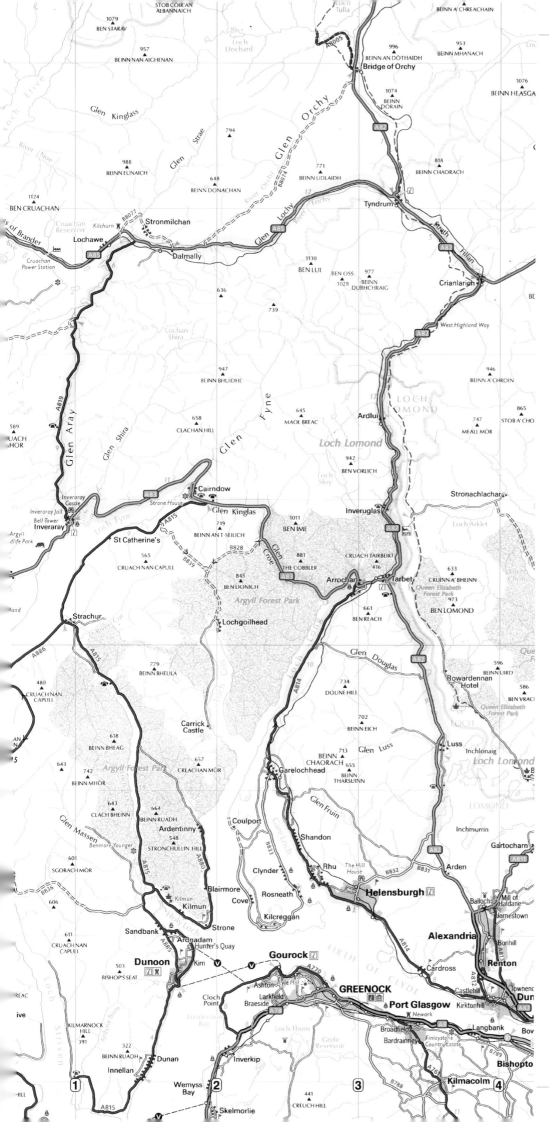

atmosphere as do the very large magnolia and rhododendron collections.

BONAWE IRONWORKS
Map ref 0132
On the shores of Loch Etive is the most complete restoration of a charcoal blast-furnace in Britain. Founded in 1753, Bonawe owed its success largely to the availability of cheap timber for charcoal. Ore was brought from Cumbria for smelting in a furnace heated by charcoal made from oak and birch gathered in the forest of Glen Nant.

FINLAYSTONE COUNTRY ESTATE
Map ref 3573
Finlaystone dates back to the 14th century. Within the house there are delightful exhibitions of dolls, Victorian flower books and Celtic art, but for much of this century the Macmillan family have been modifying and improving the gardens which are now the focus of attention for most visitors.

Covering some 10 acres with 70 acres of woodland, the garden includes a small, informal bog garden, and a formal garden partially surrounded by a castellated yew hedge. A Celtic garden maze is based on a complex geometric shape taken from the *Book of Kells*, while the fragrant garden has been planted with disabled visitors in mind.

GLEN NANT
Map ref 0226
Glen Nant, today, is a national nature reserve. However, the platforms on which charcoal was produced for the blast furnace at Bonawe can still be seen by visitors.

THE HILL HOUSE
Map ref 3084
Charles Rennie Mackintosh was one of the architects who led the movement away from the often elaborate style of the Victorians and Hill House is almost certainly the pick of his domestic architecture. Commissioned by the Glasgow publisher Walter Blackie, the outside of the house has clean lines, although it incorporates features which reflect traditional Scottish architectural design.

★ KILMUN
Map ref 1683
Kilmun Hill Arboretum has a wide range of species, most planted on steep slopes in single plots of about ¹/₄ acre, with forest walks and fine views over the Holy Loch.

TAYNUILT
Map ref 0131
There is a tradition at Taynuilt that Bonawe provided cannon balls for the battle of Trafalgar – certainly local workmen placed a standing stone near the church to the memory of Nelson.

GATEWAY TO THE HIGHLANDS

The strategic significance of this area since Roman times, and its industrial textile heritage, are well documented in its buildings. The Trossachs are a very popular holiday destination and contrast with the Fintry Hills which are remarkably quiet.

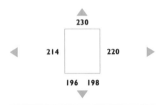

TOUR

THE TROSSACHS AND FINTRY HILLS
64 MILES

Leaving Stirling the tour follows the A84 towards Callander. Where the road turns north is Blair Drummond Safari & Leisure Park which contains wild animals, including lions and tigers, in 120 acres of superb natural settings.

On a peninsula above the River Teith is Doune Castle, built in the 14th century. Closely involved in Scottish history for almost four centuries, it fell into ruin after use as a prison by the Jacobites and was restored to something very like its original design in the 1880s.

A mile or two north is Doune Motor Museum. A permanent collection of some 40 cars – all built between 1905 and 1968 – includes rarities such as an 1934 Hispano-Suiza Ballot.

Callander is the eastern gateway to the Highlands. Easily accessible from the big towns to the south, it has become very popular at weekends with day trippers visiting the Trossachs. On the edge of the town is Kilmahog Woollen Mill; no longer a working mill, it retains its water wheel, and has a showroom selling tweeds and woollen goods.

A little way off the route, above Callander on Keltie Water, are the Falls of Bracklinn while the lovely Pass of Leny, with its famous waterfall, is north of the town.

The route passes through heavily wooded country on the lower slopes of Ben Ledi (2,873ft), beside Loch Vennacher to the small but picturesque Loch Achray, and on to Loch Katrine through the gorge of the Trossachs.

At Katrine, fine woodlands sweep down to the shores of the loch, framing the high hills in the distance. Woodland walks start from the visitor centre at the pier, and the appropriately named steamer, *Sir Walter Scott*, transports visitors the length of the loch, calling at Stronachlachar – the only other point at which a public road approaches the shores of the loch.

South from Loch Katrine the A821 starts the climb to the Duke's Road – built as a toll road in 1820, it became a public road in 1931. On the summit is a car park with notable views over Loch Vennachar to Ben Ledi. Just beyond the summit is Achray Forest Drive, the start of the 7 mile long gravel road running through mixed forest set in lovely scenery.

The main road drops steeply down towards Aberfoyle, passing the David Marshall Lodge Visitor Centre where visitors can obtain information on the Trossachs and the Queen Elizabeth Forest Park which stretches from Loch Achray to Loch Lomond.

The old village of Aberfoyle, mentioned by Scott in *Rob Roy*, lay south of the River Forth. The new village is on the north side of the river and was developed to serve the slate quarries of the Menteith Hills; it developed as a tourist centre after the Duke's Road was built.

The route now turns left and just before entering Port of Menteith, passes the only lake in Scotland, the Lake of Menteith, traditionally said to be so-called because of a mistake by a map-maker.

The picturesque ruins on the largest of the islands in the lake are those of Inchmahome Priory. Founded in 1238, this small Augustinian house is best remembered as the retreat of the young Mary Queen of Scots and her mother after the battle of Pinkie in 1547. It is reached only by ferry which is hailed by displaying a white board.

Take the B8034 due south passing Arnprior and continue to Fintry.

Spread out along the Endrick Valley between the Fintry Hills and Campsie Fells, this is now a rather fashionable village yet, for about 50 years after 1790, Fintry flirted with the cotton industry. The local family, the Galbraiths, built a mill during this period of great optimism which affected the landlords of the Highlands. Many such schemes were launched but most failed; in Fintry's case its relative remoteness was a major factor.

From Fintry the road runs beside the large Carron Valley Reservoir and Forest before turning sharp north at Carron Bridge along a minor, but attractive road with good views towards the Touch Hills and the great plain of the Forth.

On the edge of Stirling, at Borestone Brae, is the Bannockburn Heritage Centre with an exhibition and audio-visual presentation of the

Perched on top of a 250ft rock, Stirling Castle enjoys a plum position on the Firth of Forth

battle of Bannockburn. A short walk away is the fine equestrian statue of Bruce unveiled by the Queen on 24th June 1964, the 650th anniversary of the most famous of Scottish victories over the English.

SELECTED PLACES TO VISIT

♣ ★ BEN LAWERS MOUNTAIN VISITOR CENTRE
Map ref 6 I 37

Ben Lawers is the highest mountain in Perthshire at 3,984ft and is renowned for its alpine plants. The National Trust for Scotland manages some 7,500 acres of the southern slopes with nature trails and maintains an excellent visitor centre.

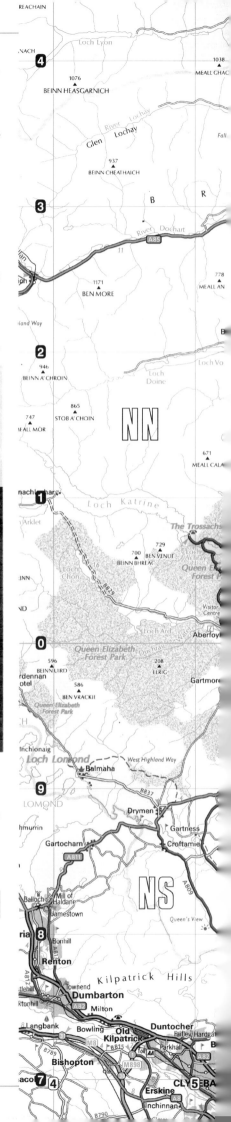

DUNBLANE
Map ref 7703

The Cathedral at Dunblane occupies a wonderful position above the Allan Water, effortlessly dominating the city. Begun by the Normans the bulk of the building is 13th-century and now houses a museum. Close by is the 17th-century Dean's house and other fine buildings of the same period.

STIRLING
Map ref 7994

Stirling was for many centuries effectively the capital of Scotland, because of its strategic position between the Highlands and the Lowlands. Two of the Scots' most decisive victories over the English were fought in the vicinity, at Stirling Bridge and Bannockburn.

The rocky outcrop beside the River Forth on which the castle stands was fortified by the 11th century, and a royal charter was granted in the 12th century. When the Stuarts came to power in 1370 Stirling Castle became a favoured royal residence; both James II and James V were born here, Mary secretly married Darnley and James VI lived here until his accession to the English throne. It is acknowledged as the finest example of Renaissance architecture in Scotland. The Museum of the Argyll and Sutherland Highlanders occupies the upper rooms of the palace while its history is displayed in the nearby visitor centre.

There are many fine buildings to seek out in Stirling. Among them are Argyll's Lodging, a superb 17th-century mansion now a youth hostel; Mar's Wark, a Renaissance house which, although partly ruined, still displays fine statues on its gatehouse; and the Guildhall. Next to Mar's Wark is the 15th-century Holy Rude Church where the infant James VI was crowned – John Knox preached the sermon. The Smith Art Gallery and Museum features a permanent display on the history of the town.

Overlooking the valley of the Forth, near Stirling lie the remains of the once magnificent abbey, Cambuskenneth.

TARTANS MUSEUM
Map ref 7723

The Tartans Museum at Comrie has a collection of over 450 tartans and contains details of over 1,000 more. There is a reconstructed weaver's cottage, and a garden where many species of dye-producing plants are grown.

WALLACE MONUMENT
Map ref 8196

At Causewayhead is the Wallace Monument. Built in 1855 – 550 years after Wallace's death – it stands on the 600ft Abbey Craig and is a further 220ft tall. William Wallace's great two-handed sword is on show and there is an audio-visual display featuring his life.

TROSSACHS

The charm of the Trossachs is that here the whole range of Scottish Highland scenery seems to be laid out in miniature; a pleasing blend of mountain, wood and loch

Some years ago the Countryside Commission for Scotland identified 40 areas considered to be of scenic significance and great beauty. These National Scenic Areas bear similarities to England's National Parks and Areas of Outstanding Natural Beauty –

Left: The crossbill, a bird typical of conifer woods

Below: The peace and beauty of Loch Katrine preserved by its isolation

their main purpose is protection against a variety of developments which could adversely affect scenic interest. Selection, as the Commission accepted, was based on the subjective judgement of a group of assessors, but the choice received general acceptance as identifying a representative spectrum of the best Scottish scenery.

Glasgow is fortunate in having two of the finest National Scenic Areas – Loch Lomond and the Trossachs – on its doorstep. The Trossachs is very small by comparison with most NSAs, extending from Ben Venue to the Menteith Hills and centring upon Loch Achray and the eastern end of Loch Katrine. The town of Aberfoyle, often used as a centre for exploring the area, is omitted.

With a View Too

Much of the boundary is formed with the Queen Elizabeth Forest Park. At the lower levels most of the trees fringing the roads, rivers and lochs are deciduous, including many oak trees, some coppiced and a reminder of the great Highland oak forests that once flourished here. This woodland extends up the lower slopes of the mountains, giving way to quite extensive conifer plantations that tend to mask the very broken, rough landscape of the Trossachs.

For many the first impression of the Trossachs is the abruptness with which the scenery changes from lowland to highland as the area is entered. The roads from the south cross the flat plain surrounding the upper River Forth – the Carse of Stirling – which, even at Aberfoyle, is only a few feet above sea level. The main road from Glasgow, the A81, is typical, appearing to run headlong at a wooded barrier, the Menteith Hills, as it approaches Aberfoyle. The route into the Trossachs is through the town before climbing the picturesque, winding road over the hills towards Loch Katrine, pausing near the summit to enjoy breathtaking views into the heart of the Trossachs (see page 216).

The approach from Stirling and the east through Callander lacks inspiration, and only as the road enters wooded country bordering Loch Vennachar does the pulse quicken with the realisation that the route is close to the heart of the Trossachs. From the terrace of the splendidly baronial Trossachs Hotel there are magnificent views across lovely Loch Achray, then, shortly after the hotel, the road plunges into deep oak woods, some at least 200 years old, leading to the pier at Loch Katrine.

Woodland Prospects

On the road back to Aberfoyle, the road passes the large David Marshall Lodge, set up by the Forestry Commission to provide visitors with information on the area and, specifically, on the Queen Elizabeth Forest Park. The Commission has long recognised the recreational potential of its large upland

forests and has been in the forefront of developments in the provision of visitor facilities. The siting of the Forest Park, so close to Glasgow and reasonably placed from Edinburgh and other centres of population, has encouraged thousands of Scots to discover an alternative environment to that in which they spend their working lives.

The Forest Park covers some 65 square miles of very varied scenery and consists of three forests – Achray, Loch Ard and Rowardennan. Included within its boundaries are large parts of two National Scenic Areas – the Trossachs and Loch Lomond. Ben Venue and Ben Lomond are the two major mountains and six lochs fall either entirely or in part within its boundaries. One final statistic: there are well over 100 miles of footpaths.

Watery Trails
Several relatively easy footpaths, including a waterfall

Moorland areas provide a perfect nesting site for the hen harrier

trail, start at the David Marshall Lodge, where trail leaflets are available. There is a very fine trail from Aberfoyle to Loch Chon. Some 7 miles long, it passes through Loch Ard Forest, touching on Loch Ard, and is enlivened by some imaginative planting, providing colourful contrasts of birch, juniper, spruce and larch.

For the less active, the B829 follows a similar route, continuing on from Loch Chon to Stronachlachar, by the shores of Loch Katrine, and the only point along the loch where it can be approached from the south. The road continues on to Inversnaid, but before it reaches this point it has entered the Loch Lomond NSA beyond Loch Arklet.

The motorist is fortunate in having another fine drive in the Achray Forest Drive, starting about 2 miles north of the lodge. It passes Lochan Reoidhte, a marvellous spectacle when the white

Left: The capercaillie can be found in the Trossachs' conifer forests
Below: Bog myrtle colonises the damper areas of the Trossachs

Loch Lubnaig lies at the foot of 2,883ft Ben Ledi and stretches for 5 miles

waterlilies are flowering in high summer, continues along the side of Loch Drunkie and drops down to Loch Achray. There are frequent stopping and picnic sites giving the motorist a perfect opportunity to study the glorious scenery.

Varied Wildlife
The area possesses a wide range of habitat, including mountain and moorland, coniferous and deciduous woodland, lochs and streams, with a correspondingly wide variety of wildlife. The open moorland around Ben Venue attracts a number of birds, including black and red grouse, ring ouzel and wheatear; the main plant on the dryer areas is crossleaved heath, with bog myrtle colonising the damper ground.

Most of the typical birds of conifer woods – capercaillie, crossbill, goldcrest and siskin – have been recorded in the forest while several species of warbler join resident species in the broadleaved areas during the summer. The lochs attract wigeon, goldeneye and pochard and have resident mallard and tufted duck populations.

Among the birds of prey buzzard, hen harrier, sparrowhawk and short-eared owl are present. Golden eagle can sometimes be seen soaring over the high northern slopes above Stronachlachar. The red squirrel is making something of a comeback, roe deer roam the forests and red deer forage on the hills.

The original popularity of the Trossachs arose partly as a result of the writings of the Wordsworths, but principally of Sir Walter Scott. Through *The Lady of the Lake* and *Rob Roy* there has grown up a folk memory which equates the scenery of the Trossachs with `the Highlands'. Wordsworth said of the area that it was `untouched, unbreathed upon' and, although hardly true today, there is still a hint of the untamed. For those who might feel uncomfortable in the bleak landscape of a truly wild area, the appeal of the Trossachs is in its controlled wilderness, through which coach parties can pass, marvelling, yet not be chilled by too much stark grandeur.

THE FORTH VALLEY

A part of Scotland that has received less attention from tourists than it merits. Here the lovely Ochil Hills, villages, castles, mills, nature reserves, lochs and the Firth of Forth, with its industrial ports, fishing villages and bathing beaches offer the visitor a rich variety.

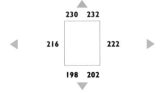

230 232

216   222

198 202

SELECTED PLACES TO VISIT

⚅ ABERDOUR CASTLE
Map ref 1985

The castle overlooks Aberdour harbour on the Firth of Forth – it was originally built in the 14th century as a tower-house for the Douglas family, who made various additions over the next few centuries. The castle fell into disrepair and the family abandoned it in 1700, but it is still in use, and the 14th-century keep has survived. Its 16th-century terraced gardens have been restored – there is a bowling green and a 16th-century doocot with perches for 600 birds.

BIRNAM
Map ref 0341

In Shakespeare's play it was prophesied that Macbeth should not fall until 'Birnam Wood shall walk to Dunsinane', some 12 miles to north. The prophecy was satisfied when he was attacked by men wearing tree branches as camouflage.

The village of Birnam developed in the 1850s after the Duke of Atholl had refused to allow the railway to cross his land on its way to Inverness. After 7 years of negotiations he finally agreed to a route, but by then hotels and villas had been built across the River Tay from the town of Dunkeld, and Birnam village was established. Beatrix Potter and her parents were among the many English people who rented holiday villas at Birnam.

BO'NESS
Map ref 0081

Bo'ness – a merciful contraction of Borrowstounness – was built at the end of the Romans' most northerly British fortification, the Antonine Wall. Last century Bo'ness was a notable port, and it is now an industrial town.

⚅ ★ CASTLE CAMPBELL AND DOLLAR GLEN
Map ref 9599

The tower, built between the 15th and 17th centuries, set in the Ochil

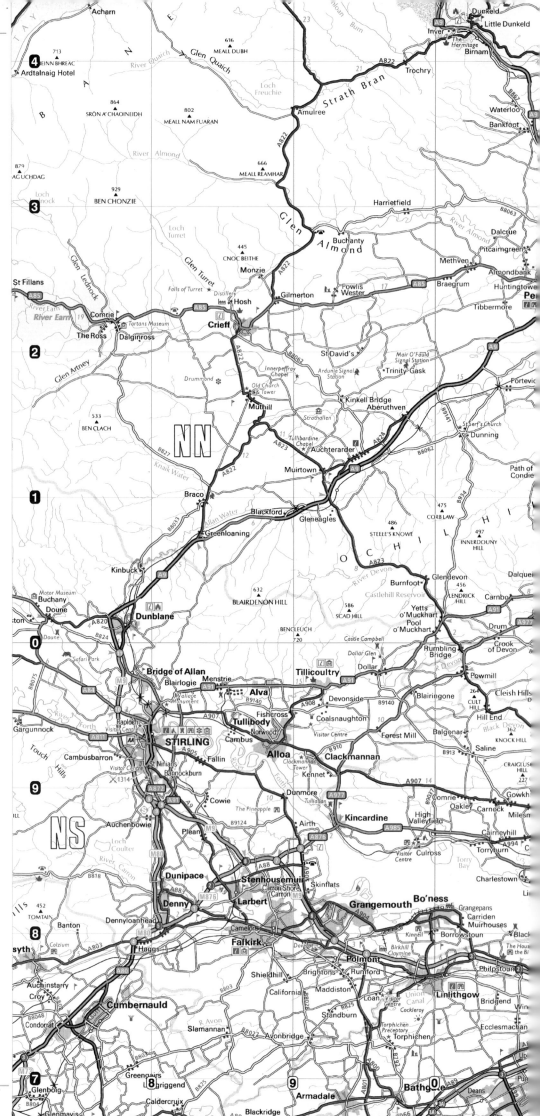

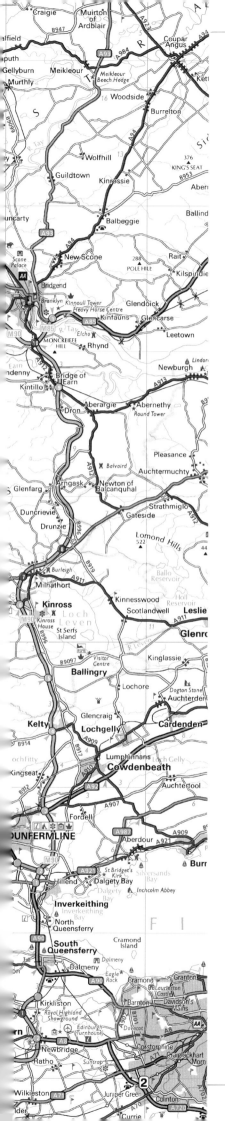

The present Scone Palace dates from 1803 but includes the earlier buildings

Hills is accessible on foot through the beautiful woodland of Dollar Glen. The earls of Argyll made this their lowland headquarters, and John Knox preached here in 1550 on a grass slope, known since then as Knox's Pulpit.

★ CULROSS
Map ref 9886

This small town on the Firth of Forth is probably the best surviving example of a typical 18th- or 19th-century Scottish burgh. The National Trust for Scotland has carried out a programme of restoration here over the past 50 years.

The 13th-century abbey was founded for the Cistercian order by Malcolm, Earl of Fife. The late 16th-century Palace is a splendid example of the house of a Scottish laird.

★ GARTMORN DAM COUNTRY PARK
Map ref 9294

Scotland's oldest man-made reservoir, directly east of New Sauchie, is now part of a 215-acre country park, popular with ornithologists because of its particularly rich bird life. Pochard, mallard and great crested grebe are among residents, with willow warblers and green sandpipers among the summer visitors.

HOPETOUN HOUSE
Map ref 0878

Scotland's greatest Adam mansion is the home of the 4th Marquess of Linlithgow. It was started to a design by William Bruce, but enlarged by William and Robert Adam.

The magnificent reception rooms have notable paintings and there are fine examples of furniture and china. The grounds are extensive and include a deer park and formal gardens. There is a garden centre.

KINNEIL HOUSE
Map ref 9880

Kinneil House has a museum in its 17th-century stable block describing the development of the nearby town of Bo'ness and its industries.

James Watt tried out his steam engine in Kinneil Park in 1764, and the Scottish Railway Preservation Society has set up a railway centre here; visitors may take a 7-mile trip from a reconstructed Victorian station to Birkhill Fireclay Mine, on veteran steam trains and rolling stock culled from Scotland's former railway companies, enjoying splendid views over the town and the Firth of Forth.

LOCH LEVEN CASTLE
Map ref 1403

The ruined castle is on an island in Loch Leven, accessible by boat from Kinross. Mary, Queen of Scots was imprisoned here for nearly a year,

and gave birth to still-born twins by her short marriage to Bothwell. The castle's 14th-century tower-house has lost its roof but otherwise is well-preserved.

PERTH
Map ref 1023

A town with mostly 18th- and 19th-century buildings occupying a strategic site on the River Tay, Perth has a colourful history, and once bid to become Scotland's capital. One of the earliest towns on this site was destroyed by flood in 1210, and subsequent rebuildings have been ravaged by a series of invaders, culminating in the Reformation, when Knox and his followers destroyed the local monasteries.

The Art Gallery and Museum has local history displays and an exhibition on the whisky industry, while visitors may tour Dewar's Distillery in the town.

PITCAIRNGREEN
Map ref 0627

Pitcairngreen was built at the end of the 18th century to house the workers in the water-powered textile mills on the River Almond. The village was planned by Lord Lynedock, who fancied it might one day rival Manchester. The mills are long-abandoned but the village survives amid rich, rolling farmland; its houses and cottages cluster around a semi-circular green, used for local events.

SCONE PALACE
Map ref 1126

Scone was the capital of the kingdom of the Picts, and its famous 'Stone' was brought here in AD843 from Iona; it was removed to England by Edward I, and is

part of the Coronation Chair in Westminster Abbey.

An early 19th-century Gothic house now stands on this ancient monastic site, where kings were traditionally crowned until James I's reign, when Knox destroyed the existing abbey and palace. The present house has French furniture, bed-hangings embroidered by Mary, Queen of Scots, porcelain, ivories and clocks.

TILLICOULTRY
Map ref 9297

There is a Mill Heritage Trail in the Ochil Hills, centred upon Tillicoultry's Clock Mill, which now houses a tourist information centre and displays of looms and other weaving equipment. The other mills on the trail were all at one time connected with the area's woollen industry, and are now in use for a variety of different purposes.

★ VANE FARM NATURE RESERVE
Map ref 1599

Many wildfowl and other water birds can be seen at Vane Farm Nature Reserve on the southern shore of Loch Leven. This reserve has a deserved reputation as a centre for education with special facilities for children.

The loch is said to contain the greatest concentration of breeding duck in Britain – at least 1,000 pairs. In autumn and winter large numbers of geese arrive, resting on the loch before dispersing to feed on nearby fields or moving south. Breeding and passage waders mass on the edges of the loch and the wet fields around it. The famous brown trout and other fish may also be found.

GOLF COURSES AND GOLDEN VILLAGES

St Andrews is one of the loveliest of all Scotland's cities, a place of learning and the home of golf. Along the East Neuk coast there are some delightful fishing villages while inland there is a Royal Palace and some delightful houses.

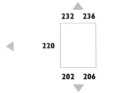

TOUR

EAST FIFE INCLUDING ST ANDREWS AND THE EAST NEUK COAST
47 MILES

The tour starts at the cathedral and university city of St Andrews. The route heads north and west towards Dairsie, with its ruined castle, and Cupar. Just off the route is the Scottish Deer Centre.

Cupar is the market town of Fife, a royal burgh with a charter dating back to 1363. Historically the stronghold of the thanes of Fife, it is the place where Mary of Guise, as Queen regent, signed the treaty which ensured that French troops left Fife.

Two miles south is the pleasant cream-coloured Hill of Tarvit Mansionhouse (NTS), built in 1696 but almost entirely re-fashioned in 1906. A monument to Edwardian taste, the house is effectively a gallery for a superb collection of paintings, tapestries and 18th-century French and English furniture. The gardens include a rose garden and woodland walk.

Part of the estate, but in stark contrast, is the plain and sturdy 17th-century Scotstarvit Tower. The early map-maker, Sir John Scot, built and lived in the tower.

The Fife Folk Museum at Ceres is a collection of rural exhibits, housed in several old weavers cottages including the 17th-century weigh-house. The village is one of the most attractive in Fife.

The tour continues south-east to the coast. Once a fishing port and market town respectively, Elie and Earlsferry have united to form a single burgh providing a broad spectrum of holiday pursuits. By contrast, St Monans remains primarily a boat building and repairing community.

The delightful church at St Monans stands on the very edge of a low cliff, just above the sea. In recent years the church has been sensitively returned to a condition close to its original.

The interior has been painted white and the large windows contribute to a lovely, light and tranquil feeling.

The East Neuk is fringed with fishing villages, each with its harbour backed by steep, narrow streets and attractive vernacular buildings. Pittenweem is typical, with a large double harbour and houses adorned with pantiled roofs over a type of gable known as a *corbie*.

The fascinating Scottish Fisheries Museum at Anstruther is housed in a number of 14th- to 18th-century buildings grouped round a cobbled courtyard. There are displays of almost every aspect of fishing in Scotland over the centuries.

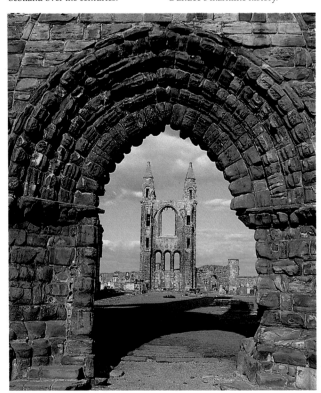

Near Kingsbarns is Cambo Country Park, based around an 18th-century farm. Return to St Andrews on the A917.

SELECTED PLACES TO VISIT

✗ DIRLETON CASTLE
Map ref 5285

A compact castle seemingly growing straight out of a rocky outcrop, parts of Dirleton date from the 13th century. Captured by the English in 1298, it was destroyed by Bruce in 1311. Added to in each of the next three centuries, the castle fell into disuse after 1651. It is now a romantic ruin, its bailey wall concealing a delightful garden and 17th-century bowling green.

Most of the cottages in Dirleton were built between the 17th and 19th centuries in a charming pink coloured stone. They, and the much older church, combine with the castle to create one of the prettiest villages in Lothian.

▨▲✗◨✦ DUNDEE
Map ref 4131

One of the oldest royal burghs in Scotland, Dundee has proved remarkably adept at developing industries and maintaining its prosperity. Displays tracing the social and civic history are contained in the Albert Institute, a fine Victorian building which houses the McManus Galleries Museum. There are important collections of Scottish and Victorian art, as well as silver, ceramics, glass and furniture.

The Broughty Castle and Museum, in a 15th-century castle, houses displays relating to Dundee's maritime history.

The ruins of St Andrews' 12th-century cathedral

✗ EARLSHALL CASTLE
Map ref 4622

Earlshall Castle is a 16th-century castle, restored in 1890. There is a marvellous Long Gallery and a large collection of armour, but the greatest treasure is the lovely walled garden, divided into a series of rooms. Topiary chessmen, a secret garden, an orchard and a kitchen garden are among the delights to be discovered in Sir Robert Lorimer's design.

▥ FALKLAND
Map ref 2506

The 16th-century hunting palace of the Stuarts is still a royal palace owned by the Queen. Following centuries of neglect the last 100 years have seen a period of careful restoration. The gardens, laid out in 1945, were once the kitchen garden where Mary, Queen of Scots played as a child. The royal tennis court is the oldest in Britain and is still in occasional use.

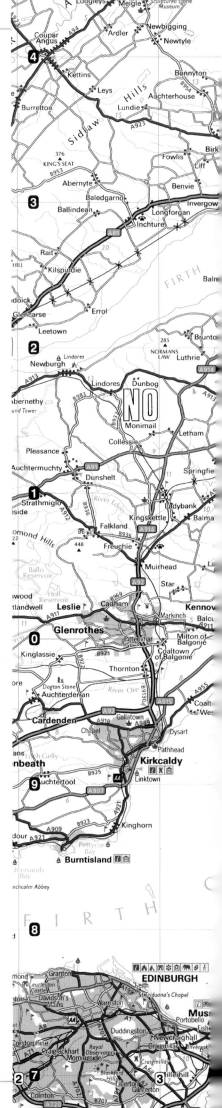

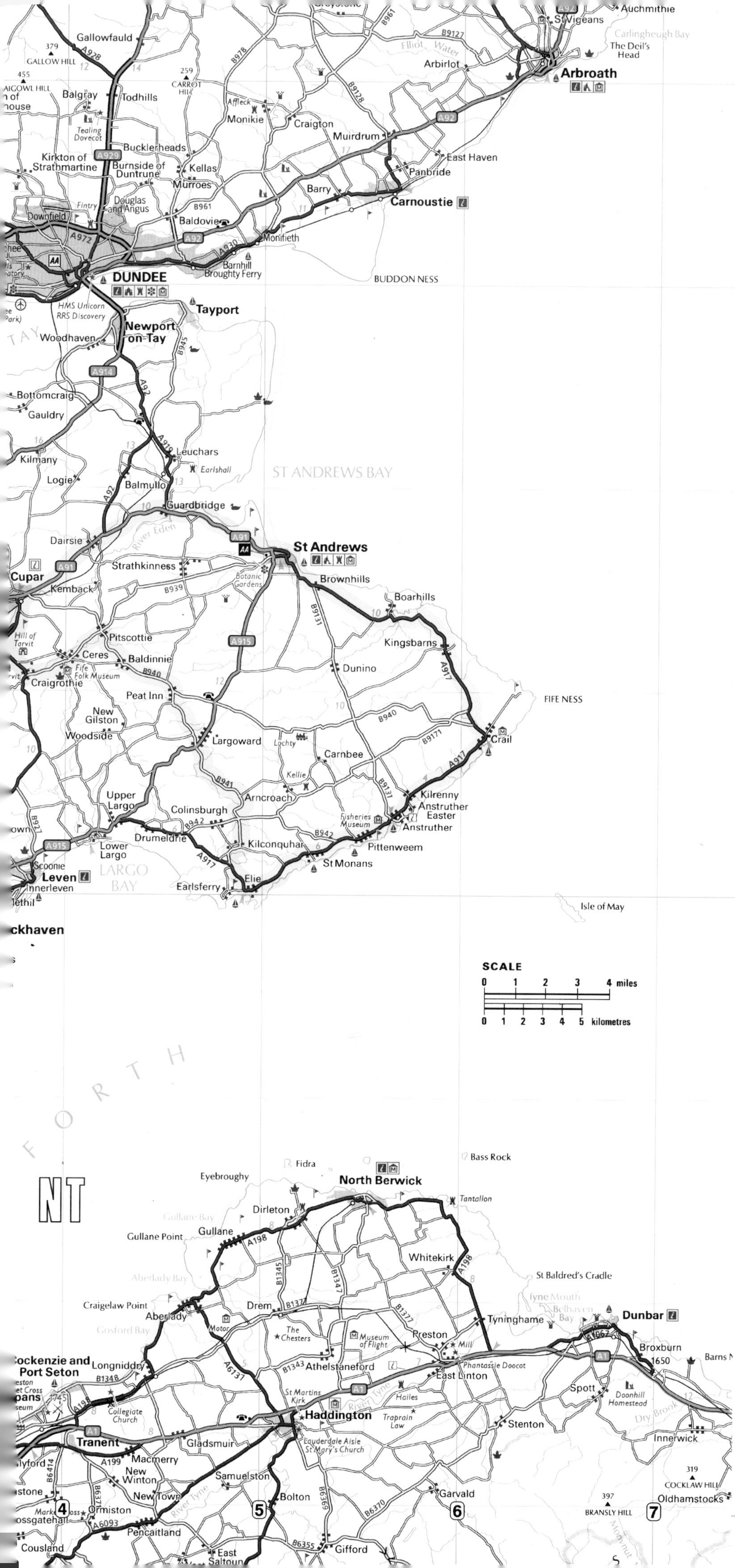

GOLF COURSES AND GOLDEN VILLAGES

Within the adjoining royal burgh there are a number of little houses now, like the palace, in the care of the NTS who have been careful to emphasise the integral relationship between palace and vernacular architecture. Falkland became the first Conservation Area in Scotland in 1970.

★ HMS UNICORN AND RRS DISCOVERY
Map ref 4230

The research ship *Discovery* has now returned to the Victoria Dock in her home port where she has joined the frigate *Unicorn*, the only example in Scotland of a wooden sailing warship and the oldest British-built ship still afloat.

✕ KELLIE CASTLE
Map ref 5205

Kellie Castle dates mainly from the 16th and 17th centuries, although the oldest part dates from about 1360. It has had a chequered history of ownership and endured a period of near ruinous neglect before it attracted the attention of the Lorimer family in the 19th century. Lovingly restored, the house and garden is now managed by the National Trust for Scotland. The outstanding 17th-century plasterwork and panelling has survived intact. The garden, created by the Lorimers, is a deceptively simple place in which to relax.

ST ANDREWS
Map ref 5116

The bones of Scotland's patron saint rest at St Andrews, the ancient capital of Fife. A bishopric by the 9th century, an Augustinian Priory was founded here in the 12th century and was consecrated in 1318. In 1559 John Knox preached a sermon against the established church, leading the townspeople to sack the cathedral. Now ruined, the fine medieval precinct wall has survived. The nearby museum contains an important collection of Celtic and medieval sculpture and artefacts. St Rule's Church, which the cathedral was built to replace, is an interesting Romanesque church, probably pre-dating the Norman Conquest.

The grim remains of St Andrews Castle stand on the clifftop near to the cathedral. Built in 1200, it had a chequered history before suffering the rather ignominious fate of being used in repairs to the harbour in 1654.

The university was founded in 1410 although the present centre, St Salvator's College, was not completed for a further 40 years.

St Andrews has a further claim to fame – golf. The most famous course in the world, the Old Course, dates from the 15th century, and for the last 100 years the R & A (Royal and Ancient Club) has been home to the controlling body of the game throughout the world.

SCALE

0 1 2 3 4 miles

0 1 2 3 4 5 kilometres

THE SMALL ISLANDS AND SOUTHERN SKYE

The Small Islands, Canna, Eigg, Muck and Rhum – while treated as a group – have sometimes obvious, sometimes subtle differences. The rocks from which they are formed are very different and so are their landscapes and climate. Their histories, though uniquely Hebridean, show marked variations and today their owners are pursuing different objectives. Yet they share, with Skye – *an t-eilean* or the island as the Gaels know it – that special attraction islands hold for the visitor.

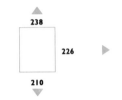

238
226
210

SELECTED PLACES TO VISIT

CANNA

Sometimes called `the Garden of the Hebrides', Canna is a lovely low island, its highest point 690ft above sea level. Now in the care of the National Trust for Scotland, it was formerly owned by Dr John Lorne Campbell, a foremost authority on the Hebrides. Canna is a Site of Special Scientific Interest – sea eagle occur here. There are a few remains of a 7th-century chapel near the original township of Cill, from which the people of Canna were transported during the Clearances.

EIGG

Owned by Keith Schellenberg, Eigg has developed its tourist trade in recent years, while retaining a crofting tradition in the north of the island. The island is dominated by the hump-backed ridge of lava known as the Sgurr, giving it the appearance of an upturned boat.

North of the harbour, at Kildonnan Church, there is the burial ground of the MacDonalds, with a broken Celtic cross. In 1577, some 200 MacDonalds took shelter in a cave near the harbour from their traditional enemies, the MacLeods of Skye. The MacLeods set a fire at the cave entrance and everyone inside was suffocated.

At the Bay of Laig when the quartzite sand is dry, it gives off a low, keening moan resulting in its Gaelic name the *Camas Sgiotaig* or Singing Sands.

MUCK

The smallest of the Isles, Muck is a sweet place, green inland and with

SCALE

0 1 2 3 4 miles

0 1 2 3 4 5 kilometres

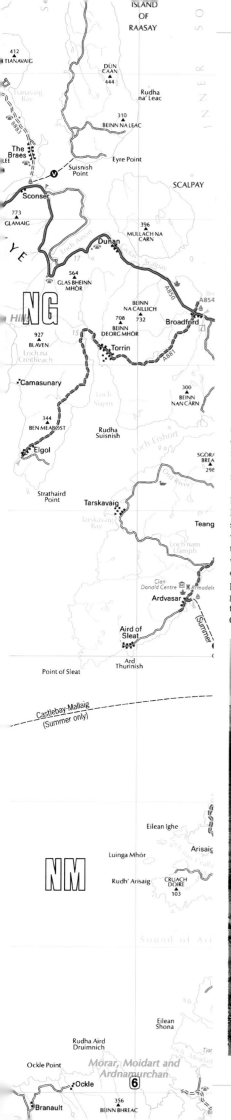

lovely, deserted beaches. It can be reached by motor boat from Eigg. The unfortunate name derives from *muc*, the Gaelic for pig.

RHUM

The largest of the Small Islands, Rhum is almost entirely mountainous, rising to 2,663ft on Askival. Rhum is now owned by the Nature Conservancy Council. The Chief Warden is responsible for a range of projects, both short and long term, concentrating on ecological research.

Rhum has a long history of human occupation, extending back to the Stone Age. Increased population made crofting untenable and, in 1826, 350 of the islanders emigrated to Nova Scotia, leaving just one family and 8,000 sheep. The island was incapable of feeding such a large flock of sheep. The next experiment was the introduction of red deer, while the rivers were stocked with salmon and trout. However, the red desert, as Rhum was known, defeated a series of owners intent on establishing a sporting estate until it passed into the hands of the Bullough family, Lancashire milling magnates.

Kinloch Castle was built by the Bulloughs in 1901 – a castellated Edwardian fantasy in pink Arran sandstone. Now a hotel, it provides visitors with a glimpse of a life style that has long since disappeared, with its orchestrion, a kind of orchestral pianola. A hooded bath provides shower waves to sooth guests before they dine at a long table in swivelling seats from Sir George Bullough's steam yacht.

Once guests were transported around the island in carriages and limousines on specially constructed roads, now visitors walk everywhere, partly because the Nature Conservancy Council so decree, partly because the heather and moor-grass have reclaimed the roads.

The geology of Rhum is varied and fascinating; the spectacular peaks of its centre and southern end are relics of its volcanic past and include a number of different rock types. The result is a wonderful flora, enhanced by the work of the Council, together with the extensive re-introduction of native trees during the last 20 years. This has led to a marked increase in woodland bird species steadily re-colonising the new plantations and feeding on the rich range of insect life for which Rhum has long been famous. The most spectacular avian success has been the re-introduction to Britain of the sea eagle. The island is home to a vast colony of Manx shearwaters – well over 100,000 pairs are estimated to nest in burrows on Askival and Hallival. The manure they produce enriches the summer grass on which the deer feed.

Deer are another of the success stories on Rhum and the culling methods introduced here – the venison is sold to offset running costs – have been widely adopted throughout the Highlands in recent years. A pure-bred herd of Highland cattle and Garrons, the Rhum ponies, add even more spice to this unique experiment, extensively monitored and reported for the benefit of other sites.

SOAY

Some years ago Gavin Maxwell, poet, painter, best-selling author and protector of seals, had the idea of setting up a factory to process the oil of the basking shark and smaller whales. The project faded gently away, leaving Soay to its solitude and lasting fame as supplier of the name of the most famous of primitive sheep breeds.

SOUTH SKYE AND THE CUILLIN HILLS

The road to Glenbrittle leads to the edge of the Black Cuillins; with Sligachan, this is the nearest the motorist can get to the mountains. However, the picture postcard views of the Cuillins are from Elgol, looking across Loch Scavaig. The Black Cuillins are fearsome, jagged-edged peaks formed from basalt and gabbro; the Red Cuillins are of more rounded red granite. None should be climbed by novices.

Close to Bracadale is Dun Beag, a typical, if rather battered, broch at least 2,000 years old. At Luib is the Old Skye Crofter's House, furnished in the style of a black house of the 19th century.

Those who prefer to study the natural history of an area should visit Tokavaig Wood, a very sheltered, and, consequently, humid site overlooking Loch Eishort. A mixture of limestone and Torridonian sandstone means that ash and oak grow profusely in the reserve and there is a fine variety of ferns and lichens.

Trekking through Glen Sligachan on Skye, with the Cuillin Hills in the background

The heart of the Western Highlands, this is largely wild, remote country with few roads and vast tracts of mountains, lochs, sea lochs and forests. Ideal country for walkers and climbers, the much fissured coastline also offers ample opportunities for fishing, swimming and sailing.

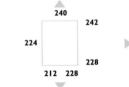

240

242

224

212   228

228

SELECTED PLACES TO VISIT

ARISAIG
Map ref 6586

This peaceful village on the Morar coast at the head of Loch nan Ceall offers superb views over a patchwork of tiny islets and reefs, with the islands of Eigg, Rhum and Muck beyond, and the Cuillin Hills on Skye in the distance. The village is a popular boating centre and there are cruises to the islands.

The Road to the Isles turns north from Arisaig past stretches of silver sand, and to the south is Borrodale Beach where in 1745 Bonnie Prince Charlie landed and embarked again from the same beach on his flight the following year.

✕ 🏛 ♨ ARMADALE CASTLE
Map ref 6304

The ruined Armadale Castle on the Sleat Peninsula of the Isle of Skye is reached by ferry from Mallaig, and now houses the Clan Donald Centre and Museum of the Isles. The visitor will learn about the clan; there is an audio-visual display, grounds with several nature trails, an arboretum and a play area for children. There are programmes of walks and talks, and a theatre in the stables for evening entertainment.

▨ BROADFORD
Map ref 6424

The popular liqueur, Drambuie, was first made at the Broadford Hotel on Skye, to a secret recipe said to have been imparted to the landlord by Bonnie Prince Charlie. The village is a busy holiday centre, built around a wide bay, patronised by large numbers of visitors in summer, and by crofters all year round.

✕ EILEAN DONAN CASTLE
Map ref 8727

Eilean Donan Castle is the archetypal fairytale castle in a most romantic setting. The castle is superbly sited on a tiny islet at the meeting point of three lochs – Alsh, Duich and Long – reached by a causeway. Eilean Donan has a

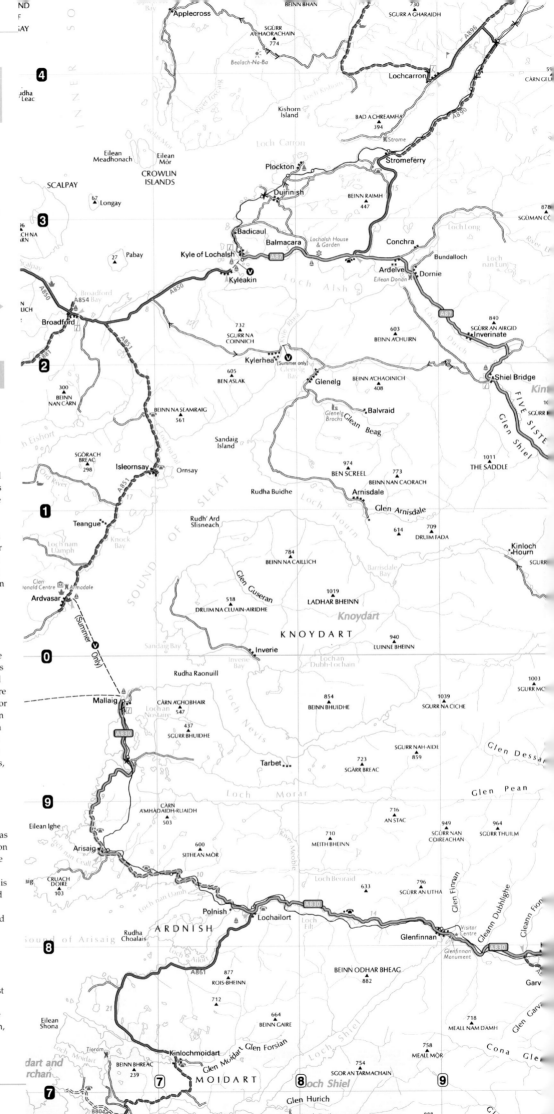

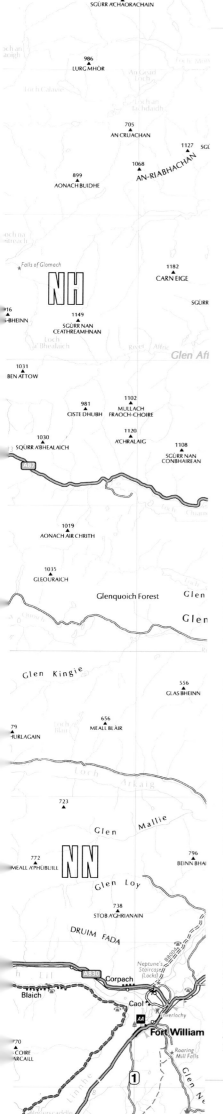

chequered history – originally built in 1230, it was blasted by English frigates in the 18th century, while held by a Spanish garrison supporting James II's son, the Old Pretender. In 1912 it was restored by Colonel MacRae, a descendant of its 16th-century constables.

★ THE FALLS OF GLOMACH
Map ref 0226

The Glomach is a high mountain burn, which sharply descends some 750ft, plunging for 300ft at the Falls of Glomach where the torrent hits a rock before falling the final 50ft. These are among the highest and most spectacular falls in Britain, but are not easily accessible – the journey, only possible on foot, takes about 1½ hours.

A spectacular mountain area at the western end of Glen Shiel, includes the dramatic Five Sisters of Kintail and abuts Glomach. The National Trust for Scotland owns 15,000 acres here, and golden eagle, peregrine falcon, raven and red grouse are among the many species of birds which live in this area. Herds of wild goats roam the mountainside, there are red deer and, in Ratajan Forest above Loch Duich, the rare shy pine marten.

⛏ GLENELG BROCHS
Map ref 8316

Glenelg Brochs are sited on the Mam Ratagan Pass beside the Glenmore River. Close by is the isolated village of Glenelg on the Sound of Sleat looking over Glenelg Bay to Skye. The road runs south of the village to the wooded Glenbeag River valley with Dun Telve and Dun Trodden, 2,000-year-old brochs or defensive stone towers built by the Picts.

♠ ★ GLENFINNAN
Map ref 9181

This early 19th-century stone column crowned with a statue of a bearded, kilted Highlander is dramatically situated on the Road to the Isles at the head of Loch Shiel. Here, Bonnie Prince Charlie rallied the clans and raised the Royal Standard in 1745 to mark the beginning of his abortive attempt to regain the British throne for the Stuarts. Nearby, the National Trust for Scotland Visitor Centre provides maps of the routes taken by the Prince's army on its way south.

❋ LOCHALSH HOUSE AND GARDEN
Map ref 8227

Lochalsh House and its lovely woodland garden with its natural history display in the coach house is part of the Balmacara estate, in the care of the National Trust for Scotland, overlooking Plockton Village. It has a network of tiny roads and small lochs. This beautiful estate includes much of the peninsula between Loch Carron and Loch Alsh and surrounds the Kyle of Lochalsh.

Looking over the rooftops of Plockton to Loch Carron beyond

LOCH HOURN
Map ref 8210

A sea-loch opposite the coast of Skye, Loch Hourn is accessible on its north side by an unclassified road which peters out beyond Arnisdale in the shadow of twin-peaked Ben Screel. A similar road approaches the inner loch terminating at Kinloch Hourn village. The loch is mainly bordered by dark, wild, remote and mountainous country, considered by many to be the grandest in the Western Highlands. To the south of Kinloch Hourn lies the trackless area of Knoydart.

LOCH NEVIS
Map ref 7596

There are no roads to take visitors to Loch Nevis; the only road is one linking two villages: Airor and Inverie. This country is strictly for well-shod walkers, and travellers by boat. The villagers can only leave the area by ferry to Mallaig. It is not, however, a gloomy place, for the mountains to the north are set well back from the loch, while to the south are the gentle hills of Morar.

⛴ MALLAIG
Map ref 6796

This busy port is at the end of the Road to the Isles, and of the West Highland Railway Line, also the mainland terminus of the islands' ferry. Mallaig harbour is surrounded by attractive white-painted stone houses and the area is very popular with tourists.

Prince Charles Edward landed at Mallaig as a fugitive in 1746, and spent some weeks in the vicinity, before taking ship from Borrodale (see Arisaig, above) to France. The summit of Carn A'Ghobhair offers views of Knoydart and Skye, Lochs Morar and Nevis, without parallel.

The 13th-century Eilean Donan Castle, beloved by artists and photographers

PLOCKTON
Map ref 8033

Formerly an 18th-century fishing community, Plockton is now a holiday resort in the care of the National Trust for Scotland. In a sheltered position in its bay on the shore of Loch Carron, its well kept stone cottages are surrounded by exotic shrubs and palm trees, made possible by the proximity to the Gulf Stream. There are views to Skye and magnificent mountain scenery all around.

⚔ STROME CASTLE
Map ref 8635

On the northern bank of Loch Carron stands the very scant re-mains of Strome Castle. In medieval times this was a stronghold of the MacDonnells of Glengarry, and one of the major fortifications on the western coast of Scotland, until, in the 17th century, it was destroyed by clan warfare. There are splendid views from the site to the Cuillin Hills on Skye, taking in the islands of Scalpay and Raasay.

PEAKS AND GLENS

This is an area of magnificent mountains, with Ben Nevis at its heart. A watery landscape of lochs and glens with very little flat land. Fort William is the centre for visitors to the area, and an important staging post on the way to the Isles, whether by road or rail.

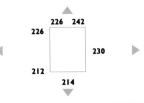

	226	242	
◀ 226			230 ▶
	212	214	

SELECTED PLACES TO VISIT

BEN NEVIS
Map ref 1672

South-east of Fort William looms the formidable shape of Ben Nevis, the highest mountain in Britain at 4,406ft. It is comparatively easy for competent climbers to reach the top, although the cliffs on its north face are best left to the most experienced climbers.

FORT WILLIAM
Map ref 1174

Situated in the foothills of Ben Nevis, Fort William can truly be said to be the gateway to the Western Highlands. The original fort was demolished last century to allow passage to the West Highland Railway, and the town has evolved around the railway.

The West Highland Museum depicts traditional Highland life and history, including a replica of a crofter's kitchen complete with equipment. There are many Jacobite relics, including an intriguing portrait of Bonnie Prince Charlie, only recognisable if reflected in a metal cylinder.

GLASDRUM
Map ref 0146

A hanging woodland rises steeply from Loch Creran at Glasdrum, just below Invercreran House Hotel. The damp lower slopes are clothed in alder; outcrops of lime-rich rocks ensure a wider range of species in the middle section with hazel and ash dominating. On the higher slopes, sessile oak and birch give way to moorland. Typical woodland flowers flourish in their preferred habitat, and there are a variety of ferns and lichens.

GLENCOE
Map ref 1058

The steep brooding mountains form a dark glen which was the scene of a massacre in 1692, when 38 members of the clan MacDonald were murdered by Campbell troops.

It was a desperate deed – a

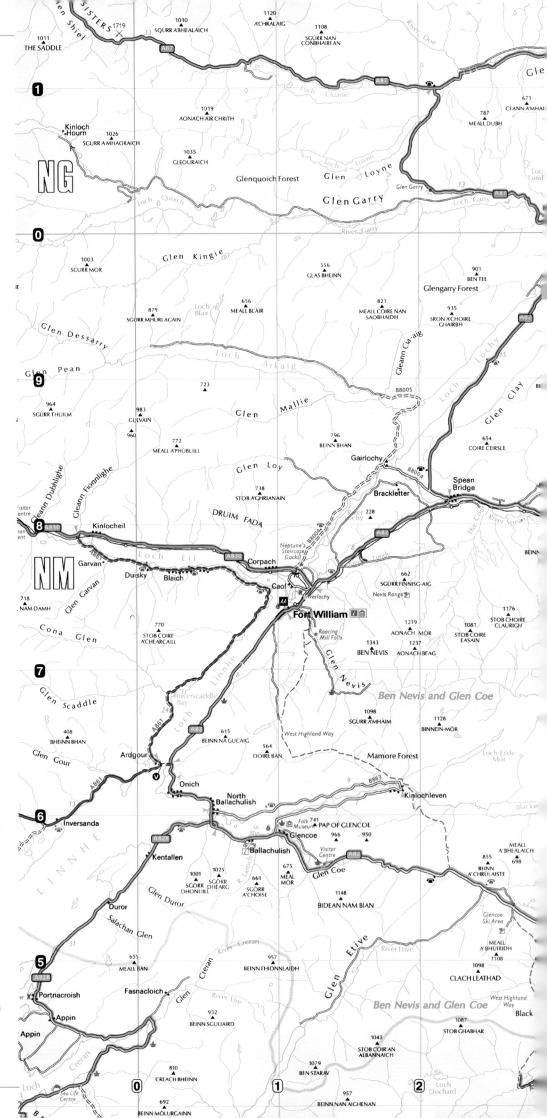

Parliamentary enquiry referred to it as 'murder under trust'. The massacre was bungled and some 400 escaped, fleeing into the mountains where many of them did not survive the severe winter weather.

The village has a monument to the MacDonald dead and a folk museum housed in cottages with roofs of heather thatch, where the visitor can see MacDonald and Jacobite relics and collections of costumes, weapons, embroidery and domestic exhibits.

At the northern end of the glen, a Visitor Centre explains the history leading up to the massacre.

☘ GLEN NEVIS
Map ref 1468
On the lower western slopes of Ben Nevis is the beautiful Glen Nevis, cutting deep into the mountains, with, at its eastern end a dramatic waterslide – 1,250ft of white water cascading from just below the summit of Ben Nevis.

Glen Nevis is a nature reserve where the visitor has a better than average chance of seeing a golden eagle. The reserve's upper car park gives superb views and it is possible to walk down from here to the glen, lined with birch and conifers.

⌘ GLEN ROY
Map ref 3089
A viewpoint in a car park in Glen Roy overlooks a curious sight – the Parallel Roads – three horizontal contour lines which show up green against the heather and stretch around the glen in a horseshoe-shaped curve. These are the tidemarks which indicate three shore levels of an Ice Age loch long since vanished, but once at least 10 miles long.

✖ INVERLOCHY CASTLE
Map ref 1175
Begun in the 13th century the castle was added to later. It is noted in Scottish history for the battle fought nearby in 1645, when Montrose defeated the Campbells.

LOCH ARKAIG
Map ref 1091
Loch Arkaig is separated from Loch Lochy by the River Arkaig. This is wild, mountain country and the 13-mile drive along the shore of the loch ends abruptly at Murlaggan; the only way to travel onwards is on foot. The loch is popular with anglers.

Where the river meets the loch is the ancestral home of Cameron of Lochiel, the chief of the Clan Cameron. Achnacarry House, which is privately owned, is set in woodland with avenues of trees. A small island in the loch is the ancient burial place of the Lochiels.

LOCH LINNHE
Map ref 0263
A 35-mile long sea-loch with Fort William at its head, Loch Linnhe is situated at the extreme west end of the Great Glen, or Glen More. It is divided into two parts by the Corran Narrows, where there is a ferry service to Ardgour.

The inner loch is dominated by Ben Nevis and the vast rift of the Great Glen begins at the eastern end of the loch. One of the best ways visitors can enjoy this splendid scenery is to take a boat trip along the loch.

✦ NEPTUNE'S STAIRCASE
Map ref 1277
There are 11 locks linking Loch Linnhe with Telford's Caledonian Canal at Banavie; eight of these interconnect to raise the canal by 64ft, and each can take vessels up to 150ft long.

The locks are collectively known as Neptune's Staircase, and were built in the 19th century. When Robert Southey, the poet, came here with his friend Thomas Telford, the canal's chief engineer, he thought the staircase was the greatest work of art in Britain. The locks are hand-operated, and the canal is now used by pleasure boats. There are two more locks at Gairlochy, and the canal then leads on to Loch Lochy.

RANNOCH MOOR
Map ref 4053
Created by an Ice Age glacier, Rannoch Moor is a vast area of high mountain moorland mostly peat and mire with bogs, burns, lochans and small pools. The nature reserve includes part of Loch Laidon, and is grazed by red and roe deer. Rannoch is a breeding site for a variety of moorland and water birds.

Only experienced walkers should venture into its trackless centre and the best way to see it is by train.

↝ SEA LIFE CENTRE
Map ref 9641
A little to the west of the village of Barcaldine is the remarkable Sea Life Centre, with a comprehensive and fascinating collection of marine life native to these coasts. Tanks display a wide variety of fish including eels and octopus; seals can be observed underwater, and there are special feeding time displays, and lectures.

THE WEST HIGHLAND WAY
Map ref 1065
The first of Scotland's long-distance footpaths runs from Milngavie, to the north of Glasgow, and ends at Fort William – a distance of 95 miles. At the start it runs through gentle farmland and woodland, but soon reaches more hilly country with a series of splendid views to Loch Lomond, where, from Balmaha it follows the loch side through oakwoods before going north to Inversnaid – landslips in recent years have made this section very difficult.

Some stout walking through Glen Falloch and Strath Fillan prepares the walker for the old military route through the mountains, giving distant views of Rannoch Moor. The most difficult part of the route is over high land from Glencoe and the Devil's Staircase to Kinlochleven, with a final climb through Glen Nevis to Fort William.

Glencoe, which is claimed to have some of the best climbing and walking country in the Highlands

THE HIGHLANDS

An area of grand mountain scenery with lochs, rivers, waterfalls and many viewpoints. The North of England Hydro-Electric scheme was begun here in the 1940s, and now encompasses much of the area, bringing reservoirs, power stations, dams and salmon leaps – new work for the resident and added interest for the visitor.

Blair Castle, at Blair Atholl, originally dates from the 13th century

The view down the length of Loch Tay at Kenmore

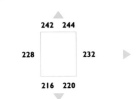

242 244

228   232

216 220

TOUR

LOCH TUMMEL, LOCH RANNOCH AND BLAIR ATHOLL
67 MILES

Beginning at Pitlochry (see page 232), the 'centre of the Highlands', set amid woodland and hillside, it is worth making an immediate detour to the Pitlochry Power Station and dam with its salmon ladder, where the fish can be seen through an observation window, making their way upstream to spawn.

The route leads north and then left on to the B8019 to Loch Tummel, passing the Queen's View, so named after a visit from Queen Victoria. This rocky spur of land gives wonderful views of the River Tummel, the loch and mountain scenery beyond. Below the viewpoint is the Tummel Forest Nature Reserve with walks and a visitor centre; the reserve contains areas of deciduous trees, lochans, and conifers – home to a wide variety of wild life.

The tour continues on the northern side of the loch through to Tummel Bridge at the western end, built in 1730. It then follows the river to Kinloch Rannoch, a famous fishing resort at the eastern end of Loch Rannoch. The route circles the 10-mile-long loch, taking first the northern road which has superb views of the high hills south of the loch, and the Black Wood of Rannoch which the route passes on its return journey.

The Black Wood is an important remnant of the Caledonian pine forest and is managed as a Forest Nature Reserve. Species such as black grouse, capercaillie and crossbill are resident here and the reserve has a reputation for the variety of its insect population.

The road rejoins the outgoing route at Kinloch Rannoch and then turns left on to the B847, a moorland road leading to Glen

Errochty. The Errochty river is part of the hydro-electric scheme and there is a reservoir and power station here.

Glen Errochty meets Glen Garry at Struan, through which the River Garry flows: there are waterfalls and a salmon leap. Just beyond the junction with the A9 at Calvine is Glen Bruar with the notable Falls of Bruar, accessible a short way up the glen by footpath.

To the east of Bruar is Blair Castle, stronghold of the dukes of Atholl since the 13th century, and one of its original towers still survives. This feudal seat is the headquarters of a unique private army, the Atholl Highlanders. Blair Castle has fine furniture, paintings, tapestries, lace, costumes, arms and Masonic regalia.

Near by at Blair Atholl is the Atholl Country Collection which reflects the daily life of local villagers in past times and, by the River Garry, the attractively restored Blair Atholl Watermill sells freshly-baked bread and scones.

The tour now turns south-east passing through Killiecrankie, where the River Garry has worn a chasm between cliffs with steep hanging woodland, managed as a reserve. Here, in 1689, the Jacobite army routed a much larger force, but lost their commander and, failing to take their next objective, Dunkeld, soon disbanded. The road winds through the pass beside the river and under two rocks almost bridging the gorge, known as Soldier's Leap. During the battle a soldier is said to have leapt from one to the other to escape a pursuer. Continue on this road to return to Pitlochry.

SELECTED PLACES TO VISIT

☑ ♣ ABERFELDY
Map ref 8648

The village is sited on the south bank of the River Tay, which is spanned by a five-arch bridge built by General Wade in 1733. Wade's commission from the British government to make Scotland more accessible with roads and bridges was fiercely resisted at the time, but much has survived as a tribute to his skills. The Black Watch Monument was built about six years later to mark the establishment of the regiment. The Birks of Aberfeldy nature trail in the ravine of the Falls of Moness, gives occasional opportunities to see roe deer, with dippers and wagtails by the river.

FORTINGALL
Map ref 7347

Thatched cottages, and a yew tree in the churchyard claimed to be about 3,000 years old make this village to the north of Loch Tay a place to visit. Fortingall lies in a narrow valley at the entrance to Glen Lyon, one of the longest and loveliest of glens. The village was restored in the late 19th century by a wealthy shipowner who lived in Glen Lyon.

★ GLENGOULANDIE DEER PARK
Map ref 7653

Highland cattle are kept in Glengoulandie park, 5 miles north-west of Aberfeldy, but the park was formed so that red deer could roam in natural surroundings. The best time to visit is in early autumn at the start of the rutting season. The

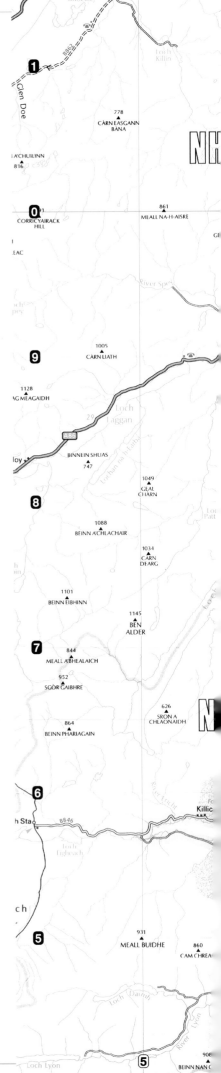

Whitebridge

778
CARN EASGANN BANA

816

861
MEALL NA-H-AISRE

CORRIEYAIRACK HILL

1005
CARN LIATH

1128
AG MEAGAIDH

BINNEIN SHUAS
747

1049
GEAL CHARN

1088
BEINN A'CHLACHAIR

1034
CARN DEARG

1101
BEINN EIBHINN

1145
BEN ALDER

844
MEALL A'BHEALAICH

952
SGOR GAIBHRE

626
SRON A CHLAONAIDH

864
BEINN PHARIAGAIN

Killic

931
MEALL BUIDHE

860
CAM CHREA

906
BEINN NAN C

1038

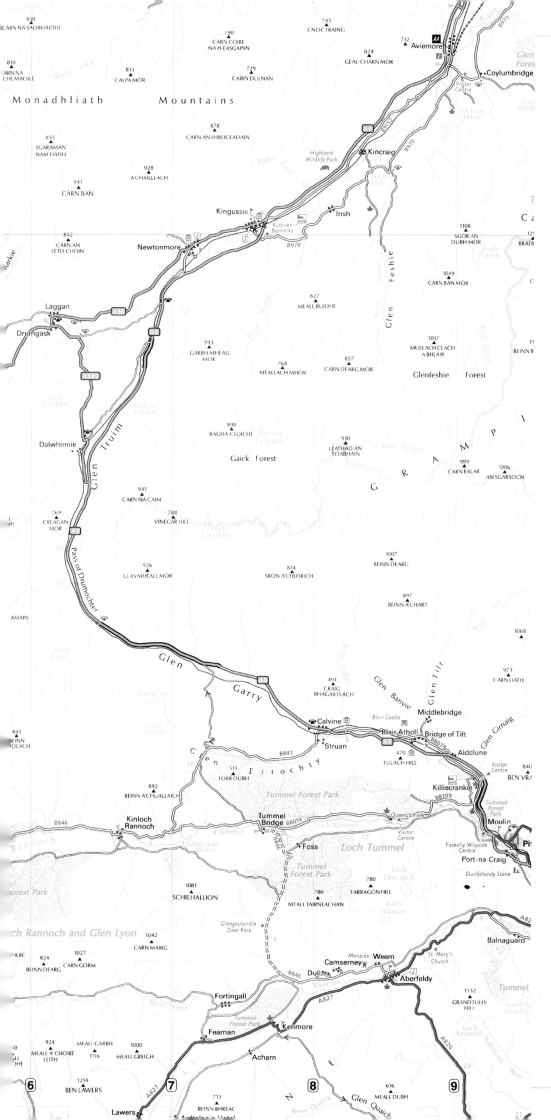

THE HIGHLANDS

park is also home to rare breeds of sheep – the tiny prehistoric Soay, and the four-horned Jacob, as well as donkeys, goats, foxes, peacocks and guineafowl.

HIGHLAND WILDLIFE PARK
Map ref 8104
In a magnificent natural setting, native animals from Scotland's past and present can be viewed; wolves, bears, reindeer, wildcats and European bison are some of the many animals that have their homes here. There is also a pets' corner.

INSH MARSHES AND LOCH INSH
Map ref 8302
Along the flood plain of the River Spey, this very large wetland area, an RSPB reserve, supports a wide variety of breeding and overwintering waders and wildfowl, including a flock of whooper swans. Buzzard, hen harrier and osprey are regular visitors and golden eagle and goshawk also occur. The area has a rich insect fauna, with over 217 species of moths and butterflies recorded. Roe deer breed in the marshland and fox and badger are also present. At the northern end is Loch Insh, where the osprey is most likely to be seen fishing.

A Celtic handbell that was once used to call people to worship is preserved in an 18th-century church above Loch Insh near Kincraig.

KENMORE
Map ref 7745
Kenmore is a popular salmon-fishing resort at the end of Loch Tay. Thought by some to be Scotland's prettiest village, much of it was built last century in a mock-rustic style by the 2nd Marquess of Breadalbane for estate workers at Taymouth Castle. There are some pleasant 18th-century houses round the square.

KINGUSSIE
Map ref 7502
The Highland Folk Museum at Kingussie is a well planned museum in an attractive grey stone town in the Spey valley. It has fascinating exhibits of reconstructed buildings, including an old Hebridean water-powered clack mill of Norse design, and a crofters black house from Lewis, as well as a farming exhibition and collections of Highland costume and musical instruments.

NEWTONMORE
Map ref 7299
This resort on the River Spey provides a good base for pony-trekking and skiing. Overlooking the site of a clan battle fought near by in 1386 is 2,350ft Craig Dhu, gathering place of Clan MacPherson. The clan MacPherson House and Museum contains relics and memorials of the clan chiefs and the Black Charter, supposedly given by a fairy to the clan MacPherson.

A ROYAL PROGRESS

At almost any point along these roads the traveller is treading in the footsteps of royalty – from Queen Victoria to successive generations of our Royal family at Balmoral, and the Queen Mother at Glamis. This is the heart of Speyside and Deeside, with grand mountains, beautiful rivers, delightful glens and lochs.

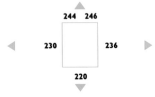

TOUR

STRATH ARDLE, GLEN ISLA AND STRATHMORE
84 MILES

Pitlochry (see page 230) is the start point of two tours – this time eastwards into the Perthshire hills by the A924, following the River Ardle over Glen Brerachan, then dropping steadily until it reaches Kirkmichael, set between hills in Strath Ardle. Here a left turn on to the B950 links with the A93 and climbs towards Glen Shee for about 3 miles before turning right on to the B951. At the head of the attractive Glen Isla are the remains of Forter Castle, built in the late 16th century and largely destroyed in 1640.

Entering Glen Isla the road passes through Kirton of Glenisla, in its forest setting on the River Isla, before running alongside the deep Loch Lintrathen. Now a reserve of the Scottish Wildlife Trust, the loch is famous for the number of wildfowl it supports during the winter – 5,000 greylag and up to 3,000 mallard roost here.

Sir James Barrie was born at Kirriemuir in 1860 in a weaver's cottage now in the care of the National Trust for Scotland; he called the town Thrums in some of his novels.

Due south of Kirriemuir is the village of Glamis, the second most famous royal castle in Scotland after Balmoral. It is said the castle has an inaccessible room with a dreadful secret, revealed to the earl of Strathmore's heir when he comes of age, ensuring he will never smile again. This is the Queen Mother's ancestral home, and here her younger daughter, Princess Margaret, was born. The Angus Folk Museum has collections of domestic and farming implements, early clothing and furniture.

From Glamis the route turns right on to the A94. Just north of the road is Eassie Church with its 8th-century carved cross-slab showing a carving of a warrior with a long spear.

The next stop is at Meigle in the Strathmore Valley where the old village school houses the Sculptured Stone Museum. This unpretentious building contains one of the most extensive collections of Dark Age sculpture anywhere in Europe. Legend has it that Queen Guinevere is buried at Meigle – Sir Henry Campbell-Bannerman, Prime Minister from 1905-08, undoubtedly is.

North-west from Meigle the route meets the A926, and continues west to Blairgowrie, the centre of a soft fruit-growing area which supplies three-quarters of the world's commercial raspberries. The River Ericht, noted for salmon and trout, runs through the centre of the town; Blairgowrie is a popular angling resort. A little off the route, just north of the town, is Ericht Gorge, where the river flows between 200ft high cliffs.

West of Blairgowrie the A923 passes several small lochs including the Loch of Clunie. Clunie Castle, a 16th-century castle which only fell into ruin this century, stands on an island in the loch; the village of Clunie lies just to the west.

Between Butterstone and Dunkeld is the Scottish Wildlife Trust's reserve, the Loch of the Lowes, famous for its resident ospreys. Reed beds fringe the loch while mixed woodland and rugged hills rise behind them creating a memorable setting. The scientific importance of the loch actually lies, not in the ospreys, but in the mixture of lowland and highland species occurring here including plants. The Trust has established a visitor centre and an observation hide beside the loch.

A mile or so away is the tiny cathedral city of Dunkeld, reached by a bridge over the Tay built by Telford in 1809. The ancient ruined cathedral by the river dates from the 12th century; desecrated in 1560 it is now being restored. The National Trust for Scotland owns a row of 18th-century cottages beside the approach to the cathedral, part of their Little Houses scheme to restore vernacular houses to modern standards without destroying their character.

Just outside the town the route joins the A9 north through the valleys of the Rivers Tay and Tummel as it returns to Pitlochry.

SELECTED PLACES TO VISIT

🏛 ✳ BALMORAL CASTLE
Map ref 2495

Set on a curve of the River Dee, Balmoral Castle is the Highland home of HM Queen Elizabeth and her family. It was bought for Queen Victoria in 1852 by the Prince Consort, who restored and enlarged it to the present baronial style – a mass of white granite with pepper-pot turrets and mullioned windows. The wooded grounds are open when the Royal family, who worship at Crathie Church outside the main gate, are not in residence.

✳ BRAEMAR
Map ref 1593

Seven miles south-west of Balmoral, Braemar lies amid spectacular

Queen Victoria loved her Highland home, Balmoral, bought for her by Albert

A ROYAL PROGRESS

Highland scenery at the meeting of the River Dee and the Clunie Water. The castle, built by the Earl of Mar in the 17th century, was burned down by the Farquharsons, who rebuilt the present castle last century. The Braemar Royal Highland Gathering is held here every September and is attended by the Royal family. The Invercauld Arms stands on the spot where in 1715 the standard was raised to mark the start of the Jacobite Rebellions.

THE CAIRNGORMS
Map ref 9900

These high, flat-topped granite mountains, the largest massif above 4,000ft in Britain, stretch from Deeside to Speyside, north-east of the main Grampian range. About 100 square miles now form the most extensive nature reserve in Britain, with rare birds like dotterel and snow bunting. Golden eagle, capercaillie, blue hare, wild cat and red deer are all found here.

GLEN CLOVA
Map ref 3373

The River South Esk flows through Glen Clova, generally considered the grandest in Angus. It can be explored by following a road from Kirriemuir which divides into a circular route, crossing the river at the north end of the glen at Clova village.

Further up the River South Esk to the north-west of Clova is the Caenlochan Nature Reserve.

Caenlochan is a large reserve with high plateaus on which dunlin and golden plover breed. The steep corries with limestone rocks support a varied flora, including alpine plants and yellow saxifrage. Red deer are here in large numbers, with fox and blue hare; golden eagle may be seen, and there are large numbers of ptarmigan.

GLENSHEE SKI AREA
Map ref 1378

Accessible from the A93 to Braemar – the highest main road in Britain – these are the nearest natural winter skiing slopes to Edinburgh and other main towns. Severe winter weather often makes the roads impassable.

TUMMEL FOREST PARK
Map ref 0563

Queen Victoria stopped here for tea on her way from Balmoral to Dunkeld in 1866. Kindrogan Manor House and woods, now a part of the Tummel Forest Park, are much as they were when she first saw them, except for some plants introduced at the end of the 19th century. There is a riverside and woodland walk.

LINN OF DEE
Map ref 0590

West of Braemar a popular 12-mile route takes visitors through the lovely wooded Dee Valley to the Linn of Dee – a waterfall caused by the river's passage down a steep gorge.

CAIRNGORMS

Visitors to the Cairngorms cannot fail to be impressed by the sheer scale of the highest and largest upland area in Britain and knowing what it is to be 'on top of the world'

Bilberry, a common plant of moorlands

The Cairngorms consist of a granite plateau; the over-riding impression is of sheer mass rather than height. There are four summits which attain a height of over 4,000ft – Braeriach, Cairn Toul, Cairn Gorm and Ben Macdhui, at 4,300ft the highest – and several others that fall not far short. Separating the first and last of those four great peaks is the steep-sided Lairig Ghru, linking Speyside to Deeside.

Accessible Wilderness

The Cairngorms have an instantly recognisable outline – long, smooth, tiered slopes, the upper levels frequently covered in snow. Great corries have been hollowed out of the slopes and mysterious passes wind away between the mountains. Around the base of the mountain range are remnants of the Caledonian Pine Forest.

At the edge of the National Scenic Area, Aviemore has grown up to cater for the great increase in skiing holidays, and the village is now a busy place throughout the year. Those planning to walk in the mountains should ensure that suitable clothing is worn and sensible precautions are taken.

A number of habitats ensure a good variety of plant and animal life. There are several lochs – Loch Insh and Loch Morlich – and Loch an Eilein is another, easily accessible, with a well signposted visitor centre and nature trail running its entire length.

Woodland Wildlife

Between Loch an Eilein and Loch Morlich lies Rothiemurchus with its mixture of pine and policy woodland. Native Scots pine growing to an upper level of about 1,500ft under Carn Eilrig represent the Caledonian Pine Forest with some 250-year-old specimens around Loch an Eilein. In places the woods contain a mixture of pine, birch and juniper with, nearer the Spey, deciduous woodland. The forest floor is carpeted by heather, blueberry and other flora, including the pinewood orchid, creeping lady's tresses, and at least two species of wintergreen. Overhead, crested tit and crossbill are present in small numbers with larger populations of siskin, redstart, chaffinch and wren; capercaillie breed deep in the pine forests. Wood ants thrive in pine forests and their huge nests can be seen throughout the area. Some of the beetles, moths and spiders found in the forest are restricted to the Cairngorms.

Rothiemurchus shades into the Glen More Forest Park with its multiplicity of forest walks leading outwards and upwards from Loch Morlich. The Forestry Commission has displayed sensitivity in its plantings here, allowing natural birch, rowan and juniper to grow along the streams and around open spaces. Plant and animal life found here is similar to that of the natural pine forests.

A view from the summit of Cairn Gorm looking to the south west

The crested tit, a bird confined to Scottish conifers, is found in Rothiemurchus Forest

Black grouse can be seen on the edges of the forest, giving way to red grouse as the heather takes over; bilberry, cowberry and crowberry grow with intermediate wintergreen and mountain everlasting on the higher moors. Where wetter areas occur it is possible to find the alpine species of lady's mantle, meadow rue and willowherb.

A Snowy Landscape

Cairn Gorm is where the ski slopes are sited, and yet there is much to interest the nature-lover within easy reach of the two large car parks below the summit at Coire Cas and Coire na Ciste. The temperature up here is often a shock for visitors who only realise as the cold penetrates unsuitable clothing that this is indeed a sub-arctic climate. If suitably clad it is possible to search for plants like cloudberry and dwarf cornel and note the variations in heather growing on exposed surfaces or in protected hollows. Lichen, which is plentiful on the rocks, is one of the main food plants of the reindeer.

On the plateaux and in the

deep corries, often snow-covered well into summer, ptarmigan can be seen and the delightful, tame, dotterel breeds. On the highest summits few flowers grow alongside the lichens and mosses that cling to the pink granite rocks, but moss campion and spiked wood-rush somehow survive, while in the corries there are a number of montane species – roseroot, purple saxifrage and alpine saw-wort – and a surprising number of rare and local plants. Even in the snowiest corries least willow and some ferns still grow strongly.

There are usually several pairs of golden eagle on the high Cairngorms although they have suffered disturbance in recent years from the increasing numbers of visitors to Glen More and other parts of the Cairngorms.

Protection Required

When, in 1978, the Countryside Commission for Scotland introduced the idea of National Scenic Areas it suggested that `for the most part [they] do not need significant recreational provisions to be made in them'. At that time no one could have envisaged the growth of recreational demand and the sort of pressure that is now exerted on areas like Speyside –

Right: *The golden eagle nests on remote crags and hunts far and wide over the moorland*
Below: *Rothiemurchus Forest floor is carpeted with heather and other flora*

the most visited stretch of countryside in Scotland – and the Cairngorms. The development of Aviemore, and vastly improved roads – Edinburgh is now little more than two hours away – have produced problems that require urgent action.

Ski-lifts, their attendant huts and car parks are one thing, the erosion of an already thin soil is quite another. With people have come avian scavengers – gulls and crows are natural predators of eggs and young birds. If eagles, breeding in relatively inaccessible areas, suffer disturbance, clearly more at risk are rare species like the dotterel, nesting closer to man. Will the widespread use of round-the-clock video cameras and barbed wire, already being used with the ospreys of Loch Garten, come to this area? Does access have to be restricted in an area like the Cairngorms or do we effectively abandon it, treating it as a giant `honeypot' and concentrate on conserving those other areas which we are confident will never be over-run?

Solutions are not easy, and it is certain that it will take more than the air of moral superiority adopted by some conservationists or the doggedly philistine attitudes of a few business people, to reconcile the needs of conservation and recreation.

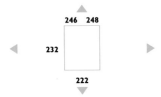

MOUNTAINS AND COASTLINE

An area of contrasts, ranging from the picturesque eastern coastline, with its ports, fishing villages and yachting resorts interspersed with nature reserves, to the mountains, hills, rivers, glens and ancient towns of the eastern Grampian Region.

246 248

232

222

TOUR

CAIRN O'MOUNTH AND HOWE OF THE MEARNS
75 MILES

Stonehaven is a fishing port and holiday resort on the east coast. Once the county town of Kincardineshire, Stonehaven has an old Mercat Cross, a 16th-century tolbooth and an 18th-century steeple where the Old Pretender was proclaimed king in 1715.

The route follows the A957 as it leads north-west passing Fetteresso Forest; known as the Slug Road, it rises steadily to about 800ft. Robert Bruce granted lands to the Burnett family, owners of Crathes Castle on the River Dee, in 1323; he also gave them a fine, jewelled horn.

Crathes is a typical tower-house of the 16th century, but with a rather incongruous Queen Anne house attached to it. There are fascinating early 17th-century painted ceilings, and the laird's gallery is the only one in Scotland to be panelled in oak. The 3½ acre formal garden is 18th-century. There are nature trails, including one suitable for disabled people.

The route continues west to the pleasant town of Banchory lying in a sheltered position under the Hill o'Fare, 1,545ft. Banchory has a small museum, a lavender distillery and, at the junction of the Rivers Dee and Feugh, a footbridge with, in season, marvellous views of leaping salmon.

Due south, beyond Strachan, the route is through wooded Glen Dye to the Bridge of Dye where the single-arch 17th-century bridge was once a toll bridge.

The road continues south over the 1,475ft Cairn o'Mounth Pass – which offers extensive views from its summit – past Fasque House. This early 19th-century castellated mansion was once William Ewart Gladstone's country home. The well preserved servants' quarters give a fascinating insight into the style of 19th- and early 20th-century country living.

Nearby Fettercairn is an 18th-century village on the border of the Howe of the Mearns, with a large Gothic arch commemorating a visit by Queen Victoria and Prince Albert. A detour just off the B966 leads to the slight ruins of Kincardine Castle, probably built as a royal palace by Alexander II, and said to be where Malcolm received Macbeth's head.

The route leads south to the pleasant village of Edzell on the River North Esk. A short way west is Edzell Castle, ruined, but indicating how fortified houses came to be adapted for a more comfortable way of life. The delightful formal walled garden, or pleasance, was designed by Lord Edzell in 1604. A range of decorative panels, based on designs obtained by the Earl in Germany, adorn the walls – unique in Scotland.

Brechin is an old town of red sandstone on the River South Esk, sheltered by the foothills of the eastern Grampians. Its one-time cathedral, now the parish church, dates from the 13th century and stands on the site of a 10th-century monastery. The building has been heavily restored but contains a fine collection of carved stone work dating back to the 8th century. Linked to the church, but originally free-standing, is a round tower, 87ft high, with an entrance door 6ft above ground, once used as a watchtower and probably two centuries older than the church. Some small fragments remain of the 13th-century Maison Dieu Chapel.

The road follows the valley of the South Esk eastwards to Montrose, a royal burgh built of sandstone – local regulations forbade any other material. It lies on a spit of land bordered by the river, the sea and the Montrose Basin. This large tidal lagoon, a popular yachting centre, is invaded each November by a tenth

The harbour at Stonehaven, which is still a working fishing port

of the world's population of pink-footed Arctic geese. Montrose has survived much while remaining a major port and now thrives servicing off-shore oil rigs.

Turning north the road follows the coast through St Cyrus. Here a nature reserve occupies 3 miles of coast, supporting a wide variety of wildlife including more than 300 species of wild flowers. There is a salmon fishery using traditional netting methods, with a boardwalk for less able people.

Inverbervie or Bervie as it is known locally, was granted a charter by King David II when he was forced by a storm to land here on his return from nine years' exile in France.

On the way back to Stonehaven, the road passes the dramatic ruin of the 14th-century Dunnottar Castle.

SELECTED PLACES TO VISIT

⬛⬛⬛⬛ ABERDEEN
Map ref 9405
Granted its first royal charter in 1179, Aberdeen became a thriving port. Still Scotland's largest fishing port, the North Sea oil industry has caused further expansion. Provost Skene's House is a 16th-century mansion with notable decorated ceilings and panelling; it is now a museum of local and social history. Another 16th-century building in the centre of the city is Provost Ross's House, which contains the Aberdeen Maritime Museum. Although Aberdeen is a centre for rose growing, the Cruickshank Botanic Garden features rock and water gardens, and fine collections of trees and shrubs with spring bulbs and alpine plants on an 11-acre site. An outstanding collection of Scottish

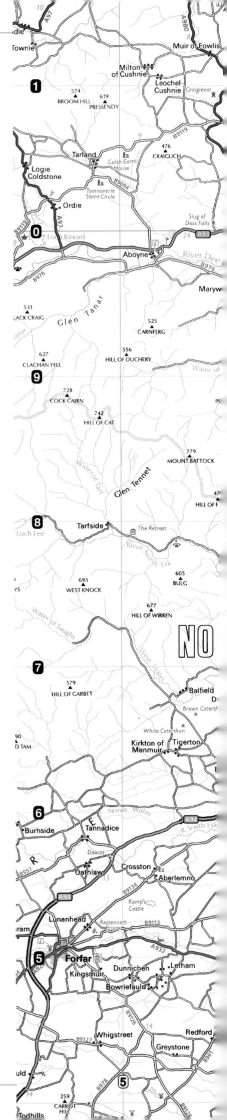

MOUNTAINS AND COASTLINE

art can be seen at the Aberdeen Art Gallery.

✗ CRAIGIEVAR CASTLE
Map ref 5609
A particularly fine, seven-storey tower-house, with fairytale turrets and conical roofs, Craigievar was built in the 17th century by William Forbes, a prosperous merchant. The classic example of Scottish Baronial and virtually unaltered, Craigievar has magnificent moulded plasterwork ceilings.

✗ DRUM CASTLE
Map ref 7901
The only 13th-century tower-house to survive in its entirety, the massive granite tower, built for Alexander III, adjoins a 17th-century mansion. Visitors can see furniture, silver and portraits, and the grounds have lawns, rare trees, shrubs and nature trails.

⌂ HOUSE OF DUN
Map ref 6659
A rather grim Palladian house overlooking the Montrose Basin, designed by William Adam, with splendid plasterwork by Joseph Enzer. The property had been in the hands of the Erskine family since 1375 but was left to the National Trust for Scotland in 1980. The recently completed extensive restoration work is a triumph of 20th-century Scottish craftsmanship.

⚶ RESTENNETH PRIORY
Map ref 4753
A lovely 13th-century ruin of mellow stone, Restenneth Priory is surrounded by green meadow. The original church was built in AD710, and its tower was incorporated into the present building by the Augustinians.

The 16th-century Provost Skene's House in Aberdeen is now a museum

SCALE

0 1 2 3 4 miles

0 1 2 3 4 5 kilometres

⑦ ⑧ ⑨

237

For those who are not climbers, this is the best part of Skye with its weird and wonderful basalt formations, splendid scenery and one of the most romantically sited castles in Scotland. More romance in the memories of Bonnie Prince Charlie and Flora Macdonald, crofters' cottages and feuding clans.

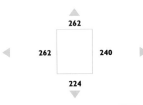

TOUR

THE TROTTERNISH PENINSULA OF SKYE
49 MILES

Sheltered by the headland of Vriskaoig Point, Portree is the only town on Skye. A fishing port and tourist resort, Portree is made up of terraces of whitewashed stone houses surrounding a natural harbour. Here, in McNab's Inn, Prince Charles Edward said goodbye to Flora Macdonald, and Boswell and Johnson stayed – the inn has been replaced by the Royal Hotel.

The tour follows the road which circles the Trotternish peninsula to the north west of Portree. The early stages present several opportunities to see Loch Snizort Beag, a most attractive sea-loch. Uig is a tiny ferry port for steamers to the Outer Isles with an exquisite setting in the lee of a great green amphitheatre, a deep bay between two grassy basalt headlands.

The road continues to Kilmuir, where Flora Macdonald is buried, her grave marked by a white Celtic cross. She brought Prince Charles to her house, Monkstadt, in the village, after he had landed nearby. The Skye Cottage Museum in Kilmuir is a group of thatched croft cottages with a weaver's house, a black house and a smithy. Documents and old photographs of crofting life are on display.

A mile or so further on is Duntulm Castle, a ruined 15th-century stronghold with a water-gate, perched on the edge of a high cliff, and once a Macdonald seat.

Turning south again the tour passes Flodigarry, where Flora Macdonald lived after her marriage and before emigrating to North Carolina in 1774. Now loyal to the Hanoverians, in 1776 Allan Macdonald was involved in the first battle of the American Revolution – against the revolutionaries. He was captured and the family later lost their lands. Flora and Allan went to Nova Scotia, then returned to Skye, where she died in 1790.

Skirting Staffin Bay the road arrives at Staffin, and 2 miles west of this village on a minor road to Uig is an extraordinary group of basalt pillars caused by a landslip and known collectively as the Quiraing which means pillared stronghold, where cattle were once driven for safety during raids.

Back to the coast road and on to Loch Mealt with its 300ft high waterfall, draining into the sea. Close by is The Kilt Rock with basalt columns resembling the folds of a kilt.

Further south are more basalt towers and pinnacles - the Storr Ridge - and in front of the ridge stands the mightiest of these, The Old Man of Storr, over 150ft high, and a much visited landmark on this coast. The route passes Prince Charles' Cave where he hid during his time on Skye, before returning to Portree.

SELECTED PLACES TO VISIT

🏛 BLACK HOUSE FOLK MUSEUM
Map ref 2148
The Black House Folk Museum at Calbost is an example of one of the earliest type of crofters' houses – with a fireplace for peat fires in the middle and the chimney simply a hole in the roof, hence the name black house. There were two rooms, one for humans, the other for their animals. A still for the illicit brewing of whisky is shown.

BORERAIG
Map ref 1855
Boreraig is the site of the piping school where the MacCrimmons of Diurinish taught piping during 300 years. The MacCrimmons were hereditary pipers to the Clan MacLeod and the site is marked by a memorial cairn.

COLBOST
Map ref 2148
Part of the Colbost Museum, 3 miles to the east, Glendale watermill at the eastern end of Loch Pooltiel is now the only thatched vertical mill in Scotland. The watermill was built some 200 years ago to grind corn for several settlements – a common practice in these remote areas. It

The harbour at Portree, chief town of the Isle of Skye whose name means 'Port of the King'

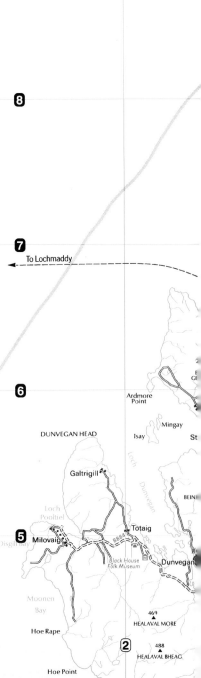

To Tarbert

Lub
Score

Museum of
Island Life

542
▲
MEALNA
SUIREAMACH

Staffin
Bay

Brogaig

Staffin

464
▲
BIODA BUIDHE

Trotternish

A855

Kilt Rock Waterfall

V

Idrigill

Uig

Valtos

BEINN EDRA
611 ▲

Rudha nam
Brathairean

Uig Bay

scrib
lands

Loch Snizort

ISLAND
OF
RONA

608
▲
CREAG A' LAIN

451
▲
BEINN A' SGÀ

214
▲
BEN DIUBAIG

719 Old Man
of
Storr
★
THE
STORR

Eilean
Tigh

Treaslane

A856

Upperglen

A850

Edinbane

Bernisdale

Tote

B8036

Borve

A850

Eilean
Fladday

Manish Point

265
▲
BEN AKETIL

271
▲
CRUACHAN BEINN
A' CHEARCAILL

ISLAND
OF
RAASAY

Portree

SOUND OF RAASAY

Colbost
Point

A863

Glen Ose

ISLE

417
▲
BEINN NA
GRÉINE

412
▲
BEN TIANAVAIG

312

ISLAND
OF
RAASAY

DUN
CAAN

Glenmore

3 **4** **5** **6**

ROMANTIC MEMORIES

ceased to work in 1902 and fell into near dereliction but was repaired in 1972.

This is a peaceful spot, with crofts dotted about the green hills, but appearances can be deceptive. In the 1880s it required the presence of a gun-boat in Loch Pooltiel to break the resistance of the crofters to the erosion of their privileges. There is a monument to their memory on the way into the glen.

✕ DUNVEGAN CASTLE
Map ref 2548

The MacLeods have held this splendid castle since the early 13th century, the longest continuous occupation by the same family of any house in Britain. The original fort was built by the Norse king Leod, forefather of the MacLeod clan. Parts of the 13th-century building remain, but the keep dates from the 14th century, and the castle was refurbished at the end of the 18th century. Portraits, arms, books and family treasures are among the contents. The wooded grounds are an unusual feature on the otherwise virtually treeless island. The flat-topped mountains to the south-west are called MacLeod's Tables where, it is said, a MacLeod chieftain held a vast banquet on one of the tables for a Lowlander guest.

ISLAND OF RAASAY
Map ref 5747

The island is a considerable contrast to the largely treeless Isle of Skye – lush arable land with pleasant birch woods, formed of Lewisian Gneiss.

The majority of the population live in the south of the island at Inverarish, near the arrival point of the ferry from Sconser on Skye. The Raasay MacLeods were the hereditary owners of the island until forced to sell up and leave in the 1840s.

The ruins of their original home, Brochel Castle, can be seen on a small promontory on the east coast. The MacLeods left Brochel in the 16th century, moving to Clachan on the west coast and building Raasay House where they entertained Boswell and Johnson. In recent years the house suffered from neglect but is now being used as an outdoor centre.

TOTE
Map ref 4249

Off the Portree to Dunvegan road on the minor road to Tote, Clach Ard is a 7th-century Pictish stone carved with a number of symbols which stands beside the road.

TRUMPAN
Map ref 2361

On the Waternish peninsula at Trumpan the ruined church was the scene of a raiding party by the MacDonalds of Uist. They found the MacLeods worshipping in Trumpan church and set it on fire, killing those who tried to escape. MacLeod clansmen appeared to defend their own and, hampered by a falling tide, the MacDonalds were unable to escape the MacLeods' vengeance.

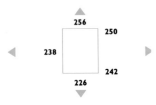

WESTER ROSS

The mountains form a commanding backdrop to the deeply incised coastline, with its sea-lochs and fjords. A wonderful panorama of coastal inlets, islands and sea is reached by precipitous and winding roads, the only means of access to this splendid mountain coast.

```
        256
            250
  238
            242
        226
```

SELECTED PLACES TO VISIT

ACHILTIBUIE
Map ref 0307

Trips to the Summer Isles (see below), and to the Coigach Peninsula can be taken from Achiltibuie, a long coastal village on Badentarbat Bay. Anglers can sample sea fishing; trips are available to the mouth of Loch Broom. There is a smokehouse, where fish, meat and game are cured, and at the Summer Isles Hotel in the village the Hydroponicum will be of interest to gardeners; it describes how to grow plants in soil-less conditions.

APPLECROSS
Map ref 7144

A lovely sandy beach lures visitors to Applecross in its sheltered bay, with views to Raasay and Skye. North of the village a monastery was founded in the 7th century by an Irish monk; it became a major centre of Christianity, but was destroyed by Norse invaders. The Applecross peninsula offers a series of splendid views to the traveller on its coastal road.

☀ BEALACH-NA-BA
Map ref 7742

The minor road to the Pass of Bealach-Na-Ba with its one-in-four gradients and hairpin bends passes wonderfully rocky scenery with lochans and burns and distant views to Skye. This was the route along which cattle were driven to markets in the east of Scotland, and it has long had the reputation of being the worst road to drive along in the Highlands although it is now improved.

♣ BEINN EIGHE NATIONAL NATURE RESERVE
Map ref 0065

On the south-east shore of Loch Maree, north-west of Kinlochewe, this reserve was established for the study and conservation of the remains of the Caledonian Forest. Mountain goat, pine marten, deer,

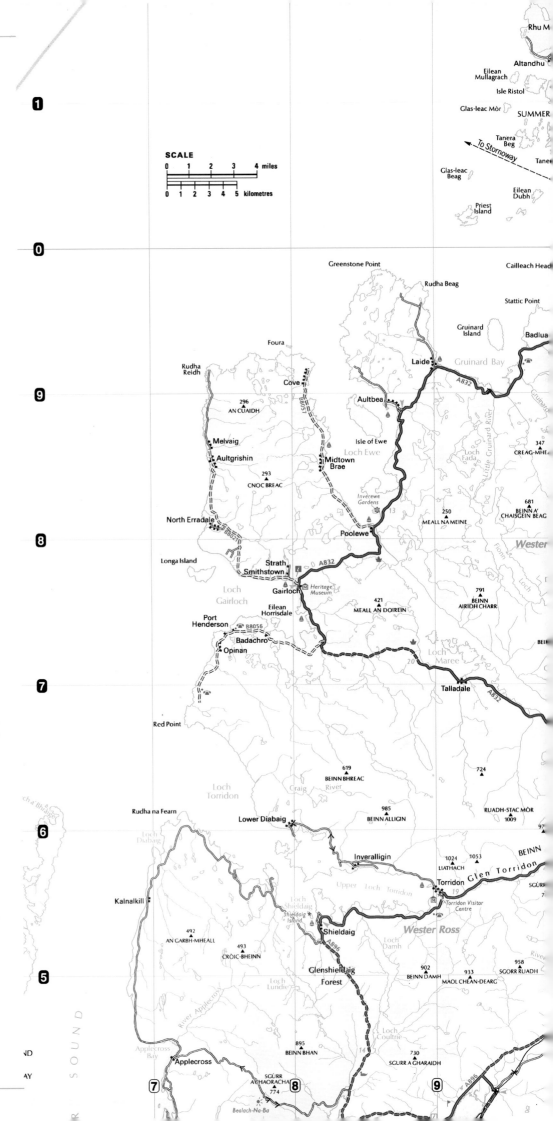

wild cat and pygmy shrew, ptarmigan and golden eagle live on the reserve. The National Trust for Scotland visitor centre provides an introduction to the wildlife and suggests walks in the area.

COIGACH
Map ref 1004
The western edge of this bleak, mountain and moorland reserve is bounded by the road through Achiltibuie and on to Culnacraig. For the hardy, it is possible to walk the 6 miles or so to Strath Kanaird, but the going is hard and not well signed. The reserve is dominated by two mountains – the attractive Ben More Coigach and twin-peaked Beinn an Eoin. Around them are great stretches of heather and grass moorland with patches of wet bogland. Behind Achiltibuie the slopes are heather-clad and in the area around Loch Lurgainn there are clumps of birchwood. A number of rare plants thrive here, including some alpines, while the bird life is typical of this habitat – ptarmigan, ring ouzel, golden plover. The rarer British mammals – otter, wild cat, badger and pine marten – all live in the reserve though are hardly ever seen, unlike the red deer which roam the area.

GRUINARD ISLAND
Map ref 9495
Gruinard Island was infected with anthrax during germ warfare experiments in World War II and has been out of bounds to visitors. In 1990 it was decided that the danger from the disease was past and the ban on the island has been lifted. Gruinard Bay has fine sandy beaches.

HERITAGE MUSEUM
Map ref 8076
The Heritage Museum at Gairloch depicts life in the western Highlands from Pictish to Victorian times. There is a reconstructed croft house with buttons to illuminate its interior and animate a model of an

old woman who sings a lullaby in Gaelic to a baby in a cradle. In an annex to the museum there is history displays and old photographs. A holiday town with good beaches and a nine-hole golf course, Gairloch boasts some of the finest scenery in Wester Ross.

✿ INVEREWE GARDENS
Map ref 8683
The architect of this famous garden was Osgood Mackenzie who spent much of his early years in Europe. In 1862 his father, the laird of Gairloch, gave him the estate beside Loch Ewe, an unpromising blend of red Torridonian sandstone, hags and peat bogs. After establishing a windbreak of Corsican and Scots pine with fences that excluded both deer and rabbit, good soil was imported in creels. Proximity to the Gulf Stream has made it possible to grow exotic plants, shrubs and trees from all over the world.

LITTLE LOCH BROOM
Map ref 0394
This lovely sea-loch carved from Torridonian sandstone and divided from Ullapool and Inner Loch Broome by a peninsula of Torridonian hills, Little Loch Broom has several small sandy bays of great beauty. The road along the southern shore is very pleasant but it has a dark history; when first built, in 1851, it was known as Destitution Road, for it gave work after the potato famine to starving crofters in return for food – not pay.

LOWER DIABAIG
Map ref 7961
Approached by a road along the north bank of Loch Torridon, Lower Diabaig has whitewashed cottages scattered around a rocky amphitheatre, and its own loch. The villagers are mostly crofters who graze sheep along the coast; wild goats roam the hillsides, descendants of those kept to provide milk when cattle were in short supply.

A view over the unusual Inverewe Gardens to Loch Ewe

SHIELDAIG VILLAGE
Map ref 8254
Once a centre of the herring fishing industry, and originally planned as a nursery to train fishermen to be sailors for the Royal Navy, Shieldaig prospered for many years as official grants were provided for boat-building and prices guaranteed for fish caught. One of the most attractive villages in the north-west of Scotland, its whitewashed cottages overlook Shieldaig island, just off-shore in the sea-loch. The road to the village from Glen Torridon, along the south shore of Upper Loch Torridon, is magnificent, with a series of wonderful views of Liathach and Bein Alligin across the loch.

THE SUMMER ISLES
Map ref 9708
This cluster of 18 flat, treeless islands and numerous tiny islets or skerries are all uninhabited, though at the beginning of this century there were crofting communities on the larger of the Summer Isles. The naturalist Frasaer Darling lived on Tanera More for a while, using the natural resources of the island. He recorded 43 species of breeding birds on Tanera More and large numbers of barnacle geese visit Glas Leac Beag each winter.

⚲ ★ TORRIDON VISITOR CENTRE AND DEER MUSEUM
Map ref 9156
The Torridon estate, owned by the National Trust for Scotland, is considered by many to be the most magnificent mountain scenery in the country. At Torridon village there is a visitor centre with an audio-visual presentation about the estate. The deer museum features displays describing the life cycle of deer in this area, stressing the need for careful management. From Torridon, the A896 runs past Liathach through Glen Torridon under the massif of Beinn Eighe.

THE GREAT GLEN

The lure of the Loch Ness Monster can only heighten the magic this part of Scotland has for the visitor. The scenery is outstandingly beautiful, and though much of it can be enjoyed by the motorist, there is good walking and climbing, fishing, boating, and many other outdoor pursuits.

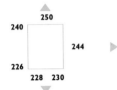

```
        250
240
                    244
226
    228   230
```

SELECTED PLACES TO VISIT

BEAULY
Map ref 5246

Beauly is sited on a noted salmon river, the River Beauly, at the point where the river widens into the Beauly Firth. The market place of this attractive village has the ruined Beauly Priory at its north end. A statue in the square commemorates the 16th Lord Lovat who raised the Lovat Scouts during the South African War.

DINGWALL
Map ref 5459

A busy small market town at the end of the Cromarty Firth with a harbour built by Thomas Telford. Dingwall was a thriving port before the mouth of the River Peffery became silted up. Macbeth reputedly ruled Ross-shire from here in the 11th century.

⌂ DRUMNADROCHIT
Map ref 5230

Situated on the River Enrick and the west side of Loch Ness, this village is a popular centre for walking, angling, climbing and pony trekking.

The Loch Ness Monster Exhibition at Drumnadrochit records all the sightings of the monster, first seen by St Adamnan in the 6th century.

FOYERS
Map ref 4921

Overlooking Loch Ness, the twin villages of Lower and Upper Foyers are set amid woodland where the first hydro-electric scheme in Britain was completed in 1896.

The Falls of Foyer are particularly spectacular after heavy rainfall. The uppermost of these drops is 30ft and the lower 90ft. However, their scenic impact was greatly reduced by the hydrolectric scheme's removal of water.

⌂ GLEN AFFRIC
Map ref 2324

One of the loveliest glens in the Highlands, Glen Affric is often depicted in Landseer's paintings.

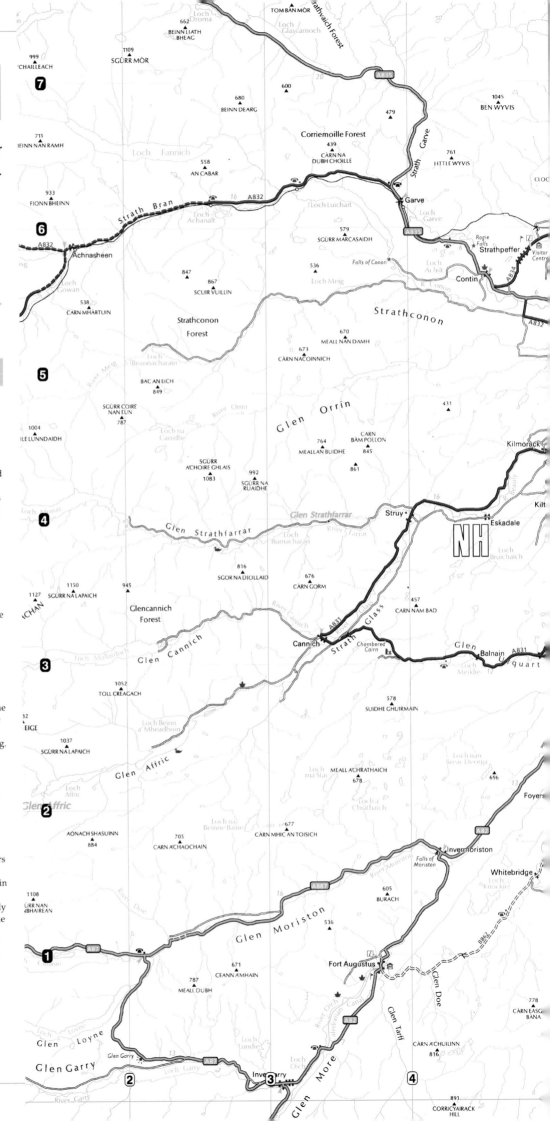

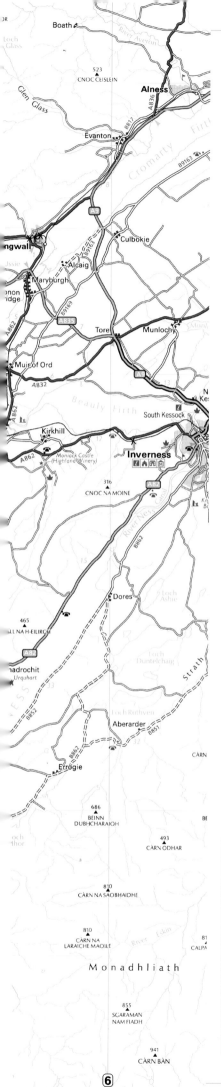

The Forestry Commission have an office at Cannich where leaflets can be obtained. The old road through the Inverness-shire hills takes the motorist through a marvellous mixture of habitats, including two lochs – Beinn a' Mheadhoin (created when the River Affric was dammed as part of a hydro-electric scheme in 1946) and Affric – a river, woodlands and waterfalls. The pine woods, containing some fine old trees, are mostly south of the lochs, with one of the best stands between them; it can only be reached on foot along one of the paths provided by the Forestry Commission. North of the road the scenery is more open, with high hills as a backdrop where red deer can be seen. Graceful silver birch grow out of a carpet of fern, and rowan supplement the pine, underscored by bilberry or heather in the open areas. Roe deer live here with red squirrel, wildcat, pine marten and badger. In the pine forests there are capercaillie and black grouse, with a wide variety of small woodland birds such as crossbill, crested tit and redstart. Dippers breed along the banks of the river, goosander are frequent visitors to the lochs, buzzard and sparrowhawk are resident and there is the chance of a sighting of a golden eagle.

GLEN MORRISTON
Map ref 3012
The wooded Glen Morriston, after some miles, emerges onto moorland and at Achlain there is a memorial to Roderick Mackenzie who, bearing a resemblance to Prince Charles Edward, allowed himself to be captured and was killed. High in the hills above the River Doe is a cave in which the Prince took refuge after his flight from Culloden in 1746.

♣ ⚲ INVERFARIGAIG
Map ref 5525
On the less frequented east bank of Loch Ness, above Inverfarigaig is a small reserve. A steeply climbing woodland trail through mainly deciduous open woodland leads to a viewpoint overlooking the Farigaig river and the loch. The trees are mostly birch with some oak, aspen, alder, juniper and hazel; heather and bilberry form the ground cover. There is a display with an exhibition on the wildlife of the woodland.

KILMORACK
Map ref 4945
South-east of this village is 19th-century Beaufort Castle, seat of the Chief of Clan Fraser. Near by are ruins of an earlier stronghold. Although the castle is not open to the public it can be seen from foot- and bridle paths that cross the River Beauly.

LOCH NESS
Map ref 5022
This 20-mile-long, narrow, deep loch is world famous for its beauty as well as for its monster. The Great Glen, created by a rift about 350 million years ago, contains Loch Ness, Loch Lochy and Loch Linnhe, connected by rivers and the Caledonian Canal. At Buloit there is a memorial to John Cobb, who died on Loch Ness in 1952 when attempting to break the world water speed record.

★ MONIACK CASTLE
Map ref 5544
An early 17th-century castle, built to an L-plan and much altered and extended, Moniack Castle is now a unique Scottish enterprise – a Highland winery. A range of country style wines is produced, including elderflower and silver birch; also mead and sloe gin.

⚲ STRATH FARRAR
Map ref 2638
A fascinating programme to assist regeneration is under way at Strath Farrar, site of one of the largest surviving remnants of the ancient Caledonian Forest. Fencing to exclude all grazing animals, wild or domestic, has been introduced and a degree of replanting is assisting the naturally slow regenerative process of old pine woods. Today, the pine woods have some magnificent 300-year-old pine trees by the river, while those growing on the rocky outcrops are probably 200 years old. Aspen, rowan, holly, birch, willow and even a few sessile oaks add to the pleasure of the woods. Wintergreen, lesser twayblade and lady's tresses grow beneath the pines, as well as wood sorrel, wood anemone and lesser celandine in the deciduous woods. Equally typical of the Caledonian Forest are crossbill and crested tit, red squirrel, roe deer and pine marten.

⚲ 🏛 STRATHPEFFER
Map ref 4758
Discovered by Dr Morrison at the beginning of the 19th century, Strathpeffer became Britain's northernmost spa, with elegant buildings and hotels.
In a renovated Victorian railway station of 1885 is the Strathpeffer Station Visitor Centre. Attractions include an audio-visual display of Highland wildlife and craft workshops where visitors can watch goods being produced. The Dolls Museum is open during the summer.
Strathpeffer also has Highland Games in early August.

✗ URQUHART CASTLE
Map ref 5329
A large stronghold, Urquhart Castle is sited at the southern end of the charming Glen Urquhart where it touches the north shore of Loch Ness. Dating to Norman times, frequently besieged and rebuilt over the centuries, the castle was finally blown up in 1692 to prevent a Jacobite occupation.

The ruins of Urquhart Castle, which mainly dates from the 14th century, overlooking Loch Ness

BATTLES, BIRDS AND CASTLES

This is a wonderfully varied area, with something for everyone. A nature reserve with reindeer; the chance to see ospreys; the site of the last battle fought on British soil; famous castles and at its centre the capital of the Highlands.

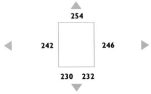

254

242 | 246

230 232

TOUR

CARRBRIDGE, LOCHINDORB AND CULLODEN MOOR
70 MILES

Leaving the ancient burgh of Inverness, the A9 soon reaches the village of Daviot, where the unusual steeple of the church is a good landmark.

The tour sweeps down through Strath Dearn and crosses the River Findhorn at Tomatin, before climbing the Pass of Slochd Mor towards its 1,332ft summit. At Carrbridge, on the River Dulnain, there is the Landmark Visitor Centre where the visitor can see audio-visual presentations on the history of the Highlands, follow nature trails or wander round a sculpture park.

In sharp contrast to the first part of the tour, the route is now north on the B9007, a lovely moorland road. Seven miles on there is a sharp right turn to Lochindorb, a small isolated loch with a bleak, ruined castle on an island. Edward I once occupied the castle as, later in the 14th century, did Alexander Stewart, known as the Wolf of Badenoch. The road runs north and east to Dava in the midst of bleak, high moors and then north-west on the A939 to Ferness.

Here the scenery softens and it is worth making a detour to Ardclach Church with its detached 17th-century belltower above the River Findhorn and on to the Bridge of Dulsie – perhaps the most beautiful spot on the Findhorn. The main route heads towards Nairn, and a detour can be made to explore this bright seaside town, essentially a holiday resort.

The route follows the course of the River Nairn by the B9090. Cawdor Castle is a fine medieval fortress with many domestic additions, surrounded by lovely walled gardens. The setting for *Macbeth*, Cawdor is in fact the family home of the Thanes, since the 14th century.

The site of the Battle of Culloden

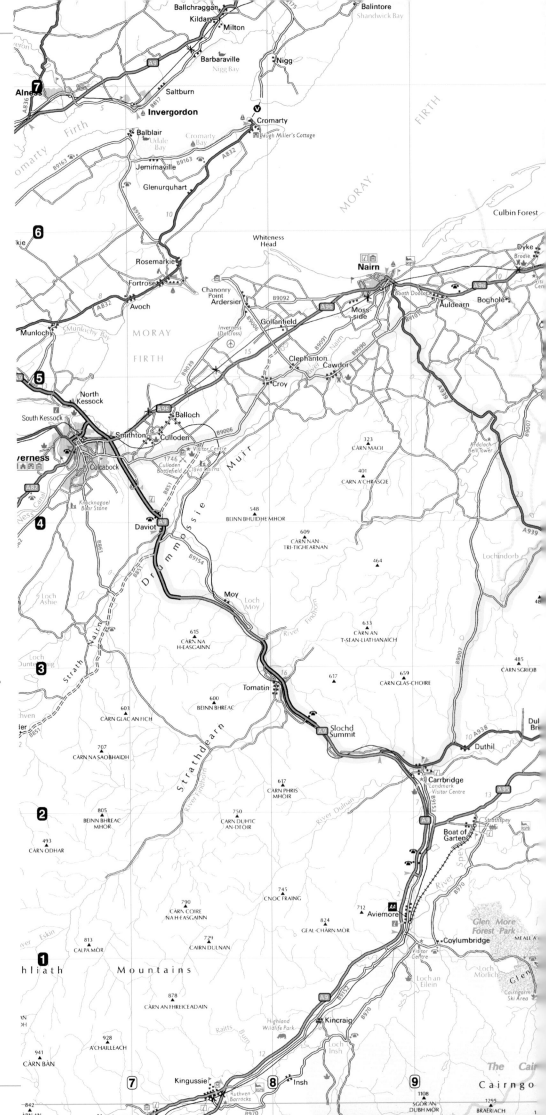

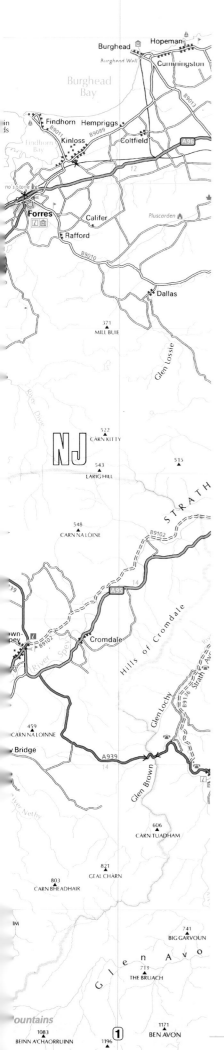

is just a few miles on, marked by a cairn built in 1881. The large visitor centre has an audio-visual display giving a vivid impression of the battle. Off the left of the road are the Clava Cairns. Burial cairns dating from about 1600, they are among Scotland's finest prehistoric monuments. Forestry Commission plantations restrict the views to the beautiful Moray Firth.

SELECTED PLACES TO VISIT

⚔ ♣ BRODIE CASTLE
Map ref 9757
The ancestral home of the Brodie family, the present building is an 18th- and 19th-century restoration. The castle contains fine plasterwork, with impressive collections of porcelain, furniture and paintings. The grounds have woodland walks, a wildlife observation hide and an adventure playground. There are facilities for disabled visitors.

★ 🏛 BURGHEAD WELL
Map ref 1268
Burghead was once a major centre of Pictish power marked by the 1st-century promontory fort – one of the largest in Scotland – extensively damaged when the present village was built in the early 19th century. The well was uncovered in 1809, and is an elaborate construction which has been variously described as a Roman well, Christian baptistry or Celtic shrine.

🏛 FORRES
Map ref 0459
The most prominent feature of Forres, an old town on the River Findhorn, is the 70ft Nelson Tower. The Falconer Museum has a particularly fine collection of fossils, as well as wildlife and archaeology exhibits. Temporary exhibitions are also held.

🏛 FORT GEORGE
Map ref 7556
One of Britain's finest 18th-century artillery fortifications, Fort George was used as a base for regiments to be equipped before they embarked for service abroad. In 1881 it became the depot for the Seaforth Highlanders now amalgamated with the Cameron Highlanders and known as the Queen's Own Highlanders. The Regimental Museum has splendid collections of medals, uniforms, weapons and pictures.

♣ GLEN MORE FOREST PARK
Map ref 9712
Loch Morlich, a small, almost circular loch in Glen More is surrounded on three sides by its Forest Park, stretching from the loch shores to the tops of the surrounding Cairngorms. More than half the park is at a high altitude, so is treeless, belying its name. Here the visitor is likely to see the reindeer herd, imported

A footbridge over the River Ness in Inverness, capital of the Highlands

Below: *The innovative Landmark Visitor Centre at Carrbridge*

from Lapland in 1950. Around the loch are Douglas fir, Scots pine, sitka spruce, alder and larch and there are several waymarked walks leading from the car park. The park supports roe deer, fox, badger, and the occasional wildcat. Whooper swans visit the loch in the winter, and golden eagle may be seen.

🏛 HUGH MILLER'S COTTAGE
Map ref 7967
A charming cottage at Cromarty was once the home of Hugh Miller, a stonemason, writer, geologist and lay leader of the Free Church. His great-grandfather, a sea captain, built the cottage in 1711; long and low, it is gabled and thatched with six rooms.

🏛 INVERNESS
Map ref 6645
Set on the junction of the Moray and Beauly Firths, Inverness is the capital of the Highlands. King David I built a castle here in the 12th century but only a well survives – the site is now occupied by a mock-Norman sandstone castle of 1835, housing the Sheriff Court. Abertaff House has a fine spiral staircase while St Andrew's Cathedral is Victorian and has a very elaborate interior.

🦢 LOCH GARTEN
Map ref 9717
A nature reserve, Loch Garten is well known for the ospreys which nest here each year.

A hide is available in summer with a camera trained on the nest so that visitors can watch the young ospreys being reared. The reserve is rich in other bird life – crossbill, redstart, capercaillie and black grouse, with teal, wigeon and other waterfowl.

♦ PLUSCARDEN
Map ref 1457
The 13th-century Pluscarden Abbey, which was originally founded by Alexander II, was burnt down, probably by the Wolf of Badenoch who also destroyed Elgin Cathedral. It fell into ruin after the Scottish monasteries were suppressed in 1560. In 1948 Benedictines from Prinknash Abbey near Gloucester began to rebuild and in 1955 the tower was re-roofed and the abbey bells rang out again. There are modern stained glass windows in the restored buildings.

🏛 SUENO'S STONE
Map ref 0459
The most important piece of Pictish sculpture in Scotland is Sueno's Stone which was discovered in the 18th century. A slender sandstone block some 23ft tall elaborately carved in the 9th or 10th century, it has a carved cross and two bearded figures with attendants, on its western face. On the eastern face of the stone – which pre-dates the Bayeux Tapestry and other narrative panels by two centuries – are four carved panels depicting a battle with equal frankness.

WHISKY GALORE!

The Ladder Hills is the local name for the north-eastern Grampian range. This part of Scotland is rich in mountain country; there is excellent fishing, skiing, walking and many other attractions – including the whisky trail.

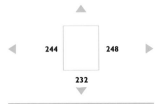

	▲	
◀ 244		248 ▶
	232	
	▼	

TOUR

THE LADDER HILLS AND WHISKY TRAIL
80 MILES

Dufftown is a pleasant town, the capital of Scotland's malt whisky distilling enterprise. The Balvenie and Glenfiddich distilleries are both in Dufftown and offer free conducted tours. The museum explains the processes involved in whisky making while, for those who wish to see the history of the area, there is a good collection of local photographs.

Two miles to the south-east is Auchindoun Castle, an imposing hilltop ruin surrounded by prehistoric earthworks. The road continues over the Glacks of Balloch Pass and past St Mary's Kirk, the ruined church of Auchindoir, with its fine 13th-century carved doorway.

The route now turns south to Lumsden, a 19th-century planned village just north of the impressive ruin of Kildrummy Castle. This 13th-century stronghold has had a colourful history, culminating in its near destruction in the 18th century, after the Jacobites had used it to

draw up their plans for the rebellion of 1715.

Soon after Kildrummy the road turns sharply west through Glenkindie, where there is an earth house open to visitors, and on to Glenbuchat Castle. This ruined 16th-century castle was owned by John Gordon, a loyal Jacobite who escaped to France after Culloden, and died in exile.

The road now winds south-west to Corgarff Castle, a 16th-century tower-house converted by the Hanoverians into a garrison post and barracks in 1748, when the striking star-shaped curtain wall was built.

Here the road turns north-west through skiing country by the Lecht road, which crosses the Ladder Hills. This is part of the military road built by the Hanoverians after Culloden; it rises steeply over bleak wild moorland to Tomintoul, the highest village in the Highlands at 1,680ft. Tomintoul is popular with anglers in summer, and skiers in winter. The Museum has displays on the social history of the area, including a reconstructed farm kitchen with old utensils and implements.

Seven miles north along Glen Livet, and a little way off the road, is the Glenlivet Whisky Distillery; from the fine, modern visitor centre there are tours of the distillery, after which a wee dram is offered to guests – as it is at all distilleries offering tours!

The tour continues north through Marypark and past the Glenfarclas Distillery, to Craigellachie, a salmon-fishing resort in the wooded Strath Spey where those two important Highland rivers, the Spey and the Fiddich meet. The splendid single-arch Craigellachie Bridge was built by Thomas Telford. Craigellachie is the home of the famous, and large, White Horse distillery (not open). From here the tour turns south-east to return to Dufftown.

SELECTED PLACES TO VISIT

◻ ⛟ ⌂ ⛿ ALFORD
Map ref 5716

The Alford Valley narrow-gauge railway takes visitors to Haughton Country Park and on to Murray Park from a reconstruction of a Victorian station. In the village there is also the Grampian Transport Museum. Here 100 vehicles of all descriptions can be seen, from horseless carriages to the *Craigievar Express* – a combined steam engine and three-wheeled cart built by a local postman in 1895.

⛿ BALVENIE CASTLE
Map ref 3341

Balvenie was originally known, in the 13th century, as Mortlach, when built by the Comyn family to guard the mountain passes. Set on a grassy hill above the River Fiddich at Dufftown, its imposing curtain wall is 25ft high and 7ft thick. Only the tower remains of a three-storeyed mansion added by later owners, using, it is said, stones from Auchindoun. This picturesque ruin has a fascinating history. Edward I was here in 1304, Mary, Queen of Scots in 1562; occupied by the Jacobites in 1689 but denied them in 1715 it was later, briefly, used as a garrison for Cumberland's troops.

⌂ ◻ BUCKIE
Map ref 4366

The important fishing port of Buckie stretches for 2½ miles along the Moray coast. It has a museum which illustrates a variety of maritime themes – fishing, sailing, life-saving, navigation, and the work of people in related industries.

⛿ CRAIGIEVAR CASTLE
Map ref 5609

An early 17th-century baronial style castle of pink harl, its walls rising smoothly from the greensward to

The Glenfiddich distillery in Dufftown was founded in 1887

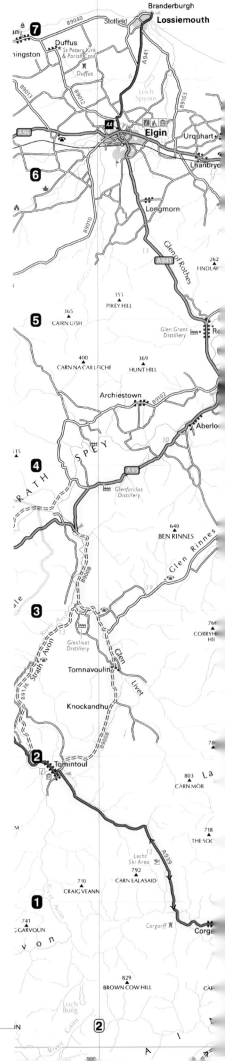

the fourth floor, above which are a hotch-potch of turrets, towers and gables. Craigievar was built for the Forbes family, and is little altered – truly one of the loveliest castles in Scotland.

✖ DUFFUS CASTLE
Map ref 1867

Originally timber, and one of Scotland's major fortifications in the 12th century, the motte and bailey castle of Duffus was re-built of stone in the 14th century. Four hundred years later it had become a ruin and was abandoned. The curtain wall survives with other parts of the building including the ground floor of the keep, part of the great chamber and the kitchen.

ⓘ⛺ⓘ ELGIN
Map ref 2162

To the east of Elgin is the shell of the beautiful 13th-century Cathedral, standing in parkland. Badly damaged by fire in 1390, with most of the town, the exterior of the building was unscathed, but Cromwell completed the destruction of the already ruined building in the 17th century, and in 1711 the central tower collapsed. The history and natural history of Elgin and Moray to modern times is related in the Elgin Museum, which also has a notable collection of fossils and reptiles.

FOCHABERS VILLAGE
Map ref 3458

Situated in a former church, the Fochabers Folk Museum has an extensive collection of horse-drawn vehicles. Other exhibits are items connected with the area and with the village, and a reconstruction of an early village shop.

✖ HUNTLY CASTLE
Map ref 5441

A ruin, Huntly Castle has a superb heraldic frontispiece over the main doorway, including the arms of the 5th Earl of Huntly and his lady, Henrietta Stewart. The castle's dungeon still has 16th-century drawings and graffiti on its walls.

⌂ LEITH HALL
Map ref 5429

The four-storeyed hall was the home of the Leith family from 1650 to 1945, and contains many relics of the family. It has a series of lovely individual gardens, each with its own theme, divided by hedges or walls. There is a flock of Soay sheep in the grounds.

⌂ TUGNET ICE HOUSE
Map ref 3566

An enormous ice house on Spey Bay, built nearly 200 years ago at the mouth of one of Scotland's major salmon rivers as part of a salmon fishing station to store the fish before they were sold. It is now home to an exhibition on the salmon industry.

THE MORAY COAST

The broad sweep of coastline above Aberdeen has many sandy beaches interspersed with fishing ports and villages, and holiday resorts, with stretches of high cliff land and an extensive dune nature reserve. Inland are forest trails, and many castles.

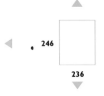

SELECTED PLACES TO VISIT

🏛️ BANFF
Map ref 6864

The fine county town of Banff is an ancient port on the Devoron Estuary. It was used as a winter retreat by Highland gentry; as a result Banff has some fine town houses. Banff Museum has an exhibition of British birds set out as an aviary. Items of local history and armour are also on display.

♣ BENNACHIE FOREST RESERVE & VISITOR CENTRE
Map ref 6719

Seven miles west of Inverurie, this reserve on an eastern outpost of the Cairngorms comprises several peaks, their lower slopes clothed in spruce, pine and larch, with lichens, fungi, mosses and ferns. There are four starting points from which paths of varying lengths and steepness wind up through the trees, becoming heather tracks as they approach the summit ridge, where there are some fine views.

⚔ CASTLE FRASER
Map ref 7313

The National Trust for Scotland cares for the vast and spectacular 16th-century Fraser Castle. One of the Castles of Mar, the Z-plan building incorporates a rectangular 15th-century tower-house and has many architectural embellishments.

CRUDEN BAY
Map ref 0937

Fine sandy beaches and golf courses make Cruden Bay a popular holiday resort. The 17th-century bridge which spans the Cruden Water is known as the Bishop's Bridge. Slains Castle, overlooking the sea behind Port Erroll, on the south of the bay, was built by the Earl of Erroll when his previous castle was destroyed by James VI.

The castle is a gaunt and intimidating ruin, thought by some to have given inspiration to Bram Stoker, author of *Dracula*, as he often stayed at Port Erroll.

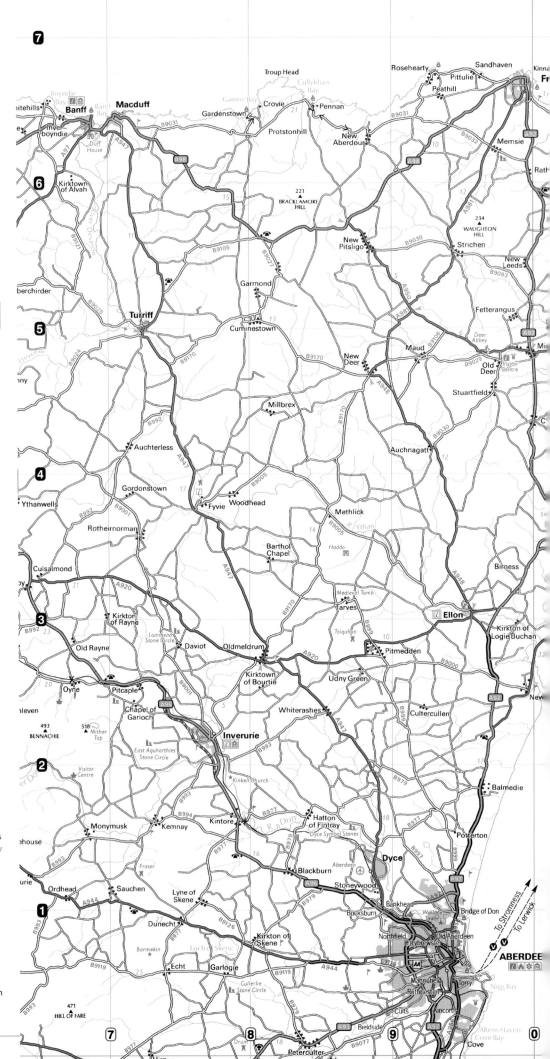

Duff House, Banff, one of Britain's finest Georgian baroque buildings

Cruden Bay, which is famous for its sandy beaches

it in the 1750s, and it was further remodelled in the 1890s by Sir Arthur Grant. Its ancient parish church with its Norman chancel arch and west doorway was built in 1140, surviving the Reformation and continuing to serve the area.

PETERHEAD
Map ref 1346
The largest town on this coast after Aberdeen, Peterhead was founded in the 16th century. Once a major whaling port, it is now important for herring fishing and as a base for the oil industry. Prisoners from Peterhead Prison helped to complete the port's vast harbour, begun in 1886 and not completed until 1958. Most of Peterhead's buildings are of locally quarried pink granite. The Arbuthnot Museum and Art Gallery in Queen Street features local exhibits and information on whaling, the Arctic, and the fishing industry.

PITMEDDEN GARDEN
Map ref 8827
Created for Lord Pitmedden in 1675, this magnificent formal garden with elaborate floral plantings in box-hedged parterres was inspired by a garden created for Louis XIV near Paris. The present house was built in 1866 and the garden was re-created by the National Trust for Scotland.

SANDS OF FORVIE NATURE RESERVE
Map ref 0127
On the east side of the Ythan estuary, 2,500 acres of dune and grassland constitute one of the most extensive dune systems in Britain; the Sands of Forvie. Inhabited by a rich variety of wildlife, including the largest colony of breeding eider duck in Britain, Forvie is now a National Nature Reserve, which includes the estuary. Four species of tern breed here and it is largely for their protection that strict controls are kept on visitors rights to wander. In autumn and winter the Ythan estuary attracts large numbers of waders and passage wildfowl. Nearby is a ruined church, all that is left of the ancient village which, threatened by the inexorable advance of the dunes, was deserted early in the 15th century. The lonely salmon netting station at Rockend looks out at the first of the oil platforms erected in the North Sea.

UDNY GREEN
Map ref 8726
Visiting this tranquil village clustered around its green, it is difficult to imagine that body snatching was so rampant here in the last century that the villagers built a mort house, to keep their newly dead for up to three months, by which time the bodies were unsuitable for sale. The circular building can still be seen. Udny Castle stands above the village, the basic structure as it was in the 17th century.

DEER ABBEY
Map ref 9748
The scant remains of a Cistercian Abbey established in the 13th century stand close by the village of Old Deer. The area has a long tradition of Christian activity and in the 9th-century gospels, *The Book of Deer*, there are references to a monastery founded in the 6th century. Unfortunately, there is no evidence as to the exact location – indeed the earliest definite evidence for Christian foundations in the area is some 1,000 years later.

DUFF HOUSE
Map ref 6864
Duff House, on the outskirts of Banff, is a fine Georgian house designed by William Adam. The interiors are as grand as the exterior and there is an exhibition on the history of the building.

FYVIE CASTLE
Map ref 7639
A magnificent castle, dating from the 13th century, Fyvie Castle is set above a bend in the River Ythan, in a wooded park. The five great towers commemorate the five families who have owned the castle in the last 500 years.

HADDO HOUSE
Map ref 8634
A Georgian house, built by Adam on the site of the former home of the Gordons of Haddo, burned down by Covenanters. Outside the house, a great stone staircase rises over the front door to the first floor.

MACDUFF
Map ref 7165
A fishing town with a large harbour, Macduff has a fish market and a customs house. Good views over the Devoron estuary may be enjoyed from the Hill of Doune near Banff Bridge.

MONYMUSK
Map ref 6815
An ancient village site, bought by the Grant family in the early 18th century; Sir Archibald Grant rebuilt

This is the most remote and breathtaking part of Wester Ross. The scenery varies from dramatic mountains to peaceful lochs and lochans; from busy fishing ports and holiday resorts to tranquil rivers and spectacular waterfalls.

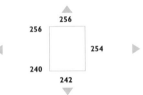

```
        ▲
       256
 256 ┌─────┐
     │     │  254
◄    │     │    ►
 240 └─────┘
       242
        ▼
```

TOUR

THE ASSYNT DISTRICT OF SUTHERLAND, LOCHINVER AND INVERPOLLY NATURE RESERVE
68 MILES

The resort and fishing centre of Ullapool is a good base from which to explore the magnificent mountain scenery of Wester Ross. It is situated on the deep and beautiful Loch Broom and offers opportunities to swim, fish, walk and climb. Boat trips are available to the uninhabited Summer Isles to study seabirds and seals (see page 241). Ullapool is an important port and has been developed by the British Fishery Society since the late 18th century. The terminal for the car ferry to Stornaway on the Isle of Lewis is here and the Russian fishing fleet uses it as a base.

Leaving Ullapool, the A835 climbs then drops down to Ardmair where there are fine views over Loch Kanaird to the Coigach peninsula (see page 241). The road now turns inland through Strath Kanaird, to the village of the same name. Beyond Drumrunnie Lodge the route passes the Cromalt Hills and leads on up to the Nature Conservancy's Knockan Cliff Visitor

The Stornoway ferry arriving at the port of Ullapool

Centre for the vast 27,000-acre Inverpolly Nature Reserve, the second largest in Britain.

The centre is above the road on the right and, granted reasonable weather, there are wonderful views of Cul Mor and, behind the peak, of the interior of the reserve. There are no roads into this wilderness area of rocky hummocks, lochans and bogs, over which loom the mountains of Suilven, Beinn Charbh, Canisp, An Stac and Cul Beag. No fewer than 104 species of bird have been recorded here: among them greenshank and golden plover on the moorland; long-tailed tit and long-eared owl in the woodland; merganser and goosander in the lochans; and fulmar, shag and black guillemot on the coast.

Trace the eastern boundary of the reserve by the A837 to Inchnadamph, a small fishing resort at the southern end of Loch Assynt.

Corrieshalloch Gorge where the river plunges 150ft over the Falls of Measach

Towering over the foreground mountains on this stretch of road is Ben More Assynt, the highest mountain in Sutherland. The road skirts the north side of the wild and lovely loch, passing the ruined Ardurech Castle, standing three-storeys high on a promontory jutting out into the loch. It belonged to the MacLeods of Assynt, and the gallant Montrose was held prisoner here in 1650 after the rout at Carbisdale, before being taken to Edinburgh to be hanged.

Leaving Loch Assynt the road turns south-west following the course of the little River Inver which flows into Loch Inver, passing through attractive woodland – a delightful contrast to the bare, grey, mountain country preceding it.

The coastal resort of Lochinver, set on its sea-loch, surrounded by hills and clusters of tiny lochans, is a popular fishing centre. To the south-east of the village is Glencanisp Forest.

South from Lochinver, the twisting, switchback, and sometimes crowded single track minor road – there are frequent passing places – leads along the wild edge of Inverpolly and back to the road to Achiltibuie and the Summer Isles. The views to seaward and landward are simply breathtaking.

The tour now turns east skirting Loch Lurgainn beside the sharply serrated mountain ridge of An Stac, with the bleak fastness of Coigach on the right before rejoining the road back to Ullapool.

SELECTED PLACES
TO VISIT

★ CORRIESHALLOCH GORGE AND THE FALLS OF MEASACH
Map ref 2078

The mile-long box canyon of Corrieshalloch Gorge is 200ft deep and best viewed from the suspension bridge built by Sir John Fowler, co-designer of the Forth Bridge. An observation platform gives a good view of the Falls of Measach, formed where the River Droma pours through the entrance to the gorge, a 150ft high cascade leaving a permanent mist of spray. The gorge has ferns, liverworts, mosses and other shade-loving plants growing from its sides and on boulders in the river. Trees that have rooted themselves in the rocky sides of the gorge include bird cherry, guelderrose, sycamore, Norway maple and goat willow. Ravens nest in the crags. Above the gorge the A832 to Gairloch has a viewpoint providing magnificent vistas of scenery unsurpassed in this and many other areas. It ranges from the heights of Meall Doire Faid to, in sharp contrast, the meadows of Strath More beyond the gorge. The River Broom flows through these meadows and into Loch Broom, leading the eye onwards, towards the sea through the hills that fall to the loch.

INCHNADAMPH
Map ref 2522

Near Inchnadamph there is a Nature Conservancy Council reserve on a limestone plateau with cliffs, screes and pavements, underground streams, caves and swallowholes. The Allt nan Uamh Caves south-east of Stonechrubie, have been occupied since the Stone Age and bones of several animals now extinct in Scotland have been found here. This outcrop of Durness limestone has a rich flora including plentiful mountain avens, holly fern and the rare dark red helleborine and toothed wintergreen.

★ ☘ ☸ KNOCKAN CLIFF
Map ref 1908

Knockan Cliff provided a new theory about the formation of the earth's crust. In 1859 Professor Nicol, a geologist, noticed that the cliff's top layer was the most compressed and altered in structure, and was probably older than the limestone at the base of the rock. He deduced from this that some cataclysmic eruption about 400 million years ago must have reversed the usual trend, throwing up the older rock so that it lay above the newer surface deposits. This lead to similar formations being recognised elsewhere and a new realisation of how the great mountain ranges may have been formed. The Nature Conservancy Council has created a nature trail here – a 1½ mile walk with 17 viewing points and a climb to over 1,000ft. Each viewing point illustrates a different aspect of the area.

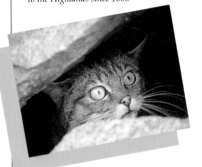

NORTH WEST HIGHLANDS

The area north of the Great Glen offers lovely, wild, unspoiled country, peopled by a fascinating mixture of races enjoying a unique way of life

The peoples of the North West Highlands are a series of settlers – Picts, Scots, Vikings and even earlier races whose very origins are obscured in ancient mists.

The earliest came by sea to settle, principally in Orkney. Trade with Ireland followed before the Romans arrived. They never penetrated the Highlands but had, on occasion, to fight off the race they termed *Picti*. The Scots came from Ireland in the 5th and 6th centuries bringing their language, Gaelic, and Christianity. The Vikings were next, settling on the mainland in Wester Ross, Caithness and Sutherland – the south land of the Viking earls of Orkney.

Throughout the Middle Ages, the clan system held sway in the Highlands, with the `children' of the chief living on his land and owing their loyalty to him, rather than kings. Even though the Stewarts had often attempted to lessen clan ties, the majority of the Highland clans supported the Stewart, or Jacobite, cause during the Civil War and again in 1689 and 1714 but, by 1745, that support had all but disappeared.

In 1746, at Culloden, the last battle took place on British soil and when it was over the Highlands were to be changed for ever. Under swingeing laws the tartan was banned, weapons confiscated, even bagpipes outlawed. Those chiefs who had supported Bonnie Prince Charlie lost their estates and most of their feudal powers. The clan system was effectively broken and, within 100 years, landowners – by no means all English – were behaving in a very different way to the old paternalism of the chiefs.

Economic Disaster

As the population expanded in the Highlands, so smallholdings became progressively less viable,

Above: *A magnificent red deer stag during the rutting season in late autumn*
Right: *Looking across Loch Torridon towards Benn Alligin*

largely as a result of the traditional habit of dividing the land among families. Four staples supported this population – potatoes, kelp, cattle and fish – and , of these , two were effectively to collapse in the same year.

Potatoes rapidly became a main crop in many areas from the 1760s, supplementing oats. After 1782-3, when the harvest failed, the potato became even more important, and the potato failures of the 1840s were a dreadful blow to an economy already in ruins.

The collapse of the kelp industry at the end of the Napoleonic Wars dealt the first blow to the communities who produced it and the Highland landlords who had invested heavily and now saw their market disappear. In 1810 the price of kelp rose to £20 a ton; in 1815 foreign supplies resumed; by 1825 new manu-facturing methods were being used in Glasgow, and by 1830 the kelp burning industry was all but dead except in a few islands.

The failure of the export trade in black cattle began to accelerate from 1815 – that fateful year – as prices slumped. Even the herring

deserted the Highlander, moving from inshore lochs to deeper water, where his small boats could not reach them. Then, later, when new towns and villages were set up to create work for displaced crofters, the price of fish slumped and the ventures failed to prosper.

The Clearances

The importation of sheep began in the latter years of the 18th century as demand for wool rose. The problem was that sheep require large areas of land to be profitable, while the Highlander lacked capital to invest in land or sheep. So Lowlanders moved in, bringing with them their Cheviot sheep. As early as 1792, the men of Ross, sensing the danger, gathered together, driving sheep and shepherds south from Lairg; the result was transportation for five men.

The idea of clearing the glens and straths to provide land for sheep farms, while providing alternative work for the

displaced crofters, took root as more and more landlords recognised that change was inevitable. The principle was sound, but the practice was not. The harsh methods employed, and a failure to understand the strength of feeling the Highlanders had for the old way of life, combined to undermine the idea. The result was a legacy of bitterness that became a part of the folklore of the North West Highlands.

The Clearances in Sutherland created most debate and continue to be an emotive subject. The Countess of Sutherland's estates, though huge, were largely barren and, as early as 1772, Pennant had noted that `numbers of the miserables of this country were now migrating'. Contrary to later opinion, widespread emigration had begun by the late 18th century and it continued, long before the Clearances drew attention to the process.

When, in 1803, Lord Stafford, the Countess' husband,

inherited a large fortune he determined to redevelop the estate. He set to work building roads, developing the new village and harbour of Helmsdale, providing new industries at Brora, enlarging small townships all round the coast, creating a fishing fleet and resettling the people on the coast.

At first, the Clearances were successful, although it was quickly apparent that the displaced crofters had little interest in fishing. In 1814, there occurred the incident which has coloured all subsequent discussion on the Clearances. Patrick Sellar, who was both factor and incoming tenant of the estate, ordered the people

Below: The mountain hare, seen here sporting its white winter coat, lives among the rocks

of Strath Naver to quit the land within six months. When they did not, he moved in, burning the little townships, violently evicting the people, destroying their crops. Five days later an old woman, burnt in the blaze, died, and Sellar was tried in Inverness for her murder. A jury of local landlords found him not guilty and he resumed his duties – and tenancy of the estate.

Nothing excuses the events at Strath Naver but the sense of outrage surrounding them obscured, and continues to obscure, an inescapable economic reality. The Highlands, over-populated and under-productive, too remote from the market place, too conservative to adapt, could not be preserved. Ironically, the Sutherlands, who tried to do

something for the economy, are remembered almost exclusively for Strath Naver.

Protecting Interests

Today the North West Highlands are being opened up to tourism by improved roads. As always, some are unhappy about this improved access, fearing the loss of the last truly wild places in Britain. Nonetheless, it seems unlikely that the heartland of the North West Highlands, areas such as Knoydart or Kylesku, will ever suffer the sort of problems faced by similar areas.

Wildlife may suffer from the intrusion of man, although there have been more gains than losses in the Highlands this century. Conservation bodies have done sterling work, with the Royal Society

for the Protection of Birds acquiring reserves in the Highlands and the National Trust for Scotland controlling some of the country. Both these charities have an excellent record in protecting the flora and fauna on their properties while the Nature Conservancy Council has identified important sites of general or specific wildlife interest, declaring them National Nature Reserves.

Naturally, there are concerns – the continuing afforestation of the Flow Country is arguably the greatest – but the picture in Scotland is hopeful. There are many who will stand lost for words, wondering, before the grandeur and beauty that is Foinaven, Assynt, Moidart, Kintail, Glen Affric and Torridon, whose 'loch, glen and the mountains on either side exhibit more beauty than any other district of Scotland, including Skye', according to an assessment of the landscape made by the National Trust for Scotland in 1961.

Left: The grey seal established its breeding colonies on western shores
Below: Looking across Loch Duich to the Five Sisters of Kintail

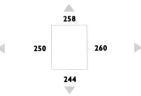

DORNOCH FIRTH

Many of the towns and villages along the Dornoch Firth and the coast of Easter Ross are holiday and fishing resorts. The area has a turbulent history – here one of the major Highland Clearances took place in the early 19th century, when crofters were brutally displaced to make way for sheep farms which, it was assumed, would be more profitable.

```
        258
250            260
        244
```

258
250   260
244

SELECTED PLACES TO VISIT

ARDGAY
Map ref 6090

Ardgay lies at the south-western end of the Inner Dornoch Firth, sheltered by hills, amid birch and larch woods. The White Stone of Kincardine, or Eitag Stone, stands in Ardgay's market square, indicating the site of the annual winter cattle market held in the village during the 19th century. Salmon netting may still be seen here in season and there is a fine 19th-century ice house for storing fish near the railway at Ardgay.

BONAR BRIDGE
Map ref 6292

This little village lies on the north side of the Dornoch Firth which is spanned by the iron Bonar Bridge. Built to a design of Thomas Telford, the original bridge was badly damaged by flood in 1892. Although rapidly replaced, the original structure known as 'spider's web in the air' was lost.

DORNOCH
Map ref 8089

A royal burgh, popular for golfing holidays, good bathing and sandy beaches, Dornoch is a charming little town of locally quarried mellow stone. The cathedral, first built in the 13th century and reconstructed after severe damage in the 16th century, is now the parish church. Dornoch (along with several other places) claims the last woman in Scotland to be burned at the stake for witchcraft; she was convicted of having turned her daughter into a pony, and taken her to be shod by the Devil. The Craft Centre in the Town Jail demonstrates kilt making and tartan weaving. Dornoch Castle was originally the Bishop's Palace; it was destroyed in 1570, leaving only the tower; a later L-plan building is now a hotel.

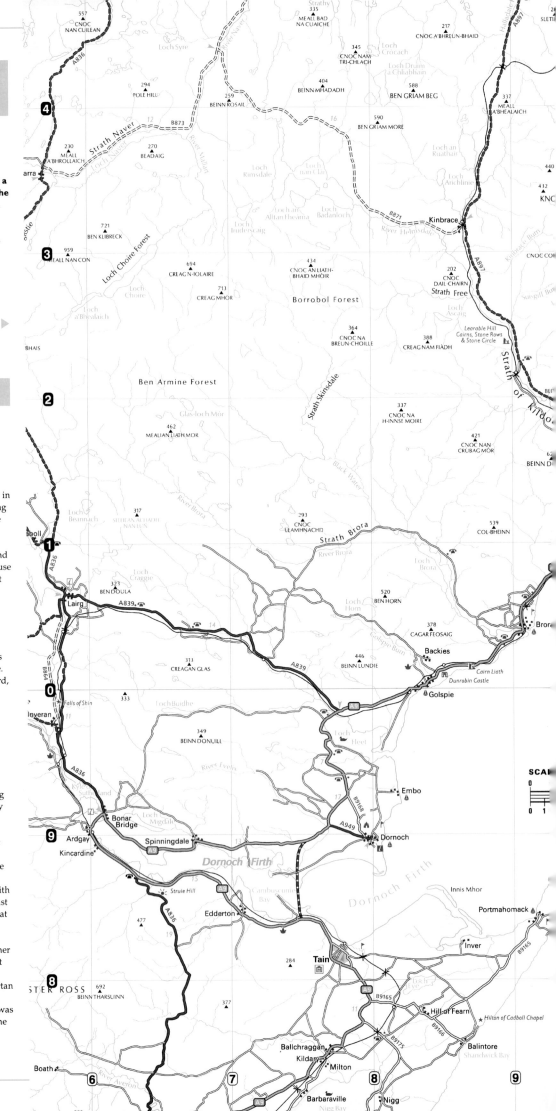

⌂ DUNROBIN CASTLE
Map ref 8501

Built on the site of an ancient broch, on a terrace overlooking the sea, with marvellous views of the Moray Firth, the flamboyant Dunrobin Castle has been the home of the earls and later the dukes of Sutherland since it was built in the 14th century. Extravagantly restored and enlarged in the 19th century by Sir Charles Barry for the 2nd Duke, the castle is a mixture of French and Scottish architecture in white stone with conical towers and turrets. In 1915 it was badly damaged by fire and further re-designed by Sir Robert Lorimer. There are fine paintings, tapestries and family relics on view, with more homely touches like the children's nursery. The formal terraced gardens are patterned on those at Versailles – the 2nd Duke lived in France as a boy and was devoted to the French style. In the grounds there is a museum of local history, a wooded park with nature trails and the castle's own railway station, built for the 3rd Duke. Near the castle are an ice house and an 18th-century dovecote.

GOLSPIE
Map ref 8399

This coastal farming and fishing village, one of several planned in the late 18th century to accommodate crofting families cleared from the interior glens, is the administrative centre of Sutherland District. It stands on a narrow strip of land, seemingly edged towards the sea by the encroaching mountain of Beinn a Bhragaidh, on whose summit is a giant statue of the 1st Duke of Sutherland. There are fine views from the summit over Dornoch Firth and Loch Fleet. Golspie is a good centre for golf, sea fishing and exploring the Sutherland area on foot or by car.

⌂ HELMSDALE
Map ref 0315

A small holiday and fishing resort at the mouth of the Helmsdale River – believed by some to be the best salmon fishing river in Scotland – in Strath Ullie, Helmsdale has a ruined 15th-century castle overlooking the natural harbour. The 1st Duke of Sutherland enlarged the village and re-settled crofters in parallel streets named after his many estates. He provided industry in the shape of curing yards, warehouses and piers, but the experiment was not a success as the crofters were not suited to the work, nor was the fishing industry any more profitable than the sheep farming.

★ HILTON OF CADBOLL CHAPEL
Map ref 8776

In this attractive village, formerly a fishing community, lie the grassed-over remains of a medieval chapel; nearby is the ruined Cadboll Castle. The Laird of Cadboll is said to have built Cadboll Mount 1½ miles to the

Dunrobin Castle takes its name from the Earl Robin – a Sutherland – who built the original keep

north, so that he could look down on MacLeod of Geanies, a neighbour with whom he was feuding.

⌂ LAIRG
Map ref 5806

A major junction for motor and rail routes to the far northern and north-western Highlands, Lairg is aptly known as the Gateway to Sutherland. It is situated at the southern end of Loch Shin, with a distant view of Ben More Assynt, the highest mountain in Sutherland. Lairg is known for its salmon and trout fishing, and is an ideal base from which to explore the mountain country of central Sutherland. There are good local walks, including one beside the River Shin for 5 miles through superb scenery to the Falls of Shin, a famous salmon leap.

⌂ LOCH FLEET
Map ref 7896

A sea-loch with a natural breakwater at the seaward end, Loch Fleet's waters are always calm and sheltered. On a ridge on the southern side of the entrance to the loch are the scant remains of the 14th-century Skelbo Castle. Near by there are several trails laid out by the Forestry Commission in Skelbo Wood.

PORTMAHOMACK
Map ref 9285

Portmahomack's peaceful harbour on the promontory guarding Dornoch Firth has a pier built for Lord Tarbat in 1697, and later improved by Thomas Telford; there are two estate warehouses now converted to dwelling houses. The village is set around a low hill facing the harbour. Tarbat old church on the hill behind the village has a tower with a stone dome which may once have been used as a sea-light.

⌂ TAIN
Map ref 7783

Tain was once an important port on the south shore of the Dornoch Firth, but progressive silting prevented development. Above the skyline of this town stands the old tolbooth tower, recalling the time when the town was an administrative centre for the Highland Clearances. St Duthus was born here in about AD1000; he built a chapel just outside the town; the ruin is still there. When he died his remains were brought back to Tain, and a splendid church was built to his memory in 1360. From its sanctuary Robert Bruce's wife was captured and taken to England.

TARBAT NESS
Map ref 9587

Tarbat Ness, with Scotland's lowest annual rainfall, is sited at the end of the low peninsula where the Dornoch Firth meets the Moray Firth. Its white painted lighthouse, one of the tallest in Britain, was built in 1830 and rebuilt some 60 years later.

THE FAR HIGHLAND

This is the wildest and most remote country in Scotland. The scenery is consistently dramatic, with deep sea-lochs and fiords, high cliffs and, inland, mountains of Torridonian sandstone and Lewisian gneiss. In contrast there can be surprising oases: noisy Handa with its huge bird colonies, peaceful Sandwood, most romantic of bays.

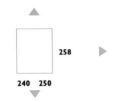

▲

◄ 258 ►

240 250

▼

SELECTED PLACES TO VISIT

☑ BALNAKEIL
Map ref 3868

Balnakeil Craft Village occupies the site of a former Ministry of Defence early warning station. In 1964 Sutherland County Council invited skilled craftspeople to move into the derelict buildings, to establish the first such village to be owned by its residents. It is the north-westernmost community in mainland Scotland. The crafts include jewellery making, bookbinding, wood and marquetry work, weaving, and pottery making. Balnakeil Bay has a ruined early 17th-century church at one end, with the grave of a highwayman and reputed murderer who paid £1,000 for the privilege of a resting place safe from his enemies, who he feared would desecrate his grave after his death.

CAPE WRATH
Map ref 2575

A headland of red Torridonian rock at the north-western tip of mainland Britain, Cape Wrath rises sheer from the sea to a height of 360ft, with its 70ft-high lighthouse built by Robert Stevenson. It is virtually inaccessible except for an 11-mile long narrow track between the lighthouse and a summer-only ferry across the Kyle of Durness. Inland, the Parph, some 100 square miles of rock, heather, scrubland and peat bog, is among the largest uninhabited tracts of land in Britain. To the east of the Cape, the highest cliffs on the British mainland rise to the Black Cliff – Cleit Dhubh – 850ft high.

★ EAS COUL AULIN WATERFALL
Map ref 2727

There are no roads and the visitor must walk or travel by boat to find the 658ft-high Eas Coul Aulin waterfall – four times the height of Niagara – set deep in the hills

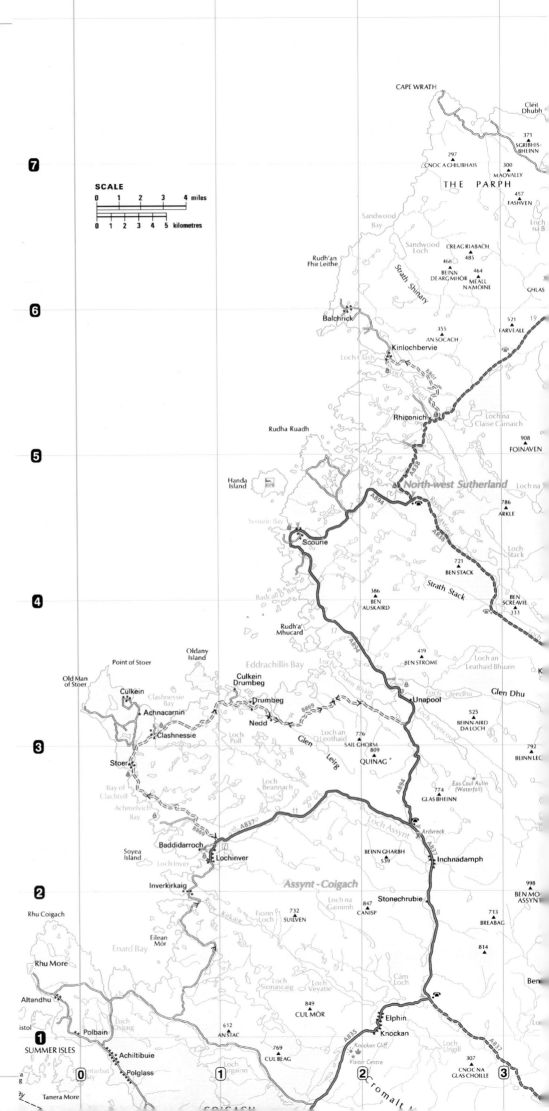

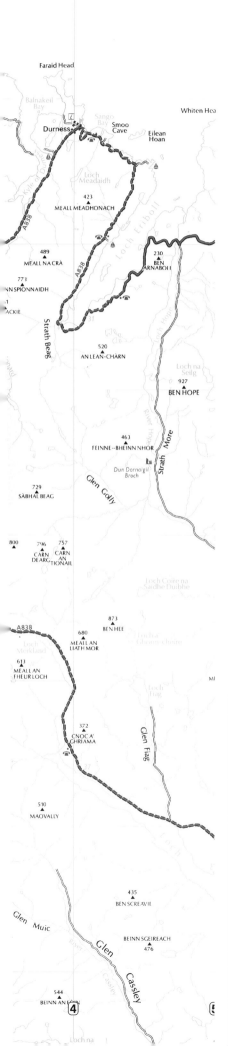

beyond the head of Loch Glencoul. A car ferry links Kylesku and Kylestrome at the narrows where Loch Glencoul and Loch Glendhu meet the sea-loch Loch Chàirn Bhàin.

EILEAN HOAN
Map ref 4567
The frequent heavy seas in this area mean that only the determined will make the trip to the Eilean Hoan RSPB reserve. Barnacle geese graze here in winter and eider, ringed plover and terns nest among the profusion of summer flowers like thrift and sea campion. Great northern divers on their way to Iceland gather off the island in spring.

HANDA ISLAND
Map ref 1347
Another RSPB nature reserve, Handa Island is separated from the mainland by the Sound of Handa and is reached by boat from Tarbet and Scourie. The island is an outcrop of red Torridonian sandstone – surprising, as the mainland shore opposite is of grey Lewisian gneiss. Crofters once inhabited the island; the remains of their dwellings can be seen. From the sea to the north and west of the island rise 400ft cliffs providing ideal nesting sites for several members of the auk family. Razorbills and guillemots nest in their thousands, with about 500 pairs of puffins. There is a large kittiwake colony while terns, notoriously fickle in their choice of breeding site, are presently increasing on Handa. Inland there is pasture, heather moorland dotted with crowberry, and bog; red-throated divers nest on the lochans in most years. The beaches are breeding grounds for many waders, and rock doves live in the caves.

KINLOCHBERVIE
Map ref 2356
The chief fishing port of the north-west Highlands, Kinlochbervie occupies a low isthmus between Loch Inchard and Loch Clash.

Fishing boats land catches of white fish for transporting to Aberdeen, Hull, Grimsby and the Continent. Kinlochbervie is a good centre for exploring this marvellous coastline.

LOCH ERIBOLL
Map ref 4358
The wild and beautiful Loch Eriboll is a cutting 10 miles into a remote part of the northern coast, in places 350ft deep, and is sheltered by steep hills. In World War II North Atlantic convoys mustered here and at the end of the war German warships surrendered to the British Navy here. Loch Eriboll is one of the few mainland breeding grounds of the grey seal; attracted by the remoteness, they can be seen around the cliffs of the south shore.

LOCH LAXFORD
Map ref 2050
Protected at its seaward end by a jumble of small islands, Loch Laxford is not easily accessible but may be seen from Laxford Bridge and other points on the A838. Inland, the views are of lochs, rocks and mountains (Foinaven and Arkle): the archetypal Sutherland landscape. Two crofting communities, Fanagmore and Foindle, survive on the loch's south shore, reached by a steeply twisting single-track road which continues to Tarbet, where boats leave for Handa Island.

SANDWOOD BAY
Map ref 2265
A little south of Cape Wrath, beautiful Sandwood Bay is perhaps the most remote part of this particularly inaccessible coastline, unless the visitor happens to have a boat or be on foot. The recommended approach is from Blairmore, along a single track road, just about possible for vehicles for about 2½ miles. The next 1½ miles must be undertaken on foot; the track is deeply rutted and can be wet and boggy. However the views will justify the effort. A freshwater loch lies behind the bay; from this a small stream threads its way

through the marram-clad sand dunes to the sea, passing rocks rich in semi-precious stones. The sand is pale pink; the rocks red Torridonian sandstone. The 2-mile long beach is one of the finest in Britain, yet it is almost always deserted. On the western flank of the bay is a huge sandstone stack known as *Am Buachaille*, the Herdsman, gathering in the waves at the end of their Atlantic journey.

SCOURIE
Map ref 1545
The gneiss landscape of north-west Sutherland can be bleak and, to compensate, the little holiday resort of Scourie does its best to comfort the traveller. Flowers – including orchids – grow in the mild climate, there is a hotel and shops, and boats to take the naturalist to Handa Island.

SMOO CAVE
Map ref 4367
The main chamber of the majestic Smoo Cave is accessible from the road, but further chambers should only be attempted by seasoned potholers. Of cathedral-like dimensions, one of the chambers is 200ft long and 120ft high. Nearby Sango Bay has wonderful white sands, in this setting of rocky limestone coastline.

STOER
Map ref 0427
Along the coast on each side of the village are several hamlets where fishermen hang out salmon nets to dry, while crofters cultivate green fields further inland. There are beaches of white sand at the Bay of Clachtoll, and at Achmelvich Bay; at Clashnessie the sands are pink. The road along the peninsula to Stoer lighthouse has views across the Minch to Lewis. Beyond the lighthouse a cliff path leads to the Point of Stoer, passing the finger of rock jutting out of the sea known as the Old Man of Stoer.

Working boats at Kinlochbervie, chief fishing port of the area

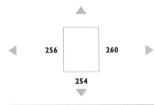
Remote, bleak, inhospitable, this is the northernmost area of mainland Britain. The last great wilderness will provide fulfilment for those who enjoy a hint of adventure. In contrast, at several points on the coast there are small, safe, delightful beaches where it is possible to relax in isolation.

```
        ▲
   256     260
◄        ▶
        254
        ▼
```

SELECTED PLACES TO VISIT

ARMADALE
Map ref 7865

A crofting and fishing village noted for sheep, Armadale has a charming bay with a good sandy beach protected by dunes.

☑ BETTYHILL
Map ref 7163

At the mouth of the River Naver, where it runs into Torrisdale Bay, is the tourist resort of Bettyhill, founded as a fishing and agricultural centre for re-settled crofters during the Highland Clearances. The crofters were forcibly removed from Strath Naver (see below) in 1814 and directed into new villages like Bettyhill, named after Elizabeth, Countess of Sutherland, whose husband was responsible for the Clearances between 1810 and 1820. The area is well known for salmon and trout fishing, while the wide sandy beach exposed at low tide in Torrisdale Bay attracts many waders and other sea birds.

⛪ FARR
Map ref 7263

A crofting museum with displays on the Clearances is housed in the little 18th-century church of the ancient parish of Farr together with exhibits related to the Clan Mackay, hereditary lords of this area. The church still has its handsome pulpit, dated 1774, the year the church was built. There is a splendid early Christian Celtic cross in the graveyard, carved on one side only, suggesting it once stood against, or close to, a wall. Semi-precious stones are sometimes found in Farr Bay.

⛵ INVERNAVER
Map ref 7060

An unusual mixture of factors led to the establishment of the Invernaver National Nature Reserve south-west of Bettyhill. It extends from the

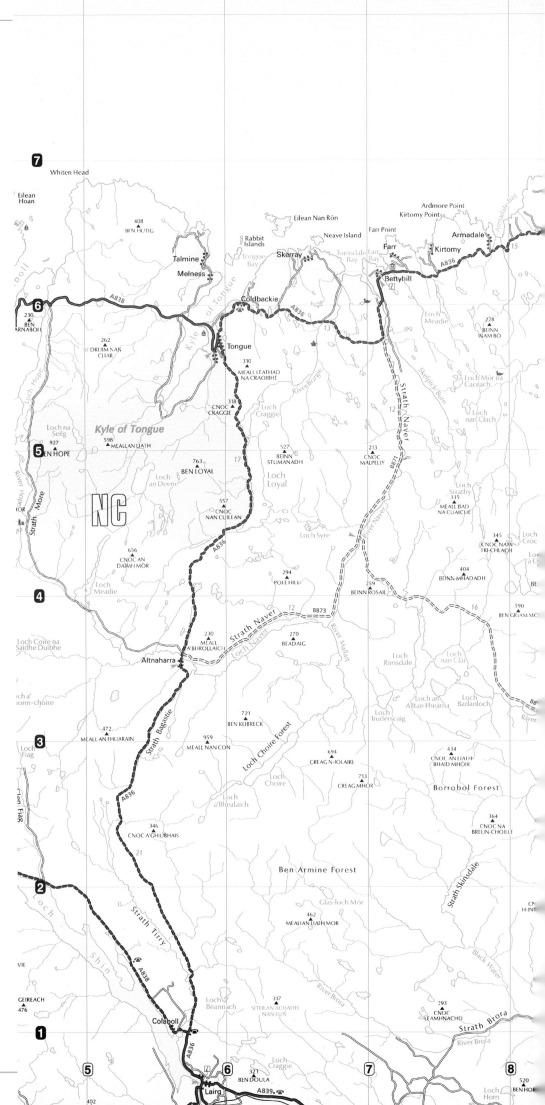

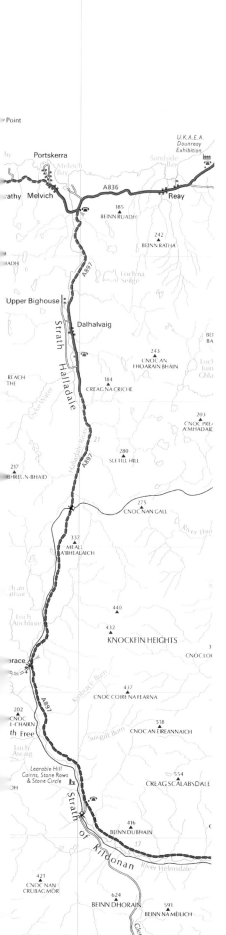

coast, across the A836 and for some way inland; habitats range from duneland, seashore and raised beach to moorland with rocks and lochans. The fierce gales, which are a feature of this area, have caused large quantities of sand to be blown inland, enriching the moorland soils and encouraging a remarkable range of plants. Oceanic and mountain species grow close to lime-loving plants and typical acid moorland species. The relatively rare Scottish primrose, restricted to the Highlands and Orkney, grows here in the damp areas, while plants as varied in their requirements as sea campion, alpine bistort and thrift flourish. The major plant of the reserve is undoubtedly dwarf juniper.

KIRTOMY
Map ref 7464
At the Aird of Kirtomy there is a long tunnel through the old red sandstone wide enough for the passage of boats. The 18th-century zoologist and traveller, Thomas Pennant, may have failed to discover Staffa on his Scottish travels of 1771, but certainly found and wrote about this place describing it as `the most curious cavern in the world'. Kirtomy Bay, with its sandy beach, is protected from the worst of the weather by the rocky promontories of Kirtomy Point to the east and Farr Point to the west.

MELVICH BAY
Map ref 8865
At Melvich the old red Torridonian sandstone rocks change abruptly to far older metamorphic rock, and the beach contains orange sand. The coast from here to the Kyle of Tongue is rocky and very beautiful, but not easy to reach. On the headland is the village of Portskerra, another of the small fishing villages established in this area at the time of the Clearances.

⌐ REAY
Map ref 9765
At the head of Sandside Bay lies Reay village, rebuilt in 1740 after being buried by sand dunes. The belfry of the 18th-century church has an external staircase.

SKERRAY
Map ref 6464
This small crofting settlement looks towards several uninhabited islands. Skerray has a pier and boats

Above: *Sand dunes at Bettyhill on the mouth of the River Naver*
Right: *An old, traditional Highland croft on Strath Halladale*

can be hired to explore the islands, or to sample some sea-fishing. The largest island, Eilean nan Ròn, was inhabited until 1938; with Neave Island it forms a breakwater protecting the approaches to Skerray Bay, with its raised beach.

STRATH NAVER
Map ref 7250
There are many reminders of man's long occupation of this bleak valley, ranging from the 6,000-year-old chambered cairn Coile na Borgie, some 2 miles south of Bettyhill, to the tragic remains of the crofts destroyed in 1814. At that time, Strath Naver was a relatively crowded place, but by 1834 a visitor could report that there were `only occasional shepherds' dwellings to be found'.

STRATHY
Map ref 8465
The River Strathy flows through this hamlet of stone cottages flanked by high piles of peat turfs. Unusually the outbuildings are often thatched here – slate is the preferred material for most of this area of high winds. A small road north leads to Strathy Point where, on an outcrop of granite – most of the area is old red sandstone – stands the newest lighthouse to be built in Britain, completed in 1958.

TALMINE
Map ref 5764
This was the centre of a cluster of small crofting communities, set up after the Highland Clearances last century. The evicted crofters learned how to fish, about quarrying, and tried to continue crofting, but the land has proved too unyielding, and the communities are in danger of dying out.

TONGUE
Map ref 5957
The road to Tongue from Altnaharra passes across lonely moorland, overlooked from the west by mountains. From Tongue the visitor can explore some of the most impressive coastal scenery in Britain. To the south of the village lies the commanding ruin of Castle Varrich, formerly the dwelling of an

11th-century Norse king. Tongue House was the seat of the chiefs of the Clan Mackay, the lords Reay, but in 1829 the 7th Lord Reay sold his estates to George Leveson-Gower, who was to become the 1st Duke of Sutherland four years later. Whatever the decision of history on Sutherland's treatment of crofters, he dramatically improved communications in this part of Scotland, laying roads the modern motorist is still using. His road across A' Mhoine, the peat bog, to Loch Eriboll, was floated on a raft of coppice wood, peat and gravel and has endured for well over 150 years.

🏛 UKAEA DOUNREAY EXHIBITION
Map ref 9866
Sand from nearby Sandside Bay has been used for building and farming purposes over the centuries, and more lately in the building of the Dounreay Reactor, Scotland's first atomic energy plant, built in the early 1950s; its 135ft steel dome is visible from many directions. The Dounreay Exhibition describes fast reactors and the story of nuclear energy.

CASTLES AND CREELS

Fishing villages, often planned to re-house and re-employ dispossessed crofters after the Highland Clearances, are part of this fascinating coastal panorama of clifftop castles and wild, rocky headlands in the far north of Britain.

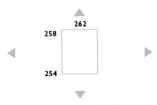

TOUR

CAITHNESS AND JOHN O'GROATS
57 MILES

The tour begins at Wick, for long a most important herring fishing port, and a burgh since the 16th century. From Wick the A9 skirts the wide sweep of Sinclairs Bay, with its 3 miles of sands. Man has inhabited this area at least since the Stone Age period. The crab-fishing village of Keiss on the north of the bay has a 16th-century castle standing in dramatic fashion right on the edge of a sheer cliff; a late tower-house, it stands four storeys high. Behind it the Sinclair family built a new castle in 1755, extending it in 1860 to a large Scottish Baronial structure.

The tour passes the spectacularly placed cliff-top ruins of 15th-century Bucholie Castle, on a much older site, passing Noss Head, to John O'Groats. The most northerly village in mainland Britain but not,

as popularly believed, the most northerly point.

Duncansby Head is a few miles east, and well worth a detour. A lighthouse guards the entrance to the hazardous Pentland Firth; from here a short walk leads to the marvellous 200ft-high sandstone Stacks of Duncansby from which the sea has carved many caves and arches.

The route leads west along the A836 to the village of Mey and its castle (see below). At Dunnet, the B855 leads due north to Dunnet Head – a high promontory of old red sandstone which really is Britain's most northerly point. Stones thrown up by severe winter tides sometimes smash against the windows of the lighthouse built on cliffs 300ft above the sea. In 1905 a pair of Fulmar petrels nested here; less than a century later this fascinating bird has colonised much of Britain's cliff coast.

The tour follows the curve of Dunnet Bay, with its large sandy beach, backed by mountainous grass-topped dunes and Forestry Commission trees, planted to stop the dunes advancing inland. Castletown was built in 1824 to house workers from the now disused Castlehill quarries.

Thurso is a fishing port and Britain's most northerly mainland town. The building of the nuclear power station at Dounreay (see page 250) more than trebled the population of the town. The narrow streets around the harbour are full of largely 17th- and 18th-century fishermen's cottages; the centre of the town has a network of fine, wide, Georgian streets planned by Sir John Sinclair. To the east of the town is Harold's Tower, a strange hexagonal mausoleum built by Sinclair to commemorate Earl Harold, 12th-century ruler of

Orkney, Shetland and part of Caithness, who is buried near by.

From Thurso the route turns inland, curving to the south and east through flat country, passing Loch Watten, famous for trout-fishing and continuing through the Wick river valley for return to Wick.

SELECTED PLACES TO VISIT

✗ CASTLE GIRNIGOE & SINCLAIR
Map ref 3755

The dramatic ruin of the castle, once the seat of the Sinclair earls of Caithness, is at Noss Head north of Wick. The tall inner tower was built in the 15th century, and the outer structure, sometimes called Castle Sinclair, in the 17th century. The castle was abandoned following an inheritance dispute in 1690.

✼ CASTLE OF MEY
Map ref 2974

The castle, set in woodland ½ mile from the coast, was bought by the Queen Mother in 1952 and is now restored. A castle has stood here for about 1,000 years, but the present structure is 16th-century with some Victorian additions. The main attraction is the charming collection of the Queen Mother's favourite flowers, many given to her and now prized additions to the garden. There was a herb garden here in the 17th century, and there is a modern herb collection in the kitchen garden which also has roses and herbaceous borders. The greenhouse has brilliant displays of cinerarias, fuchsias and begonias. This is a very personal garden, tended by its owner during her annual summer holiday.

The ruins of Castle Girnigoe and Sinclair at Noss Head

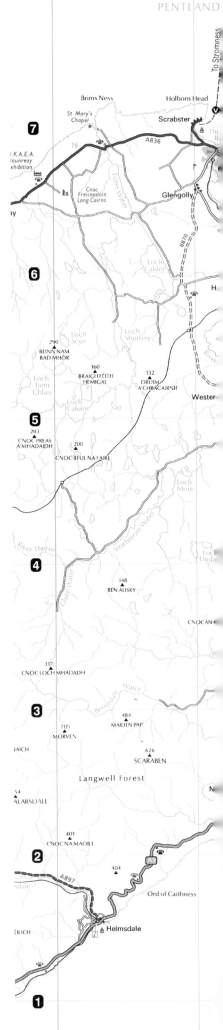

Map labels

Langaton Point
Island of Stroma
Mell Head
St John's Point
DUNNET HEAD
Briga Head
To Burwick
121
DUNNET HILL
Castle of Mey
Mey
Gills
Canisbay
DUNCANSBY HEAD
Muckle Stack
A836
Stacks of Duncansby
Dunnet
Dunnet Bay
so
Castletown
Loch Heilen
Freswick
Freswick Bay
Ness Head
Bucholie
Hilliclay
B876
Gill Burn
A9
Bower
Kirk Burn
17
Brough Head
Keiss
16
B874
B870
Loch of Wester
Keiss
B876
Sinclairs Bay
B876
A882
A882
21
Loch Watten
176
SPITTAL HILL
Spittal
B870
Watten
Bilbster
B874
Reiss
Castle Girnigoe & Sinclair
Noss Head
Mybster
Wick River
A882
Wick
Staxigoe
Papigoe
ND
23
Loch of Toftingall
Strath Beg
Wick Bay
EAG
South Head
Castle of Old Wick
145
BALHARN HILL
Grey Cairns of Camster
Thrumster
17
212
HILL OF YARROWS
Loch of Yarrows
Hill O'Many Stones
248
STERNSTER HILL
Ulbster
226
IRE NA BEINN
A895
287
BEN-A-CHIELT
Cairn O'Get
Whaligoe Steps
Upper Lybster
Loch Rangag
Halberry Head
Clyth Ness
Lybster
Lybster Bay
Latheron
Laidhay Croft Museum
Dunbeath
ally
A9
e

SCALE

0 1 2 3 4 miles

0 1 2 3 4 5 kilometres

2   3   4   5

CASTLES AND CREELS

🏛 LAIDHAY CROFT MUSEUM
Map ref 1731

North of the village of Dunbeath there is a traditional Caithness longhouse and barn, now restored as an example of the vernacular buildings of the area. Mainly early 18th-century, the house contains a stable and byre linked by a room and kitchen, with all rooms appropriately furnished; the barn has a collection of farm implements.

SCRABSTER
Map ref 1070

Originally a port for exporting Caithness flagstones in the 19th century, Scrabster is now a ferry port, with regular services to Ornkey and, in summer, to Scandinavia and Iceland.

★ ST MARY'S CHAPEL
Map ref 0370

This simple chapel near the sea at Crosskirk was built in the 12th century and is one of the oldest churches in Caithness. Roofless now, it was probably thatched; the presence of a chancel suggests that the design is derived from Orkney, then ruled, like Caithness, by Norse earls.

WHALIGOE
Map ref 3240

Telford called this 'a dreadful place' and several travellers expressed amazement that the women of Whaligoe climbed the more than 330 steps hewn out of the steep cliffs, carrying heavy loads of fish to the curing station above.

WICK
Map ref 3551

Vic (a bay in Norse) is an ancient settlement – the Viking Earl Rognvald was entertained here in 1140, and the Vikings created a coastal stronghold on the site of the Castle of Old Wick. The 'Old Man of Wick', as it is often called, still stands three-windowless-storeys high, one of the oldest towers in Scotland. There was a lot of development in the old town during the 18th and 19th centuries and very little that is older survives. Thomas Telford designed the new settlement, Pulteneytown, and built a bridge linking the two parts of the town.

The Heritage Centre near the harbour explains the history of Wick, with a photographic record of over 115 years. The Centre has a working fish kiln, a cooper's workshop and a blacksmith's shop. When the herring trade collapsed, Wick was forced to develop new industries and Caithness Glass has proved to be the most successful. Founded in 1960, the factory employs a combination of old – 15th-century glass-engraving techniques – with modern methods. The result has been steady expansion, and international recognition for the quality of glass produced in the factory. Visitors may watch glass-blowing.

OUTER HEBRIDES

The Western Isles have many differences, including their physical characteristics. They share that unhappy history common to the rest of the Hebrides, the Clearances. Both life-style and culture are fiercely defended yet contain many contradictions – not least the strict Calvinism of Lewis confronting Catholicism on several other islands. Each year visitors discover the haunting romance of the Western Isles and their uniqueness, and dream of returning.

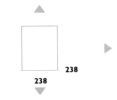

238

238

SELECTED PLACES TO VISIT

BARRA

Barra is a small island containing every form of Hebridean landscape – mountain, peat moorland, rocky shore with high cliffs, sandy beaches backed with pasture land and many reminders of long human occupancy.

✗ KISIMUL CASTLE
Map ref 6797

The capital of the island, Castlebay, with its fine harbour, is guarded by this ancient stronghold of the MacNeils, dating from the 11th century and rising sheer from the sea. A forbidding sight, the castle was deserted by the family in the early 19th century, and became derelict. In 1937 the heir, Robert Lister MacNeil, an architect, returned from America to buy back the castle and 12,000 acres of his family's lands. He began restoring the castle immediately but the work was not completed until the early 1970s; the outer walls conceal a modern complex.

The castle ruins in Castlebay, chief town of the island of Barra

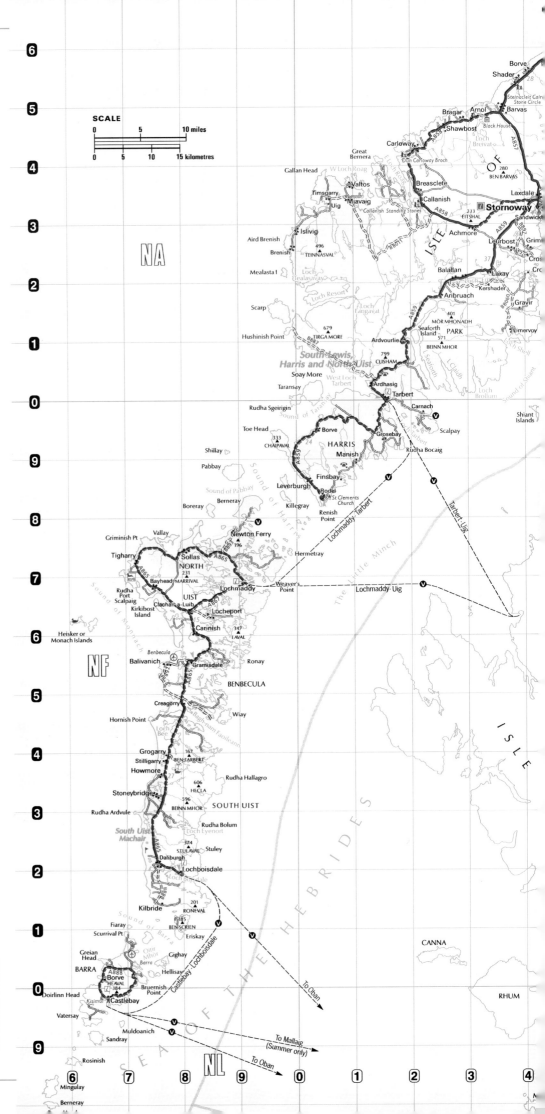

The causeway linking the islands of Benbecula and North Uist

BENBECULA

Benbecula is connected to South and North Uist by a causeway carrying the A865 over an area of quicksands. South Uist is Catholic, North Uist is Protestant – the linking island a mixture! From the only hill of any size, Rueval, there are wonderful views; on its southern slopes is the cave where Bonnie Prince Charlie hid while waiting for Flora Macdonald to bring him girl's clothing for their journey to Skye.

ERISKAY

On this tiny, exquisite island Prince Charles Edward first set foot on Scottish soil *en route* from France in 1745. He stayed in a black house which was only demolished in 1902. The island's main industries are crofting and fishing, and sweaters knitted here are much in demand.

HARRIS

The only town on the island is Tarbert, situated on a `waist' of land between East and West Loch Tarbert. Most of the population is concentrated in the south and east where they continue the crofting tradition. Leverburgh was intended as a major fishing port but the death of Lord Leverhulme in 1925, and the indifference of the islanders, frustrated the attempt.

ST CLEMENTS CHURCH
Map ref 0584
Important St Clements Church at Rodel was restored in 1873. The finest example of medieval church architecture in the Hebrides, it was built of sandstone from the Isle of Mull by the Macleods of Dunvegan at the beginning of the 16th century and is the burial place of several of their chiefs.

LEWIS

🏠 BLACK HOUSE
Map ref 3149
The Black House at Arnol, or *tigh dubh*, is a good example of its kind, although only built in the 1870s. It has 6ft-thick double stone walls and a straw thatched roof secured by rope and weighted with stones.

⌂ CALLANISH STANDING STONES
Map ref 2133
These famous stones are perhaps the most visited landmark in the Outer Hebrides. Cut from local stone and planted in the shape of a celtic cross some 4,000 years ago, they were only found and dug out in the 19th century.

⌂ DUN CARLOWAY BROCH
Map ref 1942
This Iron Age fortification is the best preserved defensive tower in the Hebrides. It has double walls 10ft to 12ft thick, rising to 30ft high. The views from the exposed top are fantastic.

ⓘ STORNOWAY
Map ref 4333
This is the largest town on the Western Isles and in the north-west of Scotland; an ancient settlement in a sheltered anchorage, it is now a major port. The merchant, Sir James Matheson, built the mock-Tudor Lewis Castle – now a technical college, but the grounds are open to the public – in the 1840s. After World War I, Lord Leverhulme bought Lewis and introduced plans to turn Stornoway into the largest fish-processing plant and fishing port in Europe. He, too, met with indifference, and he removed to Harris, although the equipment and roads he installed still exist.

NORTH UIST

North Uist is a largely flat, fertile landscape that has a long history of occupation by man. Near Carinish are the remains of 13th-century Trinity Temple, a monastery and college where the sons of Highland chiefs received their education.

One of the joys of North Uist is Balranald Nature Reserve, a relatively small reserve of marsh, dunes and lagoons surrounded by *machair*. Home to a wide variety of waders, ducks, geese and swans, it also has one or two breeding rarities, including red-necked phalarope.

SOUTH UIST

Most of the population of South Uist is gathered in the little townships on the western seaboard. Through the centre run a series of high hills and close to one of them, Ben Tarbert, is the 2,500-acre Loch Druidibeg Nature Reserve. Dotted with tiny islets it supports the largest colony of greylag geese in Britain and has a rich variety of bird life. Breeding birds include hen harrier, arctic tern and dunlin. Twite, corncrake and corn bunting live in the surrounding fields.

VATERSAY

Vatersay is a tiny hour-glass shaped island with a sand-dune `waist'. The hundred or so inhabitants live largely in the south in the village of the same name; strangely the school is in the northern half of the island. In 1906 the island was raided by men from Barra. They relied on the ancient law that squatters rights could be established by the building of a house in a day with a fire burning in the grate. Two years later 10 were arrested and given two months in an Edinburgh gaol. There was a national outcry and a year later the island was bought by a Government body and some of the raiders acquired the right to stay.

THE ORKNEY ISLANDS

'Shetland for scenery, Orkney for antiques' has some validity – Orkney abounds with prehistoric sites. The islands that comprise Orkney, with the exception of Hoy, are gently rounded, shaped `like sleeping whales'. There are some 70 islands of which less than 20 are occupied; a close society that has demonstrated the confidence to welcome and absorb outsiders. Many artists have made their home on Orkney, frequently inspired by Orcadian themes.

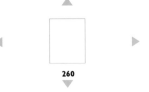

260

SELECTED PLACES TO VISIT

★ BIRSAY BAY
Map ref 2528

The extensive ruin of the 16th-century palace of Earl Robert Stewart dominates the farming country in which it is set. Uninhabited since the late 17th century, the house has a rather stark appearance, at odds with contemporary descriptions of it as sumptuous and stately. Near by is the Brough of Birsay, a small island displaying, in miniature, much of the history of Orkney, with its remains of an 11th-century Viking church which lie over a Celtic chapel, the outline of a 12th-century bishop's palace and a Norse settlement. Kirbuster has the last remaining example of a firehoose, part of the Orkney Farm and Folk Museum (see also Corrigall Farm Museum).

★ CLICK MILL
Map ref 3424

The Dounby Click Mill is Orkney's last remaining horizontal watermill, and is in working condition.

The Dounby Click Mill in the quiet, green landscape of Orkney

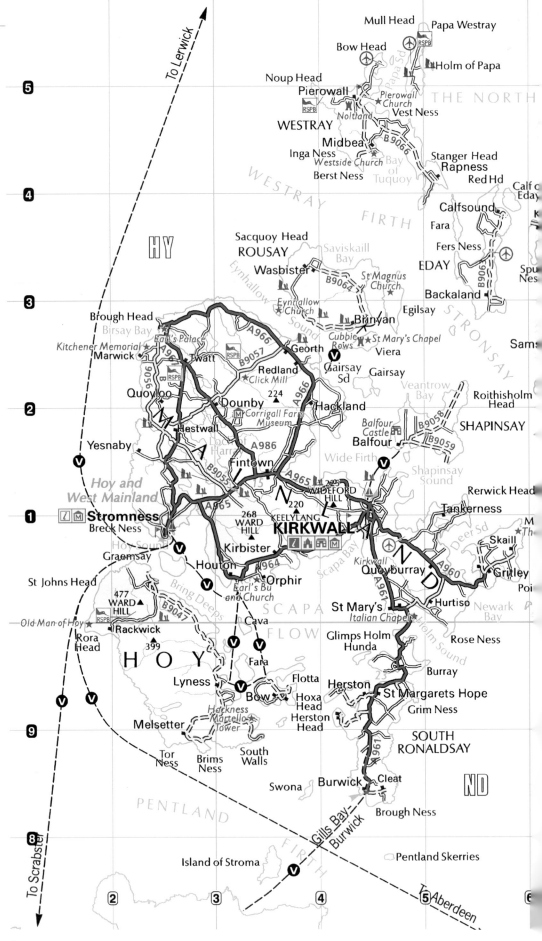

Ⓜ CORRIGALL FARM MUSEUM
Map ref 3319

Corrigall Farm Museum is an improved farmstead of the 1800s, which, together with Kirbuster at Birsay, forms the twin-sited Orkney Farm and Folk Museum. Both have period contents, farm implements and native breeds of sheep.

★ ITALIAN CHAPEL
Map ref 4800

Italian prisoners built this splendid chapel during World War II, creating a façade from scrap and driftwood around two Nissen huts. It has an arch supported by columns, a belfry and decorated glass windows.

KIRKWALL
Map ref 4311

The red sandstone St Magnus Cathedral, the most impressive medieval building in the Scottish islands, has been the focal point of Kirkwall, the capital of Orkney, for some 850 years. The Norse martyr, Earl Magnus, was murdered on

Dennis Head
North Ronaldsay
Hollandstoun   Linklet Bay
Strom Ness

UND   North Ronaldsay Firth
ANDAY
Tofts Ness
Otters Wick
Start Point
Bay of Lopness
toft
Is Ness   Bay of Newark
wick
SANDAY
SOUND

Whitehall   Mill Bay
STRONSAY
Lamb Head
uskerry Sound

Auskerry

e
say

5   10 miles
5   10   15 kilometres

7   8

cathedral stands the 12th-century Bishop's Palace, much altered over the centuries. Opposite is the splendid 17th-century Earl's Palace. Built by Earl Patrick allegedly using slave labour, it retains, even in its ruined state, a considerable Renaissance elegance.

MAES HOWE
Map ref 3312

A 4,000-year-old megalithic chambered cairn, Maes Howe is one of the most impressive pieces of prehistoric engineering in Western Europe. The corridor is aligned so that, on the day of the winter solstice only, a shaft of sunlight strikes the wall of the chamber – a wonderful, moving symbolism that bridges the centuries.

★ MARWICK HEAD
Map ref 2426

The cliff footpath at Marwick Head gives good views of this RSPB reserve, one of Orkney's prime seabird breeding sites and the most accessible. Guillemot, gulls and kittiwakes in vast numbers inhabit the cliff area with raven, puffin and skua. In 1916 Lord Kitchener set sail from Scapa Flow; his ship struck a mine and went down off Birsay. There is a grim grey monument to him on Marwick Head.

★ OLD MAN OF HOY
Map ref 1700

The Vikings named this island Hoy, the `high island'; its most famous landmark, the Old Man of Hoy, is a 450ft stack of rose-pink rock, first climbed in 1966.

★ ☒ PIEROWALL
Map ref 4448

A rather sinister looking ruin overlooking Pierowall Harbour, Noltland Castle was built on a Z-plan with 71 gun-loops which made

it a daunting fortress. There are the ruins of two churches, dating from the 12th and 13th centuries, at Pierowall.

SCAPA FLOW
Map ref 4000

Perhaps Orkney's most famous feature, the great natural harbour of Scapa Flow was the main anchorage of the Royal Navy in two world wars. The most extraordinary event in its history was the scuttling of the interned German Fleet in June 1919. During the interwar years some 25 destroyers and more than a dozen battleships and cruisers were spectacularly salvaged. Three battleships and four cruisers lie there still. Also beneath its waters are the remains of HMS *Royal Oak* sunk by a U-Boat in October 1939.

SKARA BRAE
Map ref 2920

An incredibly well-preserved Neolithic settlement, at least 4,500 years old, built from local flagstone, Skara Brae is a group of circular interconnecting houses with alley-

St Magnus Cathedral – Kirkwall's most famous landmark

ways and original paving slabs. A great sand storm buried the village, preserving much of the furniture and contents, and it was only uncovered after another storm in the 19th century. Six of the houses have been excavated.

☒☒ STROMNESS
Map ref 2510

An attractive seaside town, Stromness has a paved and twisting main street on the water's edge and gabled stone houses, some with jetties. The museum recalls the once-thriving fishing and boat building industries, and the salvaging of the German fleet scuttled in Scapa Flow in World War I. The Pier Arts Centre, in an 18th-century warehouse, is a good example of the very well developed cultural side of Orkney – it houses an important collection of paintings by notable 20th-century artists.

Primarily a port, Stromness developed in the early 18th century

Egilsay in 1116, and the cathedral was begun by his nephew, Earl Rognvald, some 20 years later. In 1919 Magnus' remains were found in a casket in the cathedral; an axe-cut in his skull bore out tales of his martyrdom, as described in the *Orkneyinga Saga*, the history of the Norsemen in Orkney. Beside the

THE SHETLAND ISLANDS

Estimates of the number of islands which make up `the Shetland Islands' vary, but there are around 100, of which 15 are occupied. The scenery is magnificent with unspoiled views and these, the most northerly of Britain's islands, enjoy the midnight sun on summer evenings.

It is a stern, bleak land, its people more Scandinavian than Scottish. The Shetlanders have made great efforts to maintain their distinctive character and have been successful in forcing the oil companies to take steps to assist in this endeavour.

SELECTED PLACES TO VISIT

CLICKHIMIN BROCH
Map ref 4640
On the outskirts of Lerwick, Clickhimin is an Iron Age broch in the form of a circular tower, once about 40ft high - the remains of a prehistoric settlement with a stone built fort.

FETLAR ISLAND
Map ref 6390
The `Fat Isle' is a green island which has always attracted human, plant and bird life. Over 200 species of wild flowers have been recorded on the island which was, for a time, the only British breeding site of the snowy owl, but the solitary male died in 1975, and two females now comprise the population. There are brochs and a standing stone known as the Giant's Grave, where eight

The impressive ruins of Jarlshof at Sumburgh

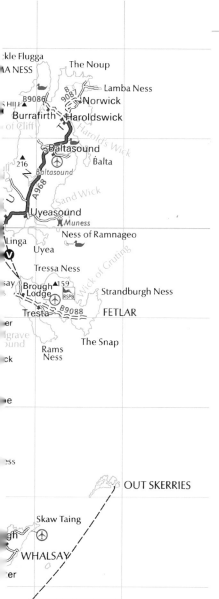

stones mark the grave of a Viking who died here after being rescued from the sea. The Tower at Brough Lodge, an early 19th-century folly, is an unexpected feature.

🔛 JARLSHOF
Map ref 4010

The impressive village of Jarlshof at Sumburgh was built in several phases – as many as eight have been identified – with Bronze Age and Iron Age dwellings, a broch, a wheel-house settlement, a Viking village, a medieval farmhouse and a 17th-century laird's house which dominates the site. The Viking remains are the most important archaeologically, though not easy for the layman to interpret. Sir Walter Scott invented the name Jarlshof for his novel *The Pirate*. For the adventurous, there is a walk from where the road ends beyond Jarlshof to Ness of Burgi, an Iron Age fort on an almost inaccessible site on a headland.

🔛🔛 LERWICK
Map ref 4840

Shetland's capital, administrative centre and main port, Lerwick is the most northerly town in Britain. Its economy depended for centuries upon the herring industry, and in the 17th century Dutch fishing fleets were based here. Now the main industry is servicing the oil rigs lying to the east and north-east of its harbour. The Shetland Museum is devoted to the history of man on Shetland from prehistoric times to present day.

🔛 MOUSA BROCH
Map ref 4624

Mousa Island has the most complete Iron Age broch in existence; the circular tower is 40ft high, probably only three or four feet less than its

original height, and within it are galleries and stairways, while from the top there are splendid views across the sea to Mainland. Why it survived as it did has never been entirely explained, but it was certainly used in a famous incident in the 12th century, recorded in the *Orkneyinga Saga*, when Earl Harald attacked it in an attempt to rescue his mother from a suitor whose marriage proposal Harald had rejected. He failed, they negotiated and all ended happily with reconciliations and a marriage.

🔛 NOSS NATURE RESERVE
Map ref 5540

Accessible by ferry, the rocky shores and cliffs of the Isle of Noss are home to more than 100,000 breeding seabirds. Noss is both a spectacular place, and internationally important. Such spaces as there are among the nesting birds in spring are bright with flowers; on the green moorland, great and arctic skua breed.

ST NINIAN'S ISLE
Map ref 3621

Christianity came to the Shetland Islands in the 6th century, and many churches were established in succeeding centuries, including one on St Ninian's. In the 1950s excavations revealed the church and the remains of an even earlier chapel. Buried in a wooden chest beneath a stone slab there was an outstanding collection of 28 pieces of 9th-century Celtic silver, including bowls and brooches, assumed to have been hidden by monks facing an attack by Viking raiders. The original treasure is now in the National Museum of Scotland in Edinburgh and copies may be seen in the Shetland Museum in Lerwick.

The town harbour at Scalloway

🔛 SCALLOWAY CASTLE
Map ref 4040

Earl Patrick Stewart built the medieval-style Scalloway Castle in 1600. It overlooks the town of Scalloway, a grim reminder of the times when the earl forcibly introduced Scottish feudal law to replace the traditional Viking law in Shetland and Orkney. His rule was ended in 1615 when he was brought to justice and executed in Edinburgh. The castle was briefly garrisoned by Cromwell's troops but then fell into disrepair.

UNST
Map ref 6301

Britain's northernmost island, Unst is beautiful and very wild – the British wind-speed record at 177 mph was recorded near Norwick. North of the island are the rocks of Muckle Flugga, with its lighthouse set on Out Stack. Completed in 1854, this was a remarkable feat of building on one of the most notorious stretches of bad weather coast in Britain. Muness Castle in the south of the island is not just the most northerly in Britain, it is very fine architecturally – simple in design, small, functional but elegantly decorated. The castle was built in the late 16th century by Laurence Bruce, a kinsman of Earl Robert Stewart.

WHALSAY
Map ref 5564

About 1,000 people live on this island which has had a thriving sea trade for centuries. A reminder of this past is the 17th-century Bremen Böd – the Hanseatic booth used for storing exotic goods.

The second largest of the Channel Islands, Guernsey is well-known for its peaceful and relaxing atmosphere. With more than 30 sandy beaches, visitors to the island have every opportunity to enjoy sunbathing, swimming, cliff walks and nature reserves.

SELECTED PLACES TO VISIT

CASTEL

Tomatoes are a major industry on the island, and at the Guernsey Tomato Centre at Castel, there are displays and audio-visual presentations on the industry since the early 17th century.

🏛 FORT GREY MARITIME MUSEUM

This white building on a tidal islet in Rocquaine Bay is a true Martello tower, today the Fort Grey Maritime Museum. Built in the early 19th

One of the many martello towers to be found on Guernsey; this one is at L'Ancresse Bay

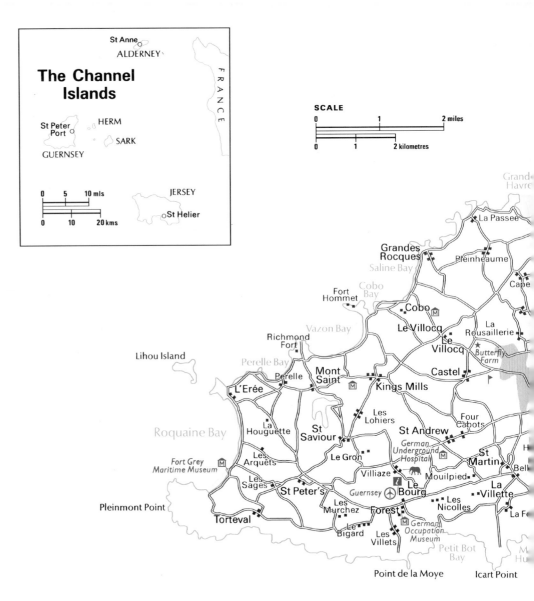

The Channel Islands

FRANCE

St Anne
ALDERNEY

St Peter Port   HERM
GUERNSEY   SARK

JERSEY
St Helier

SCALE

0   1   2 miles

0   1   2 kilometres

Grande Havre
La Passee
Grandes Rocques   Preinheaume
Saline Bay   Cape
Cobo Bay
Fort Hommet   Cobo
                Le Villocq   La Rousaillerie
Vazon Bay   Le Villocq
Richmond Fort   Castel   Butterfly Farm
Lihou Island
Perelle Bay   Mont Saint   Kings Mills
L'Erée   Perelle
                     Les Lohiers   Four Cabots
           La Houguette   St Saviour   St Andrew
Roquaine Bay   German Underground Hospital
                Les Arquêts   Le Gron   St Martin
Fort Grey Maritime Museum   Villiaze   Mouilpied   Bell
           Les Sages   Guernsey ✈ Le Bourg   La Villette
Pleinmont Point   St Peter's   Les Murchez   Les Nicolles   La Fe
                        Forest
           Torteval   Le Bigard   German Occupation Museum
                    Les Villets   Petit Bot Bay   M Hu
Point de la Moye   Icart Point

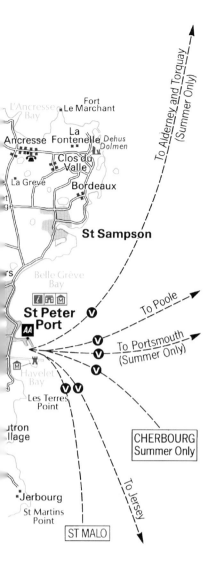

century as part of the island's defences against invasion by Napoleon and surrounded by a curtain wall, the tower houses a museum on the remains and records of ships wrecked on the Hanois rocks nearby, before the lighthouse was built.

🏛 GERMAN OCCUPATION MUSEUM

In 1940 Guernsey fell under German occupation. The German Occupation Museum at Forest vividly recalls the privations suffered by islanders through the use of tableaux containing items from a large collection of occupation memorabilia.

L'ANCRESSE BAY

One of the best bathing beaches on Guernsey, L'Ancresse Bay cuts deep into the north coast of the island, protected by two headlands. The bay has always appeared to be a likely place for an invasion and there are a remarkable number of defensive positions scattered around the area. Some 15 Martello towers were built – to a design unique to Guernsey – in the 1780s, including one on the eastern headland, Fort Le Marchant, with its Napoleonic gun battery.

★ LE FRIQUET BUTTERFLY FARM

At the Le Friquet Butterfly Farm both European and tropical species fly freely in a large greenhouse, and may be seen hatching from their chrysalides. The subtropical and tropical species are often imported as chrysalides, cooled for the journey.

The harbour at St Peter Port, part of the oldest section of the capital

PERELLE BAY

The tower overlooking rocky Perelle Bay, on the west of the island, was built by the Germans during World War II. At low tide it is possible to reach Lihou Island, just south of the bay, by a causeway from L'Eree. This exposed and treeless island contains the scant remains of a 12th-century priory, Notre Dame de la Roche.

🏛 🐘 ST ANDREW

A vast underground complex occupying 75,000 sq ft, the German Underground Hospital at St Andrew was designed for 100 patients, with a still larger ammunition store. The biggest project undertaken by the Germans during their occupation of the Channel Islands was achieved through forced labour. Imported to hack 1¼ miles of passages and rooms out of the rock, taking 3½ years, many workers lost their lives. In the event, the hospital was used to care for wounded German soldiers for about six weeks following the D-Day invasion of France in 1944.

Near by at Guernsey Zoo, the Zoological Trust of Guernsey has amassed, and contrives to breed from, a collection of rare and endangered species of small birds and animals. Possibly the tiniest church in the world, Les Vauxbelets is fashioned entirely of broken glass and china; the work of Brother Deodat, a French monk who lived at St Andrew earlier this century. He completed a grotto just before World War I and later built a chapel, which he demolished and rebuilt because the bishop who came to consecrate the first building could not get through the door.

ST MARTIN'S POINT

The De Sausmarez family have lived in Sausmarez Manor at St Martin's since 1254 with one short break in the 16th century. This feudal manor house, built on a Norman site, is a fascinating mixture of architectural styles. Its best feature is the fine Queen Anne façade, dating from 1714.

🏛🏛🏛 ST PETER PORT

The island's capital, St Peter Port is set on a steep hillside above its harbour. The Town Church in the High Street is the finest on the island with work of the 12th and 15th centuries; it is more French than English. At the harbour entrance is the large and impressive Castle Cornet, dating from the 13th century. In the Civil War the castle was a Royalist stronghold, holding out until 1651, while much later the Germans adapted its defences against possible attack in 1940. Now it houses a number of small museums – military and maritime – and an art gallery. In a rather charming ceremony, a gun is fired from the castle each day at noon – but not until the correct time has been checked using a telescope to study the clock on the Town Church! The Guernsey Museum & Art Gallery in the beautifully laid out Candie Gardens, was purpose built and tells the story of Guernsey and its people. Hauteville House was bought by Victor Hugo in 1856 and it was here that he wrote his novel, *Les Misérables*. Today, the house contains fine collections of china, paintings and tapestries while the writer is commemorated by a statue in Candie Gardens.

CHANNEL ISLANDS

Jersey, Guernsey, Alderney, Herm and Sark – these islands between England and France draw people with their wildlife, their centuries-old heritage, their beaches and their independence

Geographically and geologically part of France, historically attached to England, the Channel Islands are further set apart by their administrations, laws, flora and fauna and, most of all, by their fiercely maintained individuality.

The Channel Islands lie in the Gulf of St Malo, with the English Channel beyond. Their nearest point, Alderney, is 9 miles from the French coast, visible from all the islands. Composed of very old rocks known as Icart and Perelle gneiss, there is an underlying connection between the islands and the mainland, but each of the main islands is a separate mass. The islands were detached from Europe at about the same time as the English Channel was formed, about 8,500 years ago.

Financial Independence
The history of the Channel Islands extends back to Palaeolithic times but the earliest major historical remains are the dolmens (neolithic tombs). Given their geographical situation, it was inevitable that the islands would be invaded and Gauls, Romans, Saxons, Franks and Friesians all settled or raided them before the Viking earl, Rollo, acquired Normandy. Soon the Channel Islands were added to the duchy and, when Duke William of Normandy conquered England it became `our oldest surviving possession'.

The Channel Islands have never belonged to France, although occupied on several occasions. In the 13th century they remained loyal to King John when Normandy fell to the French, receiving their first constitution from him. The 15th century was a period of great unrest but it was followed by a period of peace lasting until the Civil War. Island loyalties were divided, Jersey standing for the King, Guernsey for Cromwell – although Castle Cornet (see page 268) was Royalist, holding out until 1651. The last French invasion,

Purple spurge, very rare elsewhere, thrives in the islands' mild climate

of Jersey, was in 1781, but the danger remained, as the Martello Towers and the remarkable range of Victorian forts of Alderney, attest.

The next invasion occurred in 1940 when, following the surrender of France, the Channel Islands were occupied by German troops; many islanders were imprisoned or deported. Imported slave labour was used to build a vast network of gun batteries, bunkers, underground hospitals and ammunition stores throughout the islands. Alderney, whose population had evacuated, became a concentration camp.

Since the war, tourism has boomed, supplemented by market gardening, but the latest, and most significant, growth has been the provision, on the two main islands, of financial services.

The Channel Islands are divided into two Bailiwicks; Guernsey is further sub-divided into Alderney and Guernsey and Sark – each group has outlying islands under its control. A form of Norman law is employed by both Bailiwicks but there are significant differences in the systems.

Natural Beauty
The mild climate ensures a marvellous diversity of wildlife; several species are restricted to the islands. Well over 1,000 plant species have been recorded, with many rarities including Jersey buttercup, purple spurge – restricted to Alderney – and Guernsey centaury. But the visitor will remember great drifts of spring and summer colour as more common, but no less beautiful, plants cover the islands.

Several mammals and reptiles are either indigenous or found in Europe and not Britain. They include two species each of shrew and vole, and green and wall lizards. Migrant butterflies include the Queen of Spain fritillary and the Camberwell beauty. Alderney and Burhou have particularly strong sea-bird colonies and the nature reserve at St Ouen's Bay on Jersey is a fine place to see both bird and plant life.

Touring the Smaller Isles
Alderney. Alderney is the most northerly of the Channel Islands and the nearest to France. Two-thirds of the island is an elevated plateau surrounded by cliffs – those around Telegraph Bay are both dramatic and attractive with a covering of sea campion, thrift and broom. The remaining eastern third is low-lying, like Braye Bay and Corblets Bay. During the German occupation in World War II, gannets colonised Les Etacs, a rocky stack at the extreme western end of Alderney – now some 3,000 pairs breed here.

The island has been inhabited since neolithic times but few early remains have survived the building of fortifications over the centuries. Alderney has more of these than any of the other islands, including the twelve forts around the coast, built in typically extravagant Victorian style as a defence against possible invasion by Napoleon III. The largest fortifications were built in World War II, by the Germans; many islanders returned to find their homes destroyed. The Hammond Memorial on the outskirts of St Anne recalls those of all nationalities who died on Alderney during the War.

Most of the population live

The wall lizard is a reptile indigenous to the islands

that Herm may have been the burial place for tribes inhabiting the other islands.

Jethou. A steep-sided island, only 600 yards across, Jethou is privately owned and not open

The Queen of Spain fritillary (top and middle) *is a migrant species and rarely reaches the mainland*
Above: *The Camberwell beauty is another migrant species*

to visitors. It was once part of Herm, but a storm in the 8th century isolated it. Flowers were grown for export on its plateau, and daffodils still bloom here. The Fairy Wood, facing Herm, is carpeted with bluebells each spring.

Sark. A little smaller than Alderney, Sark is noted for its refusal to tolerate motor vehicles – except farm tractors, essential to its economy. The world's smallest jail is on Sark, as is the smallest registered harbour, Port de Creux. Sark is the last feudal fiefdom in Europe, run by the Seigneur, Michael Beaumont; his subjects pay no duty or taxes. The island is divided into two by a slim causeway of high rocky land, La Coupé, with a sheer drop on each side. Great Sark is a fertile plateau practically surrounded by cliffs 300ft high, while Little Sark, a tranquil partner, was the scene of Sark's futile mining industry.

in St Anne with its narrow cobbled streets and white-washed houses. The capital starts as you enter the cobbled Marais Square where the history of the 'Alderney cow' can be seen over the door of the Marais Hotel. The town is built around a group of medieval farmsteads; *venelles*, or narrow lanes, run between the houses and lead out onto the agricultural land known as the Blaye. St Anne became prosperous in the 18th century as a result of privateering. In the 19th century a harbour and fortifications were built; today much of St Anne consists of 18th- and 19th-century buildings, in local sandstone. The parish church is a fine

building, arguably the best modern church on the islands.

Brecqhou. A tiny island, separated from Great Sark by the Gouliot Passage. Though the middle of the island is comparatively flat, it is completely surrounded by cliffs, some 200ft high, and access is not easy.

Burhou. In sharp contrast to Brecqhou, this island, a mile off the north-west coast of Alderney, is low-lying and flat. In fact two islands, the smaller separated from the larger at high water, both are uninhabited except for rabbits and a considerable number of sea-birds. Puffin, razorbill,

guillemot and storm petrel all breed here.

Herm. Herm and Jethou (see below) are 3 miles east of Guernsey. Herm is the larger, partly dune plain with shells and lime-loving plants. The remainder is fertile farmland, supporting about 100 Guernsey cows. Hern is about one-and-a-half miles long and about half-a-mile wide, shaped roughly like a wedge of cheese. There are cliffs to the south and a flat area in the north. Access is by boat from St Peter Port. There are less than a dozen resident families and the island depends on tourism and dairy farming. There are several neolithic burial chambers; it is thought

The largest and the most southerly of the Channel Islands, Jersey has more open land than Guernsey, the best lying behind the great stretch of sand comprising St Ouen's Bay. Primarily a tourism centre, Jersey has a flourishing financial services industry, as well as good dairy farming land and market gardening.

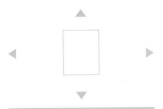

SELECTED PLACES TO VISIT

CORBIÈRE POINT

The rocks on this barren place at the extreme south-west point of the island have been responsible for the destruction of many ships, yet it was not until 1874 that a lighthouse was built at Corbiere Point. The first to be constructed of concrete, it stands 35ft high, on the highest part of the peninsula. There is a rather dramatic concrete causeway, across which it is possible to reach the lighthouse (not open to the public).

⚔ 🏰 ELIZABETH CASTLE

Elizabeth Castle is a fortress on an islet guarding St Helier harbour, named for Queen Elizabeth I by Sir Walter Raleigh. Work on it began in 1594 and was completed by 1600, when Raleigh became Governor. Charles II – proclaimed King only on Jersey in 1649 – stayed in Elizabeth Castle and Sir Philippe de Carteret later held it for the Royalists until the island capitulated in 1651. Elizabeth Castle remained the official residence of the Governor until the 18th century. It was garrisoned during World War I and re-fortified by the Germans in World War II.

⚔ GOREY

A wonderfully dramatic castle towering over the pretty village of Gorey, Mont Orgueil Castle stands on a site of great antiquity. The castle demonstrates the various stages of refurbishment necessary to maintain a defensive capability over several centuries. First mentioned in medieval times, when King John was in the process of losing Normandy, the French tried on many occasions to take it, but, with one brief exception, it withstood all attacks for three centuries. It held out for the Royalists during the Civil War before becoming the island prison until 1679, and when

Republican France declared war on Britain in 1793 Mont Orgueil became the headquarters of a British secret service force. Taken over by the States of Jersey early this century, the attractive ruins are floodlit on summer evenings.

Gorey has a charming small harbour, ringed by white-fronted houses and shops, now used by leisure craft but once the centre of a large oyster fishing industry. The harbour was built in the early 1800s; the church and some single-storey cottages for fishermen were added in the 1830s.

🐾 JERSEY ZOOLOGICAL PARK

Founded in 1959 by Gerald Durrell, Jersey Zoological Park breeds animals facing extinction, with the aim of eventually returning some to the wild. The zoo has concentrated on larger creatures.

🏛 LA HOUGUE BIE

La Hougue Bie is a Neolothic site on the east of the island, with a giant burial mound some 40ft high covering a stone-built passage grave. The passage leading to the central burial chamber is over 50ft long. Two medieval chapels stand on the mound, one containing a crypt in the form of a replica of the Holy Sepulchre in Jerusalem. Also the site of an underground communications bunker built by the

Germans, it is now one of several museums on the Channel Islands devoted to the occupation, as well as other exhibitions.

★ LA MARE VINEYARDS

A fine 18th-century granite farmhouse is at the centre of La Mare Vineyards, at St Mary, an attractive small estate where the Blayney family have been making wine for 150 years. Visitors can see the avenues of vines, the cider orchard, and discuss the making of wine and cider.

★ QUETIVEL WATERMILL

Recently restored by the National Trust of Jersey, Quetivel Mill is the only watermill still working in lovely St Peter's valley. There has been a working mill here since 1309, with a break from the late 19th century until the 1940s and again following the war.

ST CLEMENT

The herb garden of Samares Manor at St Clement has a herb maze in the form of a medieval knot garden. There are tours of the manor house, a Japanese garden with waterfalls, and an 11th-century dovecote in the extensive grounds.

🏛🏛 ST HELIER AND ST AUBIN

The capital of Jersey, St Helier is a bustling town with an excellent

shopping centre, and food and fish markets.

Traditional island trades are featured in the Jersey Museum which has a reconstruction of a Victorian chemist's shop, and a room devoted to the famous `Jersey Lily', actress and mistress of Edward VII, Lily Langtry. A sea-front road lined with hotels and boarding houses links St Helier to St Aubin, Jersey's first port. Above its 17th-century harbour are the fine houses of merchants who used the port.

ST OUEN'S BAY

A vast stretch of golden sand

SCALE

Above: *The view back to Elizabeth Castle from the causeway at St Helier*

Right: *Lobster pots on the quay at the pretty harbour at Rozel*

occupying most of Jersey's west coast, St Ouen's Bay has the finest beach on the island, but only for strong and experienced swimmers and surfers. Overlooking St Ouen's Bay is a nature area, Les Mielles, with sand dunes, scrub and other habitats; 5,000 species of insects have been identified and the area attracts a good bird population.

WESTERN IRELAND

Many Irish poets and writers have been inspired by this area of mountains, loughs, superb coastline, and sleepy towns and villages.

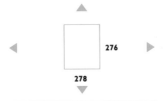

276

278

SELECTED PLACES TO VISIT

ACHILL ISLAND 1E
The largest island off the Irish coast, Achill Island is connected by a bridge to the mainland. It has superb scenery with heather-covered mountains: Croaghaun in the extreme west of the island has a sheer 2,000ft drop into the Atlantic; Slieve More, the highest mountain, has a dolmen and two stone circles on its southern slopes.

BALLINTOBER 3E
Now restored, the Abbey here has provided Mass for 750 years; it survived both the 1542 suppression of Henry VIII, and removal of the roof by Cromwell in 1653.

BALLYSHANNON 3D
Set on the River Erne Ballyshannon is the birthplace of the poet, William Allingham. North of the town is the ruined Kilbarron Castle, home of the O'Clery family, one of whom, Michael, was one of the Four Masters – chroniclers of Irish history up to the 17th century.

BUNDORAN 3D
A popular resort on an inlet of Donegal Bay, Bundoran has a wide sandy beach. The action of the Atlantic on the cliffs has caused some interesting rock formations – the Wishing Chair, the Puffing Hole and a natural arch known as the Fairy Bridge.

CLIFDEN 1F
To the east of this small town the Twelve Bens rise, creating an almost alpine-like setting. Four of the Twelve Bens are in the Connemara National Park which conserves and promotes the scenic splendour of west Galway; in that setting is Kylemore Abbey, now home to Benedictine nuns and a girls' school, but originally built for an MP, Mitchell Henry. Alcock and Brown landed near here at the end of the first ever transatlantic flight; a monument marks the spot.

CONG 2E
Cong (neck in Gaelic) is on an isthmus between the Loughs Mask and Corrib, an exquisite setting,

LEGEND

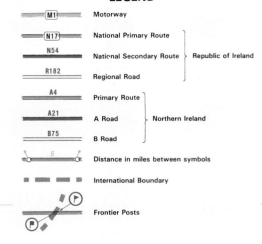

M1	Motorway
N17	National Primary Route
N54	National Secondary Route } Republic of Ireland
R182	Regional Road
A4	Primary Route
A21	A Road } Northern Ireland
B75	B Road
⊙—5—⊙	Distance in miles between symbols
▬ ▬ ▬	International Boundary
	Frontier Posts

Scale: 16 miles to 1 inch (approx)

C

D

E

F

1

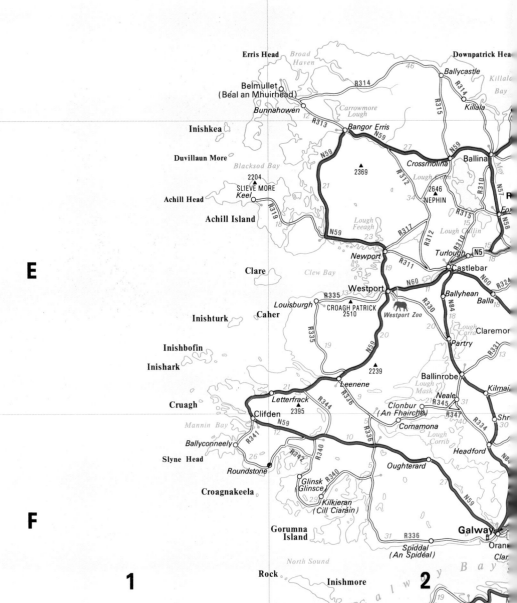

2

ideal for sportsmen. Ashford Castle, once a Guinness home but now a hotel, has the ruins of a 12th-century Augustinian abbey beside it. Cong is a good centre for explorations to Joyce's Country, the wild mountain area to the west.

CROAGH PATRICK 2E

A conical mountain on which St Patrick spent the 40 days of Lent in AD441, Croagh Patrick (also known as The Reek) has an oratory on its summit, and thousands of pilgrims climb its 2,510ft height each July for a mass. The climb begins beside the beautiful ruin of Murrisk Abbey, a 14th-century Augustinian foundation. Spectacular views await climbers at the summit; to the south the Twelve Pins can be seen, and to the north island-studded Clew Bay.

DRUMCLIFF 3D

The poet, William Butler Yeats, is buried in Drumcliff churchyard. Near by is the site of the battle in which 3,000 men are said to have died as a result of a dispute involving Columba – guilt drove him to leave Ireland and set up his community on Iona. Glencar Lough is noted for the waterfalls at its eastern end, and for two crannog lake dwellings.

DUNGLOE 3C

The Rosses are a vast expanse of land, some 60,000 acres, covered with rocks, lochans and streams. Talamh Briste is a chasm, ¼ mile-long and 12ft wide, south-west of the town.

GALWAY 2F

The gateway to Connemara, Galway is sited at the mouth of the River Corrib. Originally a fishing community, salmon may be seen in

The main town of Connemara, Clifden nestles on the edge of the Atlantic

season from the Salmon Weir Bridge leaping up the river. There are many fine old houses built by merchants, and the City Museum is housed in the `Spanish Arch' in the town wall.

In sharp contrast the old fishing settlement of the Claddagh on the other side of the river has always been fiercely independent; it is a close-knit Irish-speaking community established long before Galway city came to be built.

GLENCOLUMBKILLE 3D

A local priest founded a unique cooperative at Glencolumbkille, to dissuade villagers from emigrating from the area. It was a retreat of St Columba and his bed can be seen – it is a large flagstone! Today there is a folk museum, illustrating three periods in Irish rural life.

IAR-CHONNACHT 2F

North of Galway is a tract of bleak open moorland with peat bog, tiny lochans, occasional boulders and no trees; from its highest point near Lough Lettercraffoe there are superb views of Lough Corrib.

KILLALA 2D

The scene of one of Ireland's most significant historical events – the unsuccessful invasion in 1798 by three French warships flying British colours. They took Killala, but advancing inland were defeated by Lord Cornwallis and General Lake. The 84ft-high round tower of a very early church, possibly built by St Patrick, survives at Killala Bay, and 2 miles away are the remains of 15th-century Moyne Abbey with cloisters that are almost perfect, as are those at Rosserk Abbey 2 miles further on.

KILLYBEGS 3D

A busy fishing port on an inlet of Donegal Bay, Killybegs has a good natural harbour. Hand woven

carpets are a local industry. William Allingham, the poet, was customs officer here when he wrote his best known poem *The Fairies*.

KNOCK 2E

In 1879 it was reported that the Virgin Mary had appeared at the gable wall of Knock's small Catholic church; since then it has become a place of pilgrimage.

LISSADELL HOUSE 3D

North of Drumcliff Bay is this fine Georgian mansion, home of the Gore-Booth family. Yeats frequently stayed here and was a friend of Countess Markiewicz (*née* Gore-Booth) who was condemned to death for her part in the 1916 uprising but later became the first British woman MP – she was one of 73 Sinn Feiners who refused to take their seats at Westminster.

SLIGO 3D

Sligo is one of the most attractively sited towns in Ireland with mountains to the north and south. The 13th-century Sligo Abbey, destroyed in 1641 when the town was sacked, now has restored cloisters. Some of the buildings, including the 17th-century Baptist Church and the remarkable Gothic courthouse repay careful attention. Just outside the town, Lough Gill is Yeats' *Lake Isle of Innisfree*.

WESTPORT 2E

This market town's centre was planned by James Wyatt, who designed twin malls planted with lime trees to flank the Carrowbeg river. Westport overlooks Clew Bay with its many small islands – there is said to be one for every day of the year. The Westport House estate, the seat of the marquesses of Sligo, has an 18th-century demesne house with an exquisite interior.

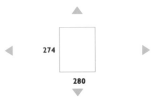

NORTHERN IRELAND

The beautiful province of Ulster is delightful. Visitors will enjoy its wealth of historic castles, beautiful country houses, loughs, nature reserves, mountains, superb coastline and miles of sandy beaches.

▲

274

◀   □   ▶

280

▼

SELECTED PLACES TO VISIT

ARDRESS HOUSE 5D

A graceful Georgian residence, near Portadown, developed from a farmhouse by George Ensor, an architect who married the heiress to Ardress in 1760. The drawing room, with its plasterwork in the style of Robert Adam, is breathtakingly beautiful and there is a collection of paintings and much fine 18th-century furniture.

BELFAST 5D

The capital of Ulster has many interesting and beautiful buildings, mostly of the 18th and 19th centuries. Victorian buildings include the City Hall, patterned on St Paul's Cathedral, the Grand Opera House with its sumptuous oriental interior and, opposite it, a fascinating High Victorian public house, the Crown Liquor Saloon. The Botanic Gardens have a strikingly designed Palm House. Belfast Zoological Gardens, on their 13-acre site overlooking the city, has all kinds of animals including a pack of home-bred wolves. East of the city are the white Portland stone Parliament buildings at Stormont.

CASTLEROCK 4C

Hezlett House is a thatched house near Castlerock with an unusual

Looking across Lough Neagh from the Battery. Petrified wood, resembling pumice stone, can be found on the shore

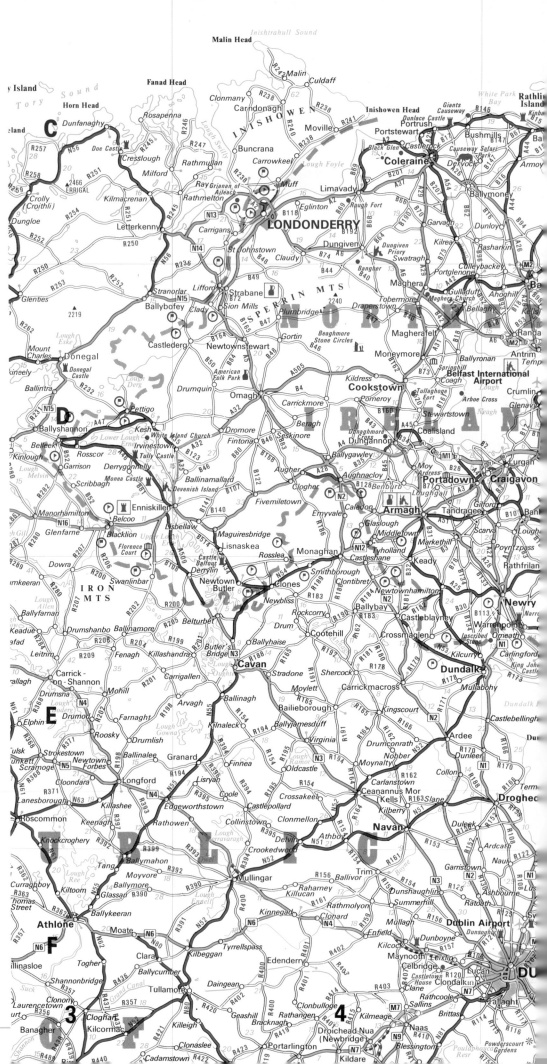

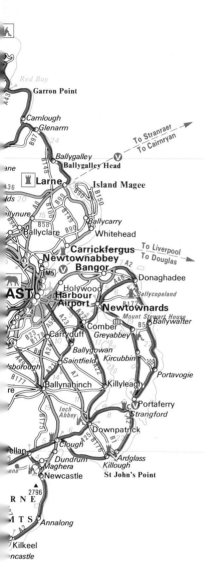

cruck-truss roof construction. Nearby is the Barmouth estuary, a good place for birdwatching as it is a stopover for many migratory species.

CASTLEWELLAN 5E
Castlewellan was mainly laid out by the Annesley family in the late 18th century. Just north of the town is Castlewellan Forest Park with its internationally famous arboretum.

DOWNHILL HOUSE & MUSSENDEN TEMPLE 4C
Built for Frederick Hervey, Bishop of Derry and 4th Earl of Bristol, Downhill was probably designed by James Wyatt. As a setting for the now-ruined house, the Earl-Bishop provided a superb landscaped park. The little Mussenden Temple, perched on the cliff edge overlooking Lough Foyle north of the house, was the Earl-Bishop's library and reflects his passion for circular buildings.

ENNISKELLAN 4D
The uncompromising neo-classicism of this James Wyatt house at Enniskillen has been re-emphasised by the recent refacing of the front in creamy Portland stone. Inside, joinery and plasterwork are of the highest quality, with Regency furnishings. Lawns slope gently down to Lough Coole, home to greylag geese, originally introduced in about 1700.

FLORENCE COURT 4D
The three-storey house, named for Florence Cole, was built by her son in about 1750 near Enniskellan. Neither the Baroque touches on the exterior, nor the stately entrance hall, prepare the visitor for the riot of rococo plasterwork on the dining room, drawing room and Venetian room ceilings.

GIANT'S CAUSEWAY 4C
No visit to Northern Ireland would be complete without a trip to this

incredible spectacle, formed some 60 million years ago by a volcanic eruption. Many of the basalt columns are hexagonal; the tallest are some 36ft high.

LOUGH ERNE 3D
Upper and Lower Lough Erne comprise 50 miles of navigable water with 154 islands; several have religious significance. The lower lake has the largest breeding colony of common scoter in Britain, and both lakes are well stocked with fish.

LOUGH NEAGH 4D
Bordering five counties, Lough Neagh is the largest inland lake in Britain; 153 square miles and an important area for duck.

MOUNT STEWART HOUSE 5D
The home of the marquesses of Londonderry, overlooking Strang-ford Lough, this 18th-century house is full of family treasures. The famous gardens were the 1920s creation of the 7th Marchioness; each garden has a theme and the formal parterres blend well with the surrounding woods and lakes.

MOURNE MOUNTAINS 5E
A range of mountains in County Down. Slieve Donard is the highest at 2,796ft; its peak is 1½ miles from the coast, and it does indeed `sweep down to the sea' as the old song says. This is good walking country.

MOY 4D
An early 19th-century two-storey house with its own acetylene gas plant, the Argory stands on a rise overlooking the Blackwater river at Moy. The interior is artfully maintained as if awaiting guests, or the return of the family. A rare cabinet organ is still in working order. The walled pleasure garden

The wonderful rock formation known as the Giant's Causeway

leads down to the river from the Victorian rose garden.

MURLOUGH NATURE RESERVE 5E
This wonderful stretch of duneland, estuary and saltings on the coast of County Down at Dundrum offers splendid opportunities to study birds, seals and maritime flora. There were Stone and Bronze Age settlements here. Guided walks, residential weekends and holiday cottages are available.

NORTH ANTRIM COAST ROAD 5C
The scenic A2 road provides a memorable experience. From Larne in the east the road clips the heads of the Nine Glens of Antrim on its way north, through charming sleepy villages. A detour can be made to the little coastal village of Cushendun, before returning to the A2, at Murlough Bay. A minor coast road leads through wonderful cliffland scenery to the tiny rocky islet fishery of Carrick-a-Rede. Rejoin the A2 which continues to the unique basalt rock formations of the Giant's Causeway (see above), and passes the 16th-century Dunluce Castle on its way to the Londonderry border at Portrush.

ROWALLANE GARDEN 5D
Begun in 1860, the beautiful Rowallane Garden at Saintfield is noted for its rhododendrons and azaleas. Also of interest is the rock garden and several areas of wild flowers which attract butterflies.

SPRINGHILL 4D
A fortified manor house near Cooksdown, built by Ulster settlers in the early 17th century, Springhill today retains many of the belong-ings of the family who have in-habited the house for 10 generations.

STRABANE 4D
Strabane was once a centre for printing and publishing. John Dunlap, who printed the American Declaration of Independence in 1776, is reputed to have learned his trade at Gray's Printing Shop. The shop now houses fine examples of old printing presses and displays illustrate the development of printing techniques.

STRANGFORD LOUGH 5D
This sea-lough is 20 miles long and sheltered by land. Two-thirds of the world's population of pale-bellied Brent geese overwinter here. The National Trust runs the Strangford Lough Wildlife Scheme and protects the entire foreshore.

No house in Ulster enjoys a finer setting, with superb views over Strangford Lough, than Castle Ward. The ultimate failure of the marriage of the 1st Viscount Bangor, and his wife Anne, is clearly presaged by the house they built in the 1760s in two utterly different styles – his half conventional Palladian, her half `Strawberry Hill' Gothic!

The south-west coast of Ireland has some magnificent wild scenery, but much that is gentle. Kerry has moors, mountains and sea; Cork is wonderfully rural. Everywhere there is a tradition of welcoming visitors, while it is possible to slip away and simply enjoy the sense of remoteness.

274

◄ 280 ►

SELECTED PLACES TO VISIT

ADARE 2G
A very pretty village, Adare's thatched wayside cottages were built in the 19th century by Lord Dunraven, as tenant homes. He built his own house, Adare Manor House, a huge neo-Gothic mansion with a profusion of turrets and castellations, in 1832 – it has recently become a hotel. In the village, the interior of the Augustinian Priory has a true medieval feel while the 13th-century Trinitarian Abbey is the only house of the order in Ireland. Both are still in use, the priory by the Church of Ireland, the abbey as the Catholic church.

ANNE'S GROVE GARDENS 3H
A 20th-century creation, Anne's grove has walled, water and woodland gardens and fine displays of rhododendrons and other plants collected by Richard Grove Annesley. Set beside the steep banks of the River Awbeg, visitors can enjoy pleasant riverside walks.

BANTRY 2H
Bantry is delightfully sited between hills at the head of its 21-mile-long bay. The superb Georgian Bantry House, set on a wooded hillside, is full of treasures including two of Marie Antoinette's bookcases, mosaics from Pompeii, Russian icons, and fine Waterford crystal chandeliers. Italian terraced gardens give wonderful views over the bay to the Caha Mountains of Kerry.

BLARNEY CASTLE 3H
This 15th-century castle at Blarney houses the famous Blarney Stone. Those who kiss the stone are said to be granted the gift of the gab.

BUNRATTY CASTLE 3G
This mid-15th-century stronghold, north of Limerick, was besieged by Cromwellian forces. Today, Bunratty Castle contains an outstanding collection of 14th- to 17th-century furniture and fittings.

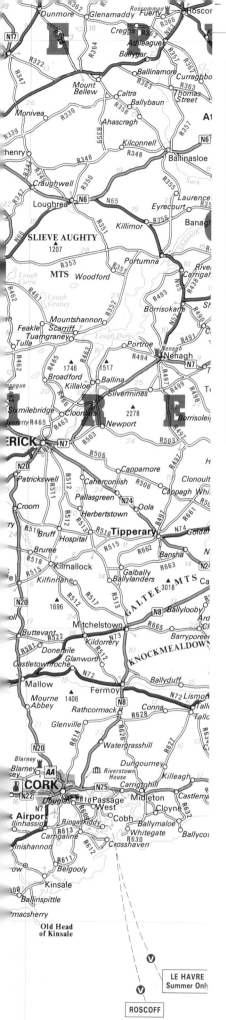

The hump-backed Parliament Bridge over the River Lee at Cork

In the grounds the Folk Park has traditional Irish farmhouses and cottages with a replica of a 19th-century Irish village street. Various old crafts are demonstrated in authentically reconstructed settings.

CASTLE MATRIX 2G

A 15th-century tower-house, built by the Earl of Desmond, Castle Matrix, west of Rathkeale, is one of the few such buildings to have survived in Ireland. It derives its name from the *matres* – a Celtic sanctuary on which it was built. There is a tiny re-created chapel on the top floor, and a medieval bedroom.

CORK 3H

The second city of the Republic, Cork claims to be the cultural capital. Built on an island formed by two channels of the River Lee where it flows into Lough Mahon, Cork was a monastic settlement in the early 7th century. Later plundered by Norse invaders, it became a thriving centre of commerce. The city centre was burned down in the War of Independence.

The lovely French Gothic Cathedral, designed by the Victorian architect, William Burges, is just one of the architectural pleasures to be discovered in the city.

FOTA WILDLIFE PARK 3H

Sited on an island 9 miles east of Cork, is the 70-acre Fota Wildlife Park with its Regency house and arboretum, administered by the Royal Zoological Society of Ireland.

GLENGARRIFF 2H

Glengarriff village is set in a deep valley surrounded by mountains which provide shelter for the native and tropical plants growing here in profusion. On Garinish Island in the large harbour there is a tropical garden designed round a central Italian garden with shaded walks through exotic and tender shrubs and trees.

KILFENORA 2F

The Burren Display Centre at Kilfenora explains the basic geology of this part of County Clare, now being developed as a National Park. A vast limestone plateau stretching over a hundred square miles, the fertile soil makes the Burren a paradise for botanists all the year round, as alpine flowering plants and Mediterranean species flourish here side-by-side. Rare plants abound, and animals, such as lizards and wild goats, also thrive. There are chasms, canyons, underground rivers and turloughs (rocky hollows which become lakes after heavy rain). The area has more than 60 Stone Age burial mounds and 400 Iron Age hill-forts.

KILLARNEY 2H

A landscape of superb lakes and hills, Killarney is east of Ireland's highest mountain range, MacGillicuddy's Reeks. In the town the Victorian cathedral was designed by Pugin. Set beside Lough Leane is the 14th-century Ross Castle, which inspired Tennyson to write his poem *The Princess*. There is a good folk museum at the 19th-century Muckross House, where skilled workers carry on traditional Kerry crafts. The extensive gardens provide wonderful mountain views. At the foot of the road leading to the Gap of Dunloe – a narrow mountain pass – is Kate Kearney's Cottage.

KINSALE 3H

A beautiful town on the Bandon estuary, Kinsale was the scene of one of Ireland's major battles in 1601 – a Spanish force took the town and held it against English armies. James II lodged here in 1689 on his way to the Battle of the Boyne. In 1915 a German U-boat sank the Cunard liner *Lusitania* off Old Head, 9 miles from the town.

KNAPPOGUE CASTLE 2G

North of Limerick is Knappogue Castle. Built in 1467, it remained in the same family for almost 350 years. Recently restored, the main feature remains the massive central tower. Franciscan Quin Abbey, two miles away, was founded in 1402 and was constructed using the remains of a Norman castle.

LOUGH GUR 3G

The centre of an important prehistoric site with two stone circles and Bronze Age, Viking and Christian relics, Lough Gur is the only lake in this area, and noted for its wide variety of bird life.

Bones of animals now extinct in Ireland have been found in caves above the lough. A Visitor Centre is housed in replica Neolithic huts.

RIVERSTOWN HOUSE 3H

Jemmett Brown, Bishop of Cork, rebuilt the originally 17th-century Riverstown House at Glanmire, north-east of Cork, in 1745 and added fine plasterwork. Nearby Dunkathel is a classic Georgian house with fine antique furniture and paintings.

TIMOLEAGUE 2H

A small village set on the Argideen estuary, its 13th-century abbey with 17th-century additions is one of the best-preserved Franciscan friaries of pre-Reformation Ireland. Timoleague Castle Gardens have been planted and maintained by the Travers family for the past 170 years.

The stepping-off point for most visitors, this area of southern Ireland has many superb castles and houses. Cashel and Kilkenny are outstanding examples of living history and Dublin requires a whole holiday to appreciate it.

▲
276

◄   278   ►

▼

SELECTED PLACES TO VISIT

ASHFORD 5F

Mount Usher Gardens at Ashford were modelled on the wild gardens created by William Robinson last century. The gardens extend along the River Vartry and contain rare shrubs and trees from all over the world. North-west of the village is the Devil's Glen where the Vartry rushes through a deep, shrub-covered chasm. The 100ft waterfall known as the Devil's Punchbowl has high-level walks nearby.

BIRR CASTLE DEMESNE 3F

The walled demesne of Birr Castle includes a lake and the meeting point of two rivers, the Little Brosna and the Camcor. The castle was besieged several times in the 16th and early 17th centuries, and was rebuilt around a ruined keep by Sir Laurence Parsons in 1620. The garden has many exotic trees and shrubs, including Wellingtonias and Cedar of Goa.

Elegant architectural detail in Dublin's Fitzwilliam Square

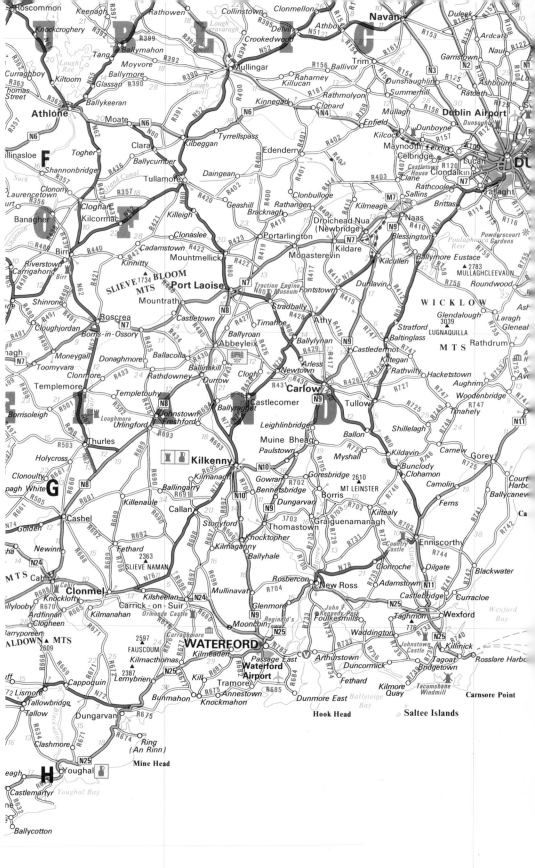

BLESSINGTON 4F

The village stands beside the northernmost reach of the Poulaphouca reservoir. Between the reservoir and the village is Russborough House, a superb Palladian mansion, built in the 16th century; it has outstanding plasterwork and houses Sir Alfred Beit's collection of paintings, amassed at the turn of this century.

CASTLETOWN HOUSE 4F

The finest Georgian country house in Ireland, designed by Galilei in 1722 for the Speaker of the Irish House of Commons, William Conolly. The interior remained unfinished, and it lacks a grand staircase.

DUBLIN 5F

On a wide and beautiful bay at the mouth of the Liffey, Dublin was originally an ecclesiastical settlement. Before the 17th century, Dublin was mostly built of wood; only a few early buildings have survived, including the two cathedrals and part of the castle. The city is largely 18th-century in plan, and most of its historic monuments are south of the river.

EMO COURT 4F

Emo Court at Port Laoise is a neo-classical house by James Gandon with lovely and extensive gardens containing specimen trees and shrubs.

HOWTH 5F

The 560ft-high Hill of Howth forms the northern part of Dublin Bay. A natural vantage point, Howth Head, gives views across Dublin Bay to the Wicklow mountains. Howth Castle gardens are noted for a splendid rhododendron display, woodland shrubs and trees. The grounds contain the Irish Transport Museum.

JAMES JOYCE TOWER 5F

The James Joyce Museum is housed in a Martello tower at Sandycove, giving a splendid view of Dublin Bay and the nearby resort of Dun Laoghaire ('Dun Leary'), best known as the ferry terminus.

JOHN F KENNEDY PARK 5G

At Dunganstown is John F Kennedy Park, the ancestral home of the family, with a comprehensive arboretum, a forest garden, a viewpoint from which six counties may be seen, and a Kennedy memorial.

KILDARE 4F

The Irish National Stud, at Kildare, has a Japanese Garden, created between 1906 and 1910 to symbolise the Life of Man from the Cave of Birth to the Gateway to Eternity. Also the site of Ireland's premier racecourse.

KILKENNY 4G

Ireland's finest medieval city, Kilkenny is small and charming with some rare Elizabethan architecture and ancient by-ways, known as slips. The 12th- to 13th-century castle houses an art gallery. The town museum is in the Rothe House, a 16th-century merchant house. Rich with ecclesiastical buildings, the town has both 13th- and 19th-century cathedrals, a ruined 13th-century priory, and two 13th-century abbeys.

LISMORE 3H

The Irish seat of the dukes of Devonshire since 1753, the remodelled 19th-century Tudor-style Lismore Castle is sited dramatically on a sheer cliff overhanging the River Blackwater. King John built the original stronghold in 1185; it was later owned by Sir Walter Raleigh. The walled and woodland gardens are open to the public. Lismore village once contained 20 churches and St Carthach founded a monastery here in the 7th century.

MALAHIDE CASTLE 5H

An historic castle, dating from the 12th century, Malahide has a splendid collection of Irish period furniture and historical portraits on loan from the National Portrait Gallery of Ireland.

NEWBRIDGE HOUSE 5F

An 18th-century house set in 100 acres of parkland, Newbridge has one of the finest drawing rooms in Ireland. There is a kitchen, a laundry and a courtyard with a coach house and some workshops.

POWERSCOURT GARDENS 5F

The vast Powerscourt estate includes one of Europe's greatest gardens, with notable statuary and

The harbour of Greystones, a seaside resort, with Bray Head in the background

ironwork. The mansion was largely burned down in 1971 but the magnificent gardens and the 400ft waterfall are open. Enniskerry, Powerscourt's estate village, near Bray, is very pretty.

THE ROCK OF CASHEL 3G

A 200ft-high limestone outcrop which overlooks the north side of Cashel, the rock is crowned with a round tower, the ruins of the lovely 12th-century Romanesque Cormac's Chapel and a vast 13th-century cathedral. This is one of Ireland's greatest historical sites – the seat of Munster kings from AD370 to AD1101, when the rock was granted to the Church. Here St Patrick preached, Brian Boru was crowned, Henry II came after he conquered Ireland and Gerald, Earl of Kildare, burned the cathedral because he thought the archbishop was inside.

SHILLELAGH 4G

This village has given its name to the Irish blackthorn stick. Timber from a great oak forest here was used to roof St Patrick's Cathedral in Dublin.

SLANE CASTLE 4E

Set on the River Boyne, the dramatic 18th-century Slane Castle features the work of James Wyatt and Capability Brown.

WEXFORD 4G

This county town is built on three levels; the long narrow main street is in the middle level. The first Anglo-Irish treaty was signed in Wexford in 1169 at Selskar Abbey. Henry II spent an entire Lent here in penance for causing the murder of Thomas à Becket. In 1838 Pugin designed the lovely chapel at St Peter's College.

References to captions are in italics.

A

Abbeydale Industrial Hamlet 139
Abbotsbury 34
Abbotsford House 206
Aberaeron 100, *101*
Aberarth 100
Aberdare 62
Aberdaron 100, 124
Aberdeen 236-7, *237*
Aberdour Castle 220
Aberdulais Falls 62
Aberfeldy 230
Aberfoyle 216
Abergavenny 84
Abergwili 60
Abersoch 124
Aberystwyth 100-1, *101*
Abingdon 68
Achamore Garden 194
Achill Island 274
Achiltibuie 240
Achlain 243
Achray Forest Drive 219
Acorn Bank 166-7
Acton Scott Working
   Farm Museum 109
Adare 278
Affan Argoed Country Park 63
Affleck Big House 198
Ailsa Craig 176
Aldeburgh 98, *98*
Alderney 270
Aldershot 70
Alford (Grampian) 246
Alford (Lincolnshire) 142
Alfriston 48
Allen Banks 184
Allerford 30
Alloway 196
Alnmouth 188
Alnwick 188
Alston 184
Althorp Hall 92
Alton 44
Alton Towers *134*, 135
Alum Bay 43
Alum Pot 166
Ambleside 162
Ampfield 38
Ampleforth 170
Andover 68
Anglesey Abbey 94
Anglo-Saxon Village reconstruction 97
Annan 182
Anne Hathaway's Cottage 88
Annesgrove Gardens 278
Anstruther 222
Ansty 47
Antony House 22
Appleby-in-Westmorland 167
Applecross 240
Appledore 28
Appuldurcombe 42
Aran Mawddwy 102
Arbigland Gardens 180
Arbor Low Stone Circle 135
Arbury Hall 112
Ardanaiseig Hotel and Garden 214
Ardclach 244
Ardgay 254
Ardmair 250
Ardress House 276
Ardrishaig 192
Ardrossan 196, *196*
Arduaine Gardens 212
Ardurech Castle 250
Ardwell House 176
Arenig Fach 126
Arenig Fawr 126
Arinagour 210
Arisaig 226
Arlington Court 28
Armadale 258
Armadale Castle 226
Arreton 42
Arundel 46
Ashburton 26
Ashby-de-la-Zouch 112
Ashdown Forest 48
Ashford (Derbyshire) 134

Ashford (S. Ireland) 280
Ashmolean Museum 88
Astley Hall 149
Aston End 94
Aston Hall 110
Athelhampton 36
Auchindoir 246
Auchinleck 198
Audley End House 94
Avebury 66
Avoncroft Museum of
   Buildings 110-11
Axminster 34
Aylesbury 92
Ayot St Lawrence 74
Ayr 196
Aysgarth Falls 168

B

Bachelor's Club 196
Bakewell 134
Bala 126
Balemartine 211
Ballantrae 176
Ballasalla 147
Ballaugh 146
Ballinaby 191
Ballintober 274
Ballyshannon 274
Balmoral Castle 232
Balnakiel 256
Balranald Nature Reserve 263
Balsham 94
Balvenie Castle 246
Bamburgh 208
Banbury 88
Banchory 236
Banff 248, *249*
Bantry 278
Banwell 64
Barbury 66
Barcaldine 229
Bardsey Island 101, 124
Bargany Gardens 176
Barnard Castle 168, *168*
Barnstaple 28
Barra 262
Barrington 34
Barrow-in-Furness 160
Barry 62
Barsalloch Fort 177
Barton Broad 121
Barton-upon-Humber 156
Basildon House 68
Basing House 68-9
Basingstoke 69
Bateman's 52
Bath 67
Bathgate 202
Batsford Arboretum 88
Battle 52
Bayham Abbey 52
Beachy Head 48
Beadnell 208
Bealach-Na-Ba 240
Beaulieu 38
Beauly 242
Beckford 86
Bede House 114
Bedford 92, *93*
Bedgebury National Pinetum 52
Beer 34
Beeston Hall 122
Beinn Eighe National Nature
   Reserve 240-1
Belfast 276
Belford 208
Belsay 189
Belton 114
Belvoir 114
Bembridge 42
Bembridge Windmill 42
Ben Arthur 214
Ben Lawers Mountain Visitor
   Centre 216
Ben Lomond 214
Ben More Assynt 250
Ben Nevis 228
Benbecula 263, *263*
Benmore Younger Botanic
   Garden 214-15
Bennachie Forest Reserve
   Visitor Centre 248
Berkhamsted 70
Berrington Hall 84
Berwick-on-Tweed 208, *208*
Beth Chatto Gardens 79

Bettyhill 258, *259*
Betws-y-coed 126
Beverley *158*, 158-9
Bewdley 108
Bexhill 52
Bickenhall 111
Bickleigh 31
Bicton Park 35
Biddenden 52
Bideford 29
Big Ben 73
Big Pit Mining Museum 84
Biggar 202
Billinghay 140
Bilsdale 175
Birdland Zoo Gardens 88
Birkenhead 130
Birmingham 110, *111*
Birnam 220
Birr Castle Demesne 280
Birsay Bay 264
Bishop's Stortford 76
Black House 263
Black House Folk Museum 238
Black Middens Bastle House 184
Black Mountain 83
Black Mountains 83, 84
Black Wood of Rannoch 230
Blackburn 150
Blackgang Chine 42
Blackness 203
Blackpool 148
Blackwaterfoot 194
Bladon 88
Blaenau Ffestiniog 126, *126*
Blaenavon 84
Blair Atholl 230
Blair Castle *230*
Blair Drummond Safari &
   Leisure Park 216
Blairgowrie 232
Blakeney Point *118*
Blanchland 184-5
Blantyre 199
Blarney Castle 278
Blessington 281
Blickling 122
Blickling 122
Blist Hill Open Air Museum 108
Blue Anchor Bay 30
Bluebell Line 49
Bluestone Heath Road 145
Bodiam Castle 52
Bodmin 20
Bodrhyddran Hall 126
Bodstone Barton Working Farm
   and Country Park 29
Bognor Regis 46
Bohunt Manor 44
Boldrewood 38
Bolingbroke 142, *142*
Bolsover 138
Bolton 132
Bolton Abbey 154
Bonar Bridge 254
Bonawe Ironworks 215
Bo'ness 220
Boreraig 238
Borestone Brae 216
Borrodale Beach 226
Boscastle 22, *23*
Boston 116
Boulby 174
Bournemouth 38
Bourton-on-the-Water 88, *88*
Bovey Tracey 26
Bovington Camp 36
Bowes Museum 168
Bowhill 206
Bowmore 191
Box Hill 47
Bradford 154
Bradford-on-Avon 67
Bradford-on-Tone 35
Brading 42
Bradley Manor 26
Braemar 232-3
Bramhall Hall 132
Brambles 54
Brancaster Staithe 118
Brand's Hatch 74
Bransdale 175
Brasted 49
Bratton Down 67
Braunton 29
Breachacha Castle 210
Breamish Valley 186
Brechin 236
Brecon 80

Brecon Beacons National
   Park 80, *80, 82, 82*-3
Brecon Mountain Railway 80
Brecqhou 271
Brenig 126
Brent Knoll 64
Bretforton 86
Breydon Water 121, *121*
Bridge of Dulsie 244
Bridgend 62
Bridgnorth 108
Bridlington 159
Bridport 35
Brighton 47, *47*
Brimham Rocks 154, *155*
Brinkburn Priory 189
Bristol 64
Brixham 26
Brixworth 93
Broadford 226
Broadland Conservation Centre 122
Broadlands 39
Broadstairs 54
Broadway 86
Brock Hole 162
Brodick 195
Brodie Castle 245
Bromsgrove 110-11
Broomfield 35
Brough 167
Brough of Birsay 264
Broughton 202
Brown Clee 104
Browsholme Hall 150
Bruce's Stone 178, *179*
Bruisyard Winery and Vineyard 98-9
Brympton d'Evercy 35
Buckfast Butterfly Farm 26
Buckfastleigh 26
Buckie 246
Buckingham Palace 73
Buckland Abbey 23
Buckland Beacon 26
Buckland in the Moor 26
Buckler's Hard 38
Bude 29
Budleigh Salterton 35
Builth Wells 80
Buloit 243
Bundoran 274
Bungay 99
Bunratty Castle 278-9
Bunyan Museum 92
Burford 88
Burgh le Marsh 142
Burghead Well 245
Burghley 114
Burhou 271
Burnby 156
Burnham Beaches 90
Burnham-on-Sea 64
Burnley 150
Burrator 25
Burrell Collection 200, 201
Burren Display Centre 279
Burrington Combe 64
Burton Agnes 159
Burton Constable Hall 159
Burton Court 84
Burton upon Trent 112
Burwash 52
Burwell 94
Bury 150-1
Bury St Edmunds 97
Butser Ancient Farm 45
Butterfly Garden 117
Buttermere 160
Buxton *134*, 135
Bwich Nant-Yr-Arian Forest
   Visitor Centre 102
Bwlchgwyn 130

C

Caban Coch 102
Cader Idris 102, *128*, 129
Caenlochan Nature Reserve 233
Caer Caradoc 108
Caerlaverock Castle 181
Caerlaverock National Nature
   Reserve 181
Caerleon 64
Caernarfon *124*, 125
Caerphilly 65
Cairn Holy Chambered Cairns 178
Cairndow 214
Cairngorms 233, 234-5
Cairnryan 177

Caister	122
Calbost	238
Calceby	145
Caldey Island	57
Caldicot	65
Callander	216
Callanish Standing Stones	263
Calshot	38
Cambo Country Park	222
Cambridge	94, 94
Campbeltown	195
Canna	224
Cannich	243
Cannock Chase	111
Canterbury	54-5, 55
Cape Wrath	256
Captain Cook Museum	170
Cardiff	65
Cardigan	60
Carding Mill Valley 105	105
Cardoness Castle	178
Carew	56
Carisbrooke	42
Carlisle	182-3
Carlton	156
Carlton Colville	99
Carmarthen	61
Carnasserie	212
Carnforth	148, 149
Carperby	168
Carradale	195
Carrbridge	244, 245
Carreg Cennen	81, 83
Carsaig Bay	193
Carscreugh	177
Carsluith Castle	178
Cartmel Priory Gatehouse	162
Castel	268
Castel Coch	63, 63
Castle Bolton	168
Castle Campbell	220-1
Castle Douglas	180
Castle Drogo	24
Castle Fraser	248
Castle Girnigoe and Sinclair	260, 260
Castle Hedingham	76, 96
Castle Howard	156
Castle Kennedy	177
Castle Matrix	279
Castle of Mey	260
Castle Rising	119
Castle Roul	276-7
Castle Rushen	146
Castlebay	262, 262
Castleton	134
Castletown	146
Castletown House	281
Castlewellan	277
Causewayhead	217
Cavendish	96
Cawdor Castle	244
Centre for Alternative Technology	102
Ceres	222
Cerne Abbas	36
Cerrigydrudion	126
Chalfon St Giles	70
Chambercombe Manor	29
Channel Islands	270-1
Chapel Finian	177
Chapel le Dale	166
Charlestown	20
Charlwood	47
Chartwell	48
Chatelherault Country Park	198
Chatham	52
Chatsworth	138
Chatterley Whitfield Mining Museum	132
Chavenage	67
Chawton	45
Cheddar Gorge	64
Chelmsford	76
Cheltenham	86
Chepstow	65
Chessington	70
Chessington World of Adventures	70, 74
Chester	130-1
Chester Zoo	131
Chesterfield	138
Chesterholm	184
Chester's Fort and Museum	184
Chicheley Hall	92-3
Chichester	44-5
Chichester Harbour	45
Child Beale	69
Chillingham	208
Chiltern Hills	90-1
Chiltern Open Air Museum	70
Chingford	75
Chippenham	67
Chipping Norton	88
Chirk	106
Chiswellgreen	71
Chittlehampton	29
Chollerford	184
Chop Gate	170
Chorley	149
Christchurch	38
Christchurch Mansion	79
Chwarel Wynne Mine	106
Cider Farm	35
Cilgerran	61
Cirencester	67
Cissbury Ring	50
Clacton-on-Sea	78
Claddagh	275
Clandon Park	47
Clapton Court	35
Clare	96, 96
Clatteringshaws Loch	179
Clava Cairns	245
Claverton Manor	67
Clearwell	84
Cleethorpes	159
Cleeve Abbey	30
Cleeve Hill	86
Cleobury Mortimer	108
Click Mill	264, 264
Clickhimin Broch	266
Clifden	274, 275
Clitheroe	151, 151
Cliveden	71
Clouds Hill	36
Clumber Park	138
Clun	106
Clunie	232
Clynnog-fawr	124
Cnoc Moy	195
Coalbrookdale Museum and Furnace Site	108
Coatbridge	199
Cobbaton Combat Collection	29
Cobham	74-5
Cockermouth	160
Cockley Cley	119
Coed Dinorwic	129
Coedydd Maentwrog	129
Coetan Arthur	58
Coggeshall	76-7, 77
Coigach	241
Coity	63
Colbost	238-9
Colchester	78, 78-9
Colchester Zoo	79
Coldharbour Mill	35, 35
Coleford	84
Coll	210
Colonsay	190-1
Colwyn Bay	126
Combe Martin	29
Combe Martin Motorcycle Collection	29
Combe Martin Wildlife Park and Monkey Sanctuary	29
Combe Sydenham Hall	30
Combestone Tor	25
Comrie	217
Conderton	86
Cong	274-5
Coningsby	143, 143
Conisbrough	138
Conishead Priory	160
Coniston	160
Coniston Water	160, 160
Constitution Hill	101
Conwy	126-7
Coombe Hill	91
Corbiere Point	272
Corby Castle	183
Corgarff Castle	246
Cork	279, 279
Cornbury House	88
Corrie	195
Corrieshalloch Gorge	251
Corrigall Farm Museum	264
Corris	103
Corve Dale	108
Cotehele	23
Cotswold Wildlife Park	88
Cotswolds Motor Museum	88
Countisbury	30
Coventry	112, 113
Cowes	42
Cowper and Newton Museum	93
Coxwold	170
Cragside	185
Craig Dhu	231
Craig-Goch	102
Craig-y-Ciliau	83
Craigellachie	246
Craigievar Castle	237, 246-7
Craigleuch	183
Craignethan Castle	199
Cranbrook	52
Cranmere Pool	24
Crarae Glen	192, 193
Craster	209
Crathes Castle	236
Creetown	179
Cregneish	146
Cremyll	23
Creswell	138
Crewe	132
Crianlarich	214
Criccieth	124
Crich	139
Crinan Canal	192
Croagh Patrick	275
Croft Castle	84-5
Cromarty	245
Cromer	123, 123
Cromford Mill	139
Crosskirk	261
Crossraguel Abbey	196
Croyde	29
Cruden Bay	248, 249
Cruggleton	178-9
Crynant	80
Cuckmere Haven	51
Cuillin Hills	225, 225
Culloden	244-5
Culross	221
Culver Hole	61
Culzean Castle	196
Cumbernauld	199
Cupar	222
Cwmcoy	61
Cwmystwyth	102
Cyfarthfa Castle	63
Cynonville	63
D	
D-Day Museum	45
Dalbeattie	180
Dalemain House	162
Dan-yr-Ogof Caves	80, 83, 83
Danebury	68
Dare Valley Country Park	62
Daresbury	133
Dark Peak	136, 137
Darlington	168, 169
Dartington Crystal Works	29
Dartmoor	24-5
Dartmouth	26
David Marshall Lodge	218, 219
Daviot	244
Dawyck Botanic Garden	202
Deal	55
Dedham	79
Deene Park	114
Deer Abbey	249
Delapre Abbey	93
Denbigh	127
Dent	166
Derby	139
Derbyhaven	146-7
Dervaig	213
Derwent Water	165
Devil's Bridge	102
Devil's Chair	105
Devil's Dyke	51
Devizes	67
Dickens House Museum	54
Didcot	69
Din Lligwy	125
Dinas	56
Dinas Bran	107
Dingwall	242
Dinmore Manor	85
Dinorwic	128
Dinting Railway	135
Dirleton Castle	222
Dobwalls	23
Docklands Light Railway	73
Docton Mill	29
Doddington	140
Dogdyke pumping station	143
Dolaucothi Gold Mines	61
Dolgellau	102
Dollar Glen	220-1
Dolwyddelan	126
Doncaster	156
Donegal	275
Donington Park	113
Donnington Castle	69
Dorchester	36, 36
Dorking	47
Dornoch	254
Douglas	146
Doune Castle	216
Dove Cottage	162
Dover	55
Downhill House	277
Drefach Velindre	61
Drum Castle	237
Drumcliff	275
Drumcoltran Tower	181
Drumlanrig Castle	180
Drumnadrochit	242
Drusilla's Zoo	48
Dryburgh Abbey	206
Duart Castle	213
Dublin	280, 281
Dudley	111
Dudmaston Hall	108
Duff House	249, 249
Dufftown	246, 246
Duffus Castle	247
Dumfries	181
Dun Carloway Broch	263
Dun Laoghaire	281
Dun Nosebridge	191
Dunadd Fort	192-3
Dunbeath	261
Dunblane	217
Duncansby Head	260
Dundee	222
Dundrennan Abbey	179, 179
Dunganstown	281
Dungloe	275
Dunkeld	232
Dunkery Beacon	30, 32
Dunkery Hill	30
Dunnet Head	260
Dunrobin Castle	255, 255
Duns	207
Dunsford	26
Dunstable	93
Dunstable Downs	91
Dunstaffnage Castle	213
Dunstanburgh Castle	209
Dunster	30
Dunure	196
Dunvegan Castle	239
Dunwich	99
Durham	170, 171
Duxford Airfield	94
Dyffryn Ardudwy	101
Dymchurch	55
Dyson Perrins Museum	87
E	
Eaglesham Village	199
Earls Barton	93
Earl's Hill	105
Earlsferry	222
Earshall Castle	222
Earsham	99
Eas Coul Aulin Waterfall	256-7
Easby Abbey	168
Easdale	213
East Barsham	118
East Budleigh	35
East Clandon	47
East Grinstead	49
East Kirkby	143
East Midlands Airport	113
East Neuk	222
East Wheal Rose Halt	21
Eastbourne	48-9
Eastwood	139
Ebberston Hall	172
Ecclefechan	183
Edinburgh	204-5
Edinburgh Castle	205
Edzell	236
Eigg	224
Eilean Donan Castle	226-7, 227
Eilean Hoan	257
Eilean nan Ron	259
Elan Valley Reservoirs	102
Eleanor Cross	115
Elgin	247
Elie	222
Elizabeth Castle	272
Ellesmere Port	131
Ellisland Farm	180
Elmstead Market	79
Ely	117, 117
Emmett's Garden	49
Emo Court	281

Enniskellan 277
Enniskerry 281
Enniskillen 277
Epping Forest 75
Epworth 140
Erddig 131
Eriskay 263
Etal 208
Evesham 86
Ewenny Priory 63
Ewloe 131
Exeter 26, 26
Exmoor 32-3, 32-3
Exmouth 27
Eyam 134
Eyam Moor 134
Eynsford 75

F

Fairbourne 102, 103
Fakenham 118
Falkland 222-3
Falls of Clyde 199
Falls of Glomach 227
Falls of Measach 251
Falmouth 18
Fanagmore 257
Fareham 45
Farndale 175
Farne Islands 208
Farnham 71
Farr 258
Farway 35
Fasque House 236
Faversham 55
Felin Geri Mill 61
Felixstowe 79
Fetlar Island 266-7
Fettercairn 236
Ffestiniog 126
Ffestiniog narrow-gauge railway 125
Ffestiniog Pumped Storage Scheme 126
Fforest Fawr 80
Ffynnon Arian 124
Filey 173
Finchcocks 52
Finchingfield 96
Fingal's Cave 211
Finkley Down Farm and Country
  Park 69
Finlaystone Country Estate 215
Fintry 216
Fishbourne 45
Fishguard 56
Flambards Theme Park 42
Flamborough Head 159
Flamingo Park 42
Flatford Mill 79
Fleam Dyke 94
Fleet Air Arm Museum 35
Fleetwood 149
Flint 131
Flixton 99
Flodigarry 238
Floors Castle 206
Florence Court 277
Fochabers Village 247
Foel Cwm-Cerwyn 56
Foel Eryr 56
Foindle 257
Folkestone 55
Folly Farm 88
Ford 208
Fordingbridge 38
Forest 269
Forest of Dean 84
Forest Row 49
Forge Mill Museum 87
Forres 245
Fort George 245
Fort Grey Maritime Museum 268-9
Fort Victoria Country Park 43
Fort William 228
Forth Valley 220
Fortingall 230
Fota Wildlife Park 279
Fovant Down 37
Fowey 18
Foxfield 135
Foyers 242-3
Freshwater 42
Fulking 51
Fursdon House 31
Fyne Court 35
Fyvie Castle 249

G

Gainsborough 140
Gairloch 241
Galashiels 206
Galloway Deer Museum 179
Galway 275
Gaping Gill 166
Garlieston 179
Garreg-Ddu 102
Gartmorn Dam Country Park 221
Garwnant 81
Gatehouse of Fleet 179
Gatwick 47
Gatwick Zoo 47
Gawthorpe Hall 151
Geddington 115
Gem Rock Museum 179
George Stephenson's Birthplace 189
German Occupation Museum 269
Giant's Causeway 277, 277
Gibraltar Point 143
Gibside Chapel 189
Glamis 232
Glasdrum 228
Glasgow 200-1, 218
Glastonbury 64
Glen Affric 243
Glen Bruar 230
Glen Clova 233
Glen Errochty 230
Glen Falloch 214
Glen Isla 232
Glen Morriston 243
Glen Nant 215
Glen Nevis 229
Glen Roy 229
Glen Shiel 227
Glenbuchat Castle 246
Glencoe 228-9, 229
Glencolumbkille 275
Glendurgan 18
Glenelg Brochs 227
Glenfinnan 227
Glengarriff 279
Glengoulandie Deer Park 230-1
Glenkindie 246
Glenluce Abbey 177
Glenmore Forest Park 234-5, 245
Glenshee Ski Area 238
Gloddfa Ganol Slate Mine 126
Gloucester 86
Gloucestershire and
  Warwickshire Steam Railway 86
Glyn Ceiriog 106
Glyn-Neath 80
Goat Fell 195, 195
Godington Park 55
Godmanchester 95
Godshill 42
Golden Hill Fort and Craft Centre 43
Golspie 255
Goodrich 84
Goodwick 56
Goodwood 45
Gorey 272
Gosport 45
Goudhurst 52
Gower Peninsula 60, 61
Grange-over-Sands 162
Grantchester 94
Grantham 115
Grasmere 162
Great Ayton 170
Great Central Railway 113
Great Chesterford 94
Great Dixter 52
Great Driffield 159
Great Malvern 86-7
Great Steeping 143
Great Torrington 29
Great Western Railway Museum 69
Great Yarmouth 123, 123
Greenbank Garden 199
Greenhow Hill 154
Greensted-juxta-Ongar 77
Gressenhall 119
Gretna Green 183
Grey Mare's Tail 183, 183
Greystones 281
Gribun Pass 213
Grimes Graves 97
Grim's Ditch 91
Grimsby 159
Grimspound 25
Grimsthorpe 115
Grinton 168
Grosmont 176
Grosmont Castle 84

Gruinard Island 241
Guernsey 268
Guildford 47
Gunby Hall 143
Gustav Holst Museum 86
Gweek 19
Gwili Railway 61
Gwydir Castle 126

H

Haddo House 249
Haddon Hall 134
Hadleigh (Essex) 77
Hadleigh (Suffolk) 79
Hadrian's Wall 184, 184
Haggs Castle 201
Hagley 111
Hailes Abbey 86
Hailes Castle 207
Halifax 154
Hall Green 110
Haltwhistle 184
Halvergate Marsh 121
Ham House 75
Hampton Court Palace 75
Hanch Hall 111
Handa Island 257
Handcross 47
Hardraw Force 166
Hardy's Cottage 36
Hare Hill 135
Harewood House 154, 154
Harlow 75
Harlow Car 154
Harrington Hall 145
Harris 263
Harrogate 154
Hartland 29
Hartlepool 171
Harwarden 131
Harwich 79
Haseley Manor 42
Hastings 53
Hatchlands 47
Hatfield 75
Hatfield Forest 77
Hathersage 134
Haughton 141
Hauteville House 269
Havant 45
Haverfordwest 56-7
Hawes 166
Hawick 183, 206
Hawkshead 162
Haworth 154-5
Hay-on-Wye 85
Hayes Hill Farm 75
Hayling Island 45
Haytor Rocks 24
Haytor Vale 26
Heacham 118
Heathfield 52
Hebden Bridge 151
Heckington 141
Heights of Abraham 139
Hele Mill 29
Helensburgh 214
Helm Crag 162
Helmingham Hall 99
Helmsdale 255
Helmshore 151
Helmsley 170
Helston 19
Hempstead 96
Hemswell 141
Hen-Gwrt 84
Henley-on-Thames 71
Hereford 85
Hergest Croft 85
Heritage Museum 241
Herm 271
Hermitage Castle 183
Herne Bay 55
Hertford 75
Hertford Castle 74
Hestercombe Gardens 35
Hexham 185
Heysham 149
Hickling Broad 120, 121
High Tor 139
Highclere 69
Higher Bockhampton 36
Highland Wildlife Park 231
Hightae's Castle and Hightae
  Lochs 183
Hill House 215
Hill of Tarvit Mansionhouse 222

Hill Top 163
Hillier Gardens and Arboretum 38
Hilton of Cadboll 255
Hitchin 94-5
HMS Unicorn 223
HMS Victory 45, 45
HMS Warrior 45
Holbeach 117
Hole of Horcum 172, 174
Holker 163
Holkham Hall 118
Hollycombe Steam Collection 44
Holy Island 208-9
Holyhead 125
Holyroodhouse 205
Honiton 35
Hopetoun 203
Hopetoun House 221
Horncastle 143
Horner's Wood 33
Hornsea 159
Horsey Mere 120, 121
Horsham 47
Houghton St Giles 118
House of Dun 237
Houses of Parliament 73
Housesteads Roman Fort 184
Howden 157
Howden Moors 135
Howth 281
Huddersfield 155
Hugh Miller's Cottage 245
Hull 159
Hunstanton 118
Hunterian Art Gallery 201
Huntingdon 95
Huntly Castle 247
Hynish 211

I

Iar-Chonnacht 275
Ickworth 96
Ightham 49
Ilfracombe 29, 29
Ilkeston 139
Ilkley 154
Immingham 159
Inch Kenneth 213
Inchmahome Priory 216
Inchnadamph 250, 251
Ingleton 166
Insh Marshes 231
Inveraray 214
Inverbervie 236
Inverewe Gardens 241, 241
Inverfarigaig 242
Inverlochy Castle 229
Invernaver 258-9
Inverness 245, 245
Inverpolly Nature Reserve 250
Iona 210-11
Ipswich 79
Iron Age Farm 45
Ironbridge 108
Island of Raasay 239
Islay 191
Isle of Arran 194
Isle of Bute 193
Isle of Gigha 194
Isle of Man 146
Isle of Whithorn 179, 179
Isle of Wight 42-3
Isle of Wight Steam Railway 42
Italian Chapel 264

J

Jackfield Tile Museum 108
James Joyce Tower 281
Jane Austen's House 45
Jarlshof 266, 267
Jedburgh 206
Jersey Zoological Park 272
John F Kennedy Park 281
John Knox's House 205
John O'Groats 260
Joseph Parry's Cottage 63

K

Kailzie Gardens 202
Katrine 216
Kedleston Hall 139
Keiss 260
Kelburn Country Centre 197

Keld 166
Kellie Castle 223
Kelso 206, 206
Kendal 163, 163
Kenilworth 113
Kenmore 231
Kennet and Avon Canal 67
Kensington Palace 73
Kent's Cavern 27
Kentwell Hall 96
Kenwood 75
Kessingland 99
Keswick 160-1
Kettering 93
Kew 75
Kidwelly 61
Kidwelly Industrial Museum 61, 61
Kilbarchen 197
Kilburn 170
Kildalton Cross 191, 191
Kildare 281
Kildrummy Castle 246
Kilfenora 279
Kilkenny 281
Killala 275
Killarney 279
Killhope Wheel 167
Killiecrankie 230
Killybegs 275
Kilmarnock 197
Kilmorack 243
Kilmory Castle 193
Kilmory Knap Chapel 193
Kilmuir 238
Kilmun 215
Kiloran 191
Kinder Scout 136
Kingley Vale 50-1
King's Lynn 119
Kings Norton 111
Kingsbridge 27
Kingston Lacy 36
Kingston upon Hull 159
Kingussie 231
Kinloch Castle 225
Kinloch Rannoch 230
Kinlochbervie 257, 257
Kinneil House 221
Kinsale 279
Kippford 180
Kirbuster 264
Kirby Hall 115
Kirby Misperton 172
Kirkbean 180
Kirkby Lonsdale 166, 166
Kirkby Stephen 166
Kirkcudbright 179
Kirkmichael 146
Kirkoswald 196
Kirkstall Abbey 155
Kirkstone Pass 162
Kirkwall 264-5
Kirriemuir 232
Kirtomy 259
Kisimul Castle 262
Knappogue Castle 279
Knaresborough 154
Knebworth House 95
Knightshayes Court 31
Knock 275
Knockan Cliff 251
Knole 49
Knowsley 131
Knoydart 227

L

La Hougue Bie 272
La Mare Vineyards 272
Lacock 67
Laidhay Croft Museum 261
Lairg 255
Lake District 164-5
Lake District National Park 160, 162
Lake of Menteith 216
Lamb House 53
Lamberhurst 52
Lamlash 195
Lamorna Cove 18
Lampeter 61
Lancaster 149, 149
Lanchester 189
L'Ancresse Bay 268, 269
Land's End 18
Lanercost Priory 182, 183
Langstone Harbour 45
Lanhydrock 20
Lanreath 20

Largs 197
Laugharne 61
Launceston 23
Launceston Castle 22
Lavenham 96
Laxey 147
Layer Marney 77
Le Friquet Butterfly Farm 269
Leamington Spa 88-9
Leeds 155
Leeds Castle 53
Legbourne 143
Legh Manor 47
Leicester 113
Leighton Buzzard 93
Leighton Hall 163
Leiston 99
Leisure Lakes 149
Leith Hall 247
Leith Hill Tower 47
Leominster 85
Leonardslee Gardens 47
Lerwick 266, 267
Les Etacs 270
Letchworth 95
Leverburgh 263
Levisham Moor 174
Lewes 49
Lewis 263
Leyburn 168
Lichfield 111
Lihou Island 269
Lincoln 141, 141
Lincolnshire Wolds 144-5
Lindisfarne 209
Lingholm 161
Linlithgow 203
Linn of Dee 233
Linslade 93
Linton 94
Lismore 281
Lissadell House 275
Little Loch Broom 241
Little Moreton Hall 133, 133
Littledean Hall 87
Liverpool 131, 131
Livingstone Centre 199
Llanbadarn Fawr 102-3
Llanberis 125
Llandovery 81
Llandrindod Wells 81
Llanfair PG 125
Llangollen 107, 107
Llangurig 102
Llanidloes 103
Llanrwst 126
Llanstephan 61
Llanthony Priory 83
Llantilio-Crossenny 84
Llanwyddyn 107
Llanystumdwy 124
Llechwedd Slate Caverns 126
Lleyn Peninsula 124
Lloyd George Memorial Museum 124
Lloyds building 73
Llyn Celyn 126
Llyn Gwynant 129
Llyn Tegid 126
Llynnau Cregennen 129
Llywernog Silver Lead Mine 102
Loch Arkaig 229
Loch Druidibeg Nature Reserve 263
Loch Eriboll 257
Loch Fleet 255
Loch Garten 245
Loch Gruinart Nature Reserve 191
Loch Hourn 227
Loch Insh 231
Loch Laxford 257
Loch Leven 221
Loch Leven Castle 221
Loch Linnhe 229
Loch Lintrathen 232
Loch Lomond 214
Loch of the Lowes 232
Loch Morlich 245
Loch Ness 243
Loch Ness Monster Exhibition 242
Loch Nevis 227
Loch Sunart Woodlands 213
Lochalsh House and Garden 227
Lochindorb 244
Lochinver 250
Lochnell 181
Lochranza 195
Lode 94
Loder Valley Nature Reserve 47
Lodmoor Country Park 37
Logan Gardens 177

London 72-3
London Bridge 72
London Colney 75
London Dungeon 73
London museums and art galleries 73
London Planetarium 73
London Zoo 73
Long Man of Wilmington 49
Long Melford 96
Long Mynd 105, 105
Long Sutton 117
Longleat 67
Longshaw 139
Looe 20, 21
Loseley House 47
Lough Erne 277
Lough Gur 279
Lough Neagh 277
Lough Neath 276
Loughborough 113
Louth 143
Lower Basildon 69
Lower Beeding 47
Lower Diabaig 241
Lowestoft 99, 99
Luccombe 30
Ludlow 109
Luib 225
Lullingstone 75
Lulworth Cove 36
Lumsden 246
Luss 214
Luton 93
Luton Hoo 93
Lyddington 114
Lydford 23
Lyme Regis 35
Lymington 38
Lyndhurst 38, 38, 40
Lynmouth 30, 33
Lynton 30
Lytham St Anne's 149
Lyveden New Bield 115

M

Mabie Forest 181
Mablethorpe 143
McCaig's Folly 213
Macclesfield 135
Macduff 249
Machrihanish Bay 195
Machynlleth 102
MacLean's Cross 211
Macquarie Mausoleum 213
Madame Tussaud's 73
Madame Tussaud's Royalty and Empire Exhibition 71
Maes Artro Tourist Village 101
Maes Howe 265
Maiden Castle 36
Maidenhead 71
Maidens 196
Maidstone 53
Malahide Castle 281
Maldon 77
Malham Tarn 151, 153
Mallaig 227
Mallyan Spout 172
Malmesbury 67
Malton 156
Manchester 133
Manderston House 209
Manor House Wildlife and Leisure Park 57
Mapperton Gardens 35
March 117
Margam 63
Margate 55
Mark of Mote 180
Markby 143
Market Harborough 115, 115
Marsden Bay 189
Marsden Rocks 189, 189
Martin Mere 149
Marton 171
Marwell 45
Marwick Head 265
Marwood Hill 29
Mary Rose 45
Matlock 139
Mauchline 199
Mawthorpe Museum 143
Maxwelton House 180
Mayflower Stone 23
Meare 64

Meigle 232
Melbourne 113
Melford Hall 96
Mellerstain 206
Melrose 206
Melton Mowbray 115
Melvich Bay 259
Menai Bridge 125
Mendip Hills 64
Merthyr Mawr 63
Merthyr Tydfil 63
Mevagissey 19
Mid-Hants Railway Watercress Line 45
Middlesborough 171
Middleton 139
Midland Railway Centre 139
Milford Haven 58
Millers Dale 134
Millom 161
Milton Keynes 93
Minack Open Air Theatre 18
Minehead 31
Mingary Castle 213
Minster Lovell Hall 88
Mirehouse 161
Mistley 79
Moniack Castle 243
Moniaive 180
Monk Bretton 155
Monkey Sanctuary 21
Monksilver 30
Monmouth 84
Monmouthshire and Brecon Canal 83, 83
Mont Orgueil Castle 272
Montacute 35
Montgomery 107
Montrose 236
Monymusk 249
Morecambe 149
Moreton-in-Marsh 88
Moretonhampstead 26
Morfa Nefyn 124
Morpeth Chantry Bagpipe Museum 189
Morton Manor 42
Morwellham Quay 23
Mosquito Aircraft Museum 75
Moss Farm Road Stone Circle 195
Mottisfont 38-9
Mount Edgcumbe Country Park 23
Mount Grace Priory 170
Mount Stewart House 277
Mourne Mountains 277
Mousa Broch 267
Mousehole 18
Moy 277
Moyses Hall Museum 97
Much Wenlock 108, 108
Muck 224-5
Mull 212
Mull of Galloway 177, 177
Mull and West Highland Railway 213
Mumbles 61
Muncaster Castle 161
Muncaster Mill 161
Mundesley 123
Muness Castle 267
Munslow Aston 108
Murlough Nature Reserve 277
Murton 156
Museum of the Welsh Woollen Industry 61
Mussenden Temple 277
Mynach Falls 102

N

Nantwich 133
National Gallery of Scotland 205
National Library of Wales 101
National Mining Museum 141
National Motor Museum 38
National Motorcycle Museum 111
National Museum of Wales 65
National Park Centre 151
National Stud 94
Neath 63
Needles 43
Nefyn 124
Nene Valley Railway 115
Neptune's Staircase 229
Ness Gardens 131
Ness Point 99
Nether Hall 96
New Abbey 180
New Alresford 45

INDEX

New Forest 40-1, *40-1*
New Lanark 199, *199*
New Milton 38
New Place 89
New Quay 101
New Romney 55
Newark-on-Trent 141
Newbridge House 281
Newbury 69
Newcastle Emlyn 61
Newcastle-upon-Tyne 189, *189*
Newcastleton 183
Newgale 56
Newlyn 18
Newlyn East 21
Newmarket 94
Newport (Isle of Wight) 42-3
Newport (Monmouthshire) 65
Newport (Pembrokeshire) 56
Newquay 19
Newstead Abbey 139
Newton Stewart 177
Newtondale 175
Newtonmore 231
Newtown 107
Nidderdale 154
Norfolk Broads 120-1
Norfolk Rural Life Museum 119
Norfolk Shire Horse Centre 123
Norham Castle 209
Norman Manor House 159
Normanby 157
Norris Castle 42
North Antrim Coast Road 277
North Devon Maritime Museum 28
North Elmham 119
North Hykeham 141
North Uist 263, *263*
North West Highlands 252-3
North York Moors National
  Park 172, 174
North Yorkshire Moors 174-5
Northallerton 170
Northam 52
Northampton 93
Northern Ireland 276
Northey Island 77
Northumberland National Park 186-7
Norton 156
Norton Priory 133
Norwich 123
Noss Nature Reserve 267
Nottingham 139
Nuneaton 113
Nunwell House 43, *43*
Nymans Garden 47

O

Oakham 115
Oare 30
Oban 212, *213*
Ogmore Castle 63
Ogof Ffynon Ddu 83
Okehampton 23
Old Beaupre Castle 63
Old Dailly 177
Old Deer 249
Old Knebworth 95
Old Man of Hoy 265
Old Man of Stoer 257
Old Man of Storr 238
Old Sarum 39
Old Warden 95
Olney 93
Onchan Head 147
Orchardtown Tower 181
Orford 99
Orkney Islands 264
Ormesby St Michael 123
Oronsay 190, *191*
Oronsay Priory 191
Osborne House 43
Osmington 36
Ospringe 55
Oswestry 107
Otley 154
Otter Trust 99
Otterton Mill 35
Oulton Broad 99
Oundle 115
Out Stack 267
Over Owler Tor *137*
Overbecks 27
Owl House 52
Owletts 74-5
Oxford 88

P

Padstow 21
Paignton 27
Paignton and Dartmouth Railway 27
Palnackie 181
Paperweight Centre 23
Parham Park 47
Parke Rare Breeds Farm 26
Parnham 35
Parton 180
Pass of Leny 216
Passmore House 75
Pateley Bridge 154
Paycocke's House 77, *77*
Peak Cavern 134
Peak District 134, 136-7
Peak District National Park 136
Peckover House 117
Peebles 202, *203*
Peel 147
Pembroke Castle 57
Pembroke Dock 57
Pembrokeshire 58-9, *58-9*
Pen Dinas 101
Pen-y-Fan 80
Pen-y-Garreg reservoir 102, *102*
Pencarrow 21
Penmorfa 124
Penrhyn Castle 127
Penrith 162
Penshurst 49
Pentre Ifan 56, 58
Penzance 18
Perelle Bay 269
Pershore 87
Perth 221
Peterborough *116*, 117
Peterhead 249
Petworth 47
Pevensey 49
Peveril Castle 134
Phantassie Doocot 207
Pickering 172
Picton Castle 57
Pierowall 265
Pitcairngreen 221
Pitlochry 230
Pitmedden Garden 249
Pittenweem 222
Plas Newydd 107
Plas-Yn-Rhiw 124
Plockton 227
Pluscarden 245
Plym Valley Railway Steam Centre 23
Plymouth 23
Pocklington 157
Polesden Lacey 47
Pollok House 201
Polperro 21
Pontypridd 63
Pool 19
Poole 36
Porlock 30
Porlock Weir 30
Port Erin 147
Port Eynon Point 61
Port Laoise 281
Port Talbot 63
Porth Neigwl 124
Porthmadog 125
Portland 36-7
Portmahomack 255
Portmeirion 127
Portree 238, *238*
Portskerra 259
Portsmouth 45
Post Mill 99
Postbridge 26
Powderham 27
Powerscourt Gardens 281
Powfoot 183
Powis Castle 107
Prescelly Hills 56, 59
Preston (Dorset) 36
Preston (Lancashire) 149
Preston Mill 207
Probus 21
Puddletown 36
Pumsaint 61
Pwllheli 124

Q

Quarry Caves 34
Quebec House 49
Queen Elizabeth Country Park 45
Queen Elizabeth Forest Park 218, 219
Queen Elizabeth Hunting Lodge 75, *75*
Queen's View 230
Quetivel Watermill 272
Quince Honey Farm 31
Quiraing 238

R

Raby 168
Railway Museum 103
Ramsey (Huntingdon and
  Peterborough) 117
Ramsey (Isle of Man) 146
Ramsey Island *56*
Ramsgate 55
Rannoch Moor 229
Ravenglass & Eskdale Railway 161
Raynham Hall 118
Reading 71
Reay 259
Reculver 55
Red Hill 145
Redcar 171
Redditch 87
Reeth 168
Regimental Badges 37
Reigate 47
Restenneth Priory 237
Restormel Castle 21
Retford 141
Revolution House 139
Rhaeadr Cynfal 126
Rhayader 102
Rheidol Railway 102
Rhinns of Islay Lighthouse 191
Rhodes Memorial Museum and
  Commonwealth Centre 76
Rhoose 63
Rhuddlan 127
Rhum 225
Ribblesdale 153
Riber Castle 139
Richmond 152, 169
Ridgeway Path 91
Rievaulx Abbey 170
Ringwood 38
Ripley 154
Ripon 154
Riverstown House 279
Robertsbridge 52
Robin Hill Country Park 43
Robin Hood's Bay 172
Roch Castle 56
Rochdale 151
Rochester 53
Rock of Cashel 281
Rockcliffe 180
Rockend 249
Rockingham 115
Rodel 263
Rolvenden 52
Romney, Hythe and Dymchurch
  Railway 55
Romsey 39
Ropley 45
Rose Green 79
Rosedale 175
Rosemoor 29
Ross-on-Wye 84, *85*
Rothesay 193
Rothiemurchus 234
Rougemont Castle 26
Rough Island 180
Round Tor 24
Rowallane Garden 277
Royal Mews 73
Royal National Rose Society 71
Royal Pavilion 47
Rozel 273
RRS *Discovery* 223
Ruddington 113
Rufford Old Hall 149
Rushen 147
Rushton 115
Russborough House 281
Ruthwell Cross 183
Ruthwell Museum 183
Rutland Railway 115
Rutland Water 115
Ryde 43
Rye *52*, 53

S

Saffron Walden 94
Sailing Barge Museum 53
St Albans 71
St Andrew 269
St Andrews 222, *223*
St Anne's 270-1
St Aubin 272
St Bride's Church 199
St Clement 272
St Clements Church 263
St Cyrus 236
St David's 56, 58
St David's peninsula 56, 58
St Fagans 63, 65
St Florence 57
St Govan's Chapel 59
St Helier 272, *273*
St Hilary 63
St Ives (Cambridgeshire) 95
St Ives (Cornwall) 18, *18*
St John's 146
St John's Town of Dalry 180
St Just 18
St Lawrence 43
St Martin's Point 269
St Mary 272
St Mary's Chapel 261
St Mawes 21
St Michael's Mount 18
St Monans 222
St Nicholas' 63
St Ninian's Cave 177
St Ninian's Isle 267
St Ouen's Bay 270, 272-3
St Paul's Cathedral 73
St Peter Port 269, *269*
St Winifred's Well 131
Saintfield 277
Salford 133
Salisbury 39
Salmestone Grange 55
Saltersgate Inn 172
Saltram House 23
Samlesbury Hall 151
Sandown 43
Sandringham 118
Sands of Forvie Nature Reserve 249
Sandwich 55
Sandwood Bay 257
Sandycove 281
Sandyhills 180
Sango Bay 257
Sarehole Mill 110
Sark 271
Savernake Forest 69
Savill Gardens 71
Saxtead Green 99
Scalloway 265, 267
Scalloway Castle 267
Scapa Flow 265
Scarborough 173
Scolt Head Island 118
Scolton Manor Museum and
  Country Park 56
Scone 221
Scone Palace 221
Scotney Castle 52
Scott's View 206
Scourie 257
Scrabster 261
Scunthorpe 157
Sea Life Centre 229
Seahouses 208
Seal Sanctuary 19
Seatoller 160
Sedbergh 167
Selby 157
Selkirk 206
Seil Island 213
Selworthy 30
Semer Water 152
Severn Estuary 64
Severn Valley Railway 108
Sewerby 159
Shaftesbury 37
Shandy Hall 170
Shanklin 43
Shap 162
Shaw's Corner 74
Sheffield 139
Sheffield Park 49
Sheldon Manor 67
Sherborne 37
Sherborne St John 69
Sheriff Hutton 156
Sherwood Forest 139
Shetland Islands 266

Shieldaig Village 241
Shildon 169
Shillelagh 281
Shipton Hall 108
Shire Horse Centre 71
Shirwell 28
Shottery 88
Shrewsbury 104, 109, *109*
Shropshire Hills 104-5
Shugborough Hall 111
Shuttleworth Collection 95
Sibsey 143
Sidmouth 35
Silbury Hill 66
Silchester 69
Simonsbath 30, 32
Sir George Staunton Country Park 45
Sissinghurst Castle 52
Sittingbourne 53
Sizergh Castle 163
Sizewell Information Centre 99
Skara Brae 265
Skegness 143
Skenfrith Castle 84
Skerray 259
Skerryvore 211
Skipness Castle 193
Skipton 151
Slains Castle 248
Slane Castle 281
Sledmere 156
Sligo 275
Slimbridge Wildfowl Trust 87
Smoo Cave 257
Snaefell 146, *146*
Snape Maltings 98
Snowdon 127, 128, 129
Snowdon Mountain Railway 125
Snowdonia 128-9
Soay 225
Solva 56
Solway Firth 180
Somerleyton 123
Somerset Levels 64
Somerset Rural Life Museum 64, *64*
South Downs Way 50
South Molton 31
South Skye 225
South Uist 263
Southampton 39
Southend Village 195
Southend-on-Sea 77
Southport 149
Southsea 45
Southwell 141
Southwold 99
Spains Hall 77
Spalding 117
Springhill 277
Squerryes Court 49
Stack Rocks 59
Staffa 211
Stafford 111
Staithes 172
Stalker Castle 213
Stamford 115
Stamford Bridge 156
Stansted Mountfichet 77
Stanway House 86, *86*
Steamport Transport Museum 149
Steeple Bumpstead 96
Stevenage 95
Stickford 143
Sticklepath 24
Stiperstones 105, *105*
Stirling 216, *217*
Stobo 202
Stockton-on-Tees 171
Stoer 257
Stoke Bruerne 93
Stoke by Clare 96
Stoke Park Pavilions 93
Stoke-on-Trent 133
Stokesay 107
Stokesley 170
Stonehaven *236*
Stonehenge 67, *67*
Stoney Middleton 134
Stornoway 263
Storrington 47
Stourbridge 111
Stourhead 37
Stow-on-the-Wold 88
Stowmarket 97
Strabane 277
Strangford Lough 277
Stranraer 177
Stratfield Saye 71, *71*
Stratford-upon-Avon 89

Strath Farrar 243
Strath Halladale *259*
Strath Naver 259
Strathpeffer 243
Strathy 259
Street 65
Strid 154
Strome Castle 227
Stromness 265
Strone 214
Stroud 87
Studland Bay 37
Studley Roger 154
Stump Cross Caverns 154
Sudbury 96
Sudbury Hall 111
Sudeley Castle 86
Sueno's Stone 245
Suffolk Wildlife and Rare
    Breeds Park 99
Sumburgh 265, 267
Summer Isles 241
Sussex Downs 50-1, *51*
Sutton Bank 170
Sutton Coldfield 111
Sutton Hoo 99
Sutton-cum-Lound 141
Sutton-on-the-Forest 156
Swaffham Prior 94
Swaledale 153
Swallow Falls *127*
Swanage 37
Swansea 61
Sween Castle 193
Sweetheart Abbey 180
Swindon 69
Symonds Yat 84

T

Tain 255
Taliesin 103
Talley 61
Talmine 259
Talybont Reservoir 83
Talyllyn Railway 101
Tamworth 113
Tank Museum 36
Tapeley Park 29
Tarbat Ness 255
Tarbert 193
Tarbet 214
Tarr Steps 30, 33
Tartans Museum 217
Tattershall 143
Taunton 35
Tavistock 23
Taynish 193
Taynuilt 215
Tayvallich 193
Telford 104
Temple Newsam 155
Tenby 57
Tennyson Down 42
Tenterden 52
Tetbury 67
Tewkesbury 86
Textiles Museum 151
Thaxted 77
The American Adventure 139
The House of the Binns 203
The Mens 51
The Pleasaunce 123
The Vyne 69
Thetford 97
Thirlestane Castle 207
Thirsk 171
Thomas Carlyle's Birthplace 183
Thornhill 180
Thornton Abbey 159
Thornton Dale 172, *173*
Thorpe Park 71
Threave Castle 180
Thrigby Hall 123
Thursford Collection 119
Thurso 260
Tideswell 134
Tighnabruaich Village 193
Tilbury 75
Tillicoultry 221
Timoleague 279
Tinkinswood 63
Tintern 65
Tiree 211, *211*
Titterstone Clee 104, 108
Tiverton 31
Tobermory 213
Toddington 86

Tokavaig Wood 225
Tolpuddle 36
Tomintoul 246
Tongland 179
Tongue 259
Topsham 27
Torosay Castle 213
Torphichen Preceptory 203
Torpoint 22
Torquay 27
Torre Abbey 27
Torridon Visitor Centre and
    Deer Museum 241
Tote 239
Totnes 27
Tower Bridge 73, *73*
Tower of London 73
Towneley Hall 151
Tramway Museum 139
Trapp 81
Traprain Law 207
Traquair House 202
Trawsfynydd 128
Trecastle 81
Trelissick Garden 21
Tremadog 124
Tre'r Ceiri 124
Tre'r-ddol 103
Trerice 21
Tretower 85
Trewint 23
Trewithen House 21
Triangular Lodge 115
Tring 93
Tring Reservoir 90, *91*
Trinity College, Cambridge 94
Trossachs 218-19
Trumpan 239
Trumpington 94
Truro 19
Tugnet Ice House 247
Tummel Forest Nature Reserve 230
Tummel Forest Park 233
Tunbridge Wells 49, *49*
Turnberry 196
Turton Tower 151
Two Bridges 24
Tynemouth 189
Tynwald Hill 146
Tyseley 110
Tywyn 101

U

Udny Green 249
Uffculme 35
Uffington 69
Ugbrooke 27
Uig 238
Ukaea Dounreay Exhibition 259
Ullapool *250*
Ullswater 162
Ulverston 161
University of Wales 101
Unst 267
Upminster 77
Upper Coquetdale 186
Upper Irwell Valley 151
Urquhart Castle 243, *243*
Uttoxeter 111

V

Vale of Evesham 86
Vale of Neath 62
Vale Royal Abbey 133
Vale of the White Horse 66
Vale of York 156
Valle Crucis Abbey 107
Valley Gardens 71
Vane Farm Nature Reserve 221
Vatersay 263
Ventnor 43
Virginia Water 71

W

Wakefield 155
Wakehurst Place 47
Wales Aircraft Museum 63
Wallace Monument 217
Wallington 185
Wallsend 189
Walmer Castle 55
Walsingham 118

Waltham Abbey 75
Walton on the Naze 79
Wanlockhead *180*, 181
Wantage 69
Wark Forest 186
Warkworth 189
Warrington 133
Warwick 89, *89*
Washford 30
Washington 189
Watchet 30
Watermouth Castle 29
Watership Down 69
Watersmeet 30, *30*, 33
Waterways Museum 93
Wayland's Smithy 69
Weaver's Cottage 197, *197*
Wedgwood Visitor Centre 133
Wedmore Hills 64
Wells 64
Wells-next-the-Sea 118
Welsh Folk Museum 63, 65
Welsh Miners' Museum 63
Welshpool 107
Welshpool and Llanfair
    Light Railway 107
Wendron 19
Wenlock Edge 104-5
Wensley 168
Wensleydale 153
Wesley's Cottage 23
West Bromwich 111
West Felton 107
West Highland Way 229
West Kennet Long Barrow 66
West Midlands Safari and
    Leisure Park 108
West Runton 123
West Somerset Railway 31
West Stow 97
Westbury 67
Westbury Court 87
Westerham 49
Westham 49
Weston Rhyn 107
Weston-super-Mare 65
Westport 275
Wetheral Priory Gatehouse 183
Wethersfield 96
Wetlands Waterfowl Reserve
    and Exotic Bird Park 141
Wexford 281
Weymouth 37
Whaligoe 261
Whalley 151
Whalsay 267
Wharfedale 153, 154
Wheal Martyn Museum 21
Wheddon Cross 30
Wheeldale Moor 175
Whinlatter Pass 160
Whipsnade 93
Whitby 172, *172*, 175
Whitchurch 69, *69*
White Castle 84
White Horse (Bratton Down) 67
White Horse Hill 69
White Horse (Kilburn) 170
White Lady waterfall 23, 24
White Peak 136-7
Whitesand Bay 56, 58
Whithorn 177
Whitland Abbey 61
Whitstable 55
Whittington (Derbyshire) 139
Whittington (Shropshire) 107
Whittlesey 117
Wick 260, *261*
Widecombe in the Moor 26
Wigan 133
Wigtown 177
Wilmington 49
Wimborne Minster 37
Winchcombe 86
Winchester 39
Windermere 162
Windmill Hill 66
Windsor 71
Windsor Safari Park 71
Winkworth 47
Winsford 30
Wirksworth 139
Wisbech 117
Wistman's Wood 24, *24*
Witney 88
Witton le Wear 169
Wolferton 118-19
Wolverhampton 111
Wolves Wood 79

INDEX

Woodbridge 99
Woodhall Spa 143
Woodstock 88
Wookey Hole 64
Wool 36
Woolbridge Manor 36
Wootton 42-3
Worcester 87
Woldwide Butterflies and
    Lullingstone Silk Farms 37

Worthing 47
Wrekin 105
Wrexham 131
Wroxdall 42
Wroxham 121, 123
Wyre Forest 108
Wythall 110

Y

Y Gaer 81
Y Gyrn-Ddu 124
Yarmouth 43
Yelverton 23
Yeovil 35
Yeovilton 35
York 156, 157
Yorkshire Dales 152-3

Yorkshire Dales National
    Park 152, 153, 166
Yr Eifl 124

Z

Zennor 18

The Automobile Association would like to thank the following photographers and libraries for their assistance in the preparation of this book:

D FORSS 275 Clifden, 276 L. Neagh, 277 Giant's Causeway, 279 Cork, R Lee.

D HARDLEY 190/1 Kidalton Cross

NATURE PHOTOGRAPHERS LTD 24 Dipper (P J Newman), 25 Pony (A J Cleave), 33 Red Deer (W S Paton), 40 Fallow Deer (R Tidman), Bog Asphodel (P R Sterry), Badger (H Clark), 41 Spruce Plantation (R A C), Lower Heath Burley, (P R Sterry), 50 Butterfly (P R Sterry), 51 Dark Green Butterfly (A Wharton), Silver Spotted Skipper (P R Sterry), 58 Grey Seal (W S Paton), 59 St David's Head (G Lycett), 72 Black Redstart (P R Sterry), 83 Lesser Horseshoe Bat (S C Bisserot), Globe Flower (B Burbidge), 90 Willow Warbler (P R Sterry), Tring Reservoir (R Bush), 91 Broad Leaved Helliborine (R O Bush), Autumn Beeches (E A Janes), Hairy Voilet (J Russell), 104 Raven (F V Blackburn), Bog Pimpernel (P R Sterry), 121 Avocet (R Tidman), Swallowtail Butterfly (E K Thompson), 128 Redshank (P J Newman), 129 Mountain Avens (R O Bush), Golden Plover (P J Newman), 136 Curlew & Chicks (E A Janes), 137 Yellow Archangel (R O Bush), 144 Dunnock (H Walker), 145 Kidney Vetch (P R Sterry), 152 Globe Flower (C Grey-WIlson), 165 Peregrine (D Smith), 165 Goldeneye (P R Sterry), 174 Bilberry (S C Bisserot), 175 Curlew (R H Fisher), 186 Siskin (F V Blackburn), 186 Short-eared Owl (E A Janes), 187 Hedge Bedstraw (P R Sterry), 218 Crossbill (F V Blackburn), 219 Hen Harrier (F V Blackburn), Capercaillie (G T Andreartha), Bog Myrtle (B Burbidge), 234 View from Cairngorms (A J Cleave), Bilberry (N A Callow), 235 Crested Tit (C Carver), Golden Eagle (F V Blackburn), Rothiemurchus Forest (A J Cleave), 252 Wildcat (W S Paton), Red Deer Stag (W S Paton), 253 Arctic Hare (H Miles), Grey Seal (W S Paton), 270 Purple Spurge (A J Cleave), Wall Lizard (S C Bisserot), 271 Queen of Spain Fritillary (A Wharton), Camberwell Beauty (P R Sterry)

A WILLIAMS (Cover) Allerford

All remaining photographs are held in the A.A. PHOTO LIBRARY

288